AMERICAN EDUCATION SERIES

GEORGE DRAYON STRAYER, GENERAL EDITOR

READINGS IN
CURRICULUM DEVELOPMENT

HOLLIS L. CASWELL
PROFESSOR OF EDUCATION
GEORGE PEABODY COLLEGE

AND

DOAK S. CAMPBELL
PROFESSOR OF EDUCATION
GEORGE PEABODY COLLEGE

AMERICAN BOOK COMPANY

NEW YORK   CINCINNATI   CHICAGO

BOSTON   ATLANTA   DALLAS   SAN FRANCISCO

38198

375
C356c1

EDITOR'S INTRODUCTION

In their earlier book on *Curriculum Development,** the authors furnish students of education with a most stimulating and valuable discussion in this most important field of inquiry. Throughout that text they list selected references, noteworthy for the care with which they were selected and for their range of point of view represented. In the present volume, *Readings in Curriculum Development,* the authors have brought together many of the most important contributions to the discussion of curriculum development, especially those that have been published during the past fifteen years.

Students in this field will be grateful to the authors for bringing together in this source book a wealth of material not easily available in many libraries. The excerpts from books and articles included are not a miscellaneous collection. The authors have sought out the most significant discussions in the field, representing all points of view. Here will be found excerpts from those who have studied the problem from the standpoint of the philosophy of education; here are reported the conclusions of the most eminent of the psychologists; here are the findings of those who have done the most significant research in the field of curriculum development.

The readings are arranged in such order as to make them supplementary to the authors' textbook on *Curriculum Development.* They are equally indispensable, however, for independent use in the study of the problems of the curriculum. No one could claim to have covered the literature of the field without reading the references which are here assembled. Whether the student is interested in the problem of relating the curriculum to contemporary social life or whether he seeks to engage in the actual process of assembling and organizing materials for the guidance of teachers, in either event he will herein find just those discussions and suggestions which will help him in his work. This book is a veritable treasure house for students of curriculum development.

GEORGE D. STRAYER

* American Book Company, 1935.

PREFACE

EFFECTIVE study of the curriculum or participation in curriculum programs requires the use of reference materials from a wide variety of sources. Much valuable material is contained in sources which can be secured only with considerable difficulty by the average student and by professional study groups. Frequently only a small section of a bulletin, magazine, or book, is pertinent to curriculum issues and problems. As a result it is difficult and time consuming to secure these materials for reference use. In fact, there are probably few public school systems and relatively few colleges in which a considerable proportion of such sources is available.

Readings in Curriculum Development presents a critical selection of such materials. Choice of materials was based on a number of considerations, as follows:

1. Authority of the source. In all selections attention was given to the expertness of the author in the field under consideration. Effort was made to secure excerpts from those most competent to deal with each problem.

2. Clarity and effectiveness. Selections were chosen where possible which presented the problems and issues in clear and effective form. Excessively long and involved statements were avoided.

3. Range of point of view. Effort was made to avoid weighting the readings to any single point of view. In the case of all controversial issues the purpose was to present a range of materials which would give the strongest statements of position available on major points of view. Weakness in presentation of some positions is due to lack of effective published statements of the positions. The compilers present no comments on the readings, their point of view being available in *Curriculum Development*.

4. Availability of the source. In general the selections were made from sources not easily accessible or in which only small sections of material were pertinent to the problem under consideration. In dealing with certain problems it was necessary to disregard this basis of choice in order to present most effectively the varied points of view on the problems.

5. Recency of the source. Relatively recent sources were canvassed with special care. It was considered particularly desirable to make easily available for general use by curriculum workers those materials which reflect the influences of social change, critical evaluations of education, and significant changes in the concepts of the nature of curriculum and curriculum making during recent years. At the same time materials of merely temporary significance were avoided and older sources were used when they presented more fundamental analyses of problems than were available in recent sources.

The readings are organized around the chapter headings of *Curriculum Development*, a text on the curriculum by the compilers. This basis of organization makes the volume a particularly valuable source for use in courses and professional study groups in which *Curriculum Development* is employed as a text. However, a reclassification of the readings can be made readily by anyone preferring a different organization.

In addition to its use in courses in the curriculum and in professional study groups the volume will be found helpful also as a general reference source for the points of view of various leaders upon many educational issues and problems. Advanced students may find a consecutive study of the readings particularly valuable as a means of gaining a more adequate understanding of the range of points of view upon many issues.

The compilers are greatly indebted to Ruth Allen Caswell and Mary Louise McGlothlin for assistance in preparing the manuscript. They are also appreciative of the permissions granted by authors, school systems, organizations, and publishers, to reproduce the materials herein presented.

HOLLIS L. CASWELL
DOAK S. CAMPBELL

CONTENTS

I. CHALLENGE OF CONTEMPORARY LIFE TO THE SCHOOL

II. THE SOCIAL RESPONSIBILITY OF THE SCHOOL

III. SIGNIFICANT INFLUENCES ON CURRICULUM DEVELOPMENT

IV. CONCEPTS OF THE CURRICULUM

V. PRINCIPLES BASIC TO CURRICULUM DEVELOPMENT

VI. AIMS OF EDUCATION

VII. SCOPE OF THE CURRICULUM

VIII. PUPIL PURPOSES

IX. ACTIVITIES FOR REALIZATION OF PURPOSES

X. SELECTION OF SUBJECT MATTER

XI. GRADE PLACEMENT AND TIME ALLOTMENT

XII. TEACHING PROCEDURES

XIII. EVALUATING THE OUTCOMES OF INSTRUCTION

XIV. ORGANIZING INSTRUCTION

XV. THE UNIT BASIS FOR ORGANIZING INSTRUCTION

XVI. THE COURSE OF STUDY

XVII–XVIII. ADMINISTRATIVE CONSIDERATIONS AND ADMINISTRATIVE ORGANIZATION IN CURRICULUM DEVELOPMENT

CHAPTER I

CHALLENGE OF CONTEMPORARY LIFE TO THE SCHOOL

1. "EDUCATION FOR SOCIAL PROGRESS"[1]

Harry Elmer Barnes

THOMAS ALVA EDISON is perhaps most significant as symbolizing better than any other American of the last half century the dominant trend and the outstanding challenge of American life. His era has been characterized, and above all else, by staggering progress in mechanical science and by equally amazing stagnation in the field of culture, institutions, and ideas.

It is this juxtaposition of an airplane technology and an oxcart society that is the outstanding threat to the further happiness — even existence — of human society. . . .

In Edison's era — say, since 1870 — we have been lifted out of the Middle Ages in our material surroundings. The Empire of Machines has arisen. Modern machinery has made possible mass production and greater factories. More powerful and rapid transportation methods have speeded up the distribution of commodities.

We have built better locomotives and cars; have added Pullman cars; have invented safety devices on railroads; have built surface, elevated, and subway lines; and have passed from the bicycle to the automobile and airplane. We have improved the steam engine, devised gas and gasoline engines, built the Diesel engine, and constructed practical electric motors.

Chemistry has wrought its marvels in the iron and steel and rubber industries, in the manufacture of dyes, in the exploitation of by-products and waste, and in the synthetic re-creation of innumerable and diverse commodities.

Modern communication has passed from the crude telegraph to the telephone, wireless, and radio station. The human voice has been preserved by the phonograph and transmitted by the radio. We build vast skyscrapers and imposing bridges with nonchalance.

In short, when it comes to science and engineering we are something to marvel at, if judged by earthly standards.

[1] *Journal of Adult Education,* 4:373–377, October, 1932. American Association of Adult Education.

But the sober observer must admit that we continue to think and behave much as we did not only when Edison was born but when George Washington was born two centuries ago.

Our social ideals are still based on pecuniary standards, snobbishness, a class system, and the worship of display. Exclusiveness and exploitation, rather than cooperation and service, dominate with little effective criticism.

In economics the reverence for wealth and property is unabated. When the dollar is no longer a prize, sheer economic power becomes such. We mouth the fallacies of the days of Adam Smith and Ricardo, still crediting a " rugged individualism " which was outmoded before Lincoln split a rail. The state is still viewed with hostility as the collective policeman rather than as the instrument of social progress and justice.

Politics is as much " air-driven " as in the days of Clay, Webster, and Calhoun, except that the quality of the air has markedly deteriorated. We trust majority rule and ostensibly believe in numerical democracy. The party system continues without notable reform. Our own party system is today a travesty and joke even with national committeemen. There is no longer any clash of vital economic and social interests in our major party divisions. Outside a few commissions, expert knowledge and direction are derided and rejected in public life. A joke is more highly regarded than a graph.

In the field of international relations, though we live in an age of world perspective and contacts, we still reverence and apply the ideals and practices of an age of quasi-isolated national states. Patriotism, war, tariffs, imperialism and the like still flourish with little abatement. The League of Nations is but a feeble first step and is built on the assumptions of nationalism and national independence. Reservations transform the Kellogg Pact into a moral defense of all probable wars.

Law is playing the game according to archaic rules that were a disgrace to the human mind even in the days of Blackstone. The rules of legal evidence are an affront to all science and logic. Even lawyers laugh when one naïvely connects law with justice.

Religion has made little progress since Tom Paine. Our modernists are only trying to find new phrases to envelop or obscure old ideas and practices. Our professional atheists are less informed and more shallow than Baron Holbach a century and a half ago. Thoroughly modernized and humanized religion has but a handful of followers. Morals are still based on theological formulas for heavenly salvation instead of informed secular guidance for happiness and well-being here and now.

Journalism is for the most part vastly successful commercialization of gossip. The murder of a harlot may be more important news than the termination of an ancient empire. Rarely does our journalism even pretend to intellectual and social leadership. Education has made some progress in theory and assumes to prepare people to live today. Actually, it is still chiefly a mechanical and punitive machine, carrying a heavy freight of antique myth and superstition, and crushing zest and ambition.

Broadly speaking, while we are frank and daring in technology, we are cowardly, evasive, and unreliable in our thought and conduct. The honest and courageous man is as rare and in as much social jeopardy as in the days of Diogenes.

Such is the challenge of our social order. We can not go on forever with one foot in an airplane and the other bound to an oxcart. We shall need sociological Edisons, or the work of the scientific Edisons will topple in the dust and snuff out human civilization beneath the scattered débris. We need some social engineering.

Social engineering today must rest upon sound education. We can not safely delay until a well-trained younger generation comes along. Adults living today must be provided with a civilized intellectual perspective, reliable and cogent information, and a technique for bringing about orderly social change.

It is frequently asserted, and with entire accuracy, that the whole problem of " salvaging modern civilization " boils down to the question of providing a satisfactory and potent system of education. It is said that we need special emphasis on the field of the social sciences, which will enable man to deal with the novel and diverse issues raised by our complicated urban industrial civilization. As a simple statement of the diagnosis and remedy this is obvious enough, but the practical solution of this matter is difficult and baffling indeed.

. . . .

It is infinitely better that social change should be presided over by trained and informed intelligence rather than by the emotions of the vigorous but untutored agitator. This is the essence of the case for education in relation to social progress. We have our choice between conservative domination, on the one hand, which means an arrested civilization and ultimate extinction; and, on the other hand, social change, driven either by indignation and emotional revelation or by sound conviction and scientific information.

With such alternatives the choice should be easy, once the necessity of making exactly this choice is driven home to the dominant elements in the community. Neither the sure ruin, which awaits conservative evasion and obstinacy in so dynamic and complex a civilization as ours, nor the wasteful change associated with violent revolution presents an alluring spectacle to sane minds.

Considerable complacency might well be generated in the minds of the fearful ones by calling attention to what the conservatives of the past have feared and what they have fought to retain.

It can be shown that in regard to the prevailing socio-economic system the dominating groups in society once defended a hunting and fishing existence and feared the transition to pastoral life; then clung to the pastoral economy and delayed the transition to agrarianism; then defended the agrarian order and were repelled by capitalism as much as the contemporary capitalist is disturbed by the socio-economic system operating in Soviet Russia. It can easily be proved that, in each great transition of this sort, those linked up with the older order of things confidently predicted the destruction of all civilization if far-reaching innovations were tolerated.

Likewise, in the field of government; monarchy, aristocracy, and democracy have in turn been greatly feared and bitterly resisted. The effort of the French to construct a limited monarchy at the close of the eighteenth century was viewed by the autocrats of that day with apprehension as terrific as that which the Bolshevik experiment of the twentieth century has created in the minds of the late Judge Gary, Mr. Hoover, Judge Hughes, and Ralph Easley. The *laissez-faire* politico-juristic system, so precious to the arch-conservative of twentieth-century America, was, no more than a century ago, regarded by the conservatives of that day as a very dubious and adventuresome policy.

This knowledge of how every advance, great or small, has been feared and resisted in the past ought to reduce the apprehensiveness of the present generation with respect to contemporary programs of social and political reconstruction. These may now be guided by a more comprehensive and scientific body of information than has previously been available to assist in any important historical transition. . . .

One of the most frequently exploited arguments of the conservatives is the assertion that all liberal proposals are impracticable because they would require a change in human nature. This position can be quickly refuted. There has been no essential change in human nature — if we mean by that the neurological equipment of man — in the last twenty or thirty thousand years. In this same period we have passed from the cave to modern urban industrial civilization, from the stone culture of the late Paleolithic period to the empire of machines, from crude tribal society to a federal republic embracing half a continent, and from the rudimentary beginnings of private property to the age of billionaires. . . .

All special problems of our age — capitalistic avarice and cupidity, depressions, unemployment, wars, armament, brutality and inefficiency in dealing with crime, sex obscurantism and tyranny, archaic types of religion, educational maladjustments, increased nervous and mental disease, and the like — all fall in as important but subordinate aspects of adapting our thought and institutions to the advanced character of our scientific achievements, our astonishing technology, and the dictates of sound esthetics.

2. "THE QUEST FOR NATIONAL SECURITY"[2]

Charles A. Beard

The American republic now tosses heavily amid the tempest of a crisis in its economy. No facts and figures are required to prove that statement. Stark evidences of the crisis lie all around us — in silent industries, in rusting machines, in the broken lives of men, women and children. But deeper than these outward signs and entangled in them is another crisis, not visible to the eye — a crisis in American thought which springs from our quest for security through national action on a national scale. This is the phase of the present national dilemma which distinguishes it from previous panics and especially concerns the teachers of the land.

When, nearly a century ago, the United States was shaken by the economic crash of 1837, the ensuing popular distress was generally taken as a passing visitation of an unknown evil. President Martin van Buren attributed it largely to the sins of greed and speculation. In a message to Congress he declared that, under the Constitution, the Federal Government could do nothing about it. Moreover, he insisted that, were the powers available, it would be unwise for Congress to meddle with the affairs of private enterprise. Such was the thought of the President during that calamity. The poor suffered in silence or fell by the wayside. In due course came a revival of business as American ingenuity was turned to building railways, opening virgin soil to cultivation, establishing basic industries and exploiting the national endowment in natural resources.

Today the republic finds itself in another economic crash, with similar signs of distress and discouragement. But the whole economic setting has been altered, and thought has changed. The continent has been rounded out; foreign trade has been pushed to the limits; the exploitation of natural resources has reached a point of decline and decay; railway construction has stopped and the mileage shrinks; basic industries have been established; and an unexplored wilderness no longer beckons youth with opportunity. The nation stands in the presence of an unparalleled equipment for the produc-

[2] *School and Society*, 41:721–725, June 1, 1935.

tion of wealth, and this equipment is nation-wide in its connections and ramifications.

In the course of a hundred years, the whole economy of the nation has been altered. The independent producer and owner of 1837 has been supplanted by the specialist, the corporation, the cooperative association and the trade union. The self-sufficing homestead and community have almost disappeared. Individuals, communities and regions have become interdependent. All have been so woven into a common economic mesh that, apart from a few primitive farmers, no one, whatever his virtues of industry and thrift, lives unto himself, or by his own efforts applied to nature's resources wins security for himself and his family. This transformation was coming about before the crisis; it is proceeding amid the crisis; the calamity itself has demonstrated the collective character of our economy and our distress. Individual energy, industry and virtue no longer guarantee a chance to make a living and attain security.

While the economic scene has been changing, thought has been changing, though lagging behind the alteration in the economic structure. When President Hoover declared that " no one shall starve in America," and took steps to check the course of the panic, he made a breach in the historic thought of America. When President Franklin D. Roosevelt, in his message of January 4, 1935, proclaimed his objectives to be security of livelihood, security against the major hazards of life and security of homes, he widened the breach opened by his predecessor. If economic security is in fact the certain reward of individual industry and thrift, if poverty is the offspring of laziness, then there is no reason why the poor should not be allowed to starve, to suffer punishment for their sins. There was a time when economists and statesmen held and celebrated this faith and practice. Charity might dole out soup, but the nation represented by its government had no moral responsibilities in the case. But thought changed. The obsolescence of the creed has been demonstrated. President Hoover and President Roosevelt have condemned it. Their measures differed, but their thought on this issue was the same. And it is inconceivable that we can go back to the philosophy of President van Buren or the economic arrangements of his day. A break has come; a return to the past is impossible; the burden of the new thought and the new responsibility will press harder and harder upon us as the future unfolds.

This change in thought did not come upon us out of a blue sky. For more than half a century practice had been preparing the way for it. Confronted by the alterations brought about in economy by machinery, specialization, integration and the multiplying ties of social living, our cities, states and the nation had been making innumerable adaptations in government to meet new problems as they arose. They did this pragmatically without much speculation in social theory. The process may be simply illustrated by reference to the substitution of a collective water-works system for the individual pump in the back yard. And, as Theodore Roosevelt remarked long ago, no one thought that his individuality was crushed when he surrendered the pump handle for the faucet in his house. Stagecoach drivers and carters felt aggrieved, no doubt, when continental railways took over long-haul transportation, but society derived benefits from that achievement of corporate enterprise. When the rates and services of railways were deemed unfair and unreasonable, government stepped in to regulate and control them. But not many citizens felt their liberty destroyed because railroad companies were compelled to heat trains, guard crossings and subject engineers to tests for color blindness.

The history of municipal, state and federal governments for more than fifty years is the history of growing interventions and actions on behalf of the public or collective interest in a quest for greater convenience and security. Compulsory public education was one of the first forms of this transformation. The individual right of parents to bring their children up in illiteracy and ignorance was denied, and the burden of supporting schools was placed upon society itself. Public health services, parks, playgrounds, hospitals, mothers' pensions and public institutions of beneficence all illustrate the increasing assumption of collective responsibility for the welfare and security of individuals. From year to year there has been an increasing intervention of government in the processes of agriculture and industry, an increasing regulation of private enterprise, an extension of government activities into new fields, a growing centralization of control and financing in the hands of the state and federal governments as contrasted with local governments — in health, education, highways, relief and social insurance, for example. To go into more detail would be superfluous. The story is told with a wealth of cold statistical description in the volumes prepared by President Hoover's Committee on Recent Social Trends. And now those findings are almost daily confirmed by presidential messages, by report after report on resources, welfare and planning, turned out by engineers, statisticians and specialists in economy and government. And the particular proposals are crowned by a great national project for state and federal cooperation in providing assurance for the aged and unemployed. The whole nation is engaged in a quest for security for all men, women and children.

Various names have been applied to this new configuration of things and efforts. President Hoover called it " associational." The term " cooperative " has been used to characterize it. The Commission on the Social Studies found the word " collectivism " appropriate. Over definitions it is not profitable to tarry long. The fact stands: We live in a society that is differentiated, integrated, centralized and interdependent in all its parts — a society in which government, representing the common interest, assumes increasing responsibilities, along with farmers' cooperatives, industrial corporations and labor organizations, in holding economy together and making it work. Individuals remain. The virtues of intelligence and industry remain. Individual responsibilities remain and will always remain. But without informed and efficient collective action, without the subordination of personal ambitions and greed to common plans and purposes, Americans can not win security, can not safeguard natural resources, can not bring an economy of abundance into full flower. This is not a theory, a mere supposition; it is the configuration of the cold and brutal facts amid which we flounder and blunder today in a search for security and the good life.

With the facts, however, our thought has not yet entirely caught up, and this discrepancy makes for tension, distress and uncertainty. The old theory that security is the simple product of individual thrift and virtue no longer corresponds to the actualities of the social situation, to our knowledge of its stern mandates. And unless we can bring our thought into harmony with established and stubborn facts, with emerging trends, American society can not be brought to the highest possible degree of economic efficiency. Nor can the forms of security required for decent living be attained.

The task is conceded, but already voices are heard, telling us that the new adjustments and institutions can not be made by thought, knowledge and common efforts; that they must be made by brute power, supported by the sword. Already tones of thunder in Europe proclaim the death of democratic processes — government by public discussion, public decision and public action, supported by the knowledge and resolve of citizens.

Amid the crumbling structures of old practice and thought and emerging practice and thought stand leaders in education, responsible for the schools and the preparation of youth for the coming years. In the nature of things they represent a public or collective interest, as distinguished from special and individual interests. Yet what are their immediate obligations, if any? They must say, of course, that this crisis in economy and thought is not their concern, that they must not be involved in the tensions and conflicts of society, that they will close their eyes and ears to the turmoil of the world, that such great public documents as the report of President Hoover's Committee on Recent Social Trends have no interest to them. They may say, " Let us go on undisturbed teaching Greek, Latin, mathematics, literature, chemistry and history in the old way, without any reference to what is taking place in society or the nature of the social order in which children are to be graduated from the school." Or, confronting the fact of a closely integrated society, they may say, " We believe that a return to the old order of 1850 is possible and that old theories and knowledge may after all work very well again." Or they may say, " We are pure scientists concerned with purveying facts and we are not concerned with the use of facts any more than the chemist is concerned whether one of his formulas is used to heal the sick or poison personal enemies." These intellectual positions are possible — as long as society can afford and will pay salaries to educational leaders who hold to such views of their present responsibility.

On the other hand, another position is possible for educational leaders. They may say, " It is our duty to give to pupils a picture of contemporary society and its trends as realistic and accurate as knowledge can make it. Let us prepare boys and girls through information and training to take part in this order of things, to contribute to its smooth and efficient functioning, to supply the knowledge and enthusiasm required to sustain the common interest, and to contribute abilities to the maintenance of the democratic processes of government and collective adjustments." If the schools are after all to serve the society which supports them, this seems to be the only position open to the educational leader who is not indifferent and defeatist in thought and spirit.

Such a position, however, carries with it imperatives. What are they? First of all, is a clarification of thought and purpose, enlarging the mind and giving it firmness without harsh dogmatism, vision without hectic illusions and guidance without bigotry; wide and deep knowledge of social development and contemporary social processes, including the history of culture; acquaintance with ideas and ideals now bidding for the loyalties of American citizens; a judicial spirit — the capacity to look around each particular issue, to listen to conflicting voices, even though their tones be hateful, and to weigh and balance evidence; a generous freedom of teaching, so that a realistic picture of American society, with its tensions and conflicts, may be squarely presented to students; a recognition by each community of the fact that schools have functions to perform in this respect which transcend special and private interests; the judgment and wisdom that pay strict attention to strategy and tactics and never lose sight of grand objectives in personal or particular quarrels. These, to borrow from Shelley, are the seals of that firm assurance which bars the pit over destruction's strength.

Suppose educational leadership, in common with all leadership, fails at its task, what lies ahead of the republic? Glimpses of its fate are to be found in the monumental report of the Mississippi Valley Committee, prepared by competent men of science under the auspices of the United States Government. After making a minute survey of the Mississippi basin, comprising all or parts of thirty-one states, the committee presents an illustrative finding:

If certain present day trends were to be projected unaltered into the future, the map (of the Valley) would be a sorry one. We would be compelled to show increasingly larger stretches of once fertile lands stripped of their life-giving humus, rivers breaking forth in floods of increasing severity as the denuded slopes permitted an ever swifter run-off, industry and agriculture becoming ever more precarious, the life of the people on the land becoming more and more disorganized, and a steady increase in farm tenancy and of economic dependency. Under such conditions local self-government would be likely to break down, and under the spell of a dire and never-ending emergency, economic and political centralization would steadily increase. The comparison of such a situation with the final days of the Roman Empire is not too far-fetched.

This is not a vague declaration of sociology, social psychology, partisan philosophy or parlor communism. It is the cold, scientific and statistical verdict of engineers, foresters and geographers, based on a study of indisputable and stubborn facts of earth and life. As one among the many great state papers of our time, dealing with the crisis in our economy and thought, it reveals an inescapable phase of the present challenge to American leadership. It lays no iron mandate upon us, but it forecasts our destiny if leadership fails. The past is closed and can not be recovered. It is for us, the living, to take up the work before us, and to meet the challenge of our time with the indomitable spirit and the inquiring mind which inspired and led the founders of the American republic.

3. SOCIAL CHANGE NECESSITATES EDUCATIONAL CHANGE [3]

John Dewey

. . . The necessity of great educational change may be indicated by sketching the changes which life has undergone in the United States.

First, one hundred years ago, our life was agrarian and rural. Agrarian civilization has always when left to itself moved at such a slow pace that, to those who lived in it, it did not seem to change in any fundamental way. It is static, based on the traditions of the

[3] From "Some Aspects of Modern Education," *School and Society*, 34:582–584, October 31, 1931.

past, and accommodated to the course of nature. During the nineties of the last century, our society became definitely urban and industrial. It moves neither at the tempo of the ox-cart nor of the horse, but at that of electricity, the motor car and the airplane. Life has to adapt itself to the mechanical inventions which control the processes of nature rather than to the cycle of nature itself. Invention rather than routine and custom determines the course of events, and no one can say what further inventions are going to modify the course of living in the years that are before us. We do know that railway, telegraph, telephone, electric light, power, transportation, automobile, radio, airplane and their multitude of accessories have revolutionized our habits of work, of amusement, of communication and intercourse. Schools which have looked upon their task as that of preserving and transmitting the classic cultures of the past have fought shy of adopting into their own aims and methods enough of the new forces, the forces which determine our life, to fit individuals to cope with them. They may wreck us unless they are intelligently regulated and employed. Our mechanical devices and processes have got far ahead of our capacity to plan and to enjoy — ahead of our minds in short. The gaps between our machines and our ability to control them for human ends is widened because education has clung to old traditions and aims of culture in the face of the new industrial situation.

Secondly, there has been a revolution in the methods by which things get done. Our fathers worked by custom and the models laid down in the past. These models and procedures have been thrown into the scrap heap, not intentionally and deliberately, but none the less effectually. For science has dictated to men new ways of doing things based upon understanding of natural energy and the relations of cause and effect. Because of scientific advance, because of the methods it puts at our disposal, a single great industrial company creates devices by which the work can be done which would occupy our entire population, men, women, children and babes, if the work had to be done with the instruments and processes of even sixty years ago. It can not be said that our schools have begun to introduce scientific method into teaching to anything approaching the part which it plays in shaping our actual lives.

Thirdly, we have altered from a population with simple political problems to one with extremely difficult and complex issues. When the outlines of our school system were formed there was no great separation into rich and poor; there was free land; there were abundant unused and unappropriated natural resources. There was work and opportunity to get on for all. Then the aims of political democracy were easily understood, since they were in harmony with the conditions of soil and occupation. Now there are vast and concentrated aggregations of wealth; there are monopolies of power; great unemployment; a shutting down of doors of opportunity, a gulf between rich and poor, and no frontier to which the hard-put can migrate. In consequence, the problem of democracy is no longer chiefly governmental and political. It is industrial and financial — economic. It is infinitely ramified, and the threads which bind the social structure together are subtle and invisible. It would be absurd to hold educators responsible for our present depression, a depression which is obviously mental and moral as well as financial. But the depression is a warning that we live in an age in which education must take on new responsibilities and come to grips with realities which it has passed by as outside its province.

Fourthly, control of natural forces by means of machinery has brought to humanity the possibility of an amount of leisure from which the mass of men and women in the past were hopelessly shut out. At the same time, popular amusements and recreation have been seized upon as means of financial profit. The combination of these two facts has created what may be truly called a crisis in our national moral life. A new conception of the uses of leisure has to be created; boys and girls need to be instructed so that they can discriminate between the enjoyments that enrich and enlarge their lives and those which degrade and dissipate. The possibilities of artistic production and appreciation can no longer remain the privilege of a select class, but must become a universal possession. Otherwise the increase of leisure time may become a demoralizing agent on a vast scale.

Not all the social changes which are going on are good and beneficial. But it is claimed that these changes are here and must be faced, not ignored; education has the responsibility of developing types of mind and character that can direct these new forces toward good and that otherwise they will surely become forces of destruction and disintegration.

The sum of the matter is that at the present time education has no great directive aim. It grows, but it grows from specific pressure exerted here and there, not because of any large and inspiring social policy. It expands by piecemeal additions, not by the movement of a vital force within. The schools, like the nation, are in need of a central purpose which will create a new enthusiasm and devotion, and which will unify and guide all intellectual plans.

In earlier days there was an aim which worked throughout the whole system. Education was the key to individual success, to making one's way in life, to getting on and getting ahead. The aim corresponded with the realities of social life, for the national need was the material subjugation of a continent, the conquest of a wilderness. There was always a frontier just beyond, and the pioneer advanced to take possession of it. It was enough for the school to equip the individual with the tools of learning and to fire him with ambition and zeal to get on. His real education came in contact with others and in struggles with the forces of nature. The aim was individualistic, but it was also in harmony with the needs of the nation.

This earlier purpose has lost its vitality and its meaning. It survives, but operates as an oppressive handicap. As President Hoover said some time ago: " We are passing from a period of extremely individualistic action to one of associational activity." Except for a favored few, there is no longer any unbounded opportunity for advancement open to individuals. We live in an epoch of combination, consolidation, concentration. Unless these combinations are used democratically for the common good, the result will be an increasing insecurity and oppression for the mass of men and women. Education must cultivate the social spirit and the power to act socially even more assiduously than it cultivated individual ambition for material success in the past. Competitive motives and methods must be abandoned for cooperative. Desire to work, for mutual advantage, with others must be made the controlling force in school administration and instruction. Instead of imbuing individuals with the idea that the goal is to sharpen their powers so they can get on personally, they must be trained in capacity for intelligent organization so that they can unite with others in a common struggle against poverty, disease, ignorance, credulity, low standards of appreciation and enjoyment. There must be a purpose and methods which will carry over the earlier ideals of political democracy into industry and finance.

Only in respect to methods of thought and judgment should the earlier individualistic aim be retained; *there* it should be intensified. Democracy will be a farce unless individuals are trained to think for themselves, to judge independently, to be critical, to be able to detect subtle propaganda and the motives which inspire it. Mass production and uniform regimentation have been growing in the degree in which individual opportunity has waned. The current must be reversed. The motto must be: " Learn to *act* with and for others while you learn to *think* and to judge for yourself."

The problem of educational reorganization is not one which it is easy to solve. But we are discovering that the problem of maintaining the democratic ideals of our founding fathers is not easy, either. The only way to attain the latter is by giving a social direction to our educational system. If the good will, the loyalty, the political faith and hope of the American people can be united with the affection which parents have for their children, and the union can be directed by the spirit of free scientific inquiry, there is no ground for fear of failure. When the ideals of democracy are made real in our entire educational system, they will be a reality once more in our national life.

4. Implications of Characteristics of Modern Life for Education [4]

A. ECONOMIC

(1) *Science and power.* — The applications of research to medicine, engineering, and industry have profoundly modified life. There has developed an amazing accumulation of knowledge. Modern power-driven machinery has transformed the home. Freed from drudgery by vacuum cleaners, electric irons, washing machines, and other inventions, families have more time for recreational and cultural pursuits. Many women have been free to enter gainful employment. Occupational patterns have been broken down by the decline of certain types of work and the creation of new jobs. Products which once were so costly as to be possessed by few are by machinery placed within the reach of many.

(2) *Potential plenty.* — For the first time in history man can probably produce enough for all. Power combined with science has developed machinery which can turn out goods with incredible speed and efficiency. Each decade fewer farms are needed to supply the necessary food. But the era of plenty is only a potential one. We need still to develop a distribution system which is coordinated with the effectiveness of the production system.

(3) *Acceleration.* — In the period of agrarian dominance of American life, the rhythm of life was relatively slow. Today, with power-driven machinery, buildings are constructed more rapidly, farms plowed in less time, distance annihilated by rapid transit facilities, and mass impressions speeded by new means of communication. Fashions created in Paris one week are on display shortly afterwards in New York, or even in Middletown. New improvements in automobiles, radios, trains, and airplanes steadily demand the replacement of old equipment. Changes come upon us with accelerated rapidity and make life more complex for increasing numbers of people.

(4) *Leisure time.* — Year by year mankind has been freed more and more from unremitting toil. Improvements in technology have

---

[4] National Education Association, *Modern Social and Educational Trends,* Research Bulletin, Vol. XII, Washington, D. C., November, 1934, pp. 284–287.

placed increasing amounts of time at the disposal of all workers. Industry is finding less need for children and youth, thereby increasing the possibilities of a lengthened period of schooling. Old age retirement systems are reducing the span of years which must be allotted to employment.

(5) *Interdependence.* — An industrial society requires first of all a supply of raw materials. Our silk mills depend upon Japan for raw silk, cotton mills rely upon southern fields, and steel mills require the coal of Pennsylvania and the iron ore of Michigan. The fabrication of automobiles, telephones, and other machinery calls for imports from all parts of the world. In financial matters the world is closely bound together. Two cases in point are the bank failure in Austria which precipitated the 1931 financial crisis, and the recent request of the Chinese government for modifications of the American silver policy. The typical pantry shelf reveals the world's interdependence for food supplies. In a thousand ways our daily lives are touched by the events in remote nations and in nearby communities.

(6) *Standardization.* — As the world becomes more closely related, ideas and ideals spread rapidly. The rhythm and ethics of life in industrial nations penetrate to all parts of the world. City culture thru the radio, newspapers, and magazines dominates rural culture. Advertising methods of Fifth Avenue are found effective on Main Street. The moral ideals of Hollywood are displayed in every city and town and, for better or for worse, set new standards of dress, manners, and conduct. Standards of living are cast in a mold that places the auto, the telephone, the radio, and the electrical refrigerator among the necessities of comfortable living. Overwhelmed by new additions to knowledge, people turn to the breezy news review, the anthologies of literature, and the digests of current periodicals.

(7) *Economic insecurity.* — In an agrarian society each family, and to a certain extent each individual, is largely independent. As America changed from an agricultural nation to one predominantly industrial, many people surrendered their economic independence. They took jobs created by invention and science. At first, those who rebelled against this new type of life moved out to the simplicity of the frontier. Today the frontier no longer exists, and youth must look to the existing industrial organization for employment. The employee's, and often the employer's, means of livelihood is dependent upon the business cycle, and economic security is threatened to an extent not known in an agricultural civilization.

(8) *Collective action.* — Freedom of the individual in many aspects of life has been a tradition of American civilization. A peculiar

type of self-reliance was required under pioneer conditions. A continent to be gained and exploited stimulated a race for property, power, and prosperity. But tho this phase of life has been greatly publicized, it was, and had to be, accompanied by collective action. The early colonists were able to exist only because people worked and fought together. The continent was won by the trains of covered wagons, welded together by railroads, educated by schools, and otherwise united by cooperation among groups of people. Today thru legislatures, conferences, committees, associations, and other groups, citizens are working together to advance the general welfare.

(9) *Centralization.* — Partly as a result of economic conditions and partly because of the demand for more collective action, there has developed an increase of government participation in everyday life. The federal government increases its control and direction of industry, agriculture, and banking. State governments increase their supervision of education, housing, police work, and other social activities. Great companies merge into larger corporations, with national and even international affiliations. Chain stores are important competitors of the independent corner stores. Credit and banking facilities reach from the smallest town to Wall Street.

(10) *Objectivity.* — The farmer planted his crops by certain traditional formulas until controlled laboratory studies displaced many of these " rule of thumb " guides with scientific principles and practices. The home has surrendered much of its traditional domination of the individual and released youth to an ever widening sphere of influences. Experience and experiments are substituted for " arm chair " philosophy. More and more people are subjecting all phases of life to the pragmatic test: " Does it work? " The demand for objectivity has set the stage for clearer thinking and more efficient action in regard to the intricacies of modern life.

B. EDUCATIONAL

What do the foregoing social and economic changes mean to education? No one can predict with absolute certainty. . . .

(1) *Philosophy of education.* — If there is to be an adjustment of education to a changing civilization, schools need to direct their efforts toward broader objectives. Education has been primarily concerned with making people literate. Book learning that developed abilities to memorize, to read, to comprehend, and to recite has been of fundamental importance. Schools have been organized, teachers trained, and instructional materials prepared with book learning as the controlling factor. It is no condemnation of the past to hold that present social conditions and objective knowledge as

to the nature of the learner make it necessary for the general philosophy of education to be enlarged. Education must be recognized as a continuous process from birth to death; from sunrise to sunset. It is not something that goes on for a few hours each day within the four walls of the school. Education arises from, exists in, and will continue to flourish as a part of its surrounding social culture. It cannot be completely isolated from life outside of the school.

(2) *Teachers.* — Teacher-training institutions have in the past produced capable technicians — well-grounded in knowledge and methods of instruction. But today society needs teachers who are zestful and capable students of social problems. If in the future training agencies have fewer, more carefully selected students, they should find new opportunities to improve the social understanding of teachers now in service and to help school systems to keep pace with an advancing social order. There falls upon the individual teacher the obligation to keep abreast of social trends and to participate actively in life outside of school. At the same time he will need to perform his professional duties in accordance with good taste, high standards of scholarship, and respect for community opinion.

(3) *Childhood.* — Constantly new discoveries are being made about the nature and the nurture of children. Educational methods that treat children as small-sized adults will continue to lose ground. More attention will be given to individual differences. The influence of the early years upon later life suggests the advisability of further efforts to remove disabilities and to stimulate potential talents. All of the activities of life are recognized increasingly as educational, altho not necessarily efficient and constructive. The new attitudes toward childhood forecast the hopes and the values that people generally, and educators in particular, expect to characterize our future American civilization.

(4) *Social curriculum.* — It follows certainly that with the extension of knowledge in all fields of human life the curriculum of the schools will be greatly enriched. Thru the recasting of existing courses and the integration of all types of subjectmatter in terms of meaningful units, the lag between the advance of knowledge and the school's offering will be taken up. The *use* of facts in social experiences within the school, such as pupil government, committees, clubs, publications, and the like, will bring a form of enrichment characteristic of but few educational programs of today. Pupils will study the interrelations between the various aspects of society, noting where inarticulations occur, exploring the causes of difficulty, and projecting possible improvements.

In many instances this social emphasis will require new school courses and activities. Better opportunities for pupils to study home life, industry, and labor conditions will tend to develop a higher type of social intelligence. Besides the addition of new units of study, there will be an increased emphasis upon the social aspects of existing courses. By tracing the history of writing, of numbers, and of spoken language, there will be gains in an appreciation of the problems and progress of group life.

(5) *Instructional methods and materials.* — Since books have been primarily places for book learning, the dominant classroom procedure has been the recitation. This method succeeded in spreading a degree of literacy among the people. It contributed little to an understanding of the problems of modern life. Recognition of the futility of the typical recitation does not minimize its contribution to American education. But thru experiments teachers have found new methods which, while utilizing the advantages of the older procedures, promise to develop the type of thinking ability required by modern life. Thru the use of libraries, laboratories, debates, conferences, and committees, students are participating in the direction of their own learning. The teacher is no longer the dictator, but a guide.

The social emphasis in education calls for the development of new materials, textbooks, and equipment. Universities, research centers, and teacher-training institutions will assume more responsibility for developing materials which can be used to enrich the student's reading. Thus, students will be constantly in touch with up-to-date and vital sources of information.

Every effort will be made to encourage the pupil to become so interested as to go beyond any formal assignments. Education will cease to be a list of activities bound between the covers of the course-of-study bulletin. It will become all of the activities of life thru which the pupil may improve himself. Schooling of this type will make for open-mindedness, tolerance, and suspended judgment as well as for initiative and decisive action. Thus equipped, the public of tomorrow should be able to make more intelligent decisions in matters of public policy.

(6) *Internal organization and management of schools.* — It seems likely that the present school system will extend its systematic efforts both downward to include younger children and upward to provide for adults. The units of the system may be reduced in number, and certainly will be more closely integrated to further the continuity of school experiences. Types of schools may become more flexible and varied — such as summer schools for workers — to take care of the requirements of social and economic organization.

The management of the school system may be expected to adjust itself to newer social needs and a broader theory of education. Artificial and unnecessary distinctions between types of teaching positions will give way before the realization that all teachers are workers in a common cause. Classroom teachers, as they become better trained and more socially minded, may be expected to bring their knowledge of child nature and needs into the formulation of instructional policies. School systems will provide further for the democratic sharing by administrators, teachers, and students of the responsibilities of management.

(7) *External contacts and administration.* — The schools will need to be organized so that educational experiences available to children may have the maximum of concreteness and reality. Educators will figuratively level the walls of the schools thru excursions, journeys, and extended trips. Experts and creative artists will enter the schoolroom in person or by means of the radio and the sound motion picture. The school will not be a world set apart, with manners, ethics, and problems different from those of the real world.

In this breakdown of isolation the school will integrate its program more and more with libraries, playgrounds, and other agencies for community betterment. Thru coordinated efforts there will develop local, state, and even national programs for cultural progress. The layman will cooperate in these activities and thereby obtain an understanding of public education which the typical " publicity program " has not yet succeeded in giving him.

The financial support of education is an administrative problem which needs to be considered in the light of social conditions. The recent depression has clearly revealed that the financial problems of education are deeply rooted. If America has passed its period of greatest prosperity, people may find it difficult to buy adequate education as well as other social services. There are relatively few, however, who are willing to accept this assumption. There is reason for believing that our national income can be increased beyond its 1929 peak, if we will make intelligent use of our natural resources, labor, and means of production. In this social advance, education, if given adequate financial support, will contribute to the vocational efficiency of individuals and the social intelligence of people generally.

(8) *Character and citizenship.* — The American public school has always been concerned with morals and character development. It has been generally recognized that the character and the social intelligence of the people generally are the basis of a more perfect and more permanent democracy. But many of the efforts for character development were formulated under a narrow philosophy of education. Helpful and valuable as some of these technics are today, they

need supplementing in the light of the known facts of individual growth and of social progress.

While the social emphasis in the social sciences and all school activities will probably constitute the chief preparation for a high type of citizenship, it is not enough in itself. We may expect the development of tests and standards whereby the individual may explore his own capabilities and defects. Continuous and careful record keeping of these surveys will supply data upon which intelligent vocational, educational, and personal decisions may be made. It is reasonable also to expect that classes in character development may be able to contribute something under favorable conditions.

Another general trend will be the shaping of the entire program so as to contribute constructively to the wholesome use of leisure. There are some who view an increase of leisure time as a threat to good character. Others view the new freedom as an opportunity for the enrichment of character. Which of these predictions will come true depends largely upon the amount of intelligence which the American people bring to the problem. If the schools develop students with the maximum ability to direct their own time along wholesome lines, the threat is not serious. To do this, the school's program must be broadened in scope and attractiveness as suggested in preceding paragraphs. The arts and crafts must be taught by artist-teachers who can awake the latent talents which exist.

5. " Education and the Economic Depression " [5]

John K. Norton

. . . Thus far we have allowed the forces set into play by the machine to run riot. There has been but little effort to control these forces and to mitigate the severity with which they fall on the individual. If " canned " music throws thousands of musicians out of work, if the type-setter is first displaced by the linotype operator, who is in turn thrown out of employment by the invention of a still more advanced machine, we are perhaps sorry, but we leave it to the individual to take care of himself.

The present economic depression is the normal outgrowth of such an unplanned economic system. Can one imagine a more irrational situation than the one in which we now find ourselves? Here is a nation abundantly supplied with the natural resources and raw materials necessary to production — land, coal, oil, water-power, iron, and all the rest. We are in an extremely favorable position as to the implements of production. No nation has gone so far in applying the machine to industry and agriculture. We possess an abundant sup-

[5] *School and Society*, 34:272–275, August 29, 1931.

ply of labor, anxious to work, and more intelligent than any other large body of workers in the world. Our 125,000,000 people enjoy an annual income which in 1929 approximated ninety billions of dollars, which is roughly equivalent to that of all the other inhabitants of the globe. Their tremendous purchasing power and general desire to maintain a high standard of living make the American people the customer market *par excellence* of the world. But what are we doing with this unparalleled situation? Hundreds of factories are completely closed down, and thousands more running at a mere fraction of capacity. Thousands of farmers are unable to sell their products at a price sufficient to pay for their production. From five to six million workers are out of work, which means, if we consider their dependents, that some twenty million persons in the United States are a prey to all the demoralizing influences which trail in the wake of unemployment.

Abundantly supplied with the raw materials and implements of production, amply provided with competent labor, inhabited by a population constituting the world's greatest market, yet the nation continues in an economic impasse in which factory wheels do not turn, farms lie fallow, the unemployed continue idle and want even for food, and the legitimate wants of many millions are but partly satisfied.

Somebody has said that if the other planets are inhabited, there seems justification for believing that the earth is their lunatic asylum. The present situation in the United States flavors the remark with something more than humor. . . .

If we, through education, are to play a major rôle in bringing about the economic adjustment and social planning which are essential if civilization is to avoid a collapse, we must become students of the society which the school seeks to serve. If the school is to play a major rôle in the coming decades it must take its cue from contemporary civilization and build its program with the demands of practical life clearly in mind. What are some of the facts of contemporary life which call for educational responses?

The first fact of contemporary life to which your attention is invited is that the environment of children in their out-of-school hours is becoming progressively less educative. President Hoover recognized the problem clearly in his introductory speech before the White House Conference when he said:

In the last half a century we have herded 50,000,000 human beings into towns and cities where the whole setting is new to the race. We have created highly congested areas with a thousand changes resulting in the swift transition from a rural and agrarian people to an urban, industrial nation. Perhaps the widest range of difficulties with which we are dealing in the betterment of children grows out of this crowding into cities. Problems of sanitation and public health loom in every direction. Delinquency increases with congestion. Overcrowding produces disease and contagion. The child's natural play place is taken from him. His mind is stunted by the lack of imaginative surroundings and lack of contact with the fields, streams, trees and birds.

Let us consider some values which the typical farm child of a generation or two ago gained from his out-of-school environment. He gained a concrete, first-hand knowledge of work. He performed the chores with which the farm abounds. As soon as he was old enough, he aided in such fundamental farm operations as sowing, hoeing, and harvesting. When the horses needed shoeing he drove with his father to the blacksmith shop and saw the glowing iron fashioned at the forge and fitted to the horse's foot. The milk bottle did not mark the limit of his knowledge as to the source of milk. He did not have to go to a zoo to see a cow. He knew all about their habits, and the chores connected' with them from first-hand experience. Nearly every hour of the day brought him increased understanding of, and training for, life. He knew how real work was done, and learned how to do it.

Compare this situation with that of the child living in the congested city. There is much less in the typical urban community that children can do. The grocer brings the eggs, machines milk the cow, and the baker bakes and delivers the bread. Actual participation in the work of the city is prohibited by child labor laws; and it is difficult to observe what goes on even at second hand, for " keep out " is posted in large letters at the entrance to the factory and shop. Often turned loose with nothing to do, children have to choose between play upon the crowded city street, association with the back alley hoodlum, or attendance at the cheap movie show.

Here is a condition which offers a double opportunity to education, first for supplying the child with the raw material out of which to build an understanding of life, and second for protecting the child in his out-of-school hours from the negative educational influences with which the city abounds. The modern school at its best has already made substantial progress in meeting the first need through its expanded and enriched curriculum. The second responsibility has not been faced as yet. We school people have been content to wash our hands of responsibility for what happens to the child, after three-fifteen on school days, on Saturdays, and during the summer vacation. We have hoped that the home would meet the problem, or that the Boy Scouts or some other agency might step into the breach. But existing social agencies are falling far short of offering the child the protection he needs in his non-school hours.

Here is an example to illustrate our point. First comes the machine, then the congested city with its many pitfalls for children. Society, and particularly the school, fails to respond to the new factors which have come into child life. It is satisfied to continue to function essentially as it did in an agrarian civilization. Juvenile delinquency, gangdom, and crime are the result. And so we have one of the strongest influences for social deterioration in modern day life, millions of children unprotected from the negative forces which play upon them in our cities during much of their out-of-school time. . . .

6. TECHNOLOGY MUST BE USED FOR SOCIAL ENDS [6]

John Dewey and John L. Childs

. . . A second basic principle is the use of technology for social ends. Modern machine industry is, of course, the product of technology, and this in turn is the result of application of the findings of scientific method. There are those who personify the machine much as our savage ancestors personified the forces of nature, and thus surrender their minds to a new form of mythological animism. In itself, the machine is of course but the effective supplementation of the energy of human muscle and nerve by the inanimate energies of heat, electricity, chemical reaction. The only basis on which the machine can be condemned logically is that of a passive and pessimistic philosophy which regards all exercise of energy as intrinsically evil. The present widespread blame of the machine for our present evils is a projection of the unwillingness of human beings to blame themselves for permitting the development and growth of legal and political institutions which make machine-industry the fountain head of widespread insecurity, poverty, fear, physical and mental crippling, with subjection of the many to the privileged power of the few.

Inherently the new technology is simply skilled control on a wide scale of the energies of nature. It contains within itself the possibility of not merely doing away with the evils which result from our present economic régime but of ushering in an order of unprecedented security and abundant comfort as the material basis for a high culture in which all and not merely the few shall share. It is as certain as any fact can be that we have within our power the means, including technical and managerial skill, by which the natural resources of the earth may be used to save all from dire want, from paralyzing insecurity, and to guarantee the essential conditions of a life devoted to higher things than the mere struggle to escape destitution for one's self and one's dependents.

[6] From *The Educational Frontier*, William H. Kilpatrick (ed.). D. Appleton-Century Company, New York, 1933, pp. 62–64.

It is not necessary to recite here all the evidence that the man-made legal and political system under which technological industry operates is the cause of our troubles rather than machine-industry itself. On the negative side the evidence is overwhelming that material success is not the attendant of superior character and that poverty and unemployment are not the results of inferior character. The sole alternative is that the social system is at fault. There have been times when it was utopian to indulge in a belief in a state of society in which all dire want and its attendant evils would be abolished. Our present technology brings the hope wholly within the region of possibility. The educational profession has therefore a direct concern in all that concerns the use of technological resources for the formation of a more secure and more humane order. Because of conditions which have been indicated, our professed and professional educational aims are fated to impotency with respect to both social advance and the systematic development of personal character unless the power inherent in science and technology is utilized for ends which are not controlled by economic institutions where competition for pecuniary gain is supreme.

The net conclusion of the discussion is:

An identity, an equation, exists between the urgent social need of the present and that of education. Society, in order to solve its own problems and remedy its own ills, needs to employ science and technology for social instead of merely private ends. This need for a society in which experimental inquiry and planning for social ends are organically contained is also the need for a new education. In one case as in the other, there is supplied a new dynamic in conduct and there is required the coöperative use of intelligence on a social scale in behalf of social values. . . .

7. TECHNOLOGY AND EDUCATION [7]

Jesse H. Newlon

. . . When we ask what are the educational implications of modern technology, many possibilities come to our minds. We may think of the use in the educative process of such instruments as the radio, sound pictures and other mechanical devices. Though they can never afford a substitute for individual experience, for study and patient inquiry, these technical appliances may work a revolution in educational method. The radio has knit the whole nation into one community. It is a powerful instrument for moulding the public

[7] From "Educational Implications of Modern Technology," *School and Society*, 37:572–573, May 6, 1933.

mind, though a dangerous one. But other implications are more fundamental . . . education will be universal to age twenty, and throughout life for that matter. Life will become one long process of education. The secrets of the universe and of life will be pursued relentlessly, and the frontiers of knowledge will be pushed farther and farther back. Education to do one's part in production will be important, but education for living will become relatively of far greater importance in the age of plenty. Two years ago former Ambassador Gerard startled the country with a list of some seventy men, who, he said, controlled America. Education was conspicuous for its absence from that list. But it will not be so when we decide to employ technology for the common good. Then education will occupy an important position in the councils of the nation. Education for living will be the most important business of society.

There are other and more immediate implications. We do not as yet know how to get from where we are to our Utopia. The transition — that is the big problem. If we follow our present policy of drift, even greater disaster will surely overtake us. We are unable to cope with the problems of industrialism and of the great world society created by the machine because the people and most of their leaders still think too much in terms of economic individualism. Our immediate task is to give youth and the entire adult population understanding of the twentieth-century industrial society in which they live. The content of education must be the social concepts and ideas of today and tomorrow. The curriculum of the school must be reconstructed and focused upon contemporary American life. Teacher training and the study of education must be redirected in the light of these changed conditions. Nothing is needed so much today as thousands of adult discussion groups scattered throughout the nation engaged in the study of the social and economic problems that technology has brought to us. In the remaking of American life, education must take its place as one of the great creative forces in society. It is a vital function of a complex, dynamic, swiftly moving social order. . . .

8. UNEMPLOYED YOUTH [8]

Lotus D. Coffman

In the past society has solved its unemployment problem for youth by sending them to school. As long as it was possible for society to profit by the labor of children, it hired them to work. But when

[8] From "Education of Unemployed Youth," *School and Society*, 38:485. 488–489, October 14, 1933.

work, due to changes in industrial life, was no longer available, the school day and the school year were lengthened, the entire educational program greatly expanded, and all because of pressures brought to bear upon the schools by special groups or by society in general.

Now the young people of America face a new unemployment situation. It arises partly out of the fact that the number of adults per one thousand children has been steadily declining; partly from the industrialization of society, and partly from the world-wide depression which threatens the very foundations of civilization itself. Millions are out of employment in this country; tens of millions more throughout the world. How the people shall be returned to work is a problem of the gravest importance to the welfare of humanity.

Of the millions who are out of work, there are several million young people who, with nothing to do, are wondering what the future has in store for them. Some of them have already broken away from the moorings of home and have become aimless drifters. I have seen hundreds of them this summer in empty box cars, riding freight trains across the country. Every highway is lined with hitch-hikers asking for rides. Every urban community has its quota of young men and young women with nothing to do. Every rural community has its share of youth who find it unprofitable to labor on the farm and who, like thousands of others, are looking for a break in the clouds. Failure to prepare these and other similar groups for the increased leisure which seems inevitable can wreck civilization.

Unemployment for any age group is always serious, but unemployment of youth is the most serious of all. It is serious because it means that the right kind of character is not being developed in young people. It is serious because the training of future leaders is being neglected. It is serious because the entire situation and the influences flowing from it will develop false notions, and bad habits and ideals, unless the proper correctives are provided. If we neglect youth in our effort to recover prosperity, we shall pay heavily for our neglect a few years from now; in fact, we shall pay more heavily than if we neglect any other age group, although, of course, no group should be neglected. . . .

Some of these youngsters who we wish to serve will desire and should be allowed to carry high-school or college work of the conventional kind. But others need something else. I ran hastily through a hundred replies of young people who need help. Some of them would choose medicine, law, dentistry, teaching, pharmacy, and the like; others would choose stage work, the R. O. T. C., cartooning, piloting, baking, beauty culture, broadcasting, orchestra and band, mechanical refrigeration, aeronautics, advertising — things that were not included in the school curriculum a few years ago and are not often included now. Any program of service we may outline should include special work along these and other lines — lines that represent the shifting needs of the times.

It seems clear to me that a heavy responsibility for the program so far outlined rests upon the public school and college authorities in the respective communities of the state. This movement represents a call to service — to community service. It involves cooperation of a high order and the willingness to accept responsibility. In so far as any feature of it can be carried on without funds, we should do so. The chief work of the more formal educational program will reside in the local communities.

This is a time when school superintendents and school principals and college authorities need to exhibit special leadership, to dedicate themselves with renewed vigor to the call of their profession. It is a time when they can help the schools develop a large and inspiring social policy which will in turn develop for the school a new enthusiasm and devotion. . . .

But I do not wish to devote all my time to those who are fitted and who wish to attend a high school or college. There is a much larger number who do not desire to attend high school or college and certainly some who should not be encouraged to do so. Most of them want a job. They would accept employment at once, if it were available. With no job in sight many of them would like some sort of a technical or vocational course. The usual high school or college is not equipped to provide this training. If it is to be provided at all it must be by the introduction of new courses, which would be difficult in these times, or by using private educational institutions equipped to do such work, or by some tie-up with industry itself. These are matters upon which we need the expert advice of those who are familiar with this aspect of the problem.

But all or practically all those who do not wish to attend school in the usual sense have some interest that may be appealed to. All of them, or nearly all of them, want to know how we got into this depression, they want to know how we are going to get out. They hear a lot of terms used that they don't understand. They may be able to spell the word " tariff," but do not understand how tariffs affect world commerce. They have heard people use the expression, gold standard, but they do not understand what it means and they have less knowledge of what " managed currency " means. They know little about intergovernmental debts and the part they are playing in world recovery. They know that revolutionary legislation has been enacted for agricultural relief, but they can not describe what the agricultural legislation actually is. They have heard the NRA referred to repeatedly, but they are not familiar with its provisions. They have heard of these and of a hundred other problems, all of which have some relation to their present situation. They want to know what caused this situation and how to prevent a similar one in the future.

Herein lies a fertile field for education that has no thought of credits, courses or degrees. It is education that is intended to make people intelligent about those problems that affect their welfare most vitally. Every one should be interested in this type of education and especially young people should be interested in it. It will help to explain things they do not understand; it will help to prevent future disaster; it will help to fit them for their citizenship responsibilities. It is, in fact, education for citizenship of the best kind. . . .

9. CHANGE IN SOCIAL INSTITUTIONS [9]

Lyman Bryson

Social control in all our institutional life is passing into the domain of larger and larger units of organization, and these units are responding to centralizing influences. This change is especially marked in industry. Production and financing very largely have gone from the hands of numerous small enterprisers into the control of huge corporations with thousands of stockholders, thousands of employees, and more or less centralized management. Whether or not the chances for individual initiative have diminished is a moot question, but there can be no doubt that invention and individual energy are now oftener the servants of accumulated capital than free competitors in the open arena. In the same way, the functions of the state have been greatly increased.

The family as a fundamental social unit may be taken as illustrative of this change. No social transformation can seriously threaten the existence of the family because biological relationships remain, whatever we do to our social structures, but the family as a unit of control has been rapidly giving way to larger units. Economic functions have been taken over by large-scale industry. There are still millions of women in our population who can be classified only as housewives, but the primary economic activities of the housewife are incessantly narrowed by the encroachments of mechanical devices. The growth of the numbers of women " at work " is more a transfer of laborers from the home to the office or the factory than it is the bringing of new laborers into production. Women are now working

[9] From "Recent Social Trends," National Education Association, *Social Change and Education,* Department of Superintendence Thirteenth Yearbook, Washington, D. C., 1935, pp. 57–59.

in food factories instead of canning food at home, or working in laundries instead of doing the family washing. It has the effect, nevertheless, of increasing the control by the industrial, that is, the larger and less personal, unit of organization.

But more striking is the enlargement of the functions of the public school. Parents have to a great extent handed over to the schools a custodial responsibility. Most educators appear to believe that society at large should, thru the school, make up to each child any element seriously lacking in his home environment, and the scope of public education grows. The present acute conflict between education and discouraged taxpayers has shown that neither the educators nor the parents are willing that this growth shall be checked.

Not only the protection of the child from contagious disease, but his nutrition, his dental care, and his mental well-being are taken over by the larger unit, the public school system. It is in the classroom that he is expected to learn social attitudes of cooperation. Instead of looking to his parents as solely charged with the duty of making him a fit member of the social order, society counts on the school to do a larger share of that job.

This surrender of responsibilities by the family to industry, the school, and the state, does not mean that it is less important as an institution. Many sociologists believe that the family may play a still greater part in forming character, in building personalities thru emotional relationships, in providing the framework for the deepest satisfactions. Marriage is increasing rather than diminishing and, altho divorce is more common, longer lives and a higher age level have maintained the proportion of married persons. Not the destruction of the family but a transformation of its usefulness is what the scientist finds from an examination of the facts.

The church as a primary institution is being subjected to similar changes. It shows the same phenomenon of centralizing control and activity in larger organizations. Total church membership shows little change, but the smaller village church is less important in the lives of most people because they can easily reach larger churches whose services they find more attractive. Whether attendance is being maintained is doubtful in spite of state membership rolls, and the automobile which makes Sunday recreation more accessible is often blamed for this failure of full participation.

The shifting of social control and responsibility to the state, especially the federal branch, is a similar development of control by larger units of organization. This change has two phases, a greater scope in the more strictly governmental functions and a larger use of socialized wealth in education, health, recreation, and general service to the people. The details of the phases and meanings of this change . . . are of primary importance from a strictly social point of view because they are to be included among the changes summed up under the rubric of centralization. When the family was a more effective unit of social control, when industrial, educational, and governmental duties were discharged by the family, the attitudes of the American people were more individualistic than they can be now. The citizen of today is caught in a wide net of interdependence. The complex forces which bear upon his individuality and among which his individuality works are more impersonal, more difficult to grasp thru direct experience. The trend toward collectivism and toward " planning " in terms of the whole society instead of in terms of the single life is a logical result. . . .

10. " EDUCATION AND THE CONSUMER "[10]

Dewey H. Palmer and Frederick J. Schlink

The idea that a healthy, wise, and working consumer — the person who eats the food, wears the clothes, and uses the appliances produced by modern industry — is an indispensable unit in our industrial-commercial complex has not entered the minds of educators and is only now being sensed by a very few of the more advanced and realistic thinkers among the economists. Students are, of course, consumers and for the most part play no other rôle in the economic order; yet educators have never, if one may judge by their activities and the products of their labors, had any concept of the student other than as a person who must at some future date take his or her place in society as a producer, or, if unlucky, as a cog in a producers' or distributors' mechanized commercial world.

EDUCATION FOR BUSINESS SUCCESS

Consistent with such views, and as an incentive to students to get more education, the schools have constantly held up the goal of an independent enterpriser's or successful employer's life as the crowning end and achievement of learning. The retired but well-heeled life of the Palm Beach or Newport capitalist is, in the average student's mind, more desirable than attempting the interesting but often financially and socially dangerous task of resolving some of our major economic or social ills.

While the schools may not promise such quick returns for a little effort as does Alexander Hamilton Institute, with its high univeristy-

[10] From *American Academy of Political and Social Science*, *Annals*, 173:188–189, 191–192, 195–197, May, 1934.

professor sponsorship, which offers a "new course and service for men who want to become independent in the next five years," yet the majority of the courses offered in arithmetic, accounting, and sales management, and some courses in economics and engineering, only train increasing numbers of individuals as processors, advertisers, and sellers of goods and securities, who will desire and take in private and personal profits as great as the market will bear. The young person who cannot select tooth powder intelligently or even know whether it serves any useful function whatever, who cannot refrain from urging his parents to purchase the latest model radio or pseudo-streamlined car (80 miles per hour on the straightaway!) is taught either directly or by implication to look forward to the time when he may be a successful department store owner, a division manager of sales, a real estate or insurance personage, a contact man for the power trust, or a chief executive engineer in some great telephone or electrical company.

Only a few years ago, much ado was made about the need to offer practical trade courses in the elementary and high schools. The skills which such work developed were all to the good, but here again the emphasis was placed on increasing one's money-making ability as a worker, or more often one's usefulness to an employer, and not at all on developing consumer skills that would tend to increase the purchase value of the worker's dollar after it was earned. Manual training schools have taught boys how to make unneeded candlesticks, taborets, and hammered copper letter openers, but none of them has ever so much as mentioned the satisfaction and savings resulting from compounding supplies of daily need that would otherwise have to be bought — shoe dressing, writing ink, or floor and automobile polish. The least one might expect from a woodwork shop course would be a careful study of woods and finishes and the construction of different kinds of furniture, to enable a person to recognize and avoid shoddy materials and cheap construction, and, when the time to set up a home arrived, to purchase their opposite as nearly as the pocketbook should permit. . . .

USELESS SCIENTIFIC TEACHING

In the main, science taught in the school system is innocuous, and pretty insignificant in its values. Except as it builds up a body of facts, some of which may be useful in helping one to hold a job, or in enjoying the abstract and economically harmless consideration of the fortuitous concourse of atoms and worlds, it is totally devoid of any purpose, social or otherwise. It is amazing to us in Consumers' Research, who have been in correspondence and in personal contact with some hundreds of science teachers in high schools and colleges, to discover how few teachers of science know anything about the methods of science: its function as an overturner of authority and tradition, and its impersonality and disinterestedness and unconcern for business interests or attitudes; or the rôle it has played as both the liberator and the destroyer of mankind.

Science is not an automatic, constructive force, as the god-finders among its more eminent devotees would make out. We may have and do have a science, so-called, of production, with technological displacement of workers, sciences of distribution, marketing psychology, war, and poisoning, which either in fact or through their potentialities are quite certainly carrying us to greater economic and social unbalance, and may bring us to complete social chaos as some of them have surely brought us to a catastrophic economic breakdown.

We might have had courses in biology, chemistry, physics, engineering, economics, and education which were closely integrated with the whole concept and trend of the social sciences, and if we had begun this course twenty years ago, we could have avoided many of our major social ills resulting from overspecialization, overspending, displacement of workers, and excessive debt burden. If consumers had received the practical technical training necessary to enable them to judge the qualities of complex goods, they could never have been pursuaded to endure the businesslike pressures that are responsible for maintaining present widespread consumer ignorance, now practically a vested right of the automobile, radio, and toothpaste manufacturers.

For instance, if science teaching were real and geared to the social and economic order, no high school boy would ever naïvely assume, after taking the required number of hours in general science and physics, that octane selectors, free-wheeling, and streamlining (as sold), are real or fundamental developments in the perfection of motor cars, or that " Interstation Tuning Silencer," " Filterizer," or " Duo-Diode-Triode Detector " represents the last word or words in the technical improvement of the radio. . . .

EDUCATION FOR CONSUMPTIVE ENDS

The era of expanding production is rapidly drawing to a close. Here and there new business ventures will rise to prominence and then subside, only because our present economic system cannot support the waste that goes into costly and planless speculation. At the moment there is a rising tide of interest and a growing murmur of dissatisfaction at the hopeless position into which the ultimate consumer has been forced by ruthless drives of competitive salesmanship and planless production and marketing.

One need hardly expect that the public schools of themselves will take up the cudgels in the consumer's behalf, but, as in similar social revolutions, consumers themselves will in time force consideration of their rights in public education. When that day arrives, science classes will find that testing electric toasters, vacuum cleaners, can openers, household rubber, leather, and paper articles, and analyzing soap, cosmetics, shoe pastes, prepared flours, and baking powders is an integral part of their work; and lo! the educators will discover that the principles and methods of science are not only being taught more certainly and more effectively, but that interest in the sciences — which are now definitely fighting for existence in many schools, against the bastard sciences and pseudo-sciences of the market place — will increase manyfold. Fundamental and valuable household and trade and consumption skills will be revived, and the amateur in this and that will come into his own and acquire the respect hitherto given the boy who "learned to play the saxophone in his own home in 10 easy lessons by mail." In the home, stamp collecting, the accumulation of glass and ivory trinkets on the mantlepiece, and new forms of bridge will give way to small work benches and chemistry laboratories where tooth powder, ink, and floor polish are compounded and made to replace inferior and costly commercial products, and where commercial products are analyzed and made to give an accounting of themselves, both technically and economically — a synthesis never yet achieved or attempted by the schools.

RISING DEMANDS OF CONSUMERS

It is to be hoped that economists, students of law, sociologists, and educators will take a keener interest in studying and participating in the consumer movement; in the activities of pressure groups to obtain consumer protective legislation; in the utilization of the boycott against dishonest and recalcitrant industry to hasten the coming capitulation of the Government to the forces demanding for consumers a place in the sun *and* in legislative halls, and in the Government's laboratories for foods, drugs, and household appliances.

Something even more fundamental must be got under way in the difficult task of educating a long befuddled public about the complex and often extremely intricate goods which they must use and work with. Teachers of economics must become familiar, at least in a broad sense, with the technical nature of consumers' goods and with the doctrine of value as measured in terms both of production and of cost of production rather than in terms of what products will bring either on the so-called free market or on the price-controlled market set up by the seller with the aid of price-fixing or "stabilizing" agreements or of quasi-monopolies due to advertising pressure.

Also, it is just as important, if not more so, that teachers of engineering and the other technologies impart a thorough and realistic knowledge — gained through intimate contact — of the social movements of their day, particularly those relating to consumption. It behooves academic professors of engineering to get over their complacent assumption that the economic corner is just about to be turned and that all will again be well for the universities' investments — public utility and other stocks — and for their graduating students in their hope of obtaining jobs.

WHOSE INTERESTS SHALL BE SERVED?

Finally, it seems to us that the time is now ripe to eliminate all those courses which wholly or in part negative or hamper the furtherance of the consumer's rights and interests. This means that the schools *must*, if they are to serve the common weal for which they are supported, throw off the dominating influence of chambers of commerce, rotary clubs, and school boards made up of business executives, and get back to the job of leading in needed social changes, and of determining their direction out of wisdom and not out of prejudice or tradition or academic inhibition or economic pressure.

The public schools have never consciously decided or even raised for discussion the question of whom they intend to serve — business enterprisers or the numerous laity of consumers. As a result of their efforts to maintain an ostensibly middle-ground position, and, in cases of doubt, to side with the business-must-be-furthered theory of public policy, they now find themselves in a time of institutional, educational, and personal crisis without staunch and militant supporters among the great group which has constituted their nominal clientele. Even the business men who have profited most and most consistently from the schools' operations have, to the educators' naïve astonishment, been the first and most vociferous to demand sharp economies and curtailments in the schools' programs, and to talk in most unpleasant fashion of the tax-eating pedagogues and school functionaries who thrive at the citizens' expense.

Consumers will, we hope, some day support an enlarged and strengthened educational program and policy; but one may be sure they will not do so, or come to the aid of the hard-pressed high school and college faculties, until university presidents, professors, school boards, principals, and teachers of the rank and file decide on whose

side they wish to cast their lot, and whose welfare, the public's or
that of trade, they are determined to serve.

11. "EDUCATION AND THE PREVENTION OF CRIME"[11]

Royal S. Copeland

We have chosen in America to turn over to the school teachers
not only those duties which are naturally theirs, but also many of
the functions which should be performed in the home. We have
come to expect the teacher to instruct our children in manners, personal hygiene, social etiquette and the household arts. We expect the
teacher to give by precept and example that moral and ethical training which in other times was imparted by the home and the church.

Certain recent experiences of my own have given me a growing belief that America must lean still more heavily upon the school teacher.
As chairman of a committee appointed by the United States Senate
to investigate crime, it has been my duty to listen to the testimony
of hundreds of witnesses. What we have learned centers upon one
point — the necessity of preventing juvenile delinquency. To accomplish this, the schools can do more than all other agencies within
public control.

The importance of what I shall have to say to you is emphasized
by the statistics of crime. In the United States today the average
age of the criminal is 23 years. The largest age group is found at 19
and the next largest group at 18. The seeds of moral delinquency,
sown and grown during school age, develop into evil plants, the fruits
of which are publicly displayed by boys and girls long before maturity of their minds and bodies. . . .

First let me present a brief statement of fact: From several
sources, apparently authoritative estimates of the cost of crime, it
appears to total approximately one fourth of our national income.
This sum . . . exceeds by at least three times our total expenditures for education. We can agree, I believe, that the cost of crime
in money and in reduced morality of the people is devastating beyond computation.

You know better than I how much the situation has been ag-
gravated by recent publicity given the activities within the law
of certain metropolitan bankers, utility heads and business executives. Such infractions of the moral law reported by the press
are dramatic presentations which must have undermined the public
morale and the morals of many individuals. Your minds will

[11] *School and Society,* 39:593–596, May 12, 1934.

quickly jump to acts within your own knowledge, where perhaps there may have been smaller monetary losses, but which are equally distressing examples of that lack of the sense of trusteeship and general public spirit which should characterize men of affairs. The anti-social conduct of persons operating within the law, ruthlessly exploiting the economic resources of the public, has inflamed the minds and emotions of criminals and of weaklings. Recognized as one of the major causes of our economic condition, those acts have added to the general social unrest.

In short, the factors that have acted to promote criminality have been added to of late because of economic conditions and what the average man believes is the chief cause of our economic distress. No matter how we approach the problem, we surely must agree that the menace of anti-social behavior and actual crime is greater than ever before.

Where does crime begin? The answer to that question will determine what we should do about it. While there are many causes, no doubt, yet there will be no dispute of the thesis that the perfect home should develop the perfect character. Most of us regard character building as the primary responsibility of the home. But, if I may jump to my conclusion on this point, I am forced to recognize that there is no immediate hope of greatly improving the home conditions of those who may later follow criminal careers. To accomplish this end is a long range process.

We think of the church as having a heavy responsibility in character building. But as regards this, I can criticize no church except my own. For any except my own denomination, I have no right to comment upon the adequacy of its character building program or to make recommendations for the extension of its work. I will say of my own denomination that I believe there is much more it should be doing. But whatever the churches may do in the future, we can not turn to them for an immediate and major attack on the problem of crime. I pause only long enough to express confidence that the church will lend support to a well-planned program of prevention.

This brings me to the schools. It is an old custom, familiar to you, to carry to the doorstep of the school all the problems that can not be solved in the home or elsewhere in the community. To blame the schools and the teachers appears to be one of the diversions of the American people. But it is not in this spirit that I approach the subject under discussion.

I could devote my available time to reviewing the forces which have tended to transfer from the home to the school almost the entire responsibility for the welfare of children. To you this is a well-known story. But when I turn my thoughts to what the schools can and should do in the matter before us, I have been wondering how the public would respond to a new plan. What would happen to a proposal that the public schools assume the responsibility for a basic crime prevention program?

In face of the alarming facts about crime and the growing anti-social conduct within the law, may not the public be wondering what has happened and why? How many are inquiring how such a state of affairs has come to pass in a country that has so liberally supported schools for the express purpose of insuring good citizenship?

Personally, of course, I do not place upon the American public school system primary responsibility for this crisis. But what shall we say in reply to those who charge the public schools with a share of the blame? . . .

One of the questions I want to ask you today is this: Does the habit of appraising the results of schools in terms of intellectual achievement and manual skill have anything or everything to do with our trouble?

To define clearly what I mean I want to make reference to two recent publications: First, the committee of the American Association of University Professors, in its report issued last May, stated that the purpose of college teaching is to " induce self-propelled intellectual activity on the part of the student." The second reference is to a report of the Commission on the Social Studies, entitled, " A Charter for the Social Sciences in the Schools," drafted by Charles A. Beard. This is intended to emphasize the value of scholarship and skill in scientific method as a primary dominating objective. This point of view is epitomized on the 99th page of the report, which I quote:

" All the way through the schools the process may be followed, *ever sharpening the mind* [the italics are mine] by increasing the complexity of the situations about which questions are asked and of the materials necessary to correct answers, rising steadily in the complexity and abstraction of the subjects considered."

The words " character," " conduct," " behavior," " attitude " and " emotions " do not appear in Beard's index. His discussion of character and the process of character building are limited to a few sentences in the closing pages of his 117-page " Charter." These two reports, financed by large foundations, seem to represent the point of view of orthodox leadership of our higher educational institutions.

Is it proper for me to ask: Have not educators tended to define the job of the schools in terms of developing tool skill and of mastering content? Have they not placed remarkable emphasis upon " sharpening the minds " of those who are to be the lawyers and the executives of the future, as well as the minds of the average run of us who pass through the school system?

Has not the habit of appraising the results of schools in terms of intellectual achievement and manual skill tended to produce a citizenry with sharpened wits and skilled craftsmanship, rather than a realizing sense of social obligation and good citizenship? Has not our attention been too sharply focused on mastery of the scientific method to the exclusion of the personal and social needs of the masses of our children?

Let me turn from this questioning process a moment to say this: Sometimes the scientist becomes so engrossed in what he sees in the microscope that he fails to lift his eye from the instrument to gaze upon the wide world about him. Other scientists may become so militant as regards their theories that they engage in wordy battle to worst their opponents. So many of these contests are going on at the same time that those of us who are onlookers are worn out in our efforts to see the whole show. Our brains no longer function as they should and we begin to suffer from a sort of creeping paralysis. In consequence, we become incapable of accurate estimate of the value of the theories proposed.

I have asked what I intended to be pointed questions regarding problems which to me as a layman are not being solved by the intelligentsia — and I use that word with perfect respect. But in all candor, I believe they are shooting over the target.

We must take society as it is. Our program of education must be suited to the requirements and capabilities of each boy and girl, according to individual need. In view of this self-evident truth, it may be fortunate that the many and no doubt brilliant suggestions of educational literature have met no more than languid and ephemeral intellectual acceptance. Far be it from me to criticize, but in humility of spirit I contend that there is something in education more vital than sharpening the mind.

12. Social Factors in Educational Reconstruction [12]

John Dewey and John L. Childs

Intellectual and practical reconstruction will be compelled to take account of the following factors in our society.

1. Society has become in fact corporate. Its interests and activi-

[12] From *The Educational Frontier*, William H. Kilpatrick (ed.), D. Appleton-Century Company, New York, 1933, pp. 68–70.

ties are so tied together that human beings have become dependent upon one another, for good or for harm, to an unprecedented degree. This is a statement of fact, whether the fact be welcomed or deplored. This interdependence is increasing, not lessening. It must be taken into account by education. We must not only educate individuals to live in a world where social conditions beyond the reach of any one individual's will affect his security, his work, his achievements, but we must (and for educational reasons) take account of the total incapacity of the doctrine of competitive individualism to work anything but harm in the state of interdependence in which we live.

2. Not merely the material welfare of the people, but the cultural and moral values, which are the express concern of the educational profession, demand a reorganization of the economic system, a reconstruction in which education has a great part to play.

3. The crucial problem is no longer one of stimulating production, but one of organization of distribution with reference to the function of consumption and use, so as to secure a stable basis of living for all, with provision against the hazards of occupation, old age, maternity, unemployment, etc., in order that an abundant cultural development for all may be a reality.

4. Strictly speaking, the idea of *laissez faire* has not been carried out for a long time. Monopolistic ownership of land and of values socially created, privileged control of the machinery of production and of the power given by control of financial credit, has created control by a class, namely, control over production, exchange, and distribution. Hence general and public repudiation of the doctrine of *laissez faire* in behalf of the principle and practice of general social control is necessary. Education has a responsibility for training individuals to share in this social control instead of merely equipping them with ability to make their private way in isolation and competition. The ability and the desire to think collectively, to engage in social planning conceived and conducted experimentally for the good of all, is a requirement of good citizenship under existing conditions. Educators can ignore it only at the risk of evasion and futility.

5. The interdependence spoken of has developed on a world-wide scale. Isolated and excessive nationalism renders international interdependence, now existing as a fact, a source of fear, suspicion, antagonism, potential war. In order that interdependence may become a benefit instead of a dread evil and possible world-wide catastrophe, educators must revise the conception of patriotism and good citizenship so that it will accord with the imperative demands of world-wide association and interaction.

6. We are in possession of a method of controlled experimental action which waits to be extended from limited and compartmentalized fields of operation and value to the wider social field. In the use of this method there lies the assurance not only of continued planning and inventive discovery, but also of continued reconstruction of experience and of outlook. The expanded and generalized use of this method signifies the possibility of a social order which is continuous by self-repairing, a society which does not wait for periodic breakdowns in order to amend its machinery and which therefore forestalls the breakdowns that are now as much parts of social activity as storms of nature are of the physical order.

13. EDUCATION NEEDS A NEW ORIENTATION [13]
Frederick S. Breed

It is a commonplace to remark that social conditions have vastly changed since the World War. We are living in a period of rapid social reconstruction. Old standards are being modified or discarded; old beliefs are being assailed or altogether cast aside. New beliefs and new standards are in the making, and nowhere is the resultant confusion more evident than in the moral life of the nation. Reports regarding recent increases in crime have become a matter of common knowledge and of deepest concern to law-enforcement agencies and to every thoughtful citizen.

An analysis of data presented in the federal census report shows that while prison commitments for drunkenness have markedly decreased since 1910, commitments for violations of the drug and liquor laws have noticeably increased. Most significant of all is the marked increase in commitments for such serious offenses as forgery, rape and homicide. The public impression is correct that in recent years there has been a rapid and alarming increase in several of the most dangerous types of immorality.

Although promising experiments have been initiated here and there and constructive measures have been attempted in certain localities, it can be truthfully said that the public schools have not yet really sensed this problem and have not yet seriously undertaken to meet it. In the face of new conditions and a threatening social situation, attributable no doubt in part to our neglect, we move along quite undisturbed in the ways of tradition and the past. If the increasing delinquencies of our people are due in part to sins of omission in the

[13] From "A Preface to Moral Training," *School and Society*, 32:273–274, August 30, 1930.

schools, it is time for educators to give serious thought to behavior problems.

The present deficiencies in moral education are due to a number of causes. In the first place, many teachers have a much too circumscribed conception of their function in relation to the behavior of youth. The limitation of their outlook is reflected in the meaning attached to such terms as " order," " discipline " and " control of behavior." As ordinarily interpreted and applied, these terms are stiff and sterile indeed. Their prominence in educational literature is no doubt explained by the fact that they express a prevailing attitude. They indicate a great absorption in intellectual training and a relative neglect of emotional and volitional training. They suggest that teachers are absorbed in developing ability in reading and arithmetic, algebra and physics, and regard discipline as satisfactory provided the behavior of the pupils is such as to permit the work in these subjects to progress. Control of behavior too commonly denotes that mastery of behavior by virtue of which achievement in school subjects is possible. Our educational system, however, is responsible not only for the development of intellectual traits, but also for the development of personal traits. Knowledge and skill are important for the welfare of the individual and the group; desirable ways of feeling and acting in social situations are just as important. The vital question is not, Does the boy's behavior meet the requirements of the class exercise? but rather, Does it meet the requirements of community life in America? A new orientation is necessary in which the problems of character training will be assigned a place of importance coordinate with those of intellectual training — coordinate with, not subordinate to. The schools exist for the training of thinking, feeling and acting — all three.

14. A Basic Task for Education [14]

George S. Counts

American education today, like American society at large, is in need of a conception of life suited to the new civilization. Most of the ideal terminology which students of education currently employ, if it is positive in quality, is the heritage from the earlier society. Since this terminology, however, is a product of a social order that has passed away, it ordinarily lacks both color and substance. Much is said in American educational circles today about

[14] From *The American Road to Culture*, The John Day Company, New York, 1930, pp. 193–194.

democracy, citizenship, and ethical character, but nowhere can be found bold and creative efforts to put real content into these terms. In a word, the educational and social implications of the machine culture have not been thought through. And until the leaders of educational thought in America go beyond the gathering of educational statistics and the prosecution of scientific inquiry, however valuable and necessary these undertakings may be, and grapple courageously with this task of analysis and synthesis, the system of education will lack direction and the theory of education will but reflect the drift of the social order.

15. Schools Must Provide a Broader Education [15]

Charles H. Judd

The United States has reached the point in its industrial organization where it is possible for the people of this country to develop a coöperative civilization based on intelligence which is far broader in its scope than any civilization that has heretofore been possible. There have been short periods in history when certain small groups of people have had the advantages of economies of plenty. The oligarchy of Athens flourished for a time. Back of the prosperity of the Athenian citizens, however, was the toil of the slaves, who were not admitted to any of the privileges of citizenship. The Italian cities grew rich through commerce and enjoyed a brief period of high culture, but they conferred the chief advantages of their culture on a small group of ruling aristocrats.

If the United States can find some way of equitably distributing the goods that it now produces in superabundance through its agriculture, mining, and manufacturing, it will be possible to create on this continent a civilization which will have the unique distinction of combining social opportunities of the highest type with democracy. The attainment of this goal depends not so much on material prosperity beyond that which has been achieved as on the cultivation of a new understanding of human relations. It is far more important for the future of this country that a way be found of raising the general level of intelligence than that the wealth of the nation be increased. Intellectual poverty is as unthinkable in an ideal state as are hunger and inadequate shelter.

If the American people are really entering, as they seem to be, on a period when there is to be no material poverty, if slums are to disappear, and if land areas which are unable to support profitable

[15] From *Education and Social Progress,* Harcourt Brace & Co., New York, 1934, pp. 265–268.

agriculture are to be abandoned by the people who are now struggling to gain a living by tilling these unpromising areas, it follows inevitably that the range and scope of education must be enlarged. When education is fully and properly organized, it will not be a means of equipping a few individuals to secure for themselves advantages which the majority of the people cannot enjoy; it will be the basis of a new political science and of a new economics. The profoundest students of the social order are beginning to teach that, unless all members of society prosper and are contented, the conditions of life can never be satisfactory even for those who have superior advantages. If the social implications of what is now being said by students of society are to be understood and are to be made the basis of a new organization of the general social order, schools will have to provide a broader education than they now give. They will have to deal in a comprehensive way with public relations and with the rights and obligations of individuals.

16. "THE PROBLEM OF THE FUTURE" [16]

George D. Strayer

Public education, organized to meet the needs of the past, has already assumed, in a halting way, many of the new responsibilities; but it will not play the vital rôle which modern society has assigned to it if it continues to advance slowly by trial and error and to lay a thin veneer of modernity upon an out-dated base. Aimless drifting has disorganized economic life. Public education must not float with the tide. We need a planned education. Whatever may be the changes made as to the mechanics of education, whatever may be the relative assignment of educational tasks to family, church, or school, these issues, important though they be, are minor compared with the problem of what public education is to attempt. It must prepare our people for the duties of citizenship. It must compensate for the injustices and unfairnesses of life. It must change itself fundamentally to attack the problems caused by the extended leisure, the unemployment, the quick tempo, the division of labor, the high standard of life, and the plenty economy of the Power Age.

But there is one problem which has not changed. For ages education has tried to make plain that there is a world of the flesh and a world of the spirit — one world where men are troubled and distressed by material things, another where they live content with

[16] From *Report of the Governor's Committee on the Costs of Public Education in the State of New York,* New York, 1933, pp. 13-14.

the best that has been thought and said; one where men are bound, another where they are free — and education unlocks the door which leads from one to the other. In the past, education of this kind has been the privilege of the few. With the rush to the schools and colleges and the tendency to stress the practical, there is danger that cultural education may not survive. Our hope is that New York may devise a plan which will guide the development of education to meet modern needs, and at the same time strengthen the best practices of the past. Confucius said " He who understands the old knowledge so as to appreciate the new, that man may become a teacher of others."

17. INDUSTRIALISM MAKES NECESSARY A NEW CURRICULUM [17]

Harold Rugg

Industrialism has transformed an individualistic order into a social one — and life in America has become compellingly coöperative. Since 1800 the peoples of the great industrial nations have been forced to adjust their modes of living to a most startling social transmutation. Communities and countries that were entirely isolated and self-sufficient have become almost completely interdependent. The peoples of the world are now so linked together that no nation can live to itself; no section lives to itself; no industry lives to itself; no person lives to himself — all are interdependent.

The evolution of the Great Mechanical Society, therefore, has raised the mechanism of understanding to a status of crucial significance. Words play a new and dictating rôle — in industry, in politics, in social life. Under industrialism goods are produced for deferred consumption; hence exchange is put upon a verbal basis. The reaches of contract have multiplied to undreamed-of ramifications. The agencies of communication — conspicuously the press and the radio — domineer over the group mind. The area of government has been stretched and politics has become a mushroom growth of hierarchical organization and confusion.

I say the current American scene, therefore, makes for the strategic position of the printed word and, correspondingly, of the school curriculum. Current conditions in America throw into sharp relief the critical need of teaching our youth to understand American life. America is attempting to carry on a great experiment in democratic government under the most hampering conditions: A heterogeneous congeries of people of less than eighth-grade education,

[17] From " A Preface to the Reconstruction of the American School Curriculum," *Teachers College Record*, 27:602–604, March, 1926.

sprawled over a huge continent of 70,000 communities, huddled (sixty millions of them) in towns and cities, existing on a bare living wage, engaged primarily in the quest for food, — many totally ignorant of and indifferent to their collective affairs.

It is especially important that our youth should develop clear comprehension of life in America because of the cleavages which dominate it. The whole continent is ablaze with the impact of groups; in this respect it merely reflects the contemporary order in other countries. Suspicion, misunderstanding, friction, pervade the social life of peoples in many parts of the earth. Successive decades of American political and economic history have been characterized by their realignments of countries, sections, and groups. The contemporary order reveals this same division of our people into cliques. They exhibit distressing cleavages; for example, that of proletarian worker and capitalist owner, of Protestant and Catholic; of producer and middleman; of black and white; of industrialist and farmer. Scores of races, nationalities, and cultures have been thrown into the melting pot of America, but the process of coalescing is thwarted. At the basis of each cleavage is lack of understanding.

The foregoing paragraphs . . . carry implications of grave import.

The American public schools confront curriculum problems that are little short of overwhelming in difficulty. Their task is no less than the creation of a generation of men and women, informed about and interested in the American drama, who tend to settle matters of controversy on the basis of reflection rather than prejudice. It is an industrial civilization which is incalculably difficult to comprehend. A candid review of the events of the past few years reveals the imperative necessity of attempting to help solve this tremendous problem. So, American life being what it is — complicated, difficult to understand, highly dynamic; the school constituted as it is — large classes, relatively uninformed teachers, early elimination of pupils, only one conclusion can be drawn. This is that the greatest hope for improvement in our generation lies in the construction of a curriculum which shall as fully as possible overcome the handicaps of the present school situation, and which shall lead the great body of pupils to an understanding and appreciation of the conditions and problems of our complex civilization.

CHAPTER II

THE SOCIAL RESPONSIBILITY OF THE SCHOOL

18. "Education an Expression of a Particular Geographical and Cultural Setting" [1]

Being a form of social action, education always has a geographical and cultural location; it is therefore specific, local, and dynamic, not general, universal, and unchanging; it is a function of a particular society at a particular time and place in history; it is rooted in some actual culture and expresses the philosophy and recognized needs of that culture. Contemporary American society of course is of vast proportions and manifests wide-reaching economic and cultural ramifications extending to the most distant parts of the world.

Although the basic biological equipment of man seems to be comparatively invariant and may therefore be expected to give certain common elements to education everywhere and at all times, human civilization has characteristics of neighborhood, region, nation, and more extended cultural areas, which lend unique qualities to every working educational program, however persistent and pervasive may be the universal elements entering into it.

19. Schools and National Ideals [2]

William F. Russell

An educational system is successful only when in all its aspects it contributes to the ends of the society in which it lives and has its being. All primitive tribes which survived found ways in which to change their boys and girls into adults completely adjusted to the environment of the tribe. Prussia a century ago devised an educational system which through two sets of schools turned out the leaders and followers that the Fatherland desired. Recent educational developments in Soviet Russia, Italy, and Bulgaria show that changes in national purpose are followed by corresponding changes in the school; not only in what is taught, how it is taught and the

---

[1] Commission on the Social Studies, American Historical Association, *Conclusions and Recommendations,* Charles Scribner's Sons, New York, 1934, pp. 31–32.

[2] From "School Administration and Conflicting American Ideals," *Teachers College Record,* 31:17–18, October, 1929.

spirit of instruction, but just as completely in teacher training and school administration. Every aspect of education must adjust itself to the national ideal.

This process of relating an educational program to a national end is neither simple to comprehend nor easy to put into practice. Education has momentum, teachers are traditional, and as a rule modifications are the result of efforts extended over a considerable period of time. The history of education does not tell the story of many sudden widespread school reforms. When they do come, they are found where the national ends are clear and distinct, accompanied by powerful governmental control.

In the United States educational changes have come very slowly. At the time of the formation of the Constitution, our educational system was an importation from England and Scotland, with sporadic primary classes, occasional academies and secondary schools, and a few colleges, practically all under the control of churches and other voluntary agencies. From this beginning a century and a half of effort has brought us to our present state of development. This advance has been almost entirely toward the realization of the ideals for which our country was founded.

20. Schools Must Clarify Social Ideals [3]

Boyd H. Bode

The social order of which we dream will be an order that is concerned primarily with the development of capacity or personality; which is only another way of saying that all our institutions will be judged, in the first instance, by an educational test. We can talk about such a social order, but we can scarcely visualize it in advance. Nor is it easy to sketch beforehand the change in outlook, in attitude, in our intellectual and emotional responses that must take place if equality of opportunity, the full development of personality, is to become, in truth, our final criterion of value. It would mean the development of motivations which, in our present competitive and commercialized conditions of industry, remain submerged. It would mean a revision of the whole mass of biological, psychological, ethical, and theological notions which at present block the way.

It's a long, long trail a-winding, into the land of our dreams. Moreover, it is quite within the bounds of possibility that when we catch a clearer view of this distant scene we shall cease to be at-

[3] National Education Association, *Our Educational Frontier*, Department of Superintendence, Official Report, Washington, D. C., 1933, pp. 57–58.

tracted by it. We may, in the end, prefer to retain the old familiar beliefs and to surrender the dream of equality of opportunity, as surely a dream of our youth. But in any case, the time has come to reexamine our tradition. We cannot afford to continue on the old basis of makeshift and confusion of purposes. The dangers threatening our civilization are too real and too imminent. There is ample basis for the faith that as the implications of our belief in equality of opportunity are more clearly understood, the idealism of the American people will rise to new levels of achievement. At present, however, this idealism is inhibited and paralyzed because there is no clarity of vision. As the prophet said of old: " My people are destroyed for lack of knowledge."

How is this clarity of vision to be achieved? At this point our thoughts turn naturally to the schools. As a people we are confused regarding our basic aims and purposes; we are confused regarding the meaning of our national tradition. This is only another way of saying that we fail to read the record of human civilization in the light of our tradition. When we review the achievements of the past in the field of the physical sciences, in biology, in industry, in government, and in the domain of art, for the express purpose of tracing the bearing of these achievements on freedom and equality of opportunity, the whole perspective changes. When we see how every important advance also created new obstacles to further progress; how truth and falsehood were intermingled; how old obstacles have not been completely removed but persist into the present; it soon becomes apparent to us that we have not thought the matter thru. We can become intelligent concerning our national tradition only by gaining an understanding of the issues and conflicts that are involved in it. These issues and conflicts extend to every important domain of life. To bring them into the open is the inescapable obligation of the schools. The schools can no longer be content to transmit the cultural achievements of the past. They must open up a new frontier. This involves a reorganization of our educational system, which, in its difficulties and perplexities, is almost as appalling an undertaking as the reorganization of the social structure itself. . . .

21. " EDUCATION FOR DEMOCRACY " [4]

J. W. Studebaker

In those foreign countries where democracy is most virile, and the possibility of success for dictatorship is most remote — countries like Sweden and Denmark — the educational base is both

[4] *The Nation's Schools,* 17:23–24, March, 1936.

broad and vital. This education is not merely vocational or cultural. It is concerned with "the pursuit of happiness" through democratic processes. Such educational programs are founded upon the proposition that democratic action must come from mass understanding of the problems the people face as citizens.

When a country has moved from democracy into dictatorship, there has been no such broad educational base for democracy as we find in Sweden today. Dictators are realistic and quick to understand how vital it is to control the educational process in the interest of a given social organization. They want obedience, unquestioning respect for their authority, ignorance of ideas contrary to their own and uniform agreement with their policies. They use the educational system to indoctrinate youth with their ideas and to train up faithful followers.

INDOCTRINATION BEGINS

More important than terror and violence is the control of the means of communication and even of the details of the educational process. Teachers and professors who cannot be persuaded to indoctrinate in accordance with the desires of the dictatorship, are summarily removed and the most trusted disciples of the régime are given the responsibility of managing education.

Whatever else may be said of modern dictators, it must be conceded that they see clearly the relation of education to social organization. They have with all haste and thoroughness organized education to make a major contribution to the authoritarian state. They have organized education on the assumption that the dictator should direct the "pursuit of happiness" and that the people should be trained to follow his directions.

The assumption in democracy is that the people shall be free to direct the "pursuit of happiness" for themselves. Democracy, more than any other form of social organization, requires a mass educational system for its perpetuation and an educational process which fits the social organization and contributes to its stability and growth. Here, I think, we must make a careful distinction between education for democracy and education under dictatorship.

FATAL TO DEMOCRACY

While the technique of planned and persistent indoctrination is a good one for the social organization of dictatorship, its widespread use is fatal to democracy for the point of view to be indoctrinated is certified by the leaders of the totalitarian state. The object of indoctrination in this case is to induce people to hold the prescribed opinions and thus become satisfactory citizens.

When the process of indoctrination is applied in a democracy, it has no legitimate point of reference in the social organization itself. Its point of reference must be some faction within the democratic social organization. That is to say, the system of education becomes the propaganda agency of some faction. When this happens, education becomes the enemy of that society and contributes to its early dissolution.

The social organization we call democracy is based upon two important principles. First, that the majority shall determine the policy with respect to any given issue at any given time; second, that the right of the minority to attempt to become the majority through the use of free speech, free press and free assemblage shall be assured.

The educational system cannot be used to indoctrinate the learners with respect to the social, economic and political issues upon which there is a difference of opinion, without either violating the democratic rights of the minority by acting as the instrument of a majority faction, or violating the rights of the majority by acting as the propaganda agency of a minority faction. If public education is used as an instrument of indoctrination, the dominant factions in our society will dictate the process.

ORGANIZING FOR SELF-GOVERNMENT

Organized education must have a point of reference. Ours is democratic self-government. I think we should analyze our educational process critically and frequently to see whether it is actually functioning efficiently as a bulwark of democracy. This is more important to my mind than our more usual inquiries concerning overcrowded classrooms, efficient budget organization, and many other problems of school management, none of which should be neglected.

I am contending for an educational technique that actually prepares and assists people, not only as children and adolescents but as adults; to function effectively in democracy. It has little to do with the " pep rally." It places no particular emphasis on constantly arguing the theoretical merits of democracy over any other form of government.

It is a technique that starts in the kindergarten and is applied in all learning processes through middle life. There is no particular formula by which it may be put down in a sentence or two. Rather it is characterized best by the philosophy of democracy that gave it birth. It is described partly by the term " scientific approach " and partly by the term " discussion method." It induces critical inquiry and the habit of validating conclusions. . . .

22. "SHOULD THE SCHOOL SEEK ACTIVELY TO RECONSTRUCT SOCIETY?" [5]

John L. Childs

Society organizes and maintains schools because it deems it necessary that specialized attention be given to the process by which the young are introduced into its manner of life. The school is thus doubly social in nature. As an institution, the school is society organized for action along a certain line, namely, the education of the young. But the school is social in another and more fundamental respect. The very materials which supply the substance of the school's program are also derived from the life of society. The group ways both of action and of thought are the ultimate sources from which the aims of the school and the content of its curriculum are drawn.

Again, although we frequently speak of society as the agency which organizes schools, actually there is no such thing as a society existing in general. The concrete reality with which the school has to do is necessarily some particular society existing at a definite time and place. Increasingly in the modern world these different societies take the form of nation-states. While these various national societies have their common characteristics, each of them also has its own unique cultural features. Today the program of the school necessarily relates to the wider life of the particular national society taken in its world relations, in which the school is organically contained. Apart from this social reference, the work of the school would literally have no orientation.

REFERENCE TO SOCIAL EVENTS INEVITABLE

The issue, therefore, is not whether the program of the American school should relate to the affairs of American society. For the school to attempt to withdraw from these social affairs would be to withdraw from the only source from which the materials of education can be obtained. Thus the *real* issue is, In what manner is the American educator to make this reference to his society? Is it to be made in a hidden manner, possibly half unconsciously, or is it to be made openly and with frank acceptance of responsibility for what is done? Are convention, habit, and immediate pressures to control the approach of the school to society, or is the reference to be made through a process of careful social analysis and reflective evaluation

[5] *American Academy of Political and Social Science, Annals,* 182:1–9, November, 1935.

of actual social conditions and trends? The inescapable fact is that in some manner or other, the reference will be made to contemporary social life. He who demands that educators stick to their last, the school, and leave current social problems severely alone, is asking in reality that they omit the conscious exercise of intelligence from their educational function.

Equally untenable is the position of those who affirm that the school is a social agency and that education is a social function, yet who protest in alarm as soon as any educator attempts to deal with concrete social problems. Education can gain vitality only as it deals with the specific affairs of modern technological, scientific, economic, political, family, and religious life. The young whose lives are to be lived in the society that is now in process of formation have a right to demand that the school which seeks to educate them shall be oriented primarily to that which lies ahead, rather than to a culture which is in process of disintegration and disappearance.

But today the intelligent construction of a school program involves more than the mere conscious recognition that educational aims and curriculum materials can have pertinence only as they relate to contemporary society. In contrast to earlier societies, modern industrial societies are exceedingly complex and include many diverse interest groups and cultural patterns. Even a single national society such as the United States is composed of many sub-groups. To be sure, the members of these various groups have many things in common, but they also have their specialized activities, interests, and loyalties. Often the special interests of one group are in serious conflict of those of another.

Moreover, much as we may deplore the fact, it is also apparent that the lines between different economic classes are becoming more sharply drawn. No generalization about American society which takes account of this conflict of interests between these economic classes can be so misleading as one which assumes that we live in an essentially classless society, in which the equality of opportunity characteristic of our earlier agrarian period still obtains.

CULTURAL SELECTION

Industrial societies are also highly dynamic, and the rate of social change is much more rapid than was formerly the case. In this complex and rapidly changing American society, the act of cultural selection involved in education becomes fundamentally important. Nothing could be more confusing to the young than that the school should seek to include impartially within its program all our different patterns of life and thought. Actually no school could succeed in doing this, even if it were fatuous enough to suppose that such a miscellaneous representation of American life constituted a desirable education.

Moreover, society expects the school to serve as an agency of cultural selection. Were the adults of any given society equally friendly to all possible outcomes, they would never bother to organize schools in order to control the process by which the young are introduced into the group ways. Hence, all intentional education is a moral undertaking; moral in the sense that it involves working for one set of social ends and a definite type of personal character as opposed to others, in a situation in which genuine alternatives are present.

Cultural selection is therefore inherent in all deliberate education. To propose a completely socially neutral school is to propose a contradiction. Schools are organized in order deliberately to weigh educational procedures and outcomes. One of the reasons why modern society makes such unprecedented investments in school education is because it is not willing to trust the education of its young to mere haphazard interactions with all its existing ways of thought and action.

Many educators have been much more willing to accept the foregoing social interpretation of the work of the school than they have been to accept the corollary that the school functions as an agency of cultural selection. At least four current interpretations of education seek to avoid the heavy social responsibility included in this latter undertaking.

EDUCATION AS AN EXACT SOCIAL SCIENCE

Of these four, the one which has enjoyed greatest prestige is the movement to make an exact science of the construction of educational policies. The leaders of this movement have perceived that the task of building a school program is a serious social undertaking. They have also discerned that ultimately the materials for the program of the school must be taken from society. They have recognized that unless this cultural selection inherent in the making of a curriculum is to be a purely personal, arbitrary affair, it must be based on a solid foundation of fact and understanding of society. They have insisted, therefore, that the one thing needful for the adequate determination of educational aims and processes is the patient, thorough, objective accumulation of social data.

What this movement to transform education into a completely objective science has failed to apprehend is that no amount of knowledge about *what now is* in existence can in and of itself determine *what should be*. But the construction of educational programs involves exactly this transition from what *is* to what *ought to be*. As Professor Cohen has indicated in *Reason and Nature,* no matter how much we elaborate premises which confine themselves to descriptions of *what is,* we can never deduce one solitary *ought to be* from such premises. A growing number of educators are beginning to recognize that, important as have been the contributions of this movement to make education an exact social science, it suffers from this radical defect. What has actually afforded the norms for education controlled by this scientific fact-finding technique has been nothing other than the established conventions of society. Now that we are entering upon a period of social transition, when it is apparent that many of those traditional arrangements are no longer adequate, the weakness of exclusive reliance upon the scientific procedure is glaringly apparent.

It is of course highly important that choices among life values should be conditioned by thorough knowledge of social conditions and trends, but experience unfortunately demonstrates that individuals and groups confronted with the same social data will often draw very contrary conclusions from these data. Human *interests* and *values,* as well as *facts,* are of the stuff of which socio-educational policies are made. Fact-gathering can make the cultural choices of educators more intelligent, but it can never relieve educators of responsibility for making these choices.

EMPHASIS ON THE INDIVIDUAL CHILD

Nor have educators found any more satisfactory escape from this difficult task of making cultural judgments and choices in another movement, which has sought to center the school around the individual child. Here, again, an important contribution has been made to educational thought and practice. No social fact is more scientifically established than that of individual differences. Individuals do vary markedly from one another in capacity, aptitudes, interests, and purposes. These individual differences, both native and acquired, have the largest significance for the work of the school. It is highly important that an educational program should respect the uniqueness of each child, and that it should be managed in such a manner as to develop his initiative and independence. Nor are these factors purely formal affairs. They rule out many types of classroom procedure, and they call for certain positive school arrangements.

But it is equally true that the norms for education cannot be exclusively derived from the uniqueness and the interests of the child. As far as the inherited native equipment is concerned, it is almost indefinitely plastic in a normal child, and can be patterned into a wide variety of possible adult selves. Which of these potential adult selves will become actual depends not only upon the organic equipment but also upon what we see in society in the form of limitations, possibilities, demands, and values. So also for the interests of the child. These interests do not develop by a process of the mere unfolding of an inborn psychological latency. They are just as surely a product of the materials and activities afforded by the environment of the child as they are of his organic individuality. What emotional, intellectual, æsthetic, and moral dispositions, interests, and allegiances are to be nurtured in the child are determined by the conception of social welfare which we as adults possess. This conception of social welfare will, in turn, be conditioned by what we prize in contemporary American culture.

No one who has grasped the educational and ethical significance of individual differences can ever be indifferent to all that they imply for educational activity, but he will not and cannot make interest in the welfare of the child a substitute for social understanding and cultural selection. On the contrary, respect for the welfare of the individual child deepens the educational obligation to be socially intelligent.

CONSERVATION OF PRESENT SYSTEM

A third group of educators accept all that has been said about the social nature of education, about the fact that education rests ultimately upon a conception of social welfare, about the futility of the attempt to develop education into an exact social science, and about the fact that respect for the uniqueness and interests of the individual child in no way relieves those in charge of the school of responsibility for adult guidance and socio-educational control. But while accepting all this, they nevertheless consider it utopian and dangerous for the educator as educator to attempt to choose between competing interest groups and rival cultural patterns. The legislature and other adult institutions are held to be the agencies for achieving social change, and it is folly to expect that the school created by society in order to transmit its values to the young can serve as an agency for the reconstruction of that society.

According to this group, the school is essentially a conserving agency in society, and it must educate in terms of the values and practices now commonly approved, not in terms of some imaginative projection of a more ideal social system. Even some social radicals, particularly communists, as well as many social conservatives, are found among those who adopt this view of the social function of the school.

Undoubtedly there is an element of truth in this position. As has been emphasized repeatedly in this article, society does establish schools in order to induct the young into its mode of life. These schools are agents of the society which creates them, and are subject to all the limitations of agents. If the good will of society be deliberately withdrawn from the school, it is difficult to see how the school can continue to function.

But does the fact that the school is an agent of society automatically preclude it from serving as an agency for social reconstruction? A growing number of educators do not believe this to be the case. In the first place, to say that the school is the agent of society is not equivalent to saying that it is the agent of the state, to say nothing of its being the mere mouthpiece for the particular group which happens to constitute the government at any given time. According to historic American doctrine, the government is held to derive its powers from the consent of the governed, and is to be altered or abolished when either the form or the manner of government is no longer acceptable to the majority of those who live under it. It is fascist, not American, political theory which identifies the will of society with the will of the government, and which gives power to the government to dictate what the members of a society shall think and say. In fact, the right of criticism is fundamental to the democratic social theory. This of course does not establish the fact that the school is one of the agencies which has the right to engage in the function of social criticism, but it at least disposes of the notion that it must teach only that which the political rulers find favorable to their interests.

Moreover, even if it be admitted that the exclusive purpose of the school is to introduce the young to the values already established in American society, it by no means follows that the school should refrain from social criticism. Many would affirm that one of the most characteristic and cherished values of our democratic society is the right of criticism. It would be a strange educational procedure, indeed, which asked the teacher to communicate to the young a living appreciation of the historic American values of freedom of expression and criticism, and which at the same time commanded the teacher to serve as the mere spokesman for the ideas of others.

Finally, the outstanding characteristic of the present situation is that many of our traditional beliefs and practices are no longer consonant with emerging life conditions. Not only is this so, but under the impact of changed economic conditions, some of the most basic American values are no longer compatible with one another. To illustrate: the doctrine of laissez faire is an anachronism in a society made so largely interdependent by our machine technology; and the historic principle of equality of opportunity is obviously no longer compatible with adherence to the equally historic doctrine of economic individualism. To ask the educator to transmit all these traditional American doctrines to the young, regardless of how well they conform to changed social conditions, and without concern for the extent to which they contradict and nullify one another, is to ask the educator to sacrifice his own intellectual and moral integrity. It is not at all clear that this is a demand that the vast majority of the American people desire to make of those in charge of the school.

The attempt to stand faithfully by the traditional positions can no longer be construed to be a socially neutral position. The forces back of the present drive for "constitutionalism" are seeking to advance the interests of a small fraction of the population. The educator who wittingly or unwittingly serves as the agent of this powerful property group is not only taking sides in a social conflict; he is also using his position for the benefit of the few at the expense of the many. Nor can it be said that those who have launched this movement to preserve the Constitution are interested in preserving all the historic American values. The ease with which they support repressive measures which aim to destroy basic American liberties is further illustration of the fact that important cultural choices are inherent even in the social movements which pretend to be devoted to the good old ways of the past.

In sum, for the educator to endeavor to stand by all the historic American values results either in futility or, more probably, in active alignment with some of the most reactionary and predatory groups in American life.

IMPARTIAL PRESENTATION OF ALTERNATIVES

Of the several educational movements which seek to find a way in which the school can serve as a positive social force and still maintain its social neutrality, possibly the most popular at the present time is that which interprets education to be primarily a process of social analysis and criticism. The leaders of this group recognize that if the school were to limit its activity to the noncontroversial areas, it would have to omit from its program much that is most educationally significant in present American life. They also believe that the public will support the school in its effort to deal with controversial social topics if the school is careful to take a nonpartisan position, merely striving to present impartially the various proposals for dealing with the confronting socio-economic situation.

According to this interpretation, the leaders of the school should be sensitive to the problem-situations in contemporary American life, they should analyze the factors involved in these situations, and they should make a scrupulously fair exposition of the various proposals for dealing with them, leaving it to the individual pupil to make his own evaluations. It is argued that this is not merely the only defensible social policy for the school to adopt, but that it also meets the highest educational standards; because any effort on the part of the educator to bias the thinking of his pupils — to dispose them to accept one conclusion rather than another — is unethical in that it fails to respect the intellectual processes of the young. The school, it is said, is interested in *process*, not in *product;* in teaching the child *how to think*, not in telling him *what to think*. The aim of the school should not be to make disciples for this or that social program, but to develop critical-minded persons, skilled in the techniques of social analysis and able to reach reliable conclusions on the basis of evidence.

Many would call this interpretation of the function of the school the educational counterpart of the liberal, democratic political and social movement. Some of the most eminent figures in American education are champions of this conception of the social rôle of the school.

That this interpretation has in it elements of great value must be admitted by any candid observer. It appropriates much that was best in the movement to center the school around the individual child. It has the same high ethical regard for the individuality of the child, and for his right to become a thinking person equipped to manage his own affairs. It believes that an adequate interpretation of respect for the personality of the child should include respect for his mind. It also is founded on a sound educational psychology which holds that we learn that which we practice, and that if we are to learn how to think about tangled social problems, we must be given freedom during our youth to engage in thought about actual social conditions. The writer finds much in this program which he not only accepts, but which he considers indispensable in any educational program which is to meet the ethical tests of democratic procedures. The question under consideration, however, is not how much is valid in this interpretation of the work of the school, but rather, is it an adequate interpretation? Here, again, grave doubts arise.

BASIS OF CRITICISM

In the first place, the foregoing is not considered to be an adequate interpretation of the school program because it does not state all that is actually involved in the process by which the young are educated. Strive as we may, we can never reduce education to a bare process of criticism. This, for the simple reason that criticism, in order to be significant, involves the use of standards, ethical judgments, and social values. Ultimately, criticism must rest on something other than criticism.

To illustrate: Two proposals are now before us for national adjustment to the ways of modern industrial life. Both proposals are realistic enough to recognize that a functioning economic equilibrium cannot be maintained in our present closely integrated, interdependent society by the mere unregulated exchange of goods and services on the open market. In other words, both recognize that the social policy of laissez faire is dead, and that some form of authoritative, planned control must be introduced into our economy. One of these proposals, concerned to maintain existing property arrangements, proceeds in the direction of the limitation of output to that which the American people can purchase under the present unequal distribution of the national income. The other suggests that property arrangements be changed, and that production be controlled not in terms of present capacity to buy, but in terms of what our people need, and what our agricultural and industrial plant can produce.

How are we to choose between these two proposals? Obviously, our choice will be determined by that which we value. If we value most present property arrangements, we shall proceed to limit output; if we value most the scientific administration of our production processes in terms of the good life for all, we shall modify those property arrangements which obstruct the maximum utilization of our material and technological resources.

Should the school leave the young neutral before these alternatives? Actually, no existing school does leave its pupils wholly indifferent to these rival social schemes. Even though it does nothing directly to influence their thought on a social problem of this sort, its total influence will incline them in one direction or the other.

Many educators believe that in a democratic society they should seek actively to nurture in the young the emotional and intellectual dispositions which will prompt them to put the welfare of the many above the privileges of the few. They manage their school situations so as to inculcate attitudes of this type. In doing this they recognize that they are using the school as a positive agency to bias the young in favor of the ethical values of social democracy. This is going beyond mere intellectual criticism. It is building the background of values and beliefs out of which the process of criticism is to operate.

Were their right to develop a definite social bias of this sort in the lives of the young to be challenged, these educators are fully prepared to refer the issue to the rank and file of the members of American society. Nor are they uneasy about the outcome of such a national referendum. They are not willing, however, that a few blinded by selfish privilege or by the unreflective acceptance of traditional economic individualism should dictate what the school is to teach on these matters. In their opinion, it is a form of self-deception to suppose that a decision on a national problem of this sort can ever be attained by a pure process of intellectual criticism which does not touch the underlying question of property and human values.

DETERMINATION OF SOCIAL SIGNIFICANCE

This conception of the social function of the school is judged inadequate, in the second place, because it fails to recognize that social problems do not automatically define themselves. Indeed, it might be argued that the heart of the present difficulty resides in the failure of the American people to sense the nature of the real problem which now confronts them. In any case, what we take to be a social problem worthy of serious study will be conditioned by our social frame of reference.

To make concrete what is here implied, it is only necessary to call attention to the fact that few if any of the American schools believe that the question of whether or no American society is a class-structured society is a social problem worthy of investigation. There are those thoroughly intelligent about American social conditions, however, who believe that the conflict of interests between these various economic classes is our most crucial national problem. Here, again, our social outlook controls our educational procedure. The areas of social strain to which we are sensitive depend upon the social frame out of which we as educators work.

A DEFENSE OF THE *Status Quo*

Finally, this conception of education is declared inadequate because it also becomes in reality a defense of the *status quo*. In spite of all that is said about social neutrality, the school controlled by this conception of its social function is not actually socially neutral. As long as the school is content merely to make an exposition of various social alternatives and to commit itself to the advocacy of no positive social policies, it tends to throw its support on the side of the arrangements and groups which are now intrenched in power. One indication that this is the case may be derived from the fact that in recent years many educators who heretofore have had little interest in either social reform or the freedom of the school to criticize social practices have, under the stimulus of present developments, become ardent defenders of this policy of making the school a neutral forum in which all views are presented without constructive interpretation by the teachers.

SOCIAL OBLIGATION OF THE EDUCATOR

After all, to give a phonographic report of different social programs does not constitute a very serious social or intellectual undertaking. Any socio-educational analysis which fails to give a definite emphasis is essentially a contradiction of terms, for intellectual *analysis* in any significant sense involves *emphasis*. Nor is it universally true that for a teacher to carry an exposition through to a conclusion inhibits the intellectual activity of pupils. Under certain conditions it may have this effect; under others it may provide indispensable intellectual stimulus.

In the physical sciences it is not considered a violation of either intellectual or educational procedure for the instructor to point to the conclusions that scientists draw from accumulated data and experiments. In fact, the building up of a body of scientific generalizations — conclusions — is the indispensable pre-condition for an individual who is to reach the level of critical or creative thought in any given field. Why is it considered so reprehensible, then, for the educator in the social field to give conclusions based on his investigations, provided he carries his pupils through a survey of the data which have led him to his conclusion, and openly indicates the values which prompt him to take the position he does? Are the materials of the social sciences so different from those of the natural sciences that we fear that an analogous procedure would destroy the intellectual independence of the young? Or is the reluctance to have teachers give positive social leads due to the fear that certain powerful minority groups may be offended thereby?

Finally, these various social proposals do not all possess equal social validity. Some of them fail to take due account of important new characteristics of industrial society — the compulsions, the limitations, the resources, and the new possibilities which are inherent in the power-economy. Others fail to take account of the democratic ideals and aspirations of the American people. Why, then, is the educator who is supposed to have respect for intelligence and for the democratic meanings of American society obliged to bow in humble deference before all these varied social proposals?

The implication of the foregoing is not that the educator should draw the blueprints of the new society and take advantage of his position to impose them upon the young. The difficulties of the social situation, and the requirements of his educational office, both alike preclude this type of procedure. It does mean, however, that the educator should frankly recognize that all educational programs rest, in the last analysis, upon a set of social presuppositions. It also implies quite definitely that he should recognize that American life has entered upon a period of social transition; that it is within the framework of the collective life-conditions which the machine has built that for better or worse we must work out our destiny; and that this interdependent society, with its potential economy of abundance, calls for the supplanting of many of our historic social presuppositions with a new set of social principles more consonant with emerging life-patterns; in fine, that in a period when the basic postulates of American society are undergoing change, the American school needs a new social orientation. During this period of social transformation, one of the most important obligations for the educator is to become intelligent about these new conditions and about the ideal aspirations of the American people, so that the school may do its share in helping the young to adjust to that which lies ahead.

23. Positions That May Be Taken in Educational Planning [6]

William H. Kilpatrick

. . . With the growth of science, philosophy escaped from theology and becomes now increasingly critical even of goals. Science has brought technology and this greatly changes the modern world. Now at last even the common man, partly from science, partly from social changes, partly from economic turmoil, is learning to criticize the fundamental structure of his culture. Criticism of the culture is even now in process of becoming a recognized part of the culture itself. It is in this region that our problem lies.

We can now the better understand our present need with its resulting dilemma. Technological developments introduce social changes which call in question our old system of life and thought. Further changes seem demanded. We must introduce better order. Intelligence is our only reliable hope of dealing with this situation. We must apply constructive criticism.

Intelligence, as we have seen, is socially built through cultural accumulation. Moreover, intelligence, as psychology teaches us, is relatively specific. To learn to deal with social change we must study social change itself and this at least partly while the change is in process. A changing civilization must then provide the means for building the social intelligence needed to deal with the fact of

    [6] From "Public Education as a Force for Social Improvement," *School and Society*, 41:523–527, April 20, 1935.

change. Else it is doomed either to ignorant blunders or perhaps to angry violence. We must provide for the wide-spread and popular study of social changes.

And thus results our present dilemma. Changes already in effect demand significant changes in goals and beliefs; but deep-rooted cultural conservatism opposes any adequate proposals for social reconstruction. This is partly mere cultural conservatism, the result of cultural indoctrination, and partly the self-protective efforts of selfish vested interests. Our essential problem is then psychological and educational: How can a nation which does not yet believe in needed changes bring itself to accept the idea, and find and make the changes demanded by the situation? The problem becomes the more difficult because the existing economic system (under which we must meanwhile live) by its very operation educates against the cooperative attitudes and habits that seem indubitably needed for the new state of affairs.

Let us now take up in order the criticism of certain typical proposals as to what the school should do.

(1) The school must be suspicious of social innovation, must indeed throw its weight against change.

This position was well stated by the Lusk Committee of New York in 1920: " No person who is not eager to combat the theories of social change should be entrusted with the task of fitting the young and old of this state for the responsibilities of citizenship."

Such sentiments are common to many groups who profess to speak in the name of patriotism. Admiral Plunkett used these words: " We have got the greatest Government on the top of God's green earth, conceived by our Maker and transmitted to George Washington." H. F. Atwood, author of " Keep God in American History " and the originator of the oratorical contests on the Constitution, said: " The writing and adoption of our Constitution was unquestionably the greatest and most important human achievement since the Creation and as an event it ranks second in history only to the birth of Christ."

A variety of motives group themselves under this general wish to keep the school unspotted from social innovation. There is an antiquarian interest in maintaining patriotic myths, holding naively and often erroneously to the letter of our revolutionary heritage as opposed to its spirit. There is a chauvinistic slant on patriotism. There is the conservative, not to say reactionary attitude toward the *status quo* as maintaining vested interests.

Underlying this general position we can distinguish certain fundamental conceptions:

(i) A denial of any significant place to change in human affairs;

(ii) The acceptance of the logic of black *vs.* white distinctions. Both of these are pre-scientific and anti-modern conceptions, usually now coupled with a general willingness not to think.

(iii) There is also a further but less well-defined belief that teaching is properly a handing down of fixed beliefs and attitudes, that is, that all teaching is essential indoctrination. These people do not conceive a modern type school.

(2) The school must teach the socially accepted culture, not try to be a factor in changing it. This position is respectably held and demands serious consideration. We must admit that historically the school has existed to teach the established culture. However, because the school has hitherto so acted, is no sufficient argument that it must forever do so. On such a theory, no existing institution would ever take on new functions, and no new institution would ever come into existence. Clearly the factor of change is not only not taken into account, but is by implication denied.

This position likewise assumes that teaching is primarily a handing down of fixed content. There is no apparent appreciation of the give-and-take of study and discussion leading to ever better independent judging such as is sought in the best modern schools.

This position assumes an accepted culture so clearly defined that the school knows what to hand down. But in a changing civilization the culture must always be in process of change. Some things are going out, while others are coming in. So again, and more clearly, the fact of change is disregarded. The school is to act as if change did not exist.

If the school is to hand down beliefs, etc., it must either itself choose what to teach or be so told from the outside. For the school to decide what to teach would be a denial of this position. If the state is to tell, we discuss that next. If not the state, the source is usually custom, the *status quo*. And this, I believe, defines this position: It means in effect to uphold the *status quo* with its privileges and injustices.

If on this theory any intelligent attempt were made to hand down a dynamic and changing culture, it would destroy this position. The fact of contemporary change would have to be noted, and the proper treatment of it discussed. But this is no longer mere handing down. Intelligently done, this would be preparation for better change. The position thus is self-consistent only on a theory of no change.

(3) The school is the agent of the state, it must therefore teach as the state directs. To do less is dereliction of duty, to do more is malfeasance.

The objections to this position appear weighty and conclusive. In so far as the state would act on this theory, it would fix and hand down an official orthodoxy. For higher education, this would destroy the conception of research and inquiry. Academic freedom would go. This position would in so far bring the totalitarian state to America. For elementary and secondary education, there would be no academic freedom, no genuine discussion of controversial issue, no conception of creative study wherever the orthodoxy had spoken. Teaching would be execution of orders, supervision would be inspection to enforce orders. Initiative, creation, experiment — except within orthodox bounds — would be denied. Such a position seems an almost total denial of all the democratic and humane trends of modern life and education. It seems to ascribe omniscience to state house officials, leaving only docile obedience to the rest of us.

This position either denies significance to the factor of change or denies to education any intentional part in making change more intelligent. There seems in it no acceptance of the need to base the state and society on the fact of continuing change.

In opposition to such a position I should wish to maintain that the state schools from the bottom up have as a chief function the bringing up of youth into a citizenship able and disposed to bring intelligence to bear upon public problems — in fact, to help create an ever higher and finer social intelligence to control and direct social change. And this is impossible unless the idea permeates the school through and through from top to bottom. And the idea will not be realized unless there is genuine discussion of controversial issues, with increasing development of personal responsibility to share in bringing about the changes that intelligent study approves.

(4) In marked contrast with the foregoing is the extreme European-bred revolutionary position, namely, that the class war is inherent and inevitable, and, being war, all available means are justifiable, including violence and deceit; victory is predestined to the workers, the owners, clinging to their privileges, will so resist as to force their own violent overthrow; for this the general strike is the all-sufficient means; meanwhile right-thinking people will drill all workers and available youth in strike tactics.

I will not comment on this further than to say that to me such a position seems for this country false and wrong in almost every detail: the class conception does not fit, nor the class war; nor is any one outcome fated; always also must means be chosen with due regard to consequences; our democratic tradition of discussion and voting seems far more promising of good results; to condition youth to any fix-in-advance and undebatable position is abhorrent.

(5) Quite antithetical to the two immediately preceding positions is one which holds that the teaching profession must accept responsibility for building up an intelligent citizenship, and do this by

having pupils study as fully and impartially as possible the various sides of the current controversial issues. The school and the teacher, however, are to take pains to remain neutral as between the opposed sides.

There is so much here in keeping with our historical traditions that we must examine it at length. It accepts the fact and factor of change and proposes a way of caring for it. The way provided lies commendably along the line of building vital social intelligence in the learners by study into the merits of current controversial questions. The hope is that this will build up youth for subsequent intelligent self-direction. Also the teacher commendably takes the part not of conditioner to prior chosen positions, but as helper to more intelligent thinking.

These things seem so far good, but there are counter considerations.

Will the kind of teacher we wish be able and content to remain neutral? If he is in fact neutral in his own mind, what kind of study has he done? Is not something lacking in the working of his mind? Is one who can not make up his mind or does not reach some pertinent convictions the kind of person we wish to put in charge of our classes? For myself, I have to answer these questions in the negative. I can not conceive how a good leader of youth can be the kind of person to study and not conclude. But suppose the teacher does have honest and growing convictions, can he as a rule so teach as really to conceal his convictions? Again for myself, I have to say no. I believe the effort would so often fail that to pretend to follow it would be a sham; and therefore, like all shams, hurtful.

We seem therefore forced to say that we can not make a program of neutrality work and should not try. For myself, I wish every teacher to have convictions. These should not be so fixed that he can not and will not be sensitive to the possibilities of reexamining them upon proper evidence. We must then somehow build our teaching program on honesty of avowal. Just how to do this, we shall later consider.

(6) A position somewhat like the foregoing is that we should recognize the need that each one build a philosophy of life as inclusive and consistent and helpful as we can effect it. In so doing, I as teacher will have my own philosophy and will not hesitate to avow it, but I shall do all I can to force each student to think for himself. I will bring to his attention the unsuspected inconsistencies of his position. If he uses what I deem bad logic, I shall argue with him. But I will respect the integrity of his thinking and leave him to conclude for himself. In particular I shall shun any and all pressures to have him conclude on other than personally seen merits. If I

can succeed in helping my student thus to build a philosophy that really integrates him within himself and with his environment, then I can feel that I have done all I could do to make him intelligently self-directing.

There is so much in this position to accept that one hesitates to criticize it, but I must point out some limitations.

This seems to contemplate college and university students and not to take sufficient account of the elementary and secondary school situation. Though of course beginnings can be made there. Also this seems to isolate the intellect as if it could function alone apart from feeling and acting; and to separate learning from the living situation — all in a way that seems highly questionable. In particular, it seems not to concern itself directly with the actual social situation as something to concern one's self constructively about.

We have now passed in review most of the positions proposed for the American school as it faces our social situation. There remains to be examined one that either includes positive indoctrination of a prior chosen situation or sounds very like it. Possibly we can examine this position as we try to draw a conclusion.

Some things seem now to stand out as necessary constituents in any satisfactory conclusion.

(1) We must take effectual account of the facts of change and the precariousness of any social planning that may be undertaken. Provision must be made for continual intelligent change as regards both means and goals.

(2) We must — so I believe and hope — hold to essential democracy and must educate accordingly.

These two taken together dispose of the indoctrination of any prior chosen plan or scheme of social reconstruction. It is a planning society we wish, not a once-for-all planned society. Democratic planning means that all must be as socially intelligent as possible in order to pass on essential policies involved. The inherent precariousness of human affairs means that intelligence must expect change and be prepared to direct it.

(3) The school has to take both prudential and considerate account of the present attitudes of parents and citizens. Prudentially so, lest we be dismissed and others less progressive take our places. Considerately so, because parents love their children and have rights and feelings in connection that we must in both kindness and justice consider. It is part of our school duty to interchange education with the parents and citizens of the community. To effect this, the road of decent consideration offers the best return.

These things do not mean that the school must not work for the right of full discussion of all appropriate topics without interference from the community. In my judgment, school people should not only work for freedom from interference but should organize to protect themselves in their just rights, especially to protect against meddlesome busybodies who profess patriotism but really mean obscurantism and unjust privilege.

(4) We school people must become socially intelligent in the highest possible degree, and we must help all others within reach to grow in social intelligence. Again it is not indoctrination or propaganda that is contemplated, but the building of intelligence. This means parent-teacher associations to study social problems; it means adult education on an unprecedented scale to give conscious study to all problems affecting life; it means that our schools must study social problems as never before. We who are now citizens must become more intelligent by much. The rising generation must be more socially intelligent by far than we now are.

(5) This means, as I see it, both the study of social problems and the participation as far as feasible in cooperative community enterprises, all of course appropriately to the age involved. Only as study contemplates actual conditions is it real. Only as we are engaged socially in actual enterprises can we build proper social habits and attitudes. Only as we have contact with actual life conditions can we make our social generalizations real and defensible. To learn how to run our schools in this fashion will be no simple matter, but we must undertake it. . . .

24. "EDUCATION AS STATESMANSHIP" [7]

George S. Counts

The historical record shows that education is always a function of time, place, and circumstance. In its basic philosophy, its social objective, and its program of instruction, it inevitably reflects in varying proportion the experiences, the condition, and the hopes, fears, and aspirations of a particular people or cultural group at a particular point in history. In actuality it is never organized and conducted with sole reference to absolute and universal terms. While the biological inheritance of the race presumably remains practically unchanged from age to age and thus gives a certain stability to the learning process, education as a whole is always relative, at least in fundamental parts, to some concrete and evolving social situation. It possesses no inner logic or empirical structure

[7] From *The Social Foundations of Education*, Part IX, Report of the Commission on the Social Studies, American Historical Association, Charles Scribner's Sons, New York, 1934, pp. 1–5.

of its own that dictates either its method or its content. In both its theoretical and practical aspects it expresses the ideals of some given society at some given period of time, either consciously with clear design or half-consciously with hidden and confused purpose. There can be no all-embracing educational philosophy, policy, or program suited to all cultures and all ages.

Hence the problem of education assumes one form in ancient Athens in the time of Pericles, another in China during the Tang dynasty, another in Mediæval Saxony, another in modern Japan, still another in Russia under the Communists, and yet another in twentieth-century America. It is clear therefore that any group, charged with the task of shaping educational theory or practice for any people, should begin with an examination of the society to be served — its natural surroundings, its major trends and tensions, its controlling ideals, values, and interests. . . .

In the United States periodic recurrence to fundamental study and analysis is especially necessary because of the highly dynamic character of American life and institutions in the age of industrialism. In a comparatively static society an educational program, if once adjusted to definite and acknowledged conceptions of social need, may remain unchanged for generations and even for centuries, and yet perform its functions effectively. As long as the balance of ideas and interests, which such a program reflects, remains essentially undisturbed, it is likely at least to be deemed satisfactory and adequate. But by common consent, confirmed by the comprehensive survey just completed by President Hoover's Research Committee on Social Trends and by countless other inquiries, American society has been and is changing rapidly in its basic institutions and relationships. The nature and extent of many of these changes have been expressed in some measure in indisputable mathematical terms.

The impression should not be given, however, that the task of formulating educational policies and programs is merely a matter of gathering social data. Facts must be selected, interpreted, and woven into patterns of utility and purpose. Also this task should not be confused with scientific neutrality, on the one hand, or with unfettered speculation, on the other. Always and everywhere genuine education is a form of practical endeavor — a form of social action. This means that the educator fails in his line of duty if he refuses to step out of academic cloisters, even leave the research laboratory, reject the rôle of disinterested spectator, take an active part in shaping events, make selections among social values, and adopt, however tentatively and broadly, some conception of social welfare and policy. No inquiry into American society, profound and comprehensive though it may be, can remove from his shoulders the responsibility of embodying in his theories and programs some interpretation of history in the making, some general outlook upon the world, some frame of reference with respect to society, some conception of things deemed necessary, of things deemed possible, of things deemed desirable in the proximate future. This responsibility he may discharge openly, deliberately, and intelligently, or furtively, impulsively, and ignorantly; but discharge it he must. He may rightly inquire what choices of purpose and direction are practicable and feasible; but being compelled to act he inevitably makes such choices, even though he may conceal his decisions from himself as well as from others. . . .

Among men of action the educators of the country occupy an important position. Consequently, in the light of the data provided by the social sciences and within the limits imposed by necessity, as revealed by the data, educational leaders are obliged to make an interpretation of contemporary history and with full recognition of all the hazards involved, submit their interpretation in educational program to the judgment of time. Since, being denied the privilege of neutrality, they must act, no other rational course is open to them. But it should never be forgotten that in acting they, in proportion to the power of organized education, mold the minds of the coming generation and thus share in shaping the future of the nation and even of world society. . . .

Education is one of the highest forms of statesmanship. The educator working in the public schools is a servant of the state. As distinguished from the educational jobholder, he is under obligation to foster the most complete development of the capacities of the citizens, upon whose powers the state depends for its existence, its security, and the fulfillment of its ideals. And since the American state, at least in theory, is not the government or some independent authority standing above the masses of the people, but rather the whole body of citizens functioning in their collective capacity, the educator, besides discharging mandatory obligations, is required to provide educational leadership for the nation and to assume general responsibility for the formulation of educational philosophies, policies, and programs. . . . In the light of the dominant and emergent ethical and aesthetic values of the age and on the basis of the potentialities of the natural endowment, the technological resources, the cultural heritage, and the great social trends of the time, he must define problems, make choices, and decide upon courses of action. This is the supreme task which the educational profession faces today in America.

25. Schools Should Participate Actively in Social Progress [8]

Bruce Raup

The long-abiding consensus that the very agencies fitted to give social perspective, such as the schools, must maintain judicial detachment without the opportunity even of venturing the judge's decision, that they must hear and present all sides and stop there, is not suited to the age in which we live. It must yield. Perhaps it is already yielding to a view that takes the " all sides fairly " principle as a guide in seeking better conclusions and convictions, not as a substitute for this quest.

The National Education Association made an official investigation and pronouncement at the time of the Federal Trade Commission's exposure of the utilities' propaganda. A pamphlet known as the Broome Committee's Report on Propaganda in the Schools is the pronouncement referred to. This study, excellent in many ways, simply reiterates the traditional consensus when it faces the crucial point which has concerned us here:

". . . the propagandist and the teacher embody two extremes as to attitude and method. The propagandist's mind is made up on a particular subject. He seeks to inculcate the viewpoint. The teacher's mind is open on all subjects. He seeks to present all viewpoints. The function of propaganda is to gain acceptance of a particular opinion, doctrine, or course of action, under circumstances designed to curb the individual's freedom of thought and action. The function of education, on the other hand, is to acquaint the individual with a variety of opinions, doctrines, or courses of actions, so as to equip him, intelligently to do his own thinking and to select his own courses of action. The main purpose of propaganda, therefore, is to teach *what to think*, while the guiding purpose of education is to teach *how to think*." [*]

In summary, there are more than the two alternatives cited by this committee. There is a third, namely that the function of the schools is to participate actively and positively along with other agencies in society, in the process of generating and regenerating the aims, principles and policies by which we manage living together. Fair-mindedness is a condition of doing this well, not a substitute for doing it at all.

[8] From *Education and Organized Interests in America*, G. P. Putnam's Sons, New York, 1936, pp. 38–39.
[*] *National Education Association Addresses and Proceedings*, Atlanta, Georgia, June–July, 1929, Vol. 67. " Report of Committee on Propaganda," Edwin Broome, Chairman, pp. 206–207.

26. Education Cannot Lead in Social Progress [9]

Nathaniel Peffer

When H. G. Wells pronounced his well-known dictum that the future was a race between education and catastrophe, he may have been speaking merely in an expansive mood or out of a psychology of despair, or only committing a logical fallacy by over-simplification. But in any event he won converts in America beyond his hope, perhaps beyond his intention. American education is stripped and on the mark, about to outrun catastrophe.

It is the kind of challenge that makes an appeal in America, and the times are such as to lend force to the appeal. Religion has lost its hold on us. We no longer really believe in the traditional democracy. Salvation by prosperity is newly proved delusive. Thus the three cardinal American articles of faith have lost substance. But the American nature abhors a vacuum of belief in panaceas. We must have a magic key to the riddle of life, a master key, rather, to all its riddles. Now one is being fashioned out of education.

I have had occasion in the last two years to observe from within something of the spirit which animates the world of education. I have seen it not in its workaday aspects but on the higher levels where the philosophy of education is mooted, where its objects are formulated and grand strategies laid down. I refer to such circles as the National Educational Association, the American Council on Education, the Progressive Education Association, the Association of American Colleges, and the schools of education and teachers colleges from which emanate the researches and philosophical systems which are the tablets of Sinai to contemporary education. I have examined the written record in which the educational profession expresses itself with deliberation and for preservation. As I have pored over the voluminous literature of education, the books, monographs, reports, " surveys," journals and, most of all, the published proceedings of multitudinous educational conferences, I have felt a gathering sense of awe. No one can read what educators write or hear what they say on official occasion without being awed by the amplitude of their assumption and the altitude of their ambition. They mean to save the world, at least in America — a prospect which would never occur to anyone who knows the world or America or the results of American education in recent years.

This exalted ambition is not altogether new-sprung. It has roots in the soil. Education has always had a kind of sanctification with

---

[9] From " Educators Groping for the Stars," *Harper's Magazine*, 168:230–232, January, 1934.

us, if only as an institution. Heretofore, however, the belief in education has been a corollary to the belief in democracy. There was the inherent right to equality of opportunity for all cultural advantages and, furthermore, only a literate people could fulfill the political duties of a democratic state. Education was, therefore, the instrument with which to make democracy effectual. Now, however, education is giving itself wider scope. It has taken Mr. Wells to heart and conceives itself an agent of universal solution.

How? Broadly speaking, there are two main bodies of opinion on the frontiers of educational thought. One is centered on what may be called social reconstruction, the other on what is loosely and largishly called personality. The first sets the making of a new social order as the goal of the school. The second sets as its goal the prophylaxis and remedy for all the ills that make men unhappy in their personal lives. It would not only educate individuals to extract the full development of their capacities but correct their personal deficiencies.

These two camps are by no means inclusive, for when educators let themselves go by tongue or pen, universality alone sets their bounds. I have, for instance, heard a college president boast with pride in a speech to other educators that he had introduced into the curriculum of his institution courses on leadership. Business men had told him that what they needed most was leaders; his own reflections on life had convinced him too that the world had drifted into a morass for lack of leadership. Asked how he could choose which boys of eighteen would be leaders at forty, what the prerequisites to admission were and how the contents of the courses in leadership were distinguished from other courses, he answered that he was not clear as yet; he was certain only that the world needed leaders and that they could be trained. Half of which is indeed true and has been true since there has been a world.

The two main roads by which the educators hope to lead the advance, however, are by way of social reconstruction and by way of the development of personality. It is easier to discuss the first, since that can be put with definiteness, while the proponents of personality are seldom inhibited by the need for exact definition. Also, the proposals for social reconstruction have intrinsic substance. There is some reality to the controversies to which they have given rise. It is proposed that education become a process of indoctrination for a new social order. The race must be prepared for a socialized way of life, for a society in which collectivism is progressively supplanting individualism, and social control is supplanting individual autonomy. Individualism is already an anachronism, since the individual is no longer an effectual unit in a world of large-scale production, chain distribution, and concentrated credit. We shall have collectivism in any case. We must, therefore, re-shape the social order in conformity, and we must make the transition as smooth as possible by preparing the younger generation to live in such a society. Therefore, it follows, we must take the school as the most effective instrumentality to hand and use education to indoctrinate the coming generation with the principles of collectivism and social control. In the words of Professor Harold Rugg, of Teachers College, Columbia University, one of the more modest advocates of this philosophy, "Nothing less than thoroughgoing social reconstruction is demanded, and there is no institution known to the mind of man that can compass that problem except education." Professor George S. Counts of the same institution, the most vigorous advocate, bluntly entitles the pamphlet carrying his pronouncement " Dare the School Build a New Social Order? "

To this argument, which can be put impressively, at least in the abstract, it is generally answered that education would then become merely a form of propaganda. To this in turn it is replied that that would constitute nothing new in theory or practice, since education is and always must be propaganda, if only by the process of selection of what shall be taught. Our present education is no less a form of indoctrination. It differs only in that it indoctrinates for the *status quo*, the regime of laissez faire and individualism. And thus the controversy is waged, with much heat and telling blows on both sides.

Impressive as the case may be in the abstract, it lacks reality of course. True or not, what of it? Granted that we are going into a new society, that it is more efficient to prepare by education for the kind of world we shall live in, and that the school ideally is the best agency for such preparation — granted; but who believes this? How large a proportion of our population now believes that we must have a collective society — or any other society essentially different in form from the one we have? More important, how large a proportion of that part of the population which makes opinion and sets values? View all these considerations against the setting of the recent quarrels in Washington over the right of labor to collective bargaining! The boards of trustees of our largest universities are composed of bankers, corporation lawyers, owners of large industries. Let the economics department of a university attempt deliberately to instill the principles of a communistic or socialistic society as preferable to the regime of private property and how long will the members of the economics faculty remain in the university? The school board of a city of one hundred thousand is composed of a prominent real estate dealer, the president of the First National

Bank, a Presbyterian minister, the vice-president of the Chamber of Commerce. Let them hear that high-school teachers in their town are teaching the evils of capitalism and private enterprise and pointing the lessons by laudatory descriptions of Soviet Russia and how long before the teachers are dismissed and proscribed from the teaching profession?

When indoctrination for a new social order is practicable it will no longer be necessary, for then the new order will already have arrived. Those who control the present order will have surrendered or been converted. Whatever education may be culturally or as a concept, as an institution it is not independent or self-sufficient. It cannot create; it can only reflect. It cannot generate new social ideas; it can transmit only those which are already accepted. It must always bend to the collective will around it. In social ideas it can rise no higher than the source of the thought, feelings, and beliefs of the dominant groups in the society in which it finds itself. Having regard to how ponderously and wastefully societies move, this is a regrettable fact, but it is a fact nevertheless. For educators to debate the merits of new social indoctrination in schools and universities is either an interesting but meaningless intellectual exercise or it is to clothe themselves with a fictive importance. They are followers, not pioneers. To attempt to endow themselves with a grander role is to waste motions or court heartbreak. . . .

27. Schools Not an Agency of Reform [10]

Franklin Bobbitt

The school is not an agency of social reform. It is not directly concerned with improving society. Its responsibility is to help the growing individual continuously and consistently to hold to the type of human living which is the best practical one for him. This should automatically result in an enormous improvement in society in general. But this improvement is not a thing directly aimed at. It is only a by-product. If we visualize the conditions of a perfected society wherein further improvement is not possible, the responsibility of education is not changed or diminished thereby. . . .

[10] From " Orientation of the Curriculum Maker," National Society for the Study of Education, *The Foundations of Curriculum-Making*, Twenty-Sixth Yearbook, Part II, Public School Publishing Company, Bloomington, Ill., 1927, p. 54.

28. SOCIAL OBLIGATIONS OF TEACHERS [11]

In the great battle of ideas and values precipitated by the advance of industrial civilization the teachers of the country are inevitably and intimately involved. They cannot stand apart and at the same time discharge their professional obligations. This is due to the fact that they are guardians of childhood, bearers of culture, and, presumably, loyal servants of the masses of the people. These three considerations compel the teachers to action.

As guardians of childhood teachers cannot be indifferent to the operation of social institutions. In normal times they are keenly aware of the injustice and the misery wrought by the existing economic system. They know that capitalism, with its extremes of poverty and riches and its moral degradation of millions, makes an empty farce of our democratic professions and dooms multitudes of children to lives of severe privation. They know that these children will have to forego, not only the luxuries which are literally showered upon their more fortunate brothers and sisters born to wealth and privilege, but even those things demanded by the laws of physical and mental health. Teachers can never be reconciled to a social order that even in days of " prosperity " needlessly violates the deepest loyalties of their calling. Then in years of depression they see additional millions of boys and girls deprived of their social birthright, denied the most elementary material and cultural necessities, and crippled beyond hope of redemption in body, mind, and spirit. They see the youth of the nation bewildered by the deep chasm separating precept from reality and embittered as they beat vainly against the closed doors of occupational opportunity. They even see that no defensible theory of education can be practiced successfully in contemporary society. Consequently, if they are but interested in the lives of children — the central responsibility with which they are charged by the state — they must work boldly and without ceasing for a better social order.

Teachers are also bearers of culture. In their own persons, in their selection of the materials of instruction, in their organization of the life of the school, in their connections with the community, they must give expression to some set of values. Education itself is essentially a process of cultural transmission and transformation. It therefore cannot be neutral toward the great issues of life and destiny without becoming completely formalized and losing all contact with the world. If the school is to live, some vital and growing

[11] Committee of the Progressive Education Association on Social and Economic Problems, *A Call to the Teachers of the Nation*, The John Day Co., New York, 1933, pp. 18–20.

tradition must provide it with nourishment, some conception of worth must course through and animate and integrate its organs and tissues. This is clearly sensed by the American people in their insistence that the young be reared on the democratic ideal. But the difficulty arises out of the fact, already noted, that the ideal has lost much of its meaning and requires reformulation in the light of vastly changed conditions. *To teach the ideal in its historic form, without the illumination that comes from an effort to apply it to contemporary society, is an extreme instance of intellectual dishonesty. It constitutes an attempt to educate the youth for life in a world that does not exist. Teachers therefore cannot evade the responsibility of participating actively in the task of reconstituting the democratic tradition and of thus working positively toward a new society.* The simple discharge of their professional duties leaves to them no alternative.

Finally, attention should be directed to the fact that teachers are at the same time the loyal servants and the spiritual leaders of the masses of the people. This does not mean, however, as some have maintained, that teachers are to regard themselves as mere tools in the hands of the state; nor does it mean that they are constrained to defend the existing social system and serve the interests of the dominant class. To do either would be a gross violation of trust. Such arguments are purely legalistic or mechanistic in character and fail utterly to express the nature of the educative and social processes. Even the taxpayers have no special claim on the schools; they are but the tax collectors of society; ultimately school revenue comes from all who labor by hand or brain. This the teachers should never forget. Their loyalty therefore goes to the great body of the laboring population — to the farmers, the industrial workers, and the other members of the producing classes of the nation. They owe nothing to the present economic system, except to improve it; they owe nothing to any privileged caste, except to strip it of its privileges. Their sole duty is to guard and promote the widest and most permanent interests of society. Though seeking alliance from time to time with those groups that can be relied upon to work for the establishment of a genuine democracy, they can take dictation from none. They must always be in a position to place their faith, their intelligence, their idealistic fervor, and not merely their professional skill, at the service of the masses of the people. Today, when life seems so freighted with possibilities, these broader responsibilities should receive the most earnest consideration of teachers. As never before in their history they should recognize their social obligations and be prepared to participate in the struggles of the day. . . .

29. A Criticism of "A Call to the Teachers of the Nation" [12]

I. L. Kandel

Society in the past has established and everywhere continues to maintain schools in order to create new generations in its own likeness. As the Committee * states repeatedly " education itself is essentially a process of cultural transmission " and teachers are " the bearers of culture "; education in the broadest sense is also a process of cultural transformation, as the Committee claims, but not in the sense that the school as a formal institution creates new cultural patterns but that it develops or should develop that intellectual training which combined with social and other conditions leads to cultural transformation. In other words, as the Committee in another passage says of the teachers, "their sole duty is to guard the widest and most permanent interests of society," but it is society which determines what these interests are, and not the teachers.

Should teachers, then, remain neutral in times like these? As teachers they can do nothing else! To suggest that they can take a lead in the schools in a direction not already agreed upon by society is to capitalize discontent on the one side and to disrupt the educational system on the other. The school, the American school, is the institution of all the people for all the children of all the people. (It is not unfair nor does it detract from their sincerity to point out that the majority of the members of the Committee are not now engaged in public school work.) There are vital issues of life other than the economic on which teachers must remain neutral. One hundred years ago it was decided that sectarian religious instruction, still a vital issue for the majority of people, should not be given in public schools. Teachers may be Protestants, Catholics, or Jews, agnostics or atheists, but in the schools, for good or ill, they must remain neutral; they may be Republicans or Democrats, Socialists or Communists, but in the schools they must be non-partisan politically. And yet neutrality does not and cannot mean that pupils should not be taught to consider all the facts in a situation and be allowed to make up their own minds, but the teachers themselves must know the facts and not shelter behind a specious plea of academic freedom to excuse digressions into fields in which they are not masters. The Committee is not as clear as was Dr. Counts in his

[12] From "Mobilizing the Teacher," *Teachers College Record,* 35:476–478, March, 1934.

* Committee of the Progressive Education Association on Social and Economic Problems in *A Call to the Teachers of the Nation,* a pamphlet published by The John Day Company, New York, 1933.

Dare the School Build a New Social Order? but the implication running throughout the *Call* is that all the teachers must have one mind and one point of view and insist on the right to present that in class.

The schools and the product thereof are society's, and society determines when changes shall take place in them. The school does not precede the cultural transformation but follows it. When society, whether by the slow process of evolution or by the rapid cataclysm of revolution, decides that the time for a new order has come, it will determine, as did Lenin, Mussolini, and Hitler, what shall go on in the school and what the teachers shall teach in them. A year ago it would probably have been dangerous for teachers to preach the mild collectivism of the New Deal; today American society (at least until the next election is in prospect) may demand that the New Deal be propagated through the school. I have sufficient faith, however, in liberalism and democracy to prefer neutrality to imposed ideologies, if a choice has to be made. . . .

30. KANDEL AND THE "CALL" [13]

William A. McCall

The issue between Kandel and the Callers is of fundamental significance. Shall teachers *lead* society or *follow* it? A teacher is a citizen and as a citizen dealing with other mature citizens he has an undoubted right to lead or follow as he chooses or as he can. I assume that neither party to the controversy questions this right and hence that this is not the real issue.

Shall teachers use the public elementary and secondary schools to lead society? This is the real question, and Kandel's answer is an emphatic NO. And so is mine, and for the following reasons:

First, my proposed survey of human purposes will reveal irreconcilable ideas concerning what constitutes " a better social order." Since it is not feasible to maintain separate public schools for all the important *isms,* teachers *as teachers* should be strictly neutral.

Second, the hope of the future lies in maintaining at least one agency of instruction for the young that is capable of guiding youth in a dispassionate consideration of controversial issues. With respect to such issues, most homes nurture children in an atmosphere of prejudice, and the churches are established on definite emotional commitments which necessarily limit the possibilities which may be considered.

Third, if teachers insist upon the privilege of leading the young in specified directions or even of " expressing opinions as a member of

[13] From " My Philosophy of Life and Education," *Teachers College Record,* 36:315–316, January, 1935.

the class," I predict that the time is not far distant when theirs will be the fate of teachers in Japan, China, Russia, Italy, Germany, and a growing number of other countries. They will not be left free to decide in which direction they will lead or whether they will lead or follow or be neutral. They will be ordered to lead in a dictated direction or resign.

Fourth, it is of paramount importance that controversial issues be made a part of the school curriculum. This will not be possible until teachers agree and widely publicize their agreement to strive to maintain strict neutrality in the consideration of controversial questions.

While my philosophy of education compels me to agree with Kandel's contention that teachers should not exploit their positions to lead society, it compels me to disagree emphatically with his contention that teachers should be mere followers, mere purveyors of society's culture, mere transmitters of the relatively dead by-products of society's vital activities. The Callers' school would, at least, be *alive*. Their schoolhouse could not be appropriately located in a graveyard, nor could their curriculum consist mainly of reading the runes carved on decaying gravestones. As previously indicated, a survey of human purposes would not reveal a static society — would not show most individuals most of the time sitting squat and satisfied, surveying the past. Rather it would reveal the most persistent and characteristic purposes to be those which press upon the future. And not the least or least universal of these purposes would be the desire to achieve " a better social order." Kandel offers teachers just two choices: *to lead* or *to follow*. There is a third, *to guide*. Life is lived on the line which divides the past and the future. If I may conclude a serious discussion with a slang expression, that should be the teacher's line.

31. SOCIAL RESPONSIBILITY OF TEACHERS [14]

Charles A. Beard

All about us are signs of stresses and strains. Optimism can not overlook them. Nor can indifference deny their exigency. East and west, war looms on the horizon, while the President and Congress of the United States seek ways and means of keeping the nation out of impending conflicts. At home ten million men and women search hopelessly for a chance to make a decent livelihood, and millions of young people hunt vainly for opportunities in which to try their

[14] From " The Scholar in an Age of Conflicts," *School and Society*, 43:278–279, February 29, 1936.

talents. With staggering burdens forced upon government and society by an economic crisis, there can be no doubt about the gravity of the issues before us.

In such a time it is above all things fitting for us, on this occasion, to inquire, with the powers of mind we can command, into the present duties and responsibilities of the teacher and the school in America. Taking account of these stresses and strains, and painfully aware of the perplexities involved, I venture to lay before you my opinions on the subject for your consideration, and at the conclusion to suggest a program of action appropriate to the challenge of the hour.

At the very outset we face this pertinent question: What is the primary function of the public school system in American democracy? It is, as I see things, the training of minds and the dissemination of knowledge — knowledge useful in the good life, in the conduct of the practical arts and in the maintenance and improvement of American society. The teacher is not a physician, a nurse, a soldier, a policeman, a politician, a businessman, a farmer or an industrial worker. These officers have their rights and duties, but the rights and duties of the teacher's office are marked by special features. To be sure, all citizens of the United States have many common responsibilities, but we are concerned here with the immediate interests of the profession. The teacher's principal business is the training of minds and the dissemination of knowledge.

For the training of minds, a trained mind is required. For the dissemination of knowledge, a mastery of knowledge is required. The union of the trained mind and knowledge makes scholarship. So the teacher is under obligation to be a scholar — not a pedant, but a scholar dedicated to the cultivation of the mind and the transmission of knowledge useful in the good life, the arts and the management of social affairs.

There are many, no doubt, who deny this conception of public education. They look to the schools to correct all the ills of humanity. Society creates conditions that foster crime; the schools must serve as crime prevention agencies. Society sends undernourished, ill-clad and sick children to school; teachers must feed and nurse the unfortunate. Parents quarrel and fight at home; teachers must make saints of children so trained at the fireside. Parents refuse to read good literature and insist on maintaining an intellectual and moral vacuum at home; teachers must turn the victims of the vacuum into wise and good men and women. Parents surround children with trashy newspapers, flashy movies and radio nonsense; teachers must overcome the distempers and follies of such a life. Special interests in society demand this or oppose that; teachers must bow to the winds of these passions and pressures.

Self-constituted professors of all righteousness think they have the way of universal salvation; teachers must force the creed upon the rising generation. These views of education run counter to my notion of its duties in American society.

If the primary function of the public schools is the training of minds and the dissemination of knowledge that is useful to individuals and society, then the teacher can not be a fire warden, policeman, soldier and politician combined. On the contrary, the teacher is another kind of person, with other duties and responsibilities — the duties and responsibilities of the scholar. It is right and proper, of course, that any individual teacher may feel bound to assume the obligations of the soldier, propagandist or politician. In this case let the teacher take up the profession with which such obligations are properly associated.

32. Role of the School in Social Progress [15]

Thomas H. Briggs

Although propaganda has been popularly feared and deprecated, it is popular now for those who term themselves " progressive " in education to assert that the schools should be used to reform society, to bring about desirable social changes, and even to incite a social revolution. There is doubtless general agreement that " desirable social changes " shall be effected, the ambiguous word " desirable " insuring that, but many would balk at the assumption that a revolution is necessary. I myself would stickle at neither reform nor revolution; whatever is necessary to cure current ills and to set us anew on the path of democracy leading to social good should be welcomed. But the assertions mean precisely nothing unless the desirable changes are specified, their approval by the public secured, and machinery for accomplishing them set up. Phrases like these quoted sound impressive, especially to those not critically minded and to those without imagination to envisage the changes consequent on them; and the " progressives " make a brave show until challenged to manifest in their own lives social practices obviously better than those observed in the lives of less pretentious men. They are themselves challenged to manifest a convincing higher life, and also to set forth with some specificity the details in which society should be reformed or revolutionized. Many such details most men have doubtless already approved. It is the novel and minority details that would manifest issues.

[15] From " Propaganda and the Curriculum," *Teachers College Record*, 34:470–480, March, 1933.

My experience with reformers is that they agree well enough in condemning the world as it is, but that no other group of men and women so bitterly dissent among themselves as to details of what needs reform or as to methods that should be used. If they mean in their frequent demands for social reform by education that any and every teacher has the right to advocate and to "propagandize" whatever theory of change he sees fit, regardless of what the employing social group approves or accepts, then I am forced to conclude that the principle is unsound, illogical, absurd, and impudent. I am unwilling to permit a teacher whom I select and pay for educating my child to warp his judgment, to set up ideals, and to direct practices contrary to those in which I believe and which I endeavor to exemplify in my own life. Should you not be? Society is just a plural " I."

THE TEACHER'S RESPONSIBILITY

The real question, then, is who shall select the issues to be taught and determine the bias to be sought through teaching? At once the principle of academic freedom is adduced by the so-called progressives. That abused and often perverted principle is still in its original sense sound. But there is a difference, a vast difference, between the freedom that a scholar must have to declare the results of his investigations and of his reflections in the field in which he is competent and the freedom of any and every classroom teacher, employed as he is to promote the interests of society, to advocate idiosyncratic ideas unapproved by the employing society and unsubstantiated by accepted facts or philosophy. It is altogether irrational to argue that any teacher, however biased his attitude, however partial his consideration of inadequate data, however erratic his judgment, has the right to use his influence for the subversion of the society that has entrusted him with responsibility and pays him a wage to perform his duties loyally. He may be sincere in believing that monogamy is not the best practice or that democracy should be replaced by communism or by fascism; but the society that pays his salary does not think so. Consequently he has no right to advocate in his classes such doctrines. Society has often been wrong in its ideals, no doubt; but when such is the case one's challenge is to convince society that another ideal is better and not, as its agent, to betray in the schoolroom the trust imposed on him.

For several reasons there has been little trouble from public school teachers who perverted their responsibility to undermine the ideals of society. In the first place, when such perversion becomes known there is a swift reaction on the part of the public, and the offender offends no more. Such a reaction very properly came to the teacher

who distributed in his classes a bibliography of pornographic literature, called by him " modern," with such an annotation of some of
Whitman's poetry as " tinkling castanets of passion." But the relatively infrequent subversion of commonly accepted ideals usually is
subtly carried on and when considered " smart " by adolescents is
approved by them and is not reported. The threat of popular protest
ordinarily prevents or holds in check the tendency of erratic teachers.
So far, so good. But more important, from a large social point of
view, are the effects on teachers with high ideals and sound convictions of the constant threat of vocal and often very potent minorities
who will not tolerate the teaching, or even the consideration, of problems in which they have a selfish or an unsocial interest. The protection that such a teacher should have will be proposed presently.

The fear of public protest, whether by the respectable majority
or by a minority that is annoyingly vocal, deters many teachers
from attempting to teach what they are convinced would be real education that would affect the ideals and the consequent actions of
their pupils. With the imminent threat of protest and no assured
protection, they find that the easier way is to confine themselves to
the dates of the Egyptian dynasties or the succession of the Mero-
vingian kings. Let us illustrate by a fable. A man with convictions
that education should seriously affect life was chosen to organize a
school with an abundance of resources and a minimum of restrictions. In his first address to prospective patrons violent opposition
was voiced by a sarcastic member of the audience to one of the
sound proposals. In his second address that proposal was dropped,
but another one was attacked by an emotional critic. That, too,
was dropped; and so by a succession of concessions to minority
criticism the program became entirely conventional, and the school
opened as just another conveyor of the bricks out of which education could be made. How frequently we have seen the fable exemplified.

Probably the most important reason why little trouble results
from attempts to modify the ideals, attitudes, and actions of pupils
in important matters is that the very business of teaching tends to
make men and women conservative. Reiterating undisputed facts,
cultivating open-mindedness, so absorbed in their work as to be
largely divorced from aggressive citizenship, fearing to offend, and
devoted to narrow duties, the great mass of teachers set a pattern
that few of the independents dare transgress. They become what I
have elsewhere called " academic ladies of Shalott," watching the
world go by, but sharing little in its important activities. In their
conservatism they are, of course, like the great mass of the citizenry.

However comfortable and undisturbing such teachers may be, do we want as teachers or as citizens in a democracy those who are " learned, yet without opinion "? Is it worth all the great cost of the schools if they merely keep children and youth happily out of mischief a few hours of the day when in session, teach them a mass of facts that are largely forgotten as soon as they leave the classroom, and pass them unprepared to the conflicting and irresponsible propaganda of the world? This too pessimistic query is meant to emphasize the necessity of a preparation — an indoctrination, if you please — to meet in the best manner possible the unavoidable challenges of active citizenship. When everybody believed in " the trained mind," which as a result of abstract education could effectively function in any situation, the problem was relatively simple. If we could ignore the facts of experience, to say nothing of laboratory results, and concentrate our efforts again on " training the mind " while neglecting the challenges of life, the teacher's job would not be endangered, but real education would pass into the hands of the newspress, the politician, the radio, and the movie. But the old gods are dead. Lacking faith that they can develop minds so trained that they will be competent to adjudicate all issues equally well, the schools must accept the responsibility for propaganda for the democratic way of life. . . .

OBLIGATION OF THE SCHOOL TO REPRESENTATIVE DEMOCRACY

That our social, economic, industrial, and political life does need radical change many of us are convinced. Bewildered by excesses, misery, paradoxes, and political malfeasance, we seek leadership — within the democratic way, however, until it is made plausible that some other way is wiser, more equitable, and more substantial. When leadership convinces society what should be done, it should be and doubtless will be eager to pass on the use of the potent machinery of the schools for patterning the minds and the hearts of youth in a better way. Our sin is not so much in being recalcitrant before the shouting of those who fill our ears with the din of criticism and the noise of vague proposals for an indefinite betterment, as it is in not ourselves using education seriously and systematically to teach childhood and youth what the public believes to be sound and sane in the good life. We must be conservatives until democracy is convinced of the wisdom of radical change. Whatever society believes to be good the schools should teach so that it is effective in the lives of the new citizenry.

The weakness in democracy is, of course, that so small a fraction of those who have the suffrage are interested in the issues that affect its perpetuation and its prosperity. This weakness necessitates representative leadership that makes tentative decisions as to what is best for society, and inaugurates a program of action. It interprets the public mind or anticipates its decisions. In most instances when leadership is agreed, the general populace acquiesces and conforms to the new order, often coming to incorporate it into the national mores. But in other instances the change is not convincing, and democracy asserts itself to demand a reversion to older or to different ways of procedure. Democratic leadership is thus restricted by the more potent necessity of convincing the people that change is desirable, of educating them to accept and to approve that about which they have not thought or toward which they have previously been hostile. Democratic leadership has to make the people try change and like it. On the heads of the school systems, then, the administrative officers and the boards of education, rests constant responsibility to determine, by interpretation or by anticipation, what advances are good for society and to propose means for propagandizing for them with children and youth. They may have to retrace their steps many times and to start anew in directions for which they can gain popular approval. But that is entirely as it should be in a democracy. If we had such leadership, unceasing and untiring in its efforts to provide an education that promotes the good of society, constantly seeking to convince the public mind, and modifying the program when necessary to conform to the general popular sentiment, education would actually be the potent force that philosophers have always dreamed it would become. With such a program each teacher would know his responsibility and both the direction and the limitation of his freedom. He could then with safety to himself use his strength to direct youth to an acceptance of ideals that have the approval of representative democracy.

Other nations have seen the wisdom of using the schools for propaganda to establish and to promote the philosophy on which they are established. It was by the use of propaganda in the schools beginning early in the nineteenth century that Prussia became the head of a great federation of a powerful people; it is by means of school propaganda now that Italy is being confirmed in fascism and that Russia hopes to substantiate its novel dream. Without it neither monarchy nor fascism nor communism nor democracy can integrate its peoples and thus succeed. We see and marvel at the results in other nations; but because they are Germany, Italy, and Russia, with ideals far different from ours, we are foolishly afraid of the same means. But be assured that democracy needs an integrated people, too. Integration in the principles on which this nation was conceived and on which it was built is an extreme necessity of democracy. Most of the social and political ills from which we suffer urge our attention to the crumbling foundations of democracy as conceived by generations lacking the essential indoctrination. Like the teetotalers, we have assumed that having gained the form we could cease our efforts to inculcate into the younger generation the sustaining principles. What happened to prohibition should be a lesson to democracy.

There can be no sound and comprehensive program of propaganda through education, however, until national ideals are clarified and generally accepted by the people. The lack of clarification and integration is the chief trouble today in the new Germany, as well, it may be suspected, as it was in the tottering ruins of several venerable nations that thought they could " muddle through " by transmitting vague ideals to only the leaders, leaving the great mass of populace uninformed, unconvinced, and loyal only to dimly perceived and outmoded traditions. Until the people of Germany agree on the meaning of *Deutschtum* and passionately believe in it, it will be futile for the various and varied leaders to attempt to popularize it through the schools. It cannot be otherwise with us in the United States. Democracy must be practiced as well as professed before it can become a part of the wise propaganda of the curriculum.

It is a terrifying thought that perhaps the chief obstacle to a curriculum of propaganda is that already we have no unity in a clearly conceived and passionately approved democracy. Without that we as a public cannot agree on the important larger things that shall be taught in our schools. Without that no government, least of all a democracy, can continue to prosper or even to exist. Whenever a progressive educator, his eyes clearly seeing the need of a curriculum that affects the fundamental theories of social and political life, attempts to introduce an appropriate but novel teaching unit he inevitably learns that some potent element of the public will not permit that which runs counter to its beliefs or its fancied interests. How long will it take us to learn that public education cannot run far ahead of public ideals? How long will it take those who would reform the nation through its schools to learn that they must first convince the supporting public not only of the rightness of their ideals but also of the soundness of their program? If Counts is correct in saying that " we are moved by no great faiths; we are touched by no great passions," we are challenged to define " that ideal factor which gives meaning, direction, and significance to life . . . that element of faith or purpose which lifts man out of himself and above the level of his more narrow personal interests."

PROBLEM OF THE CURRICULUM MAKER

Granting that we should have propaganda in our curricula, that no education socially worth while is possible without it, and granting further that the propaganda should promote the ideals accepted by the supporting society, we realize the situation in which the real curriculum maker finds himself. If he avoids the challenge with its large promise and equally large dangers, he only perpetuates an academic tradition already to a great extent obviously outworn for a modern democratic society, or introduces superficial variations. If he accepts the challenge to devise a curriculum that will promote in the younger generation the ideals accepted by their elders, he is bewildered to find that there is no general agreement on the fundamental ideals — indeed that there is little popular thought about or interest in them.

What, then, is he to do? It is not only futile but also foolish to leave the most important elements of the curriculum to the individual teachers, many of them immature and without definite convictions of their own, some with ideals significantly aberrant from the democratic way of life. For his immediate guidance he can first define his terms, beginning with *democracy,* and seek an acceptance by his public of the definitions; then he can analyze the problems that are important — the problems that center in such phenomena as the family life, the economic structure, the relations of capital and labor, political rights and obligations, and the church in the state, to mention but a few — and ascertain with the help of teachers and varied representatives of the public on what there is general agreement by unselfish leaders; and, finally, he can introduce into the curriculum teaching units that promote the ideals that are approved. By such procedure he moves in the direction of making education vital and important; and by it he sets up a defense against the minorities who inevitably will object. Every clash will serve still further to interest the public, to clarify its ideals, and to hasten the larger program, which will next be proposed. Beyond the agreements he may attempt to present the facts and the arguments on both sides of issues as fairly as possible, being certain that by the compromise he is inviting criticism by affected minorities, and these criticisms should be used to foment public discussion leading to wholesome understandings and a measure of popular agreement. I suspect that there is much more agreement than we realize on many issues ordinarily avoided as dangerous.

Ultimately, I think we shall be wise enough to attempt the formulation of a larger program by some such means as I proposed two years ago before the North Central Association of Colleges and Secondary Schools. Each clash of minorities over an attempt courageously made to provide a curriculum contributing to the solution of important current problems will forward this larger program. It will provide for a permanent commission of the best minds of our nation — of statesmen, economists, sociologists, publicists, philosophers, and educators — that will attempt to formulate the ideals of democratic society and to popularize them with our heterogeneous public. Such formulated ideals will be the foundation on which all the important parts of the new curriculum will be built. The details of its procedure could be worked out if the need were realized. There are obstacles, of course, but none of them insuperable. . . .

33. EDUCATION AND SOCIAL CHANGE [16]

Henry W. Holmes

The problem is not new. It is under discussion everywhere and has been the central problem in scores of meetings and published statements. It is the problem of the relation between education and social change. To deal with it adequately in a few pages would, of course, be impossible; and therefore I can here attempt only a very compact statement of my personal convictions and reflections on the points at issue.

Some of these are negative. I do not believe that the schools should attempt, in practice, to " build a new social order." This does not mean that teachers should have no social vision or that they should make of themselves a conservative force, opposing change, bolstering old institutions or practices, or maintaining curricula and pursuing methods that lead to stuffy, snobbish, illiberal attitudes or ideals on the part of their pupils. But building a new social order — actually building it — is simply not a job for teachers. It involves problems teachers in general cannot handle. Teachers, as teachers, have no special insight into financial problems: they cannot lead the country to the correct answers to the questions that face Congress, the Treasury, and the President with respect to the monetary standard, banking, the tariff, and taxes. Teachers are not competent to decide whether the N. R. A. should stay, or go, or be modified. They cannot advise Secretary Wallace as to the continuance of his policies under the A. A. A. They are not experts on relief. There is no problem outside of education itself on which teachers as a body, or any group of their leaders, can justifiably seek to advise the law makers, the political executives, or the courts. To *build* a new social order is wholly outside the competence of educators.

Even to plan a new social order, in any immediate sense, is *ultra vires*, so far as teachers are concerned. In their professional organi-

[16] From " Ultimate Values in Education," *Progressive Education*, 12:114–116, February, 1935.

zations the teachers have enough to do — perhaps more than they have proved that they can do with any degree of mastery — to discuss the issues that arise in education itself. Not even in the N. E. A. ought teachers to declare themselves on such questions as the payment of the bonus, public ownership of power plants, the redistribution of wealth through taxation, old-age insurance, the maintenance of the profit system, birth control, or the social management of medical care. Every teacher ought, of course, to interest himself in such things. If he can form an opinion on any present social, economic, or political problem, he ought to insist on his individual right, as a citizen, to express it in any proper way and on any appropriate occasion. If his teaching covers any such problems he ought to defend his right to deal with them freely, with due regard to the maturity and intelligence of his pupils. But he ought not to use his professional prestige or his professional organizations for political purposes.

A strict or legalistic division between what is educational and what is political is not, to be sure, either desirable or possible. If teachers can think so deeply, clearly, and connectedly about the values that education should serve, and can be made to serve, as to be quite sure that certain measures of social reform are essential — measures, for example, looking toward economic security — they might well be justified in setting forth their views in the name of their own professional interest. But, in general, the interests of education provide insight only as to the *direction* of social change, not as to the measures needed for the building of a new social order.

Teachers have enough to do to think out such " directions." Their moral ground in politics is clear enough. They are the guardians of values higher than the values of the physical organism, as such. They know that people must live, if they are to be educated: therefore they should stand for social change in the direction of security, social justice, and higher economic productivity. But they should not be satisfied to look toward comfort, conventional morality, the safe discharge of instinct, social conformity, or the mere spread of opportunity for pleasure and excitement. The social gospel of education is more positive than utilitarianism. It is a gospel of creative effort, a shared spiritual purpose to develop the positive resources of humanity and press forward in the mastery of nature.

To translate such views of education into measures affecting the schools themselves is a sufficiently difficult task. I say " such views " as if the views themselves were sure to be acceptable as I have stated them; but, of course, that is quite the reverse of the truth. Teachers have the task of getting *some* views of educational values accepted and then working out their social implications. My point is that they ought not to jump at conclusions about social measures that are educationally desirable. Their first task is to analyze their own business. What sort of a world does education require? What society will best minister to the values education seeks? If teachers can begin to answer these questions they can begin to lay down a social policy for education. They can work toward changes in the schools that will help to create a new social order and they can begin to see the direction of social changes that will foster education.

Education seems to me to require peace, the abolition of involuntary poverty, social justice but not equality, and the social conservation of excellence in all its forms. These social conditions and processes — there may be many others — seem to me to be goals at which education can aim. The task of elaborating the educational consequences of accepting these goals is a long business; and equally long is the task of connecting educational vision with the conflicting social changes going on about us. Fortunately, as in most human affairs, we do not need to have everything clearly mapped out before we begin to work. The business of thinking can go forward along with attempts to put into effect such insight as we have. To avoid mere explosiveness, however, and a progressivism that rides off in all directions at once, we must do and demand only what we have really thought through. I cannot yet see further than the goals I have here named.

34. CURRICULUM CHANGES NEEDED [17]
Charles H. Judd

My diagnosis of the reason why society has not kept up with education is that education has not concerned itself as fully as it should with the exposure of the retarding influences that hold society back. The schools have taught in a few advanced courses and somewhat timidly that outworn taxing systems are wrong in principle and inadequate, that they originated in a bygone age and need to be reconstructed in the light of present-day experience. I am here to advocate that the schools begin, with the sessions of next autumn, to prepare lessons on taxation and present these in vigorous form to the citizens of the next generation. I am in favor of such a reconstruction of the curriculum, worked out cooperatively by educators, that the American people will be compelled to talk at the dinner table with their children about taxes and legislators and tax-reduction associations.

[17] From "Educational Trends and the General Social Order," *School and Society*, 38:260–261, August 26, 1933.

I am further in favor of the discussion in schools of the governmental organization of cities and states. If it is said by those who are afraid to have light thrown on our national inadequacies that young children will be harmed by such discussion, my answer is that they are now harmed beyond measure by popular ignorance and lack of initiative in seeking reform.

The teachers of this country have a responsibility for the training of young people and for the protection of the interests of youth. There will be some who will say that the proposed program of civic education is radical. There will be some who will accuse teachers of seeking to serve selfish interests. The answer to these charges is that no other organized group is competent to represent youth.

35. Secondary Schools Must Assume An Important Social Role [18]

Harold C. Hand

In the light of certain actual or highly probable developments apparent to all who can and will take a realistic view of the present social and economic situation, there can be little doubt that the secondary school administrator will shortly be called upon to undertake tasks of a degree of complexity and difficulty never before attempted by any similar group of schoolmen. The present assignment of imparting to an approximate half of the adolescent population a content of admittedly little real value either to the individual or to society will very quickly be replaced by a demand on the part of the investing state far more difficult to satisfy. Very properly, those in charge of secondary schools will soon be given the alternatives of (1) making available to practically *all* adolescents a type of functional training essential to intelligent action in a society faced with a choice between reconstruction and chaos, or (2) being highly discredited and ignored in their requests for financial support.

One does not have to seek far to find evidence in support of these contentions. The pathetically ridiculous and shameful spectacle of dire poverty in the midst of plenty, now so familiar to all who have not willfully shut their eyes to the easily observable facts of the present situation, suggests to every thinking individual that our disjointed social and economic system must quickly be realistically examined and brought under control. That this examination must be undertaken by adolescents as well as by adults seems obvious in view of the fact that in our rapidly changing order this matter of examin-

[18] From "Social Reconstruction: Its Implications for Secondary Education," *Teachers College Record*, 34:587-592, April, 1933.

ing the structure must, if optimum social good is seriously to be striven for, become a continuous process in which every normal adult in a democracy participates. This suggests that the exceedingly technical task of controlling the order, though it will of necessity be conceived and executed by highly skilled individuals, must, in the face of certain deeply rooted and very powerful American traditions. have the real consent and intelligent coöperation of the governed and thus be rooted in a mass or democratic base.

If *all* normal adults are thus intelligently to participate in the considering, accepting, rejecting, and, in some cases, the formulating of schemes or systems of planning, it follows that *all* normal (that is, above the intellectual level of a moron) adolescents must be given a type of training which will prepare them for activities of this description. Consequently, the writer feels reasonably confident of the two assumptions underlying this discussion; first, that the democratic tradition of free secondary education will continue to find expression in the extension of educational opportunities to increasingly larger proportions of underprivileged adolescents and, secondly, that a type of training appropriate to the social task confronting the investing state will replace much, if not most, of the present offering. It is the purpose of this article to examine the more important of the implications for reorganization inherent in this situation, particularly as they touch upon or suggest enlarged responsibilities for the secondary school administrator. . . .

This very necessary but difficult shift from our present secondary school's offering to a more completely functional type of training geared to the realities of the times and designed for *all* adolescents would profoundly modify practically every item in the school program. The present curriculum would have to be so thoroughly reorganized as to be almost, if not entirely, unrecognizable. The scope of the guidance service would have to be enormously expanded. The problems associated with the classification, grouping, and promotion of students would assume staggering proportions. The corporate life of the school would need many modifications, chiefly in the direction of adding supplementary activities. The appropriate organization of the school day would be no small task. The employment of excursions and various forms of visual aids would become an absolute necessity. Library facilities would have to be enormously expanded and enriched. The important problems of optimum class size and optimum school size would then, as now, be thrown wide open. A new type of better-trained teacher would have to be produced. If the practice of assigning school marks survives the shuffle, their administration would be far more difficult than the very vexing problem which they now present. The necessary task of interpreting the program of the new school to *all* the parents would be far more complicated and more difficult than the present problem of providing adequate facilities for interpreting the present program to half the parents. . . .

It has already been suggested in this discussion that the problem of providing a curriculum appropriate to the individual needs of each and every adolescent and in harmony with the needs and purposes of an investing state immediately faced with the necessity of reconstructing its economic and social framework is truly one of staggering proportions. It is highly probable that many of the more alert minds in every secondary school and in every graduate school of education in the country are today vigorously attacking this gigantic task. It is with considerable humility that the writer ventures to make a few remarks relative to one phase of this problem, namely, the common core of the curriculum.

It seems obvious that no investing state acutely in need of an informed citizenry for the maintenance of its very life will long continue to support an institution of learning which permits and encourages youth to dictate its own educational destinies and refuses to admit that there is any appreciable common core of experiences, information, appreciations, and insights which it should provide for absolutely all its students regardless of the whims and passing fancies of the individual pupil. It is becoming painfully apparent that our 250-item offering has not been a very intelligent one from the point of view of the investing state. Boys and girls who have spent their years in the secondary school becoming inducted into the mysteries of algebra and Latin, and learning the little tricks of accounting, duplicating, multigraphing, and typewriting have not emerged with the ability to take anything even remotely resembling a realistic view of contemporary social, economic, and political life. They are accordingly almost totally worthless to the investing state as it faces the alternatives of building a new structure of social control in harmony with the realities of the new and inevitable economic order or sinking deeper into the paralysis of social chaos.

I propose, therefore, that this matter of equipping every normal adolescent to take a realistic view of contemporary life is one task which the American secondary school should, indeed must, assume. Somehow, all adolescents must be led to examine the existing traditions in economics, religion, morals, and politics in the light of the actual movements of the social life of the day and to prepare themselves to be intelligent in revising these collective beliefs to bring them into harmony with the realities. When one reflects that our technology has for the first time in the history of the race completely solved the problem of poverty so far as production is concerned, and that we could all live on a vastly more elevated scale were we but able to devise an appropriate structure of social control, it is unthinkable that any system of secondary education could almost completely ignore the problem. There can be no denying that leisure and a superabundance of physical goods have been forced upon us by the machine, that an increased leisure and an increased super-abundance of physical goods will continue to be forced upon us, and that much of this leisure will be in the form of destitute unemploy-ment unless we very quickly address ourselves to the task of build-ing new and appropriate forms of social controls. Clearly, we have no alternative but to set ourselves to this all-important task. Cer-tainly, the investing state has every right to demand that the sec-ondary school curriculum be so conceived as to prepare every adoles-cent to play an intelligent part in working toward the solution of this great social problem.

36. CURRICULUM REVISION ENDANGERS SOCIAL STABILITY [19]

William C. Bagley

What is the task of education in a period of rapid social change? I should say that the most important function of education in such a period is a stabilizing function. The very time to avoid chaos in the schools is when something akin to chaos rages in the social environ-ment. The very time to emphasize in the schools the values that are relatively stable and abiding is when the social environment is full of uncertainty and when standards are crumbling.

The most marked defect of American education today is its con-fusion as to aims and content. Like big business, American educa-tion went on a regular jamboree during the Golden Decade. About 1920, certain college professors of education proclaimed themselves to be specialists in curriculum revision. Now professors of educa-tion have much to account for, but some of the particular professors who became curriculum specialists succeeded in messing things up worse than all of the other members of the guild put together. Their technique was interesting. As guides of committees of teachers in local school systems they would direct the reconstruction of the programs of study, generally from the standpoint of the needs of the local community. A favorite procedure was to have the teachers draw up long lists of what they designated as educational " objec-tives." Some of these lists will be amusing reading to the future his-torian of education. The curriculum-revision fad, however, spread

[19] From " The Task of Education in a Period of Rapid Social Change," *Educational Administration and Supervision,* 19:568–569. November, 1933.

quickly throughout the country and today there are *no fewer than thirty-five thousand different curricula* on file in the curriculum library of Teachers College, Columbia University, most of which have been prepared by committees of teachers during the past ten years.

37. The Functions of the Educational System [20]

The fundamental functions of the State educational system are to educate the people to greater and greater competency, in performing

First, the general social obligations of citizenship or membership in American civilization required of all men and women and,

Second, the particular or specialized services to society allotted to different occupational groups, membership in any one of which is a matter of individual choice and fitness.

These educational functions correspond with the two types of requirement which modern social life lays upon every citizen. Every person has social, political, or other responsibilities which he should bear in common with other persons, as in his membership in the family, the neighborhood, the local community, the State, the nation, and humanity at large. On the other hand, every person has, under our economic system of subdivision of work or services, a particular obligation which he meets, usually by the services he renders through his special remunerative occupation.

A. THE FIRST FUNCTION OF THE COMMON SCHOOL SYSTEM

It is the primary and fundamental function of the common school system extending from the earliest years of schooling, through kindergarten, elementary school, junior and senior high school, and the junior college, to educate the citizen for effective participation in all those common understandings and cooperations which are necessary to sustain the best in our complex contemporaneous civilization which is American.

Our common schools must be dedicated primarily to educating men and women so that they may work and live together more successfully in and through the institutions of a civilization that must be constantly adapted to changing conditions. Failure of citizens to understand many of our current problems and their tragic inability to cooperate in the solution of them constitute one cause that has led to breakdowns in our current civilization.

A common school system rededicated to the original social pur-

[20] From *State Higher Education in California,* Report of the Carnegie Foundation for the Advancement of Teaching, California State Printing Office, Sacramento, June 24, 1932, pp. 17–21.

poses which warranted tax-support by all the citizens of the State, must aim mainly at the fullest possible development of a social rather than a selfish personality. It will seek to develop an enlightened citizenship, rather than an enlightened selfishness. Much of the current criticism of the behavior of citizens as the product of schools is based on the fact that the common schools, above the elementary school are not really utilized by the student nor fully managed by teachers and administrators for this fundamental civilizing purpose. When this ideal is realized, subject boundaries will be less sharply defined. New and more practical groupings of materials will be devised, and the process of learning will be reorganized, much as is now being done in comprehensive courses at some 160 institutions in the United States. Problems will become more important than topics, libraries than textbooks.

The points at which public and professional criticism are now mainly directed are the secondary rather than the elementary stages of general or common schooling. That reform has been at work for some time in the field of secondary education is attested by the increase in junior high schools, senior high schools, and junior colleges. Modifications of the curriculum, changed methods of teaching and learning, educational and vocational counseling are merely additional symptoms of the attempt to meet current dissatisfaction with the schools as they are or have been. A complete reconstruction, somewhat similar to that which began in the elementary school in the '80s and '90s seems now well inaugurated in the secondary stages of general education.

The reconstruction of secondary education, necessarily a concern of this Commission which deals with its later stages in the junior colleges and the lower divisions of the teachers colleges and the university, will involve several marked changes from the traditional outlook and method.

In the first place, secondary education will be not less intellectual but more social and adaptive. It will be directed toward giving the student an understanding of the natural and social world in which he lives. The mastery of the academic letters, arts, and sciences will be no longer the end of his school mastery, but the educational means of understanding life. Whatever other resources of experience lie outside of the traditional disciplines, such as industrial arts and fine arts, will be utilized with full scholastic respectability as valued aids in realizing the new and broader conception of the human and social purposes of the common schools.

In the second place, secondary education will focus its attention more steadily on contemporaneous life, with its oncoming problems. The lag between what the school teachers and what present and impending citizenship requires will be decreased. Scholarship, once chiefly related to the past, will now be related to the present, with study of the past still highly valued to the extent that the contributions of the past inevitably persist in the present.

Thirdly, schooling will not be thought of as practically the end of education or learning, now too commonly and so fatally the case. Education will be regarded as a continuous process, coterminous with life, to which schools merely give impetus for further and continuous personal inquiry and growth. An education at school will be regarded as preparatory to continuous adult learning. How much academic ground is covered in the school building under a licensed or accredited teacher, will no longer be so important as it has been. What one learns anywhere in life, and the degree to which one has the impulse and power to continue to learn and think accurately will be far more important to all concerned — to the world, to the university, and, most of all, to the student himself.

B. THE SECOND FUNCTION OF THE COMMON SCHOOL SYSTEM

It is a second and equally important function of the educational system to prepare young people for productive living. In so far as the individual differences of students — intellectual, social, economic — warrant, this end will be accomplished through occupational training of different types.

The most significant body of psychological fact concerning human nature that has recently influenced our thinking or our action is that which reveals the astounding range of individual differences in a social or school population. People are not all alike. To believe they are and to treat them as though they were is to commit a grave human injustice to many individuals, and to deprive society of the use of their full powers. Social and educational justice is far more nearly realized by treating students differently than by treating them identically.

Differentiated treatment is necessary the moment individual differences begin to assert themselves in such a manner as to make inadequate the traditional curriculum and method of common schools. It may first express itself in allowing or providing a different mode of approach to the study of the world and civilization.

Inability or lack of interest exhibited by a pupil demand a redirection of intellectual interest and provision for a shift of educational emphasis. A change of emphasis from the academic to other domains of arts, letters, or science, on the part of a student, often salvages a school career and acts as a spur to continuous learning. After some years of common schooling a considerable portion of students in compulsory attendance show a lapse of interest. The fact that such persons display limited ability in liberal studies may indicate that their chief powers lie in other directions than the purely literary or mathematical. Here arises the necessity for providing vocational courses of a quality and value equal to and coordinate with those of an academic nature. This situation involves growing numbers of cases as larger and larger groups of the population move through the school system toward the upper levels of common schooling. New intellectual opportunities and new opportunities for specialized, vocational training are then plainly indicated, the more so because little by little the school has been forced to assume responsibilities that the home and industry can not or will not longer perform. But in all such cases the trade or industrial teacher still has the responsibility of socializing or civilizing the student through connecting in the fullest possible extent his vocational activity with the rest of civilized life. Sometimes late, sometimes early, the readjustment just implied takes place for every student. 38198

C. THE MAIN FUNCTION OF THE UNIVERSITY SYSTEM

It is the main function of the university system, which includes the upper divisions of colleges, the graduate schools, and the professional schools, to educate specialists for the strategically important social services which modern civilization requires, and to do this with full regard to the number of such specialists that society can utilize. Among the specialized callings for which the university system educates are research, teaching, the ministry, the law, medicine and surgery, engineering, and similar professions.

Provision for general education in the United States commonly closes at the end of the second college year, or at the end of the lower division or junior college. Certainly, it is a very general practice throughout the United States, particularly in most institutions west of the Appalachian Mountains, to begin scholarly concentration in the arts, sciences, and letters with the third (or junior) college year; that is, with the senior college proper, and to begin either professional or specialized preprofessional education at the same stage in school progress. The exceptions, though conspicuous, merely accentuate the general trend of current practice.

In California both the university and the teachers colleges recognize a functional articulation between the lower and upper divisions, and legislative enactment recognizes that the local, but state-aided, junior college (or college, as it perhaps ought to be termed), is a part of the provision for tax supported secondary education.

A profession may be provisionally defined as "a vocation involving relations to the affairs of others of such a nature as to require for its proper conduct an equipment of learning or skill, or both, and to warrant the community in making restrictions in respect to its exercise." The effective or ineffective performance of professional duties is preservative or destructive of some fundamental potentiality, right, or other value of crucial importance to society or the individual. For this reason ethical practice is as important as expert practice. This is obviously true respecting a career in law, medicine, teaching, engineering, or the ministry, and ought to be true respecting journalism and business management. Complete devotion to professional specialization is not now usually regarded as the major undertaking of the student until the conclusion of the period of liberal, general, or civilizing schooling.

Since expert practice is essential to make devoted ethical interest effective in result, special preprofessional training is often required in studies basic to professional understanding. Mastery of practical skill is usually acquired under mature supervision in either an internship or an apprenticeship. In further protection of society, the State finally licenses only those graduates who meet its standards.

The selection of those students who are promising material for such specialized professional education and the determination of the nature of their preliminary or professional education, should rest not with the common schools, but with the university. The university should utilize the advice of its professional teachers and those actively engaged in professional practice, as well as the findings now available from modern personnel studies.

The right to admit to specialized courses is properly lodged in the university system, but in so far as the university method of judging the ability and educational promise of the applicant is antiquated and inadequate, injustice ensues to the individual and therefore ultimately to society. Of such injustice the layman has a right to complain.

The right of the university to refuse admittance to a professional course requiring special and high qualifications rests in some measure upon other grounds than that of personal fitness. The Commission is not unmindful of the necessity of giving some attention to the relation of supply to the probable demand in the several professions. Only a limited number of certain types of professionals can be utilized by society, and overproduction in these particular fields may readily become a social and professional evil, as well as an unwarranted cost to the university and the public. For this reason, admission to some professional schools will soon become, if it is not already, a matter of discriminative selection. Every large consideration involved in this problem of professional school admission — whether it be personal or social, financial, or professional — confirms this policy. The selective functions of a university system are primarily social in purpose, and the individual is and ought to be of secondary consideration.

What has been said of admission to specialized professional schools in the university may not at first thought seem to apply to all those who seek admission to the senior college of arts, letters, and science. The university should be concerned not only with clearly professional subject matter but also with the various fields included within the division of letters, the arts, and the sciences, which from their very nature prepare through special mastery for superior civic service. The same discriminative and selective principles must be exercised in admitting students to the senior college as are applicable in respect to the professional schools.

CHAPTER III

SIGNIFICANT INFLUENCES ON CURRICULUM DEVELOPMENT

38. DISINTEGRATING INFLUENCE OF SPECIALIZATION [1]

Charles A. Beard

IN the universities and colleges, specialists in subject matter — in science, history, economics, civics, and sociology, for example, showed a tendency to sharpen their specialties rather than to broaden their interests. They organized numerous associations representing the several divisions of learning. The way to fame and fortune for the young teacher lay through the production of some minute work which would command the respect of his superiors in specialization. Hairs split many times were split again. Courses were divided and subdivided. Whereas, for example, it had once been deemed possible for an intelligent mortal to know enough American history to give a college course in that subject covering the period from Columbus to President William McKinley, such a conception was now regarded with suspicion as superficial. In this fashion higher learning disintegrated into thousands of courses, without any center of gravity in intellectual or moral purpose, and each specialty became a sort of vested interest which often brought pressure to bear on the schools to secure the insertion of its offerings into the curriculum.

In outcome the disintegrating influences of the university spread to the colleges and from the colleges into the public schools, multiplying courses and special interests. Although many gains were made in detail, the general tendency was to make education increasingly " academic," that is, to divorce it from the realities of home, community, economy, life and labor. Even where efforts were made to introduce vocational training and guidance, emphasis was laid on the creation of niche-filling employees rather than many-sided, creative, adaptable personalities; and, owing to the kaleidoscopic character of changing business and industry, vocational training and guidance often led up a blind alley. When the great crisis of 1929 burst upon the country, the individual and collective helplessness of millions of persons who had been educated in American schools dem-

---

[1] From *The Nature of the Social Sciences,* Charles Scribner's Sons, New York, 1934, pp. 137–138.

onstrated the inadequacy, if not the futility, of their training in methods and subject matter.

39. A PROGRAM OF ISOLATED SUBJECTS LEADS TO CONFUSION [2]

John Dewey

In this difference of meanings within the terms "study" and "learning" is implicit the point I wish to make. The titles we find in a school program, such as history, geography, algebra, botany, assume that learning is already at hand, set in proper summaries and needing only to be divided up into proper doses. They assume that this material which is unified through its isolation from other things is the natural occasion for the act of studying. This assumption has broken down through the expansion of knowledge and modes of expert skill; this breakdown has caused the immense variation in actual subject-matter which has come about even when the nominal titles remain the same. The content changes; titles persist. The persistence of names is of little account. What is important is that segregation also persists.

The name is a tag but it operates as though there were something definitely fixed underneath it. The same adherence to an outworn idea explains the multiplication of subjects. When there is too much material to be "covered" in one course, the logical thing, given the premiss, is to break the unwieldy material into pieces. This fractionizing is inevitable as long as the educational mind is dominated by the notion that studies are identical with traditional divisions of subject-matter. The fragments become first smaller cabins and then hardly more than pigeon-holes for odds and ends.

In the actual advance of knowledge and the arts, there is much more than mere extension of facts and principles. It has been attended by constant development of cross references, of interdependencies and interrelations. When we compare the actual situation with the scholastic, we find growing divergence, till now there is a split. The extension of knowledge in scope has had an effect of multiplication of courses; its movement in complex intricacy of relationships has had little effect. The scholastic and the actual now sustain an almost inverse ratio to each other. If we take a glance at only the titles of the latter we come upon many which are designated with hyphens: astro-physics, bio-chemistry, and so on. And there are many more where an adjective is prefixed to the noun that names the old subject-matter, such as physiological chemistry, physiological

[2] From *The Way Out of Educational Confusion,* The Inglis Lecture, Harvard University Press, Cambridge, 1931, pp. 13–18.

psychology, physical chemistry, etc. These names also testify to the breaking down of dividing walls between subjects. And quite apart from the emergence of these connecting links, every subject now borrows from others; it can be pursued only by using material drawn from other subjects in order to throw light, and by using methods developed in other subjects as tools of inquiry. The connection between physics and mathematics is very old; in spite of this fact in schools the two are taken up independently, and too often the student of physics does not see the bearing of what he has learned — that is to say, memorized — in a subject labelled mathematics; while his mathematics remains a vexing set of operations and of merely symbolic formulae apparently devised *ad hoc.* It is no wonder under such circumstances — and physics and mathematics is the field in which interdependence is best, not least, recognized — that subjects grow superficial and barren, and that their multiplication brings weariness to the spirit and the flesh.

What has been said about interdependence in branches of knowledge holds equally well in those technical activities of use of knowledge that we call industrial or practical arts. In operation they are often immensely specialized in detail. But back of the operations there lies a concentration of knowledge derived from many sources, an integration of many processes which originated in separate arts. Consider the multiplicity of problems that have to be met by a city architect, problems not just of building, but of lighting, heating, plumbing, ventilation, elevator service, perhaps electric power, decoration, and so on. The individual architect may not be master of them all but he has to know enough to coördinate the activities of specialists in these departments. The illustration is typical of what goes on in every modern factory.

I hope my point has become reasonably clear. In a situation where the skills or arts and the subject-matter of knowledge have become interwoven and interdependent, adherence to the policy forming the studies of secondary and collegiate instruction on the basis of many isolated and independent subjects is bound to result in precisely the kind of confusion we have at present.

40. Results of Logical Treatment of Subject Matter [3]

Neal Billings

This isolated and factual handling of social materials is part and parcel of that same point of view that has confused teachers and learners alike with artificial and academic distinctions. It has re-

[3] From *A Determination of Generalizations Basic to the Social Studies Curriculum,* Warwick and York, Baltimore, 1929, pp. 13–15.

sulted in slurring over the important interrelationships between these facts — the interrelationships without which no true understanding of the intricacies of modern life is conceivable. What good is it to memorize the amount of imports and exports of the United States (facts of economic geography) if one does not see the systems of trade, transportation, credit, diplomacy, and social life which intertwine with these facts. Children study the geography of Great Britain many times, but not until college or graduate school is England's great dependence on the rest of the world for food and the consequent fear of starvation that caused her to impose on herself the task of building the world's largest navy made clear. Seldom in twelve to sixteen years searching for the truth does any one call to the attention of pupils the relationship between missionary and business activities. Not because teachers do not want them to know, but because the textbooks they teach from do not tell them and they teach " by the text."

Facts are learned, instead of the things that facts stand for and that explain these facts — the broad, integrating relationships of life. Around the facts of the industrial and scientific revolutions are gathered the nebulæ of what is probably the most significant trend and movement which explains on the one hand, and on the other hand gives rise to, the problems and conditions of modern social life. We live in an age of growing industrialization — of work, of play, of religion, of thought. In spite of its profound importance few students hear of the industrial revolution and its consequences until they are in college and then perhaps only in a vague sort of way. Here is a movement the understanding of which fuses a heterogeneous mass of detail into a vital unity but which remains largely unnoticed in the school curriculum.

This Encyclopedic Treatment Results in Lack of Interest on the Part of the Students. — This panoramic arrangement and teaching with its emphasis on facts, isolated and soon forgotten, causes lack of interest on the part of learners. Why should they be expected to get anxiously enthusiastic about the number of carloads of grain that are shipped into Chicago in a year if that fact is unrelated to others of geographic environment and the transportation problem involved in feeding many millions of people. There is nothing lively, adventuresome, or appealing in that cold fact. For years the captivation of interest in the classroom has been recognized as a major educational problem, but little has been done toward solving it.

Encyclopedic Treatment Results in Impermanence of Learning. — The factors mentioned also combine to produce impermanency of learning. Fundamental items are not selected for stress and planned recurrence in the courses. Facts are memorized in order to pass an examination. The result is rapid forgetting of the contents of the texts and lessons. Furthermore, there is no great stimulus to make the items learned a part of the pupil's permanent mental organization since they are not taught in a relationship which makes them appear useful and valuable to him.

Encyclopedic Treatment Precludes the Possibility of Carry-over of Learning to Life Situations. — The emphasis on factual learning has a final result of great consequence — such learning can not carry over into life situations. Life situations in the social studies are not purely factual situations. They are complicated situations such as deciding for whom to vote in an election, deciding which candidate's policies will be most serviceable to the community, with whom to sympathize in industrial strikes, what attitude to take toward the disposal of public water power rights, toward railroad and public utilities regulation, toward the civil war in China and the actions which our government takes towards the contending parties, and so on. These are problem situations. Such situations require something very different from the mere memorization of a few facts, to which the encyclopedic treatment of materials lends itself and almost compels.

41. THE DOMINANCE OF THE TEXTBOOK IN HIGH SCHOOL [4]

John L. Blair

A great deal has been said during the past decade about the social function of education, and at the parlous present the voices are becoming more numerous. Concerning the high school the argument has taken the form of a plea for an extension of the time devoted to the social studies other than history.

In response to this plea some attempts have been made to incorporate studies of American society into the high school program. For the most part these have been sporadic and attenuated and, with perhaps a very few exceptions, have failed to attain the possibilities visualized for them by their exponents. In the light of the claims of many of our most cogent thinkers that the misshapen mass miscalled modern society can be moulded into coherence and organization only by an intelligently goal-conscious system of education, it becomes pertinent to inquire why the social sciences do not enjoy a greater repute amongst educational administrators.

Without overlooking the fact that the full answer to the question will include explanations of many aspects, and without wishing to minimize the importance of other explanations, it is my desire to point

[4] From "Social Studies and the Textbook Complex," *Educational Administration and Supervision,* 19:613–615, November, 1933.

out here that a large share of our troubles is due to the fact that the high school is still afflicted with a malignant sort of textbook-mindedness: That is, the idea that for every subject there should be one book — and not much else.

This is due, I suspect, to the fact that the high school curriculum is largely made up of relatively " fixed " courses, the subject-matter of which can apparently be squeezed between two book covers in such a way that the teacher and her class can spend the year in concentration on the one book with never a glance outside; achieving as a result at least the outward semblance of success. A survey of the high school fields may make this apparent.

Mathematics shows this in the most extreme form. A relatively small algebra textbook provides ample bewilderment for a whole yearful of exhilarating pleasure, for a certain type of mind, and excruciating torture, for another type. A page of formulae on quadratic equations will last for weeks when applied to a few pages more of problems. Fifty pages of a geometry text tell all that needs to be said about circles and throw in a month's worth of problems besides.

Foreign languages have tended, in the main, to constitute a group of book-of-the-year clubs. Long ago the editorial committee on Latin awarded the selections in perpetual rotation to Latin Grammar, Caesar, Cicero, and Virgil: The club idea is more or less maintained in the modern languages although with less fixity of selection. I recognized, of course, that a vast amount of lip-service, and a small amount of practical attention, have been given to the idea of wider reading; but even here it is safe to state that any excursions from the favored text have been incidental rather than fundamental.

The work in English composition hinges upon a book of rules and principles, to be applied to the writing of themes. In the study of literature the textbook idea might seem to break down in view of the nature of the subject, which requires reading from different authors. Even here, however, the anthology has crept in and become a text: Where this has not been the case the work of a course has often been limited to a certain few " classics " which are required of all, are studied in concentration *ad nauseam,* and thus become themselves a series of textbooks.

The sciences are no less textbooked. Physics, chemistry, biology contain virtually all their subject-matter within the leaves of the text. Even the laboratory work too often becomes a cut-and-dried process of supplementing the subject-matter of the text, instead of an adventure into the unknown through the avenue of direct experimentation. There are even laboratory manuals which virtually do the student's experimenting for him!

History, except in the rare situations in which it is vaguely disturbed by a sort of social-mindedness, concerns itself mainly with the dried shell of war, politics and dynastic succession which surrounds the real people of any epoch, probably because that sort of thing lends itself most easily to the exactitude and finality of the textbook form.

The foregoing paragraphs should not be misconstrued. I do not imply that the statements made apply to secondary schools without exception: I recognize that the indictments are applicable to particular schools in varying degrees. Nor am I concerned to maintain that the procedures cited are necessarily undesirable for the subjects concerned: I stand ready to admit that in certain subjects, at least, the textbook approach may be essential. I have been concerned, up to this point, to demonstrate the dominance of the textbook idea in the high school.

42. " On the Use of Textbooks "[5]

Boyd H. Bode

We are told from time to time that textbooks have a much greater importance in American schools than in the schools of Europe. The reason for this difference, so we are informed, is that our teachers are less well trained. They do not know enough to venture far from shore. Their general knowledge of the subjects which they teach is enveloped in a fog, and so they cling to the haven of the text.

The comparison of our teacher training with that of Europe is a matter which may be left to the experts. It may be pointed out, however, that our fondness for textbooks may have other sources besides ignorance or helplessness. In part, at least, this predilection may spring from misdirected piety. The business of the schools is supposed to be limited to the preservation or perpetuation of our civilization. Consequently, we should teach the subjects in the curriculum as we teach the catechism, not to encourage a spirit of independence and inquiry, but to insure a set of correct responses.

Principals and superintendents sometimes feel it incumbent upon them to admonish teachers to stick closely to the textbook. It is a fine thing for a teacher to have a rich intellectual background, provided that he makes no use of it. The disposition to engage in explorations beyond the limits of the textbooks is regarded as evidence of intellectual frivolity, if not of irreverence or bolshevism.

Our worship of the textbook, then, appears to be a joint product of plain ignorance and an ignorant veneration of tradition. A com-

[5] Educational Research Bulletin, 7:10–11, January 11, 1928.

bination of this sort can scarcely fail to make the world safe for the textbook. Some persons will doubtless be disturbed by this outlook, but they may be reassured by being told that the modern textbook can present a certificate of character to show that it is entitled to confidence. The older textbooks were to a considerable extent the product of guesswork, but our up-to-date textbooks aim to leave nothing to chance or opinion. They have the indorsement of science. Every precaution is taken to make sure that the evil which they contain is kept below the danger line of one half of one percent. We need no longer fear to take our textbooks straight.

We are all aware of the efforts that are being made at present to construct textbooks on scientific lines. Objective tests are employed to keep the language of the text within the range of comprehensibility, and to determine what material shall be selected, in what order of difficulty the contents are to be arranged, and how provision is to be made for drills and reviews. It would be strange, therefore, if our modern textbooks were not much more serviceable as instruments for imparting a certain body of desirable information than were those of the past, nor would it be strange, if this advance in textbook-making were to strengthen the old idolatry. If the modern textbook has such high scientific sanction, why not follow it without deviation? The old combination of ignorance and traditionalism thus gives promise of growing into a triple alliance for safeguarding the supremacy of the textbook.

Perhaps one might hazard the suggestion that the appeal to science in the present case settles nothing in particular. Science, like the textbook itself, is only a tool. It can be used for all sorts of purposes, and the use of scientific principles in textbook-making may be for the sake of a questionable aim. The fundamental question in the present case is — if a certain amount of exaggeration may be permitted — whether the textbook is written to make the teacher unnecessary or whether it is written to make the textbook itself unnecessary. In other words, does it intend to limit the function of the teacher to the business of " learning " the pupil what is in the book, or does it aim to assist the teacher in drawing extensively on his own resources in order that the contents of the textbook may be translated into terms of " vital " experience? Is the textbook intended primarily to develop certain skills and to facilitate the acquisition of a certain body of factual knowledge, or is it designed chiefly to cultivate appreciation on the basis of insight, the power to think in terms of a given subject-matter?

That there has been much improvement in textbook-making may be cheerfully conceded. But, this improvement should be taken for what it is worth. A good textbook is like a well-trained servant who knows his place. Overemphasis of the textbook is evidence that the controlling purpose is to give a more or less automatic control over a certain body of subject-matter. Such overemphasis not only fails to develop intelligence, save incidentally, but may actually weaken intellectual power. A physician once made a remark to the effect that it is an open question whether the practice of medicine, taken through its entire history, has saved as many lives as it has destroyed. It is of course impossible to decide such a question, just as it is impossible to ascertain to what extent the intellectual power of children has been destroyed by the wrong use of textbooks. Teachers are held even less responsible than physicians in the practice of their profession, but the time may come, as Dewey once suggested, when it will be possible to bring suit for educational malpractice.

43. " The Relation of the Curriculum to the Textbook " [6]

B. R. Buckingham

The relation of the curriculum to the textbook is by no means simple. On the one hand the curriculum furnishes causes which find their effects in the textbooks. On the other hand the textbook may with equal propriety be said to stand in a causal relationship to the curriculum, or at least to the course of study. The play between curriculum and textbook is intimate in both respects.

The causal relationship of the curriculum to the textbook is, however, more fundamental. When we say " the curriculum " we use an abstract term. We are therefore justified in asking its meaning in an abstract way. With a certain lamentable lag, the curriculum is a reflection of the times. In the days of the close association of school and church the school had a strong religious tinge. School teachers and the public expected a considerable amount of money and effort to be expended in the schools upon religious doctrine. Similarly the curriculum in reading reflected the morality of the times. Patriotism, prudence, thrift, and piety were expected and were provided for in the curriculum.

Various movements, big and little, could be instanced. The curriculum in reading has reflected the belief in the efficacy of whole compositions, of classical literature, of silent reading, of learning to study, and so on. When a given period becomes conscious of itself historically, history is to the fore in the curriculum. A scientific era produces a scientific curriculum — not necessarily a curricu-

---

[6] National Education Association, *Reconstructing Education Through Research*, American Educational Research Association, Official Report, Washington, D. C., May, 1936, pp. 146–148, 149–150.

lum scientifically made, but a curriculum in which science is featured.

Where does the textbook belong in this picture? There are a great many reasons why the textbook has assumed so prominent a place in American education. One of the most fundamental reasons is the rapidity with which changes have taken place in the culture of the people in this country. The only practicable alternative to textbook teaching is personal teaching, and in a society where vast movements are taking place and the roots in the storied past have not been struck, the development of a learned profession of teaching becomes very difficult. Personal teaching, in the absence of profound scholarship, is viewed with suspicion.

Accordingly the curriculum, taking its color from the times, depends for its inculcation upon the book as an instrument for guaranteeing scholarship of the sort that the situation demands. In the early days of the Republic it was apparently felt that only a few people possessed the requisite qualities, including scholarship, to make the curriculum effective. On the other hand, the American plan called for a widespread common schooling. This meant far more teachers than there were scholarly men and women. What could be more natural than that the best scholars should produce books for the guidance of those less talented than themselves? And so it comes about that the textbook as an adjunct to personal teaching, or as a substitute for it, enters the American school as a means of supplementing the shortcomings of teachers.

It is a mistake, however, to suppose that this is merely an episode in the early history of American schools. It is my judgment that the rank and file of teachers today is, in scholarship, in charm, in skill, farther behind the requirements of today than the rank and file of teachers was in comparison to the needs of the time fifty or one hundred years ago. It is not that the teachers are not more capable than they used to be. No one in his senses would say that teachers are not better prepared now than ever before. The real point is, however, that society is demanding so much more of its schools today that even with the advances which teachers have made, they have not been able, by their unaided efforts, to meet the need. If textbooks were introduced into the American schools to guarantee what the teacher could not personally supply, they are now being maintained in the schools for precisely the same reason. In our huge educational organization it becomes increasingly clear that the best thought of the most gifted teachers is needed to supplement the talent of the usual classroom practitioner.

So we find the curriculum, originating in the culture of contemporary society, although lagging behind as has been admitted, depends for its transmission not only upon the teacher but upon the textbook. Under these circumstances the textbook is an effect of the curriculum, not a cause. And this I should like to present as the more fundamental relationship. Authors and publishers of textbooks are constantly seeking to find out what the curriculum is in its essentials in order that the textbook may be acceptable.

From what I have said it is clear that the dignity and importance of textbooks depend squarely upon the dignity and importance of the curriculum. Moreover, if the courses of study which embody the curriculum are trivial, crotchety, uninspired, then the textbooks which depend upon these courses of study will be similarly affected. Again, if the curriculum-makers, when they get down to writing courses of study, differ widely among themselves in their interpretation of the *Zeitgeist* by which they are supposed to be guided, then confusion results. Textbooks are then made which meet only a limited need. Although a certain amount of diversity in curriculums is a symptom of health, it can easily happen, and it sometimes does happen, that educators by their disagreements merely darken counsel with words and leave both teachers and authors in helpless perplexity. I suppose we should be entering a publisher's paradise if educational thinkers and writers were to agree on the fundamental aspects of the curriculum. . . .

Permit me to indicate briefly some of the ways in which textbook teaching actually surpasses the type of teaching which emanates from the teacher and which I shall call personal teaching. Please note in this connection that I am by no means denying important advantages to personal teaching. It happens that what I am about to say is on the other side.

First, it is evident that when a child learns from a book he is able to do so at his own rate. Children differ enormously in their speed of thinking and learning. The book allows them to adapt their pace to their capacities. On the other hand, personal teaching is conducted not at the learner's rate but at the teacher's rate. However skilfully this may be adapted to the pace of some pupils in the class, it cannot be in the very nature of things a challenge to the bright child and at the same time a stimulus to the dull child.

Second, when the child learns from a book he can repeat the learning as often as he wishes. Topics which present difficulty, ideas which are apparently in conflict, obscurities, passages of high interest and importance — any of these may be repeated at the will of the learner. It is not so with personal teaching. What repetition there is is done at the will, not of the learner, but of another person.

Third, a considerable amount of psychological research supports the idea that in learning *recall* is even more important than repetition. Recall is that act of the learner in which he turns away from the material he is learning and tries himself on it to see if he has mastered it. Normally he then returns to it to piece out a defective recall. All this is at once possible when the material to be learned is offered in a book; it is quite impossible when the material is offered by the teacher.

Fourth, the learner can take notes on material presented in a textbook. He can do so at leisure. He can take time to make outlines and to extract quotations. This is all done with less success and with greater difficulty when one must learn from personal teaching.

Fifth, the book, especially the modern textbook, makes much more effective use of pictures than is normally possible when the teacher is the source of the learning material.

I see then these five important advantages which learning from a textbook has over learning from personal teaching — thinking at one's own rate, repeating as one wishes, recall, note-taking, and using pictures. These advantages are by no means small. They undoubtedly permit the textbook to be an important carrier of the curriculum.

44. ANALYSIS OF TEXTBOOK USE IN AMERICAN EDUCATION [7]

William C. Bagley

The textbook system, as we all know, has been developed to a far greater extent in American schools than in those of other countries, and the alleged domination of the work of the schools by the textbook has been severely criticized, both by our own educational leaders and by foreign observers. It seemed important to determine, if possible, whether the formal textbook methods had been affected in a significant degree by these criticisms and by the emphasis which has been given to the more informal methods of teaching in the teacher-training institutions and especially in the extension and summer-session courses to which apparently an overwhelming proportion of our public-school teachers have been exposed during the past ten years.

While the data which we gathered are not sufficiently representative to warrant sweeping generalizations, they show an internal consistency which justifies the inference that they give a fairly typical picture of the types of teaching that prevail in the schools of urban communities. Outstanding features of this picture may be summarized as follows:

1. While more formal types of textbook work still characterize many of our schools, there is a quite appreciable use of the more informal procedures. There is an increasing tendency to use more

[7] From "The Text-Book in American Education," *School and Society,* 33:356–357, 358, 359–360, March 14, 1931.

than one textbook in a given course, to use reference books, and to supplement and in some cases to supplant the textbook recitation by the so-called " socialized " recitation in which individuals or groups report to the class what they have learned from various sources. Our data suggest, too, an appreciable use of the project method. Indeed, in the reports of our observers, the socialized recitation and the project method taken together are mentioned slightly more frequently than is the " straight " textbook recitation — that is, the more or less literal reproduction of textbook assignments by the learners. Again it should be emphasized that our data were gathered chiefly in town and city schools and may not be at all representative of practices in the rural school.

2. The formal textbook methods are much more frequently reported as characterizing high-school instruction than as characterizing instruction in the elementary schools. For example, the socialized recitation and the project method, taken together, are reported three times more frequently from the elementary schools than is the formal textbook recitation, while in the reports from the high schools, the informal procedures appear 25 per cent less frequently than the formal textbook method.

3. Quite contrary to our expectations, the tendency to use the more informal methods is significantly more prevalent among teachers with five years or more of experience than among the younger teachers. The beginners tend very strongly toward the more formal methods. There is a similar relationship between the length of training of the teacher and his tendency to use more frequently the informal methods. There is an exception here, however, in that the teachers with four years of training beyond high school use the formal methods more frequently than do those with two or three years of training. It is probable that most of the four-year teachers are college graduates teaching in the high schools. On the other hand, teachers with more than four years of training (presumably those who have had some graduate work) make very frequent use of the informal methods. These teachers, I believe, represent largely those who have taken summer-session and extension courses in which professional courses in education are likely to be emphasized, as they are in the normal schools and teachers colleges attended in all probability by those reporting two years and three years of training. In any event, I am venturing the hypothesis that it is professional training rather than mere length of training that predisposes teachers toward the use of the more informal methods. If this hypothesis is substantiated by further studies we shall have convincing evidence of something about which there has been a considerable measure of doubt — namely, whether educational theory, as taught in our pro-

fessional schools, both graduate and undergraduate, affects in a fundamental way the practice of the elementary and high schools. If our data are in any way significant, educational theory in the present organization of American education with its really vast facilities for in-service training exerts an almost immediate and fairly profound influence. In fact, I venture the guess that the oft lamented " lag " between theory and practice is a good bit of a myth in so far as American education is concerned.

4. The development of the textbook as the principal agency of instruction in American schools came about largely because the teachers until very recently have been as a group immature, undertrained, and short lived in the profession. Our findings indicate that this condition is rapidly passing. Of the " random sampling " of five hundred-odd teachers whose classwork formed the basis of our study, nearly half had had the equivalent of four years or more of training beyond high school while only a negligible proportion had had less than two years of such training. In fact, those who had had more than four years were four times more numerous than those reporting less than two years. Within the decade we have made almost unbelievable progress toward a stable, permanent, and generously trained teaching-personnel. . . .

Whatever the evils of the textbook system may be, it is fairly clear that it is about the only force in American education that reflects a systematic and orderly procedure. Our teachers are not trained to give that type of systematic and thoroughgoing oral instruction that characterizes the best European practice. Our teachers are not even trained in the relatively simple techniques of using textbooks effectively. For more than a generation, theory has frowned upon the use of textbooks and has declined, in effect, to have any commerce with them. Textbooks, of course, have been used in the training institutions themselves, in part because of the prejudice against oral instruction; but as P. G. Chandler has recently shown in an extended study of the methods of teaching used in normal schools and teachers colleges, the instructors in these institutions, while using textbook methods almost exclusively, exhibit a minimum of skill in textbook teaching. Controlled experiment, for example, has abundantly confirmed the hypothesis that the most important phase of textbook instruction from the standpoint of the teacher is that which has to do with the assignment. Yet in more than one hundred class exercises observed and analyzed by Chandler in six representative state teachers colleges, an overwhelming majority of the instructors, although they were using textbook methods almost exclusively, apparently regarded the assignment as the least important phase of their teaching. The recitations too, practically without exception, were of the dreary, time-wasting " question-and-answer " type. It is scarcely to be marveled at that teachers brought up under such ineffective methods of using textbooks make the dismal failure in the use of textbooks in the lower schools that another recent investigation reports.

The trouble with the use of textbooks in our schools is not that the methods of using them are " formal " but that these methods are so often unintelligent and even stupid. I believe that this contrast holds pretty generally in our efforts to cure the ills of education. We condemn the lecture method *in toto,* when the real object of our condemnation should be the poor lecture. We condemn the textbook teaching out of hand, when what we should condemn are the numberless stupid ways of using textbooks. Within a decade we have embraced in close succession problem teaching, then project teaching, then the contract plan, then the activity program, then the unit plan — ever on the hunt for a foolproof formula. There is no such thing in teaching. Every one of these patterns or procedures has its virtues and the probability is that no one's schooling should be entirely dominated by any one or any two or any three of them. The only solution of the problem lies, not with the system nor with the pattern nor with the method, but with the teacher.

If I were a supervisor I would sedulously avoid judging teachers by the methods that they used. I would judge them rather by the results that they achieved. If one teacher could do a really fine piece of work on the socialized-recitation plan, I would say use that plan; if another did passing well with the contract plan, I would say use that plan; if still another demonstrated his ability to give direct, systematic, oral instruction in a stimulating and effective way, I certainly would not condemn him on the ground that his instruction was by word of mouth or on the ground that his instruction was direct, straightforward, and systematic and therefore clearly out of date according to our American standards; and if still another teacher could teach textbook lessons as did the teacher that I described, I would say, in effect, God bless you, keep it up; I should not condemn him merely because other teachers foolishly expect the textbook automatically to do all their teaching for them and naturally bring the whole system into disrepute.

Our profession would stand aghast if any one seriously suggested that all children should be fitted to an identical educational mould; yet in our attitude toward classroom procedures we apparently believe that there is just one good way to teach if it can only be found and that every teacher ought to follow the particular pattern that happens at the moment to be proclaimed as the final word, with firm faith that here at last is the pot of gold at the foot of the rainbow.

The rapidity with which these patterns have arisen and enjoyed their brief hour of glory and then sunk out of sight ought in itself to awaken us to the futility of this attitude. We decry the prevalence of formalism in our schools but by far the most serious type of formalism is that which is based upon the assumption that any one teaching procedure can be made to fit all educational materials, all teachers, and all learners. I should like to plead for intelligent teachers in the choice of their teaching methods at least a small fraction of that freedom which our educational theorists would grant to children in choosing the lessons that they are to learn.

45. " FORCES THAT CONTROL THE SCHOOLS " [8]

Howard K. Beale

Among the noisiest, though not the most effective, outside pressures are those exerted by the so-called patriotic organizations: ancestor-worshipers like the Daughters of the American Revolution, military organizations like the American Legion, and various other organizations set up to further patriotism of the one hundred per cent variety. These groups have several characteristics in common. They stand for a common brand of chauvinism and super-nationalism. They advocate huge armies and navies, imperialism, isolationism. They tend to hold reactionary economic, social, and political views. They are stimulated to panic or patriotic oratory at the mention of anything they consider radical or even liberal. They hate pacifists, whom they regard as traitors. They attack an opponent's ideas by denouncing his motives, his morals, his loyalty to America. They fight " radicalism " in the name of ancestors who were themselves radicals. They deny freedom to opponents and practice repression in the name of early Americans whose great claim to fame was their love of freedom. They talk freely of protecting American ideals and traditions, but they have never studied the writings of men like Lincoln, Madison, Jefferson, Franklin sufficiently to know that they themselves perpetually violate the ideals for which these men struggled. One wonders if they have ever read Jefferson's first inaugural address or the Declaration of Independence. If Thomas Jefferson were alive today and tried in an American school to interpret the Declaration of Independence in terms of modern America, the patriotic organizations would get him barred as a dangerous radical.

Many of these " patriotic " organizations make suppression of freedom in the schools a chief purpose. They seek to use the schools for propaganda for their own views of patriotism, war and peace,

[8] *Harper's Magazine*, 169:604–610, 611, October, 1934.

economic and political theory. They try to force teachers to indoctrinate children with " correct " views. They go farther and try to suppress as radical or prejudiced any contrary views a teacher may hold. If they are successful education will become a process of memorizing shibboleths, going through outward forms of patriotism such as flag salutes and oaths of allegiance, and then learning to render blind, unthinking obedience to the behests of a small minority who have taken upon themselves an un-American censorship of the speech and ideas of all of their fellow-citizens.

How successful these groups are in controlling the schools is difficult to determine. They have succeeded in getting some of their wishes incorporated into school curricula. They have forced the modification of some texts and secured the banning of others. Occasionally a teacher is disciplined to please them. Thousands of teachers refrain from self-expression because of fear of them. They keep pacifist and liberal speakers out of many schools. They force teachers to hypocrisy. They keep popular opinion unfavorable to freedom. Yet their influence is small in proportion to the commotion they create. The American Legion is most powerful. The D. A. R. and United Daughters of the Confederacy share second place. In the South feminine patriotism owes allegiance to the Confederacy, not to national heroes. Hence the D. A. R. is relatively inactive, but its position as guardian of the schools is adequately filled by the U. D. C.

Some of the newly organized patriotic groups — not the descendant organizations or the military brotherhoods — are very closely related to reactionary " big business " and are heavily financed by timid men of great wealth who use these " patriotic " organizations as disguises under which to crush reforms that endanger their economic power. Furthermore, some of the professional " patriots " find it quite profitable to feed the fears of these men of wealth by discovering for them a red in every schoolhouse and church. There can be no doubt of the sincerity and the devotion to country of the D. A. R. and the Legion. Their motives are not bad. But they are dangerous to the schools because they will never admit the purity of their opponents' motives, because they depend upon threats and force and are unwilling to allow questions to be settled by free speech and free debate, and because they look upon teachers as automata hired to impose upon the next generation the views of whatever group is powerful enough to control them.

There are other groups who seek to control teachers for specific purposes: anti-Britishers who make political capital or personal gain out of rekindling the traditional hatred of Britain; Irish-Americans who besides twisting the British lion's tail seek to emphasize in the schools the contributions of the Irish to American life; German-

Americans who have added to their old interest in glorifying German-American heroes the new purpose of barring from classrooms all material derogatory to Germany's part in the War and all truths unpleasant to German ears, even official pronouncements of President Wilson; Negro organizations that not only labor tirelessly for fair and equal treatment of Negroes, but when this is attained, like all such groups, go farther and seek to eliminate from the schools all unpleasant reminders of the Negro's past. Religious groups put occasional pressure upon teachers. In smaller communities this comes from Protestant sects that are usually eager to control schools not only in order to serve their own religious ends but to bulwark the present social order as well. In the cities Catholics are often powerful enough to prevent the expression of views " dangerous " to their faith.

For several years the Ku Klux Klan was a power in the schools of the Middle West, South, and Border States in persecuting Jews, Catholics, Negroes, " radicals," persons with foreign names. Teachers and superintendents who would not do its bidding were driven out. Today the old Klan element is still often the motive power behind attacks upon freedom in teaching, upon Negro schools, Catholics, and the teaching of evolution.

The W. C. T. U. has long been powerful in education. Chambers of Commerce and local bar associations interfere with teaching for the sake of protecting things as they are. The American Bar Association in 1922 appointed a committee on American citizenship, which included Wallace M'Camant, attacker of historians, red-baiter, and anti-Britisher. The citizenship creed drawn up by the lawyers began, " I believe that we Americans have the best government that has ever been created — the freest and the most just for all the people." " The schools of America," reported the committee, " should no more consider graduating a student who lacks faith in our government than a school of theology should graduate a minister who lacks faith in God."

The American press is one of the worst restraints upon schools. It is largely owned or controlled by wealthy and conservative men. Its keenness for news sometimes overcomes its desire to serve its masters. Occasionally when thoroughly aroused, public opinion must have a victim, and the press turns on a Mitchell or an Insull. But ordinarily it " soft-pedals " news fundamentally derogatory to the rich and the powerful who continually menace freedom in the schools. The damaging revelations made during the Federal Trade Commission's investigation of public utility domination of the schools got very little publicity except in the liberal weeklies and an occasional independent daily. Cases of violation of freedom are usually ignored or written from the conservative or the administration point of view in all but a few papers like the Scripps-Howard chain.

Besides, the press often leads the attack upon freedom. Frequently it is impelled thereto merely by its appetite for news. The story of some " queer " or " radical " teacher or, above all, a juicy bit of gossip, harmless perhaps in itself but fatal to the teacher, whets that appetite and tickles the public's fancy. Stories that injure teachers are, in short, " news," whereas the fine but quiet work and influence of these same unconventional teachers through long years of service are not " news." In other cases, honest conviction or a desire to please its masters leads the press to attack teachers or the schools. The *New York Times,* generally more fair-minded than many, has attacked teachers' unions and radicalism. The *Los Angeles Times* has been a large factor in maintaining business and political control of Los Angeles schools. The Hearst papers not only carried the Charles Grant Miller attacks upon history but have persistently baited " reds " and attacked freedom in teaching in other ways. The *Charlotte Observer* has led attacks on freedom in its State and has carried on deadly warfare against the liberalism of the University of North Carolina. The *Chicago Tribune* rarely loses an opportunity to attack teachers' organizations and " radicalism " in the schools. A newspaper is in a position to publish falsehoods and then ignore the corrections, which it may admit privately. Corrections of misstatements are not news. During the depression a large part of the press has led the cry for economy, not at the expense of business and political corruption but at the cost of crippling the schools and thereby depriving teachers of the economic security that is basic to their free participation in solving society's problems.

Abundant evidence exists that schools and their teachers are often the football of politics. All too often attacks on schools, or something taught in them, or the conduct or views of their teachers, make excellent ammunition for the demagogue. Evolution and radicalism would have been much less serious issues if it had not been so profitable for politicians to capitalize on them. When politicians are in danger of losing on real issues or when they wish to turn public attention from their own misdemeanors, socialism or some other bogey serves as a red herring. When once an appeal is made to emotions of this sort then, whatever their own convictions and however great their regret at the raising of the issue, few politicians dare stand out for the schools in the face of popular feeling. Moreover, schools provide rich spoils for the political bosses. For schools to criticize abuses of local politicians is ordinarily impossible.

Recently A. O. Roorbach was dismissed from the Harrisburg, Pennsylvania, schools because he attacked boss control. In 1931 two of the nine machine school directors, dominated by the Republican county boss, had inspired the organization of a High School Teachers' Association. At a secret session hand-picked officers were elected. Then an effort was made to bully all teachers into joining this politician-controlled Association. A blanket dismissal of all teachers sixty days before the close of school was used as a whip threatening refusal of reinstatement to any who refused to join. The Association's president boasted that all teachers who stayed out would be fired. One teacher critic of politician control was demoted. Others were intimidated. Teacher opposition to the Association was so strong, however, that the teachers were finally reinstated without joining. Roorbach led the opposition. He co-operated with leading citizens in obtaining a financial and pedagogical survey of the Harrisburg schools by outside experts who reported that "petty politics of all sorts is ruining the school system." In June, 1933, Roorbach was dismissed. But Harrisburg was aroused. Mass meetings were held. A Citizens' Committee was formed. Members of this Committee were threatened by politicians with business ruin. The Board evaded action and finally refused to restore Roorbach. Then a "citizens' no politics" ticket was entered in both party primaries. In September, 1933, all of its school-board candidates were nominated on the Democratic ticket; three out of four of them on the Republican. A reform school board was elected in November. Roorbach was triumphantly reinstated in February.

Such temporary defeat of boss control, however, is rare. It was made possible in Harrisburg only by an unusual combination of an aroused public, a friendly press, and unusually courageous teachers.

Labor, too, seeks to make teaching serve its purposes. Labor groups have interfered on a number of occasions — sometimes successfully — with curricular matters. Some of its leaders fought the junior high schools, the platoon system, separate vocational schools, psychological tests — all of which it regarded as devices to discriminate against labor's children. It also sought to obtain from teachers a fairer attitude toward labor and some attention to labor's part in economic development. Unlike most pressure groups, however, labor has aided both the social studies and freedom in teaching. It has insistently demanded that more attention be paid in the schools, even in the lower schools, to a realistic study of economics and social problems of the new industrial order. Furthermore, labor has long fought the teacher's battle for freedom. It has pleaded for emancipation of schools from propaganda and the teachers from pressures of particular groups. It opposed the Lusk Laws and loyalty tests. But it has not the money nor the influence of some of the other groups.

The increasing tendency toward government control of education threatens to become one of the great menaces of the future. The last two decades have seen an appalling increase of legislative regulation of schools. /Legislatures prescribe mandatory courses on the federal and State constitutions, on State history, on the federal government, on the State government, on " civil government," on citizenship, on community civics, on the Declaration of Independence.) Many legislatures require flag salutes, patriotic oaths of children, special loyalty oaths of teachers, the singing of the " Star Spangled Banner " or other patriotic songs. The number of commemorative celebrations prescribed by law is sufficiently great to interfere seriously with the educative work of the schools. (The identity of the wording of prescriptions in widely separated States indicates that these are sponsored not by the educators of the State concerned but by national lobbying organizations)

Politicians and pressure groups have secured the enactment of laws making mandatory the inculcation of certain qualities of character and conduct such as Americanism, benevolence, business integrity, chastity, cleanliness, common honesty, courtesy, economy, frugality, gentility, good behavior, honesty, industry, integrity, justice, kindness, love of country, manners, moderation, moral courage, morals, neatness, obedience to law, obedience to parents, order, patriotism, piety, politeness, professional integrity, promptness, public spirit, purity, refinement, regard for others, regular saving, respect for government, respect for the home, respect for labor, respect for laws, respect for the national flag, respect for parents, safe investment, sobriety, temperance, thrift, truth, and wise spending. Special instruction is made mandatory in Bible reading, fire prevention, accident prevention, disease prevention, traffic laws, proper conduct on the streets, forestation, kindness to birds and animals. In almost every State, laws sponsored by pressure groups like the W. C. T. U. require instruction in the nature of alcoholic drinks, narcotics, and stimulants and their effect upon the human system. Many States make special exercises mandatory in observance of Arbor Day, Bird Day, Conservation Day, Temperance Day, Flower Day. Many of these provisions are harmless enough or perhaps highly desirable, but they are so numerous as to interfere seriously with the normal educative process. Frequently, too, the law necessitates a special course on the Constitution or " good citizenship " unrelated to a modern course in the social studies and, therefore, tiresome to the student and contrary to sound pedagogy. Surely if any or all of these provisions are to be included in school curricula, it should be teachers and other experts in education, and not politicians or lobbying groups like the W. C. T. U. or the " patriotic " societies, who prescribe them.

Federal aid to schools, now eagerly sought by educators, is likely to carry with it federal control over schools. A federal Department of Education would open the way for making the schools merely an effective instrument of national propaganda. People who talk glibly of using the schools to put over the New Deal or some particular Utopian scheme of their own need to study the schools of Hitlerite Germany and then pause for reflection. Yet the New Deal is being "taught" in a number of our schools in 1934. The theory that the people who pay the taxes or the State that maintains the schools should control the schools has wide acceptance. Schools controlled by the party in power or the social order of the moment can never help create a better order. It makes no difference whether the controlling power is fascism, capitalism, or a utopian state sponsored by social reformers.

Perhaps the most dangerous, because the most general and most subtle, control is that exercised by business. Business men dominate most school boards. In his study of school boards George S. Counts discovered that professional groups, particularly lawyers, merchants, manufacturers, and bankers, representing a very small proportion of the population, control the boards. A recent analysis of several school boards found them to include the wife of the manager of a cement company, a retired hay and grain merchant who said he "was tired of playing golf and wanted something to do," a lawyer whose firm floated school bonds and fought government ownership of utilities, a chemical manufacturer who made a fortune out of government contracts during the War, a manufacturer of cigars, a tobacco merchant, an engineer connected with a coal company from which the board purchased coal, a lumber merchant, a grain speculator prominent in anti-labor fights, a retired mining engineer, a retired storekeeper, a contractor, a traction company president bitterly opposed to unions, a jeweler, several corporation lawyers, several bankers, several wealthy old ladies. Boards of trustees in private schools read like a selected list of America's better known business leaders and corporation lawyers.

The influence of these business men gives them power over superintendents and teachers and subjects taught in the schools. They see that certain subjects are tabooed: government control of railroads in a railroad town; conditions in the mines in a mining town; labor questions and company police in a steel town; criticism of the mill owners in a textile town; the fact that a particular local business is not paying its share of school taxes. In Winston-Salem, North Carolina, for example, no teacher would dare criticize the tobacco industry's practices or advocate a tax on tobacco. Economic views contrary to the business interests of interested wealthy benefactors would not be expressed in most private schools. This power of business men comes partly from the fact that their gifts finance private schools and their taxes pay for public ones. It arises also in part from the respect that schoolmen in a society dominated by material values feel for the man of affairs who has been successful in accumulating wealth. . . .

Manufacturers' associations and other business groups have been successful in concealing most of their activities. In 1928 an investigation by the Federal Trade Commission brought the activities of the utility companies into the open and revealed an amazingly well organized and extensive set of controls by which teachers' freedom of thought and teaching was being restrained, often in subtle fashion. Committees of " education " were set up all over the country which, under the guise of " helping " the schools, put utility propaganda into the hands of teachers and pupils, sought to control texts and curricula, sent propagandists into the schools as " lecturers," supplied material for the private ownership side of debates and distributed an enormous amount of printed matter. The purpose was to obtain higher rates and effectively to prevent government control by creating " good will " in the coming generation while their minds were still " plastic." " Future generations of Americans," the American Gas Association was told, " will be staunch friends of the public utilities . . . if the work of the information committees continues to function in teaching the youth of the land that the utility men are neither bugaboos nor bandits, but public servants." " Working the schools," said one utility agent, " is something that must be handled very carefully. . . . You cannot afford to let the public think . . . that the . . . companies are trying to circulate propaganda through the schools." Pleased with his shrewdness, one utility propagandist wrote, " Will not the public look upon us as educators rather than as propagandists before the year is over? "

In general, the outside forces that shackle the schools are not vicious persons but almost always the community's " best citizens," its good church members, its civic and business leaders, the most " respectable " people.

46. " PUBLIC OPINION AND EDUCATION " [9]

Jesse H. Newlon

Many instances could be given of the control of teaching by overt pressure from without the school.* During the War a powerful public opinion practically drove German from the curriculum of the sec-

[9] From National Education Association, *Social Change and Education*, Department of Superintendence, Thirteenth Yearbook, Washington, D. C., 1935, pp. 149–150.

* See: Beale, Howard K. *Freedom of Teaching in the Schools.* Report of the Social Studies Commission, American Historical Association, Part XII.

ondary schools. In those hectic war and post-war years, powerful groups brought pressure on the schools to inculcate in youth a militant nationalism and faith in the established economic, political, and social order. Many teachers were driven out of the schools because powerful groups were displeased with their attitude toward the War or their views with regard to political and economic problems. In the state of Tennessee, under pressure of certain religious groups, a law was passed some years ago forbidding the study of the theory of biological evolution in the schools. In many communities teachers belonging to particular religious faiths have long been virtually debarred from appointment to teaching positions. Patriotic societies insistently demand that the school teach youth the ideals of patriotism and of nationalism to which these societies give allegiance. Organized labor, chambers of commerce, manufacturers associations, and other groups have on occasion brought pressure to bear upon the schools to prevent the study of particular economic and political problems, or to secure the study of these problems in the schools. For several years following the World War powerful pressures sought to prevent the study of the Russian experiment in schools both public and private. A good illustration of the use of schools to buttress a private or corporate interest is found in the attempts, successful in many instances, of the utilities group to insinuate into the schools sheer propaganda against public ownership of utilities. The sharpest conflicts center around critical economic and political problems.

If we would fully comprehend the forces that control the schools, we must also examine the social attitudes of members of boards of education, of school executives, and of teachers. Every individual is influenced by the interests and attitudes of the class or group to which he belongs. As various studies have shown, most of the members of our boards of education are drawn from the upper classes in society, from the professional and business classes.* Labor has but small representation; only in rural boards composed of farmers may it be said that all classes served by the school are adequately represented in its direct control. School executives and teachers are drawn for the most part from the middle classes and most of their social contacts are with the middle and upper classes. It is important that those who serve on boards of control and fill administrative posts be persons of broad social understanding and sympathies.

What shall be the policy of the educational profession with regard

New York: Charles Scribner's Sons. (In press.) ¶ Waller, J. F. *Outside Demands and Pressures on the Public Schools*. Contributions to Education, No. 542. New York: Teachers College, Columbia University, 1932. 151 p.

* Counts, George S. *The Social Composition of Boards of Education.* Supplementary Educational Monographs, No. 33. Chicago: Department of Education, University of Chicago, 1927. 100 p.

to these pressures? A policy of drift or opportunism in this conflict of social forces is disastrous. It means that the school becomes futile. Under a policy of drift the school can but reflect the points of view of the most powerful groups in society, for these groups will control it — even tho they be opposed to the best interests of the mass of people and thus to the true interests of democracy. If education is to give youth a realistic understanding of society and of its problems, the school must be conducted in accordance with a considered social-educational philosophy. Such an objective is inconsistent with a policy of drift and evasion. As a matter of fact, education is always conducted in accordance with social principles. It cannot be otherwise. The crucial question is whether education must always be merely a reflection of the status quo, whether the school must, in the very nature of the case, always be controlled by those dominant classes and groups who believe that their selfish interests are best served by preventing change.

In this connection it should be pointed out and emphasized that there are powerful forces working on the side of a forward-looking program of social education in the United States. The tradition of democracy is strong. Freedom of thought and of speech is not only guaranteed in the federal Constitution and in the constitutions of the various states, but it is one of our most cherished American ideals. The public school administrator should remember that the schools serve *all* the people. He should make his appeal not merely to the most powerful groups and individuals in the community but to the rank and file of people. In a democracy the people can control thru the ballot. There is no interest closer to the hearts of the American people than the education of their children. Already nearly thirty million youths are enrolled in the schools, and we are on the verge of universal education to the age of eighteen or twenty. In one way or another the school touches every individual in his most impressionable years, and it touches virtually every family in America. The profession of education has unparalleled access thru the schools to the American people. This opens up a great opportunity to educational leadership and imposes upon it a heavy responsibility.

47. Controversial Issues and the Curriculum [10]

We believe, therefore, that curriculum-makers are obligated to consider definitely the merits and deficiencies of American civilization. In so far as this consideration is in conformity with the domi-

[10] National Society for the Study of Education, *The Foundations of Curriculum-Making,* Twenty-Sixth Yearbook, Part II, Public School Publishing Company, Bloomington, Ill., 1927, pp. 15–16.

nant public opinion, little, if any, difficulty will be encountered in introducing materials into the curriculum for the purpose of using the school as a conscious agency for social improvement. But when controversial issues are raised in the school curriculum (as they must be raised), opposition may be encountered. At this point the curriculum-maker must take care that the material presented and the treatment given shall be fair to all sides. The chief aim will not be to reach final solutions for such problems — still less to establish any prior chosen position — but to build in the children methods of attacking controversial issues and increasingly to develop attitudes of open-mindedness and sympathetic tolerance. In the raising of controversial issues for consideration in the school, careful attention should be given to the educative effect upon the children and to the sensitivity of the community.

In this connection, we respectfully suggest that it is not the function of legislative bodies to prescribe the detailed contents of the school curriculum. The people, through their legislative representatives, may properly formulate a general statement of the aims and purposes of education. The task, however, of discovering appropriate materials of instruction through which to achieve those aims and purposes, is a technical one of great difficulty, demanding special professional preparation. Neither the general statement of the aims and purposes of education nor the task of discovering appropriate materials can safely be left to organizations which represent minority interests. The propaganda and interference of these minority groups in school matters constitutes one of the greatest menaces in modern education.

48. ILLUSTRATIONS OF THE INFLUENCE OF MINORITY GROUPS ON THE CURRICULUM [11]

Bessie Louise Pierce

To achieve their goal, the D. A. R. have urged " the necessity of compulsory education of children of school age," in institutions in which foreign languages be prohibited up to and including " what is usually known as the eighth grade." * During the World War, it was inevitable that this antipathy toward a foreign language should be focused upon German. Just as other patriotic groups voiced their objection to the languages of the enemy in arms, the Daughters of the

[11] *Citizens' Organizations and the Civic Training of Youth*, Part III, Report of the Commission on the Social Studies, American Historical Association, Charles Scribner's Sons, New York, 1933, pp. 17–19, 35–37.

* " National Board of Management," *The Daughters of the American Revolution Magazine*, Vol. LII (April, 1918), p. 264.

American Revolution gave expression to their opposition in resolutions such as the following:

" Whereas, in school communities where Germans control the schools the German language is being taught exclusively or is given preference and German newspapers are keeping alive the spirit of fidelity to German autocracy, resulting in weakening our national spirit, fostering a hostile propaganda and undermining the patriotism of the American people; therefore, be it

" Resolved, That we call upon the President and the Congress and Legislatures of the several states to enact such laws as may be necessary to prohibit the publication and circulation of any periodicals in the languages of the various countries with which we are at war, and to prohibit the teaching of any such language in the primary grades of our schools and to require all public records and notices to be written in the English language." *

The teaching of American history and government in a way to " lay a foundation for the best citizenship " is in no less degree of immediate concern to the members of this group. To encourage an interest in these subjects there are sponsored contests in the highest grades of the schools in the study of history and civics, as well as in composition on historical subjects.† Local chapters abet this national policy by offering prizes for the best grade attained by pupils,‡ sometimes giving their support to state essay contests on a subject such as " Men and Women in the Service of the United States." § Indeed, it is the policy of the Daughters of the American Revolution to endorse wholeheartedly attempts made to prescribe courses in citizenship, government and history. For they believe " the enemies of our institutions have always recruited their ranks from among those ignorant of the true meaning of the principles of justice, liberty and equality under law — the cardinal tenets of our national confession of political faith." They hold it their " high privilege to serve as sentries, guarding the Nation against such peril from within; to foster and to protect and to pass on unimpaired the sacred heritage bequeathed us in the Declaration of Independence and the Federal Constitution." ¶ . . .

* " Twenty-Second Continental Congress," *The Daughters of the American Revolution Magazine*, Vol. LII (June, 1918), p. 339.

† *Twenty-Second Report of the Daughters of the American Revolution*, in *Senate Document*, Vol. IV (1918–19), p. 83.

‡ For example, in 1921, the chapter at Georgetown, Ohio, gave a five dollar gold piece as a prize. *The Daughters of the American Revolution Magazine*, Vol. LV (October, 1921), p. 585.

§ *The Daughters of the American Revolution Magazine*, Vol. LV (December, 1921), p. 702. This refers to the Menominee, Michigan, chapter.

¶ Cook, Lora Haines, *Address and Annual Report of the President General, National Society of the Daughters of the American Revolution, Thirty-Fifth Continental Congress*, April 19, 1926, p. 5.

In the public schools the Legion has manifested a variety of interests. Like many of their compeers the Legionnaires insist that "public education is one of the absolutely essential pillars of our form of government. Where every adult has the vote it is vital that all should have such education as shall enable them to comprehend the rights and wrongs, the whys and wherefores of the questions that come before the electorate." *

As early as its first convention the Legion adopted a resolution recommending that " a course in citizenship constitute a part of the curriculum of every school in this country, and that all our schools be thrown open to aliens for night courses, and all other persons who care to take advantage of the same." The Convention held that " the spirit of this resolution is the Americanization of America, and we feel if the above demands and recommendations are followed, the next generation will see this country rid of the undesirable element now present in its citizenship, foreign colonies a thing of the past, the spirit of true Americanism prevailing throughout the length and breadth of our country, and our ideals of Government secure." †

The Second National Convention and succeeding meetings of the Legionnaires reaffirmed the stand taken in 1919 and urged members to work in their respective states for the enactment of laws requiring not only the teaching of American history and civil government, but also that these subjects be required for graduation from all high schools.‡ Indeed, it was their purpose that these subjects be so taught that they would develop in the child " adequate respect and love for his country," for " education in citizenship is the keynote of Americanism.§

In 1921, the Americanism Commission fashioned a resolution for presentation to Congress for passage and dealing with the teaching of the " English language, American ideals, the history of our country and its form of government."

" Whereas," they resolved, " a shameful condition exists in many of the schools of the nation which makes it impossible for them to build a patriotic citizenship founded upon understanding; therefore,

" Be It Resolved, That we, the representatives of the people of the United States, in Congress assembled, recommend to every state in the Union that it enact into law immediately, measures to the end that the English language be the controlling medium of instruction in

* Woods, Arthur, " Practical Americanism," The American Legion Weekly, Vol. II (June 11, 1920), pp. 5–6.
† Committee Reports and Resolutions, loc. cit., p. 42.
‡ Summary of the Proceedings of the Second National Convention of the American Legion, Cleveland, Ohio, September 27, 28, and 29, 1920, pp. 54–55.
§ Summary of Proceedings of Third National Convention of the American Legion, Kansas City, Missouri, October 31, November 1 and 2, 1921.

our elementary and high schools and schools of high standing, both
public and private, and that all such schools shall be required to teach
at least one year of American history and civil government and all
pupils attending such schools shall attend upon these studies; and
" Be It Further Resolved, That every college and university of the
United States, both public and private, be required to give merited
credit for these subjects in their entrance examinations." *

The Americanism Commission at the same time drew up a law for
passage by state legislatures which would meet their approval, similar in sentiment and phraseology to the proposal made Congress. It
is undoubtedly true that the influence of the Legion and other patriotic groups in the enactment of such laws has not been negligible.
In March, 1925, the Senate passed a House resolution expressing " the
earnest hope and desire that every educational institution, whether
public or private, will provide and maintain as a part of the required
curriculum, a course for the study of the Constitution of the United
States. . . ." † Since the World War in substantially all our com-
monwealths such statutes have been passed.‡

The study of American history and government as proposed by the
Legion was designed to develop a citizenry of tomorrow who would
" stand forth, faithful to America's cause, ready to serve her and to
sacrifice for her," and able to say, " We learned at school to love our
country." § It was their opinion that such subjects when taught according to their proposals would implant in Americans a reverence
for the ideals of the forefathers, and " a willingness to work, fight and
die for them." ¶

49. The Influence of Private Interests and Patriotic Organizations on the School [12]

Bruce Raup

The apparent dilemma of the educator is that he must have convictions, while on the other hand these must be subordinate to the
process of " fair-mindedness." But is this not a false dichotomy?

* " Americanism Body Asks Better Schools," The American Legion Weekly,
Vol. III (February 4, 1921), p. 11.
† Congressional Record, 68th Congress, 2d Session, Vol. LXVI, No. 77, pp.
5396–5398.
‡ See Pierce, Public Opinion and the Teaching of History in the United
States, Chap. IV. See Summary of Proceedings Seventh Annual Convention
of the American Legion, Omaha, Nebraska, October 5, 6, 7, 8, 9, 1925, p. 33.
§ " The American Legion and Education," The American Legion Weekly,
Vol. III (January 5, 1921), p. 10.
¶ " Americanism Program," The American Legion Weekly, Vol. III (June
10, 1921), p. 19.
[12] From Education and Organized Interests in America, G. P. Putnam's
Sons, New York, 1936, pp. 36–38, 48–49, 69–72.

The educator has to select and choose. He must have convictions. He must not weaken his pedagogical effectiveness by subordinating it to the vague nothingness of an " open mind."

The stress on " all sides fairly " is really a good thing gone wrong. Seeing all of the aspects of a problem is an attendant condition of good choice and decision. We have erroneously allowed it to become a substitute for choice and decision. Shall we not be forced to conclude that, with conditions in society as they are, the business of education is not just to provide the means for arriving at choice and solutions but rather to take its place in the whole of society in the actual imperative business of making choices and achieving solutions?

The utilities charge that the schools and colleges are supporting campaigns in the interest of the " socialization of industry." This is a correct charge, in part. There are spots in the schools and colleges where such emphasis has been made and such convictions proclaimed. But is the proper reply to this, that the educators have thereby done amiss? May this not be precisely what should be expected of educators? Are they merely a " clearing house " of " all sides " with no responsibility for making a choice?

But if they are to be admitted to this function of making choices, the utilities publicity official retorts that his side too must be presented. And is not this the crux of the whole matter? Why do people frown upon a private business enterprise when it seeks to promote in the schools the social and economic theory in which its present status is entrenched, and upon which its very existence may depend? The reply is that we do not readily trust people who have something private to gain. We suspect the philosophical generalizations of those who have much to gain privately by their acceptance. Moreover we have learned that an orthodoxy, whether it be religious, economic, or political, is all too often the defense of some intrenched special interest. When, therefore, a special interest embarks upon a warfare in defense of an economic orthodoxy, as did the utilities, there is good ground for suspicion. The utilities did not proclaim their interest in profits. They sought even to deny it.

In a word, can a private profit interest be expected to get a clear view of the kind of social and economic arrangements which will best be calculated for the general good?

Presumably, the educators are less involved in the restrictions which beset the private profit interest. They view the problems in light of the common good; they make it a point to get all sides fairly represented. But they are properly withheld from proposing convictions thus arrived at. Who shall have and propose such convictions if not those thus commissioned? Can it be left to private interests?

Thus does the question of propaganda in the schools become one of the most acute questions before American society today. Can private profit interests be trusted either to make or to carry out plans calculated for the common good? Popular resistance to the utilities campaign in the schools bespeaks a definite doubt in the public mind that they can. . . .

It is clear that the influence of the patriotic organizations bears a freight of conservatism on the most fundamental matters which move the American people. This must always be remembered when as educators we face the issues raised by them in the schools. It is most significant, for instance, that a survey of their actions and expressions should have revealed so predominant a concern for those institutions which we call economic. For the present, at least, our nationalism is prevailingly an economic nationalism. Regardless of what it may have been in the past or what it may be in the distant future, it is for today and tomorrow integrally involved with national and international economic relations. The educator should be aware of this when nationalism is proclaimed and urged by the patriotic interest. He will also be aware that this crucial matter of consensus is at stake when textbooks, students and teachers are pressed and exhorted by patriots to measure up to their standards of national loyalty. . . .

Another means used to influence the mind of America through the schools is the censorship of textbooks. The following evidence comes from a study of the preparedness groups:

A few years ago *The National Security League* was interested in having certain textbooks barred in the schools, but failed in New York State and has not pursued the matter. It has furnished testimony in cases where compulsory military training was objected to.

The Sons of the American Revolution has conducted two investigations of textbooks, one by Judge Moore of Seattle. Their tenor is indicated by Judge Moore's report:

" The books seem to be written to gain the approval, active support and influence of ' pacifist ' school teachers, for about all of the dramatic and heroic incidents which made such a lasting impression on our youthful minds, are omitted. The present generation will never thrill with the words of the dying Captain Lawrence, — ' Don't give up the ship.' The gallant Decatur will be a total stranger! "

There should be more on heroes so that pupils " will have more respect for the principles for which they fought, and the Constitution they adopted. They will not so easily lend an ear to imported radical ideas; with more heroes we will have less young criminals."

" There should be emphasis on the effect of von Steuben's drill. ' The men who ran away from the British regulars, before he taught them by thorough drill to depend on each other.' "

In 1925 the *American Legion* approved a textbook, *The Story of the*

American People, and published a report on textbooks preceding the approval. The report is not now easily available, but its tenor is said to be somewhat that of other investigations by patriotic societies.

And the peace groups take an opposite position:

The *American Association of University Women,* Committee on Cause and Cure of War, in its investigation of United States History textbooks used in the schools of the United States, listed the " ideals for textbooks — adapted from twelve proposed by the World Federation of Education Associations." These ideals were stated as follows:

" In presenting the events representing conflicts between nations, the facts should be given with no attempt to determine the justice or injustice of either, the student satisfying himself from the facts.

" Always there should be an attempt to relieve national jealousies and racial hatreds. . . .

" The study of wars need not be avoided. They were an instrument or means among the primitive peoples and of use where nations had little other contact. It should be kept before the student that civilization and its advance is marked by the turning away from the military and accepting the civil rule."

In the conclusions of that investigation were the following statements:

" The older books all show what is considered today too great an emphasis on military history. The texts of recent date have cut down the proportion given to military history and substituted economic and social history. . . .

" An average of the proportions suggested was worked out as follows:

High school texts: Military History 10–15%; Social History 15–20%; Economic History 15–20%; Political History 50–55%.

Grade school texts: Military History 16⅔%; Social History 33%; Economic History 33%; Political History 16⅔%.

" There was considerable indirect self-glorification. It is just to praise the good deeds of Americans, but sometimes unfair to omit foreigners who have also benefited America, or to take credit by implication to America for things not entirely our own. Quoting from one of the readers, — ' Historians need to dwell more on the good traits of citizens of other countries. We need to develop along with patriotism a spirit of internationalism — an interest in, and a respect for other countries.' . . .

" There should be a more definite handling of the subject of war in relation to the general nature of reasons why nations fight, the way disputes arise, the costs and meagerness of the gains. There should be a better understanding of how public opinion works, of nationalism and of the opportunities of the United States in assisting to maintain peace." *

* *Report, Committee on U. S. History Textbooks Used in Schools of U. S.,* American Association of University Women, Washington, D. C., pp. 5, 14, 15.

The question of the control of textbooks involves the problem of forming the young mind — how shall he conceive of the history and tradition of the nation of which he is a part? Is his primarily a country where military heroes accomplished great and heroic deeds, or preëminently one in which a people painfully attempted a long and hard road toward a better kind of life? Which are the virtues most needed by the child in relation to his country? Those favoring the development of an attitude for peace would propose as follows:

The military achievements of the past are not the answer to the contemporary riddle of how to preserve the tradition which is the ideal America. If the child comes to conceive of his tradition predominantly in military terms, he will be unprepared for a constructive rôle in the creation of a satisfactory new and growing concensus.

If education is to train minds to be ready for the accomplishment of unquestioning military exploits, it will require one kind of treatment of history. If, on the other hand, it is to educate for the building of a new consensus, it will have to use all of its instrumentalities, including the written word, for giving the necessary insights, understanding and information. What information about the history of our country is most important for an intelligent building of a society which will realize our highest traditional ideals under contemporary conditions? And how can such information be conveyed to the end of helping the child to feel himself an intelligent and directive element in the furtherance of desired goals? Such are questions which an increasing number of people today want to use as the test of the desirability of a history textbook. They would not stress insistence upon this great deed or that, nor do they fear posthumous affront to any hero who did much in some settled cause. They choose rather to raise the question of how best to enlighten and inspire the child with the cause of an America made always new in the light of the abiding ideal of human happiness and worth.

In conclusion, the impact of the ardent nationalist upon American social and educational development is seen to involve beliefs and attitudes on practically every fundamental issue in the social mind and heart of America. It takes a stand on such basic matters as religion, morals, economic institutions, government, education, and methods of social change. This stand is almost without exception the same throughout, namely, resistance to basic change and anathema to all those who too vigorously advocate change; no compromise, but simple, single-hearted devotion to things as our fathers left them. The prevailing emotion is fear, and the prevailing attitudes, suspicion and belligerence. This is the powerful element in American society which makes itself felt when the " patriots " turn their attention to school affairs. Yet we have seen and felt the opposition to this element. Which of these contending forces will dominate the emerging new consensus?

50. ILLUSTRATIONS OF LEGISLATIVE CONTROL OF THE CURRICULUM [13]

J. K. Flanders

In most instances the prescription for teaching the history of the United States is found in the same section with the other fundamental subjects and no special emphasis is given to it. This was uniformly true in 1903 and 1913, and in a majority of the cases in 1923. However, in a number of states in 1923 supplementary laws are found and the prescription is more detailed and specific. An extreme case is that of Wisconsin, where a censorship of history textbooks was established in 1923 by a law which provides that —

No history or other textbook shall be adopted for use or be used in any district school, city school, vocational school or high school which falsifies the facts regarding the war of independence, or the war of 1812, or which defames our nation's founders, or misrepresents the ideals and causes for which they struggled and sacrificed, or which contains propaganda favorable to any foreign government.

Upon complaint of any five citizens, filed with the state superintendent of public instruction, that any history or other textbook contains any matter prohibited by the foregoing subsection, that official must arrange for a public hearing within thirty days; and within ten days after the hearing must make a finding upon the complaint. Any textbook found to contain prohibited matter shall be removed from the list of adopted textbooks and withdrawn from use prior to the opening of the following school year. State aid shall not be

" paid for the support of any district school, city school, vocational school or high school during any year in which any such textbook is used in such school after the finding of the state superintendent."

This law would seem to give fullest opportunity for the operation of local prejudice and ignorance. Other states have laws which doubtless work to the same end. In Oregon no textbook shall be used which " speaks slightingly of the founders of the republic, or of the men who preserved the union, or which belittles or undervalues their

[13] From " Curriculum Making by the State Legislatures," National Society for the Study of Education, *Curriculum Making: Past and Present*, Twenty-Sixth Yearbook, Part I, Public School Publishing Company, Bloomington, Ill., 1927, pp. 409–410, 418–419, 421–423.

work." In Mississippi " no history in relation to the late civil war between the states shall be used in the schools of this state, unless it be fair and impartial." In Texas a textbook in the history of the United States must be adopted in which " the construction placed upon the Federal constitution by the fathers of the confederacy shall be fairly represented." It is hardly probable that a book which satisfies Oregon as giving sufficient credit to the " men who preserved the union " will at the same time be regarded by Mississippi as " fair and impartial," or that a book which meets the requirements of Texas will at the same time be acceptable to Wisconsin. Such laws must inevitably foster sectional misunderstanding. In the teaching of history or science or any other subject, truth does not change at state boundary lines. . . .

Of the prescriptions regarding Bible reading, one was mandatory in 1903, two in 1913, and eight in 1923; there was no increase in the number of permissive laws. The term " Social and Ethical Outcomes " is here used to denote various virtues, attributes, and qualities the " teaching " of which was required. A composite list of the qualities and habits desired would include the following:

Benevolence	Justice	Piety
Chastity	Kindness	Politeness
Cleanliness	Love of country	Promptness
Economy	Manners	Public spirit
Frugality	Moderation	Purity
Gentility	Moral courage	Refinement
Good behavior	Morality	Regard for others
Honesty	Morals	Respect for labor
Honor	Neatness	Sobriety
Humanity	Obedience to parents	Temperance
Industry	Order	Truth
Integrity	Patriotism	Truthfulness

A corresponding list to be avoided would include Falsehood, Idleness, Intemperance, Profanity, Vulgarity. Certain other objectives and outcomes are enumerated, such as " the true comprehension of the rights, duties, and dignity of American citizenship," " their own responsibilities and duties as citizens," " the principles of free government." North Dakota amended her list in 1911 by adding to it " international peace," a change worthy of note because of its exceptional character; we have here an express recognition by lawmakers, when dealing with instruction in the public schools, of a world which extends beyond the boundaries of the United States. The following was adopted in Arkansas in 1923:

Whereas, Training in morals and patriotism is important to child life and education, and to the welfare of the State, and

Whereas, The prevalence and persistence of crime and immorality indicates a lack of such training in our present-day citizenship, and

Whereas, The present course of study for our State public schools does not provide especially for such training; therefore

Be It Enacted by the General Assembly of the State of Arkansas:

Section 1. That a course in morals, manners, patriotism, and business and professional integrity be, and is hereby, included in the course of study for the State public schools.

Section 2. That the State Textbook Commission is hereby authorized to adopt suitable textbooks on such subjects, for use in the public schools.

There has been very little change in the number of prescriptions in this group during the twenty years. The gain was somewhat larger in the second decade. The most significant change is the increase in mandatory legislation regarding the reading of the Bible. Whether this growth has been due to a popular demand or to an aggressive campaign by a small zealous group is, of course, not evident from the law. The legal provisions found in connection with these subjects illustrate with especial clearness a characteristic which is common to much of the legislation affecting the curriculum; namely, a tacit disregard of the laws of learning and an implicit faith in the efficacy, for character formation, of mere exposure to ideas. Those who promote the sort of legislation that is found, for example, in connection with " Morals " and with " Social and Ethical Outcomes," appear to be actuated by the assumption that desirable habits, attitudes, and ideals can, with certainty, be imparted by the written or spoken word.

No merely quantitative statement . . . will show the most significant aspect of the recent legislation, namely, the change in the character of its provisions. The recent enactments are, on the whole, more definite and restrictive. They embody more detail. Recent legislation reveals an increase in assurance on the part of the law-makers. Apparently, they are more conscious of their authority and more determined to insure the realization of their will. Time-allotments are much more common than they were twenty years ago and there has been a decided increase in the number of provisions imposing a penalty for failure to carry out a particular mandate. Responsibility is more definitely fixed. It is much more common than formerly to specify that an approved textbook must be used and that the teacher shall have had special training for the imposed task. In addition, the duty may be placed upon the teacher to include in her monthly report a statement that this special law has been complied with, her salary being withheld until she does so, and a similar obligation may be placed upon the administrative officers. Sometimes, also, state aid must not be paid to a community that has failed to carry out the provisions of one particular law. " This device is a powerful weapon. There might be twenty different laws creating obligations which rest upon a community and that community might fully meet nineteen of those obligations. If she should fail in the twentieth, she would forfeit not one twentieth of her share of the state fund but twenty-twentieths of it. This practice is such an effective means of forcing a local community to do the bidding of the central authority, especially when a large portion of the support comes from the state, that it could easily develop into virtual dictatorship." *

It must be acknowledged that coercive measures and time-specifications are still the exception rather than the rule. The situation is alarming, not so much because of the distance we have traveled as because of the direction in which we are going. The tendency, as has been pointed out, is not only for laws affecting the curriculum to multiply, but for them to become more mandatory and definite. If the process which is well under way keeps on, it is only a question of time when the curriculum will be fully determined by the members of the state legislature.

Legal provisions in the different states regarding the teaching of a given subject are not infrequently similarly phrased. ' Model ' laws are promoted by certain national organizations and by groups, often small, but interested and resourceful. Evidences of this are to be seen in connection with Bible reading, stimulants and narcotics, the constitution of the United States, and some others.

51. LEGAL CONTROL OF THE HIGH SCHOOL CURRICULUM [14]

W. W. Keesecker

Legal prescriptions — legislative or regulatory — may be regarded as representing those beliefs and aims of the citizens to whom they apply, and the frequency of their appearance in determining subjects to be taught in high school may be taken as some indication of the importance assigned to them. Legislators and school officials have insisted that secondary-school youth be instructed in those subjects which make a special contribution to the physical and moral welfare and good citizenship of the future voters of the State. Where the

---

* Flanders, J. K. " Lawmakers Encroach Upon the Schoolmen," The New York Times, September 6, 1925.

[14] From Legal and Regulatory Provisions Affecting Secondary Education, National Survey of Secondary Education, Bulletin No. 17, Monograph No. 9, Government Printing Office, Washington, D. C., 1932, pp. 110, 111, 114.

legislature and school officials have prescribed that all high-school pupils shall receive instruction in certain subjects the parents or pupils are as a rule not at liberty to exercise a choice in that regard. In current practice, however, and in line with prevailing educational theory, sufficient elective courses of instruction are generally offered; consequently there is only a small degree of compulsion in the matter of what pupils must pursue in high school. There are also few legal restrictions in this respect. The principal restrictions governing subject matter to be taught provide that no sectarian, partisan, or unpatriotic instruction shall be given, nor any instruction which is prejudicial to individuals because of race or color. . . .

Certain State control over the high-school curriculum is in general expressly or impliedly given by the State department of education and the degree of that control tends to become similar to that exercised by the State over the elementary schools. However, one of the important differences which remain is that State control over the subjects to be taught in elementary schools is primarily by legislative prescriptions while State control over the high-school curriculum is by State board or State department regulations. The prescription of the curriculum and subjects for use in high school is generally regarded as an undesirable method.

The State legislature should state only major educational objectives in general terms. Laws should be fundamental and general to insure adaptability. In most instances the basis of law should be the ideals to be attained rather than the subjects to be taught.*

Legislative provisions concerning free high-school textbooks and their adoption play an important part in the administration of the high-school curriculum. More than half of the States now require or authorize free textbooks for high-school pupils; and approximately a third of the States require that high-school textbooks be free. Twenty-three States provide for State adoption of a multiple list from which local school authorities must select. In 5 States county adoption of high-school textbooks is provided for, and in the remaining 20 States high-school textbooks are generally adopted by local high-school authorities.

State legislatures have absolute power to control secondary schools unless limited by constitutional provisions. No constitutional provisions specifically restrict legislatures in this respect. It follows that legislatures are free to adjust State school systems to meet changing conditions. Present conditions of secondary education emphasize

* Quoted also by Troxel in his " State Control of Secondary Education," p. 51, from the Research Bulletin of the National Education Association, vol. 1, no. 5, p. 324.

the need for legislators to consult with educational authorities. It seems desirable that educational legislation should conform to the best opinion of authorities in education and that it should follow carefully worked-out systems which have been found to be producing good results.

Fewer statutory prescriptions accompanied by extension of discretionary powers in State school officials would apparently enable the development of more flexible and adaptable programs in the administration of secondary education, including its support and curricular services. Laws which require uniformity in the administration of education to all may stifle the natural educational processes, especially as it affects the individual. Legislative prescriptions which adjust the school to individual needs are to be preferred to those prescriptions which attempt to adjust the individual to the school. For example, the admission to secondary schools and junior colleges may be based on the suitability of the school to meet the educational needs and desires of the individual. A number of States have made provisions for the admission of individuals to evening schools of secondary grade on this basis. Patty supported this practice in the following language: " While standards of work in secondary schools should not be lowered, the tendency to admit individuals who have capacity to profit by the instruction and training, irrespective of their mode of developing that ability, whether in the usual formal preliminary grades of public schools or elsewhere, is to be commended and fostered." *

52. INFLUENCE OF STANDARDIZATION ON THE CURRICULUM [15]

Walter A. Jessup

Few of us realize the rapid growth in power which has been exercised by this organization [North Central Association]. Our current budget is in sharp contrast to that of the early years. The first commission for the study of English included five members with an expense account of $50, which had been raised from $25! Since that modest beginning, we have witnessed the development of standards that have affected almost every conceivable phase of school work. We have standardized school years, school months, school weeks, school days, school hours and school minutes in terms

* Patty, Willard Walter. Legal Basis of the Public Secondary Education Program of the United States. Albany, N. Y. 1927. p. 227. (Ph. D. Thesis, University of California, 1925.)

[15] From " Standardization and Achievement," *Educational Record,* 13:115–116, 118–119, April, 1932.

of units, credits, points, majors. At the rate we have been going in recent years, we will soon interpret education in terms of split seconds.

We have set up standards of study for all phases of subject matter, including the classics and English and Physics and Chemistry, Music and Dramatics. We have set up standards for textbooks, for supplementary material, including fiction to be read and songs to be sung. We have set up a program of procedure ranging from the teaching load and clock hours to library and laboratory equipment. We have sought to standardize the preparation of teachers, ranging from the number of years of college attendance to the subject matters studied. We have challenged the length of the course, the number of hours, and the title given in the catalog.

The recent experimental studies and other scientific data suggest that the standards that have been set up for size of class, either in high schools or in colleges, seem to be ill adapted to all classes. The latest University of Chicago plan proposes to limit the size of certain classes to the size of auditorium and the carrying power of the professor's voice.

In the last twenty years literally thousands of classrooms have been built in this territory in such a way as to make it well nigh impossible to take full advantage of the present implication of the scientific inquiry relative to the size of classes. The North Central standards have been dominant in the erection of practically all of the laboratories in the high schools of this area. Last year Professor Downing, of the University of Chicago, succeeded in getting permission from this Association to prepare students for college with a sharp reduction in laboratory material. The Stephens College experiment has gone far enough to convince most of us of the fact that there is no special merit in the North Central standard of eight departments in an accredited college. . . .

We ourselves have hardly realized the powerful implications of the current standards. This past quarter of a century has been a period of expansion. Schools have been growing, wealth has been increasing, and since these standards for the most part sounded reasonable, they were seized upon and adopted for the purpose of improving school buildings, increasing the size of staff, multiplying equipment, improving the preferential opportunities for favored subjects in high schools and colleges, so that there was relatively little challenge. In the meantime, there has been a growing disposition on the part of the professional educationist to subject isolated standards to scientific inquiry, and it must be admitted that more than one of our standards that seemed to be satisfactory from the standpoint of opinion have not been able to withstand scientific experiment. Size of classes and the use of laboratory material are cases in point. Now comes the statewide contest in Iowa which certainly casts doubt upon the effectiveness of the whole system as a basis for selecting the best high schools. The fundamental theory back of the organization and the development of the North Central Association as a standardizing agency was that by applying the yard stick of its standards, the best high schools could be selected. In Iowa it is a fact that, measured by test of students in fourteen subjects, the variation between these high schools is as great as or greater than high schools not on the list.

53. Harmful Effects of Standards [16]

Max McConn

It is easy to see now that the gospel of standardization was based in part on a tacit, uncriticized, and unwarranted assumption: the assumption, namely, that all men and particularly all children are equal and alike, or nearly equal and nearly alike, not only in their right to Life, Liberty, and the Pursuit of Happiness, as the democratic doctrine declares, but also in kind and degree of intelligence and capacity. In short, we quite overlooked the little matter of Individual Differences — of which, in fact, little or nothing was heard thirty and forty years ago. And we who were making the Standards were, of course, educators, automatically selected in the main on the basis of considerable scholastic or bookish aptitude. Quite naturally (and quite unconsciously) we created our Standards in our own image. We provided for such equipment and curricula and methods as would have been fine for us when we were in school, and prescribed such degrees of attainment as we should triumphantly and joyfully have met if they had been set for us. And all this was excellent and greatly beneficial for that part of the oncoming generation which was like us. But we entirely missed the fact that the great majority of the children in schools, and even a substantial minority of the undergraduates in colleges, were not at all like us, but were endowed with quite other kinds of capacity and often with lesser degrees of capacity of any kind.

For those others — the majority! — our generalized uniform Standards were all wrong, in that they gave exclusive sanction and exclusive prestige to tasks which were unsuited to their kinds of capacity or impossible for their degrees of capacity or both. As a consequence, the Standards have caused, and are now causing, un-

[16] From " Examinations Old and New: Their Uses and Abuses," *Educational Record*, 16:381–382, October, 1935.

told damage and untellable misery to vast numbers of children in the elementary schools and high schools and even in colleges, thwarting and warping and beating down young lives.

We vaguely imagined that in providing and enforcing substantially the same kind of instruction for all children we were serving the democratic principle already cited: Life, Liberty, and the Pursuit of Happiness for everybody. But in fact our uniform and exclusively intellectual Standards have deprived a majority of our pupils of the last two of those rights.

54. "Beyond Standardization" [17]

Howard D. White

There has never been serious dispute as to the value of standardizing agencies on promoting and protecting a measure of acceptable achievement. We agree that their effect is wholesome, that they encourage rather than repress, and that their conserving influence must continue.

But educational standards, like many others, are subject to revision, and are intended rather to protect institutions from a too meager program than to indicate authoritatively the best line of future development.

Those responsible for standardization must continue to carry that responsibility so that nothing of present value will be lost. Certain tolerable minimum levels of achievement, equipment, teacher qualification, curriculum content, and the like must be maintained by adequate inspection, supervision, and reports.

But it is not to be assumed that standardization will tend toward improvement, once that tolerable minimum level is reached. The very nature of standardization with its implication of finality is against such an assumption. Schools must change, and we cannot consistently advocate the development of liberal programs, adaptations based on experience, and a curriculum of activity while frowning too darkly on deviations from current or customary or mediocre practice. Standardization, at best, is a counsel of mediocrity. Mediocrity is normal, but it is not excellence. To encourage deviation from it in the right direction is the duty of every standardizing agency. It should be the function, therefore, of those who prescribe standards to permit responsible officials of excellent schools to undertake promising experiment. If the undertaking involves departure from current practice, or even from prescribed standards, the stand-

[17] *The High School Quarterly*, 18:135–136, April, 1930.

ardizing authority should encourage it to the extent of authorizing provisional exceptions to accrediting requirements, in order that reports of the results of progressive procedures may be made available to other schools.

To determine what schools are strong enough to depart from uniform standards in search of improved practice and what schools need the continued support of definite prescription should be the duty of the standardizing agency.

No matter how burdensome that duty it should be assumed, for experimental practice must be encouraged if only that more satisfactory standards may be desired. Uniformity will always stand in the way of improvement no matter how satisfactory our present stage of attainment.

It is difficult to see any practical way to avoid irresponsible experiment on the one hand and mere endorsement of current " normality " on the other unless we can maintain research functions as a part of the equipment of every standardizing agency.

55. " THE ' UNIT ' IN ADMISSION TO COLLEGE " [18]

Henry Suzzallo and William S. Learned

In recent months the question has been raised informally whether the Carnegie Foundation for the Advancement of Teaching would look with friendly eye upon a modification of standards of admission to colleges that might be based upon a cumulative record revealing the candidate's achievement, interests, and aptitudes in preference to the formal satisfaction, by examination or otherwise, of the requirement of a fixed number of entrance units. An answer to this question involves two considerations, one immediate, the other historical.

In the first place, the Rules of the Foundation for the Admission of Institutions to the Associated List, 1929, although they follow the definition of a college in force in the State of New York in saying that " an institution to be ranked as a college . . . should require for admission not less than the usual four years of academic or high school preparation, or its equivalent . . ." make no mention of " units," or, indeed, of any credit-counting. The inclusion of institutions upon the associated list of the Foundation stands therefore upon a basis sufficiently flexible and forward-looking to give no concern to institutions that desire to admit candidates truly prepared to do college work of good quality.

As for the history of the so-called " Carnegie unit," in the early

[18] Carnegie Foundation for the Advancement of Teaching, *Twenty-Eighth Annual Report of the President and Treasurer*, New York, 1933, pp. 37–38.

days of the Foundation the most serious question encountered was that of definition. The query, " What is a college? " was seen to depend in large measure upon the student material that the institution received. Then, as now, for this reason the Foundation emphasized suitable preparation of the students accepted by institutions on its associated list. In the schools whence these students came the greatest confusion prevailed. There were no accepted units of measurement for work completed. The question of units of credit was answered partly in terms of the unit of the College Entrance Examination Board, " a unit being a course of five periods weekly throughout an academic year of the preparatory school." * At that time it was believed that if a college required fourteen such " units " for admission it was maintaining the proper distinction, according to educational practice of 1907, between the work of the college and the work of the high school. The following year brought an increase in the number of " units " required for admission by many institutions, both associated and non-associated.

As early as 1906 the National Conference Committee on Standards of Colleges and Secondary Schools had been constituted. This committee was composed of the United States Commissioner of Education, *ex officio*, and delegates from the following organizations: The New England Association of Colleges and Preparatory Schools, the New England College Entrance Certificate Board, the Association of Colleges and Preparatory Schools of the Middle States and Maryland, the College Entrance Examination Board, the North Central Association of Colleges and Secondary Schools, the Association of Colleges and Preparatory Schools of the Southern States, the National Association of State Universities, and the Foundation. At a meeting held in April, 1908, the subject of the definition of the unit for the measurement of admission requirements was discussed at length. Partly as a result of this discussion, a conference was held between representatives of the National Conference Committee on Standards and the officers of the Foundation, and the following statement of the " unit " was proposed: " A unit represents a year's study in any subject in a secondary school, constituting approximately a quarter of a full year's work." This definition was published by the Foundation in its Fourth Annual Report. However rigid it may now appear, twenty-five years ago it seemed both satisfactory and

---

* First Annual Report, Carnegie Foundation for the Advancement of Teaching, 1906, pages 38 ff. Further definition appears in the Second Annual Report, pages 69 ff., and the Fourth Annual Report, pages 132 f. For the use of " units " by the Foundation, see the Third Annual Report, pages 65–71, 74–77, and *passim*; the Fourth, *passim*; the Sixth, page 64; the Seventh, page 101; the Ninth, page 54. Although the First, Second, Third, and Fourth Annual Reports are now out of print, copies may be consulted in most college libraries.

liberal. In its day it represented a distinct advance over what had gone before, and it performed an indispensable function in aligning the school forces of the country in what was as near a common understanding as, under the existing circumstances, could at that time be achieved.

To-day, none recognizes more clearly than the Foundation that these standards have served their purpose. With changed conditions and sharper and more wieldy tools, such expedients become obsolete. They should undoubtedly give place to more flexible, more individual, more exact and revealing standards of performance as rapidly as these may be achieved. The Carnegie Foundation for the Advancement of Teaching looks with favor upon any and all means of judging qualifications for college admission which recent widespread experiment, scientifically and practically appraised, reveals as distinctly better than previous methods. A system of continuous individual records, including information about every phase of student interest and accomplishment, represents a decided advance over any basis for college admission previously in use. Certainly it is a marked improvement upon the " unit " system which in the early years of the present century began to bring order into the much confused situation respecting admission to college.

56. Need for Replacement of Present Standards [19]

Thomas H. Briggs

Standards can be of two kinds. The first is the kind set up some years ago by our associations of colleges and secondary schools and generally copied by every state department of education. These " present wooden standards," as Commissioner Zook in his recent masterly paper calls them, concern the attendant machinery of education. They are easily used in evaluation; they were much needed at the time when they were formulated; and they have proved of great value in the period when the nation was multiplying schools and improving the facilities for education. It seems now unfortunate, as we look back over the past fifteen or more years, that they were not supplemented by other standards that served to direct education itself. But let us not be too severe in our condemnation. Such standards have served useful purposes. We all agree that they need to be replaced by better ones.

[19] From " What Constitutes a Good Secondary-School and by What Standards Shall it be Evaluated? " National Education Association, Proceedings of the Eighteenth Annual Meeting of the Department of Secondary School Principals, Department of Secondary-School Principals, Bulletin No. 50, March, 1934, pp. 15–16.

Another kind of standard measures adequacy in terms of objectives, the competence of a school to do the work for which it is established and maintained. There have been many attempts, both here and in other countries, by central authorities to measure the accomplishment of students who have pursued the courses offered. The principle is sound enough, but it has been so administered as to thwart sound educational purposes. Almost if not entirely without exception the set examinations have attempted to measure the extent to which pupils have mastered traditional subject matter, and as a result they have unfortunately emphasized in the minds of both the profession and the laiety the importance of that subject matter and of perpetuating it. This has been the result of our College Entrance Examination Board, of the New York Regents, and of the various agencies in the several European countries. Recent studies stimulated by the international Conference on Examinations have impeached both the validity and the reliability of the European examinations, and those commonly given in our own country have long ceased to command the respect of those who know the facts.

57. Reconstruction of Standardizing Movement Desirable [20]

Charles H. Judd

When the North Central Association of Colleges and Secondary Schools was organized in 1895, one of the first questions which the Association attempted to answer was the same as that which we are assembled to discuss at this meeting. After due consideration the Association formulated a definition of a well-organized high school. The items which entered into this definition came later to be called standards. The list of standards has in the course of time been greatly enlarged. Agencies such as the Carnegie Foundation and numerous regional associations have contributed new standards and many so-called interpretations have been agreed upon until now a formidable array of requirements confronts any secondary school which asks to be recognized as worthy of approval.

While the North Central Association and other regional standardizing bodies have been active in developing lists of approved schools, state universities, state departments of public instruction and, in some instances, individual institutions of higher education have found it necessary to extend the scope of their approval so as to include secondary schools which do not conform to all of the requirements of

[20] From " New Standards for Secondary Schools," National Education Association, Proceedings of the Eighteenth Annual Meeting of the Department of Secondary-School Principals, Department of Secondary-School Principals, Bulletin No. 50, March, 1934, pp. 7–9.

the general regional standardizing associations. There are as a result a number of different kinds of approved schools. In fact, one may say that classification of schools depends on the classifier to such a degree that one is forced to question the justification for the use of the word " standard " in describing the bases of the different kinds of approval.

The disposition to be critical of standards is further reinforced by such well-known facts as the following. Graduates of secondary schools which cannot meet the standards of any of the regional associations not infrequently succeed in college quite as well as do graduates of approved schools. It also happens in a distressingly large number of cases that graduates of approved schools fall by the way when they attempt to carry college work. Furthermore, reports regarding graduates issued by two secondary schools which conform fully to the most rigid standards are often of such different degrees of reliability that one finds it impossible to believe that standardization has achieved the result hoped for when the system was inaugurated.

It is a generally accepted view that the time has come when a reconsideration of the standardizing movement will have to be undertaken. The North Central Association has been working for several years on the problem of reconstructing its system of approval of colleges and has arrived at some very interesting conclusions with regard to the inadequacy of its old standards for colleges. The Commission on Secondary Schools of that Association, following the example of the Commission on Institutions of Higher Education, is preparing to make a thorough study of its standards. The United States Commissioner of Education, who was largely influential in initiating the studies of college standards in the North Central Association, has organized a national co-operating committee to deal with the problem of devising new methods of approving secondary schools.

58. Influence of the Quantitative Method on Education [21]

Harold Rugg

Where, then, did the intermediaries who, after 1900, took the quantitative method over into education, get their concepts, their points of view, their techniques? *From the physical sciences.* Captivated by the perfection of the quantitative elements in the scientific method, enamored of the precision of measurement achieved in late

[21] From " After Three Decades of Scientific Method in Education," *Teachers College Record,* 36:114–117, 119–120, November, 1934.

nineteenth century physical science, and inspired by the aesthetic charm of the mathematics of probability, these intermediaries between the older sciences and the technology of education threw themselves enthusiastically into the task of making a quantitative description of American education. Working on implied or stated assumptions which we shall note in a moment, they concentrated most of their efforts on measurement and statistical analysis. As a consequence, in thirty years they succeeded in counting and recording the superficial characteristics of American education and in effecting certain reorganizations in its administrative framework.

For example, in an orgy of quantitative tabulation and measurement they collected and classified facts concerning:

a) Child accounting — retardation and elimination; not less than several thousand studies were made following Thorndike's original study of "Elimination of Pupils from School" in 1907.

b) The teaching staff — economic and social background, training, experience, what-not, of the teachers; hundreds of investigations have been made since Coffman's *The Social Composition of the Teaching Population*.

c) Finance — the question-blank analysis of receipts, disbursements, budgets, standardization of accounting forms, what-not, under the leadership of Strayer, Ayres, Mort, and a host of others.

d) Buildings — the systematic analysis of design, materials, costs, all of which led to standardized methods of evaluation and of construction.

e) Pupil attainment in skill and factual knowledge — thousands of studies of attainments within the established school subjects (arithmetic, writing, spelling, what-not) — made under the leadership of Thorndike, Judd, Freeman, Gray, Horn, Courtis, and others.

f) The content of courses of study and of textbooks was tabulated, the present writer contributing his mite.

g) Anthropometrical, mental, and other separated traits of the pupil population — measured and classified by Whipple, Terman, Freeman, Gates, and a host of other educational psychologists.

h) Educational reconstruction via the reorganization of classification, marking, and promoting systems engaged the energies of another army corps of educational scientists.

The past thirty years, then, have constituted the initial stage of the development of education as a technology. This period marked the initial use of the elements of scientific method — that is, of observing and collecting facts, of developing and using measuring instruments, of statistically and mathematically classifying data, of setting up controlled experiments, of inference and deduction of law from observed relationships, and thereby of the achieving of new hypotheses.

It was perhaps to be expected, therefore, that much of the initial work would be based upon whatever data, methods of work, and assumptions were at hand, and had the greatest prestige. The most respected concepts and methods were those of the physical sciences and those were taken over. And with them were taken the theory, the outlook on life and education, and the assumptions of the physical scientists.

Every phase of the quarter century of educational investigation illustrates the point — the history of the movement, the problems which were selected for study, the techniques which were employed, and the interpretation of data. Most of the work has either stated or implied four outstanding assumptions:

a) That human nature is mechanism and not organism; that human personality is indeed the sum of all its traits.

b) That "whatever exists, exists in some amount, and can be measured"; that is, that we know a thing only as we can measure and describe it quantitatively.

c) That human traits which are quantitative-qualitative fusions can be reduced to quantitative measures.

d) That certain traits of an organism can be held constant, and changes which are produced in others can be measured by the use of the statistical method of correlation.

This is not an exhaustive list but it indicates the character of the point of view that the students of education took toward human nature, namely, that it was mechanism rather than organism. Nevertheless, careful review of the evidence that has accumulated from forty years of research in the biological sciences leaves no doubt as to the organic, the integrative character of the structure, and the behavior of human beings. . . .

But the study of the bases of the scientific movement carries us even deeper than the psychological point of view of the measurers. It calls up the question of the rôle of their educational and philosophic outlook. Most of them, at least certainly throughout the first quarter century, assumed a kind of education which in our day is increasingly being discarded as unsound. They assumed or implied that industrial civilization as it had developed in Great Britain, France, Germany, Japan, and the United States — especially on the basis of private-capitalism, laissez-faire, and the rights and immunities of the individual — was essentially sound. Correspondingly, they assumed the soundness of the kind of education that had been set up in those countries. This latter assumption was that "education" was something:

a) That went on in a schoolhouse five hours a day, a hundred and ninety days a year, and was more or less isolated from the social-economic life of the community.

b) That one did before entering " life."

c) That one did with words and other abstract symbols, and with sensory-motor skills.

Correspondingly, the curriculum was a " given " body of skills, facts, and principles; education consisted in " learning " these by the methods most approved by the results of experimental studies. That these assumptions were implicit in most of the scientific work of the last quarter century is revealed by the fact that:

a) The experiments in learning and in curriculum reorganization were largely carried on within the framework of specific school subjects. There was little or no questioning of these subjects.

b) The outcomes of education were stated in terms of specific skills and items of knowledge which were acquired within the subjects (for example, arithmetical, handwriting, and spelling skills, the facts of location, the time facts of geography and history, and the facts of the physical and natural sciences).

c) Tests and scales were designed definitely in terms of these " subject-matter-set-out-to-be-learned " outcomes.

d) A widespread tendency existed among the quantitative workers not to state explicitly the assumptions and other backgrounds of their work.

e) Many of the leaders took no part in the critical discussion of educational theory; in conspicuous instances they refused to include such critical discussions of theory in the offerings of graduate schools of education.

f) Their preponderant emphasis was upon the study of administrative problems of rearrangement. As a single illustration note the assumption underlying scores of investigations of the relation between school efficiency and size of class; namely, that specific skills and items of factual knowledge are the real outcomes sought in school instruction.

g) The quantitative workers in education carried on, aside from " intelligence," very little measurement of such generalized traits as the powers of organizing material, of organizing people, of taking part in group activities, of appreciations, of general insights, and the like.

CHAPTER IV
CONCEPTS OF THE CURRICULUM

59. MEANING OF THE CURRICULUM AND COURSE OF STUDY [1]

Walter D. Cocking

WHENEVER curriculum and courses of study are discussed today, it is always necessary to define exactly what is meant by the term used, as there is considerable difference in the meanings ascribed to the terms. A few years ago the term *curriculum* was generally used as meaning a group of subjects leading toward a particular end; while by *course of study*, on the other hand, was meant what was taught in one of the subjects in a particular curriculum.

During the past few years, however, there has come a new conception of the term *curriculum* as it is ordinarily used in modern educational parlance. It seems to be a much more inclusive term, as well as a much more general term.

In order to determine what meaning is being given these terms by those in charge of curriculum programs in public schools, the question was raised: What is the difference between *curriculum* and *course of study* as used in your program?

The most interesting fact in relation to the replies is the rather large number of different meanings ascribed to the term curriculum. The following terms are some of the suggested meanings which cities testified are being given to their programs:

TABLE 3
MEANING OF THE TERM CURRICULUM

1. " The curriculum means an organized program of studies for specific purposes."
2. " The curriculum represents all of the activities through which a child learns."
3. " The curriculum is inclusive."
4. " The curriculum is an organization of courses."
5. " The curriculum is the entire program, or what is taught in the schools."

[1] From *Administrative Procedures in Curriculum Making for Public Schools*, Contributions to Education No. 329, Bureau of Publications, Teachers College, Columbia University, New York, 1928, pp. 41–43.

6. " The curriculum is used to apply to the specific materials taught in different subjects."
7. " The curriculum is made up of several courses of study."
8. " The curriculum as now used applies to the whole fabric of education."
9. " The curriculum has to do with the entire teaching process as carried on in the schools."

Two of the above definitions, 4 and 7, relate to the older idea, while in the case of the others there seems to be a definite attempt to use *curriculum* as a general term applying to the organized work of the school. One city reports that no distinction has been made between the terms *curriculum* and *course of study*.

When we turn to the term *course of study* as used in the curriculum program of these twelve cities,* we find much more uniformity. *Course of study* is commonly described as referring to a single subject-matter field. Houston puts it well: " The *course of study* corresponds to a blue print of an architect," while Long Beach and Oakland state that " the *course of study* is the teacher's specific guide book." Madison replies, " The *course of study* is the content material in each subject."

It seems evident, then, from the replies received that the term *course of study* is fairly well standardized in use, while on the contrary, the term *curriculum* is not only used in many different ways but even those in charge of the program of curriculum making are not exactly clear themselves as to just what this term does or should mean. As a result there is no uniformity of use. From the replies received and from a study of writings involving this term, it would seem clear that the term is being used to include all that has to do with the instructional work of the school.

60. THE CURRICULUM CONCEIVED AS DESIRED LEARNINGS [2]

A. Gordon Melvin

There is a host of school teachers and principals throughout the country who are trying to be progressive without being willing to admit it. They find themselves between the upper and nether millstones of modern school practice. On the one hand, almost everything which they study, and approve, and lecture on, and write about is stamped with progressive positions, which are the inevitable

* Denver, Houston, Long Beach, Madison, Minneapolis, Oakland, Oklahoma City, Port Arthur, Rochester, San Antonio, Sioux City, and St. Louis.
[2] From " Current Confusion Concerning the Curriculum," *School and Society*, 33:730–731, May 30, 1931.

result of modern scientific education. On the other hand they behold the obvious unsuitability of certain of the practices of the modern experimental schools for public school life as it is organized in their institutions. What is there for them to do but to give a half-hearted support to certain half-baked and seemingly broad-minded innovations in classroom practice. There is thus an unrest abroad in the school systems of the country, some of which have committed themselves to a comparatively thoroughgoing reform in the direction of organizing school life in terms of conduct, the majority of which, however, are somewhat blindly groping about in half-hearted reform. The movement for curriculum revision is part and parcel of this widespread change in current school life. It is this which is really at the root of current curriculum reform.

CONFUSION BETWEEN THE FIELDS OF CURRICULUM AND METHOD

Now it is to be noted that this reform, half-hearted or thoroughgoing, is basically a reform in method of teaching. It concerns itself with the organization of school life in terms of conduct rather than in terms of subject matter. It is a return of the old Greek plan of " learning by doing." It conceives of learning in terms of the activities of children rather than those of teachers. It denotes, with respect to *the children's learning process*, comparatively active children and comparatively passive teachers. It looks askance at children who sit and listen, and smiles upon those who get up and make. For second-hand experiences through books it tends to substitute first-hand living through experiences. All these things are primarily matters of method, matters not of *what* the children learn, although this is to a certain extent involved, but chiefly matters of *how* they learn it. In other words, the modern movement in the schools is fundamentally a reform in method.

On the other hand, it is impossible to separate completely the fields of curriculum and method. To a certain extent when children learn in a different way they learn different things. When method changes curriculum must inevitably change. It is in an effort to meet this change in method of teaching that the movement for curriculum revision has found its soundest and most real justification. In other words curriculum revision should not go on in and for itself, but rather to bring the curriculum into line with the needs of an improved method of teaching. What is most unfortunate, however, is the fact that so far from thoroughly realizing this, many of those who have sponsored and been engaged in curriculum revision have lost sight of this distinction. In the minds of many of those who are concerning themselves with re-writing curricula there still exists considerable confusion concerning the fields of curriculum and method. There are those who tend to pool these two concepts, with the most unfortunate results for their thinking, and the practices of teachers to whom they are giving guidance.

ACTIVITY CURRICULA OR ACTIVITY PROGRAMS?

The evidence of this confusion is to be found in the publication of various accounts of school life which are called " activity curricula." This term is a misnomer. It will be obvious that this is so if we pause to consider the contents of books labeled " activity curricula." One of a number which come to mind gives an account of activities suitable for the earlier grades. It includes among many descriptions of activities accounts of work carried on by children in studying bees, using fire extinguishers, holding an Easter sale, and in the cutting and sewing of sun-bonnets. The way in which these activities are carried on is given in detail. A certain public school system, to give a further example, publishes a series of " curriculum bulletins " which really give an account of units of work which have been carried out in the schools. In other words these so-called curricula are not curricula at all. They are really books on method. To call them " activity curricula " is to confuse the two fields of curriculum and method in a way which may result in teaching which is careless and inefficient. As contributions to the discussion of educational practice they are invaluable. If they are to be used, however, without confusion of thought, they might more properly be called " activity programs." This allows for the separate use of the word curriculum to denote something different, something theoretically separated from method, something without which the activity program may easily result in wasteful and unfinished teaching.

THE MEANING OF CURRICULUM

The word curriculum means a *race course*, and is the Latin form of the English phrase *course of study*. It should present for the teacher, in tentative suggested form, the learnings which children should attain while in her care. In a theoretical sense the curriculum should list those learnings independent of the method of the teacher who is to help the pupil attain them. In reality the listing of these goals or attainments in a form which will relate them to the teacher's method is desirable. This lack of an adequate listing of the goals of the curriculum in a form which is but slightly related to method, has done much to injure the teaching in activity schools. Concerned chiefly with the initiation of activities by the child, and with their guidance by the teacher, the progressive movement has only too frequently left the educative process dangling in air. It has started to build the bridge between the child and the curriculum and has left the job unfinished. It has begun psychologically with the child's responses, it has organized them into activity programs and stopped there. *It has failed to carry the teaching process a step farther to completion,* and to insist that children actually reach the goals of the curriculum.

This confusion of thinking and practice has been largely due to the confusion in the minds of many between the realms of curriculum and method. In their enthusiasm for activity programs teachers have sometimes forgotten curricula. There is the most urgent need for the revision of curricula as curricula, for a statement of curriculum goals in a form which will make them suitable for use with activity programs. It is this type of curriculum revision which is most valid today, and revision which is carried on to meet this need is no mere fad, but a sound contribution which is in line with developing educational progress in our schools.

61. CURRICULUM IDENTICAL WITH EXPERIENCE [3]

Hilda Taba

The curriculum cannot be regarded as a dead and summative body of all the materials, experiences and activities contained in the educational process. It is a living whole, comprised of experience actually going on in school. As such it is what it becomes in practice. Its content is identical to the content of the actual experience of the learners.

Education being an evolving process, the sequences of its experiences and their contents are at least partly determined by the process itself. They cannot be fully seen or outlined in advance. So it follows that curriculum building cannot be completely segregated from educational practice without certain limiting effects on the curriculum and on education itself. To the extent that the nature of educational experiences and of their subject matter is progressively determined by the structure of the process itself, it cannot be prescribed prior to, or apart from, that process.

[3] From *The Dynamics of Education,* Harcourt, Brace and Company, New York, 1932, pp. 243–244.

62. THE LINCOLN SCHOOL CONCEPT OF CURRICULUM [4]

L. Thomas Hopkins

. . . Lincoln School conceives of the curriculum as the way in which the school aids boys and girls to improve their daily living. Under this conception, life and living constitute the content of the school day and the school endeavor. How to live is learned in and through the process of living. Whatever is best in the process of living and how best to attain it at each year level become objects of inquiry and of study by teachers and children. This means that the curriculum is composed of all those activities or aspects of the living of children which are directly influenced by the school. Since life is not confined to a classroom, to a building, to books, to conventional school subjects, the curriculum cannot be confined to these and other limiting areas. It goes on in the school, the home, the school bus, the playground, the museum, the theater, and other places too numerous to mention. With this emphasis on the enrichment of actual living, Lincoln School early in its history recognized that it could not achieve its purpose by reëxamining existing subjects, subject matter, materials, and methods which were selected and organized primarily for remote use. Rather, it must shift its orientation from subject matter in school subjects or " studies " to individuals and groups of individuals facing courageously, meeting intelligently, and satisfying more effectively their needs or wants in daily living. . . .

. . . Lincoln School assumes that administration exists for the purpose of making possible the best environment in which to foster the type of living which is basic to its curriculum. This means that administration becomes a means toward the end of promoting the best possible conditions for learning of teachers, pupils, parents, and all others involved in the direct radius of influence of the school. It is not conceived of as an end in itself and it never assumes a superiority over the process of learning, since there are other aspects of learning which are much more crucial for everyone concerned. To that end, administration has no fixed patterns which cannot be modified from time to time in the interests of learning groups. Its keynote is flexibility, not regimentation. It is constantly in the process of evolving creative responses to meet new needs in the novel aspects of living, and is constantly examining the record of its refined experiences as interpreted in schedules, records, reports, and the like, to make sure of their continued value in promoting rather than hindering the expansion of the viewpoint upon which it rests.

[4] From " Curriculum Development," *Teachers College Record,* 37:441, 444–445, February, 1936.

63. THE CURRICULUM A RESERVOIR OF KNOWLEDGE [5]

William S. Learned

American tradition has plentifully quoted, but never acted upon, Garfield's epigram on Mark Hopkins as the epitome of a university apotheosized in the teacher. Few have considered the real point of the scene, however — the wise head of a little college pausing on an afternoon's ramble with one of his students for a bit of intimate conversation. The lad certainly sat on that log willingly and not for credit. What caught Garfield's imagination was the moment, probably one of several, when he could listen, not to a veiled oracle dispensing the curriculum, but to a rich thinker and observer of the world talking alone to a lad whom he liked and thoroughly understood.

As the importance of formalized instruction recedes, so likewise the curriculum will, I believe, revert to its normal and effective status — a mammoth reservoir of ordered and accessible knowledge in books, laboratories, and museums ready to be drawn upon by minds capable of grasping and interpreting its contents. Fascinate young students with the real wonders of this paradise by direct contact, instead of presenting them with desiccated elements disguised under the appearance of so many term units or semester hours required to buy a degree, and one has taken the first and indispensable step in their education. Certain it is that an education will never be theirs until this illusion has been dissipated and they learn to grapple for themselves with ideas in all their bewildering complexity, magnitude, and charm. Moreover, it is precisely this that a goodly proportion of these young minds are eager to do. One awaits with few misgivings the daring college that will say to a group of its most capable beginners: " This institution with all its resources is yours, particularly the time of any and all of the faculty for advice and discussion. We make no requirements of you except that you remain four years, keep well, and behave yourselves. But we shall expect to test and examine you frequently and in all fields in which you are likely to display growth, and we shall record with all possible accuracy the results of these measures or of any others that may reveal your actual knowledge and achievement in any direction. This is your opportunity and we are here to help you."

[5] From *Realism in American Education,* The Inglis Lecture, Harvard University Press, Cambridge, 1932, pp. 45–48.

64. THE TWOFOLD NATURE OF THE CURRICULUM [6]

Harold Rugg

The " curriculum " — an ugly, awkward, academic word, but fastened upon us by technical custom — is really the entire program of the school's work. It is the essential *means* of education. It is *everything* that the students and their teachers do. Thus it is twofold in nature, being made up of activities, the things done, and of the materials with which they are done.

1. *Activities.* On the side of activities the curriculum is the very life of the school. It includes the activities of clubs and other organizations, the assemblies and other group meetings, the work of class committees and student councils, the carrying on of newspapers, magazines, and " annuals," the sports and plays. It encompasses, furthermore, the researches and excursions in both school and community, the reading and study, the discussions and dramatizations, the aesthetic appreciation and creative expression, as well as the practice of innumerable techniques. The curriculum is, in short, *everything the young people and their teachers do.*

2. *Materials.* But the curriculum is more than this; it is also the materials which are used in these activities — books, the drama of both stage and screen, painting, sculpture, architecture, lectures, music, the physical equipment of laboratory and shop, of studio and lecture room. Thus the curriculum is not only everything that is done but also the vast range of materials employed in the doing.

This twofold nature of the curriculum reveals it as the very heart of the school, the great intermediary between growing human beings and the culture in which they live. It cannot, therefore, be separated either from the children and youth or from the total society of which they are a part. Its content and organization spring, on the one hand, from the needs of learners for orientation and direction and, on the other hand, from the physical civilization, the institutions, and the psychology of the people. The needs of the learners are, however, in large part social, owing to the fact that a child's life is lived almost entirely in human groups. Hence the content of the curriculum must be built directly out of group needs, that is, out of the culture of the people.

But the culture of a people is found in the interests, aptitudes, and activities of the children themselves, as well as in those of out-of-school elders. Thus curriculum-making will recognize the twofold nature of the people's culture; it will take account not only of its

[6] From *American Life and the School Curriculum*, Ginn and Company, Boston, 1936, pp. 18–19.

social characteristics but also of the individual needs of its component members. That is, young people shall study not only the problems of their local and national groups but also their own personal childhood problems. So far as is possible, their activities shall be merged into the natural activities of community and nation. In the fullest sense, therefore, the curriculum constitutes a first-hand study of the culture of the people.

65. DEFINITION OF THE CURRICULUM [7]

Florence Stratemeyer

The school curriculum, here defined to include the whole body of experiences which condition and make up the total activities of the child for which the school assumes responsibility, has been one of the latest of the great social agencies to be markedly affected (in its total aspect) by (1) changing conditions in social, economic, and political life and (2) a changing philosophy and psychology of education.

66. THE CURRICULUM AND THE PROGRAM OF STUDIES [8]

Henry C. Morrison

In thinking about the curriculum, we are very prone to confuse the curriculum with methods of teaching. This outcome is found when a series of bound volumes entitled " Curriculum of —— Public Schools " is primarily a manual for teachers. Still more often perhaps is the curriculum confused with the program of studies.

PROGRAM OF STUDIES

The program of studies, or course of study, is a list of courses properly organized in learning units, intended to be pursued by pupils, and presumed to be the best method of attaining the objectives set up by the curriculum.

Thus, the issue whether reading shall be taught at all or not is a curriculum question. Where, in the school career, it can most advantageously be taught is a program question.

Whether or not and why history and geography shall be taught,

[7] From *The Effective Use of Curriculum Materials,* Contributions to Education No. 460, Bureau of Publications, Teachers College, Columbia University, New York, 1931, p. 3.
[8] From *Basic Principles in Education,* Houghton Mifflin Company, Boston, 1934, pp. 49–50.

what kind of conception of the subject matter shall be held, what learnings are essential — all these are curriculum questions. Where the courses shall be placed and how they shall be organized for teaching purposes are problems in working out the program of studies.

On the other hand, circumstances may make it impossible for a given local school system to cover the curriculum of general education. What devices shall be adopted to cover as much as possible is a program problem.

Finally, we know that some pupils, as we find them and are obliged to deal with them, are incapable of education to the full extent of the curriculum. In most cases, incapacity resides in meager cultural background. For these pupils, we must devise special programs and sometimes special schools.

The curriculum is thus determinate and in its nature a reasoned inference from education itself and from the structure of civilization. It is experimental only in the sense that the products of all cultural evolution are experimental. The program, on the other hand, is variable as circumstances decree. It is experimental in the sense that it should in its nature be modified in accordance with the results obtained in fitting the school to the requirements of the curriculum.

67. GENERAL OUTLINES AND THE CURRICULUM FOR THE INDIVIDUAL [9]

Franklin Bobbitt

The major curriculum-makers of modern education — when we can get it modernized — will be those who are planning the *individual* curriculums of the children and youths entrusted to their care. The generalizing of these individual curriculums in the formulation of a general curriculum is but an incidental after-result. The quality of the general curriculum will be dependent upon the qualities of the several individual curricula which are generalized.

Shall the curriculum be made currently or long in advance? Quite obviously, the individual curriculum can only be made currently. And this, by the way, is the only kind of actual curriculum which should be planned. What we have here called the " general curriculum " is but the formulation of the general outlines of the educational science which is to be employed in the planning of the actual curriculums for the individuals. It is like the chart employed with profit by the master mariner. The chart may be prepared long in

[9] From " Orientation of the Curriculum Maker," National Society for the Study of Education, *The Foundations of Curriculum-Making*, Twenty-Sixth Yearbook, Part II, Public School Publishing Company, Bloomington, Ill., 1927, pp. 51–52.

advance, and used over and over again; but each course in its details must be managed according to the conditions met with at the time.

A good general curriculum may be made for the nation as a whole and employed with profit in any state or city. It may be made by the educational authorities of the state, and employed in any portion of that state, whether urban or rural. It may be formulated by the central authorities in a city and employed in all of the schools of that city. But whatever the type, it is only a general chart which is employed by those who are actually planning the curricula as they guide education. It is not a thing that can properly be imposed upon those who should be the authorities in the education of any given child by virtue of the fact that they best know him and his actual situation.

Those who participate in the formulation of the general curriculum should be primarily specialists in life itself, and not specialists in any special subject. They should be primarily generalists in education and not specialists in some portion of it.

That the general curriculum is not to be made or planned by subjects, it seems should go without the saying. The continuous, diversified, and abundant intellectual life which is desirable is not mainly a matter of learning subjects.

Thus far, national committees of subject-specialists have in the main made but meager contributions to the modernization of their departments. Their vision appears to be so completely confined to their particular subjects that they are mostly unable to get out of the deep ruts of the storage conception. Where exceptions are found, it is to be noted that the committee has succeeded in taking the general human behavior point of view first of all and then viewing their responsibility in terms of that general behavior.

Curriculum-planning is not to assume that the educational world is made up only of specialists in particular subjects or lines and that the educational generalist does not exist, and ought not to exist. It is not to assume that all we have to work with is a series of partial insights and that the technique of curriculum-making is mainly a technique of compromise. Quite the reverse: we need the technique of the comprehensive balanced vision. It is as necessary to have the technique of the generalist as to have that of the specialist. The latter has a vital responsibility to discharge. But no number of them can do the work of the generalist.

68. CURRICULUM REVISION INVOLVES COURSE OF STUDY [10]

In this process of curriculum-making, it is necessary that a teacher have at hand at any stage of his teaching an outline of the general attitudes, the finer appreciations, the important concepts and meanings, and the generalizations which he wishes to secure as part of the outcomes of his instruction. Not only must he have this outline of attitudes, appreciations, meanings, etc., which he sets as the goals of instruction, but, to be reasonably sure that these come out of the instruction, the activities of children (including all the kinds of work we do in the school) should be planned in outline form in advance.

Another way of stating the matter is that that part of the curriculum should be planned in advance which includes (1) a statement of objectives, (2) a sequence of experiences shown by analysis to be reasonably uniform in value in achieving the objectives, (3) subject matter found to be reasonably uniform as the best means of engaging in the experiences, and (4) statements of immediate outcomes of achievements to be derived from the experiences. That part of the curriculum from which selection of supplementary experiences and materials are to be used as conditions locally suggest, should be planned partly in advance and should be made partly as new materials become available. That part of the curriculum which represents the daily life-situations and interests from which the immediate specific needs of students arise, should be — can only be — made from day to day.

Because of partially equipped teachers, and of heavy teaching programs, large classes, and inadequate research facilities, it will be necessary to utilize persons specially trained and experienced in the study of society and of childhood to organize suggestive activities, readings, exercises.

The tasks of curriculum-making stated in the foregoing paragraph require special training and experience in the scientific analysis of social needs on the one hand and in the experimental study of the learners' interests, activities, and methods of learning on the other. Education is progressively adopting the methods of science. Curriculum-making, correspondingly, is creating a progressive demand for specialization and for professional, scientific training, and experience.

School practice, both past and present, has conceived too generally of curriculum-revision as a task for intermittent administrative reorganization. The Committee believes, on the contrary, that be-

[10] National Society for the Study of Education, *The Foundations of Curriculum-Making*, Twenty-Sixth Yearbook, Part II, Public School Publishing Company, Bloomington, Ill., 1927, pp. 19–20, 23–25.

cause of the dynamic nature of modern society and of the steady accumulation of truth concerning learning and child growth, school systems and colleges should make provisions for the continuous study, evaluation, and testing of the materials of the school curriculum, and the importation of new materials or the elimination of old kinds whenever this proves to be justifiable.

In local school systems it is particularly important that adequate central machinery be created for the continuous study of the school curriculum. In this work, the coöperation of experienced teachers should be secured, together with that of specialists in curriculum-making. The Committee heartily commends the practice of releasing efficient teachers from active class work to participate in the study of the content and organization of the curriculum materials within their chosen fields of work.

Curriculum-study should not only be carried on continuously; it should also be comprehensive. The curriculum has grown up, subject by subject, as specialized knowledge has accumulated. The history of curriculum-making, therefore, has revealed the corresponding tendency to revise the curriculum, subject by subject. Almost always local school officers and national committees appointed by organizations of subject-matter specialists have revised the curriculum by this method. . . . It appears from time to time needful to bring about regroupings of subject matter.

The Committee believes that curriculum-makers should seek on every possible occasion to develop sympathetic, broad views of the world. Especially should the treatment of human relations be of a type which will include as many lines of consideration as can efficiently be brought together in the experience of pupils. If this principle is to be carried out in the reconstruction of the curriculum, schools and national organizations, in organizing curriculum committees, should guarantee that the personnel of such committees view American life and the task of curriculum-making in a broad way. This means especially that the personnel of committees shall be constituted of persons of varied interests and equipments. They should include some person interested and equipped for the scientific study of learners' interests, activities, and methods of learning, others trained and experienced in the scientific study of society, and still others who are subject-matter specialists, experienced in the authentication of material. It should be recognized, therefore, that the tasks of curriculum-making are varied and difficult, demanding the coöperation of specialists of the several types. In curriculum-making by committees great care should be taken to insure that a rounded view of the modern world will be reflected in the curriculum through the representation of each of the primary interests involved, and that the material shall be organized so as to insure economical and effective learning.

69. CURRICULUM MAKING A TASK FOR SPECIALISTS [11]
Thomas H. Briggs

During the past fifteen years there have been many ambitious attempts at curriculum reorganization, usually by cities and less often by states. Although many of these efforts have contributed materially to the improvement of secondary education, they have for several reasons accomplished far less than is needed. In the first place, each and every effort has been handicapped by an inadequate staff and by inadequate time. Though the teachers selected for the work were doubtless the best available, they seldom had the background of knowledge of education both in the United States and in other lands, of the psychology of heterogeneous youth, of the complex changing civilization, and of the needs, both cultural and utilitarian, that exist in modern society.

The making of adequate new curricula and courses of study is a tremendous job. It can not be done adequately by any but the best minds of our nation, and they will need far more time than has ordinarily been realized. As a matter of fact, the task is unending. As soon as any unit is perfected for one set of conditions, those conditions will have to some extent changed, and consequently new units must be made or old ones modified. The curriculum revision committees have also been handicapped by a lack of time. For the most part they have been expected to perform the complex and unending additional task assigned them in the interstices of their other duties. High credit must in justice be given for their use of time which was properly their own, during the regular school year and during vacations. But there should be no surprise that results of their labors are for the most part only improvements in conventional and traditional courses of study — better than the old, without doubt, but woefully inadequate for the program that modern society demands.

Another weakness in the attempts at curriculum revision has been the economic waste of repetitious work. Every group of committees in every city or state has laboriously read the same theoretical materials and then, bewildered by the immensity of the challenge, has attempted with varying degrees of success the same tasks, often in realized helplessness falling back on the old scissors and paste with

[11] From "If There Were Millions," *Teachers College Record*, 35:636–637, May, 1934.

the unjustifiable assumption that other teachers elsewhere have presented in their printed materials solutions of the common problems. Of course it must be recognized that by their own readings and attempts at revision the teachers participating in the curriculum work have profited greatly and that as a result they are more professionally minded and more conscious of the need of a real curriculum reconstruction. This by-product is highly valuable, but it probably could have been secured much more economically by other means. It has made the participating teachers receptive, but it has not produced the necessary fundamental curriculum reconstruction. Who can doubt that the time, money, and labor expended by the hundreds and perhaps thousands of local communities if provided for a single group of the most competent possible workers would have resulted in a vastly better curriculum?

70. " WHO SHALL MAKE THE CURRICULUM? " [12]

George S. Counts

In the first place, curriculum-making is a task of great difficulty. None of the older professions face a task which is more arduous. Indeed, the thesis might very well be defended that the curriculum-maker has a more difficult task than the engineer, the lawyer, the physician, or the clergyman. If this contention is granted, it naturally follows that the curriculum should be made by persons specially and intensively trained for the task. The job can be intrusted to neither the tyro nor the mountebank nor the special pleader.

In the second place, curriculum-making is a task of great complexity. It requires the utilization of wide ranges of knowledge and experience and the service of many special abilities and forms of training. This means that the curriculum must be made co-operatively. No single individual or type of individual can carry the burden alone. It cannot be borne by the superintendent, the principal, or the teacher, or even by all three working together. The task of curriculum-making must be recognized as a great co-operative undertaking in which the efforts of many different persons and groups are brought to focus on a common problem. If properly accomplished, it must tax to the limit the entire resources of the profession.

To whom, therefore, shall we turn for the performance of this difficult and complicated task? Perhaps the first approach to this question should be from the negative side. What persons should not be permitted to make the curriculum? What agencies already inter-

[12] *School Review*, 35:333–339, May, 1927.

ested in the problem lack the necessary qualifications? We need not deceive ourselves with the thought that this task is necessarily going to be left to persons professionally trained for the task. There are literally hosts of individuals and groups striving today, as they have striven in the past, to shape the educational program. Many of them are sincerely devoted to the public welfare but are convinced that they alone hold the key which will unlock the doors to social salvation. They are ready and eager to make the curriculums of elementary school, secondary school, and college. Moreover, these forces feel no diffidence with regard to the matter; they have no doubts concerning their own competence; they are restrained by no traditions of professional courtesy; they are already at work. Among these agencies which are interesting themselves in the curriculum and which are not qualified for the task are the following: state legislatures, boards of education, powerful minorities, colleges, and persons concerned with the defense of special subjects. Here are five agencies which should not make the curriculum. A word of comment regarding the qualifications of each of them will be of interest.

The state legislatures seem to be increasing their interest in the curriculum. The bills and laws prohibiting the teaching of evolution reveal the temper and competence of these bodies. Flanders * has recently reported on their activity from 1903 to 1923 in making the elementary-school curriculum. His study shows no tendency on the part of the ordinary legislator to make a modest appraisal of his own powers. Yet that the legislator is unqualified to make the curriculum goes almost without saying. His personal competence, of course, is not being challenged here. The point being made is merely that he is totally lacking in the professional training and experience necessary for the discharge of this task. This deficiency, however, because he is unaware of its existence, will not cause him willingly to forego the pleasure of expressing himself through the high-school curriculum.

Boards of education should be placed in much the same category as state legislatures. They are, in fact, minor legislative bodies bearing certain general responsibilities with respect to the schools, but their members are not qualified to perform the specialized educational tasks. In so far as the curriculum is concerned, their legitimate function pertains to the determination of general educational policy. Beyond this they should not go. Even in the discharge of this function they are likely to exhibit an undesirable and even dangerous bias. To a very large degree, boards of education are com-

* Jesse Knowlton Flanders, *Legislative Control of the Elementary Curriculum.* Teachers College Contributions to Education, No. 195. New York: Teachers College, Columbia University, 1925.

posed of representatives of the favored classes in American society. Therefore, in the formulation of policy and in the making of the curriculum, they will be tempted to use the schools to defend the interests of these classes. Perhaps a measure of bias of this order is inevitable, but it should be reduced to the lowest possible proportions.

This discussion of state legislatures and boards of education suggests the third type of influence at work on the curriculum, namely, the powerful minorities in the community. The ordinary industrial city or state is literally alive with these highly organized and articulate groups. Bessie L. Pierce * has recently shown in scholarly fashion how various groups have sought to influence the teaching of history and the social studies in our schools. According to her report, the United Confederate Veterans, the Grand Army of the Republic, the Daughters of the American Revolution, the Knights of Columbus, the Steuben Society, the American Bar Association, the American Bankers Association, the American Federation of Labor, the American Legion, the National Security League, and many other organizations have endeavored to modify the curriculum. Every one of these groups is interested in pleading some special cause in the schools. If they are permitted to write our histories, the high schools might as well close their doors.

Regarding the rôle played by the college in making the highschool curriculum, little needs to be said. We all recognize the power of this agency and the way in which this power has been used in the past. The college must be ranked among the most potent influences which have shaped the curriculum of the secondary school. During the past generation the bonds with which the college has held the high school in servitude have gradually been loosened, but even this elementary struggle for institutional freedom is far from won.

The individuals interested in the defense of particular subjects constitute the fifth agency of curriculum-making lacking the necessary qualifications. Because of the departmentalization of work in the high school and the emphasis in the training of high-school teachers on a narrow allegiance to subject matter, the secondary school has been greatly hampered in its efforts to reconstruct its program. Intense loyalty on the part of teachers to their subjects has been a chief factor in the retention of obsolete materials in the curriculum. It has likewise constituted a major obstacle to an attack on the curriculum as a whole. The work of the great national committees of subject-matter specialists has revealed the limitations of this type of agency. A large proportion of the effort which is going into curriculum-making in the secondary school today is rendered futile be-

* Bessie L. Pierce, *Public Opinion and the Teaching of History*. New York: Alfred A. Knopf, 1926.

cause of the protective behavior of these special vested interests. Unless definite safeguards are provided, the ordinary program of curriculum revision is likely to degenerate into a conflict among these vested interests. Increasingly, we must have teachers who are more than specialists in subject matter. If they are to have a voice in determining the place of their subjects in the curriculum, they must be students of secondary education.

If, then, the making of the high-school curriculum is not to be intrusted to state legislatures, boards of education, powerful minorities in the community, college boards of admission, and persons interested in the defense of particular subjects, who should perform the task? To the writer, it would seem that the co-operative efforts of at least seven types of persons are required. We shall have to secure the services of the psychologist, the sociologist, the philosopher, the specialist in the selection and organization of the materials of instruction, the classroom teacher, the expert in the appraisal of the curriculum, and the high-school administrator. The contribution of each of these persons will be considered.

That the services of the psychologist are required, no one would question. At every level education has to do with the nature of the learner. Consequently, our knowledge concerning the adolescent and the factors that condition the learning process at this age can hardly be too complete. We must know much more than we do today regarding his abilities, interests, and aptitudes; and the high-school curriculum must reflect this knowledge.

Equal in importance to the psychologist and playing a correspondingly fundamental rôle is the sociologist. Whatever else it may be, education is the process whereby the individual is inducted into the life of society and into the use of its institutions. A knowledge of modern social life is therefore just as important to the curriculum-maker as a knowledge of the nature of the learner. The high school must serve the adolescent in his efforts to adjust himself to the conditions of life and to gain control over the instruments which constitute his social heritage. It can perform this service only as its program reflects a thorough knowledge of American civilization.

The contribution of the philosopher is also of a fundamental character. His is the task of developing a coherent system of values and of formulating the purposes of society and of education. This task cannot be evaded. As soon as we make a choice between alternative programs which represent two different approaches to life, we face the problem squarely. We may not recognize the source or nature of our own formulations, but we all have them. One of the greatest needs in the field of secondary education today is a restatement of purposes, but this restatement must not be derived by the armchair method. It must, rather, rest on the most complete synthesis possible of science, aesthetics, and ethics. In this formulation of purposes no division of human experience may be ignored.

After the purposes of secondary education have been formulated, we shall have to turn to persons expert in the selection and organization of the actual materials of instruction. The findings of psychologists, sociologists, and philosophers must be translated into materials to be used in the school. In the choice of these materials the entire range of knowledge must be placed at our disposal. Moreover, these materials cannot be determined by inspection. They must, rather, be derived from actual experimentation in the school.

The last statement suggests the need of securing the co-operation of the classroom teacher. Until it has become the possession of the teacher, the curriculum is just so much inert material the educational value of which is unknown. It is but pigment, brush, and canvas without the painter. Not only does the teacher make use of the materials of instruction provided by others; he also throws these materials into forms which are as necessary as the materials themselves for the successful achievement of the purposes of the high school. Moreover, the teacher is much more than a specialist in some division of subject matter. At his best, he is an artist in guiding the process of learning and in developing personality.

A function closely related to that of teaching is the function of appraisal. We must have persons who are trained for the task of appraising the curriculum. As a matter of fact, we can go but little beyond the work of the psychologist, the sociologist, and the philosopher until we have devised ways and means of appraising the curriculum in terms of the accepted purposes of secondary education. At this point our technique of curriculum-making is particularly faulty. At the present time we must admit that our methods of appraisal are totally inadequate. We know how to measure more or less well in terms of classroom procedure what goes on in the classroom, but at the high-school level a technique for measuring the influence of the school in terms of social life is almost wholly lacking. We can make guesses and draw inferences, but we do not know how the present high-school program is affecting American society. If we did know, we might be frightened. This freedom from anxiety is perhaps one of the consolations of ignorance.

We come finally to the work of the administrator, or, shall we say, the high-school principal. At least within the limits of a particular high school someone must organize, co-ordinate, and integrate the efforts of these different types of specialists. Moreover, the work of these specialists must be made to live in the school and in the teaching staff. Then, there is the additional task, perhaps the most difficult of all, of carrying the community along in the support of a program of curriculum reconstruction. The successful discharge of these several functions requires a high-school principal of unusual gifts, but there is no one else to whom we may turn. He is the logical candidate for the position. If a vigorous, scientific, and creative attack on curriculum is to be made, an attack that differs qualitatively from the numerous compromises of the past, the high-school principal must recognize this as his major responsibility. The more mechanical aspects of his job will have to be delegated to others. He alone can supply that co-ordinating quality of leadership on which the successful reconstruction of the curriculum in terms of modern needs absolutely depends.

71. RELATION OF ADMINISTRATION AND SUPERVISION TO THE CURRICULUM [13]

Jesse H. Newlon and others

THE curriculum policy that has been outlined will be effective only under favorable administrative and supervisory conditions. A coöperative type of administrative procedure is required.

This raises the question of whether genuine teacher participation in the determination of policies is consistent with the principle of responsible administration and the control of school policy by the public through their chosen representatives, members of the board of education. Does a policy of participation permit of the utilization of most expert knowledge? How far will the power of the teacher extend? It is impossible to answer some of these questions now because of lack of experience and study of the problems involved. But we have had sufficient experience with a coöperative type of administration to know that it is not inconsistent either with responsibility or with the utilization of expert knowledge. The power of approval or veto will rest with the administration, subject only to review by the board of education and ultimately by the community. The specialist, the expert, under a line-and-staff type of administration, should serve not only the administrative and supervisory staff but the teacher as well. The administration that seeks the coöperation of all members of the staff, and that places corresponding responsibilities upon them, accomplishes three desirable purposes. In the first place, the policies decided upon will be wiser, for they will

[13] From "The Curricula of the Chicago Schools," *Report of the Survey of the Schools of Chicago, Illinois,* Vol. III, Bureau of Publications, Teachers College, Columbia University, New York, 1932, pp. 98–99.

have been better considered, and they will be carried out more effectively by a staff that understands them. Second, such a policy will be most conducive to the professional growth of every member of the staff. In the third place, the work and the needs of the schools will be better interpreted to the public.

It follows, of course, that participation will vary with respect to different matters. The location of a building may be left to the judgment of staff building experts. The experience and judgment of teachers should be secured with reference to certain aspects of the design and equipment of the building. Teacher judgment would play a much larger part in the determination of what and how to teach in the school to be housed in the building.

The important consideration is that the spirit of coöperation permeate the whole corps. This requires understanding and honest endeavor on the part of the administrator. It requires equal honesty, devotion to duty, and willingness to coöperate on the part of the teacher. If the administrator and teacher are set off in separate castes the policy will not succeed. Willingness and eagerness to study education, to attend meetings without too much regard for the clock, are essential. The administration must be sensitive to the conditions under which teachers work and to the contribution which they can make. The appointment of able classroom teachers to many important committee chairmanships, notably of curriculum committees, should be a settled policy. Such a policy will result in wiser decisions and will do much to develop the potential leadership always available in any corps of teachers.

Voluntary organizations of teachers and administrators can contribute much. The important consideration is that such organizations be primarily concerned to coöperate with other groups, with the school administration, and with the public in the improvement of education. Such an attitude is entirely consistent with attention to the interests of their members by these organizations. These voluntary organizations can do much to interpret education to the public. But reliance cannot be put upon machinery. Elaboration of machinery will kill. The spirit will keep the process of coöperation vital.

It is perfectly clear that an inspectorial, routinistic type of close supervision that gives attention to details of method is utterly inimical to such a coöperative policy. Administration and supervision become problems in leadership. While close supervision will have some place, especially for the beginning teacher, its usefulness will be very narrowly restricted. Where teachers engage seriously in the study of their problems, improvement in teaching will result. The necessity for supervision of the conventional type disappears.

72. Concept of the Curriculum Employed in Los Angeles [14]

William B. Brown

A program of curriculum-making involving many radical departures and new view-points has been under way in Los Angeles for several years. This program has been the natural outgrowth of the newer educational view-point based upon the principles of dynamic and creative education combined with a due regard for the necessities of the age and society in which our young people are to live. This has resulted in a conception of the curriculum much broader and more inclusive than heretofore. No longer is it possible to think of the curriculum as fixed, rigid and made up of definite bodies of knowledge for the training of the mind. Rather is it necessary to think of it as including all activities and experiences in the school which are calculated to modify the behavior of pupils toward clearly foreseen, socially desirable goals. In its broadest sense, the program includes all aspects of school life which in any way contribute to the learning attainments of the pupil. Even though we accept this view, it is obvious, nevertheless, that for purposes of practical revision in the instructional fields we must work in rather limited or defined areas. Curriculum strategy demands that our approach be rather opportunistic. We must move into those fields which seem favorable to revision and most in need of development at any one particular time. In a word, we make no attempt to rebuild every phase of the instructional program with one sweeping reformation.

As the program has developed in this city, every effort has been made to avoid that authoritarian approach generally characterized by intensive planning and preparing in research offices of detailed, logical outlines of subject-matter in which there is often little regard for the interests and needs of the classroom. This approach may be further characterized by an emphasis on superimposition of adult materials and the covering of definite amounts of prescribed subject-matter in a previously determined space of time. It is in every way contrary to the aims of our program. We know that it creeps in on occasion, but every effort is made to avoid it, for we realize fully that pupil initiative and creative effort can not develop under such circumstances. . . .

Curriculum workers are encouraged to use every opportunity to aid teachers in breaking down subject field boundaries and in developing materials which will provide a more creative, informal type

[14] From " New Approaches to Curriculum Building in the Los Angeles City Schools," *School and Society,* 42:332, 333–334, September 7, 1935.

of classroom experience. In selecting significant areas of human experience and bringing in necessary materials from many fields, it is possible to help in numerous ways to build units of work out of which units of experience will grow. Teachers tend to be subject specialists. So curriculum workers, to be of real service, must point the way out of subject specialization into areas of human activity more significant for elementary and secondary pupils.

It is obvious that the questions how to teach and what to teach can never be answered separately. There are some phases of research in the field of contemporary problems and in the discriminative selection of desirable background materials which demand a more isolated treatment. However, even here, the pupil and the classroom must be kept constantly in mind, or the resulting product is of little value for teaching purposes. Both the materials and the methods applicable to a classroom program of work are determined by the goals and expected outcomes. They are thus closely related and can not be considered one apart from the other. In a large school system, such as that of Los Angeles, a certain measure or division of responsibility is essential. This requires that the materials of teaching be developed under the direction of curriculum specialists and research groups, placing minor emphasis upon classroom procedures. Methods are given primary consideration by instructional directors and supervisors in the field. This latter group places little emphasis on preparing materials, giving most of its time to furthering and improving the classroom teaching. Needless to say, there must be a close liaison between the research and field groups. Joint committees, joint research and joint endeavors of many types are common procedures.

In the final analysis, it is manifest that the real curriculum must grow and develop in the classroom. This necessitates an orientation of all instructional development to the needs and interests of particular teachers and classes. For this purpose, the directional work of a central curriculum office must concern itself primarily with indicating broad fields and areas of work rather than the details of subject-matter. Through its research activities, attempts must be made to point the general direction, suggest possible goals, indicate themes and units for development and provide the necessary continuity of the program of studies from grade to grade. Mutual planning, cooperative endeavor and exploration carried on between teachers and curriculum specialists are without doubt the most essential factors. Much can be done in central offices to provide alternative patterns and suggestive outlines and to prevent repetition and overlapping; however, this is not the major part of the revision program. Teachers and pupils receive as much guidance and direction as is feasible under the circumstances, but this merely supplements and in no way replaces the healthy natural development of the child-centered program of activities, problems and projects.

In a city which contains over 300 schools, each of which has had a great measure of freedom and local authority, there can be no great amount of uniform development. Nor can there be any standardized procedure for carrying out policies and programs which are widely accepted. The variations in communities within the city, the diversity of economic and social settings and the traditional influences in each school act as powerful factors in making curriculum revision a broadly generalized rather than a specialized and detailed plan of procedure. Concrete, organized materials are suggestive, tentative and subject to adaptation and adjustment in different sections and schools of the city. This empirical process of development has proved highly satisfactory, avoiding much wasted effort, useless courses of study and the conflicts which inevitably grow out of superimposed content and activities.

Undoubtedly there is no more important service that can be rendered by curriculum groups than the provision of materials dealing with contemporary life and affairs of the present age. Needless to say, teachers tend to emphasize prepared background content, neglecting the vital problems of to-day. To adapt current materials to the classroom requires an intensive study to determine which problems should be emphasized, an analysis of the trends of civilization which will be of meaning and value to pupils, and an ever-vigilant effort to ferret out, develop and make available to teachers content material dealing with important aspects of community life. Such a program must be highly flexible and must be adjusted each year to changed conditions and new outlooks. This is a job for master teachers; ever incomplete, and ever requiring revision and constant searching for the most significant in community achievement as a basis for learning activities in the schools. Our aim, in a word, is to help teachers collect those materials which will make it possible to interpret to youth society as it is to-day.

And lastly, it should be emphasized that a thoroughgoing revision of the instructional program requires a vigorous leadership centering in a director or assistant superintendent who is that rare combination of the idealist, the versatile scholar and the man of practical educational achievements. Such a director, and a group of assistants, are needed for the carrying out of certain broad functions and providing an educational guidance which is seldom found in the individual school. As the starting point for reorganizing activities on a more informal and functional basis, there must be initiated a comprehensive program supported by a clearly expressed educational view-point. Courses of study must be developed as an outgrowth of successful procedures undertaken in selected classrooms and through the aid of production and steering committees of teachers. Their purpose should be to indicate the general framework and the limits within which specified groups may work. Beyond that the units and materials included should be purely suggestive, nothing more. Briefly, the main function should be to provide every encouragement and facilitate in many ways the development by teachers of genuine functional units of work.

A continuous program of revision must be anticipated, with many adjustments to new conditions. While we feel that it is generally not possible to proceed in all fields at any one time, our plans are nevertheless made largely in terms of a fundamental, thoroughgoing reconstruction of the entire program. We shall hope and strive for wider teacher interest and participation. We will insist that the curriculum must never become static and unchangeable. We look to an expansion of the revision programs to fields of work which now lie dormant. We expect every field to undergo drastic submission to educational surgery. For some time to come we shall think largely in terms of future hopes, while working in terms of present inadequate facilities. We hope to proceed much more rapidly when school plants are made more adaptable to learning needs, when library facilities are expanded, when text-books are less needed, when teaching loads are lighter, and when pupil groups have become adjusted and trained in terms of creative, dynamic education.

Anticipating these many drastic changes, new relationships and patterns of procedure, we believe that we shall still be thinking and building largely in terms of the same fundamental concepts which motivate the present program of revision. We shall be constantly concerned with the needs and interests of youth in terms of the society in which they will have to live and make their living.

CHAPTER V

PRINCIPLES BASIC TO CURRICULUM DEVELOPMENT

73. Philosophy of Education Should Afford Direction [3]

H. Gordon Hullfish

Education must develop individuals who not only realize the ways in which human intelligence, operating through the medium of science, has introduced change into the material and social world, but who also emerge from the educative process with a realizing sense of their own obligation to use intelligence in dealing with their fellowmen. In the moral field this need is apparent at a glance. During these recent years of heightened change, man, working more and more out in the open, has made constant adaptations of his standards of conduct to the circumstances of his environment, a fact that has introduced, in some measure, insight into situations which were previously met but blindly. Rules of action, in these instances, have been used as guides, or means, to intelligent behavior; they have not been permitted to substitute for it. Our almost universal willingness to tell " the white lie " in situations where circumstances dictate it is a case in point. In this process of substituting flexible standards for fixed rules man has been forging out a program by which he might live — a program which, because of the queer admixture of standards which it includes, leaves him in a situation that is highly precarious.

The business of forging a program to live by is a serious undertaking, and, unless the individual is to be left quite frankly to the chance buffetings of a swirling world, educational philosophy must come frankly to bat for the purpose of providing a sense of direction. This is the chief business of philosophy of education and it is made necessary by the fact of change itself. The educator, if he is to main-

[3] From " A Crucial Problem for Philosophy of Education," *Educational Administration and Supervision*, 16:247–248, April, 1930.

tain his high estate, needs to take the lead in bringing a functioning conception of the good life into the world of today, and tomorrow.

Thus far we have been concerned with making the point that the crucial issue for philosophy of education in a world of change is to work out an educational program that will introduce the individual to his world in such a manner that he will leave the schools with at least an emerging philosophy of life. This the student clearly lacks at present. What is needed is that the schools envisage a social program and organize their activities, the curricula and teaching methods, with reference to this end. If change, as we have discussed it, is granted, at least this much is implicated for a program: the student, as he advances through the educative process, should grow increasingly sensitive to the problems of the present, through a procedure that stimulates him to feel a personal concern for their solution.

When philosophy of education places the emphasis at these points, as I believe it must if it is to deal in any adequate manner with the present situation, it is apparent at a glance that the schools will find it impossible to deal with a fixed future, even though that future is placed no farther away than the period of 1940 to 1980. That man-made instrument, scientific method, has permitted the individual to work and experiment with a strictly human world. And this work and experimentation, introducing as it has constantly new and unique social situations, has brought an inevitable change in standards of conduct. In general, the trend in this shifting of standards is in the direction of providing for improved and more significant social living. Specifically, if we want to deal in these terms, the schools can focus on the liberation of intelligence for the purpose of fostering progressive change in the direction of shared interests, of social betterment. Beyond this point specificity is not only impossible, it is positively dangerous. We neither know the tools that man may next fashion, nor do we know what they will demand of the individual who seeks to foster the good life.

It is in such a situation that philosophy of education must formulate a program, using the educative materials available in all reaches of education, from the elementary school to the university, to further its end. The program, if we may consider for a moment its construction, will spring from a consideration of the changes science has wrought in the realms both of (1) discovery and invention, and (2) human responsibilities and standards of conduct. In this last sphere, lies the significant lead for education. This we may realize most fully by noting first, that socially, change has introduced us to a new view of man's relationship to man, social good has replaced both the older conception of divine right and the more recent one of natural right; and second, that individually, change has brought us a new conception of the moral nature of the individual, views of inherent goodness or badness have been relinquished in favor of one that reads off the human infant in terms of moral neutrality. Obviously, a new view of life has resulted; and, perhaps also obviously, both society and the individual house these divergent views in one body. The student, therefore, should be placed in educative situations which are designed to bring him to a realizing sense of the ways in which life values have been forged and to equip him with the means of evaluating his changing social agencies. And finally, each activity of the school should be organized definitely for the purpose of making a maximum contribution to this end. It might be easier, and it surely would be less disturbing, to deal with a more specific, measurable and predictable educational program; but in that event, philosophy of education would be dodging what is clearly the most crucial problem that it faces at the moment.

74. STATEMENT OF EDUCATIONAL PRINCIPLES RELATED TO A BASIC SOCIAL PHILOSOPHY [4]

Educators stand to-day between two great philosophies of social economy: the one representing the immediate past and fading out in actuality, an individualism in economic theory which has become hostile in practice to the development of individuality for great masses of the people and threatens the survival of American society; the other representing and anticipating the future on the basis of actual trends — the future already coming into reality, a collectivism which may permit the widest development of personality or lead to a bureaucratic tyranny destructive of ideals of popular democracy and cultural freedom.

If education continues to emphasize the philosophy of individualism in economy, it will increase the accompanying social tensions. If it organizes a program in terms of a philosophy which harmonizes with the facts of a closely integrated society, it will ease the strains of the transition taking place in actuality. The making of choices cannot be evaded, for inaction in education is a form of action.

Within the limits of an economy marked by integration and interdependence, many possibilities, many roads stand open before education. The making of choices by either evasion or positive action also cannot be avoided in the development of an educational program.

The road which the Commission has chosen and mapped in the

[4] Commission on the Social Studies, American Historical Association, *Conclusions and Recommendations*, Charles Scribner's Sons, New York, 1934, pp. 36–39.

preceding chapter is one which, it believes, will make possible the most complete realization, under the changed conditions of life, of the ideals of American democracy and cultural liberty: the recognition of the moral equality and dignity of all men; the abolition of class distinctions and special privileges; the extension to every individual, regardless of birth, class, race, religion, or economic status, of the opportunity for the fullest development of his creative capacities, his spiritual qualities, his individuality; the encouragement of social inquiry, inventiveness, and tolerance; the protection of all liberties essential to defense against the exercise of brute power; the development of resistance to appeals to racial and religious passion and prejudice; the establishment of those standards and securities set forth in *A Charter for the Social Sciences in the Schools.*

Such an affirmation of human values in education, the Commission holds, is peculiarly imperative in a society moving toward economic planning and control. Recognizing the necessity of living in an integrated economy and aware that such economy may be made to serve either some privileged minority or the entire population, the Commission deliberately presents to education, and affirms the desirability of, an economy managed in the interests of the masses, as distinguished from any class or bureaucracy.

From this point of view, a supreme purpose of education in the United States, in addition to the development of rich and many-sided personalities, is the preparation of the rising generation to enter the society now coming into being through thought, ideal, and knowledge, rather than through coercion, regimentation, and ignorance, and to shape the form of that society in accordance with American ideals of popular democracy and personal liberty and dignity.

75. PRINCIPLES SUBJECT TO CHANGE [5]

Boyd H. Bode

There seems to be no doubt that the old sense of a super-sensible reality, which constitutes a sort of fourth dimension and which is the traditional basis for moral and religious authority, is passing away. The consequence is that men are learning to judge of good and bad, of right and wrong, in terms of consequences rather than in terms of a set formula. We see this attitude of mind expressing itself in connection with all sorts of questions which formerly were settled by appeal to authority, as, for example, such questions as observance of the Sabbath, enfranchisement of women, property rights, prohibition, and the like. It is interesting to notice that the great bulk of

[5] From " The Most Outstanding Next Steps for Curriculum Makers in the United States," *Teachers College Record,* 30:183–184, December, 1928.

comment on Judge Lindsey's scheme for companionate marriages, while overwhelmingly unfavorable, seemed to be based altogether on the results which might be apprehended to follow from the innovation and not on any alleged violation of divine regulation or the eternal fitness of things. In addition to all the other changes, science is bringing about a secularization of attitude which is of profound significance for the future of the race.

Let us linger for a moment on the meaning of this latter change. It makes all the difference in the world whether we hold that the basic principles of civilization are laid down in advance, either by divine ordinance or by immutable cosmic law, or whether we assume that man creates the rules of the game, in the form of new ideals and new aspirations, as he goes along. In the latter case man's advent on this planet takes on the quality of a great experiment, which has no assignable limit and which gives no assurance that anything which we now hold sacred and essential will be permanently so. From this standpoint all our institutions and customs are just instruments for the realization of mundane ends. There is only one thing that counts and that is the continued, progressive liberation of intelligence for the improvement of human life.

My purpose so far has been to show that we are in process of developing a new type of civilization, a new *Kultur*, a new temper of mind or outlook on life. This development is largely unconscious, but it is a direct and inevitable outcome of the application of science to life. If we permit men to get their hands on the tools by which they can control their environment, the rest must follow as the night the day. The attempt will then be made to translate the old transcendental values into terms of everyday human experience, and the underlying principles of associated living will then have no more intrinsic claim to finality and perfection than have the rules of football. These underlying principles are gradually being deprived of their old protections and claims to infallibility and thrown open to critical examination. The whole center of our spiritual life is shifting. We are developing a pragmatic, experimental attitude of mind. A new humanism is on the way.

76. TENTATIVE NATURE OF PRINCIPLES [6]

Hilda Taba

The traditional notion of laws and order is fallacious in many respects. One of the fallacies lies in the belief that laws are ultimate, final, and exact formulae of actual events or phenomena. These laws

[6] From *The Dynamics of Education*, Harcourt Brace and Company, New York, 1932, pp. 55–58.

are conceived of as having been " discovered," not as having been constructed by human effort in the desire to create systems. To these laws the characteristics of ultimacy and finality have been attributed.

A closer investigation of the nature of so-called fixed laws reveals that there is no reason to think that any set of laws presents an exact picture of how things really happen. Laws are completely dependent on the sets of facts available and on the types of observation possible. Reality, especially a becoming reality, is too rich in possibilities to warrant any belief in an exhaustive knowledge of it. New tools for observation discover, and at the same time introduce new sets of facts, and these require a new set of laws to deal with them. Such a revision of laws long held as final has occurred repeatedly in the history of science, yet — until recently — without having shaken the faith of scientists in the finality of laws themselves. The ruling ambition of science still is to " discover " a final set of exact laws to serve as exact formulae. The validity of its laws — as expressed chiefly by their exactness — has served as a standard by which the scientific value of any discipline has been measured, and by which the acceptance or non-acceptance of a discipline into the family of sciences has been decided. The inability of human sciences to " discover " a set of laws conforming to these demands has been the reason why there is so much doubt and argument as to the scientific nature and value of these studies.

It seems reasonable to think of laws as working tools, the product of human construction, which fit and systematize our observations, the validity and usefulness of which can be measured by the degree they render unity and clarity to the diversity of single facts and single processes. In fact, it is now among exact scientists themselves that we find expressed the view that our present laws are nothing more than the expressions of a system of our own construction, built for our own satisfaction and our own sense of security; and that we might have built just as easily in some other fashion and have discovered some other laws in the process.* We are justified in believing in the usefulness of natural law because we can find no tolerable alternative, although there is no reason for thinking in so far as finalities are concerned the law we have chosen is more probably true than false.†

Laws being of our own construction, it is evident that they share the limitations of our knowledge, and therefore are far from presenting an absolute, final picture of natural events.

Still less reasonable is the claim to their absolute exactness. A sort of numerical accuracy has been postulated as the sole standard of scientific thinking, largely because the quantitative tools of inves-

* Cf. Eddington, *The Nature of the Physical World*, p. 241.
† Ritchie, *The Scientific Method*, p. 85.

tigation in the exact sciences have rendered the numerical accuracy fairly convenient and also because it is satisfying to the natural need for clearness and simplicity. Thus it was so easy for the atomistic viewpoint to conceive of reality as a quantitative re-arrangement of a limited set of final entities and to manipulate them numerically. Other sciences less adapted to the use of numerical measurements have uncritically accepted the same standard.

There is no reason why phenomena of different character should not be systematized in ways more suitable to their peculiar characteristics, stressing adequacy in preference to numerical exactness, and still be exact in a more general sense, that is still be able to render an accurate account of actual phenomena. Phenomena are not made any more exact by numerical manipulation. It is necessary to express the subject matter in terms of laws suitable to, and best expressive of its character, granted that the system as a whole fits intelligibly together and does not blur further vision in the same field. To subject a description of phenomena to the standards of exactness and finality when they do not possess those characteristics, is to import something into the system that is alien to the phenomena themselves. Such a process hampers further productivity of thought.

It is evident that in dealing with phenomena, the basic characteristics of which are not recurrence and stability, much less exactness, it is imperative to employ a standard of scientific validity different from that used for phenomena possessing such aspects. Finality and uniformity should not be sought for their own sake but for the sake of clarity, consistency, and unity in treating the phenomena under consideration. Our thought, in order to be productive, adequate, and satisfying, requires some central idea to serve to unify the diversity of reality, or a central way of looking at things to enable us to see relations among the variety of phenomena. And a system of thought may just as well be built on the basis of the continuity of events as on the basis of a pre-arranged framework of stable recurrences. Yet from the standpoint of the dynamic universe, the latter is preferable, because it brings order and consistency to thought without limiting its specific contents and without doing violence to certain phenomena of life.

As it is now, or at least, as it was until quite recently, all phenomena which exhibit the characteristics of becoming are essentially excluded from any scientific systems. . . . Here . . . we have the question of whether the nature of events is to be misinterpreted in order that they may fit a standard alien to them and raised on false pre-suppositions, or whether we are to construct laws to suit these events. Since laws as they are predominantly conceived at present, deal pre-eminently with things already become, with the outcomes of events, with substantive and stable aspects of phenomena, and not with the processes themselves, not with change, all events that represent real change in their essentials, are either excluded from any rational treatment at all, or they are represented in partial or distorted form so as to make them fit the laws and rules fixed *a priori* to the events themselves. Laws as tools should keep their functional relationship to the events themselves and should represent change to the same degree that the events do.

77. "EDUCATIONAL SOCIOLOGY AS A SOURCE OF FUNDAMENTAL ASSUMPTIONS IN EDUCATION "[7]

Charles C. Peters

The general topic for this program is, "Where Shall We Go for Our Fundamental Assumptions in Education?" The term, "fundamental assumptions," is a very strong one to use in this connection. There are very few really fundamental assumptions that education needs to make and we do not go to educational sociology or to any other university study for them. One of these fundamental assumptions we make in educational science and practice is that human nature is reasonably uniform, just as all physical science presupposes the uniformity of nature. Trusting that there is a certain regularity in the activities of persons, we conduct scientific experiments to determine what is the most economical way of teaching a body of material to a certain group of persons and then generalize from our findings, expecting that other groups in the future — *all* groups of the same kind — will behave as our experimental group has been found to behave. But we do not go to philosophy or to psychology or to any other branch of science for this faith. We get it from experience in everyday living. Except as one assumed the uniformity of nature he could not plan ahead for any of the problems of life — could not know how large a store of coal to lay by for winter, how to approach his friend so as to avoid offending him, how to adjust himself in his social relations, how to plow his field and whether to plow it, how to count upon the sun rising the next day, or even how to take his next step. The uniformity of nature is one of the axioms that men must assume if they are to live purposively at all, and belief in it is a momentum that one inevitably acquires without teaching — certainly without the tutelage of any such stilted discipline as philosophy, psychology or sociology.

[7] *Educational Administration and Supervision*, 14:385–386, 389–390, September, 1928.

And the same thing is true of the other fundamental assumptions involved in education: That certain things have value and that of these some have more value than others, that it is possible to hasten the learning of individuals by some kind of teaching, and perhaps a few more.

But, while these assumptions fundamental to educational practice and theory arise basically out of experience, the faiths and convictions thus accruing can, of course, be modified somewhat by propaganda. In large measure people find in their experience what they expect to find — what they look for. Thus if scientific workers succeed in discovering apparently universal laws within certain fields, and continually assert their belief that we shall extend the discovery of such uniformities into other realms, popular belief in the mechanistic nature of reality is likely to be accentuated. On the other hand propagandism for such philosophies as idealism and pragmatism, with their evidence that certain so-called laws are only *approximately* true generalizations, and their insistence that all laws *may* be merely working conveniences near enough to the truth to serve practical purposes, may tend to break the popular faith in the uniformity of nature as a theoretical concept. Thus confidence in a science of methods of teaching, in educational measurements, in formulated codes of morality, in accepted systems of values, may be *affected* by what goes on in the academic circles of philosophy, psychology, and sociology. But the fundamental assumptions by which men live and act can only be *somewhat influenced* in balance by what goes on within the realms of science; they can not be created there. In the last analysis they arise inductively out of experience, and all that philosophy or psychology or sociology can do is to describe this experience in its empirically given nature. . . .

Values are relative to the conditions under which men live and act; they are determined largely by the necessities of adjustment to environment. In the long run sensed values are the outcomes of sensed needs, in spite of the fact that temporarily they can be modified by propaganda. Valuations arise, therefore, out of the clash of living and the surest way in which to find them is to isolate and formulate what is making for survival in this struggle. That is what we attempt to do in an inductive study of social valuations. The effort that Professor Bobbitt and Charters and numbers of others of us are making to determine norms from a study of the present has often been criticised as an attempt to fix and perpetuate the *status quo*. It is not that. If we studied average men as the basis of our analyses that criticism might be valid. But we fix our eyes on the men who are in the van. We ask for descriptions of the better individuals in contrast with the worse and attempt to formulate perfected goals in those directions in which the better deviate from the worse. We are, in other words, trying to catch the trend of progress toward that which represents the best aspirations of the race, and to formulate these aspirations into specific educational objectives. And in picking these " better " in contrast with the " worse " we are *not* moving in a circle. We are merely using the fact that people have a subtle sense as to who are really " fit " as cultured men or as citizens even when they could not articulately define culture or citizenship, just as a highly skilled mechanic can sense what to do in the presence of a difficulty when he could not reduce his technique to a formula. By analyzing the examples to which this mute sense for " fitness " points we can make articulate in the form of detailed lists of educational objectives the particulars which are required to constitute the " fitness."

78. "Psychology as the Source of Fundamental Assumptions in Education "[8]

Frank N. Freeman

In order to discuss the question as to the source of the assumptions in education, one must have some notion what these assumptions are. It would perhaps be a rather large undertaking to draw up a list of all the assumptions. The task is somewhat simplified by the qualifying adjective which is used in our title. Perhaps it will not be so difficult to lay down the *fundamental* assumptions.

Obviously, one of the fundamental assumptions is that education is possible. One can hardly proceed in the attempt to carry on any form of education without making this assumption. This assumption of the possibility of education has to be made not only with respect to education in general, but with respect to each form of education which is undertaken, and with respect to the education of the various individuals in the various forms of training. Stated in this way, the assumption concerns the extent and the limitations of the possibility of education.

It must be obvious, I think, that this question, both in its general and its special forms, is psychological in nature. We can only determine what education is possible by making a scientific study of individuals under various forms of training, and measuring the results. No amount of philosophical speculation, no consideration of the desirability or the ethical obligation of different forms of training, and no consideration of social demands will give us the information we need on this point.

The problem concerning the possibilities of education becomes

[8] *Educational Administration and Supervision,* **14**:371–373, September, 1928.

presumptive in proportion as we consider it in detail. Consider the question in this form: To what extent is it possible to bring about a fundamental improvement in general function as distinguished from the superficial acquisition of knowledge and skill? If we are considering the most general type of intellectual ability, the question appears in this form: Can intelligence be increased and to what extent can it be increased? The assumptions we make on this point as recent educational discussions have shown will have a marked bearing upon our procedure. It is only through psychological analysis, experimentation, and interpretation that we are able to advance our knowledge on this important issue.

Take again the time-honored question, " Is general training or only special training possible? " Some have thought this question to be dead and deeply interred. Nobody, however, can escape it. The best one can do, . . . is to assume it without being aware that he is doing so. While a philosopher may do us a service by calling our attention to the existence of the problem, it is only as a psychologist that he can aid us toward its solution.

Take again the question of individual differences. How far are these differences inherent and ineradicable, and how far can they be modified or even removed by education? The debate concerning the classification of children revolves about this point. This is clearly a fundamental assumption and as clearly a question for psychological investigation, and is to be settled by psychology. The same is true about the question, " How far can special abilities be developed? " If a child cannot carry a tune, is its inability due to lack of proper training or to lack of some innate characteristic? Finally, we may ask a similar question regarding the non-intellectual traits: " How far can character and temperamental traits be developed or eradicated by proper methods of education? " Psychology has recently been addressing itself to this problem and promises to contribute very largely toward its solution in the near future.

I can think of only one other general assumption which is equally fundamental with that concerning the possibility of education. This second fundamental assumption is that education is profitable. The proponents of the other disciplines would grant perhaps without debate the claim of psychology to the problems which have already been outlined. It is the business of psychology, they would say, as a science, to determine what is possible. It is only the normative disciplines, however, which can determine what is desirable. It is to them we must go to find out whether education in general promotes human well-being and whether particular types of education promote well-being more than do others. . . .

The assumption in question, in its general form and in its special form, may be stated thus: " Education in general or some special kind of education in particular increases human well-being, happiness, or usefulness." In order to determine the truth of this assumption, we must, of course, know what human well-being, happiness and usefulness are and what promotes them. At this point, it is a common practice to make a distinction between psychology on the one hand and the normative disciplines, such as philosophy and ethics, on the other hand. Philosophy and ethics, it is said, determine the ends or aims of human life or the norms of human living. They enable us to say what is worth striving for and what is not worth striving for. They set the values of life. They give us the basis for the distinction between the good and the beautiful and the bad and the ugly. After the ends or the norms of life have been set, psychology may enable us to determine the means by which these ends may be secured or by which these norms may be attained. Philosophy sets the ends; psychology determines the means for attaining these ends.

79. " An Educational Platform for 1936 "[9]

Grayson N. Kefauver

This educational platform has grown out of the deliberations and discussions of the Conference on Curriculum and Guidance held at Stanford University July 6–10, which dealt with many of the important problems and issues in education. The following statement represents a selective summary of the thinking of the Conference on developments and problems in curriculum and guidance. The positions taken on controversial issues are those which appeared to the writer to receive strongest support by the Conference participants. They reflect the best judgment of the writer of this statement.

1. The educational program in a democracy should be in harmony with the dominant democratic social values and aspirations. The educational philosophy should grow out of the democratic social philosophy, and the organization and methods in education should reflect the highest conceptions of the democratic way of life. The school system should be thought of as society's chief formal agency to develop in its people the vision, the creativeness, the initiative, the critical-mindedness, the understanding, the philosophy, and the discipline which will enable them to live noble personal lives and, jointly, to build a culture and a society which give expression to the democratic social ideals for which the people share responsibility in defining and in reconstructing as new conditions emerge and as our

[9] Stanford University Press, Stanford University, California, 1936, pp. 2–8.

civilization is raised to higher levels. Other groups and forces in American life may depart from the democratic philosophy; the school has an unequivocal mandate to vitalize the democratic social ideal and to develop an educational program in harmony with it.

2. The present period in the development of civilization represents a period of unusual progress. In the United States the conquering of the physical frontier has led to the development of a highly interdependent, complex, industrial, and urban society. Thrilling achievements have been made in the application of science, in the improvement of health, in the production of goods, in the development of transportation and communication, and in many other aspects of life. The process of utilizing and controlling the natural environment has advanced a considerable distance but it can still be said that the process is only well begun. The frontiers of the chemistry laboratory have replaced the frontiers of the forests and the plains. These material developments have fundamentally changed the way of life of the American people. They have changed our personal values, our cultural interests, our vocational activities, and what we do in our leisure time. The world of 1936 is in a real sense a different world from that of a third of a century ago.

3. The rate of progress has not been uniform in all divisions of our life. Extremely rapid advances in the application of science, in the mastering of our material environment, in the substitution of electrical power and automatic machinery for human labor, and in the development of a truly remarkable system for communication and for the production of goods have not been accompanied by advances equally great in the cultural and social fields. The insecurity in the modern world; the poverty, undernourishment, and slum life in the midst of potential plenty; the extreme contrast in welfare levels with a large proportion of national income going to a small fraction of the population and a very large proportion of the people living below a level of decency and comfort; the absence of democracy in the relation between employer and employee; the intolerance toward minority groups; the open and secret connivance of law-enforcement agencies with criminal groups and with groups which seek to overthrow orderly government to crush groups with ideas and activities in conflict with their interests; the illegal actions of secret groups and societies; the disease and ill health which could be corrected or postponed if the health knowledge and services were more widely used; crime; divorce; and the failure to realize cultural possibilities of the motion picture and the radio should be sufficient to illustrate the need for basic advances in the social and cultural areas. Material developments have produced new conditions, new opportunities, and new problems. These material changes have

made ineffective highly successful social arrangements of earlier years. They have jarred existing social institutions to their very foundations. The unevenness of developments has created a strain, which has caused much confusion and conflict in the modern world. This conflict and this confusion have prevented the people from making full use of the material advances. They constitute a real threat to the preservation of our democratic social objectives and the democratic way of life. The pressing need of this period is the development of social insight, social creativeness, and loyalty to democratic social values, so that rapid advances can be made in the social realm sufficient to bring our social arrangements into harmony with the needs of the people living in the modern world. Advances along social lines require active participation, understanding, and support by the great mass of people to a greater extent than do material advances. Hence, the new need for social advance calls strongly for a highly effective program of universal education.

4. In a period of rapid and fundamental social change, the place of the study of the past takes a form different from that which exists when the social changes are slight and relatively unimportant. In periods of rapid change, the future society can be expected to differ from that of the present and the past in many important respects. Consequently, the social institutions and practices which functioned well in the past may be ill-adapted to the present or to the future. The educational program can appropriately allow greater stress on the study of conditions of the present and of the potentialities of the future in a period of rapid change.

Basic trends and movements can best be defined by a careful study of the past. Society is evolving and the present takes on greater meaning when its origins are known. Through a study of the past, the present can be seen as one step in an evolutionary process and the inevitability of continued change can be recognized. The future of American society will be influenced by the developments to date, by new material factors which will be introduced, and by the vision of the people of potentialities for further development. Whether the onward movement of events will be advantageous or disadvantageous to man and what direction the movement will take will be determined by the vision of the people and their energetic participation through utilization of democratic processes in efforts to shape conditions along lines considered by them to be desirable and profitable.

5. Education should be a positive force for stimulating and giving direction to social changes along lines desirable in a democracy. When education shifts its focus from a study of the past to a study and an appraisal of contemporary life with a consideration of the

potentialities and desirable lines of development, it shifts from a position of mere transmission of information about things which have been done to one of dynamic influence in social evolution. The canvass of contemporary life involves an appraisal of the different phases in relationship to a carefully-thought-through democratic social philosophy, thereby identifying aspects in need of fundamental change. Consideration of the nature of the changes desired, with an analysis of the various proposals which have been made by social pioneers, and a weighing of the validity of the claims of proponents on both sides of major controversial issues, will make the educational program a positive agent in developing loyalty to major democratic social goals and in contributing to their attainment. To develop an educational program which informs students of the past and the present with the assumption that all that exists today is good and likely to be retained in the future is to admit ignorance of contemporary life and historic fact or deliberately to falsify. Education should clearly be shaped in a manner to contribute to the elevation or improvement of individual and social life.

6. The freedom of the teachers to work with students in a study of all aspects of contemporary life and all problems should be guaranteed. Individuals and minority groups in the community should not be allowed to force avoidance of consideration of important problems in order to create public ignorance of important issues so as to serve the personal interests or to humor the prejudices of those exerting the pressure. If individuals and minority groups are given free way in preventing or controlling the teaching in important areas, educators are forced to give a distorted picture of modern life or to retreat to a study of the past where conflicts will not cause embarrassment. Boards of education and trustees and school administrators have no more important function than to resist these pressures and to protect the teacher in his right to develop an educational program in harmony with the real needs of our democratic society. Those legally in control of schools should not turn control over to extralegal individual and minority groups by responding to their requests and pressures.

Developments in recent years indicate that teachers cannot always depend upon boards of education and administrators to resist these outside pressures. Consequently, it becomes obligatory for teachers to effect a strong professional organization to give group resistance to these interferences with desirable operation of the educational program and to protect the tenure of the teacher. The social and educational developments in recent years make professional organization essential. The individual teacher cannot cope with the negative forces now operative. At the present time many teachers consciously avoid the study of many of the most important problems in the social field because of the examples of able individuals throughout the country who have been crushed by public attacks of individuals and minority groups or by an irresponsible or prejudiced press, or who have been dropped by boards of education who proceed as though they believed their authority should be used to force perversion of the educational program in ways to support their own thinking, their personal interests, or the interests of the social group of which they are members. The public should be alert to the quiet maneuvering of minority groups to place one or more of their members on the board of education the better to control the educational policies in a way to serve the interests of the minority group they represent.

Teachers should themselves provide a judicial consideration of all important points of view and all pertinent data when considering important issues. For the teacher to hold students ignorant or to distort viewpoints in order to secure student acceptance of the teacher's thinking likewise runs counter to democratic social theory. However, professional workers and the public should not be misled by the extravagant falsification by individuals and minority groups who charge radicalism in schools to serve either as a smokescreen for their own selfish activity or as a technique for arousing public sentiment against socially desirable but to them objectionable teaching activity.

7. Social welfare and the interests of the individual are served best when human talent is distributed according to social need and the individual is engaged in activity which makes full use of his talent, in which he can succeed, and in which he is happy. This generalization holds not only for the vocational phase of life, but also for the social-civic and recreational. A sound educational program calls for a guidance service which aids the student in defining major life goals — vocational, social-civic, recreational, and health. These personal objectives can be wisely defined by the individual only when he has knowledge of the conditions, opportunities, and needs in the various fields, his own capacities and interests, and the factors which should be considered in developing a well-planned life program. The guidance service also aids the individual in his planning of his education. In addition, the program he plans under guidance carries more meaning and importance than when part of his program is determined by administrative prescription and the remainder left to casual unaided selection, since he himself selects it in relation to goals and values which are important to him.

The possession of goals, the participation in meaningful activity, and the freedom to shape one's education in terms of needs and interests together make highly important contributions in the motivation of school work. When students are indifferent or resistant and only a modicum of participation is secured through external pressures by such devices as marks, honor lists, and societies, merit systems and weighted credit, it can safely be assumed that satisfactory results are not being secured. Instead, it can be assumed that there are important undesirable learnings. The necessity for extrinsic motivation should be interpreted as a symptom of maladjustment. When the most desirable learning conditions exist, artificial extrinsic motivating techniques are not only not necessary but they constitute serious obstacles to most effective operation. While it may not be possible in a particular school situation to remove extrinsic motivation entirely, its undesirability should be recognized, and intrinsic motivation should be developed to as great an extent as the general conditions and the ability of the teacher make possible.

8. The educational program should be concerned with the growth and development of individuals along all desirable lines. The almost exclusive emphasis on knowledge in the past cannot be defended. Of equal importance are interests, attitudes, goals, loyalties, mental and physical health, and the capacity to combine these elements into a well-integrated, stable, effective, and happy personality. Regardless of the desire of the teacher, his handling of students will affect their development along the different lines. It is not possible to isolate one segment of the life of the student for training and leave the other segments unaffected. The individual always participates as a whole person. Consequently, it is important that the educational program be arranged in the light of the total group of effects on the development of the individual.

9. An educational program which is concerned with the all-round development of the individual will need to provide for a variety of experiences. Textbook and library study is well adapted for certain types of learnings but not for others. Such experiences should be supplemented by the different types of experiences which make up desirable normal living. Among the types introduced by the best schools are student participation in defining the goals of the school and in shaping the program; student participation in the management of the school; student participation, along with adults, in attempting to improve important aspects of the life of the community; creative activity in art, music, writing; testing of ideas in the laboratory, in the shop, and on the farm; student planning of their own life and their own education; in short, actually doing under supervision the things which constitute desirable living in this period. This active participation provides the occasion for meaningful student reading and discussion.

10. The classroom and the school site are no longer considered to be the only location of educational activities. Modern schools are taking their students out into the community, to study community conditions at first hand, to identify community problems and, where feasible, to participate in a program looking toward community betterment. Such a program is being developed not only on the elementary and secondary-school levels, but also on the adult level. The interest in community life involves recognition by educational workers that the community's conditions and activities of community agencies, such as the press, the radio, and the motion picture, may be highly educative — at times along lines socially undesirable. The use by the school of community situations and agencies, and the techniques developed by these agencies, gives promise of helping youth to become an integral part of the life of the community and to become active participants in socially significant enterprises.

11. Education in a democracy involves a close relationship with the people of the community. They finally determine the nature of the education which will be carried forward by professional educators. They pay the cost of the program which is developed. Professional educators are obligated to accept a mandate of the people on the type of education which is desired. However, the nature of our present society makes it extremely difficult to distinguish between the voice of the people and the voice of articulate minorities. The educational workers should carry a leadership role, join with the people in the study of educational need, build on their own part and on the part of the public an understanding of the type of education needed by youth in the modern world, and secure from adults the assistance they can give in shaping the educational program. Many new educational developments involve participation in community enterprises along with adults. Desirable co-operation can best be secured when adults understand the purpose and value of such participation. An understanding on the part of parents of the type of education needed by modern youth is of value also in securing parent co-operation in working with their children and in securing a handling of students at home in ways in harmony with the policies which are being adopted in the school.

This study by the people of the educational needs represents one example of adult education in which the adults study systematically under technically trained leadership the needs in this important area of social activity. There is urgent need of equally systematic study in all major areas of social activity. The modern world is highly complex and our democratic social system calls for participation on the part of all in shaping major social goals and practices. This cannot be done wisely without careful study of the problems being considered. Provision should be made in the school system for such study. In the future, we can expect the program in adult education to constitute a major division of the total educational service. Programs of adult education in the past have placed major or exclusive emphasis on vocational training and on the tool subjects. The social crisis through which we are passing makes training of the social-civic type imperative on the adult level. The issues before the American people will not wait for the youth of the land to attain adulthood and full citizenship status. Also, training in the period of youth cannot be expected to suffice as preparation for intelligent handling of adult problems. The cultural, recreational, and vocational phases of life should also be given major consideration.

12. The educational activities should be shaped in relation to the educational and social objectives and the characteristics and needs of the individual. Problems studied, situations met, and activities carried forward should be treated comprehensively. These learning experiences should not be regimented and restricted by subject lines. Such regimentation is particularly objectionable when the administrative policy requires the teacher to adhere closely to a text or a course of study outline and to cover a prescribed body of subject matter during a semester or a year. This subject-matter requirement, set without reference to the experiences, interests, or needs of the group, forces the teacher to place stress on subject mastery instead of on well-rounded student development. The formal subject organization with content determined by the logic of the subject field should give way to an organization in terms of the problems, needs, and activities of students. The separate learning of the different subjects with the thought that students will put them together in their later life is in violent conflict with the organismic nature of the individual and the manner in which most effective learning occurs. A sound principle of organization of learning experiences cannot be derived from the subject matter alone. To teach students well requires that the educational program be shaped in terms of their life and their needs in our developing democratic society.

A major "scope and sequence" of learning activities should be tentatively planned in advance after careful study of social needs and the needs of students at the different maturity levels. The general outlines aid in securing order in the educational program, in guaranteeing consecutiveness in the experiences of the individual, and in preventing the omission of highly important aspects of training. Within this general framework provided by the "scope and sequence," the teachers and students have great freedom in shaping the learning experiences appropriate for a particular group of students. The "scope and sequence" should not be considered to be ironclad but teachers should consider desirable modifications with their supervisor or administrator if the needs of the students cannot be fully served within the general framework which is provided. Also, the " scope and sequence " itself should be subjected to continuous review with modifications made as new evidence indicates changes to be desirable.

13. The educational program appropriate for the present age requires teachers with deep human sympathies, broad social understanding, rich cultural interests and experiences, personal courage, stable and well-integrated personalities, special scholarship in several broad areas of experience, and knowledge of how children learn and develop. Narrow training and limited cultural and social experiences foredoom the teacher to the doing of an inadequate piece of work. Teacher-training institutions should insist upon broad social understandings, a variety of rich cultural experiences and interests, broad training in general teaching fields, knowledge of how children learn and develop, and desirable personality characteristics.

Boards of education, administrators, and supervisors should provide conditions favorable for the maintenance and further development of these characteristics. Among the conditions requisite for the continued development of teachers while engaged in teaching are reasonable security in tenure, a non-restrictive intellectual climate which allows, and in fact calls, for independent creative thinking, democratic sharing of responsibility for shaping educational policies — general policies as well as those which affect their work more directly — opportunity to participate in the cultural and social life of the community with the same freedom accorded the " best " citizens of the community; a program which is not loaded with deadening routine and detail, and not so heavy as to cause a continuous feeling of dissatisfaction with what can be done in the time available and to induce a continuous fatigue, favorable for personal disintegration and physical illness; and a salary sufficient to enable him to associate with the most highly cultured people, to travel, to buy books and magazines, to attend the theater and the concert, to make fully adequate use of the available medical services, and to dress in a manner which exemplifies good taste and which sets a good standard for students' observation and possible imitation. Some people may be deluded into thinking that salaries can be cut or maintained at low levels without lowering teaching efficiency, but those who are informed know that the reduction in enriching cultural experiences because of reduced income seriously lowers teaching efficiency.

14. The task of reconstructing the educational program is a complex and difficult one and one which must be made gradually by the educative process. The early attempts involved appointing com-

mittees to write new courses of study or to adopt courses of study developed in other situations with little or no modification. While these activities were probably not entirely without value, they represented feeble beginnings. The sounder programs now in process include course-of-study writing but not as the most important phase. The basic problem is one of stimulating education and growth of teachers. Teachers can improve the educational service only by experiencing real personal growth along significant lines. Shifts in thinking must be made not only by the teachers, supervisors, and administrators, but also by the parents. Some promising educational developments have failed because parents did not understand the new program and consequently did not accept it. Because the problem of educational reconstruction is not now seen as a task as simple as conceived when the curriculum first moved into the center of professional interest should not discourage professional workers. The magnitude and importance of the task should constitute an ennobling challenge. We have an important social responsibility. Through courageous attack upon the problem we may be assured of a growth and development on our own part which will bring our powers more nearly up to what American education sorely needs. The maintenance and further development of our democratic society places a heavy burden upon the school. No group of professional educators ever faced a greater task. Few will remain complacent in the face of such a challenge.

80. " THE CHILDREN'S CHARTER " [10]

PRESIDENT HOOVER'S WHITE HOUSE CONFERENCE ON CHILD HEALTH AND PROTECTION RECOGNIZING THE RIGHTS OF THE CHILD AS THE FIRST RIGHTS OF CITIZENSHIP PLEDGES ITSELF TO THESE AIMS FOR THE CHILDREN OF AMERICA

I For every child spiritual and moral training to help him to stand firm under the pressure of life

II For every child understanding and the guarding of his personality as his most precious right

III For every child a home and that love and security which a home provides; and for that child who must receive foster care, the nearest substitute for his own home

IV For every child full preparation for his birth, his mother receiving prenatal, natal, and postnatal care; and the establishment of such protective measures as will make child-bearing safer

[10] White House Conference on Child Health and Protection, called by President Hoover, Washington, April, 1931.

V For every child health protection from birth through adolescence, including: periodical health examinations and, where needed, care of specialists and hospital treatment; regular dental examination and care of the teeth; protective and preventive measures against communicable diseases; the insuring of pure food, pure milk, and pure water

VI For every child from birth through adolescence, promotion of health, including health instruction and a health program, wholesome physical and mental recreation, with teachers and leaders adequately trained

VII For every child a dwelling place safe, sanitary, and wholesome, with reasonable provisions for privacy, free from conditions which tend to thwart his development; and a home environment harmonious and enriching

VIII For every child a school which is safe from hazards, sanitary, properly equipped, lighted, and ventilated. For younger children nursery schools and kindergartens to supplement home care

IX For every child a community which recognizes and plans for his needs, protects him against physical dangers, moral hazards, and disease; provides him with safe and wholesome places for play and recreation; and makes provision for his cultural and social needs

X For every child an education which, through the discovery and development of his individual abilities, prepares him for life; and through training and vocational guidance prepares him for a living which will yield him the maximum of satisfaction

XI For every child such teaching and training as will prepare him for successful parenthood, homemaking, and the rights of citizenship; and, for parents, supplementary training to fit them to deal wisely with the problems of parenthood

XII For every child education for safety and protection against accidents to which modern conditions subject him — those to which he is directly exposed and those which, through loss or maiming of his parents, affect him indirectly

XIII For every child who is blind, deaf, crippled, or otherwise physically handicapped, and for the child who is mentally handicapped, such measures as will early discover and diagnose his handicap, provide care and treatment, and so train him that he may become an asset to society rather than a liability. Expenses of these services should be borne publicly where they cannot be privately met

XIV For every child who is in conflict with society the right to be dealt with intelligently as society's charge, not society's outcast; with the home, the school, the church, the court and the institution when needed, shaped to return him whenever possible to the normal stream of life

XV For every child the right to grow up in a family with an adequate standard of living and the security of a stable income as the surest safeguard against social handicaps

XVI For every child protection against labor that stunts growth, either physical or mental, that limits education, that deprives children of the right of comradeship, of play, and of joy

XVII For every rural child as satisfactory schooling and health services as for the city child, and an extension to rural families of social, recreational, and cultural facilities

XVIII To supplement the home and the school in the training of youth, and to return to them those interests of which modern life tends to cheat children, every stimulation and encouragement should be given to the extension and development of the voluntary youth organizations

XIX To make everywhere available these minimum protections of the health and welfare of children, there should be a district, county, or community organization for health, education, and welfare, with full-time officials, coordinating with a state-wide program which will be responsive to a nation-wide service of general information, statistics, and scientific research. This should include:

(a) Trained, full-time public health officials, with public health nurses, sanitary inspection, and laboratory workers

(b) Available hospital beds

(c) Full-time public welfare service for the relief, aid, and guidance of children in special need due to poverty, misfortune, or behavior difficulties, and for the protection of children from abuse, neglect, exploitation, or moral hazard

For EVERY child these rights, regardless of race, or color, or situation, wherever he may live under the protection of the American flag

81. POINT OF VIEW IN DEVELOPING THE VIRGINIA CURRICULUM PROGRAM [11]

Brief statements are here presented of the more important concepts that have controlled development of the Virginia curriculum program. Analysis of the materials and procedures will reveal how these concepts are expected to be made operative in the curriculum. It will be obvious that experience makes possible more complete interpretations of some concepts than of others in a program such as this.

(1) The American system of free public schools has been devel-

[11] Virginia, *Tentative Course of Study for Virginia Elementary Schools, Grades I–VII,* State Board of Education, Richmond, 1934, pp. 1–2.

oped to assist in perpetuating, improving, and realizing democratic ideals. The entire school program should be projected to this end. The school should be democratic, not only in its instructional program, but also in its organization and method.

(2) Democratic ideals can be realized only as democracy is seen to be a way of living. Consequently, the school must guide pupils in the development of types of behavior compatible with democratic ideals.

(3) Conditions, however, are constantly changing. Material and social developments create new problems and complicate our efforts to develop a democratic way of life. Solutions to problems cannot be taught as the means of realizing our social ideals. Rather, emotionalized attitudes or general patterns of conduct must be developed which will serve as guides in meeting new situations according to the dictates of democratic concepts.

(4) Development of emotionalized attitudes that will function in desirable ways in actual living requires that social life in its functional relationships be the primary point of orientation for the educational program; that the pupil be acquainted with social realities as well as theory; that he be guided into more effective and extensive participation in the activities of the social group of which he is a part; that he have opportunity to engage in many lifelike activities which possess for him a maximum of meaning and purpose.

(5) Emotionalized attitudes, being integrations of specific habits and knowledge, become more generally applicable as the number of specific habits and the extent of knowledge forming the attitude is increased. Consequently, the pupil should be guided in a wide variety of situations in which the desired attitudes have opportunity to function.

(6) The effectiveness with which attitudes function is conditioned by the facility with which the pupil can use the specific habits and knowledge involved. Consequently, provision should be made to assure necessary mastery of such abilities. But the approach should be from the whole situation to its respective elements or parts and back again to the whole situation. Memorization of isolated facts and mastery of unrelated skills do not assure desirable modification of behavior. Attitudes are changed by reorganizing whole behavior patterns, not by piecemeal additions to them. Thus, integration of specific habits and knowledge into attitudes is a process which goes forward before, during, and after specific efforts to master skills and knowledge that are needed.

(7) The attitudes a pupil develops are materially conditioned by the success he experiences in the activities of school life. In other

words, as opportunity presents itself the pupil will continue to do the things out of school in which he succeeds in school and will evade the things in which he failed. Consequently, activities, materials, and instruction provided by the school should be so varied as to provide opportunity for successful participation by children of all abilities, capacities, and in all environmental surroundings.

(8) As the individual increases the general applicability of the various emotionalized attitudes, he increases his opportunity for greatest individual realization, for this is the outcome of development of a more democratic way of living.

(9) Many forces bear on the education of the child. The motion picture, newspapers, magazines, the home, the church, and the street, all exert great influence. Only as all of these agencies contribute to common ideals can education be fully effective. The school, being society's organized educative agency, has greater responsibility than others. It should endeavor to coordinate as many educative influences as possible and provide for the pupil an educational program as broad as life itself.

This point of view is based in general on the following principles:

The school is an agency of society for its perpetuation and re-creation.

Growth processes in individuals and in society are resultants of continuing interaction between individuals and society.

Individuals differ in interests, abilities, attitudes, appreciations and understandings, habits and skills, and in capacity to learn.

Growth is continuous.

All learning comes through experience.

An individual tends to avoid experiences which annoy and to seek experiences which satisfy.

The school can serve as a creative institution only as it succeeds in controlling through its curriculum the experience of learners so that cultivated, integrated, and individualized personalities are developed.

82. Informal Statement of the Point of View in the Wilmington, Delaware Curriculum Program [12]

One task of the group was to formulate a philosophy of education for the Wilmington Public Schools. This activity was very fundamental and worthy of careful, thorough study because a sound philosophy of education supplies the guiding principles and theories of the entire educational program. It is the resultant of accumulative, reflective, critical, analytical and continuous thought directed upon the educative process. It differentiates between good and bad prac-

[12] Wilmington, Delaware, *Cooperative Curriculum Revision,* Board of Public Education, Wilmington, Delaware, 1935, pp. 24, 26, 28.

tices and points the way to the conservation of the desirable and the elimination of the undesirable. It defines the nature of the educative process and supplies the underlying motivating forces. It furnishes the stimulating basis for improvement of curricular offerings. Without it there can be no improvement. In the first year's work in curriculum revision, the following tentative philosophy of education was developed for the Wilmington Public Schools:

" There are two vantage points from which education is usually viewed. One is the remote needs of adult life and the other is the immediate needs of the learner on his level of experience. The former has given us the present school curriculum with its subjects; subject matter set out to be learned; recitation, budget and mastery techniques of teaching; standardized tests, uniform requirements, concentration on the tools of an education, such as skills, and specific habits, resulting in a passive learner, an educational conformist in an age of activity, iconoclasm, and rapidity of social change. To emphasize the needs of adult life when these needs cannot be determined or even anticipated, to specify subjects and subject matter when there are no guarantees that the selection is valid and the materials will ever be used, to follow methods which are ill adjusted to the teaching of subject matter and are contrary to the known processes of desirable learning, to insist upon uniformity of achievement when variability is more desirable, to measure results objectively when individual functioning is the true criterion, — seem to involve much wasted educational effort for the learner, for the teacher, and for society.

" Examining education through the immediate functional needs of the learner gives us education as a psychological process of growth in purposes, power, attitudes, techniques, enjoyment — a full rich, whole life. Transferring the emphasis from the sociological needs of remote adult life to the immediate psychological process of growth is not without its dangers both to the tradition and to the learner. Progress, however narrow or broad be your meaning of the word, has never come about by adherence to tradition, by conformity, by accepting complacently the existing mores, but has been associated with a revolt from tradition and a sharp denunciation of the mores. As Rousseau in his " Emile ", published in 1762, fired the guns that battered down the walls of tradition and destroyed the fortifications of social and educational intrenchment by inviting people to look at life and education from a different viewpoint, so progress in the present can be real, permanent, and of greater magnitude only as the commonplace activities of the present are examined from a new position. To this end is proposed a new philosophy of education written around the present genuine interests and needs of the learner.

" A number of important emphases in this philosophy should be mentioned.

" 1. Education is conceived as a process of remaking experience.

" 2. The process of remaking experience is vital to the learner.

" 3. Each year the learner should increase the area, depth, and height of his experience consistent with his ability.

" 4. Each year the learner should improve his technique of controlling the remaking of his experience.

" 5. The processes of education go on continuously from birth until death. The school has no monopoly over them. The school is not expected to encompass education within its walls or within its twelve years.

" 6. Experience, the fundamental basis of all learning, is no respecter of time, place, equipment, teachers, or subjects.

" 7. In the process of acquisition of experience the growing organism reaches out into all areas of life to gather the materials necessary for the satisfaction of its needs. Those that satisfy needs have values, but criticized values are superior to the uncriticized.

" 8. The most important elements in experience for the growing youth are:

    A. Setting up preferences to be satisfied.

    B. Distinguishing between recurring and novel elements in a situation.

    C. Selecting materials adequate to the satisfaction of the preference.

    D. Forming conscious decisions.

    E. Putting the decisions in practice in changed behavior.

    F. Evaluating the results in the light of the preferences or relating the consequences to the preferences.

" 9. Learning through experience best takes place when the control of the experience is increasingly held by the learner; i. e., control over what is to be experienced, the process of development and the evaluation of results.

" 10. Creative power to deal adequately with problems arising in the experience of the learner on any present level gives best preparation for dealing with unforeseen problems on any subsequent level.

" 11. As the experience of the individuals are variable and the methods of enriching them are variable, so the social heritage must be variable as to the amount, kind, place, and use.

" 12. Since the individual must continuously make contact with social groups his learning should grow out of social situations and should therefore relate to group contacts, group working conditions, and group stimulation." *

This statement of philosophy has been tentatively approved and is regarded, for the time being, as the official philosophy of education for the Wilmington Public Schools. It suggests the general direction which the educative process is to take but it does not indicate the specific ends to be achieved. It is the function of the aims of education to indicate what accomplishments are desired through the controls of the philosophy. The aims of education harness the underlying motivating forces of the educational philosophy and direct them into productive channels. Aims are essential to determine the proper sequence in the use of various materials and methods of instruction.

* The content of this report was developed by the Curriculum Committee in May, 1932. The final statement was made by Dr. L. Thomas Hopkins.

83. FORMAL STATEMENT OF PRINCIPLES FOR FORT WORTH PUBLIC SCHOOLS [13]

EDUCATIONAL PRINCIPLES
A. Content and Activities
  a. Nature

1. As to specific content the curriculum should provide situations and experiences requisite to (a) develop the necessary skills, correct habits, and right attitudes; (b) provide the necessary knowledge, or information, as to where that knowledge may be obtained; (c) reflect the social, political, and economic problems of the modern world; (d) prepare the child to choose wisely his own life and occupation; (e) develop the child's aesthetic nature for proper enjoyment of leisure; (f) provide amply for health and character education.

2. The curriculum should provide for all phases of behavior — acting, thinking, and feeling.

3. The curriculum should consider definitely the problems of economic, political, social, and individual life.

4. Certain portions of the curriculum should appeal primarily to the emotions.

5. The school curriculum can profitably be made more social in content; first, by emphasizing humanistic studies and second, by stressing the social implications and applications of the facts learned.

6. Fundamentally important material must be taught, even though intrinsic interest and evident utility are lacking to the child.

7. To neglect the development of character is to neglect the most important phase of education.

8. Moral education is not a separate kind of education, but is an aspect of all education.

9. The forms of learning that should be encouraged are those that lead on the intellectual side to generalizations; on the habit side to the cultivation of useful skills; and on the side of attitudes and appreciations to the recognition of those relationships which are permanently satisfying.

10. The curriculum must provide for the development of adequate skill with the necessary fundamentals.

[13] Fort Worth Public Schools, *Language Arts, A Tentative Course of Study for Grade Six,* Curriculum Bulletin No. 146, Fort Worth, Texas, 1935, pp. iii–viii.

b. Selection

1. Materials selected for the curriculum should approximate life situations and at the same time include elements shown by social analysis to be desirable.
2. A particular subject, unit, or experience should find a place in the curriculum on the basis that it can satisfy certain aims better than any other.
3. The various subject matter fields are to be considered as sources of material from which to draw in carrying out experiences rather than as ends.
4. The curriculum must be based upon the needs, interests, and activities of both the child and the adult.
5. Nothing should be included in the curriculum merely because it is of interest to children, but whatever is included should be brought into the closest possible relationship with their interests.
6. Materials of instruction should be selected with a view of making it possible for the learner to acquire that development most helpful in meeting and controlling actual life situations.
7. The data of important problems — social, industrial, political — must be found and organized in thought-provoking form.
8. Economy in learning requires that the educational resources of local life be utilized.

c. Organization, presentation, and teaching

1. In the organization of subject matter, a psychological order should be used; i.e., it should be organized with special reference to the previous experience, present needs, and interests of the students for whom it is intended.
2. The intellectual work of the school should be focused upon definite, clear-cut problems providing concrete, interesting, and intelligible examples. Arguments representing equitably all angles of the problem shall be supplied and accompanied by many suggestions for intelligent research by the pupils. Extreme care should be exercised to avoid dogmatism. Group discussion of the problems shall be organized on an open-forum basis, and the crux of the matter shall be: " What do you think? "
3. To stimulate thinking there must be devised an arrangement of activities and other materials of instruction by which the pupils will be confronted constantly with problems to be solved. It is not the learning of texts, but the solving of problems that will enable one to become a critic of validity.

4. Activities, experiences, and materials should be so arranged as to give the learner carefully planned assistance.

5. It should be not only the privilege but also the obligation of each generation to learn clearly why the forms of conduct which it adopts are desirable and why those which it rejects are undesirable.

6. To guide teachers the courses of study should suggest the approximate time to be spent on each unit.

7. The course of study should provide for the teacher an outline of the general attitudes, the finer appreciations, the important concepts and meanings, and the generalizations which he wishes to secure as outcomes of the experiences provided.

8. Courses of study should always be considered tentative and should be modified whenever and wherever good reasons appear.

9. Courses of study should be so made that any normally intelligent and industrious pupil can succeed.

10. The teacher's judgment of what is real to the pupils is an important force behind the organization and development of units of work. A unit of work is real to the child only as long as the child himself continues to see possibilities in it.

11. Subject matter should be so presented as to recognize that
    (a) General transfer is not automatic and inevitable.
    (b) There is no general desirable discipline from what is merely difficult or distasteful.
    (c) Individual differences exist and must be cared for in so far as is possible.
    (d) Social education is of increased importance.
    (e) It is a means to an end.

12. The materials of instruction must be approached in terms of the child's interests and experiences.

13. The curriculum should provide for both individual differences and increasing participation in life.

14. It is of surpassing importance to provide facilities which will stimulate the most able children to the attainment of their fullest development.

15. Learning is active. The laws of learning should control the organization and the presentation of subject matter.

16. To learn is to acquire a way of behaving.

17. Learning is never single. Every learning situation involves concomitants.

18. Purposeful self-activity is fundamental to learning.
19. Material should be organized so as to insure economical and effective learning according to the principles of interest, use, and difficulty.
20. Reorganization of subject matter should conform to the true learning process without too much regard for existing subject boundaries.
21. Reactions established in one situation will not carry over to all other situations, but they may transfer to other settings which have a great deal in common with the one in which the reaction was built up.
22. Each subject should be taught so as to insure the greatest amount of transfer, but no subject should be included for transfer value only.
23. Any ability developed apart from the place where it is to be used suffers a heavy loss. The automatic application of skill to remote life situations is not now accepted.
24. Teaching is not merely training in subject matter, but it is the cultivation of a body of ideas and a series of reactions in every member of the class.
25. Teaching should at times be free and informal, at other times carefully controlled and regulated. It should never be stereotyped.
26. Habit is a unit element of character. To build character is to build right habits of thinking and feeling, as well as outward behaving.
27. Mere inhibitions never build a strong character. Strong character is mainly positive.
28. Education dealing with life itself can never be so thoroughly mechanized as to make it possible to furnish a classroom " mechanic " with recipes and specific methods of procedure appropriate to every situation.
29. We must assist our children to the point where they can and will think for themselves.
30. A type of method which emphasizes how to think rather than what to think should be developed.

B. The Teacher
1. The teacher should be concerned primarily with the accomplishment of the pupils, i.e., with what they do in terms of the ability that they possess.
2. It is the role of the teacher, as an expert guide, to secure for each child his maximum growth.
3. One important function of the teacher is to capitalize special interests and capacities and to organize the work

so as to encourage the individual pupil to make his own particular contribution to group undertakings.

4. The teacher must have ready in advance information, sources of information, and specific procedures to use if the occasion demands.

5. The teacher must have sufficient quality of sympathy and discernment to understand individual pupils, the ability to understand the ends that are to be attained, and a quality of resourcefulness, which will enable him to keep his methods of procedure flexible enough to meet the needs of the occasion.

6. The training of the teacher should enable him to adjust the plan that is made in advance to the situations and conditions of day-to-day needs.

84. Principles Basic to the English Curriculum [14]

Experience is the best of all schools. Certainly no one learns so thoroughly, and few learn so rapidly, in any other. And experience need not be a dear school, if it is competently organized and is conducted by a capable teacher who illuminates each situation in prospect and in retrospect. School and college curriculums should consist of experiences.* The school of experience is the only one which will develop the flexibility and power of self-direction requisite for successful living in our age of swift industrial, social, and economic change. To inculcate authoritarian beliefs, fixed rules of conduct, unreasoned and therefore stubborn attitudes, is to set our youth in futile and fatal conflict with the forces of modern life. By meeting situations, modifying conditions and adapting themselves to the unchangeable, our boys and girls will learn to live in a dynamic and evolving world. Today, more than ever, the curriculum should consist of experiences.

The ideal curriculum consists of well-selected experiences. The first step in constructing it is to survey life, noting what experiences most people have and what desirable possible experiences they miss.

---

[14] A Report of a Commission of the National Council of Teachers of English, *An Experience Curriculum in English,* W. Wilbur Hatfield, Chairman, Monograph No. 4, National Council of Teachers of English, D. Appleton-Century Co., 1935, pp. 3–9.

* In the proverb about experience as a dear school, the word *experience* evidently refers to *meeting real situations,* with all that may be involved. The proverb assumes that the experience includes a more or less free decision, action, and taking consequences. It implies that the natural consequences of an act, when they are recognized as such, will cause learning. *To learn* obviously means *to modify* one's *future behavior,* in psychological parlance, to acquire changed tendencies to act. The words *experience* and *learn* are used much in this report, always with these proverbial, everyday meanings.

From this display the curriculum builder must select typical examples, distributed as well as possible throughout its entire range.

It is true some kinds of experience cannot well be imported into the school — marriage, for example, and such experiences as grief, wrong-doing, and the suffering of injustice which we would eliminate if we could from life as well as from the school. Such experiences, which for one reason or another our young people cannot or should not have in actuality but which they must be prepared to have later, we should offer indirectly through literature.

The program just presented constitutes, of course, the entire school curriculum, in which each department participates when and as it can. The place of English in this program is obvious: to provide the communication (speaking, writing, listening, reading) necessary to the conduct of social activities, and to provide indirect (vicarious) experiences where direct experiences are impossible or undesirable. Perhaps no other subject gains so much as does English from an integration of the school with everyday life.

In schools which have not yet adopted an integrated experience curriculum the course of study in English must consist of more limited, though still genuine, experiences. (Because in most schools each subject is studied in practically complete isolation from the others, this pattern curriculum in English is designed to suit that condition. It will also fit, without major change, into an " activity " program.)

An effective program in school English must make provision for carrying the literary and linguistic activities beyond the confines of the English classroom.

1. Since the quality of the reading and of the speaking and writing determine, to some extent, the pupils' progress in other subjects, improvement of the English arts must be sought in all the studies and activities throughout the school day.

In the elementary school this is not difficult, since generally the teacher has the same children most of the day and can readily correlate the reading and language activities with the work of the other subjects. A reasonable general plan for this is: first, to concentrate in the English period on the opening up of new ideas about language, discussion of principles and technical details, and practice for skills; and second, in the other subjects to apply and illustrate.

In the secondary school the problem of correlation is more difficult. Perhaps the most useful concept is to regard efficiency in the English arts not as an English department objective but as an institutional objective. All the teachers of all the subjects should be, to some extent, teachers of English. Science teachers who require students to keep notebooks, history teachers who expect " outside " reading and oral and written reports, mathematics teachers who depend upon pupils' reciting and demonstrating, all teachers who cause pupils to employ reading and language, must assume some responsibility for the quality of the reading and the language.

But it is unwise for the English department to attempt to force upon the other departments any plan of coöperation, no matter how well formulated. The principal of the school, together with the representatives of all the departments and probably with the English teachers carrying the major burden of the work and responsibility, must devise and guide a program of correlation and coöperation. Such a plan is in use in many schools of the United States; it is quite indispensable in a successful high-school English program.

2. Most of the formal and informal groupings and activities in the co-curricular life of the school necessitate the use of many types of language and reading. The parties and " social " affairs, the clubs and organizations (and not merely the specifically " English Clubs "), the school and class enterprises, the assembly programs, the school paper and magazine, the library and reading room — all the rich, varied life characteristics of the modern American school — place the children in situations wherein language and reading must be employed and wherein their effective employment is socially motivated and socially rewarded.

The teacher of English can ask for observations and for class discussions of the language activities in these out-of-class situations and she can gradually educate her pupils to regard their English activities in these situations as illustration, demonstration, and extension of the work of the English class. She can also utilize the class as a tryout situation, where the pupils may present, for example, readings or speeches they are to make on some school program, or " stories " they are writing for the school paper, and may profit by class discussion and criticism. A resourceful English teacher will find and utilize many such opportunities for tying in the work of her class with the language and reading situations throughout the co-curricular life of the school.

3. The pupils of the elementary and high school are also frequently engaged in personal and community enterprises which involve them in language situations. If the English teacher can contrive means of " following " them out into these situations and connecting up the school work in English with the actual scenes in which English is employed, she will widen her classroom to community dimensions. This can be done in much the same way as is indicated above. The pupils can be led to take note of their own and others' uses of language and to report successful and unsuccessful examples. Pupils who are, for example, on a Young People's Soci-

ety program in their church or at a Father and Son banquet may try out and improve their talk or their reading in the English class.

The program of experiences must be well balanced. Accordingly this pattern curriculum presents each major field of English subdivided into " experience strands " and asks each teacher to lead his class each year through at least one unit in each strand.

Since the principal objective of creative expression in school is the individual pupil's joyous realization of the values of his own experiences, *creative expression* is put on the same footing as communication or literature, as a *major phase of every pupil's work* every year.

In daily living, *techniques are essential* — as instruments; consequently, in school life techniques should receive adequate attention — as instruments. Some study of principles and even practice exercises are needed, but such academic procedures must be kept in their proper place as accessories to the life experiences. (In simpler societies, where children might participate in the serious employments of their elders, it was perhaps sufficient for the school to give formal training, because out-of-school experiences supplied both motive for and application of school subject-matter. That day has long since passed, and in too many instances neither motive for nor application of school " study " or " drill " remains. The school of today and tomorrow seeks to bring outside activities within its walls and to step out with its students to participate in many community activities. In connection with these activities it finds the best occasions for teaching the information, ideas, and skills which obsess the old-fashioned pedagogue.)

These technical and factual matters are incorporated in the units as *enabling* objectives. They are not to be left to chance, nor are they to be taught separately as valuable in themselves. They should be incidental, but not accidental.

Moreover, *techniques are to be cumulative.* A skill or fact learned in one unit of a strand is to be employed whenever it applies in all subsequent units of that strand. Techniques of general application are collected at the end of each strand, with the suggestion that by the time the strand is completed they should have become habitual.

The term subject-matter, as traditionally used, is here avoided, though the three paragraphs just preceding this provide most adequately for the reality which that term represents. Subject-matter is merely the collected and organized, too frequently also desiccated, solutions to problems which the race has met and mastered. This social heritage is priceless, but preoccupation with its transmission makes the teacher a formalist and a drillmaster, and by inhibiting or distorting the normal development of the pupils develops a static or retrograde civilization. Pupils' use of subject-matter to solve their own problems is at once the most economical way for them to assimilate it and the indispensable condition of developing their own capacities.

The program of experiences must be orderly. In order that the pupil may gain the confidence and the clarity of mind that come from success, his experiences must be arranged in a carefully graded order of social and intellectual difficulty. No experience unit should require too many new techniques, or any technique which is beyond the maturity of the pupils. The various committees have graded the units in this pattern curriculum very carefully, but local circumstances may call for a changed order.

Because of the great variation in ability of different classes even within a single school, specific units cannot wisely be allocated to definite grades. . . . The teacher and pupils must remain free to proceed as rapidly or as slowly as their situation and ability may require.

Experiences must be adapted to the needs and capacities of individual learners. The classification of pupils according to their abilities or achievements — not necessarily according to intelligence quotients, and certainly without any labeling of sections as " fast " or " slow," " bright " or " dull " — is highly desirable as a partial solution of the problem of adaptation. Strong classes may move more rapidly through the curriculum, and may engage in some of the " optional experiences " listed; weak classes may repeat or prolong certain experiences which are particularly important. And even where grouping is not intentionally practiced, classes differ widely in breadth and speed of learning. Accordingly, definite allocation of units to specific grades is abandoned and the teacher is directed to take each class where she finds it in each strand and to proceed with it as far as time and ability permit.

Adaptation, however, includes other elements besides acceleration and retardation. In each unit there appear opportunities for leadership, for reaching out into other subject-matter and other activities; and for some pupils there is need of simpler materials to use in experience of the same general nature. The curriculum, besides discussing this problem in general, should offer in every expanded unit suggestions both for enrichment and simplification. . . .

Measurement of the growth resulting from the experiences in the curriculum is desirable. Occasionally such measurement may be helpful in determining whether an individual should go with his class on to new experiences or should repeat those he has just had. Chiefly, however, these measures are needed to help the teacher evaluate his own procedures and the curriculum maker his choice of experiences. Incidentally, until satisfactory measures are devised and applied, the standing dispute between the advocates of the experience curriculum and the traditionalists who cling to formal subject-matter and methods of instruction cannot be conclusively decided. Such measures must cover something more than progress in the mechanics of composition and the incidents in and facts about literature; they must measure composition power, social spirit and poise, perception of beauty, and habitual choice of worthy literature. . . .

A curriculum in English is necessarily multifarious in content and complex in statement. Imperfections in its construction are inevitable and confusions in its interpretation are to be expected. The guiding idea for both builder and user is the conception of the curriculum as a body of *guided experiences paralleling present and future out-of-school experiences.*

85. " PRINCIPLES GOVERNING THE DEVELOPMENT OF THE SOCIAL STUDIES CURRICULUM FOR THE SECONDARY SCHOOL " [15]

Paul R. Hanna

Before a pattern for social studies instruction can be formulated, certain principles must be accepted as guiding the instruction. The more important principles follow:

1. The program of instruction must accept as basic such psychological principles as (a) *learning is conditioned by the maturation levels of pupils,* (b) *learning takes place as the pupil carries out his purposes,* (c) *the integrity of the complete learning experience demands freedom to test the validity of thought through its application to situations.* The social studies materials and activities must be suited to the ability of the pupils and so selected and constructed as to aid in the continual increase of ability as the pupil proceeds from one school level to the next. Concepts, attitudes, and skills which are " taught " are not " learned " by the pupils unless the concepts, attitudes, and skills are essential tools and materials needed by the pupils in executing " study " in response to their drives or purposes.* The teacher must be aware of the essential place that testing-the-consequences-of-thought has in the complete learning experience.

---

[15] From " Functional Social Studies, A Symposium," A Program for a Social Studies Curriculum for the Secondary Schools, *California Journal of Secondary Education,* 10:423–424, October, 1935.

* Dewey has said it is as misleading to say you have " taught " when no one has " learned " as it would be to say you have sold when no one has bought.

2. Social studies instruction must constitute *a sequence planned in broad outline* from the first contacts in school to the culmination of " formal " instruction in the secondary school or institution of higher learning. In other words, the social studies program of the secondary school cannot be sketched without a full and intimate knowledge of the experiences which the students have previously had in the elementary school. Similarly, a clear picture of the learning experiences which will touch the life of the student, either through college or adult education, must be obtained before a defensible program of social studies instruction can be formulated for the secondary school.

3. A planned sequence in broad outline must not be the inflexible type that will not permit the student from capitalizing on his developing interests. The social studies curriculum must make *provision for incorporating the day-by-day happenings of human beings* in the locality and in the broader national and world community. The focus of the curriculum must be study for the purpose of more fully understanding and improving these current affairs. Because of its unpredictability and its sensitiveness to popular opinion, nothing is as important and nothing is as difficult to achieve as instruction of this type.

4. At the same time that instruction is focused upon studying the insistent problems facing us today, there is the obligation of planning a pattern, *a scope and sequence chart*, by which the teacher can be assured that the pupil will have experiences *in all the major social functions* as he progresses through the elementary and secondary school. There are certain key concepts running through the pupil's entire school career. Planning within broad areas is necessary if grasp of such concepts is to be assured at the culmination of the secondary school period. It is within these broad areas as a framework that the teacher develops a dynamic and flexible program as suggested in 3 above.

5. In the development of these key concepts there are *numerous types of content and activities, various combinations of which will equally well develop the concept under consideration.* For example, it is not necessary to review all of the culture patterns, historic and contemporary, to illustrate how climate conditions the adjustment which man makes to his environment. Single illustrations drawn from cultures existing in hot, temperate, and frigid regions will demonstrate the far-reaching effect of climate on dress, food, shelter, religion, recreation, etc.

6. The sixth principle which should guide in the construction of a program of social studies instruction is concerned with the other areas of the school curriculum and the time allotment available for experiences in this broad field of human relations. The social studies can

be thought of as one of the three great areas of human existence, and, therefore, roughly one-third of the time of the school might justifiably be given to such instruction. But the social studies are not unrelated to the other two areas, science studies and general arts, and must not be so developed that restrictive departmental categories are built in pupils' minds. For instance, the development of science during the later years of the 18th century was causal to the social revolution and to the expression in literature, music, and fine arts of the period. It is impossible to understand any one of these aspects when it is lifted out of its context in the total culture pattern of that day. *The instruction in social studies should be related to the other broad fields of the secondary school curriculum.*

86. General Curriculum Principles for Character Building [16]

The Tenth Yearbook of the Department of Superintendence describes an adequate character-building curriculum briefly as follows:

Any curriculum that makes a sincere, intelligent, and courageous approach to the real problem of living is a character education curriculum.*

A curriculum which brings to youth a consciousness of the problems of life, some understanding of these problems, a sense of personal responsibility in contributing to their solution, a reasonable degree of technical efficiency of procedure, and a rich personal life in harmony with the good of others, is achieving the end of character education.†

These statements need much more elaboration than is possible in a bulletin of this scope. It may be helpful, however, to review here certain pertinent principles which have been stated or implied in the recent writings of curriculum specialists and others.‡ These prin-

[16] National Education Association, *Education for Character,* Research Bulletin, Vol. XII, Washington, D. C., May, 1934, pp. 96–98.

* National Education Association, Department of Superintendence. *Character Education.* Tenth Yearbook. Washington, D. C.: the Association, 1932. p. 179.

† *Ibid.,* p. 192.

‡ In selecting these principles, the following sources were consulted: Almack, John C. *Education for Citizenship.* Boston: Houghton Mifflin Co., 1924. p. 80. ¶ Bobbitt, Franklin. *Curriculum Investigations.* Supplementary Educational Monographs No. 31. Chicago: University of Chicago Press, 1926, p. 4. ¶ Bobbitt, Franklin. *How to Make a Curriculum.* Boston: Houghton Mifflin Co., 1924, p. 7–8, 41–42, 44–59, 61–62, 280–86. ¶ Bonser, Frederick G. *The Elementary School Curriculum.* New York: Macmillan Co., 1923. p. 1–25. ¶ Charters, W. W. *Curriculum Construction.* New York: Macmillan Co., 1923. p. 12–25, 97–102, 152–54. ¶ Davis, Calvin O. *Our Evolving High School Curriculum.* Yonkers-on-Hudson, N. Y.: World Book Co., 1927. p. 140–45, 149–63, 230. ¶ Germane, Charles E., and Germane, Edith G. *Character Education.* New York: Silver Burdett and Co., 1929. Part I, p. 28–32. ¶ Hopkins, L. Thomas. *Curriculum Principles and Practices.* Chicago: Benjamin T. Sanborn and Co., 1929. p. 9–11,

ciples are presented with full realization of the fact that educators are not entirely agreed in regard to all of them. In the brief statement accompanying each principle, an effort is made to resolve conflicting viewpoints so far as possible.

1. *A character-building curriculum will provide for the needs, interests, and potentialities of each individual child.* This principle requires that careful attention be given to individual differences among children, and rules out the lock-step type of educational program designed for the hypothetical " average " child. It calls for such differentiation in subjectmatter and teaching methods as will enable each pupil to make the most of his capacities and to adjust himself harmoniously to his physical and social environment. There is, of course, a common body of abilities, knowledges, and appreciations which ideally should be shared by all. Provision must be made, however, for those who have special incapacities and for those whose abilities and interests are greater or more varied than the average.

2. *A character-building curriculum will consider the requirements of adult society as well as the needs and interests of children.* There is a school of educational theory which would base the curriculum almost entirely upon child interests and desires. Most authorities, however, view the growth of personality as a continuous process, whose ultimate goal is the most satisfactory participation in life on the mature or adult level. The relative immaturity of children must be taken into consideration thruout the educational system, but the basic needs of individual and social living appear to be the same for children as for adults. During the limited time spent in the school, therefore, it seems unwise to permit transitory or relatively unimportant interests of children to crowd out activities of more permanent and fundamental importance. Even more objectionable is the inclusion of activities which have no significant relation to either child or adult life.

14–15, 27–31, 129–33, 135–37, 139–42, 193, 292–99, 304, 608–10. ¶ National Education Association, Department of Superintendence. *The Nation at Work on the Public School Curriculum.* Fourth Yearbook. Washington, D. C.: the Association, 1926. p. 10–11, 13–18, 407. ¶ National Education Association, Department of Superintendence. *Character Education.* Tenth Yearbook. Washington, D. C.: the Association, 1932. p. 179–90. ¶ National Education Association, Department of Superintendence. *Research in Constructing the Elementary School Curriculum.* Third Yearbook. Washington, D. C.: the Association, 1926 (reprint). p. 18–22. ¶ National Education Association, Research Division. " Keeping Pace With the Advancing Curriculum." *Research Bulletin* 3: 115, 117–18; September and November, 1925. ¶ National Society for the Study of Education. *Foundations of Curriculum-Making.* Twenty-Sixth Yearbook, Part II, Bloomington, Ill.: Public School Publishing Co., 1926. p. 12–25, 73–75, 85–87, 154–55. ¶ Rugg, Harold, and Shumaker, Ann. *The Child Centered School.* Yonkers-on-Hudson, N. Y.: World Book Co., 1928. p. 55–67, 112–23, 128–30. ¶ Williams. L. A. *The Making of High School Curricula.* Boston: Ginn and Co., 1928. p. 184, 195–96, 201.

3. *A character-building curriculum will undertake to transmit our heritage of common culture and experience; to consider contemporary issues and achievements; and to develop a generation of people who will contribute to an improved social order.* Since the aim of education is to improve individual and social living, children must be given the benefit of mankind's previous experiences and achievements insofar as these are valuable for present and future living. A curriculum is inadequate, however, if it deals exclusively with past occurrences and achievements. It must present significant issues of the present day, point out current trends in social, economic, and political life, and attempt to develop in pupils the desire and the capacity to help direct these trends for the welfare of all in the future.

4. *A character-building curriculum will be concerned primarily with the weighing of values and the solution of real life problems, and secondarily with the acquisition of routine skills and factual subjectmatter.* The importance of fundamental knowledge and skills is not to be underestimated, but these should be selected and organized with reference to the practical needs of modern social life. These practical demands are not limited to the unthinking performance of certain actions which have received general social approval. They require the willingness and the ability to consider relative values and to solve problems of living for which no ready-made solution is at hand. To meet this requirement, the curriculum must present abundant opportunities for choosing among different values, not among adult values alone or childish values alone, but among all values in such a way that life for everyone will be made as rich as possible from beginning to end. Such a selection of values cannot be made without the acquisition of certain skills or the knowledge of pertinent facts. The latter are tools, however, rather than major objectives, and this fact must influence profoundly the selection, organization, and presentation of subjectmatter in the curriculum.

5. *A character-building curriculum will be planned in advance, but will be flexible enough to permit the introduction of new materials and first-hand pupil experiences whenever these are available and useful.* Generally speaking, those who believe that the curriculum should be limited to the spontaneous interests and activities of childhood also assert that such a curriculum cannot be formulated in advance. They contend that it must develop from day to day in accordance with the desires of the pupils. On the other hand, those who believe that education should prepare for both child and adult life contend that this is impossible without careful selection and organization of educational materials in advance. Most curriculum

workers have adopted the latter view, with the proviso that the planned program must be subject to interruption and modification whenever necessary to capitalize the current interests and life-situations of the pupils.

6. *A character-building curriculum will be constructed with the cooperation of all parties concerned — pupils, teachers, curriculum specialists, subjectmatter specialists, and society in general.* A curriculum developed without the aid of all parties concerned can hardly make a " sincere, intelligent, and courageous approach to the real problem of living." Competent laymen should be consulted because they have a knowledge of adult social needs and responsibilities. Curriculum and subjectmatter specialists are needed to insure that materials are authentic, wisely selected, and organized for economical learning. The assistance of capable teachers is essential because of their intimate contact with, and knowledge of, the classroom situation. Teachers may help in the actual writing of the formal courses of study, but even more important, they must transform the cold outlines of these courses into a vital influence among children in the classroom. Last, but by no means least, is the contribution which should be made by the pupils themselves. Without the liberal injection of their personal observations, experiences, and problems, the curriculum stream becomes sluggish, artificial, and devoid of relation to child life outside the school.

7. *A character-building curriculum will be continually reconstructed and brought up to date.* In a world of changing social and economic relationships, it is imperative that the curriculum be modified whenever any part of it ceases to have significant relation to life. This principle is especially important because most school systems find it impossible to effect a thoro revision of their teaching materials all at once. If such revision were possible, and if the job were very well done, the resulting curriculum might need only minor changes for a period of five or ten years. Under present conditions, however, a policy of continuous curriculum reconstruction is necessary to bring and to keep school work in close relation to life outside the school.

CHAPTER VI

AIMS OF EDUCATION

87. The Nature of an Aim [1]

John Dewey

It is assumed in earlier chapters that the aim of education is to enable individuals to continue their education — or that the object and reward of learning is continued capacity for growth. Now this idea cannot be applied to *all* the members of a society except where intercourse of man with man is mutual, and except where there is adequate provision for the reconstruction of social habits and institutions by means of wide stimulation arising from equitably distributed interests. And this means a democratic society. In our search for aims in education, we are not concerned, therefore, with finding an end outside of the educative process to which education is subordinate. Our whole conception forbids. We are rather concerned with the contrast which exists when aims belong within the process in which they operate and when they are set up from without. And the latter state of affairs must obtain when social relationships are not equitably balanced. For in that case, some portions of the whole social group will find their aims determined by an external dictation; their aims will not arise from the free growth of their own experience, and their nominal aims will be means to more ulterior ends of others rather than truly their own.

Our first question is to define the nature of an aim so far as it falls within an activity, instead of being furnished from without. We approach the definition by a contrast of mere *results* with *ends*. Any exhibition of energy has results. The wind blows about the sands of the desert; the position of the grains is changed. Here is a result, an effect, but not an *end*. For there is nothing in the outcome which completes or fulfills what went before it. There is mere spatial redistribution. One state of affairs is just as good as any other. Consequently there is no basis upon which to select an earlier state of affairs as a beginning, a later as an end, and to consider what intervenes as a process of transformation and realization.

[1] From *Democracy and Education*, by permission of The Macmillan Company, publishers, New York, 1916, pp. 117–121.

Consider for example the activities of bees in contrast with the changes in the sands when the wind blows them about. The results of the bees' actions may be called ends not because they are designed or consciously intended, but because they are true terminations or completions of what has preceded. When the bees gather pollen and make wax and build cells, each step prepares the way for the next. When cells are built, the queen lays eggs in them; when eggs are laid, they are sealed and bees brood them and keep them at a temperature required to hatch them. When they are hatched, bees feed the young till they can take care of themselves. Now we are so familiar with such facts, that we are apt to dismiss them on the ground that life and instinct are a kind of miraculous thing anyway. Thus we fail to note what the essential characteristic of the event is; namely, the significance of the temporal place and order of each element; the way each prior event leads into its successor while the successor takes up what it furnished and utilizes it for some other stage, until we arrive at the end, which, as it were, summarizes and finishes off the process.

Since aims relate always to results, the first thing to look to when it is a question of aims, is whether the work assigned possesses intrinsic continuity. Or is it a mere serial aggregate of acts, first doing one thing and then another? To talk about an educational aim when approximately each act of a pupil is dictated by the teacher, when the only order in the sequence of his acts is that which comes from the assignment of lessons and the giving of directions by another, is to talk nonsense. It is equally fatal to an aim to permit capricious or discontinuous action in the name of spontaneous self-expression. An aim implies an orderly and ordered activity, one in which the order consists in the progressive completing of a process. Given an activity having a time span and cumulative growth within the time succession, and aim means foresight in advance of the end or possible termination. If bees anticipated the consequences of their activity, if they perceived their end in imaginative foresight, they would have the primary element in an aim. Hence it is nonsense to talk about the aim of education — or any other undertaking — where conditions do not permit of foresight of results, and do not stimulate a person to look ahead to see what the outcome of a given activity is to be.

In the next place the aim as a foreseen end gives direction to the activity; it is not an idle view of a mere spectator, but influences the steps taken to reach the end. The foresight functions in three ways. In the first place, it involves careful observation of the given conditions to see what are the means available for reaching the end, and to discover the hindrances in the way. In the second place, it suggests the proper order or sequence in the use of means. It facilitates an economical selection and arrangement. In the third place, it makes choice of alternatives possible. If we can predict the outcome of acting this way or that, we can then compare the value of the two courses of action; we can pass judgment upon their relative desirability. If we know that stagnant water breeds mosquitoes and that they are likely to carry disease, we can, disliking that anticipated result, take steps to avert it. Since we do not anticipate results as mere intellectual onlookers, but as persons concerned in the outcome, we are partakers in the process which produces the result. We intervene to bring about this result or that.

Of course these three points are closely connected with one another. We can definitely foresee results only as we make careful scrutiny of present conditions, and the importance of the outcome supplies the motive for observations. The more adequate our observations, the more varied is the scene of conditions and obstructions that presents itself, and the more numerous are the alternatives between which choice may be made. In turn, the more numerous the recognized possibilities of the situation, or alternatives of action, the more meaning does the chosen activity possess, and the more flexibly controllable is it. Where only a single outcome has been thought of, the mind has nothing else to think of; the meaning attaching to the act is limited. One only steams ahead toward the mark. Sometimes such a narrow course may be effective. But if unexpected difficulties offer themselves, one has not as many resources at command as if he had chosen the same line of action after a broader survey of the possibilities of the field. He cannot make needed readjustments readily.

The net conclusion is that acting with an aim is all one with acting intelligently. To foresee a terminus of an act is to have a basis upon which to observe, to select, and to order objects and our own capacities. To do these things means to have a mind — for mind is precisely intentional purposeful activity controlled by perception of facts and their relationships to one another. To have a mind to do a thing is to foresee a future possibility; it is to have a plan for its accomplishment; it is to note the means which make the plan capable of execution and the obstructions in the way, — or, if it is really a *mind* to do the thing and not a vague aspiration — it is to have a plan which takes account of resources and difficulties. Mind is capacity to refer present conditions to future results, and future consequences to present conditions. And these traits are just what is meant by having an aim or a purpose. A man is stupid or blind or unintelligent — lacking in mind — just in the degree in which in any activity he does not know what he is about, namely, the probable consequences of his acts. A man is imperfectly intelligent when he contents himself with looser guesses about the outcome than is needful, just taking a chance with his luck, or when he forms plans apart from study of the actual conditions, including his own capacities. Such relative absence of mind means to make our feelings the measure of what is to happen. To be intelligent we must " stop, look, listen " in making the plan of an activity.

To identify acting with an aim and intelligent activity is enough to show its value — its function in experience. We are only too given to making an entity out of the abstract noun ' consciousness.' We forget that it comes from the adjective ' conscious.' To be conscious is to be aware of what we are about; conscious signifies the deliberate, observant, planning traits of activity. Consciousness is nothing which we have which gazes idly on the scene around one or which has impressions made upon it by physical things; it is a name for the purposeful quality of an activity, for the fact that it is directed by an aim. Put the other way about, to have an aim is to act with meaning, not like an automatic machine; it is to *mean* to do something and to perceive the meaning of things in the light of that intent.

88. THE NATURE AND FUNCTION OF AIMS OF EDUCATION [2]

Hilda Taba

The question of educational aims and the problem of an adequate method for their finding and formulation are at present in a state of confusion. The traditional philosophic systems, together with the structures of ideals, values, and social institutions which ordinarily have served as a basis from which the educational aims have been derived, have crumbled. Familiar standards thus have lost their value as educational directives, and the new educational theories, as yet unable to translate their general principles and outlooks into practicable principles, find themselves torn by numerous conflicting trends.

A common verdict pronounced on present-day education is that it is shiftless and without direction, without *an aim*. To some extent this criticism is true. The aims proposed by different trends of education are many and often conflicting. A clarity of principle and conscious direction are lacking. Aims represent an aggregate of various more or less immediate ends rather than a unified and unifying body of views regarding crucial educational issues and the ways of dealing with them. They range from the definite objectives provided by specific subjects or vocational activities to broad speculations on cul-

[2] From *Dynamics of Education*, Harcourt Brace and Company, New York, 1932, pp. 190–194, 212.

ture and civilization; from specific habits and skills to the ideal of self-realization of personality; from a sum total of all things learned to general abilities and powers of the individual to participate in the business of living.

Because of this lack of a consistent and critical philosophy concerning the values of life and the direction education should take, there are no generally accepted standards to go by in educational choices and evaluations. The perspectives are blurred, and any one of many accepted objectives can easily acquire an importance equal to or superior to any of the others, according to the emphasis that one chooses to give. As a result, we frequently find major and fundamental educational values confused with the specific and minor objectives, and authorities in specific subjects or in specific vocations attempting to determine general educational aims in terms of their own particular fields.

But to a far greater extent the feeling of instability in education comes from the fact that educational thought cannot reconcile itself with the impossibility of subordinating all educational activities under one single, ultimate and absolute aim, *an* aim, as was done by traditional theories. Our mentality unfortunately has grown accustomed to expect static unity and singleness of direction provided by final and absolutistic standards. Consequently, a varied and apparently conflicting multiplicity of aims immediately connotes lack of direction in the educational outlook possessing them.

It is evident that, in view of the philosophy of life predominant at present, it is impossible to find an aim or an ideal for education which, when understood as a final end-state, or a final end-achievement of educational efforts, will be perfect enough and inclusive enough to cover all our educational values and to represent all educational efforts in the form of one single unit. Whenever educational aims are conceived as contentually determined end-states of achievement, a multiplicity of disorganized objectives is unavoidable. Educational values are many; cultures, social organizations, and institutions change; personalities are of a very different type, and so contentually there can be no ultimate ideal end-state to serve in the orientation of either the society or the individual.

Nor does it seem possible to unite the diversity of definite and contentual ends or aims in one logically consistent and closed system of values. Even if such a thing were possible, it would be quite undesirable as it would ultimately mean a limitation of future possibilities imposed by present actuality.

Contentual aims are of necessity pluralistic, as is, in fact, any concrete actuality. The unity, and the logical as well as the philosophical consistency that is sought in educational directives, are not to be looked for in the contents of any particular aims held; they are to be found in a balance of divergent directions effected by criticism based on functional and methodological standards of judgment. This involves a consistent thinking through of the meanings and consequences of different particular aims in relation to each other, in relation to what at any particular moment is held as most valuable in life, and in relation to the liberating power of the educative experiences promoted by the aims held.

It is in such a functional approach to educational aims, in such a basis for a continuous re-evaluation, that education has to look for the organization and direction of its thought and practices.

In this functional approach no effort would be made to attempt to fix a final contentual end-state as an ultimate educational aim; effort would be directed to the formulation of unifying and stabilizing standards of criticism, applicable as methodological tools in evaluating all evolving, temporary, and specific contentual aims. Educational aims thus considered could not be attached to any particular achievement. They are to be pictured as moving aims, applying themselves to new forms, to new outcomes and values as the educational situations change.

The function of an aim in ordinary behaviour is to organize activity, to render a basis for choices, valuations and different courses of behaviour, to unify effort, and to help evaluate partial activities in the light of the whole act. Dewey has pointed out three major functions of an aim:

" In the first place it involves careful observation of the given conditions to see what are the means available for reaching the end, and to discover the hindrances in the way. . . In the second place, it suggests the proper order or sequence in the use of means. . . In the third place, it makes the choice of alternatives possible." *

From the standpoint of one isolated act the end-aim seems to be the sole directive. However, from the standpoint of long-span continuities of behaviour, it is not the end-aspect of aims that is important, but their role as organizing agents. An aim as an end-state has only passing value, while its influence on the organization of behaviour entails more or less permanent effects on behaviour yet to actualize. And the more comprehensive the aims, the more extensive is that effect.

Educational aims in this respect do not differ from those of everyday behaviour. They are temporary and changing moments in a continuous process, and consequently are to be regarded primarily as agents, the outstanding value of which is not their role as end-
* Dewey, John, *Democracy and Education*, p. 119.

states, as final and ultimate achievements, but their capacity to free, direct, and organize activity, to help evaluation and choices.

Aims, when understood as continually limited end-states, necessarily limit activity. But educational aims should serve chiefly to liberate activity. In order that the major educational aims may be truly liberating forces, they must be stated in functional terms, in terms of values that are not finalities but which, when achieved, will serve as means for producing new values, whatever their specific nature. Their formulation should be such that they can be used as criteria for criticism and choices irrespective of the specific content or nature of the educational process or its outcomes. In other words, one should conceive of major educational aims in terms of the methodology of critical educational thought, in terms of ever new appraisals of a multitude of specific aims in relation to a unifying direction and a consistent outlook; they cannot be viewed as attached to any definite outcome or end-state.

The problem of educational aims, therefore, is not to find one ultimate aim but to build a basis for sound judgment, for a clear and consistent educational outlook. It involves sifting from the multitude of temporary contentual values those which are challenging and productive, and which offer liberating and organizing effects on educational thought functioning in theory and in practice. . . .

Major educational aims cannot be formulated by aggregating the specific aims of various subject matters. They need to be constructed from the guiding principles evolved in the analysis of experience as an educative process, having its individual quality, and carrying its social and moral implications within itself. To start with the analysis of the values of subject matters means to subordinate the values and aims evolving in the experience of the learner to those of subject matter. It is too easy to accept the values implicit in existing subject matters without seeing them concretely in terms of their significance to living and evolving experience.

It is quite generally accepted that it is impossible to find and formulate educational aims either on the basis of the analysis of the social heritage only or on the basis of the analysis of the needs of the development of the individual only. Unfortunately the tendency to separate these two inseparable agents in education is so deep-rooted that the problem has been viewed as a conflict between the needs and interests of the child and the demands of the objective social and cultural values. In other words, the problem of educational aims is set up in terms of a conflict between the immanently valuable, and therefore educative, experience of the learner on the one hand, and, on the other, the continuation of the cultural heritage, the preservation of social institutions and values, and the preparation for participation in future adult society. The solution to this impossible question is then sought in the correlation of the customary curriculum materials with the needs and interests of growing individuals, and the necessity of such a correlation is stressed with almost equal insistence by the advocates of the subject matter type of curriculum, by the proponents of the " scientific education," and by some, at least, of the sponsors of a creative, active, and integrated educative experience.

89. FACTS AS OBJECTIVES OF EDUCATION [3]

Edward Lee Thorndike

What shall the content of adult education be?

I shall not, within the space of a magazine article, try to give a complete answer to this question. What I shall try to do is to present the case for something which is now despised and rejected by many of those active in adult education and in education in general; namely, mere knowledge of facts, mere habits of conduct, mere skill and good taste in small particulars of art.

It is customary among the élite of educational reformers to disparage these particular, small, specialized items of achievement in favor of higher and more far-reaching powers, such as the ability to discover and organize and apply knowledge, versatility, readiness to change to fit a changing world, and creativeness. And probably a certain amount of such disparagement is healthy. But some of it seems to me to deserve attack as uninformed, ill advised, and misleading. In any case, it is only fair that someone should defend the humdrum details of knowledge, behavior, skill, and taste. This I shall try to do. Limits of space confine me to the case of knowledge, but the arguments will in general apply throughout.

Mere knowledge is out of favor for many reasons. One is that the schools were indiscriminate, heaping up task after task for learning just because the task was something that could be learned, and neglecting training in organizing and using what had been learned already. Another is that where the schools did exercise discrimination, it was too often in favor of facts valuable only or chiefly as preparation for later advanced study. So the beginner in physics was taught methods of making exact measurements; the beginner in zoology learned elaborate details about the frog, the earthworm, or the grasshopper. A third reason is that much of the supposed factual information was not factual but verbal and, hence, as learned, carried very little information about reality. For example, at the tender age of

[3] From " In Defense of Facts," *Journal of Adult Education*, 7:381–383, October, 1935.

five, according to traditions of the Thorndike family, I was taught in school to reel off a list of a hundred or more words naming the bones of the human body. But such achievements are not factual; they are of the nature of liturgy or incantation. These unfortunate associations of pedantry, propaedeutic exercises, and verbalism with factual knowledge have prejudiced us illogically against it.

It is also customary to contrast mere knowledge, habit, skill, and the like, unfavorably with intellectual power, character, and personality. What we should do, it is said, is to give men and women power to think, not a package of ideas; to make their characters good and strong and benevolent, not to improve petty habits; to develop healthy, integrated personalities adjusted to the real world of things and men, not to work piecemeal at this, that, and the other detail of behavior and attitude.

This contrast of general or total powers, qualities, and tendencies with particular detailed facts, habits, and attitudes, and derogation of the latter, is guilty of three cardinal errors. It assumes that such general or total powers exist as unitary traits or entities which can be changed throughout in something the same way that a man's skin can be made black all over by dipping him into a vat of ink, or that his entire blood stream can be influenced by certain drugs. The evidence goes to show that, on the contrary, specificity is the rule, and that the words naming general or total powers, qualities, and tendencies usually refer really to statistical averages and summations of particulars. The power to resist typhoid is fairly unitary; we can create it or strengthen it by a single procedure. But the power to resist temptation is, to the best of present knowledge, only the statistical average of a host of detailed powers to resist rather particular temptations in rather particular situations. And the probability that any educational inoculation will transform it throughout is extremely slight. Even the most unitary traits, such as ability in abstract intellectual operations — Spearman's General Intellectual Factor or something closely approximating it — are much restricted in their spheres of operations and conditioned by cooperating specific factors.

The contempt for mere knowledge assumes that the general or total powers, traits, and the like are easily amenable to educational influences. On the contrary, the more unitary they are, the more they are rooted in the person's original constitution, given to him by nature as is the color of his eyes, or the type of his blood, or the number of neurons in his brain, and the less amenable they are to educational influence. The general intellectual factor just mentioned — the general intellectual ability of ordinary educational discussion — resists efforts to increase it so obdurately that some of the most competent investigators of the matter deny that it can be increased at all. It is idle to argue that we should give men power to think, in so far as that power is given or withheld by biological causes that are beyond our control.

The third error is neglect of the fact that whatever general total powers, qualities, and tendencies there may be, either as unities or as aggregates, they are modifiable only by specific ideas, habits, attitudes, and the like.

An educational reformer can talk about improving a man's character as a whole, but the only way he can do the job or any fraction of it is by improving the actual responses the man makes to the situations of life. The only holds he can get on character are by way of ideas, ideals, acts, and desires, and their connections one with another and with the events of the physical and social world.

Furthermore, the facts which are best as facts seem the likeliest to improve mental powers. The habits which are best as habits seem the likeliest to improve character. The detailed emotional and attitudinal tendencies which one would recommend as the sound treatment of particular personal problems seem the likeliest to give health and balance to a man's personality as a whole. What is known about intellectual discipline of the mind indicates that the study of physics, economics, and law is better than the study of logic, Latin, and argumentation as a means of general improvement of mental power. A subject does not gain in disciplinary power by being barren of intrinsically valuable facts.

As a consequence of these three errors, the degradation of facts and habits below powers and traits has, I think, done much more harm than good. I hope that adult education will avoid it. The only positive lesson it has for us, in my opinion, is the reminder that all facts and habits are not of equal value and that those which are useful over a wide range and variety of situations, which propagate other useful ones, which concern issues of great moment, or which are otherwise notably beneficial in the mind should be preferred.

90. OBJECTIVES AND OUTCOMES [4]

Florence Stratemeyer

Attention is called to an element of difference between the commonly used terms " objectives " and " outcomes." From one point of view they are the same, the word outcome connoting the end

[4] *The Effective Use of Curriculum Materials,* Contributions to Education No. 460, Bureau of Publications, Teachers College, Columbia University, New York, 1931, pp. 128–129.

product and the word objective the goal to be reached. The objective is the end toward which the activity is to be directed, while the outcome is the goal actually attained. So conceived the objectives of education may be determined in advance and school activities planned toward their accomplishment, while educational outcomes, as the actual resultants, can be known only after the activity has been carried forward. For example, the particular purpose of a person visiting New York on a given occasion may be to hear and come to know a certain opera. Contingent upon this experience he may come to better understand congested traffic conditions and the polyglot nature of New York's *populus*. The latter are resultants or outcomes brought about by the interaction of the individual and curriculum materials which were selected, however, to fulfill other purposes or goals. At another time they may be the objectives directing experience.

91. "Objectives of Education" [5]

Franklin Bobbitt

If different persons were asked what the greatest single need of education is at present, the replies would vary according to their several specializations. From their different points of view they would name: improved financial support, better-trained teachers, improved organization of school systems, modernized methods of teaching, a better curriculum, and effective supervision.

These are all essentials, and our schools will not give the needed kind of service except as they are supplied; but to the present writer, from his specialized point of view, the effective working of each of them rests upon a need that is still more fundamental, namely, that of defining the results to be achieved by education. In other words, we need to establish our objectives, purposes, aims, ends, goals, projected outcomes, or whatever we may choose to call them.

It seems incredible that this should not have already been done. It is the essence of labor of any kind to aim at a specific product or result. It seems impossible that schools could have operated at all without aiming to produce some result or other.

As a matter of fact, the schools have very definite objectives. These can be ascertained by discovering the "achieved results" for which the pupils are given "credit." They are shown also by the kinds of instruments, methods, and standards employed in the measurement of the results.

[5] *School Executives Magazine*, 54:99–100, 122, December, 1934.

ARTIFICIAL ACADEMIC OBJECTIVES

Achievement tests, whether old-type examinations or new-type tests, are designed in the main to measure two kinds of things: (1) The kind and amount of knowledge implanted in the memory; (2) The level of skills attained, chiefly in language and mathematics, but in minor degree also, in certain aesthetic and practical arts. Some tentative attempts are made in the measurement of appreciations, attitudes, character, traits of personality, and the like; but in schools in general, as objectives, those are not taken seriously. Not often do they receive " credits," required and accepted by higher institutions. Except here and there, tests and credits show that the basic and genuine objectives of public education are only stored academic knowledge and the artificially fostered academic skills. The objectives are things that can be produced and measured.

These objectives are not held in any halfhearted way. They are the foundational determinants of all arrangements and labors. Everything is adjusted to, and focused upon, their attainment. The teachers are trained to teach academic information and skills. Except for a bit of sentimentality about appreciations, culture, and character, they hear and have heard of nothing else that they are to teach. The program has that in view. The courses of study outline the subjects, topics, units, and drills. The prescribed textbooks provide the materials. The classes are organized with a view to an effective and economical teaching and learning of just those things. The modern tests measure them with uncanny accuracy. The supervision sees that the teachers bring the pupils up to the standards. The succession of grades and schools from primary to college are built upon each other with a view to advancing just these two matters of academic knowledge and skills.

It is difficult to find anything in human affairs that has been more thoroughly institutionalized than these objectives of the schools. Every feature of the public school system has been built around them; and how solidly, one realizes only as one attempts to change any fundamental thing.

The teachers have never known any other kind of objectives. They were the things aimed at in their own schooling on elementary, high school, and college levels; and these were viewed then as the only things worthy of credit. They were the teachers' actual educational objectives during their twelve or fifteen most impressionable years, and for their most serious labor during all those years. Their later professional training has only deepened these earlier impressions.

As they come to their teaching positions, they are prepared with the greatest thoroughness imaginable to hold to these same academic objectives. They cannot conceive of any other kind.

In the recent and current campaigns of curriculum reconstruction, the usual attempts to formulate the objectives of education seem rarely to have been taken seriously. The task has seemed unreal to the teachers. In the background of their consciousness, they *know* — and with a certainty that is absolute — that the objectives are just those which they have always known, and that there is nothing else that the objectives *can* be. As they are then asked by the supervisory officials to formulate the projected outcomes of the subjects, they find it a novel and sometimes stimulating experience to toy with the problem of finding reasons or rationalizations that justify the teaching of what they know they intend to teach anyway. They pretend that they are setting up objectives; but in their hearts, they *know* that when school opens on Monday morning at nine o'clock, they are not going to pay any attention to those pretended objectives. With the pupils before them, they get down to the real job of teaching; and that is simply to have the pupils study their lessons in preparation for recitations and examinations. They are thankful to have labors so definitely demarked by the real purposes and not confused by the pretended ones.

The schools have continually sought improved methods of attaining their academic objectives. In the beginning, when teaching materials were meager, the method was memoriter learning of the textbook, and an artificial system of drill. With increased financial support, the methods are greatly improved by the use of parallel texts, interesting supplementary books, libraries, laboratories, and a wealth of diversified and stimulating drill materials. Recently, the abstractness of the subjects has been ameliorated by combining or "integrating" them so as to teach materials together that belong together, as for example, history and geography, or the several fields of natural science as integrated into "general science." Most recent has been the development of a great number and variety of "integrated units," in which informational subject matter and practice activities are organized around problems and natural centers of interest. Its culmination is the activity program.

This vast improvement in the ways and means is not a change in the general character of the objectives. This is proved by the tests. When the efficacy of the activity curriculum is challenged, its defense is to show that, by the use of standardized tests, it is as effective as other plans in achieving mastery of the approved information and skills.

THE REAL OBJECTIVES

And yet, more and more, this test of the activity curriculum is coming to be but a concession to those who cannot yet see, or use as a criterion, any other kind of objective. The leaders in the activity movement are coming to see that *continuity of activity* is the substance of life, and that the business of education is to guide this continuity into wholesome and fruitful channels during childhood and youth, to the end that it may continue in channels of that character throughout adulthood. It accepts with literalness the world-old educational doctrine: " Train up a child in the way he should go and when he is old he will not depart from it." Guide the footsteps of childhood and youth along the pathways justified by modern science, and when adulthood is reached he will continue along the farther and higher stretches of those same pathways.

Increasingly the objective of education that they set up is *continuity of right living*. The child or youth who carries on all his current daily activities for twenty-four hours each day in the manner best for him is achieving the end of his education. He continues to achieve it as long as he continues to hold to that standard. If he can hold to it consistently to the age of twenty, he will by that time be stabilized and securely launched into a lifetime of high-grade human living.

The activity-curriculum proclaimed first as a step forward in the pedagogics of method, is bringing us back to sanity in the matter of objectives. It is discarding the artificial academic objectives and is setting up *life itself properly lived* as the objective. The movement is ultra-conservative, in the sense that it is a return to the type of educational purpose that ruled in the world for ten thousand years before schools were ever invented. It is ultra-progressive in the sense that it would help the young people of today properly to guide their behavior through the bewildering mazes of this complex science-directed age.

The change in the objective is proved only when the test is correspondingly changed. When the objective is right living, the proof that one has achieved right living is that it be visible in his current day-by-day performance when he is operating under his own self-direction. It is *how he lives* when he is outside of school that proves his education. This new objective promises to sweep a whole raft of academic standardized tests into the discard.

One of the strangest misconceptions of a large portion of the educational profession is that human life, the current life of a man in this world, is a disreputable unworthy thing, and beneath the dignity of a profession of exalted purposes; and that it is therefore a lowering of our lofty standards actually and seriously to aim at human living. They would aim at the superhuman things of high academic knowledge, the austere techniques of advancing such knowledge, and certain related ideals, appreciations, and aspirations. One can admire the loftiness of their purposes, but he cannot greatly esteem their knowledge of the actual realities and their values.

As a matter of fact, there are no aspirations that are higher than those involved in the highest type of concrete living. There do not exist any ideals, appreciations, or purposes that are higher than those that operate at their best in the daily affairs of men. There is no knowledge in this world that is more exalted than the current vision of the best of those enlightened men and women who live in human homes and carry on concrete human affairs. To aim at human life at its best is to aim at the best of everything that this world can show.

DISCOVERING THE REAL OBJECTIVES

The trouble largely arises from the definition of the term *activity* which has grown up among persons of unmatured minds who are unaccustomed to viewing the intangible doings of the subjective life. To them, activity is that which is revealed by the senses. But with humans, the basic activities of civilized living are those that can be seen only with the " eyes of the mind " as they view the stirring inner life of man. This goes on all the time, sometimes calm, sometimes tumultuous. Actually, this invisible continuity is one's life. Outward performance is mostly its externalization. One who sees only this outer portion sees, as a child or an animal, the less fundamental part. One is indeed blind to the nature of human action if he does not see it basically as activity of the human spirit manifesting itself, according to its inner nature, in outward action.

The activities of the good life are: (1) The intellectual ones: direct observation, indirect observation through pictures and language, reading, listening to others, expression, problem-solving, reflective thinking, planning, and using thought in directing the execution of plans; (2) Those of physical living and health care; (3) The numerous ones, on both play and work levels, involved in family life; (4) The activities of the good citizen: participation in public opinion, lifelong maintenance of civic enlightenment, wise " consumer " performance, and public-spirited cooperation with one's fellows in promoting the general well-being directly and through governmental service agencies; (5) Wholesome and fruitful leisure occupations: intellectual, social, aesthetic, and physical; (6) As adulthood is reached, the activities of one's calling; (7) To prevent misapprehension, we should mention the use of the several essential techniques of intellectual living: for all, reading, writing, spelling, grammatical sentence construction, and arithmetic; for a few, certain techniques of rare use, such as algebra, drawing, or French.

The greatest present need of the schools is to formulate in considerable detail *the activities* that constitute the good life and to adopt them as its objectives.

It is actually well on the way toward doing just this thing. The break-up and confusion of the formerly standardized subjects in the recent formulations of " life-interest units," and the abundant use of non-academic activities are rapidly weaning the profession from the ancient " organized knowledge " obsessions, and at the same time helping them to see that life zealously and abundantly lived is a thing of worth in itself — even of more worth than going about as walking containers of desiccated information. It is giving teachers the idea that to live — when properly defined — is both worth while, and an objective well worth aiming at as the goal of education.

The profession is at least breaking through the hitherto impenetrable barriers. In such matters as health and safety education, clearly we are rapidly everywhere coming to aim, not only at a way of living, but at an actual holding to right living as the aim. In the training in household occupations, in the free " recreatory " home reading, and in various kinds of civic campaigns and cooperations, the schools are energetically breaking through to life itself. They will not be stopped. The movement is sanctioned and guided by an enlightened view of human needs, whereas the ancient academic objectives lack such sanction.

Education stands bewildered by the unwonted vista, and yet confident, at the dawn of a new day. If one has acquired a more or less justifiable phobia for all things exploited as " new," there is another phraseology that is both more congenial and more true: Education, after its long sojourn in isolation from life and reality, is emerging from its cloisters to discover in the needs of men its responsibilities for service, and then to give this service to all ages according to needs.

To aim at the improvement of human activities will probably be much more effective in improving them than was the old way of aiming at something else. The result of the change of objective will undoubtedly be a large increase in educational efficiency.

In spite of the clearness of the trend and the certainty of its ultimate consummation — assuming that our national institutions do not collapse in the meantime — it is a long program of readjustment that we face. Fundamental changes in educative process call for equally basic changes in the means, machinery, and labors to be employed. In previous paragraphs we called attention to the number and the solidity of the arrangements and procedures that have been brought into being by the long-held academic objectives. These exist, and are not to be dismissed merely by asserting that they are no longer needed. Realities are not so easily modified. When an obsolete building is replaced by a modern one, it is only in long sweat and grime that the change is slowly effected. But the obdurate and obstructive educational realities are far more fixed and sound than any building. To change them will require a long time and incalculable labor.

Herein we find an explanation of the fact that after the profession's two decades of intensive work upon the curriculum, it has scarcely yet made a start. It cannot advance until it has first discovered its objectives. The discovery of these is the greatest responsibility that now rests upon the profession.

92. Analysis of Aims as the Basis of Curriculum Planning [6]

Charles C. Peters

Similarity between educational procedure and engineering. . . . The engineer first plans the object he wishes to make—the house, the bridge, the electric transformer, the railroad bed. He sets up his plan in the form of a detailed blue-print and studies the adequacy of each of its parts from the standpoint of established theories. After he has perfected his blue-print in every detail, his next step is to have the plan embodied in concrete materials. Now precisely the same procedure characterizes the new education. Our first step is to get a blue-print of the individual of the society we want — a detailed picture of the good citizen, the man of culture, the vocationally efficient person, etc. — indicating the specific ideals, skills, bodies of information, attitudes of mind, prepared judgments, abilities to reason which are needed for getting on in his life. Our second step is, then, by using such instrumentalities as school subjects, discipline, and example as tools, to forge out individuals to conform to these blue-prints. In searching for means through which to attain clearly conceived ends, the educational engineer determines by scientific experiment which will most economically serve his purpose. When he is obliged to choose between a course in economics and one in history as a means of developing abilities needed in citizenship, he does not make his choice on the basis of tradition or of arm-chair philosophizing, but sets up an experiment in which he uses one kind of subject-matter with one group and the other with the other group,

[6] From *Objectives and Procedures in Civic Education,* Longmans, Green and Co., New York, 1930, pp. 21–24.

keeping all other conditions the same for the two contrasted groups, accurately measures his results from the two kinds of materials, and chooses for future uses the one which more largely achieves the ends he is seeking. Similarly he chooses between methods of handling his subject-matter — for example, between the project method of teaching economics and the logically organized, textbook method — not on the basis of *a priori* reasoning but on the measured outcome of scientifically controlled parallel-group experimentation. On the whole, there has been a considerable amount of this sort of scientific experimentation in the field of education, but unfortunately very little in the field of education for citizenship. Most of our questions there as to which of alternative procedures is better must still be answered on the basis of impression and of argumentation of a theoretical sort. But throughout the whole range of education we are moving toward the time when we shall have subjected to scientific tests all of our vital alternatives.

Education as social engineering. The possibility of handling education as a form of social engineering gives to it almost unlimited potentialities. We need only know what is wanted and, given time enough and sufficiently intelligent purposiveness, we can supply it within any reasonable degree. Does acceptable clerical work require the typing of fifty words a minute with not more than two errors per page? We can turn out graduates able to meet that demand if we are willing to pay a sufficiently high price in terms of properly motivated drill. Does citizenship threaten to break down because people succumb to the leadership of cheap and selfish demagogues? There are ways of effectively fortifying them against the wiles of such demagogues: we can, by narration and by argument, show our pupils the social dangers involved in demagoguery; we can, through case studies, train them to recognize demagogues by their methods and can build up emotional revulsions against the tactics of such parasites. And we can make this aversion to demagogues as strong, and the ability to recognize and combat them as complete, as the urgency of the case demands. If a certain ideal is needed, there is a technique for developing it: clarification of the idea that lies at its center through conviction of its high claims, and strong emotionalism of the idea by one or more means the teacher has at his command. There are, likewise, techniques for developing skills, others for developing concepts, others for prepared judgments, and others for every psychological component that enters into any form of social efficiency except for those traits which are inherited as instinctive or physical bases upon which ability rests, and these can be reached through vocational or eugenic selection.

As long as education was conceived as general discipline, it could guarantee nothing except undirected momentum; one could only hope that this momentum would carry the individual through to good conduct instead of bad. But when education is conceived as many particular readjustments for the particular problems of life, it can guarantee whatever conduct is demanded, since it can mature techniques, as suggested above, for getting the individual under training formed into ways our plans require. The only factor that can curtail this unqualified control over the future conduct of the educand, and that can impair the force of our guarantee to meet specifications, is imperfect engineering — lack of sufficiently clear-cut objectives on the part of the teacher, lack of sufficient intelligence and purposiveness in selecting materials and methods, lack of sufficient time, interference or education in counter directions by parents and other out-of-school factors, and, in the case of abnormals only, lack of the physical bases upon which to build. Of course in practice these limitations are now very powerful, but it should be our aspiration continually to lessen their potency as time goes on.

Reconstruction of social institutions. We have been speaking of educational engineering in the sense of ascertaining what are the demands society makes upon the individual and then so using educational materials and methods as to bring it about that the youth shall be sent out equipped to meet these demands. But social engineering can go still further than that; it can purposely remake society itself. We are at present, in respect to our social institutions, as much the victims of undirected forces as our grandfathers were in respect to their health and in respect to the material processes with which they struggled. Our social institutions have grown up haphazardly. They are the result of accidental beginnings, which have been forged into shapes more or less " fit " by the grim necessity of survival in the struggle for existence. As might be expected, they contain many vestigial elements which have not yet been eliminated and which are the cause of much present unhappiness. It is the function of social engineering to apply human purposes to the untangling of this knotted web, and to the reweaving of parts of it into a social fabric that embodies more consistently the legitimate aspirations of mankind. And evidently our technique will be the same here as in the cases where we wish to forge out *individuals* according to order. We shall need, that is, first a blue-print of the institution that we want — a blue-print for the organization of the state, the family, the church, the community. Then we shall need to put into play agencies for the realization of these plans. Our social engineers are our economists, our sociologists, our political scientists, eugenists, and constructive statesmen; our social mechanics, who must be expected to embody in practical outcomes the plans made by the constructive leaders, are our teachers, preachers, newspaper editors, motion picture producers, voters, and politicians. If such engineering technique can be applied to the improvement of our social institutions throughout the next century as the technique of mechanical engineering was applied throughout the century just passed, it ought to increase the spiritual wealth of mankind by as large a margin as other types of scientific direction have increased the purity of our water supply, our control over yellow fever, the comfort of our homes, the proper hygiene of our eyes and throats, our general health, and our material wealth.

93. A Criticism of Educational Blueprinting [7]

William H. Kilpatrick

The professed theory of the book [*Objectives and Procedures in Civic Education*] under review we wish especially to study because it is a theory widely held in this country, particularly among those who hope to make education into " a science." We may thank Professor Peters for stating it so clearly. The implications are thereby the more easily seen. These implications cut very deep into life, so deep that we must postpone their " civic " bearings while we study their more fundamental bearings on experience narrowly considered.

This professed theory may be stated in general terms as follows: " Science " is even now establishing a " new education." The new plan and bases are analogous to those of mechanical engineering. Life and our world of affairs is the kind of thing that can in time — granted probable increase of knowledge — be foretold with fair accuracy. Man as a behaving organism can, also in fair probability, become similarly well known. So that we can expect to be able to foretell with sufficient accuracy the " preadjustments " man will need in this about-to-be-foretold world of affairs. In this view of life, the problems and uncertainties will gradually be solved by the capable few and the solutions as " preadjustments " be taught to the many. This is to be the " new education." Science is here put forward as all inclusive. The bearings of the underlying and conditioning presuppositions of the theory seem hardly if at all sensed. Curriculum making becomes on this basis a social engineering, a blue printing of whatever may be decided (by the same few) to be appropriate (for the same many).

That this is in fact the theory put forward by the author as the basis for the book seems clear from many explicit statements. In a

[7] From " Hidden Philosophies," *Journal of Educational Sociology*, 4:60–66, October, 1930.

chapter on " the meaning of education " we find (p. 21) a section on
" education as social engineering." Note these key sentences and the
spirit they breathe. " The engineer first plans the object he wishes
to make." " He sets up his plan in the form of a detailed blue print."
" After he has perfected his blue print in every detail, his next step
is to have the plan embodied in concrete materials." Note here for
later use the words, " has perfected his blue print in every detail."
And see how the illustrations of what is dealt with exclude any regard
for self-directing personalities — " the bridge, the electric transformer, the railroad bed," all entirely physical, all completely under
outside control. " Now," says the author, " precisely the same procedure characterizes the new education." And he goes on to tell (pp.
21–23) how the " educational engineer " will determine subject matter and method by " scientific experiment " " on the measured outcome of scientifically controlled parallel-group experimentation."
Note throughout the scientific exactness of every procedure. We are
dealing with practical certainties.

Throughout this presentation as the correlative of exact procedures
the author thinks consistently in terms of exactly foretold wants.
For such an education with its " almost unlimited potentialities,"
" we need only know what is wanted and, given time enough and
sufficiently intelligent purposiveness, we can supply it within any
reasonable degree." And the conclusion in blackfaced type: " In
order therefore to plan a functioning education we need to know
what the preadjustments are the individuals in question will need."
" This necessitates blue printing the outcomes we want, just as the
mechanical engineer blue prints the house or the electric transformer
he wishes to build " (p. 26). And elsewhere (p. 23) the words pregnant with social implication: " The only factor that can curtail this
unqualified control over the future conduct of the educand, and that
can impair the force of our guarantee to meet specifications, is imperfect engineering." And the discussion recognizes no permanent or
inherent imperfection in the engineering.

From the foregoing we get the following reasonably implied characteristics of this theory: (a) Education is fairly analogous to mechanical engineering. (b) We can know the child's future and his
future needs in the same sense that the engineer knows the needs
which the house or the electric transformer are to meet and in much
the same degree. Blue printing is an equal possibility in both cases.
(c) The child is the kind of material to be molded to suit our wishes
in the same sense that the house-building materials are at the disposal of the engineer. Or at least, the molding in the one case is
analogous to molding in the other case. The one is now already
exact, the other can become so. Psychologically and ethically the

two cases are parallel and analogous. (d) It is reasonable to expect that the new " science of education " will by sufficient procedures tell us precisely (a) what " preadjustments " the child will need and (b) how to get them. The fact that many educators as above suggested accept substantially the presuppositions here made, makes it all the more important that we examine into their validity. Of the four characterizing features above listed the middle two, foretelling the future and molding the child to our will, contain the crucial presuppositions. The other two follow in greater or less degree from these.

Can the future be foretold? Consider life, experience, the ongoing stream of human events. Can this be foretold in the way needed by the theory under consideration? Is this stream such that thinking can exhaust its possibilities? Shall we in time become able to foretell what difficult situations the child will later meet so as to be able to provide him in advance with " preadjustments " to fit them? Or may it be objected that " preadjustment " is not the right term or concept to use. Considering life as we know it, are " preadjustments " the way of meeting it? Do we not rather need an intelligent grappling with events as they come? Could any aggregate of such " preadjustments " (contrived by somebody else's prechoice and predecision) without intelligent readaptation enable one to grapple with life's succession of difficulties? Do we not need to consider the life process more closely and see wherein and how it can and cannot be foretold? And accordingly wherein and how its successive situations can or cannot be met on the " preadjustment " theory?

To any one who looks with open eyes, life presents an on-going stream of novelly developing events. In each such event we shall recognize familiar elements, many such frequently recur. Two parts or aspects or elements we must then recognize in life, the novel and the recurring. If we consider the stream of events more closely, we can see that it is a " one-way " affair. Time always goes forward. What has been once done can never be undone. And if we consider the *total* content of the stream, no one cross section ever exactly repeats a preceding. In very literalness each successive total content of experience is novel.

Now what about foretelling? For one thing the continuance of the recurring elements can be foretold better than can the events in which they will figure. That my chair will be here to sit in for a good while to come is fairly certain. How long I shall sit in it much less so. The telephone may ring at any minute. In general the simpler the recurrent element the surer can its future conduct be foretold, in uncertainty man ranking highest. As regards events, the longer in general the interval of prediction the greater uncertainty as to detail. Also the more complex the situation, the greater in general the uncertainty of prediction. Putting together all we know, it seems reasonable to say that if we disregard total contents and fix attention on chosen and limited features, some events, as the needs of food, clothing, shelter, etc., we can foretell with fair certainty. But these had to be consciously limited before we could foretell them. When I shall become hungry, how hungry, where I shall be, what food will be available, how it will be cooked, who else will be there, what will be said, etc., — if we consider the *total* content we can foretell the future hardly if at all. In the stream of time the recurrent elements are always present but they swim along in more or less abiding but still ever-shifting combinations within the waters of uncertainty.

What then do we conclude about fore-preparing or " preadjusting "? In any precise sense it must in general be limited to the recurrent elements. It can be applied to events as such only in very limited degree. The farther we can get from man the better will preparing — in the sense of devising precise procedures in advance — apply; namely, best of all in dealing by machinery with nonliving matter, the ordinary manufacturing. Among human affairs we can best prepare in advance with the simplest elements, as spelling or the mechanics of typewriting, in which individual choice has little or no place. Beyond these, preparation in the sense of preadjustment is less and less possible the more complex the recurrent element dealt with. *Always, however, preadjustment is to an element not to a whole (typical) situation or event.* This means then that preadjustment is (in general) limited to those activities which we expect to use as tools or means in dealing thoughtfully with a novelly developing situation.

We come thus to dealing with the unpredictable, with the novelly developing event. A very simple case will perhaps serve for all. I am walking north. As I am about to cross an east-and-west street I see a motor car that looks as if it might swing into my street. I pause to see. It continues south. I then walk on. Here I could not have planned my walking in advance because I did not know about the motor car; and when I saw it, I had to adapt my movements to the development of its program. In this instance there are many recurring elements which I know, principally for present purposes the street arrangement and motor-car movements. Walking, recognition of streets, and of motor-car movements I had prepared in advance. I had learned these in such a way that I could use them as instrumental elements in dealing with such a situation as that described. But I had to contrive on the spot, in terms of things then occurring, my plan of action. Both in contriving and in executing I used tool procedures prepared in advance by means of which I could so contrive and execute. Preadjustment holds then of instrumental unit-element adjustment procedures but not of the inclusive plan of action. For dealing with the novelly developing, plans (except as possible construction units) cannot be made in advance. The actual working plan must be made at the time as the novel situation develops itself. The process of actual contriving as the situation develops to view is thinking (in any proper sense of that term). What we need then as preparation for dealing with the novel and unpredictable is thought materials (concepts, etc.) and a stock of instrumental unit procedures from which selection can be made as necessity demands. But this is not " preadjustment." For the novelly developing situation preadjustment in any inclusive sense is impossible.

We are now prepared to say why we reject Professor Peters's professed theory. The future cannot be " blue printed " — never can be in the sense demanded by the theory. " Preadjustment " in that sense is impossible. No educational theory based on prepared in advance, ready-to-use, preadjusted solutions can take care of the life we live. Life in any sense that interests us, even the humblest of us " allowed to go around loose," consists of a stream of novelly developing events, with many recurrent elements to be sure, and we have to deal with these novel situations each on the basis of intelligent grappling at the time. Using unit elements prepared beforehand, yes; using suggested plans made by experts, yes; but at every significant juncture each must contrive for himself as best he can, how he will meet the situation confronting him. If we are to meet life successfully, we have to meet it intelligently. And that means that the remaking of old patterns of all sorts is a never-ending affair. Preadjustment, no, impossible. Remaking patterns, yes, continually.

94. Implications of the Organismic Concept of Learning for Determination of Aims [8]

Hollis L. Caswell

Determination of the aims of education is generally considered one of the major tasks of curriculum making. A variety of procedures has been employed to determine and organize aims for use. The fundamental concepts underlying the large majority of these procedures are mechanistic. Aims are determined deductively but are assumed to be achieved on an inductive basis. For example, general or ultimate aims are analyzed through a varying number of steps into

[8] From " Practical Application of Mechanistic and Organismic Psychologies to Curriculum Making," *Journal of Educational Research*, 28:17–20, September, 1934.

specific or immediate aims. The specific aims are allocated to grade levels according to difficulty. The task of instruction is to achieve each specific aim, adding it to those achieved before, until finally at the close of the elementary school period the aims of the elementary school have been achieved, at the close of the junior high school period the aims of the junior high school have been achieved, and at the completion of high school the general aims of education are at last realized in full.

This may sound like an overly simplified statement of the procedure, but it is nevertheless essentially what is attempted in one form or another in many curriculum programs. It is true that the procedure is carried through with varying degrees of thoroughness, as is evidenced by statements of aims in courses of study, but there appears to be a common tendency to state general aims and to deduce from them more specific ones for grade levels. An illustration from a course of study in which the analytical procedure for determining aims was followed with great care and thoroughness will show the point to which the procedure may reach.

One of the aims for reading as stated in this course of study is " to fix and to expand desirable reading habits." On the first grade level under the development of right habits of eye movement are specific objectives such as:

1. To acquire the ability to read the entire line before returning to the beginning of the next line.
2. To acquire the ability to read in large word groups.
3. To develop the ability to progress regularly.

On the second grade level some specific objectives are:

1. To develop the ability to recognize increasingly longer units within a single eye pause.
2. To learn to decrease regressive eye-movements.
3. To develop further the ability to read with shorter periods of fixation.
4. To learn to acquire accurate return sweeps from the end of one line to the beginning of the next.

In the third grade objectives such as the following are found:

1. To increase the ability to recognize a short group of words at a single " eye-pause."
2. To develop the ability to recognize the sentence as the unit of thought in oral reading.

In courses of study in which the procedure has been employed we find very general use of expressions such as, " To further develop " and " To continue to develop." Some of the statements are quite ingenious in getting around difficulties of analysis. For example, here are specific aims stated for fifth grade language in another course of study:

1. A little firmer holding for accuracy of form, not, however, at the expense of fluency and originality.
2. Some increase in written work, but with the oral work still receiving the greater emphasis.
3. More definite attention to paragraph building.
4. Teaching of other correct-usage tables, with review drills on those already given in the fourth grade.
5. More exercises in enunciation and in punctuation practice.

This technique of analysis is applied with generalizations as well as with skills. On each level a particular concept is supposed to be developed to a certain stage until finally the total concept emerges.

The extent to which analysis of objectives is sometimes carried is suggested by the findings of the committee on social studies of the National Survey of Secondary Education. One course of study for seventh grade social studies lists 135 objectives. One course in another subject contains 85 objectives. One course for junior high school contains 47 pages (mimeographed) of objectives.

Such a conception of aims appears to be incompatible with the organismic point of view. According to this concept the inclusive pattern of conduct or ability as a whole must be functioning for the pupils on all grade levels. Out of the whole certain parts may tend to be individuated on certain grade levels, but the whole is always the base and foundation. Thus, it becomes impossible to assign to particular grades or parts of grades portions of general objectives to be achieved. To revert to our previous illustration, the ability to read, according to this point of view may not be broken up into eye span, return sweeps, and regressions to be treated separately. Rather, reading must be considered as an evolving whole at all times. Each part must function in some way with all other parts from the very beginning. The problem of teaching is to get a suitable rhythm of all the parts rather than performance of isolated parts. Consequently, according to the organismic point of view, it appears undesirable to break down general aims into specific or immediate aims and to endeavor to locate these parts on grade levels for sequential development. Rather, aims, stated in terms of general patterns of conduct or of abilities arranged in those relationships in which they function normally become the guide throughout the development of the child. There would be one general list of aims for an educational program. Each step in the education of the child would be a process of reconstruction or refinement of the modes of behaving which were employed in the beginning in cruder form. Thus, aims from the organismic point of view cannot be broken down and conceived as goals to be reached progressively by the pupils, as has been done so generally in interpretation of the mechanistic point of view.

It is interesting to note that in some schools where detailed statements of aims have been used, changes have been made to the more general form of statement. " The Denver course of study, published in revised form in 1926, contains lists of classified objectives for each grade and long lists of standards of attainment for each course, while the latest tentative revision includes only brief unclassified lists of objectives for each grade and a series of ' general understandings ' for each course. The Oakland course of study, published in 1923, provides lists of classified objectives for each semester, while the latest tentative revision includes only brief lists of unclassified objectives for each unit. In both cities, then, a simpler formulation of smaller lists of unclassified objectives seems to have displaced rather detailed classified lists found in earlier courses of study." * This suggests that, from practical experience some curriculum workers have found unprofitable the elaborate analysis implied by full application of the mechanistic concept to the determination of aims of education. In my judgment this is precisely what has happened. Observation of curriculum committees struggling to analyze aims and place them on grade levels so as to provide for sequential development leads to this conclusion. I suspect from examining courses of study that most committees have been unable to achieve the task satisfactorily and have included a statement of aims on grade levels largely because it is the customary thing to do in curriculum making.

95. SOCIAL-ECONOMIC GOALS FOR AMERICA [9]

The committee sets forth the social-economic goals of America in terms of the things we regard as most desirable for (and presumably as most desired by) the individual American. We believe that the best measure of our social, economic, and political policies and practises will be found in their effectiveness in providing these desirable things for individuals. But culture, personality, and social living are not distinct entities. Their problems have common roots. We would emphasize, therefore, the mutual inter-play of personality and culture upon each other. Culture molds personality; and conversely, in personality we find the materials and motive powers that make pos-

* *Instruction in the Social Studies,* Bulletin No. 17, 1932, Monograph No. 21, National Survey of Secondary Education, U. S. Office of Education, p. 9.

[9] Committee on Social-Economic Goals of the National Education Association, " What Are Desirable Social-Economic Goals for America? ", *Journal of the National Education Association,* 23:6–11, January, 1934.

sible change and improvement in culture. *To accept as the approach to our national goals the enrichment of individual personality is, then, not solely to seek a richer and more satisfying life for every individual; it is also to seek the refinement and enlargement of culture with resultant benefit to social living.*

In approaching its assigned task, the committee had to reach agreement upon certain tenets of social philosophy. It now affirms its faith in democracy; its faith in the orderly steps of social evolution, guided dispassionately by intelligence, as a method of adjustment to any social change; and its faith in the efficacy of education to assure an understanding of and zeal for the essential ideals of American life.

PART I.   THE NEED FOR A RE-STATEMENT OF NATIONAL GOALS

The brief span of 150 years cannot have extinguished the zeal of the people of the United States to establish justice, insure domestic tranquillity, promote the general welfare, and secure the blessings of liberty to themselves and their posterity. Nor do we of today admittedly value less than did our fathers freedom of worship, of speech, and of the press, the right of petition, of a speedy and impartial trial, and the sacredness of life and liberty, against impairment without due process of law.

These historic ideals still constitute the foundation upon which must rest any presentday statement of the social-economic goals of America. But the times demand a translation of these ideals into terms charged with new meaning. Forces of disintegration, alarming in their power, are making Americans aware of the need for a restatement of our national social-economic goals around which we can rally with enthusiasm.

Our nation was founded that government might serve equally the needs of all people, with special privilege for none. But concentrated wealth has resulted in the formation of a power that often overshadows government and bends it to its purpose.

Our nation was inspired by the ideal that every individual should have opportunity for the full development of his own capacities unhindered by accidents of birth and social status. Today, extreme inequality in distribution of wealth and control by the few of the instrumentalities of production have closed to many the doors of opportunity.

Our great natural resources once held out to all the promise of useful work and security of living. Millions are now without opportunity to labor and are demoralized by an uncertain and scanty life dependent on charity.

Early conditions fostered friendly cooperation with common participation in life's values. This friendliness has been largely destroyed by brutal competition for private pecuniary gain. Our fathers looked forward to a time when all should have the opportunity to share in the good things of culture. Now, in spite of immensely increased technical resources, multitudes have no chance to enrich their lives with art, science, and worth-while companionship. Conditions oblige many to keep their minds on material things and limit their aspirations to material ends.

In early days faith in democratic institutions as the effective guarantee of a freer and nobler life was all but universal. Now many of the interests that largely dominate public opinion decry the democratic faith. They preach defeatism or the doctrine that an impoverished life, poor in spiritual and cultural attainment as well as in worldly goods, is inevitable for all but the few.

Basic in all this change has been the apparent weakening in certain of the time-honored virtues which constitute ethical character. Honesty, sobriety, chastity, obedience to law, and other elements of high ethical character were once the common attributes of most leaders of society. Now, with the shift of certain sanctions, these are absent too often in high places, so that the powerful influence of emulation is largely lost.

Most of our social maladjustments spring from conditions hostile to the realization of our native American faith and purpose. In interpreting this faith and purpose for the life of today we re-affirm as our most cherished ideal the opportunity for all our people to develop free, cooperative, rich lives, to stand, confidently on their own feet, to judge clearly and effectively by means of their own trained intelligence, to act vigorously as occasion requires, to enjoy the highest values that modern life now offers to the most privileged, to engage joyously in the free exchanges of a shared life. This ideal determines the nation's social and economic goals.

PART II.   TEN DESIRABLE SOCIAL-ECONOMIC GOALS OF AMERICA

Social and economic policies and practises must be judged by what they do to enrich the lives of individuals. Therefore the desirable social-economic goals of America are stated in terms of the things we covet in the highest degree for the largest possible number of Americans.

(1) Hereditary strength — The development of rich personalities depends first of all upon the innate strengths and capacities of the individuals. Whether experiences which are socially desirable produce personal satisfactions is often at base a biological question — a question of the level upon which motives make an effective appeal.

Furthermore, proposals for social betterment are often limited in practise by the level of innate capacities of those among whom the proposal is to operate. The development, therefore, of individuals capable of the deepest enjoyments, and the building of a culture designed to enrich the personalities of great numbers of individuals, are alike conditioned by the biological endowment of the people.

Rapid and significant changes are now taking place affecting the hereditary strength of the American people. The birthrate is diminishing in widely varying degrees among many of the groups composing our population. The resulting changes are probably influencing profoundly the nature and quality of our human stock. Many students of the problems of population believe that these changes on the whole are making for biological deterioration.

It would seem that in an enlightened society cultural influences exerted upon mating and conscious control of reproduction might be instituted in such wise as to increase constantly the percentage of our people who are " wellborn," and thereby to raise steadily the average level of innate capacity. While admittedly difficult, progressively larger attainment in this direction is clearly within our reach if we may judge by the positive steps already taken.

(2) Physical security — To be born with superior innate capacities is but half the picture; to have these capacities conserved and developed is the other half. A strong hereditary base can be ruined by poor medical attention at or before birth, poor nourishment, improper home care, contaminated milk, a speeding automobile, a gangster's bullet, or any one of a thousand other conditions largely outside the control of the individual.

Physical security today hinges largely upon social regulation. Contagious diseases which once decimated entire populations are fast yielding to medical science. The commercial interest in impure drugs and unwholesome food is slowly but surely yielding to the public interest. The witch doctor's shadow in the form of foolish traditions and superstitions is vanishing before the knowledge with which parents are fortifying their instinctive care of their children. These and other like gains in the care and protection of individuals mark our progress in attaining even greater physical security.

But much remains. Thirty thousand lives a year sacrificed to the speeding automobile; ten thousand trapped by fire; millions improperly nourished even in normal times; other millions underfed in times of depression; as few as 2 percent of children in some communities vaccinated against smallpox — these are but a few of the many evidences that physical security is yet far from realization.

(3) Participation in an evolving culture — Every newborn babe is an intricate bundle of latent potentialities, each ready to develop

when touched by the sunlight of experience which culture provides. It follows, then, that if a rich and integrated personality is to be attained, the individual must be able to participate effectively in the cultural life that surrounds him. Society must assure to each individual the fullest possible opportunity to come into fruitful contact with culture. All the agencies that play a part in selecting and transmitting the culture of the race — the family, the church, the school, the playground, the library, the newspaper, the theater, the radio, the workshop, and all the rest — share in this task and should recognize their respective responsibilities in it.

(a) *Skills, technics, and knowledges* — Every individual must have command of those skills, technics, and knowledges that will enable him, to the limit of his innate capacities, to use and enjoy the culture of the group. Basic to all others are the arts of communication — language, spoken and written, numbers, music, drawing, and the like — with provisions for facilitating intimate and far-flung contacts with men, goods, and ideas. To this end agencies used in accomplishing these far-flung contacts, such as the radio, the newspaper, the cinema, should be trustworthy, not used for purposes subversive of social living.

The individual should know the essential features of social living. This calls for a substantial understanding of our institutional life; for a working acquaintance with problems of the day and the appropriate solutions; for a grasp of the history of the race. It calls for all these interpreted in terms of a working philosophy of life.

(b) *Values, standards, and outlooks* — There are values, standards, and outlooks that reflect the experience of the race and — *most important* — regulate the attention of the individual, determine his choices, organize his activities, and shape his personality. The basis of human motivation is found just here — what is right, what is wrong; what is good, what is bad. Responsiveness to motives which harmonize selfinterests with social interests will grow by virtue of better appreciation of the values, standards, and outlooks which actuate human conduct.

In this realm lies one of the most perplexing problems faced by society today. For individuals to reject racial standards *in toto* means chaos; to accept them all means stagnation. How to cultivate a critical attitude without nullifying the controling influence upon conduct of all standards and values is the problem. The role of the expert in social science is little understood. That the energies of many are being dissipated in fruitless attempts to be critical of values and standards which they are not prepared to appraise, is quite obvious. It seems clear also that with the present enormous amount of information and experience bearing upon almost any one of these standards and values, no one person, however competent and critical, can encompass the whole field. Each must accept values as established by others in whom he has confidence. Furthermore, to see each value clearly in the pattern of the whole social fabric calls for many critical minds brought to focus upon the mutual interrelationships of all these standards and values.

Apart from intellectual values and standards there is a large group at the emotional level of our experience. Non-rational behavior growing out of one's feelings is far more characteristic of man than his hard-won and recently acquired rationalism. The enrichment of personality in terms of esthetic and emotional values and standards is a vital need, and properly the concern of the social order.

Since, in default of constructive, planned action, the personality will be shaped by habitual, customary, and traditional standards, thus impeding both social progress and individual selfrealization, society must provide for the proper derivation and utilization of values, standards, and outlooks in the enrichment of life.

(4) An active, flexible personality — Participation in our cultural resources should promote personalities who are active, not passive and inert; who are motivated by intelligently chosen purposes, not by unguided impulse from within or casual pressure from without; who are not set and rigid but who re-adapt flexibly to social change and to the consequences of their own prior conduct; who express their individual differences, but who do it in ways that are cooperative and socially contributory, not selfcentered and egoistic.

In view of the social maladjustments that work against these ends economic and social goals must be consciously pursued that will foster:

(a) *Personal initiative* — At present multitudes are engaged in mechanical and monotonous pursuits that thwart the exercise of initiative. They engage chiefly in carrying out plans made by others with no original activity on their own part. Only automatic routine habits are encouraged. Initiative is deadened and power to welcome and to carry responsibility correspondingly paralyzed. The resulting enfeeblement of personality extends its influence into political life and threatens the success of democratic institutions. Opportunities should be multiplied to share actively in the formation of industrial and social plans and to accept personal active responsibility for their realization.

(b) *Discriminating judgment and choice* — Integrated personality and a coherent social order can be maintained under present conditions only as individuals are trained to think clearly and to the point, and to act in accordance with the outcome of their thinking. This demands that all individuals shall seek for the facts concerned, weigh evidence honestly, and resist prejudice and class interest. To achieve this end the channels of information must be kept clear, and individuals must learn to protect themselves from the flood of meaningless or biased material that now pours in from so many quarters.

(c) *Flexibility of thought and conduct* — Our society is characterized by rapid pace and constant change, while generally speaking our minds have been attuned to expect that things will remain practically unchanged. The consequence is great friction, with undue disintegration and disorganization. Stability becomes rigidity. Our people are not taught to understand how habits are formed and changed and how they are modified thru flexible re-adaptation to new occasions. Mental disorders and personal disintegrations are so on the increase as to create a major social problem. The situation demands more than merely curative measures. Only individuals habituated to adjust to changes and to integrate them into their own personality can meet the necessities of the situation. Society must recognize the difference between stability and the preservation of what has been. They must see that change is normal. Personalities must be habituated in flexibility.

(d) *Individual differences* — Traits that are distinctive and unique are not only the sources of one's own keenest satisfactions, but also the ultimate source of all fruitful social change. Present social conditions too often suppress these qualities in the many by enforcing regimentation and conformity, while in the few they are stimulated into one-sided egoistic activity at variance with the needs and rights of others.

(e) *Cooperativeness* — As a rule, the extent to which people resort to mutual voluntary cooperation is far below the point of maximum advantage. Continually people fail to cooperate when they would greatly benefit by so doing, and abandon cooperative efforts because of petty bickerings, suspicions, jealousy, and bossism. The young should be so educated that as adults they will readily resort to democratic cooperation. In home, classroom, workshop, and on playground, the young should become habituated to smooth, effective, and enjoyable teamwork until cooperation becomes " second nature."

(5) Suitable occupation — A congenial life work is a first requisite of a rich personality. Society can help in three distinct ways to make this possible:

(a) *Guidance* — Society should provide counsel as to what vocations youths should fit themselves for, taking into account the gifts, aptitudes, and tastes of the individual as well as the prospects of the various callings.

(b) *Training* — With appropriate regard to what guidance efforts reveal, society should make available to all youths, according to individual liking and social need, the chief skills and technics which underlie current reputable modes of obtaining a living.

(c) *Placement and advancement* — The individual worker today is in many cases so far removed from the control of his own occupational fate that society has a stake in connecting him with a fitting job and in seeing to it that progress in his occupation results normally from efficient work.

(6) Economic security — The deplorable economic conditions of today are apparent to everyone. How utterly devastating to personality, and how completely destructive of most of the things we cherish, is a breakdown of our national (and international) economic machinery! Recent amazing revelations of the connection of certain industrialists, financiers, and organizations with practises inimical to public welfare make clear the sinister power which may reside in vast accumulations of wealth. This same sinister influence has infected financial and industrial life thruout the country. Even the many aspects of our ugly plight which seem not to be the result of selfish manipulation point to the need for greatly increased economic planning in the public interest.

We have, to be sure, set up certain standards of economic security; some legal, some with such extra-legal sanctions as public opinion, conscience, and our ideas of common decency. At the wretched lowest, there are poorhouses, paupers' graves, private " charity," public " reliefs " — mention of which serves the useful purpose of emphasizing how far we have advanced from being content with such makeshifts. Increasingly, we think in terms of the right to a job, the minimum wage, the legal dismissal wage, security of tenure, mothers' pensions, compensation for industrial accidents and disease, old-age insurance, unemployment insurance, and similar devices.

The same outlook guides the establishment of certain minimum standards of " safe " participation in business enterprise. In particular, as business risks have developed, we have arranged for various types of " limited liability "; for bankruptcy proceedings which in some sense wipe the slate of business mistakes and disasters; and for debtors' exemption laws that leave the business debtor at least a modicum of economic security.

It is obvious, tho, that the devices and agencies currently employed to confer economic security are wholly inadequate. That they fail to meet the wishes or the needs of large numbers of persons may be seen in the strenuous efforts of many individuals to provide private means of security in old age, in unemployment, and for their children; and in the large number of cases of mental disorder chargeable, allegedly at least, to worry over lack of economic security. Still more striking and pitiful are the conditions of the unemployed, with all the well-authenticated perils to personality.

(7) Mental security — " What, indeed, may we believe? " Individual personality and public welfare depend upon a satisfactory answer to that question.

Above our heads, giant profit-seeking concerns fight for the privilege of writing on our minds something that will help them make money. Truth-seeking and truth-telling organizations abound, but they cannot offer as much for an opportunity to enlighten the people as Mammon will pay for an opportunity to fool them.

Society has had great success in finding disinterested truth lovers and enlisting them in its service; but their voice is feeble these days in comparison with the commercialized press, screen, and radio. If amid the din of advertising ballyhoo the public knew where it could hear a clear trustworthy voice, would it not listen in? The air channels should not be monopolized as now by gainseekers; more of them should stand open to educational institutions. The fact that some educational instrument, the cinema, for example, is under private control does not absolve the owner from responsibility to use it with regard for public interest.

The more we are plied with untruth, the more we need truth. We Americans ought to go in fear of the powerful commercial interests that are trying to exploit as thru gaining control of our thoughts and opinions. What irony that at the time when the truth is being discovered at a rate never before known, the truth about matters essential to our welfare is being systematically obscured as never before! Just as society has brought pure drinking water to the houses and the highways, so it ought to bring pure truth within our reach at every point and on every matter where non-social agencies are interested in hoodwinking us.

(8) Equality of opportunity — Our nation had its birth in a struggle for equality as opposed to special privilege. Its birthcry, the Declaration of Independence, began with the statement: " We hold these truths to be self-evident — that all men are created equal; that they are endowed by their Creator with certain unalienable rights; that among these are life, liberty, and the pursuit of happiness."

In the light of modern knowledge of individual differences, we do not construe this to mean equality of powers and abilities or of other innate or acquired personal traits. But equality as a social principle means equality of rights and opportunities, therefore no special privileges; it means the equal chance to attain to one's fullest possible development; it means accepting duties, responsibilities, and service in proportion to abilities; it means compensation in proportion to services rendered; and it means the general diffusion among the people of the knowledge, the ethics, the idealism, and the spirit which as nearly as possible shall make this equality actual and effective.

Political power exerted by influential men or organizations, not responsible to the people, causes marked inequalities in the rights and powers of citizens to participate in the benefits of government and other institutions of society. The use of political power or money to obtain special privileges, such as unworthy appointments to public office, freedom from taxation, unfair franchises, or other means of obtaining unearned riches at the expense of the public, violates the principle of equality of opportunity.

Education is a function of the state, and certainly the state ought to render its services and extend its benefits equally to all children. But everywhere we find inequalities in the services and benefits of the public schools. Some children have excellent educational facilities in good, sanitary buildings, with ample equipment, long terms, and well-trained and well-paid teachers. Others have poor, unsanitary buildings, meager equipment, short terms, and young, untrained, and poorly-paid teachers. The bitter fruits of this inequality of opportunity endure thruout the lives of the generation affected.

Equality of opportunity, the birthright of every American, should involve for each individual the opportunity to live a healthy, happy, satisfying life, to have a comfortable, sanitary home, to have useful employment that yields a comfortable living for self and dependents, to be surrounded by the beauty and truth that are inspiring and elevating rather than by the ugliness and deceptions that are discouraging and degrading, to enjoy the same rights under the law as are enjoyed by those more powerful or more favored by fortune, and to have the benefits of such educational facilities and other means of proper development as will enable the individual to become the happiest, most efficient, and most useful member of society possible with his natural endowments.

(9) Freedom — Historically the struggle for freedom has seemed to center in the effort of one group to free itself from oppression by another. Dynastic and hereditary tyranny have been largely overcome, but domination of the economically less-favored group by the economically more-favored group still persists. The yearning for personal freedom, moreover, dwells in every human spirit. Self-expression is the source of our keenest satisfactions, and freedom is basic to selfexpression.

How to preserve the fullest possible measure of freedom at a time when social living is necessarily surrounding each of us with a network of prohibitions which the welfare of our neighbors imposes upon us, is a very real problem. The deep sense of satisfaction experienced in making one's own decisions, fundamental as it is in preserving selfrespect, should be kept in mind by society as it endeavors to assure to every person the widest sphere of freedom compatible with the equal freedom of others and with certain paramount public interests such as safety, health, decency, and quiet. Plans should be taken to assure to all at least freedom of choice of mate, of occupation, of movement, of place of residence, of manner of life, and of industrial, political, religious, and cultural affiliations.

The greatest stress, however, should be laid on what may be termed *the agitative liberties*, i. e., freedom of speech, of the press, of the screen, of broadcasting, of assembling, of demonstrating, of organizing. In our day these are under constant heavy attack because ultimate political power rests with the voting public and the last hope of victims of wrong is to lay their cause before this public. Hence, groups enjoying some lucrative form of exploitation will resort to any high-handed measures to hinder their victims from gaining access to the public ear. Just as, in the decade before the downfall of the slave power, the violations of the right of free speech became constantly bolder, so, since the World War, the assailants of the agitative liberties have evinced an unprecedented determination.

Particularly to be cherished and defended are freedom of research, of experimentation, and of teaching; for they are the means by which new truth is revealed and grafted upon old truth. Furthermore, with a lessening influence of erstwhile forms of education such as the soapbox, the neighborhood store, and the debating society, formal educative agencies such as the school and church have an added responsibility to become the forums for the discussion of the most pressing problems of the day. More and more should teachers become community leaders of thought. In that rôle they will need group solidarity and the support of public opinion, aroused to appreciate the fundamental importance of this aspect of freedom. The vested interests connected with certain elements of society will surely throttle liberty of inquiry and of teaching unless friends of the undiscovered truth and of the cause of free speech rally to their defense.

(10) Fair play — By fair play as a social virtue, we mean not only the justice defined by the courts but also the good sportsmanship that should be practised by the individuals constituting our society in all their relations with one another.

It is apparent that there are many violations of the principle of fair play as thus defined. The frequent handicap of the poor man in the courts; the helplessness at times of the individual employee when in conflict with his employer; the exhibitions of race prejudice; the filing of false assessment schedules or the employment of " tax fixers "; the disregard of sanitation in the erection or maintenance of tenement houses; the sale of adulterated foods; the placing by a public utility corporation of a much higher valuation on its property for ratemaking purposes than for taxation purposes; the issuance of " watered stock " in order to collect unearned profits — these but illustrate a long list of situations in which we are obviously far from the goal.

Fair play is simply the Golden Rule boiled down to two words. It is the practise by the individual of his duty as a member of society to act in conformity with the highest good of all other members of society. It rests upon mutual respect for the rights of others and must depend for its attainment upon goodwill more than upon law.

Of special significance at present is the ever-widening circle of those whom each individual admits tacitly into his fair play group. Fair play with one's family is common. Fair play with one's close neighbors is rather easy. As the circle widens to include unseen neighbors across the tracks, those in a nearby state, or members merely of the great impersonal " public," the tax upon our sense of fair play grows heavier. Of late, we are called upon to widen the circle to an unprecedented degree, to include among those with whom we are to play the game, all the nations and races of the earth. Taught to be enemies from the dawn of history, nations are striving now to write their codes of ethics in worldwide terms. This is the supreme test of the depth of our sense of justice and fair play.

96. THE AIMS OF PUBLIC EDUCATION IN ARKANSAS [10]

One of the tasks of curriculum development is to aid teachers in the effective use of aims. This may be done in part by preparing a statement of aims against which teachers may check the adequacy of the aims which they employ in directing instruction. It is difficult, however, to develop such a statement because, in the final analysis, the teacher must be concerned at all times with all aspects of the conduct of the individual. It is impossible to divide conduct into segments and to deal with one segment at a time. The individual reacts as a total organism in every situation which he encounters.

However, the characteristics of the well-rounded individual, or of the integrated personality, may be described. Such a description

[10] Arkansas Co-operative Program to Improve Instruction, *A Teachers' Guide for Curriculum Development,* Bulletin No. III, State Department of Education, Little Rock, Arkansas, 1935, pp. 31–41.

may be made in a variety of terms. One rather satisfactory way of describing the individual is in terms of general patterns of conduct or of the attitudes and appreciations.

Such a description is one phase of a statement of aims that should be of assistance to teachers. The material which follows indicates in this manner the type of individual which it is considered desirable for the schools in Arkansas to develop.

Suggestive Attitudes and Appreciations

The individual who lives in a democracy with greatest satisfaction to himself and good to his fellows will be characterized by the following attitudes and appreciations:

He will have a high degree of personal integrity. He who possesses this attitude will:

Hold self-respect above group approval

Adhere under varying circumstances to the same principles of thought and action

Face reality

Tend to watch for and to avoid self-deception

Be sincere, trustworthy, and dependable

Be faithful to promises

Accept responsibility for his acts

Persevere in undertakings

Believe in the worth of his own personality

Tend to carry forward all undertakings to the best of his ability.

He will have strongly imbued in his being an attitude of respect for personality. Possessing this attitude, he will:

Be inclined to believe in the integrity of others

Recognize the right of all people for a fair chance for optimum development of their potentialities for happy and successful living

Tend to admire the fine qualities and achievements of others

Be free from prejudices against persons because of race or nationality

Respect constituted authority

Be considerate of the welfare and convenience of others

Respect the point of view of others

Be courteous and tactful

Follow rules and regulations which promote the common good and assure fair play

Be tolerant of customs and beliefs that vary from those he practices.

He will have the scientific attitude. An individual who possesses this attitude will:

Hold conclusions tentatively
Base judgments on facts when available
Endeavor to increase the reliability of conclusions
Evaluate evidence critically
Be free from superstitions
Tend to seek explanations, causes, and consequences of social and
     natural conditions
Be willing to entertain new ideas and points of view
Seek and accept improved ways of doing things
Be accurate and impartial
Tend to attack problems with confidence and dispatch
Be inclined to welcome suggestions.

*He will be characterized by the attitude of constructive social
participation.* An individual who possesses this attitude will:
Be inclined to forego personal benefits for the good of the group
Tend to rely upon orderly methods of achieving social ends
Be patient in dealing with others
Assume the responsibilities of leadership in fields in which he is
     competent
Accept a position of followership in fields where others are more
     competent
Be industrious
Cooperate in group enterprises.

*He will have a deep appreciation of the beautiful in human rela-
tions.* If he possesses this appreciation he will:
Seek friendships
Prize high standards of conduct
Be optimistic and cheerful
Respect self-sacrifice
Prize a sense of humor
Be sensitive to ideals, motives, and virtues
Seek contacts with groups which are organized around cultural
     interests.

*He will have an appreciation of the artistic in its many mani-
festations.* An individual with this appreciation will:
Enjoy music, literature, and art
Enjoy nature
Tend to be neat and attractive
Tend to express himself creatively
Use good taste
Support artistic enterprises.

Basis of Attitudes and Appreciations

Teachers sometimes think of attitudes and appreciations as more
or less mystical qualities that an individual develops apart from

other phases of growth. This leads to the separation in the use of aims of the intellectual aspects of learning from the emotional aspects. As a matter of fact attitudes and appreciations involve both the intellectual and emotional aspects. Attitudes develop only as feeling is associated with knowledge and specific habits. Consequently, teachers must at all times be concerned with the knowledge and specific habits that will permit the desired attitudes to function. For example, a child cannot exhibit satisfactorily the attitude of personal integrity if he is given too much change at the store and lacks the ability to count change. This ability is absolutely essential for his use in this situation. Similarly other attitudes function through knowledge and specific habits.

Consequently, the teacher who uses aims effectively must be concerned, in addition to the attitudes which it is desirable to develop, with the knowledge and specific habits which will permit these attitudes to function. Such knowledge and habits will vary from situation to situation and with different individuals. Yet there are certain abilities of these types that have been found generally useful. Suggestive ones are presented in the following list. Especially valuable knowledge is best suggested by generalizations that have wide applicability while specific habits are suggested by the indication of abilities which involve relatively complex organizations of specific habits.

Suggestive Generalizations

All Forms of Life Are Related and Interdependent.
> Individuals are dependent upon other individuals and have responsibilities to them.
> Individuals are dependent upon social groups and have responsibilities to social groups.
> All types of groups are dependent upon one another and have responsibilities to each other.
> Optimum satisfaction of man's wants is dependent upon the wise use of natural resources.
> Industrialism increases the interdependence of people.
> War is detrimental to all concerned.

Group Organizations and Regulations Are Necessary for the Protection of the Individual.
> Individuals cannot live apart from groups.
> Group life must be based upon regulations.
> The greatest freedom for the individual is accomplished through regulations that are for the common good.
> Violations of regulations that are for the common good operate to the advantage of the strong and to the disadvantage of the weak.
> Group organizations make possible the care of dependents.

Human Life Is Sacred.

Human life may be taken justifiably only in self-defense.

Carelessness costs many lives.

The lives of many people are shortened by others for selfish purposes.

Man's inability to rationalize misfortunes impairs life.

All Aspects of Life Are in a Process of Change.

Man's conception of the truth changes.

Much knowledge yet remains to be revealed.

Forces in nature are operating continuously to produce changes in physical and biological environment.

Man's concepts are limited by the customs, ideas, and knowledge of his time.

Social institutions and habits tend to crystallize and cause social maladjustment.

Social change tends to lag behind material developments.

Man Constantly Endeavors to Improve His Living Conditions.

Man has continually increased his means of self and group protection.

Man has increased his efficiency and joy in living by increased knowledge of the principles of health and sanitation.

Man's inventions and use of power have improved his home conditions, increased his earning capacity, and lightened his occupational load.

Man tends to move from place to place in search of better ways of living.

Man tends to move from place to place to free himself from religious and political oppression and to escape social obligations.

Man employs numerous methods to protect himself from the uncertainty of the future.

The Masses of Men Struggle Constantly to Gain Freedom from Domination by the Few.

Individuals and powerful minorities have always sought to control and to subjugate the masses.

Human rights are gained through individual suffering and sacrifice.

Industrialism tends to exploit the masses.

The few tend to control means of production.

Minority groups attempt to control government for selfish advantage.

Education frees men from the domination of other men.

The Physical Universe Is Balanced and Orderly in All Its Aspects.

Matter and energy cannot be created or destroyed.

Spatial and time relationships occur with mathematical precision.

Nature's laws are invariable.

Through the interdependence of species and the struggle for existence a balance is maintained among the many forms of life.

All life comes from life and produces its own kind of living organism.

Chemical changes are accompanied by energy changes.

Chance relationships conform to a uniform probability distribution.

Patterns set by nature are inherently symmetric.

Animal and Plant Life Are Influenced by the Forces of Nature and Tend to Adapt to These Forces.

Species have survived because by adaptations and adjustments they have become fitted to conditions under which they live.

Density of population is influenced by climate, topography, and availability of natural resources.

Types of food, clothing, and shelter employed are determined by the forces of nature.

The sun is the source of energy and light.

Man's customs, ideals, and ways of making a living are conditioned by the physical environment.

Man Exerts Control over Nature.

The nature of plant and animal life may be modified through artificial selection.

The nature of plant and animal life may be modified through control of environmental surroundings.

Use of power increases man's ability to control nature.

Man controls his environment by use of physical and chemical change.

Man controls plant and animal life by using certain organisms to destroy other organisms.

Man increases his control over nature through discovery and invention.

Man controls nature through the discovery of cause and effect.

Man Is Dependent upon Natural Resources for the Satisfaction of His Wants.

Food, clothing, and shelter are secured from natural resources.

Power is derived from natural resources.

Recreational needs of man may be cared for through contact with nature.

Man Is Dependent upon the Experience of the Race for the Solution of His Problems.

Mechanical inventions are the outgrowth of much race experience.

Social institutions are developmental in nature.

Each generation adds to the social heritage.

Customs and ideals are transmitted from group to group.

Each generation creates very few of the means of satisfying its wants which it employs.

Knowledge is cumulative.

Suggestive Special Abilities

The Ability to Read.

The ability to use the mechanics needed in reading.

The ability to analyze, interpret, and evaluate reading materials.

The ability to use reference books.

The ability to interpret thought in oral reading.

The ability to use silent reading as recreation.

The Ability to Speak.

The ability to express one's thoughts clearly, forcibly, and correctly in all forms of oral discussion.

The Ability to Write.

The ability to express one's thoughts clearly, forcibly, and correctly in all forms of written discourse.

The ability to spell needed words.

The ability to use handwriting.

The Ability to Study.

The ability to begin work promptly.

The ability to ignore both internal and external distractions.

The ability to get a clear insight into the meaning of the material to be learned.

The ability to concentrate on the important elements of a discussion.

The ability to review in spare moments material which has been learned.

The ability to apply newly acquired principles in wider fields.

The ability to take notes which will insure ready availability of material or ready reference to sources.

The ability to concentrate on a problem until it is completed.

The ability to make skillful use of such aids to study as tables of content, indexes, card catalogues, reader's guides, etc.

The ability to keep in mind that work is not being done for teachers.

The ability to provide external conditions of work — light, temperature, humidity, chair, desk, etc. — favorable to study.

The ability to provide the tools of study.

The ability to form a place-study and time-study habit.

The Ability to Use Quantitative Symbols and Procedures.

The ability to use integers, measures, measurements, fractions, and graphs.

The ability to check answers.

The ability to think through the solution of a problem before computation.

The ability to make computations accurately.

The ability to work with reasonable speed.

The ability to interpret problems carefully.

The ability to estimate quantities.

The ability to become sensitive to the uses and values of the quantitative aspects of life of whatever sort.

The Ability to Use the Common Objective Materials and Instruments of the Social Heritage.

The ability to use the common objective materials found in home and school.

The ability to use maps.

The ability to make maps.

The ability to use conveyances of transportation.

The ability to use institutions of the community.

The Ability to Maintain Certain Objective Materials of the Social Heritage.

The Ability to Maintain Health.

The Ability to Express Oneself through Music.

The ability to sing correctly and pleasingly with good singing habits.

The ability to express in bodily movement the rhythmic element in music.

The Ability to Maintain Economic Competence.

HOW TO USE AIMS

Certain general considerations which should receive attention in using aims have already been discussed. It is the purpose of the material herewith presented to suggest more specifically how aims may be used in planning and directing instruction. Use of aims differs somewhat in the unit of work and direct teaching phases of the instructional program.

Aims in Units of Work

In developing a unit of work the first step, of course, is to select a unit that appears appropriate for the group of children being taught. Several considerations require attention in making this selection. Among these considerations is the possibility provided by the unit of development of the desired type of conduct on the part of children. This is the point at which teachers should turn to the aims of education. They should survey with care the aims that might function in directing the unit of work, and on the basis of this survey should judge the probable educative value of the unit.

The following illustration serves to show how aims that the teacher believed would guide a particular unit were stated. In a section of the State in which lumbering is the principal industry, a forest fire occurred during the school year. This served to call the attention of the children to the necessity of maintaining adequate forest resources. It became clear to the teacher that a unit of work could be developed on the problem of forest conservation. The purpose of the children was formulated around the objective of determining how forest resources could best be conserved. With this dominating purpose on the part of the children, the teacher listed the following aims as being suggestive of the opportunities for valuable educational outcomes through the unit of work.

Aims to direct unit:
It should be possible to develop attitudes of:
    Trustworthiness in regard to camp fires, disposal of trash, and preservation of trees
    Respect for the work of forest rangers and state officials concerned with conservation
    Respect for rules governing forests
    Responsibility for protecting forest resources
    Appreciation of the beautiful in forests.
Generalizations that may be involved are:
    Man is dependent on forest resources for the satisfaction of his wants
    Wise use of forest resources depends on the cooperation of many people
    Group regulations are necessary for the protection of forests.
Special abilities of practically all types may be involved in such a unit. Special emphasis may be placed upon:
    The ability to use source material
    The ability to use and make maps
    The ability to organize facts.

As the unit of work developed the teacher found it necessary to modify the aims suggested in the original list. In certain cases new aims were added. In other cases aims in the original list were found to be inappropriate. This modification of aims took the form of rough notes jotted down by the teacher in the aims column of the plan sheet. Certain of these notes follow:

" Check inability of John G. to cooperate in group work. Provide special opportunity for him to engage in cooperative activities."

" Visit to reforestation project provides special opportunity to emphasize generalization concerning man's control over nature."

" Participation of children in planting trees provides opportunity to emphasize attitude of constructive social participation."

" Check inability of Dorothy M. to use reference materials. Emphasize use of index and table of contents."

It will be observed from the foregoing notes that the teacher was giving emphasis to his aims, to the *attitude of constructive social participation,* to the generalization that *man exerts control over nature,* and to the *ability to study.*

97. THE GOALS OF PUBLIC EDUCATION IN MICHIGAN [11]

The Michigan Educational Planning Commission consists of officials of certain influential state organizations representing agriculture, business, commerce, education, industry, and labor, and certain organizations of women. The Commission was named by the State Superintendent of Public Instruction in February, 1934, and has held numerous conferences for the consideration of problems in the field of public education. The members are convinced that certain problems in public education arise from the confusion in the thinking of citizens regarding the goals of public education. The Commission has therefore prepared a statement concerning the goals of the educational system established and maintained by the State of Michigan. It recommends that this statement of goals be used as the basis for the discussion and the appraisal of the program of public education. It is believed that such discussion and appraisal will help to solve certain educational problems that now face the State of Michigan.

DEMOCRACY AND THE SCHOOLS

The success of American civilization depends on the capacity and the desire of the people to maintain democracy, which is "government of the people, by the people, for the people." The essential idea in a democracy is that of respect for personality. The principles of democracy are defined in the Declaration of Independence and the Preamble to the Constitution of the United States. Numerous pronouncements regarding the necessity of schools in a democracy are

[11] Michigan Educational Planning Commission, June 22, 1934.

set forth in the famous Ordinance of 1787, in the Constitution of the State of Michigan, and in various decisions of the Supreme Court of our State. From these pronouncements it is clear that schools should be regarded as an essential element in the education of a democratic electorate, a means of state preservation, and a line of national defense of vital importance. It is not an exaggeration to declare that the school and democracy are most intimately related, and that the failure or success of one is reflected in the failure or success of the other.

In a democracy the people must ultimately decide important questions of local and state policy with respect to education, because the public school touches the everyday lives of citizens so intimately and so frequently. Important questions concerning the scope and nature of public education are being raised daily, and because our citizens must ultimately decide these questions, they should be prepared to decide wisely. To make wise decisions, the people must have an understanding of the purposes and goals of public education.

In order to preserve and improve our democratic civilization, and to provide educational advantages for all, in accordance with the American principle of equality of opportunity, the State of Michigan has the right and the obligation to provide a system of public education at public expense. In such a system it should be the aim to seek to achieve the following nine goals at the appropriate levels of the public school system — elementary, secondary, and higher.

ONE. *To cultivate a deep regard for democracy and an intelligent appreciation of democratic institutions.*

This goal implies that effective democratic institutions constitute the best means for insuring justice and liberty; for maintaining the equality of political, social, and economic opportunities; for fostering growth and progress; and for furthering truth and honesty.

1. Should teachers be obligated to teach that democracy is, or can be made, the best type of government?

2. Does the school devote sufficient time to instruction in social, economic, and political problems of American life?

Two. *To develop those qualities of character which are of special significance in a democracy.*

This goal implies that citizens in a democracy must possess certain qualities of character that are not required in other forms of society. The preparation requires the development of a personality that will find expression in responsible self-direction, self-control, and self-appraisal in both individual and cooperative endeavor. This goal implies emphasis (*a*) on understanding and appreciation instead of blind obedience; (*b*) on fair and honest dealings instead of exploitation; (*c*) on investigation instead of thoughtless acceptance; (*d*) on openmindedness instead of prejudice; and (*e*) on the promotion of the common good instead of selfish advancement of the individual.

1. Are there additional qualities of character that should be emphasized in training pupils for a democratic society? Why?

2. Is there a type of discipline that trains the child to direct himself rather than to be dependent on the autocracy of forced obedience?

THREE. *To develop the willingness and the ability to cooperate effectively in a democratic society.*

Democracy succeeds in proportion to the capacity of the people to solve their problems through voluntary self-directed cooperation. This goal requires a system of education, in organization, materials, and method of instruction, which will provide in the school an environment that will most nearly approximate an ideal democratic society. In such a school pupils and students may participate actively in the life of the school, molding it to their needs and aspirations and adjusting themselves to it.

1. Do children need special training in cooperation?

2. What are some of the activities of a school that afford training in cooperation?

FOUR. *To develop the ability to use the most effective and reliable methods in searching for truth as a basis for the discovery and solution of problems.*

In a democracy, new generations should be prepared to discover new truths and to revise their practices accordingly. The training proposed in this goal will furnish necessary preparation for the cooperative discovery and solution of the problems created by the complexity and interdependence of our social, political, and economic relationships. It will also increase the power of citizens to cooperate successfully in creating the best conditions of living for all.

1. Is it better to emphasize that the social world grows, changes, and improves, rather than to teach that " whatever is, is right " in the community or state?

2. Is it possible to have classroom activities that will enable children to discover truths for themselves?

FIVE. *To develop the effective use of the fundamental knowledge and skills required by all.*

This goal demands effective training in the arts of reading, writing, spelling, language, and arithmetic. Such arts are essential tools of common understanding and communication.

1. Why do some people believe it would be sufficient to make this goal the sole purpose of the elementary school?

2. How thorough a mastery of these fundamental skills should be required of all pupils?

SIX. *To insure an abundant social and individual life in accordance with each individual's capacity and ambition.*

This goal involves provision for proper and adequate training in problems of health, in desirable home membership, and in the worthy and constructive use of leisure time. It also calls for the general and specific vocational training required for economic sufficiency.

1. How much vocational training should be provided in the elementary school? In the junior high school? In the senior high school?

2. Is it likely to be too costly to provide health training for all?

SEVEN. *To provide training in the specialized and professional services which are requisite for society.*

Society must have the services of persons specially equipped in the preservation and further development of the knowledge, skills, and techniques vital to the advancement of society as a whole. This goal recognizes that the valuable and useful accumulation described as " the social inheritance " must be preserved and transmitted from generation to generation. Through research and experimentation this inheritance should be increased.

1. How valuable to American civilization are specialized services such as those of the physician, the engineer, the metallurgist, and the scientist?

2. How many persons should be trained for specialized services and how should these persons be selected for such training?

EIGHT. *To provide for the enrichment of adult life.*

This goal is receiving attention because our increased leisure demands provision for continued education for adults, and the changing social and economic conditions require the provision for retraining for both the vocational and the avocational aspects of life.

1. Is it proper to use public funds for this purpose?

2. How would emphasis on this goal tend to decrease crime and unhappiness?

3. Should society re-educate the workers thrown out of employment because of technological changes?

NINE. *To plan for the continuous appraisal and readjustment of the educational program to fit changing conditions.*

When scientific discoveries and inventions force us to set aside old ways of living, the schools should provide new activities which give definite practice in making adjustments to new situations in order that society may be modified through the process of orderly change rather than through revolution. This goal is important in a democracy because social and economic conditions change and education must also change accordingly in order to make its contribution at each stage of social progress.

1. Are you convinced that democratic educational training decreases the danger of costly revolutions or dictatorships?

2. Since your experience in school, has the school changed as much as the social and economic conditions have?

CHAPTER VII

SCOPE OF THE CURRICULUM

98. Subject Organization of the Curriculum Inadequate [1]

James Harvey Robinson

THERE is a still more fundamental obstacle than those already mentioned which interferes with the proper interplay between the so-called natural and social sciences. Each of these grand divisions of human knowledge, which belong so intimately together, dealing as they do with man and his world, are artificially separated by old boundary lines, defended against invaders by jealous vested interests.

At present vital knowledge is broken up into fragments; shuffled into large piles labelled history, philosophy, psychology, philology, anthropology, ethics, politics, economics, astronomy, physics, chemistry, biology, geology, geography, botany. And each of these is divided into smaller piles — stellar physics, bio-chemistry, embryology, thermo-dynamics, optical mineralogy, prehistoric archaeology, epistemology, Latin epigraphy. But even these are too cumbersome and distracting and miscellaneous for the real specialist, who finds his life work in classifying the white corpuscles of the human body, in the oscillations of the electrons, or German hymnology before Luther.

These departments of knowledge, great and small, correspond to a necessary division of labor, and have, of course, a great significance in *research*, but they form one of the most effective barriers to the cultivation of a really scientific frame of mind in the young and the public at large. In the enterprise of humanizing knowledge it is necessary first to recognize that specialization, so essential in research, is putting us on the wrong track in education. This has been suspected for some time; nevertheless a recent and carefully considered scheme of educational reform proposes that we continue to classify our instruction under social sciences, natural sciences and language.

Representatives of these branches were summoned to testify as to the significance and setting that should be assigned to their particular sciences in a new attempt " to enable our youth to realize what it

[1] From *The Humanizing of Knowledge*, by J. H. Robinson, copyright 1923, 1926 by Doubleday Doran & Company, Inc., pp. 62–64, 66–68.

means to live in society, to appreciate how people have lived and do live together, and to understand the conditions essential to living together well; to the end that our youth may develop such abilities, inclinations and ideals as may qualify them to take an intelligent and effective part in an evolving society." * This is surely the great aim of modern education, excellently expressed; but I wonder why we should think of history, economics, politics and geography as distinctively social sciences; language is pretty social too; and why is geography more social than chemistry or physics or botany? The importance of all of them lies in their relation to ourselves and our fellow men. . . .

Is not our habit of transplanting into our educational plans the technical divisions of scientific research chiefly responsible for our many disappointments? For our scientific courses in school and college rarely produce either of the important effects that they should. They neither engender in the student a discriminating and exacting tendency of mind — that combination of open-mindedness and caution which should be the finest fruit of successful scientific training; nor do they foster such a lively understanding of the workings of nature that the fascination of discovering ever new wonders will endure through life and mitigate sorrow, boredom and disappointment. Of course, judged by this standard, the failure of education is no less conspicuous in the fields of literature, history, language and philosophy.

Our problem has apparently two phases. One, how is human knowledge to be so ordered and presented in school and college as to produce permanent effects and an attitude of mind appropriate to our time and its perplexities? the other, how is knowledge to be popularized and spread abroad among adults who have become dissatisfied with what they know and are eager to learn more? Since, however, there is no great difference in the ways in which the overwhelming majority of young and old really learn, these two phases need not be discussed separately. Both the text books and manuals used in formal teaching and the various popular presentations of scientific facts written for adults tend, almost without exception, to classify knowledge under generally accepted headings. They have a specious logic and orderliness which appeals to the academic mind. They, therefore, suit the teachers fairly well, but unhappily do not inspire the learners.

When one has " gone through " a text book and safely " passed " it, he rarely has any further use for it. This is not because he has

---

* Preliminary report of the Joint Commission on the " Purpose of Social Studies in Our Schools." This committee represented several associations devoted to the various social sciences.

really absorbed it and so need not refer to it again. On the contrary, it is associated with a process alien to his deeper and more permanent interests. And it is usually found by those who embark in adult education that text books make almost no appeal to grown-ups, who are free to express their distaste for them.

Teaching is one thing, learning, as we are slowly coming to see, quite another. Teaching aims to be logical; learning is strangely illogical, or rather, has its own logic and its own effective methods which have hitherto been almost completely disregarded.

Let anyone review what he has learned in life. We will find that his effective and living knowledge has come in the most informal and seemingly casual manner. It has crystallized about unexpected nuclei. Chance happenings have aroused interest, and interest has bred curiosity, and curiosity has begotten learning. Most of what passes for learning is a kind of pitiful affectation. The student says, " I have had " Latin or chemistry, or " I took " science or literature. All is safely in the past or the perfect tense, as if it were an attack of pleurisy or a boil.

The " principles " or " elements " of a branch of science are really the ultimate outcome of a knowledge of it, not the thin edge of the wedge which insinuates it into our minds.

99. IN DEFENSE OF A SUBJECT CURRICULUM [2]

It is natural for curriculum makers to want something new. Hence we hear a great deal, from workers in this field, of an activity curriculum, a project curriculum, or a large-unit curriculum. The above terms are practically synonymous, though there may be a difference in emphasis, the first emphasizing physical activity, the second the pupil's purpose, and the third the size of the teaching unit — especially the correlation and integration of all the elements involved. The " project " devotees would say the pupil's purpose determines the size of the activity and brings about correlation and integration, and the " activity " people would have no quarrel with either, so long as there was evidence of enough pupil activity. The advocates of each of these points of view toward the curriculum oppose the subject curriculum.

Let us see how what they have to substitute works out. There has for several years been great activity in working out curriculum " units." These constitute particular topics, activities, problems, projects. They all relate to " experience " and " life " in some way. However, each is worked out originally, independently, and individually. The elements within the " unit " are all related to each other and to the pupil, but the various units are not related to each other. Hundreds of these " units " have been worked out. It would seem perhaps thousands would have to be worked out before the elementary school curriculum would be complete. When this is all done, we are offered thousands of individual " units " of work as a substitute for the subject curriculum. It is quite evident that this great mass of unsatisfactorily related " units " would be unacceptable as a curriculum.

What is a " subject " as far as the curriculum is concerned? It is merely one phase or division of " phenomena," " life," or " experience," set apart for systematized investigation and study. Man has built up his scientific knowledge by concentrating his attention on one field of knowledge at a time, so that relationships and principles in this limited field could be discovered. So it has been as to physics, chemistry, biology, psychology, sociology, and other sciences. So these sciences were built up. Is it not reasonable to suppose that a student of today could most effectively discover relationships and build up his concepts in the same way? Knowledge, to be useful, must be organized, classified, and systematized. Can this be done apart from the study of the various sciences as such? What are our curriculum experts going to do with all these thousands of " units " which they have built up *psychologically*, but not *logically?* After they have them, they must organize, classify, and systematize if they are to make the knowledge serviceable and satisfying. When they do this, they will establish *subjects* again. They may not establish the same subjects we now have, but they will have subjects just the same. It is clearly evident that a large mass of unrelated " units " will be wholly unacceptable. The Herbartian theory of teaching was a great advance in that the relationships of things in the outside world to one another were systematically and thoroughly developed. What was lacking was that these things were inadequately related to the pupil in a vital way. This was accomplished through the " problem method " as developed by Dewey and McMurry and the " project method " as developed by Kilpatrick. But why abandon all the gains made toward establishing adequate relationships and order among things and events in the outside world, just to establish the child's relationship to individual situations? Let us keep the problem and project concepts and practices in teaching, but let us also keep a systematic organization of knowledge on a subject basis, for effective service in solving the problems of life.

Until a new set of subjects is proposed, and until it is evident that the new subjects possess superiority to the present list, it might be well to hold on to our present list. It may be well to remember, too, that the biggest problem in education is a *teaching* problem, not a *curriculum* problem. Even with the *subject curriculum*, by the introduction of the " project," " problem," " activity," and " large unit " procedures in teaching and learning, within the subjects, together with the introduction of certain correlating and integrating activities in addition to the work in the regular subjects, all essential purposes and ends of the " project," " problem," " activity," and " large unit " theories of teaching can be realized without the necessity of an entirely new curriculum. What we need is reform in teaching procedures rather than a new type of curriculum. We need reform in the use of the textbook, not the elimination of the textbook and the abandonment of the subject curriculum.

Modern teaching, with a subject curriculum, seems to give greatest promise of meeting our needs satisfactorily.

F. M. U.

100. Shall Experience be Organized Under Subject Categories? [3]

The Committee's Summary. If the " investment theory " is sound — and its validity has not been challenged — then the curriculum should show both in form and content a direct, positive, and specific effort to protect and promote the interests of the State and to make it a better place in which to live and make a living. No one claims that conventional subjects came into use as curricular categories with this purpose in mind. The oldest and most representative of the conventional subjects entered the curricula of public secondary schools in America through uncritical acceptance of European educational tradition. The newer and less conventional ones entered largely through demands of the public for a " more practical " education, and, therefore, can lay some claim to being " fundamental " according to the definition above. The reluctance with which these newer offerings have been accepted by the advocates of the traditional curriculum, however, does not augur well for depending upon revising the subject-curriculum as a method of making it harmonize with the demands of the " investment theory."

1. It would, therefore, seem that the best claim that the advocates of conventional subjects can make for them is that a good teacher can *make* them perform many of the functions demanded of the school by the " investment theory." Considering their origin, it

[3] National Education Association, *Issues of Secondary Education, Report of the Committee on the Orientation of Secondary Education,* Department of Secondary School Principals, Vol. 20, No. 59, 5835 Kimbark Ave., Chicago, January, 1936, pp. 275–281.

is too much to expect that conventional subjects will be of great assistance to teachers in achieving the function of the school as proposed by the " investment theory " except by mere chance. The content of these subjects was selected without reference to any such function. Each item was primarily selected because of its importance in and to the subject itself and with reference to its use and value in further study of similar subject-matter. The test was " does it help to cover the subject? " Inspired teaching of these subjects has helped and will, to some extent, help achieve the proposed function of the school, though chiefly through concomitant learnings, but to expect teachers to attain satisfactory results under such conditions is like expecting a tap-dancer to perform in rubber boots. All of this is to say that good teachers get good results of a kind, in some measure, in spite of the organization of the curriculum. A good curriculum organization should assist, not handicap, the teacher in achieving the schools' functions. The " more fundamental " (as defined) the categories are, the more nearly will this be true.

2. If the plan sometimes proposed by advocates of the subject-organized curriculum of gradually bringing the content of the present curriculum as organized more into harmony with the demands of the " investment theory," is followed, the argument of the " more fundamental " category group has been admitted in a sort of " left-handed," indirect manner. By such a process the conventional subjects are made less and less conventional in order that they may become more and more functional. They thus try to conform to the proposed categories. As an *ad interim* practice to be followed during a period of transition from the present form of the curriculum to one using " more fundamental " categories, this proposal might be accepted, but it is a tacit admission of the weakness of conventional subjects as curricular categories. The necessity for a period of adjustment between present curriculum practice and the proposed plan is admitted. This should be long enough to permit teachers to develop power to handle the new type of teaching materials and situations and to permit of other necessary adjustments in equipment, buildings, text materials, etc. Allowing for the gradual introduction of the new program evaporates most of the arguments against it based upon cost and impracticability.

3. The advocates of conventional subjects as curricular categories must seek refuge in the illogical position that the curriculum need bear no fundamental relation (as defined above) to the functions of the school as set up in the " investment theory " and as applied by this Committee to the American secondary school or they must propose and secure approval of another function for the schools in this country and show that conventional subjects are the fundamental

curricular categories when such a function is assumed. Until the proponents of conventional subjects do this, their position is unsound and subject to attack on its social and educational philosophy.

4. Conventional-subject organization of the curriculum is weak because there is no essential and inherent relation between subject-categories and the kinds of growth in youth which the accomplishment of the proposed function of the school requires. Effective and economical efforts to produce these kinds of growth call for categories which bear a relation to what it is proposed to accomplish through the curriculum. Attempts to produce these growths on a subject basis mean that some kinds are not attained at all, while some are sought through two or more subjects at needless duplication of expense. Frequently the natural learning situations of school life are butchered up and divided among the several departments and subjects so each may have at least a little really " live " subject-matter. Therefore, from the viewpoint of sociology, since present subject-categories were not established on the basis of their relationship to the desired kinds of growth they should be abandoned in favor of "more fundamental" categories which more effectively achieve the functions of the school because selected with the promotion of certain desired kinds of growth definitely in mind.

5. Conventional-subject organization of the curriculum is weak psychologically because there is no essential relationship between its content and the life youth is participating in, either directly or vicariously. Experimental psychology, as previously explained, affirms that the best learning situations — leading to most growth — are intrinsically bound up with living. Present subjects are not, therefore, necessarily the best means for promoting desirable growth. Many subjects when originally included in the curriculum did serve such a function, at least in part. The conditions of life which accounted for the inclusion of some of our best examples of conventional subjects in the curriculum have so changed that they no longer serve such a purpose to any respectable degree. Some other subjects now do so to an extensive degree, but in none has or can the full possibility of interrelating living, learning, and growing be as fully realized as it can be when the curricular categories bear an intrinsic relation to the kinds of growth demanded by the approved functions of the school as set out by this Committee.

6. The logical organization of content involved in conventional subjects is not defensible. Even if subjects had been selected with present approved functions in mind, they would still be subject to attack because in a conventional subject the content is usually arranged logically chiefly with reference to facilitating the learning of such subject matter. The chief value of logically organized knowl-

edge is for the use of a learner as a convenient source of reference when and as necessary to the attainment of a desired goal in action or in thought. Used thus, a learner turns aside from his main activity to acquire the needed information just as any other worker pauses momentarily in his work to pick up the tools or materials he next needs. This pictures a vastly different use of logically arranged subject-matter than obtains in conventional subject-courses where " picking up tools and materials " frequently becomes, for most students, an activity without any purpose unless it be to become more expert in picking up similar tools and materials. They pass through what to them are unreasonably difficult mazes of subject-matter toward remote, poorly seen, and often little desired ends for achievement in which they sometimes find the skills acquired in threading the maze to be of little consequence. This logical arrangement of content is inherent in conventional subjects and their adoption as categories requires acceptance of this arrangement of content without the necessity of providing a validating purpose for the learner. If the proponents of conventional subjects deny this, and suggest rearrangement of content of *each* subject into a better order for learning they then propose to accept the psychology of their opponents as it applies to the arrangement of the content of each subject but to reject it as it applies to the arrangement of all the subjects of the curriculum. This is a fatal admission, because if the desirability and necessity of arranging the content of each subject so that it is functional for the learner — that is, useful in and related to his living and growing — is admitted, then it can hardly be denied that the whole curriculum ought to be functionally organized. Such an admission automatically precludes the use of conventional subjects as well as their logical arrangement of content and admits the necessity of " more fundamental " categories. If the need for other categories — more fundamental with reference to the functions of the school — is admitted, then by the same logic the content of each division (subject) under each category should be selected and organized to be maximally functional and the curriculum and all its parts will thus be consistently focused upon the task of achieving the accepted functions of the school.

Conventional-subject advocates, however, commonly accept as their criterion for the selection and arrangement of content the logical and orderly coverage of the subject. This is not necessarily — in fact, is not likely to be — a good order for accomplishing the learnings required by the functions of the school. Actually, the typical content-arrangement of a conventional subject is often a poor order for learning, even if knowledge of subject-matter were accepted as the criterion, because it was instituted before the laws of learning were identified, and never did and does not now represent a sound effort to promote learning. This conventional order and arrangement is, therefore, psychologically weak even if subject-matter learning were accepted as the criterion. It cannot, therefore, be expected to be defensible as the best arrangement of content for the accomplishment of the proposed functions of the school.

In general, then, this Committee holds that the first step toward a curriculum, sound because it promotes rapid and effective learning, is the acceptance of "more fundamental" categories as defined herein. The second step is the organization and selection, for each such category of content, of experiences which are pregnant with the kind of learnings needed to produce the kinds of growth required by the functions of the school.

It is, therefore, the opinion of this Committee, that, if the school curriculum is to become an effective agency for achieving appropriate functions in a school operating under the "investment theory," the conventional-subject organization of the curriculum will have to be abandoned in favor of the categories which are more fundamental to the task imposed upon the school by these functions.

ORGANIZATION OF THE CURRICULUM INVOLVING "MORE FUNDAMENTAL" CATEGORIES

The General Outlines of a Plan. The argument in support of "more fundamental" curricular categories demands the reorganization of both the form and content of the curriculum in harmony with the proposed functions of the secondary school and consistent with present-day psychology. The proposed functions of the secondary school derive from the "Golden Rules" and the "investment theory" of Briggs. Interpreted by this Committee and applied to the sort of social order which it conceives to be desirable in America, these statements require that the schools and all other educative agencies in a society have the double function, first, of developing ability and creating the will in each person so to organize and maintain human relationships that maximum opportunity for growth, development, and well-being can and will be available for all, and second, of creating and developing the ability to use and manage the natural resources of society's physical environment so that they will contribute maximally to the growth, development, and welfare of all. We have shown that effective education in any society is a plan of growth, control, modification, and stimulation along directions approved by that society and that this process results in most growth in power to think, feel, and act when it is sought through a planned program of experiences which appeal to the learner as important to the present and immediate future welfare and well-being of himself and others for whom he is concerned. The problem of the curriculum then becomes one of arranging such experiences as are or can be made meaningful to the learners and which in the experience of the educators in such a society are provocative of maximum amounts of growth in power to think, feel, and act in the life situations which eventuate when this social philosophy begins to act on the physical environment.

This leads to the inevitable conclusion that the curriculum has two major concerns which give rise to two major categories under which its content should be organized. *The first of these should be devoted to society's need for the growth of ability and willingness to sustain and improve the mutually helpful relationships with other human beings which a democratic philosophy of life assumes should characterize group living.* School experiences should, therefore, include a group dealing with this major social need. These should provide for study of, observation of, and practice in sustaining and improving social relationships. This is the first major category under which school experiences must be classified if the schools' function is purposefully and systematically attained. There are many fields of competence under this major head, each representing a kind of growth needed if competence in solving the problems underlying the major social problem represented by this category is to be secured. Ethics, for instance, is involved here, as no plan for human relationships can be set up except in reference to an ethical criterion.

The second major category should include those experiences concerned with supplying society's need for the growth of ability so to manage and utilize the potentialities of our natural physical environment that it may make its maximum contribution toward the attainment of the high levels of human living which a democratic society seeks for all. School experiences should include a group dealing with this major need. There should be study, observation, exploration, and experimentation in the use of our physical and biological universe for the promotion of human welfare. Here, also, there are fields of competence, each representing a kind of growth needed if competence in solving the problems underlying the second major category is to be secured.

101. PLACE OF SUBJECTS IN NEWER PRACTICES IN SECONDARY SCHOOLS [4]

Samuel Everett

There is *the issue as to whether, in the new American high school, the curriculum should be reorganized in more functional and mean-*

[4] From *A Challenge to Secondary Education*, D. Appleton-Century Company, New York, 1935, pp. 343–347.

ingful ways or should be confined within departmentalized subjects. On this question there is entire agreement among members of our Committee on Secondary Education of the Society for Curriculum Study. No one is confining his thinking to the specialized-subject curricula now found in the conventional American high school.

This does not mean that many members of the Committee have not made provision in their plans for the highly specialized type of study now contained in such courses as physics, chemistry, European history, economics, American literature, and the like. In a large number of plans such subjects may be elected by students who wish them.

Some students will enjoy and benefit by spending part of their time in this type of study. Undoubtedly in the minds of a number of the authors, provision for such specialized study represents something of a compromise with parental demands and college-entrance requirements. However, as has already been said, no author would confine the curriculum to such conventional practice. All are interested in an integration of subject-matter content and experience which is not possible within specialized subjects. All are concerned with setting up a type of curriculum which will help pupils see the interrelationships of problems clearly enough to deal with them intelligently.

The authors differ widely in the ways and means to be used. They all agree, however, that providing for such a type of experience is absolutely necessary in the new American high school.

In providing for a democratic type of education which shall meet the needs of American youth, the authors of these plans face *the issue as to whether a core curriculum shall be provided for all pupils, or whether the curriculum shall follow the individual interests and needs of children without recourse to a core experience.*

The preponderance of opinion is in favor of providing a core curriculum for all. Those who take this position would provide for individual differences within the common core experience. Teachers would stimulate pupils to work on their own frontiers of experience. In general, this group would provide also for meeting individual differences through various types of electives.

Those authors who rely upon an individual interest approach in building a curriculum, stress the importance of personal counseling in order that each pupil may be guided in such a way as to build up a broad background, and provide the wide variety of experience which is so necessary to achieving the well-rounded individual.

One core curriculum program which is being worked out on a statewide basis represents a challenging departure from the present-day secondary-school curriculum. In the planning of this program certain major functions of social life have been worked out which include: protection and conservation of life, property, and natural resources, production of goods and services and distribution of the returns of production, recreation, expression of esthetic impulses and education. These and other " social functions " coupled with " centers of interest " for each grade level determine the areas and content of both the elementary and high-school curriculum program.

One plan, which provides for a common core curriculum, would in a six-year high-school program require that all pupils go through a common experience in the first four years. In the fifth and sixth years, however, the program is elective but subject to careful adult guidance. The core program includes arts and crafts, language arts, physical activities, science and social-economic studies. Provision is made for the counseling of individual students throughout the program.

One plan outlines in detail certain required orientation courses in the areas of biological science, personal and group guidance, the humanities, physical science, social science and home economics. These courses are given in the 10th or pre-junior college year, and in the 11th and 12th years of the junior college. The last two years of this program are elective under guidance.

Another plan provides a common core curriculum to run throughout a four-year rural high school. This core includes community problems and English, world history and world literature, American history and American literature, and American problems and creative expression. In this program the emphasis throughout is upon meeting present-day needs and stimulating young people to participate in the current community life about them.

One plan quite definitely makes the interest approach but builds a core curriculum based upon it. " We must start from a consideration of the teacher and the pupil," writes this author. " The characteristics of the human material (in the American cultural situation) in terms of interests, needs, capacities and the like, are the bench mark from which we start." The author would construct a core curriculum using this interest approach.

Among the few who make the individual-interest approach, without recourse to a core curriculum, one would have individual pupils study a series of units constructed for this purpose. These units would fall into seventeen distinct areas, such as: keeping physically fit, choosing vocations, maintaining desirable social relations, and exploring leisure-time possibilities. All would deal with some important aspect of modern life; while the choice and sequence of these units for every pupil would be guided carefully through a counselor system.

Another plan would orient young people of high-school age to the life about them, and seek to help each person find his place in this life through making it possible for him to follow his art, science, or business interest, and to approach the study of other subjects and fields through the relation they bear to the all-consuming, developing interest.

102. CURRICULUM PLANNING SHOULD NOT PROVIDE EXACT CHARTS [5]

Hilda Taba

Curriculum thinking should not attempt to provide exact charts for educational experiences, nor give any rigid prescriptions as to the materials to be used in connection with educational activities. Instead it should try to provide principles and materials to think with in a creative manner in dealing with educational practice. The value of curriculum planning does not so much lie in its ability to provide exact maps to be followed, as it does in furnishing those guiding the learning process with a broad and critical outlook, sensitivity to possibilities that lie in each evolving situation, and ability to see the relations that the particular experience has with as many possible general principles and implications involved in every single experience.

Planning conceived of as a mapping out of experiences and particular objectives is conducive to a static education. What is desirable is planning in the sense of developing broad and thorough knowledge as to the way certain experiences foster certain outlooks, as to how certain bodies of facts grouped in a certain way will influence thought and conduct; as to what cues towards better and fuller experience can be found in the situation at hand. An outline of major objectives, major concepts, experiences, is very helpful, but it should not serve as an exact map, and it should not become a substitute for a living curriculum that is based on insight into the workings of the mind and the particular cues as to possibilities of growth that spring from the individual character of each experience.

There is no doubt that many practical difficulties are connected with this programme. In the first place, the whole basis of curriculum thinking has to be shifted from concrete materials and subject matter to the functional principles of thought, organizing concepts, and leading ideas. More emphasis is to be given to the methods of experiencing than to the finished and completed contents

[5] From *Dynamics of Education*, Harcourt Brace and Company, 1932, pp. 249–250.

of experience. The practicability of this programme demands, too, a teacher with a preparation very different from the present training available, as well as greater co-operative thought between educational theory and practice, and continuous vigilance as to possibilities for the reconstruction of the curriculum in the process of its practice.

103. The Curriculum Should Not Be a Preplanned Sequence of Units of Work [6]

Laura Zirbes and Lou LaBrant

The policy of conserving the integrative quality of purposeful experience not only preserves the program from the encroachment of formal subjects and the extrinsic motives with which they must usually be bolstered up; it is also responsible for the more natural sequences and subdivisions of the school day and week into periods for group discussion, planning work, play, lunch, rest, trips, and other types of shared experience.

The acceptance of a fixed curriculum or a preplanned sequence of units of work would obviously contradict the policies herein stated and give priority to specific content and arrangement of subject matter. The assumption that this makes the selection subject to caprice and whim does not recognize the possibilities of other more defensible types of intelligent guidance and control. The further assumption that failure to specify subject matter or to predetermine the sequence of units of work makes for a neglect of significant content may be countered by indicating how prior concern for subject matter inevitably leads to the employment of extrinsic motivation, and devious insincere devices for putting fixed requirements across.

Four years have demonstrated the feasibility of developing content sequences out of the ongoing experiences of each particular group. The fact that similar learning values accrue from any one of several possible units, if guidance is sensitive to leads, does not warrant the conclusion that one unit is as good as another for any given group; nor does it follow that the sequence of activities, developed in the course of experience by one group, may be expected to produce equivalent effects when prescribed and followed by another group. Four years have demonstrated the wisdom of setting the environment and guiding pupils in a way which does not lead inevitably to a given point of departure or to a predetermined course. The preferable

    [6] From " Social Studies in a New School," *Progressive Education,* 11:89–90, January-February, 1934.

procedure is to set the environment to include a variety of challenges, any one of which may lead to responses that reveal common backgrounds and growing margins of experience. The important considerations are continuity and extension of experience through whole-hearted participation.

Guidance operates by providing various outlets for individual initiative, meanwhile developing also some concrete unifying group concern which enlists shared interests and responsibilities; by moving the margins of first-hand experience out from their center on any sector which seems to need extension and gives promise of whole-hearted participation; by using this first-hand group experience as a basis for guided group discussion, so that it clarifies and extends meanings, generates problems and purposes, and sensitizes the group to related purposes and experiences which may add to the intrinsic satisfaction of whole-hearted activity and coöperative endeavor.

Guidance opens up vistas of pertinent information, makes sure that experience is in process of continuous extension, use, reconstruction, and reorganization, so that an increasing awareness of relationships develops insight, while growing ends of experience make for peripheral development.

Instead of setting fixed dates and points of arrival, guidance paces experience with reference to particular groups. It adjusts to the child's maturity and capacity for understanding and effort, with due provision for rest and recreation to avoid the evil effects of failure, strain, and excess fatigue. It cultivates intelligent self-direction and responsible action by letting the child infer suitable action from actual situations, whenever that is possible without undue risk, thus avoiding the use of explicit direction wherever it can, and substituting a more suitable morale for impulse, fixed habits, implicit obedience, personal domination, fear, force, nagging, policing, appeal to authority or tradition, persuasion, bribery, expectation of reward or punishment, permissive indulgence, personal approval, and social pressure.

Guidance cultivates developing standards of thoroughness and workmanship, by relating all effort to purposes which have meaning and immediate significance to the child and the group, instead of fostering an educational régime which not only fails to develop desirable drives but actually cultivates responsiveness to undesirable ones. By exercising continuous constructive concern for the integrity and educative quality of individual and group living day by day, guidance facilitates the gradual emergence of integrated and socially sensitized personalities.

104. " THE PLANLESS-CURRICULUM PANACEA " [7]

William C. Bagley

I turn now to the more radical proposals for educational changes to meet social changes. These involve a complete rejection of adult control of the educative process. The movement just now goes under the name, " activity curriculum," and is sometimes called the " planless curriculum." Until the past two years of the Great Depression, it was sweeping through the country as preceding movements have swept — for American communities like nothing less than to be out of fashion; they must keep up with the educational Joneses at whatever cost.

Back of this movement are several theories and postulates. One I have already referred to as a conviction that there are no eternal verities or values. Another is the conviction, especially upon the part of some of the younger leaders of the left wing of educational theory, most of whom have strong Communistic leanings, that the curricula of the lower schools have been dictated by the capitalistic class to conserve its own interests and prevent the rise of the proletariat. A third is the discovery, made, it seems, by some of the psychiatrists, that anyone who does anything or is made to do anything that he does not want to do at the moment of doing, is in grave danger of disintegrating his personality. In any case, this interesting and most attractive theory has been spreading among the teachers of the younger generation and has given acceleration to the movement under discussion.

These three beliefs I shall discuss briefly.

1. First, consider the notion that there are no eternal verities and the added belief that the future configuration of society cannot be predicted, so why try to prepare for it.

Because new configurations are unpredictable, however, it does not follow that there are no permanent, or at least relatively permanent, elements of culture. It is true that the world of to-day is a different world from the world of 1913 and from the world of 1929; it is even different to-day from what it was yesterday; but this does not mean that everything has changed. Two and two still make four; the square on the hypotenuse is still the sum of the squares on the two other sides of the right-angle triangle; light and radiation still vibrate through interstellar space at the rate of 186,300 miles a second; the winds that blow still follow the laws of storms; *Huckleberry Finn* and

---

[7] From " The Task of Education in a Period of Rapid Social Change," *Educational Administration and Supervision*, 19 :565–568, November, 1933.

Treasure Island still delight youth; and the Sistine Madonna is just as beautiful as of yore.

From the point of view of social welfare and progress, too, there are some virtues that have not lost their value. Frugality and thrift may not be so significant as they once were, but respect for life, respect for law, consideration for the rights and feelings of others, and plain every-day honesty are still important. Though fewer people believe in a literal hell, there are other means of holding passions within leash. Even in the past, many men and women who rejected religious dogmas lived honest, considerate, decent, and respectable lives. Ideals of duty, loyalty, and devotion are usually conditioned by one's early training, and so in the past usually reflected religious dogmas, but they are capable of being aroused by, and enlisted in, causes that have nothing to do with dogmatic religion. The emotive energies that the teachings of Mohammed aroused on a theistic basis were probably no more powerful than the emotive forces that the teachings of a Marx, a Lenin, and a Stalin have aroused on the most radical of atheistic bases; and to many a scientist who has rejected religious dogmas the quest of truth has back of it and through it a devotion and a fervor which are cut psychologically from the same cloth as the devotion and the fervor with which St. Francis of Assisi sought to achieve virtue and eternal life.

2. The notion that capitalists have dictated the curricula of the lower schools in their own selfish interests is as absurd in its way as are the capitalists' fears of the Red Menace. Except for variations due to differences in national cultures, the elementary and secondary curricula are about the same in Democratic England, Fascist Italy, and (since last year) Communistic Russia. . . .

It is significant the theory which now dominates American education, which is exemplified in the schools that are regarded generally as the best and the most up-to-date, and which has increasingly softened the fibre of American education over more than a generation is the theory that has been discarded in Russia after a twelve-year trial, under the most favorable conditions — for the Soviets adopted this theory as thoroughly in harmony with Communistic ideals. It may be consistent still, but the Soviets need results, and the theory does not get them.

3. As to the contention that one must never learn anything unless one has a yearning for learning (lest one should disintegrate one's personality), I am told that reputable psychiatrists do not hold this view but would rather insist that one test of a well-integrated personality is the willingness to do necessary but unpleasant duties willingly and cheerfully. This notion that doing things that one does not want to do disintegrates personality seems to be a misinterpre-

tation (not necessarily insincere) set forth by educational theorists because it supported their doctrines of child freedom.

If it is desirable to prevent the " disintegration of personality " by the means suggested, it will be necessary to subtract from human endowments one of the chief characteristics that differentiate Mankind from the subhuman animal species — namely, the ability to work systematically and steadfastly in the face of immediate impulse or desire. It is precisely because normal human beings can learn to do this that human progress has been and still is possible. Young children must needs follow the impulse of the moment, but the time comes when, with the proper training, they can hold themselves to tasks that are initially distasteful, and then they are on the road to volitional maturity. Of course, there are some persons who never grow up volitionally. There are volitional morons just as there are intellectual morons.

105. CURRICULUM ORGANIZATION NECESSARY [8]

John Dewey

While what has been said may have a tendency to relieve educators in progressive schools from undue anxiety about the criticism that they are unscientific — a criticism levelled from the point of view of theory appropriate to schools of quite a different purpose and procedure — it is not intended to exempt them from responsibility for contributions of an organized, systematic, intellectual quality. The contrary is the case. All new and reforming movements pass through a stage in which what is most evident is a negative phase, one of protest, of deviation, and innovation. It would be surprising indeed if this were not true of the progressive educational movement. For instance, the formality and fixity of traditional schools seemed oppressive, restrictive. Hence in a school which departs from these ideals and methods, freedom is at first most naturally conceived as removal of artificial and benumbing restrictions. Removal, abolition are, however, negative things, so in time it comes to be seen that such freedom is no end in itself, nothing to be satisfied with and to stay by, but marks at most an opportunity to do something of a positive and constructive sort.

Now I wonder whether this earlier and more negative phase of progressive education has not upon the whole run its course, and whether the time has not arrived in which these schools are undertaking a more constructively organized function. One thing is sure:

[8] From " Progressive Education and the Science of Education," *Progressive Education,* 5:200–201, July-August-September, 1928.

in the degree in which they enter upon organized constructive work, they are bound to make definite contributions to building up the theoretical or intellectual side of education. Whether this be called science or philosophy of education, I for one, care little; but if they do not *intellectually* organize their own work, while they may do much in making the lives of the children committed to them more joyous and more vital, they contribute only incidental scraps to the science of education.

The word organization has been freely used. This word suggests the nature of the problem. Organization and administration are words associated together in the traditional scheme, hence organization conveys the idea of something external and set. But reaction from this sort of organization only creates a demand for another sort. Any genuine intellectual organization is flexible and moving, but it does not lack its own internal principles of order and continuity. An experimental school is under the temptation to improvise its subject-matter. It must take advantage of unexpected events and turn to account unexpected questions and interests. Yet if it permits improvisation to dictate its course, the result is a jerky, discontinuous movement which works against the possibility of making any important contribution to educational subject-matter. Incidents are momentary, but the use made of them should not be momentary or short-lived. They are to be brought within the scope of a developing whole of content and purpose, which is a whole because it has continuity and consecutiveness in its parts. There is no single subject-matter which all schools must adopt, but in every school there should be some significant subject-matters undergoing growth and formulation.

106. Pupil Needs Do Not Provide an Adequate Source of Curriculum Orientation [9]

Boyd H. Bode

It is precisely at this point, however, that the progressive movement exhibits its greatest weakness. The deeper implications of the movement get scant consideration. It can scarcely be claimed, for example, that the progressive movement in the past has been inspired by any burning zeal for social reconstruction or reform. On the contrary, it has shown an unmistakable disposition to operate within the limits of the existing social order, in the sense that the area within which the "reconstruction of experience" was to take place was

[9] From "The Next Step in Elementary Education," *Education*, 55:515–517, May, 1935.

sharply limited in advance. Our national habit of identifying democracy with certain political and economic forms was so firmly fixed that the reinterpretation of democracy was hardly a serious problem. This limitation is doubtless in large part responsible for certain serious aberrations of the movement, such as the one-sided and unhealthy absorption in the " interests " and " needs " of individual pupils, the insensitiveness to the importance of sequence in the school program, and the failure to give proper recognition to the significance of " logical organization " in knowledge. To emphasize the need of dealing with the " whole child " is not likely to get us anywhere unless we have a respectable notion of what is meant by " wholeness." If wholeness means in Matthew Arnold's phrase " to see life steadily and see it whole," the admonition to deal with the " whole child " becomes an appeal to direct the process of reconstruction towards those basic points where authoritarianism and " progressivism " came into conflict with one another.

The upshot of all this is that we must have a definite and philosophical point of orientation for the interpretation and exploitation of pupil needs. Without such point of orientation we are likely to engage in random activities and to end in frustration. The term " needs " is a weasel word. Examining a youngster to ascertain his needs is different from examining him, say, for adenoids. Whether, for example, a pupil with a pronounced talent for business needs a commercial course, or a comprehension of the defects of the capitalistic system, or a realizing sense that the love of money is the root of all evil will not be revealed by any educational microscope. Yet this seems to be assumed whenever curriculum making is centered so largely on intensive studies of pupil needs. There is reason to fear that the greatest danger to the progressive education movement at the present time is within its own household. Social extremity is the educator's opportunity; but this opportunity will fade away if the demand for a more adequate educational philosophy is deflected towards a renewed emphasis on pupil needs.

Assuming all this to be granted, however, how are we to proceed? To the casual eye we seem to be confronted with a practical dilemma. Social patterns must not be imposed, yet there is no way of preventing it. A closer examination shows, however, that the situation is not quite so desperate as may appear on the surface. These social patterns which exploit the loyalties of children so ruthlessly do not present a united front. They are divided among themselves. Our social environment is not dominated by any central tendency, but is made up of a welter of tendencies. This is the case in all the important areas of life — in economics, in government, in religion, and in our social institutions generally. This conflict of tendencies confers upon the individual a certain measure of freedom or independence, if he once learns how to capitalize it. A first step in this direction is taken when the discovery is made that the conflicts and contradictions which characterize our modern society reappear in the beliefs and conduct of the average man. The chief danger of imposition lies in the fact that it tends to keep these discrepancies out of sight. The average man tends to be serene and to regard himself as a thoroughly reasonable person, because he is unaware of his intellectual sins. Let education set itself the task of acquainting him with himself and it will come into possession of a far-reaching guiding principle. Incidentally, also, it will discover a new meaning and application for the dictum that education should center on the continuous reconstruction of experience.

Our next consideration is to determine how this general approach which was so sketchily indicated bears on elementary education. It goes without saying that the discrepancies and contradictions in the beliefs of adults are no proper diet for small children. At the outset the interests and activities of children relate chiefly to acquaintanceship with their immediate physical and social environment. This immediate environment is progressively brought into relation with things that are remote in space and time. As we go afield in this fashion, there must be increasing reliance on some principle of selection, in order to prevent our excursions from degenerating into irresponsible joyrides. It is the teacher's job to develop a background of experience and understanding for the emergence, at higher levels, of those problems and issues with which the educated person of today must come to terms, if he is to be oriented in his world. For example, does morality have its roots in expediency, or is it something more? If this question is present in the mind of the teacher, special attention will be given to the variations in the standards and values that are cherished by different communities under varying conditions. Is economic organization subject to revision, and, if so, for what ends? Here again there is a wealth of material that falls well within the competency of pupils in the elementary grades. What are some of the distinguishing traits of scientific method and how has this method operated to displace earlier beliefs? Once more we find an abundance of suitable material at our disposal. Problems of this character can give a purposiveness and definiteness to the work of the elementary school which it does not usually have at the present time. Such problems serve not only to give continuity and direction, but they will tend to emerge in various forms as problems to the pupil and thus provide a basis for the unification or integration of his experiences.

One further comment may be added. The lack of a guiding philosophy has frequently resulted in protests against " subjects." In education as in politics we are disposed to look for a scape goat. Let us grant that the mechanical teaching of subjects is indefensible. This concession is by no means identical with the notion that subjects are responsible for every form of educational evil. Or, to put it differently, a school program does not automatically acquire vitality and purposiveness if subjects are abolished. A more sensible view, it seems, would be that subjects should be introduced whenever the pupils are ready to give more special and intensive consideration to certain aspects of their experience. There is an appropriate time for dealing directly with the special relationships which we designate as mathematics. The same may be said of other rubrics, such as language, geography, history and science. In a properly organized educational system there will be a progressive differentiation into subjects, in somewhat the same way that teeth, a bass voice, and whiskers make their successive appearances in the development of a physical organism. This insistence does not mean that subjects may be introduced at random, or that subjects, may be taught in isolation from a guiding educational philosophy. There is a lot of middle ground between the traditional teaching of subjects and the indiscriminate phobia against subjects with which we are afflicted at the present time.

In conclusion, the next step in elementary education lies in a more adequate recognition of the far-reaching implications which are contained in the doctrine that education means the continuous reconstruction of experience; it means that education must acquire a deeper sense of the need of interpretation in the intellectual and spiritual life of individual pupils. A more adequate sensitiveness to this responsibility in elementary education will have a direct bearing on the selection of subject matter, on the progressive differentiation of the curriculum into subjects, and on the transformation of our entire educational system into an instrumentality for social progress.

107. Ways of Making Education Realistic [10]

Bruce Raup

First, there is the emphasis upon putting felt needs and self-initiated problems at the heart of the educational program. This has been, certainly, an indispensable step toward making education more realistic for the pupil. It recognizes that things will be real to him only as he senses them in relation to his own purposes, and

[10] From " ' Realistic ' Education," *Progressive Education*, 11:40–43, January-February, 1934.

that his education will result from meeting and solving his own problems. This conception of education, however, does not seem adequate. The vital problems which the pupil meets and formulates get their character largely from the community of which he is a part. But the modern community is usually divided within itself, and our several communities are often different from each other. Consequently the way into the future is confused. Shall we then just trust to the growing intelligence of the young to find the problems of most worth? Is this abstract " faith in intelligence " the only resource we have? Is there no other basis of selection — nothing more concrete? The persistent reply to these questions is that there *must* be something more concrete and more definitely unifying, and that attention must be directed to generating this more nearly common basis of selecting among all the varied possibilities of the modern social order. There is a belief that something must be said and done regarding *what* problems are initiated, *what* conclusions are reached by the young, and *what* they regard important. Pursuing this belief, some educators have either held on to or have retreated to the traditional ways and the traditional subjects. Others, not willing to do this, are still reaching out for the answer to the question. For these educators, there is still something important to be sought for, lacking which the problem-theory of education is not entirely realistic. Indeed, they proclaim that it is far from realistic. They press us with the questions: What problems? What conclusions? What attitudes, in the concrete? These demands are louder today than they have been at any time within the progressive movement.

A second proposed road to realistic education has been the policy of encouraging almost complete *laissez faire* individual self-expression. Who today will wish to question the importance of the regard for individual personality out of which this emphasis sprang? This regard has been near the heart of the whole progressive movement. The gains for richness in living which have come through it we cannot afford to lose.

Why, then, is there the strenuous resistance to this particular proposal for realistic education? Evidently to many people there is something important which the " self-expression " education seems to neglect and consequently to them it falls far short of being real education. What, they insist, is to become of standards of decency and social consideration? What has become of the values of " discipline "? What of the virtues of order? How provide the stalwart defense of the common good in the race heritage? What meaning, at all, has character? Life is not merely an arena for self-expression, and education which is so oriented is not realistic.

Here again, there is a cry for some more enduring body, for some greater definiteness, in the educational program. It comes from conservatives and from radicals. The former would go back to the old, the tried, and true; the latter are attempting to see the *what* of education as a formulation looking to a new future. Clearly we are not together on what we consider important. If education is to be, in any commonly accepted sense, realistic, this confusion about what is important becomes a primary problem.

A third way for getting away from unrealistic education has been proposed and promoted by those who believe that education must have a definitely selected subject-matter. The most effective among these educators are the ones who have emphasized faithful description of the actual society in which the young live and grow up. On the one hand, this emphasis reaches into history to show the genesis, the roots, the background and the trends of the culture in which we move. On the other hand, it focuses upon the potentialities of this social order as we look into the future. Books and pamphlets, outlines and courses of study, for young and mature, are issuing forth in admirable rate and quality. The foundation belief in this movement is that the young and the elders must have a realizing sense and an accurate knowledge of the forces at work in the society of which they today are a part.

Contrasted with the academic histories and social studies wherein are stressed not this society but society in remote abstractions, this movement is indeed realistic. But why then the resistance to it which comes from both conservatives and radicals? The answer is clear. For the former, the movement is too disturbing of traditional forms, too ambitious, too "impudent." For the latter, it is too much a continuation of the traditional, abstract study *about* this society, rather than corrective operation *within* this society. To these it seems to be just another subject-matter.

What is to save this most commendable movement from becoming academic, or "just another subject-matter?" The objectors to it, whom we have just cited, gave the clue to the answer. Why do they object? Fundamentally it is because they disagree with the social philosophy which underlies the movement. No one can describe this society or any other without revealing his own preferences, his own standards of selection, his own points of view. It is to these that there is resistance. What these authors regard as important, others disagree with. What they criticize, others praise and wish to retain. What they would change, others, with interest intrenched, insist upon preserving.

Plainly, we miss the basic problem here when we see the issue as concerned only with whether or not the new descriptions of society are just a new subject-matter. Subject-matter of some kind there will always be. The important problem concerns the points of view, the social philosophy, and the social vision, according to which the subject-matter is given form and emphasis.

Who then shall decide which is the realistic education? No one can decide this for the others. Each may propose and his proposition may be accepted or rejected. Sooner or later one or the other emphasis or some combination of them wins out. And then there may be agreement on what is real education because there is some consensus of view on what is desirable to have by way of a social order.

Fourth among the ways for making education realistic is the emphasis upon creative art. Closely related to the movement in the interest of self-expression, this has been one of the leading themes of progressive education. There does seem to be in it something of almost universal appeal. People of every nation have arisen to greet it as tidings of a new way of life. But why, then, the resistance to it? Why has it not been more completely accepted?

There are several conditions which seem to resist it, but the one of concern to us here is the reluctance of many to admit a separation between the " practical " things of life and creative artistic expression. They insist first, that art, though perhaps at times legitimately an escape, is a danger if allowed to become a *drug* against the ills which lie deep in the order of our society; second, that there may be artistic living in the basic processes of the world's work, and that we must not yield to a system which tends to reduce man's participation to mere drudgery and routine.

In brief, the conflict over the central place of creative art in the educational program is due, in no small degree, to differences with regard to what should be done with basic conditions of living in this present order of society. Art and artistic living must have their roots in basic conditions of the social and physical life process. Art is not to be merely an adornment, but a creative and appreciative character which may attend the control and expansion of any or all of life's relationships. The place of art in making education and life realistic depends then on the type of accord which is reached on just such basic matters.

There is much to convince us that creative, artistic activity *is* at the heart of humanity's most preferred experiences, and thus central in realistic education. But these preferred experiences, cannot be dissociated from the physical and social conditions in which they emerge. We are right back, therefore, to the dependence of realistic education upon what we regard important among the potentialities of this society.

108. CURRICULUM SHOULD BE PLANNED AROUND SIGNIFICANT PHASES OF SOCIAL LIFE [11]

Glenn Frank

To me it is incredible that, in a world of tragically unfilled human need, we should now set out upon the Quixotic attempt to increase welfare by destroying wealth or declining to create it. Our ancestors fought valiantly over the centuries to conquer famine. Are we now to say that their conquest has been too decisive? After the sweat and science of generations have brought us out of an economy of scarcity into an economy of plenty, are we to confess that we are incapable of managing plenty, and deliberately legislate a modified famine? I think history will pass a bitter judgment upon us if, in the midst of such manifest need, we take this road in dealing with the difficulties now confronting our farms and our factories.

Two things must, I think, be done in our schools and research establishments to help prevent our taking this suicide's road.

First, from one end of our school system to the other, we must rebuild our curricula around a spinal column of political, social, and economic studies which reduce to utter simplicity and intelligibility the plain principles of organization and operation that must govern the work of an age of science and technology if its magnificent mechanism for producing abundance is to serve instead of sink us. These studies must be organized, not in terms of traditional academic objectives, but for the avowed social purpose of training a generation of citizens to play a productive role in the creation, comprehension, and control of a workable social and economic order in an age of plenty.

109. USE OF THEMES IN CURRICULUM PLANNING [12]

Neal Billings

If the curriculum-maker recognizes certain central themes, he can guide the selection of the materials of his social studies course by the contribution which these materials make to an understanding of these themes which he desires to utilize. If he does this, his course will possess a unity and coherence not otherwise attainable. As

---

[11] " Learning to Live With Plenty " from an address to a conference of leaders in science and industry called together by Alfred P. Sloan, Jr., President of the General Motors Corporation at the Century of Progress Exposition, Chicago, May 25, 1934.

[12] From *A Determination of Generalizations Basic to the Social Studies Curriculum,* Warwick and York, Baltimore, 1929, pp. 213–214.

an example, the "problem of taxation" and the "extension of the suffrage" are themes an understanding of which help to explain a wide range of contemporary civilization. They are applicable to all excepting the so-called "backward" countries. Contemporary world affairs can not be thoroughly understood without a comprehension of such other themes as the "influence of geographic environment on human activities," the "rise and spread of industrialism," the "urbanization of modern life," the "growing emancipation of women," etc. Many other themes of great current importance amount to brief and incisive phrasings of central problems of national and world-wide concern as the "prevention of war," "prevention of overpopulation," "provision of proper education," "establishment of the best form of government," "determination of the most desirable organization of industry (economic life)," "development of a sound culture," etc.

Central themes, therefore, serve as summarizing strands around which can be woven the data of the social studies; the data explain the themes, the themes give meaning to the data. As summarizing strands, they designate the salient points which should be carefully considered both by those who wish to be known as fully educated and by those preparing curricula to provide a complete education.

110. Functional Phases of Social Life as a Basis for Curriculum Planning [13]

Hollis L. Caswell

It appears that the building of an educational program which may reasonably be expected to contribute significantly to development of social understanding will require procedures fundamentally different from those that have been employed in developing the current program. The procedure of compromise upon which the existing program is based — compromises with the demands of logically organized subject matter, compromises between the various subjects, and compromises with traditions — must be cast aside. In place of the patchwork which has resulted from these compromises, a major controlling plan must be set up in which the scope of the curriculum will be defined with consistency and in which due consideration will be given to the demands of society upon the school for developing understanding of the various phases of group life. This comprehensive plan should look to social life for its major points of reference and emphasis. It should provide for the organization of

[13] From "Developing Social Understanding in the Elementary School," *The Elementary School Journal*, 36:341–343, January, 1936.

the curriculum around phases of social life that are functional in nature. Opportunity should be provided through the plan of organization for the child to be introduced to all the important areas of activity in real life and for his gradual induction, starting in the elementary school and continuing through the secondary school, into participation in these activities.

What procedure will accomplish such a fundamental social orientation of the educational program presents one of the challenging problems of curriculum development. It is possible that the approach of the cultural anthropologist to study of social life may be suggestive. The need in such studies is to avoid a piecemeal attack which overlooks the wholeness of a given culture and the intricate interrelations of its many aspects. At the same time, it is necessary to reduce such studies to a basis that will provide for an orderly procedure which guarantees that all aspects of a culture are considered and which permits objective treatment. This need for dealing with social life as a functioning concern and, at the same time, providing an orderly plan of attack which encourages thoroughness and objectivity is essentially the same problem faced by the curriculum worker in endeavoring to give the curriculum a fundamental social orientation. The approach of the cultural anthropologist is suggested by the following statement from *Middletown*.

There are, after all, despite infinite variations in detail, not so many major kinds of things that people do. Whether in an Arunta village in Central Australia or in our own seemingly intricate institutional life of corporations, dividends, coming-out parties, prayer meetings, Freshmen, and Congress, human behavior appears to consist in variation upon a few major lines of activity: getting the material necessities for food, clothing, shelter; mating; initiating the young into the group habits of thought and behavior; and so on.*

These " major lines of activity " may be looked on as functional phases of social life.

This point of view suggests that a direct analysis of group life might indicate certain functional phases of such permanence as to warrant their use as a basis of curriculum orientation. Study of group life shows that there are certain major centers about which the activities of individuals and the plans and problems of the group tend to cluster. These centers tend to persist and to be common for all organized groups. For example, certain of the activities of primitive tribes tend to center in protection of the lives and the property of the group. In civilized group life protection of life and property is also an important function, about which many activities cluster and

* Robert S. Lynd and Helen Merrell Lynd, *Middletown*, pp. 3–4. New York: Harcourt, Brace and Co., 1929.

from which a group of related problems and issues arise. Since these centers or functional phases of social life represent points about which real life-activities tend to gather and organize, it seems reasonable that a curriculum which is concerned with preparing children to participate effectively in the activities of social life should use these functional phases of social life as points for emphasis and orientation in outlining the curriculum. As the individual develops an understanding of the efforts to discharge these functions in the past, an appreciation of the problems of the present, and ability to anticipate somewhat the problems of the future, and as he actually participates in the discharge of the functions in the present, he will develop that social understanding which makes him an effective member of the social group, participating satisfactorily in the many activities required of him. In this way the program of the school does not stop at merely providing contact and acquaintance with phases of culture, as is the prevalent procedure at the present time. Rather, emphasis is placed on the relations of knowledge, facts, and principles to social situations in which they are continuously used.

A plan of organization of this type would provide a spinal column of such social, political, and economic significance as to vitalize the entire curriculum and to make the whole school program contribute ultimately to development of effective social understanding and to participation in the activities of social life. Organization of the curriculum would not be required in terms of the past or the present or the future alone, but that vital element, a functional phase of social life, would be employed which ties the three together in meaningful relationships.

Attack on the problem from some such approach as that outlined will eliminate artificial distinctions between the elementary and the secondary school and will provide a common center of reference about which the curriculum throughout the common-school period may be projected. In this way the development of an educational program that makes adequate provision for developing understanding of social life may, at the same time, further the development of a unified program of general education that gives due regard to the continuous nature of the child's experience and growth.

111. Activity Analysis as a Means of Defining Scope [14]

W. W. Charters

But though in all the educational classics, the writers have begun with the statement of aim, none has been able logically to derive an

[14] From " Educational Aims, Ideals, and Activities," *Journal of Educational Research,* 3:322–325, May, 1921.

adequate curriculum from his aim. In every case there has been a mental leap from the aim to the subject matter, with no adequate principles to guide in the selection of material. This may seem to be a sweeping statement but a few illustrations will demonstrate its accuracy. In Plato's *Republic*, the author states his aim as follows: " Then in our judgment the man whose natural gifts promise to make him a perfect guardian of the state will be philosophical, high-spirited, swift-footed, and strong." Proceeding he says, " This then will be the original character of our guardians. But in what way shall we rear and educate them? " And answers his query as follows: " What then is the education to be? Perhaps we could hardly find a better than that which the experience of the past has already discovered, which consists, I believe, in gymnastics for the body, and music for the mind." He then proceeds to analyze gymnastics and music and argues for the inclusion of narratives, fables, and poetry in his course in music, which present certain proper ideals in the proper form, and of the proper types of melodies and songs. In his course in gymnastics he mentions little of the content but devotes his attention to the ideals of temperance, hardness, and health of body.

But this line of reasoning leaves much to be settled. Can the philosophical disposition be best trained through music? What parts of censored literature are to be selected? What gymnastic exercises are to be included in the curriculum? When the warrior has exercised in the gymnasium is he adequately trained for war or does he need some additional curriculum not mentioned by Plato?

This curriculum is not an adequate system of instruction for warriors. Within the last few years we have seen " a million men spring to arms," " high-spirited and strong," but they were not soldiers. Before they became the perfect guardians of the state their curriculum came to include much besides fables and poetry, melodies and songs. They had to learn to march, to shoot, to thrust with the bayonet, to fight in aeroplanes, and to sail the seas. Nor for the warriors of ancient Athens, who needed much specific training in the field and camp before they could perform the acts of protection or aggression mentioned incidentally in the arguments of the *Republic*, was Plato's curriculum adequate.

The aims and curriculums of Comenius present the same insufficiency. This great educator assumes the aims of education to be to bring to maturity the seeds of learning, virtue, and piety implanted within us by nature. He then outlines his course for the vernacular school as follows (after Quick): " In this school the children should learn — first, to read and write the mother-tongue *well*, both with writing and printing letters; second, to compose grammatically; third, to cipher; fourth, to measure and weigh; fifth, to sing, at first popular airs, then from music; sixth, to say by heart sacred psalms and hymns; seventh, catechism, Bible history, and texts; eighth, moral rules with examples; ninth, economics and politics, as far as they could be understood; tenth, general history of the world; eleventh, figure of the earth and motion of the stars, etc., physics and geography, especially of native land; twelfth, general knowledge of arts and handicrafts."

Comenius sets up a threefold aim — learning, virtue, and piety. If we consider learning first, and ask whether it is possible to learn everything, the answer must be negative. Even though the Orbis Pictus was supposed to be a compendium of all knowledge, the compiler selected a few facts from the total mass. But when we ask for the basis of selection of facts no answer can be given. So far as the aim of learning is concerned with the selection it provides no criterion. Learning is learning and one fact is as good as another. If, however, we say that virtue and piety are the subsidiary aims which determine what facts should be learned we are still without a basis of selection. Will ciphering, or singing, or economics assist in any peculiarly valuable way to promote these two ends? Or, to carry the question further, what details of ciphering or economics will be most valuable in promoting virtue and piety? None, since one is as virtuous as another. Obviously, subject matter cannot be derived from learning of virtue and piety.

The impossibility of deriving subject matter from these aims is due to the fact that they are ideals isolated from activities. A virtuous carpenter does not perform the same actions, nor meet the same problems as a virtuous cook. A pious blacksmith receives a different education from that of a pious doctor. A virtuous and pious Chinaman thinks and acts on different matters from those which engage the attention of a virtuous and pious American. The ideals are the same; the lives are widely different. It would be futile to teach a Chinaman the same curriculum as an American unless the intention were to Americanize him.

The curriculum is derived from both ideals and activities. Virtue, swift-footedness, piety, or social efficiency must be set up in a system of education; but in order to select the material to which these shall apply it is absolutely essential for the teacher to know the activities, problems, thoughts, or needs in connection with which these ideals are to operate.

Plato had a golden opportunity to set a new style in curriculum construction when he posited the perfect warrior as his ideal. If, instead of resting content with an enumeration of his qualities, he had analyzed the duties of the soldier, made what we call a job analysis, and had decided to teach swift-footedness, strength, high spirit, and the philosophic mind *through* these activities, he would have most profoundly influenced the education of two thousand years. But when he had stated his aim, he slipped back into the rut of the traditional subjects of his day as the best means of developing his aims. If, in like manner, Comenius had inquired into the activities of the French or English citizenry, had found out the important daily problems they had to meet and then had sought to make them virtuous and pious in their performance of these, he would have had a curriculum of demonstrable validity. He would then have known what ciphering, or economics, or political science, what music, sacred songs, and Biblical passages to learn. In other words, he would have been able to determine not only what subjects but what parts of subjects to include in his curriculum.

Ideals are both goals and standards. As goals, good taste, virtue, health, eloquence, and completeness of life are expressions of valuable ends for which men reach and whose attainment spells satisfaction. Discover the ideals of a nation and the trend of its action is known. As standards, ideals are arbiters of actions. One action may be discarded because it does not promote the ideals, while another may be accepted or modified because its performance leads toward the goals. But no man who sets ideals as goals is able to build his life in a vacuum and order his actions to suit his plans. He is born into a social group in situations over which he has no original control. He is confronted by the actions of other men actuated by different ideals. Thrown into one situation he develops a set of actions different from those he would have had in another. With both his situation and his ideals in mind he is compelled to perform actions whose character is determined by both the ideals and the situation. Instead of possessing ideals and inventing a situation which will further them, it is more nearly accurate to say that he starts with situations and modifies them so as to realize his ideals as fully as circumstances will permit.

For this reason the curriculum by which he is trained to perform the important activities of the group in accordance with the highest ideals is necessarily based upon both activities and ideals. And obviously any aim of education expressed only in terms of ideals must fail to function.

Today the same procedure is necessary if the curriculum is to be modified intelligently. We suffer from the failure to distinguish between ideals and activities in the current aim of social efficiency. On some occasions we think of it as social efficiency, as an ideal in the sense that ideals of social service are advocated. But on other occasions we think of the activities carried on by those who are socially efficient, such activities as voting, beautification of the city, and the observance of community health regulations. And the result has been that only spasmodically and incompletely have we been able to modify the curriculum. What should be done by those who advocate social efficiency as the aim of education is to determine, first, the ideals of socially efficient individuals; second, the fundamental physical and mental activities carried on by people in the United States; and third, by a process of laborious analysis to discover exactly what important specific activities shall be taught and what ideals shall control in the performance of each. Until the objectives of education are broken up into these two elements it will be impossible to make an adequate reorganization.

112. Curriculum Planning Based on Social Trends [15]

Charles H. Judd

By way of christening this child of my enthusiasm, I shall call my theory the theory of a scientifically constructed curriculum based on the study of social trends. You will recognize at once that I am impressed, I think not unduly, by the importance of the recent publication entitled *Recent Social Trends in the United States.** When the social sciences severally and collectively turn their searchlights on American life and ask what has been happening in recent years to make that life distinctive and significant, the student of education must realize that his task of charting the future of education has been greatly facilitated. After all, the future will certainly be greatly influenced by the trends which characterize the immediate past. Society may undergo radical reforms, but even radical reforms must start from somewhere, and that somewhere is determined in its character by the course which society has been following in past years.

The theory that the curriculum should be based on the study of social trends does not limit its consideration to the recent trends in the United States; it goes back through the long centuries and asks what has made man the distinguished member of the animal kingdom that he is. If one can discover by a study of civilization whither man has been tending, one can determine what to offer the younger generation in the way of training for the future, for the future must

[15] From " The Curriculum in View of the Demands on the Schools," *School Review*, 42:20–25, January, 1934.

* *Recent Social Trends in the United States*. Report of the President's Research Committee on Social Trends. New York: McGraw-Hill Book Co., Inc., 1933.

be in an important sense the projection onward of established social trends.

Let us consider certain illustrations. There was a time when men's thinking was not precise nor comprehensive of great quantities. Then men began to count. Long ages passed, and men invented one system of numerals after another until finally the Arabic numerals supplied an almost perfect device for precise and unlimited quantitative thinking. Since the arrival in Europe of the Arabic numerals, precision has penetrated every domain of Occidental life and thought. To the student of social trends it is unthinkable that instruction in number should be omitted from the school curriculum.

A second trend which has made itself increasingly manifest in all civilized countries is the trend toward the broadening of individual experience through written records. There is a long history of accumulation of records. Only in modern times have these records been regarded as the property of the common people. In recent centuries, specifically since the Protestant Reformation, books have been put into the hands of all the people, even those of the humblest ranks of society. It would be unthinkable to cut off the common people from access to written and printed records after the social developments of recent centuries.

I can well imagine that some of you are beginning to wonder when the theory which I am expounding will come to grips with the really difficult problems of curriculum construction. I suppose some of you will ask what answer this theory has to the question whether the high-school curriculum shall include algebra, which is certainly a part of the race's technique of dealing with quantitative ideas. Or you will ask whether the written records left by the Greeks and the Romans are to be included in the catalogue of historical documents to which adolescents are to be introduced. Someone will perhaps say that it is easy to prove by any theory that instruction in number and reading must be offered in the schools.

I confess at once that I am not at the moment able to meet all the demands which I should like to see the theory of social trends meet. I am disposed to think, however, that the present inadequacy of the theory is due not to fatal inherent weakness but to the fact that the techniques required for its full application have not been completely matured. I shall attempt to carry the analysis somewhat further than it was carried in the foregoing references to number and reading, but I do not promise that I shall be able at once to satisfy all the legitimate demands which are to be made on a valid theory of curriculum construction.

I note several trends in human society which seem to me very significant for education. There is certainly a trend in the direction of greater equality among men. The days of slavery and of aristocratic domination of society are not altogether past if one takes into account the whole world, but there can be no denying that, in the main, equality among men is much nearer attainment in the society of today than it ever was before. Equality of opportunity means access to the higher ranges of knowledge for an ever increasing number of people. Equality of opportunity means also that the dictates of government will have to be generally and voluntarily accepted. It is not possible any longer for any government to deal ruthlessly and arbitrarily with human rights. Even a dictatorship in these modern times must prove itself beneficial for the life of the people or it cannot survive.

It seems to me clear that this trend toward equality dictates that a very large share of the energy of the school shall be devoted to cultivating an understanding of governmental and other social institutions. Men who are equal in opportunity need not all follow the same vocational and avocational routes in life, but they must have an appreciative understanding of one another or the social structure will fall to pieces.

If the implications of what I have said are accepted, it is clear that the school curriculum of our day is grossly deficient. We do not train pupils to understand the general social order; we leave the understanding of social institutions to be cultivated largely by the accidental experiences of individual life.

The foregoing advocacy of a new social core of the curriculum allows me to introduce a principle of selection which will help to remove some of the difficulties encountered by the theory of curriculum construction through the study of social trends. If we accept the social trend which dictates that pupils shall be made intelligent about social institutions, we shall have to surrender the possibility of including in the curriculum certain traditionally approved or highly esteemed bodies of knowledge. It is not here implied that all tradition is to be disregarded. The fundamental traditions of society coincide with the fundamental social trends. Thus, as was pointed out earlier, no modern man can be truly in contact with civilization who is not precise in his thinking and who is not able to take advantage of the written records of racial experience. The point to be made is that tradition as such is not a safe guide. There are traditions which are indefensible, such as those which have in the past dictated that children in certain American communities shall be taught in public elementary schools the languages of their immigrant parents. Tradition is acceptable as a guide only when it has the support of a dominant social trend.

I am sure that a canvass of all social trends will put civic intelligence in a pre-eminent place in the curriculum along with number and reading, and I am sure that training in civic intelligence will replace in a rationally organized curriculum much that is there today. In other words, there is a hierarchy of values in the curriculum, and the determination of the subjects which the curriculum is to include will depend on attention to those social trends which are of greatest immediate importance in any given situation. Our technique of selection of social trends will require that we canvass all social trends and evaluate them in terms of their application to present-day life. The range of inclusion of the curriculum will be determined by securing a total conspectus of what might be included and dividing this total into inner circles and peripheral circles. The inner circles will represent the trends which must be recognized in the curriculums of all schools; the outer circles will represent the trends which may be recognized in the curriculums of schools which educate pupils who have the time for extended training. Perhaps what I am now saying will explain why the theory of curriculum construction in accordance with social trends is at the moment unable to answer all the questions that arise. This theory will operate effectively only when all the information has been collected which is necessary for the general conspectus I have attempted to describe. There must be a collecting of all trends before one can evaluate any particular trend.

There is one definite negative statement which should perhaps be made. The principle of selection which I am attempting to describe is not the principle of emphasis on direct practical utilities. The inner circles which represent universal need are not the circles of individual trade skill or practical knowledge of one's immediate surroundings. I come back to the original statement that the trends which must be taken into account are the trends of social evolution. The large social advantages are to be recognized and followed, not the petty personal needs of the individual. The individual is, to be sure, to be specifically prepared for his individual life, but his specific preparation is to be subordinated to initiation into civilization. The theory of curriculum construction in accordance with social trends is wholly opposed to the view of education, which has gained currency in some quarters, that all education is specific practical training of individuals in lines for which they are peculiarly adapted.

There is one broad general trend of civilization which cannot be omitted in even an outline sketch of the kind that I am attempting to offer. Society has diligently sought for the causes of the phenomena observable in the environment. From the early days when men sought the explanation of thunder in myths about a being like man but superior in strength and power down to the present time, when the physicist attributes thunder to the operation of electrical forces, there has been a steady pursuit of causes. The scientific developments of our day are the outcomes of trends long operating in human thinking. The cultivation of the scientific attitude on the part of individuals is essential to sympathetic participation in modern civilization. The school curriculum cannot escape the responsibility for cultivating the scientific attitude in pupils. Note that I am not speaking of scientific information. The social trend is not a trend toward the piling-up of series of verbal statements. The reason why much science-teaching is unproductive is that it does not truly initiate pupils into social modes of scientific thinking. There is need of reform in science-teaching, and I believe the theory of selecting subjects on the basis of social trends supplies the formula which can be relied on to guide the needed reform.

I must rest my case with these few examples. I am quite sure that what I have said will not be convincing to those who are wedded to one of the older and more familiar methods of curriculum construction. My function will be served if what I have said excites discussion rather than furnishes final solutions. I am content, therefore, to leave the theory which I have suggested to be attacked by anyone who holds that there is something more important for education to accomplish than the initiation of young people into the major ways of civilized life.

113. Curriculum Planning Based on a New Synthesis of Knowledge [16]

Harold Rugg

The first change . . . imperatively needed in the school curriculum is a change in the character of its content. Paralleling this there is a second: the critical need for a sweeping reconstruction of the *organization* of our entire school curriculum. America is an integrated welter of forces; essentially it is a unit. It must be studied *in toto*. It cannot be comprehended by studying its forms separately or by considering, one at a time, the operations of its underlying forces, problems and agencies. These forces, problems and agencies — in part psychological, in part economic and political — are welded inextricably together: the ownership of land, the control of credit, industry and trade, the standard of living, the fatigue of home life and the correlated mental attitudes of conformity and desire for

[16] From " A Preface to the Reconstruction of the American School Curriculum," *Teachers College Record*, 27 :606–608, March, 1926.

social approval, the hierarchical organization of community life, the dazed indifference of the public, and, strangely aloof from it all, a giant only half awake to its potentialities — the public school.

In spite of the need for studying our national order as a unit, curriculum-making in American schools has always been piecemeal. The materials of instruction from which children obtain their understanding of American life are presented in conventional " subjects ": history, geography, civics, economics, English, nature study, chemistry, what not. These subjects are narrow academic compartments of knowledge, representing bodies of technical facts and principles; they have been assembled for school use by specialists in subject matter. Their sponsors, those indeed who have constructed our curricula in the past, are experts in research, documentation, authentication. Curriculum-making utilizes this technique but it plays a subordinate rôle.

As one views American life as a whole in the light of the composition of the curriculum of our great school system, one conclusion presses insistently: We must invent a new synthesis of knowledge and make it the basis of the entire school curriculum. The conventional barriers between the existing subjects must be ignored in curriculum-making. The *starting point* shall be the social institution, or the political and economic problem, — not the subject. Psychological forces must oust economic and political form as the directing themes of organization.

The principal of reconstruction is so far-reaching that it should be illustrated voluminously. Since there is space, however, for only one example of the need for redepartmentalizing the materials of the school, I shall choose as that single illustration the story of how Europe came to the doleful condition in which we find her to-day. Consider, in studying its successive compact phrases, each dealing with events fraught with world significance, to what extent any existing school subject can give growing youth understanding of such crucial matters.

The story of the causes of the World War is very complicated and difficult to understand; nevertheless, from the recent researches of historians and scholars we can piece it together. The steps in that story are succinctly summarized as follows:

The story of the causes of the World War is the story of the industrial revolution and its consequences. It is the story of the steam engine and how men learned to use engines to turn factory wheels and the wheels of trains; how people were brought together in cities; how one part of the world became dependent on another; how each industrial nation needed more coal, more iron, and more lands from other parts of the world; how each one sought to build up its trade with other regions; how colonies were needed and how pathways of trade had to be kept open between the home country and the colonies; how ships — bigger and faster ships — and trains — longer and swifter trains — were built to transport the goods of the industrial world; how island coaling stations and midway ports were necessary to keep the ships going; how each industrial country competing with others for trade and colonies, and for iron, coal, and oil lands feared and suspected all the others; how these industrial countries conspired and allied themselves, one with another against certain others, so as to keep a very tipsy " balance of power " between them — that is, so that no one country could dominate them all; how the masses of the people, as they came together in cities, demanded and got more education; how more and more people were given the right to vote and how they tried to exercise a larger control over their governments; how governments saw that they must have greater navies, larger battleships, and guns that would shoot farther, also that more men must be taught the art of war; how conscription for universal military service came to European countries; how Prime Ministers and Foreign Offices secretly made military alliances, alliances about which people and their representatives were denied information; how the spirit of national pride, distrust, and hatred of other people grew; how Europe, from 1900, became an armed camp, hostilities nearly breaking out in 1905, and 1911; how at last the fuse was lighted for the great World War explosion in the summer of 1914, by the murder of the Archduke Ferdinand of Austria and — the greatest catastrophe in the world's history had come.

Will it be granted that the foregoing story affects the life of America so vitally that her youth should become possessors of a rich understanding of it before leaving the school? If so, how — under the existing organization of American history, European history, medieval history, English history, even world history, geography, economics, or civics — can the economic, political and social interrelationships underlying the present world situation be really understood? I do not believe it possible that these subjects, as now constituted, *can* develop an integrated understanding of the deep-lying forces which operated to bring distress to the current order.

Only one criterion should be permitted to dominate the organization of the materials of instruction: learning, not subject-matter sequence or authentication. We should ask constantly what facts and principles do young people need assembled in close relation in order to understand and to practice themselves in reflection upon American institutions and problems? What kinds of examples, episodes, graphic and pictorial presentations, problems, statistics, facts, do they need to comprehend the interdependence of the modern world, the problems of Americanizing millions of foreign born, the wise use of coal, iron, oil, and land, the improvement of education, the culture of the American people? Certainly to understand such matters they need data that are not now to be found in any one school subject. Hence the demand for a new deal — a new synthesis of knowledge.

114. Suggestions for Scope from the Commission on the Social Studies [17]

In the elementary school major attention would be devoted to a study of the making of the community and the nation, although materials bearing on the development of world society and culture would by no means be excluded. The program would begin with the neighborhood in which the child lives. Starting from a first-hand study of the life, institutions, and geography of the community, it would proceed to an examination of social changes taking place in the locality, of the history of the place, of the civilization of the Indian in the same area, of the contrasting elements of European and Indian culture and of early and later American culture. Emphasis would be placed throughout on actual participation in the social activities of school and neighborhood, and every part or phase of the program would begin and end in the contemporary and surrounding community which the child knows directly. Thus the pupil would develop an active interest in the fortunes of society and acquire a stock of ideas which would enable him to go beyond the immediate in time and space. He would then be led by natural connections — genetic and functional — to the study of the making of the region and the nation. Through such an organization of materials the elementary school would acquaint the child as fully as possible with the evolution of American culture — local and national — and to some extent with the origins of American culture in the Western world.

In the secondary school the central theme would be the development of mankind and the evolution of human culture, . . . with constant reference to the present and to American civilization. This program might culminate in the study, through concrete and living materials, of regional geography, of comparative economics, government and cultural sociology, of the major movements in social thought and action in the modern world, of the most recent developments on the international stage — a study in which the experience, the knowledge and the thought of all the preceding years would be brought to bear, by means of comparison and contrast, upon the emerging problems, tensions, and aspirations, the evolving social programs and philoso-

[17] Commission on the Social Studies, American Historical Association, *Conclusions and Recommendations*, Charles Scribner's Sons, New York, 1934, pp. 59–62.

phies of mankind and of the American people in their regional and world setting. Also special attention would be given in the secondary school to the reading of historical and social literature, including newspapers and magazines, great historic documents, classics of social thought, and to the achievement of familiarity with the methods and instruments of inquiry in the social sciences, with historical criticism, analysis, verification, and authentication. This program should embrace both the junior and senior divisions of the secondary school and reach into the years of the junior college.

In the organization of all social science instruction an effort should be made to develop in the pupil the concept of the principle of continuity — the concept that nothing ever did or does exist in isolation, that everything is always in process of change or becoming, that no event is without antecedents and sequences. Through such a study the pupil should acquire a realistic outlook upon the world and a broad perspective for the appraisal of persons, events, programs and ideas.

115. A Core Curriculum for Secondary Schools [18]

Butler Laughlin

. . . We are ready to outline a course of instruction for all secondary school pupils. First, we shall need to undertake a reorganization of the social studies in terms of modern needs. For the dubious and highly indirect approach represented by a succession of courses in history, we shall substitute a direct attack upon the problems of modern life, beginning in the seventh and eighth grades, with a realistic study of the immediate community, and continuing with a study of the larger problems of present-day society. Historical materials will be drawn upon generously to illuminate the backgrounds and causes of current trends. Around this sequence of crucial problems the rest of the curriculum will be built. The prevailing techniques will be exploration — direct, wherever possible — discovery, and discussion. Instead of beginning in the remote past, and leading up to the present in a final brief section of a course which most secondary pupils do not reach, we shall begin at once in the immediate present, and go back to the past for information that will shed light upon contemporary life.

In addition to the systematic study of modern problems, provision should be made for the regular informal discussion of the events of the day. Alternative interpretations of the day's news should be

[18] From " A New Program for the High Schools," *Chicago Schools Journal,* 16, 17:59–62, March–December, 1935.

provided by the teacher from sources other than the daily newspaper and the popular news magazine, insofar as these sources are not available in a form suitable for reading by the pupils. The discussions must be free, frank, and open, so far as possible, like the informal comment of the family at the dinner table. All reasonable points of view should receive a hearing in these discussions. Examinations and the usual coercive measures should be resolutely barred from this portion of the social studies program. Nothing but the genuine and compelling interest of the pupil is a safe incentive or an adequate safeguard against sterility in this instruction. All the advantages of the modernized curriculum will be lost if the shadow of the treadmill reappears in the classroom.

The Reorganization of English. Much misguided though sincere effort is currently expended in the teaching of English in the secondary school. It has been said that, although this subject is practiced all the pupil's waking hours, and although it receives the lion's share of the time in the daily program, it nevertheless is notoriously lacking in effectiveness. The excellent report on Reorganization of English, published in 1916, has had relatively little influence upon the actual teaching of English in the public schools. In the new high school curriculum it will be necessary to challenge ideals and procedures of English instruction, and to bring this field into closer relation with the actualities of present-day living.

Since the appearance of the report on the Reorganization of English in 1916, there have been numerous developments in the social and educational areas which impose new responsibilities upon the teacher of English. The rapid rise of the radio and the photoplay, for example, presents an educational problem which the schools have hardly begun to attack. The need of teaching English in situations in which it is normally used has even today been only sporadically recognized. The study and minute analysis of yesterday's classics still occupies the time that should, in large measure at least, be devoted to current periodical and book literature.

In the new high school curriculum all this will need to be changed. Each week's activities should minister directly to the pupil's specific needs in the whole field of the communication of ideas. The most obvious of these needs are suggested in the following general principles basic to a modern curriculum in English:

1. Throughout the entire secondary school period, from the seventh grade to the fourteenth, pupils should be kept in touch with articles, stories, and poetry in current issues of the better magazines, and with new books appropriate to the pupil's level of understanding.

2. Pupils entering the secondary school have in most instances failed to master the more complicated reading skills. Group instruction in these

skills, and individual remedial assistance, where needed, should form a regular part of the English program.

3. Throughout the entire secondary school period, radio programs and current photoplays should be given attention with a view to the development of discrimination and independence of judgment concerning the basic assumptions inherent in the performances.

4. Pupils who show reasonable facility in the accurate use of the mother tongue should be exempted from instruction in the English language, regardless of grade level.

5. The speech and writing in all in-school and out-of-school situations are legitimate occasions for the performance of advisory service by the English teacher.

6. Standards of effective expression for the entire school should be established by the English department.

7. Standards of correctness in English should be based upon conventions of the living language rather than the bookish traditions of the textbooks.

8. Formal instruction in literature should be replaced by systematic guidance in the reading of books of every description, from every period and every nation.

9. Individual tastes and interests of pupils should be respected as a first principle in reading guidance.

10. Course credits and grades have no place in the teaching of literary appreciation.

11. Independence of judgment and critical discrimination in reading constitute a primary objective of teaching in secondary school English instruction.

Science in the New Curriculum. The rapid rise of science in the course of the last century and its incredible influence upon the conditions of human living point unmistakably to the importance of an intelligent program of science instruction. Again it is necessary to refer to our basic principle, that the public high school is a school for the masses. We are obliged to distinguish between the science needed in the preparation of scientists and the science needed for the training of the intelligent citizen. Six objectives stand out as the directive principles of the science curriculum which all pupils should follow in the secondary school:

1. Understanding of the essential biological principles basic to the maintenance of health.

2. A general acquaintance with the plant and animal world from the point of view of the cultivated layman rather than that of the laboratory worker.

3. Understanding of the physical principles operative in the daily life of the learner.

4. A general acquaintance with the more popular aspects of geological and astronomical sciences.

5. Mastery of the scientific method in the solution of problems.

6. Skill in the use and care of mechanical devices and instruments involving the application of scientific principles.

Briefly, the science instruction for the rank and file should improve and diversify the learner's life interests and qualify him for the performance of the practical activities demanded by the conditions of modern living.

Field trips, lectures, demonstrations, laboratory experiments, abundant and diversified reading, and home performance of the practical activities should be the prevailing techniques. Question and answer recitations should be the exception rather than the rule. Free discussion and reporting of findings, either in the larger class groups or in the smaller committee circles, should be the rule rather than the exception. Specialized courses for the rank and file must be abandoned in favor of surveys organized in terms of human experience rather than the logical classification of subject matter. The gruelling drills upon scientific nomenclature must give way to interesting experiences in the biological and physical worlds, and to a frank encounter with the biological realities that affect human happiness.

A Rational Plan for Mathematics. More than ever we need a revamping of the curriculum in mathematics, which, perhaps as much as any other subject, has thus far resisted the impact of educational intelligence. The dead hand of past generations still dominates the content of the mathematics courses. Little or no effort is made to relate materials to life needs, or even to correlate them with the mathematical situations arising in the science class. By some incomparable superstition it is assumed that the solution of an equation or the proof of a theorem will contribute to the happiness of the individual or the welfare of society.

Required mathematics in the modern curriculum will be purely and simply the mathematics of every-day life. It will supply those skills required by quantitative thinking in the pupil's normal experience. Much of this mathematics may be taught in the science classes in association with the problems for which it is used. Much of it may be taught in the social studies sequence in those social situations requiring computation. Special courses in mathematics should be organized solely for the teaching of those things which can not be cared for well enough in the social and physical science sequences.

Pupils entering the seventh grade should finish the fundamental arithmetical processes in common and decimal fractions. If the more complicated processes were left to the secondary school period, particularly grades seven and eight, the pupil would have less difficulty in mastering them. Increased maturity will eliminate much of the failure and unhappiness which now attends so much of the elementary school mathematics instruction. The mathematics instruction should, however, be strictly adapted to individual needs, and the program should be limited to the barest essentials. The major portion of the core curriculum in mathematics should be concerned with quantitative thinking in genuine social situations.

A limited number of students will elect to continue the study of mathematics after the ninth grade. Formal courses in algebra, geometry, and advanced mathematics should be provided for these. Admission to the elective courses should be upon recommendation of the mathematics department only. The usual course in algebra plus the semester of advanced algebra could then be condensed into a single year. Plane and solid geometry should also be given intensively in a year's course. All this would be entirely feasible if formal mathematics were taught only to pupils whose capacities and interests fitted them for this field.

Art and Music Appreciation in the High School. The courses in art and music in the secondary school, like the course in literary appreciation, will be organized chiefly from the point of view of the cultivated beneficiary, or consumer, rather than the creative worker, or producer. Art and music appreciation can not be compelled; it can not be achieved by the device of course grades and credits. Illustrated lectures, displays and exhibits, recitals, radio listening, excursions to art museums and collections, as well as small group discussions and the opportunities provided by the extra-curriculum activities, are examples of the basic techniques in the art and music instruction intended for all pupils. The procedure will be, so far as possible, to approximate the conditions of normal living outside of school, with the sole exception that the school will seek to enrich the art and music content of the pupil's day, and to make the observation of a great work of art and the hearing of a great musical composition meaningful experiences. The courses ought to be required only in the sense that all pupils are to be expected to participate in the activities; they are not to be required in the sense that credit in them is necessary toward graduation.

116. "A Suggested New Secondary Curriculum"[19]

William H. Kilpatrick

The proposals for remaking the curriculum discussed in the preceding articles have found readier acceptance in the elementary school than in the secondary. Probably it is the existence of de-

[19] *The Journal of the National Education Association,* 25:111–112, April, 1936.

partmentalized teaching that has opposed the spread of the " activity " movement to the highschool. Many secondary-school people admit readily enough a strong argument in favor of basing education on the life process as hereinbefore discussed, but they do not see how they can give up the concentration and specialization that departmentalization of teaching allows. So far these have accordingly been unwilling to follow a procedure that ignores subjectmatter lines.

Without discussing here how much of this devotion to teaching by distinct subjects is the inertia of tradition and how much of it is justified on sounder grounds, let us admit outright that some pupils can and will profit by at least some of the concentration and specialization which is permitted by existing highschool departmentalization. But it does not follow that all pupils profit equally by such a regime nor that any pupils of secondary age need to have their whole school time so split into separate subjects. For one thing, there are strong reasons why some one teacher should have such continual and extended acquaintance with each distinct pupil as to permit a degree of personal counseling and guidance denied under a complete regime of departmentalization. It appears exceedingly doubtful that demands either of mental hygiene or of proper educational guidance can be adequately safeguarded on the usual basis of departmental teaching.

Furthermore there are many highschool pupils for whom the need for extended specialization is far from clear. Especially is this true where anything like all pupils of highschool age continue in school. If the considerations advanced in the preceding articles for remaking the curriculum are granted to hold for the elementary school, as they increasingly are so granted, there appears no obvious reason why the argument should suddenly fail of cogency as children get to be around twelve or fourteen years of age. In fact if the arguments hold for the elementary school, the burden of proof would seem to lie with those who claim a difference for the secondary school.

It is from these considerations that the proposals are herein made for a new type of secondary school. The aim is to contrive a school program that will keep education for all the pupils on a basis of living for most of each day at the beginning of the highschool period and grant the privilege of specialization only as an affirmative case is made out for each individual concerned.

To fix ideas, suppose the 6-3-3 plan is in operation with the elementary school run on the basis advocated in the preceding articles. In the sixth grade the teacher has had charge of all the pupils certainly most of the day, and this teacher has tried to manage the education of her pupils on a thorogoing living process basis as has been discussed in the preceding articles. This means that the various sides and aspects of life suitable for rounding out life for pupils of this age have been cared for by the on-going curriculum. And the teacher has sought to have the pupils grow each in ever more adequate self-direction as they have faced the successive situation-experiences that have constituted the activity curriculum. Each pupil has meanwhile been to the teacher a distinct personality, studied and guided as such so that always the "whole child" might grow best into ever fuller and more adequate participation in the surrounding cultural life. As the children have thus been studied, the teacher has known that they had different abilities and widely varying tastes and interests. Within certain social-moral limitations, it has been a definite aim of the teacher to cultivate each such individuality for all it was worth. James has been encouraged to study electricity, and Henry butterflies, while Mary has been encouraged to follow her special interest in music and Susie her interest in drawing and Lizzie her wish to write poetry. All such special interests have been cherished and cultivated as choice instances of budding individual life.

Now according to the plan herein proposed the seventh grade would be run in much the same way as was the sixth. One teacher will be in principal charge of all the children. The main part of the class work, perhaps three-fourths of it, will be common to all the pupils; and this will be guided, as was done the year before, so as to care for all the sides and aspects of the well-ordered life. There are two differences between the seventh grade this year and the sixth grade last year: one, the pupils are a year older and have got further along in knowing and managing life; the other, some of the pupils are ready by special taste and aptitude to take up seriously one or more lines of specialization. James wishes to carry his electricity further in the direction of a more general science and John wishes to join him. Henry's butterflies now call for a wider study of biology. Mary's music is ready for further and more consistent study, as is Susie's art work. Lizzie's poetry now reaches out into a closer study of literature as well as more adequate writing. Other pupils wish to begin algebra, and some others typewriting.

When the sixth-grade teacher had sent these pupils on to the junior highschool, she had told in her records of the various interests and abilities so far as she had known of them. The more definite and pronounced of these had been talked over both with the preceding year's fifth-grade teacher and with the principal. So that this year's seventh-grade home room teacher is prepared in advance to give approval for some tryout specializations, and during the quarter of the day set aside for such specialization these pupils will go to other rooms to work under teachers especially qualified to give the needed advice and help. As any such tryout justifies itself it may be continued and expanded, under the joint advice of the home room teacher, the parents, the subjectmatter specialist, and the school's general counselor (dean, principal, or other guidance officer).

Those pupils who have as yet found no special task or interest will continue to work together during the specializing period at any matter that seems best to teacher and pupils, possibly in one large group, possibly in smaller groups, possibly at individual projects. It is the business of the seventh-grade teacher to help the pupils here as elsewhere and always to use their time to best advantage.

When the same pupils reach the eighth grade, they will find the same general state of affairs. They are now a year older and still further along in insight into and control over life. More will have developed individual tastes and interests worthy of specialized pursuit, and some will need more extended periods of study. Possibly one-third of the day may now be devoted to these approved specialized interests. And similarly for each succeeding year to the last, always for a large part of the day all the pupils are together under one home room teacher, while an annually increasing proportion of the time will be available for approved specialization. What proportion of the work of grade twelve will be common may well be debated. My own opinion is that from one-third to one-fourth may well be so spent. For pupils going on to colleges which are still so backward as to specify precisely their entrance requirements, possibly a large part of the day given to departmentalized work may be needed. But this now seems, to me at any rate, not the best use of their time.

Such an arrangement as that here sketched contemplates that practically all pupils of secondary age will soon be enrolled in secondary schools. In the degree that this is so, in like degree should all be as a rule " promoted " (if this old-fashioned term be still retained). At the end all will as a rule " graduate," with whatever recommendations for further work that fit the conditions then obtaining.

Two reasons then especially support the plan outlined above. First, all pupils will (so I believe) profit by giving a good portion of their school time to such a life process program as ignores subject divisions. Only thus can they learn to study and work as life requires. Second, many pupils, just as many adults, have no need to specialize in the way and along the lines set out by existing school subjects. In fact, it probably hurts most of such pupils to spend time on such logically organized subjectmatter. In the years gone by these pupils have usually dropped out of school. Now, they continue to the embarrassment of all concerned. Such pupils need more of the problems of life itself and less of the formal school work. The plan proposed allows adjustment to meet each particular case, and thus allows the more intellectual and the more interested to pursue their work under conditions more favorable to them.

A word now about the more practical side of the problem. This plan is here proposed for study and experimentation. So far as is known it has never been tried. It would appear to be feasible both for small and for large highschools. Just what changes actual trial would require in the plan we can, of course, tell only upon such trial. Two things would seem necessary for a beginning, first, that there be a will to try the plan, and second, that teachers be found who can carry on the activity program on the highschool level. In 6-3-3 school systems that already have the " activity " program in the elementary there could easily be found sixth-grade teachers who would like to carry on the life work on seventh- and eighth-grade levels. And similarly in many 8-4 school systems, there can be found seventh- and eighth-grade teachers already carrying on " activity " programs who would like to go forward into the ninth grade. It would be comparatively easy for the larger institutions that prepare both elementary and secondary teachers to take on the new work of preparing activity home room teachers for the highschool. This need involve no heartburning since the present specialized preparation for highschool teachers could continue much as hitherto. However, teachers expecting to go to small highschools would have to prepare both along the " activity " line and one or more subjectmatter specialties.

That we need to change the secondary school rather drastically is admitted by an increasing number of American educators. The foregoing plan is proposed as both easy to try and promising of good returns.

117. Tentative Outline of Scope Developed in Mississippi State Curriculum Program [20]

GENERAL PLAN OF CURRICULUM ORGANIZATION

. . . The committee decided that an adequate program of education should make the following definite provisions.

First, it should provide for the development of social understanding and understanding of the physical environment. As was developed in the Point of View, the basic obligation of the school is social in nature. Its essential function is the development of individuals who can participate effectively in the various aspects of

[20] From Mississippi Program for the Improvement of Instruction, *A Guide for Curriculum Planning*, Bulletin No. 3, State Department of Education, Jackson, October, 1936, pp. 41–49, 70–72, 78–79.

social life and contribute to general social improvement. Consequently, in planning a curriculum organization, consideration should first of all be given to the development of understandings of social life and of the way we are influenced and conditioned by the physical environment. This phase of the curriculum may be looked upon as the core of the entire curriculum. It is in this area that major instructional units will be developed. Other phases of the curriculum should be so organized and developed as to contribute in a maximum way to the enrichment of this phase of the program.

Second, it should provide special opportunities for developing individual interests and aptitudes as rapidly as such interests and aptitudes become clearly differentiated as the child matures. The phase of the curriculum concerned with developing social understanding and understanding of the physical environment will contribute greatly to the development of individual interests and to the cultivation of individual aptitudes. However, as the child matures, interests and aptitudes tend to develop to the point that they cannot readily be cared for in a heterogeneous group. Consequently, it is necessary and desirable to make special provision for the development of these interests and aptitudes. When they become clearly differentiated it is possible and desirable to organize special courses to care for them. In this way, pupils with common interests may be grouped together and more effective instruction provided. Until this stage of development has been reached, it is necessary for teachers to make provisions for the development of special interests and aptitudes through special assignments, committee work, and the provision of opportunity for individual enterprises.

Third, it should provide special opportunities for children to engage in creative, aesthetic, and recreational activities. While units of work designed to develop understanding of social life and of the physical environment will involve many activities of a creative and recreational nature, they will not provide an adequate opportunity for children to engage in such activities. It is desirable for boys and girls at all times to have opportunities to engage in group singing, in individual art projects, in playing games, and in developing hobbies. The school should foster these activities through special provisions which will encourage regular participation in them.

Fourth, it should provide opportunities for the mastery of basic skills and techniques. As was pointed out in the section of this bulletin on Aims, there are certain abilities, techniques, and information which are of very general use. Many of these abilities are of a complex and intricate nature. If children are not given careful guidance in the development of these abilities, they may never achieve mastery of them. Special emphasis, consequently, should be given to the systematic cultivation of abilities which have wide and general use. This part of the curriculum should be related closely to the other phases of the curriculum and to out-of-school activities.

While it is necessary in curriculum planning to indicate general areas of emphasis such as the foregoing in order to be sure that certain phases of the child's development are not overlooked, the curriculum should not be organized into discrete parts. The good teacher will so relate all phases of the curriculum that the work during a given day will develop without noticeable breaks and that one day's work will lead into another with smoothness and rhythm.

On the basis of these requirements a general plan of curriculum organization was projected. This plan is indicated in Chart I in terms of a possible division of the time of the school day. It should be emphasized that Chart I is intended only to be suggestive of an approximate division of the time of the school day which might desirably be given to various phases of the school program. The chart should not be interpreted, necessarily, as a schedule of classes but rather as an approximate distribution of time. The scheduling of classes would depend upon the local school situation. The chart seems to be self-explanatory with respect to units of work on problems of physical environment and social living, skill aspects of various subjects, recreational and aesthetic expression, and approximate amount of time for electives.

A careful study of the Chart should be made by all teachers and administrators in the State. It will be noted that it is proposed to give approximately one-half of the school day extending through the entire period of education to the phase of the program devoted to the development of social understanding and understanding of the physical environment. This is referred to as the core curriculum. It will involve subject matter from all fields and will be organized, as is pointed out later, around aspects of social life which are truly functional in nature. As pupils become more mature, however, and their interests become somewhat specialized, the tendency will be to give special emphasis to the social studies and science with English correlated with the two.

Approximately one-fourth of the day in grades one through nine is to be devoted to the mastery of certain general abilities and information of particular significance. This time will be given to the direct teaching needed for developing the ability to read, write, speak, use numbers effectively, and similar abilities. Terminal courses will be provided in these fields during various years of the junior high school. The amount of remedial work needed by certain pupils in various kinds of skills should be provided in grades ten

CHART I

GENERAL PLAN OF CURRICULUM ORGANIZATION AS RELATED TO THE SCHOOL DAY

Amount of Time	Grades		
	1–6	7–9 *	10–12 †
One-half of Day	Units of work on problems of physical environment and social living. Utilizes activities and information from various fields of knowledge which will help solve the problem or attain the goal. In Grades 7 to 12 the core area may include all the literature required of all pupils, and in Grades 10 to 12 it includes all the skills in English required of all pupils.		
One-fourth of Day	Skill aspects of reading, writing, English, mathematics, etc., needing special attention in order to provide adequate mastery for effective use in units of work in life outside the school.	**Electives** Courses, clubs, and sports to provide for special interests, aptitudes, and needs. Not required of all pupils. Some of these courses may be required in certain curricula such as college-preparatory, vocational, or general.	
One-fourth of Day	Recreational and aesthetic expression including games and sports, art, music, literature, etc., in addition to such expression in units of work in the core curriculum.		

* All pupils could well be required to elect some type of recreational or aesthetic expression in Grades 7 through 9.

† In Grades 10 through 12, pupils ranking in the upper 25 per cent of the class may be permitted to elect three subjects.

through twelve in connection with the units of work on problems of physical environment and social living and to some extent in certain elective courses.

The remaining fourth of the day in grades one to six is to be devoted to recreational and aesthetic activities as is pointed out in the discussion presented heretofore. Many such activities are included in the core curriculum but additional provision is needed for them. Recreational and aesthetic expression would be continued beyond grade six through the units of work and through elective courses and club activities. All pupils might well be required to elect some type of recreational or aesthetic expression in grades seven through nine.

It will be observed by studying the Chart that one-fourth of the day in the junior high school and one-half of the day in the senior high school is to be devoted to electives. These electives serve two functions. They will permit pupils who develop special interests and aptitudes in the core curriculum or in out-of-school situations to select courses especially designed to cultivate such interests and aptitudes. They will permit, as well, pupils who become interested in organized subject fields to pursue the study of such fields. Also, pupils wishing to secure vocational training may use this opportunity to do so by electing vocational courses.

DEFINING THE SCOPE OF THE CORE CURRICULUM

If real understanding of social life and of the influence of the physical environment upon man is to be accomplished through the work in the core curriculum, it must be organized in such a way as to provide a view of social life as a vital going concern. Pupils must come to see the problems which men face as individuals and groups. They must understand the conditions relating to these problems, the race experience out of which they have developed, and the proposals for solving them. This requires that the curriculum be organized around phases of life which are sufficiently dynamic to require knowledge of the present, understanding of the past, and a consideration of the possibilities of the future. In studying the problems and activities of man as analyzed by research investigations, students of society and educational leaders, it was discovered that all problems and activities tend to fall in certain major areas. For example, a considerable number of our problems and activities group around the purpose of making a home, others around our effort to preserve and protect life, and still others around making a living. These aspects of life represent dominant group and individual purposes which are present in any civilized society, and which have persisted through many ages.

After careful consideration, the committee decided that these functional aspects of life would provide the most dynamic basis of organization for the core curriculum. Consequently, the first step in defining the scope of the core curriculum was to indicate these major phases of life. The following phases were selected:

1. Protecting Life and Health
2. Making a Home
3. Conserving and Improving Material Conditions
4. Cooperating in Social and Civic Action
5. Getting a Living
6. Securing an Education
7. Expressing Religious Impulses
8. Expressing Aesthetic Impulses
9. Engaging in Recreation.

In order to indicate more clearly the points about which the curriculum would be organized, the committee made an exploratory analysis of important problems which fall under each of the aforementioned aspects. A complete analysis of such problems would indicate an optimum scope for the core curriculum.

DEFINING THE SEQUENCE OF THE CORE CURRICULUM

Having determined the basis of the scope of the core curriculum, it next becomes necessary to make provisions for some order of sequence so that the understandings which children develop will be sequential and cumulative. It is proposed to define the sequence of the curriculum by use of the following procedure. It will be observed that the various aspects of life are influenced by a variety of factors. Prominent among these factors are social institutions and organizations, tools which civilization has developed, inventions and discoveries, and other such factors. Understanding of the various phases of life will involve consideration of the ways in which these influences condition living. Consequently, the sequence of the curriculum may be defined by employing such influences as a basis for determining the scope of the work in various divisions of the school.

The following criteria were used in determining which influences to employ as centers of interest for the various grades:

1. The center of interest should exert significant influence on the functional phases of life.

2. There should be numerous objects and activities within the area of the centers of interest that are of interest to children on the level for which the center of interest serves as a limitation.

3. There should be adequate instructional materials of suitable difficulty to develop the center of interest on the level for which it serves as a limitation.

4. The center of interest should provide for maximum growth of desirable concepts and should offer opportunity for participation by the pupils in significant undertakings.

When a particular influence on our living, whether an institution, a movement, a tool of civilization, or an invention, meets these criteria it may appropriately be referred to as a center of interest for a given grade.

The committee made a careful study of the characteristics of children at various stages of development and of the major influences on life. On the basis of this study, they defined centers of interest which they deemed desirable for the respective administrative divisions and grades of the school. The centers of interest as selected for the respective grades follow:

Lower Elementary Grades: Life in Home, School, and Community
  Grade 1, Life in Home and School
  Grade 2, Life in the Immediate Community
  Grade 3, Life in the Extended Community
Upper Elementary Grades: Relation of Life to the Physical and Social Environment
  Grade 4, Life in Markedly Different Physical Environments
  Grade 5, Influence of Discoveries and Travel upon Living
  Grade 6, Development of Inventions, Agencies, and Tools of Civilization
Junior High School: The Individual's Adjustment to and Use of the Physical and Social Environment
  Grade 7, Improving the Home and School
  Grade 8, Finding a Place in the Community and Social Life
  Grade 9, Using Science and Social and Governmental Agencies
Senior High School: Problems and Trends in Living
  Grade 10, Problems in Improving Biological and Material Conditions through the Ages
  Grade 11, Problems in Improving Social, Economic, and Business Conditions through the Ages
  Grade 12, Influences and Trends in American Life.

DEFINING THE SCOPE OF RECREATIONAL AND AESTHETIC ACTIVITIES

The persistent impulses to play and the desire for expression of aesthetic impulses has assumed a new importance in education today. Man's improved conditions brought about by his utilization of machines for production has created greater leisure for larger numbers of people. Recreational and aesthetic activities will become social necessities if the newly created leisure is to enrich the lives of our people. The responsibility of the school in educating for leisure is more pronounced today than at any other period of democratic education. Therefore, the individual teacher should feel the responsibility of properly guiding the experiences of his pupils to this end.

Recreational activities and aesthetic qualities are aspects of all activity. It is possible to group the general activities in which children may engage around the following suggestions:

1. Reading for pleasure.
2. Playing.
3. Appreciating beauty in line, form, and color.
4. Enjoying music.

Children's interests, abilities, and all-round development should be the only criteria for defining the Scope of recreational and aesthetic activities. Creative expression should be fostered in these activities. Broad opportunities should be provided at all stages of the child's development to engage in such activities as: playing games and sports; singing songs; playing musical instruments; telling stories; reading beautiful literature; reading for pleasure; drawing; coloring; painting; observing the beauties of nature; expressing beauty in rhythmic motion; participating in plays, pageants, operettas, clubs, hikes, parties, and picnics; visiting art museums, beautiful parks, and other beautiful spots of nature; and developing hobbies.

There should be no formal program organized in this area but rather the child should be surrounded with an environment which will encourage and stimulate him to engage in such activities. Care should be exercised to see that children are introduced to reading materials, games, songs, and other opportunities for creative and recreational expression which are adapted to their particular stage of development.

DEFINING THE SCOPE OF THE PROGRAM FOR DEVELOPING SKILLS AND TECHNIQUES

Several of the most important abilities which involve complex patterns of specific habits develop through fairly well recognized stages of growth. Through careful experimentation and study, teaching materials and methods have been developed to provide most effective guidance in directing growth through these various stages. Consequently, the Scope of the curriculum insofar as it relates to the systematic development of a particular ability must be projected in terms of the growth characteristics of the ability. It will be necessary in outlining the Scope of this phase of the curriculum to indicate the general stages of growth through which the various abilities to be emphasized progress. This analysis will provide a basis about which instructional materials may be organized.

This does not suggest that the development of these abilities is unrelated to the core curriculum and to events in everyday life. In fact, the opposite is true. The abilities selected for emphasis in the direct teaching program will be used continuously in the core curriculum and in out-of-school experiences. In a large proportion of cases the need for particular emphasis in the direct teaching program will grow out of an experience in the core curriculum.

This phase of the curriculum must be very flexible in nature and readily adaptable to individual differences. Some children need much more systematic instruction than do others. Some teachers can accomplish effective use of such abilities in a much shorter time than others. Consequently, as this phase of the program is planned it will be held in mind that it should be readily adaptable to the individual needs of pupils and to the ability of various teachers to guide pupils.

One of the early tasks of production committees in this field will be to define the general abilities which should receive systematic emphasis and to outline the general stages of growth through which they move.

DEFINING THE SCOPE OF COURSES TO CARE FOR INDIVIDUAL INTERESTS AND APTITUDES

As was pointed out in an earlier discussion provision should be made throughout the core curriculum for encouraging the development of individual interests and aptitudes. However, according to the general plan of curriculum organization as indicated in Chart I elective courses are to be offered in the junior and senior high school to provide special opportunity for the development of interests and aptitudes which have become strong as the pupil has matured. It will be necessary to define the Scope of each of these courses separately. The procedure for defining Scope should be planned so as to utilize to the fullest possible extent the interests and aptitudes of pupils enrolled in the course. It should also be planned so as to contribute whenever possible to the development of understandings of the physical and social environment emphasized in the core curriculum. As production committees for these various courses begin work one of the early tasks which they will face is the outlining of the Scope of the curriculum in their respective courses.

The number of such courses which may appropriately be offered depends upon the variety of interests which pupils develop and upon the teaching facilities of the particular school involved. Obviously, a small school will not be able to go as far in providing for the development of such interests as will a large school. The core curriculum offerings should always be provided first and beyond that the courses to be offered should be determined so as to meet the needs of the largest possible number of pupils.

There is special need in this phase of the instructional program for competent educational and vocational guidance because this phase of the program should contribute to choice of fields for further study and of vocation.

118. Organization of the Curriculum of the Eleventh and Twelfth Grades in the Ohio State University High School [21]

This year a progressive step was taken in the organization of the school experiences of the students in the eleventh and twelfth grades. Our efforts of previous years with rigidly sectioned and scheduled student-groups and teachers carrying a heavy educational load led to a radical solution of our chief difficulties.

Since it had been especially in the areas of English, social science, and science that we had tried vainly before to achieve sufficient flexibility for our purposes, we decided to assign a two-and-a-half-hour block of time and the use of from two to four rooms in the English, social science, and science laboratories to a unified-studies program for the eleventh and twelfth grades (50 students each), with the guidance of an eleventh- and twelfth-grade faculty staff (which finally comprised two full-time teachers, two full-time interne teachers, and two part-time teachers) from English, social science, and science.

Six faculty members, then, one hundred students, two to four rooms, two and a half hours each morning: within those opportunities — a program to be worked out flexibly, to achieve the purposes of our educational philosophy, to achieve this supreme value, integration.

We achieved a paradox. Purposing flexibility, we drew up a most complicated and dove-tailed schedule. Our students then divided themselves into four sections, each of about twenty-five, two sections to each grade. This achieved a maximum of use, potentially, of the available laboratories, and a teacher-student ratio in which the individual, while enjoying the stimulation and experiencing the responsibilities of a group, could not easily be lost to teacher guidance.

But we did not desire to limit the contacts of the students with one another to these four discrete roll calls. So that the autonomy of the larger grade-group should be preserved, we arranged that each grade would be able, when advisable — notably in the planning of a unit of work and in the summarizing of a unit of work or in their own self-government as a group concerned with specific grade problems such as social functions, participation in inclusive school events,

[21] From " Programs of the Six Upper Classes," *Educational Research Bulletin*, 15:45–50, February 12, 1936.

graduation and so forth — to meet together as a unit. The schedule achieved this for each of the three subject areas.

Again, we realized from past experience the desirability for varying purposes (planning, laboratory activity, research involving reading, trips, presentation of reports, demonstrations, and lectures) of scheduling periods of varying lengths. This was achieved in each area for both entire grades and separate sections.

The possibility of having both eleventh and twelfth grades meet together or with other grades for some inclusive purpose lies in recognizing that there is no particular sanctity to the claims of the subject areas for their scheduled periods. At any time an activity or a program considered in traditional educational circles as extra-curricular can become curricular and supersede all other matters of schedule, if it can justify the use of the time by its probable worth.

Originally our week of mornings was partitioned rather equivalently among the three areas. Before long it was evident that this was not the best arrangement. Our students have (at least to date in our experimentation) been required to work with teachers who are specialists, each in his own of the following areas of educational experience: social science, English, science, mathematics, physical education, and arts, during at least six consecutive years. Languages are electives for the last four years; the elementary experience also involves work in all those areas. As teachers we are anxious to have as little home work or outside preparation as possible, both so that the preparation can be expertly supervised and so that the many educational experiences of the home and the community, such as leisure reading, art lessons, hobbies, lectures, radio, press, theater, forums, church, social functions, out-of-door activities, work, and the like, can be realized without conflict from assignment. Because of the two factors just presented we agreed to include within our morning block of time all the opportunity for preparation necessary, except for the minority of slow students and students who have been absent and for the minority of students with a highly specialized interest, for science and social science.

Now preparation in the two fundamental features particular to the English program, free reading and creative writing, cannot be scheduled, must be done outside of school hours. (The reading that a student does evenings, week-ends, and during vacation is the content of his English program!) The other fundamental features of the English program are: the discussion of the reading and writing done outside and the conference and guidance necessary to the individual's reading and writing level; and the functional use of tool English — as a means of communication: deriving information from verbal sources, speaking effectively in discussion, organizing written notes and written reports. The discussion and conference are allotted time on the schedule as English periods; the functional use of tool English is made a vital educational experience by means of releasing the English specialists on Monday completely and on other days partly to participate in the work of the science and social-

TABLE II

SCHEDULE FOR ELEVENTH AND TWELFTH GRADES
CLASSES IN ENGLISH, SCIENCE, AND SOCIAL SCIENCE

8:45	9:30	10:00	10:20	11:10
Monday				
Science XI-x		Social Science XI-x		
Science XI-y		Social Science XI-y		
Social Science XII-x		Science XII-x		
Social Science XII-y		Science XII-y		
Tuesday				
Science XI-x	English XI-x			Social Science XI-x
Science XI-y	English XI-y			Social Science XI-y
English XII-x		Science XII-x		
Social Science XII-y				English XII-y
Wednesday				
Social Science XI-x		Science XI-x		
Science XI-y		Social Science XI-y		
Social Science XII-x		English XII-x		
English XII-y		Science XII-y		
Thursday				
English XI-x		Social Science XI-x		
Science XI-y				English XI-y
Social Science XII-x	English XII-x			Science XII-x
Social Science XII-y	English XII-y			Science XII-y
Friday				
English XI-x		Science XI-x		
English XI-y		Social Science XI-y		
Social Science XII-x		Science XII-x		
Science XII-y		Social Science XII-y		

science areas. Therefore there is an apparent, but not an actual slight to the English program in the schedule as it appears later.

The schedule just described, although it appears to be complicated, has proved its worth and its actual flexibility in practice. Potentially there are opportunities for each specialist in each area to be free for visiting his students in their other classes.

There are four hour periods after lunch for eleventh- and twelfth-graders. One of these is scheduled for mathematics and for mathematics preparation. The last hour is scheduled for physical education. The remaining two periods are partitioned by each student individually among the various arts and languages, electives, and the preparation necessary to a language elective.

It has seemed desirable to conclude this statement of the eleventh- and twelfth-grade work with an account of one strikingly successful experience in the integration of the three areas for our Seniors. As is evident in the statement in this BULLETIN of the social-science program through the junior and senior high-school grades, twelfth-graders return to a year's consideration of contemporary problems, looking also to the future and its demands upon them as citizens coming into responsibility. As they were discussing their plans for their year's work last October, they became involved in certain questions which reduced themselves ultimately from prejudices and vague generalizations about personality and about the individual in society, to a need for an understanding of certain biological and, particularly, psychological principles.

This need was brought out, because of the flexibility of our schedule, in the presence of teachers from all three areas. Almost immediately, within the science planning periods, we embarked upon an organization of the needed experience. A unit of work in biological, particularly psychological fundamentals! We were at that point fortunate in having in the person of one of our English specialists, a psychologist who not only had received advanced degrees in that area, not only had taught the subject and had done research in the field, but who had proved invaluable to our faculty because of her continued, current contact with that field. Furthermore, both in the analysis of the reading done by her English classes of novels, plays, poetry, biography, essays dealing with conflicts in the living of individuals in society, and in the intimate, counseling function of conferring with students in the light of their personal conflicts as revealed in their free, creative writing, she had also come to the point where she welcomed an opportunity to organize such a unit of study (especially fortunately, in the characteristically objective atmosphere of the science laboratory) as a really significant experience to serve as a foundation for the remaining months of the secondary-school experience of these boys and girls.

A glance at the schedule will indicate how it was possible for this English teacher to meet the entire twelfth grade for discussion of these matters during a long science period on Monday and a shorter science period on Thursday and each section separately for a more individualized discussion for a long period each, one on Wednesday and one on Friday. She built her discussions directly upon the biological foundation laid during October by the science teacher and upon the questions of the students which had been stimulated, as we have related, in the English, science, and social-science areas separately. In addition to discussion periods, we organized the selection by each student of an individual reading or laboratory research which we assisted him in limiting to the scope of his powers and of the school facilities.

Most rewarding of all have been the rapidly accumulating evidences of the value of this unit which lasted until Christmas. Discussions in English classes and the papers written now show a new understanding of personality and of human conflicts, of the relation of the individual to others and to society. In science and in social science is evident a new precision of speech, a new freedom from the confusion consequent upon ignorance of the psychological factors which result in the folly of prejudice.

Perhaps a clearer example of the integration of an educational experience within three ordinarily distinct subject areas could hardly be selected than our twelfth-grade excursion last fall into these fundamentals of biology and psychology which serve as a basis for understanding the conflicts of human personalities in society.

119. SCOPE OF THE CURRICULUM IN THE BRONXVILLE SENIOR HIGH SCHOOL [22]

I. D. Taubeneck, Frank Misner, and Willard W. Beatty

In planning the new curriculum for the tenth, eleventh, and twelfth years, with the new freedom gained under the Commission on Secondary School and College Relations, the Bronxville staff laid out its basic work in three broad interlocking fields — those of natural science, human relations, and literature and the arts — which are each to be studied for three years.

Planning an experimental curriculum, we escape the necessity of dividing the work in the field of human relations into ancient, modern European, and American history. We have chosen instead the broad problem of understanding human relations in their manifold aspects, with a group of major concepts to guide us rather than a chronological study of historic facts.

In the case of the majority of our students, who have come through our own Elementary School, we are able to build upon a foundation of a three-and-a-half-year world-history course, taught from the point of view of understanding human beings rather than of remem-

[22] From "History Begins With the Present," *Progressive Education,* 11:85–87, January-February, 1934.

bering dates. This course is followed in our Junior High School by a three-year study of the _____ Social Science series. We are able, therefore, to assume that certain information and ideas are in the background of our students.

While we have barely begun the analysis of the basic concepts toward which our classroom experiences will be aimed, a few may be stated to indicate what we mean by the term basic concept.

A widespread diffusion of property interests makes for stability in government.

Any tendency to dispossess large portions of the populace makes for unrest.

Unreasonable repression tends to produce violent outbursts.

Causes for social phenomena tend to be many and complex.

Many tend to over-simplify the explanation of social phenomena.

Governments are created to promote the well-being of society and its members.

As we have disregarded the usual divisions into Ancient-Medieval, Modern European, and American history, so we have eliminated the artificial lines between economics, sociology, history, and civics in our work on the problems of human relationships. These problems do not divide themselves nicely and exclusively into economic problems, civic problems, or sociological problems. Nor is the information which will lead to the better understanding of the subject under discussion exclusively from the field of history, of economics, of sociology, or of civics. Almost inevitably information is needed from two or more of these fields.

As in the case of the pupils studying history, the pupils in the class of human relations start with the present. The first few days are given over to a consideration of the problems facing society today. The pupils are invited to suggest such problems or to tell of important events they have read about or have heard discussed. One pupil reports that the government in Cuba has just been overthrown. Immediately questions begin. Shall we intervene in Cuba? Will the new government be able to preserve order? What will happen to American investments? What should we do if American citizens were killed in Cuba? What would happen if some other country tried to protect the property and lives of its citizens by intervening in Cuba? Finally a boy who thinks more clearly than some of his classmates asks whether we should intervene in Cuba or leave the Cubans free to work out their own problems. We realize that we shall have to devote more time to a study of Cuba, and we pass on for the present, to decide what other problems are vital at the moment.

A sport enthusiast volunteers the information that the Giants have won a double header. Another pupil reports that a certain major industry has accepted its code under the N.R.A. Immediately there comes a flood of questions and comments. And so we proceed until the blackboard is well filled with topics, statements, and problems.

Our next step is to weigh the value of the various events and questions, and to discuss them briefly. The class soon rules out such items as the winning of a ball game and events of a freakish nature as having no permanent value. The pupils are beginning to recognize relative worth in news. The class discussion also serves to bring into sharp relief the gaps in the knowledge of the group concerning various problems, and to aid the individual in deciding what problem he would like to investigate further.

In a few days the members of the class are ready to make such a choice. Committees of three or four pupils are allowed to work on a topic. In general, each pupil is to serve on some committee, though under some circumstances a pupil may be allowed to undertake an investigation alone. The committees report to the class, and these reports form the basis for further class discussions. The natural unit of study, therefore, is the problem; the contemporary problem proves to be the most vital.

In this procedure the function of the teacher is to guide, to encourage, to balance, to suggest relationships, but not to supply a detailed plan of work. That is to be avoided. If the teacher yields to the importunities of the pupils to organize the work for them and to supply data, he will deprive them of the real value the work might have for them.

As in the case of the study of current problems in the history classes described earlier in this paper, so in the class in human relations, habits and skills must be developed in the use of newspapers, magazines, and books of all sorts.

Studying current problems, using current sources of information, tends to develop the habit of thinking about current problems and of using current sources of information. The individual, therefore, will become increasingly intelligent concerning social problems and will avoid that tragedy, so often encountered, of a citizen who tends to think concerning social problems in terms of conditions which existed when he studied ancient history, but which have long since been materially changed.

120. THE SCOPE OF A RELATED PROGRAM OF ENGLISH AND SOCIAL STUDIES IN THE UNIVERSITY OF CHICAGO HIGH SCHOOL [23]

THE ENGLISH PROGRAM, ASSOCIATED WITH THE SOCIAL STUDIES

Year	Language-Composition	Reading-Literature	Social Studies
Sub-Freshman	English Usage	The Literature of American Life — Associated Work — Related Courses	United States
Freshman	Community Life-English — An integrated course: language, composition, social science, reading, and literature		Modern World I
Sophomore	English Grammar and Composition	The Literature of the Modern World — Associated Work — Related Courses	Modern World II
Junior	Grammar Review and Advanced Composition	Correlated Courses — The Literature of Early Civilizations — Associated Work — Correlated Courses	Economic Society — Early Civilizations
Senior	Advanced Composition and Rhetoric	Correlated Courses — The Literature of Western Civilization — Associated Work — Correlated Courses	American Political Institutions — Western Civilization

[23] The University of Chicago High School, The English Program, May 15, 1935.

CHAPTER VIII

PUPIL PURPOSES

121. IMPORTANCE OF PURPOSE [1]

William F. Book

NUMEROUS experiments have shown that if a learner can be given a clear idea of the end that is to be attained, his progress will be facilitated and his ultimate success made more certain. To make learning truly economical, there must be a definite purpose and some planning to achieve it. A defined purpose guides the learner's work, serves as a means for checking his reactions, and serves as an additional stimulus that elicits pertinent suggestions and successful trial responses.

A learner's purpose, therefore, not only supplies additional motive power but also guides his responses to an end that is clearly sensed before he begins to work. Few persons are willing to work blindly. When a learner knows exactly what is to be achieved and sees that success is being attained, his progress is satisfying to him. This inner drive toward successful activity, which any definite purpose inevitably provides, is in reality one of the most essential factors in economical learning, since it recognizes the need for the particular type of activity that is required to solve the problems involved.

If this conscious factor can be successfully introduced into a given case of learning so that the learner sees exactly what he is to achieve, and if in addition he can be made to see just what he must do to attain this desired result, the learning process will be lifted to the truly purposive level that yields the greatest possible results.

122. PURPOSE AS AN INTEGRATING INFLUENCE [2]

Daniel A. Prescott

It is the major thesis of this paper that mental hygiene, as taught to teachers, needs a new point of focus. At present teachers are given the idea that integration, the single-minded condition of mental

---

[1] From *Economy and Technique of Learning*, D. C. Heath and Company, Boston, 1932, p. 405.

[2] "Realism, Purposing, and Integration," *The Peabody Reflector and Alumni News*, 9:15, January, 1936.

health, is achieved through absence of conflict, through the avoidance of situations that might involve unpleasant emotions. But this is really a negative attitude. I wish to stress the point that integration is secured more surely and permanently by the development of a positive, purposive outlook on life — even if some measure of frustration is experienced more or less continuously as the individual works toward his goals. Then I have a second thesis. It is the extension of this first principle to that great social entity, the nation. I feel that a nation is mentally healthy only when it has great collective purposes that it is seeking to accomplish. Even a cursory examination of history or of contemporary world conditions will show that the greatest vitality and vigor of national effort is found in the countries challenged to accomplish collectively certain definite and consciously stated objectives. Finally there is a third proposition. It is that individual citizens can best feel a sense of their own personal worth as they apply themselves realistically to the task of furthering the great rational goals of their nation. In other words, I hold that people should state their own personal purposes in terms of the larger objectives of their nation. To sum up — the thesis of this paper is that mental hygiene should shift its perspective away from the analysis of the individual and his needs. Instead we should study the collective interdependence that exists within our society and that is *reality* for all of us. When this is done it will surely be discovered that individual purposing of a constructive social type must replace the anarchistic personal purposing that has been fostered traditionally in our time.

Weigh the fairness of the following analysis and see whether one is not forced to these conclusions. Under the impetus of a strong belief in the efficacy of science and growing out of the observation of the industrial applications of science, our curriculum makers have analyzed life's various activities to discover what to teach. They have tried to learn what specific knowledges and skills are necessary to successful individual functioning in the vocational, avocational, personal, and civic phases of our existence. When they have discovered the words used most frequently in our language, the eye-movement habits essential to speedy silent reading, the skills necessary to an efficient typist or stenographer, the dates and events that marked the turning points in our history or the ideals that our forefathers found adapted to their times, they have told us to teach this agglomeration of items to the pupils in our schools. They have suggested that we " form the necessary stimulus-response bonds," or that we " condition " our children to these habits or ideals by clever psychological set-ups, just as one might train animals for a circus performance. They believed that this was " scientific " education.

They had seen these specific knowledges and skills in use and could prove it: they had Professor Thorndike's word for the neural bonds (that is, until Professor Lashley spoke up) so they turned the schools into assembly lines. Each child as he was carried along the slowly progressing line had a number combination nut added here, a loose historical screw tightened there, and the motor of "desire for personal success" assembled independently along another line on the birthdays of our eminent statesmen and soldiers. This process of forming stimulus-response bonds to meet life's various activity needs was to produce the "adjusted individual," the smoothly functioning car in the crowded traffic of our urban life.

How has it worked out? We have the highest incidence of nervous breakdowns, insanity, divorce, and crime of any nation on earth. In other words they turned the cars over to crazy drivers, drunken drivers, drivers who didn't know where they were going and had had no experience with driving before. Our scientific educators forgot that every car made has been turned over to an intelligence to be used purposively. They forgot that driving a car successfully implies constant control over it, exercised by a mind continuously evaluating the changing panorama, figuring out the purposes and intentions of fellow drivers on the highway and cooperating with them to help them get where they are going as well as striving to arrive himself. Our scientific-educators forgot all about the driver. No wonder we have had smash-ups. Stated in other terms, we have forgotten that knowledge and skill have no value or meaning except in terms of the purposes for which they are used. Our schools have too often failed to provide this integrative core of a *purpose*, about which to bind all the knowledge and skill into a smoothly functioning, self-directing unit. The error came through the stimulus-response fallacy, for we are not machines controlled by external stimulation but living organisms behaving in response to internally originated desires, aspirations, longings. In fact, external stimuli have meaning for us only in terms of our internal needs. Education cannot afford to neglect purpose longer.

123. THE NATURE OF PURPOSIVE BEHAVIOR [3]

Boyd H. Bode

This brings us squarely to the problem of purposive behavior. As was said a few pages back, we start with an organism that is already active. The activities that are already under way are de-

[3] From *Conflicting Psychologies of Learning*, D. C. Heath and Company, Boston, 1929, pp. 245-247.

termined in part by the inborn connections of the nervous system and in part by habits. As a convenient illustration, let us take a hungry boy whose attention is attracted by an apple on a tree. The fact that he is hungry makes him sensitive to stimulations that have reference to eating. The craving for food involves reactions or habits that he has established previously with reference to apples, since these have to do with eating, and so the apple on the tree catches his attention easily. The apple when seen becomes a stimulus to reaching and eating. But there are difficulties in the way. Perhaps the apple is too high to be reached, or there is a difficult fence to be got over, or there is a dog in the yard that must be taken into account. Consequently there is a conflict of responses and need of reorganization. The manner in which this reorganization of responses is brought about is characteristic and distinctive of purposive behavior. It is accomplished through a reorganization of the perceived situation. As the boy stands and looks, he notices a shed near the tree upon which he can climb and thus circumvent the dog, or he sees a ladder in the yard that can be used for securing the apple. The whole situation is transformed. Instead of just seeing apple and adjoining shed, he sees " shed-that-can-be-climbed-to-get-the-apple-out-of-reach-of-the-dog." Psychologically this mode of perceiving the situation is as different as can be from the original perception. The stimulus is made over into something else. The ability to secure adaptation in this way is what we mean by intelligence. We reorganize the responses by reorganizing the stimulus. The fact that this reorganization of response is made on the spot and is not determined beforehand by the inborn connections of the nervous system is what distinguishes purposive behavior from the adaptive behavior that results from reflexes.

There are two factors or traits in this process that merit special mention. One is the part that is played by habit. It is evident, for example, that the suggestion of climbing the shed could not have occurred unless the boy had already acquired habits of climbing. The other is the act of reconstituting the situation into a new whole by the introduction of new relationships. The boy may never have picked apples in this particular manner before, and so it is necessary for him to see the situation in a new way. Persons that are quick to do this are called " bright "; those who are slow are called " stupid." But whether it is done with facility or not, the act when it occurs is an act of sheer creation. Things are put together in a new relationship or according to a new pattern. The situation is continuously made over as the act proceeds. Perhaps the boy has to find a box before he can get on the shed; perhaps he needs a stick after he is on the shed in order to bring the apple within reach. The peculiarity of conscious behavior lies precisely in this progressive making over of the stimulus. This is the everlasting difference between purposive and mechanical behavior. In mechanical behavior the stimulus merely starts the activity; in purposive behavior the stimulus undergoes continuous reconstitution throughout the whole course of the activity. Both the stimulus and the response are being shaped up as the act proceeds.

124. PURPOSE AND CONSCIOUSNESS [4]

Ephraim Vern Sayers

In the common use of the term, purpose implies consciousness. In the analysis of the adjustive process that is necessary to understand purpose, we need, however, as was the case in the attempt to find the general nature and place of thinking, to go back to the process as it appears below the level of consciousness. Here is seen the aspect of equilibration that is at the base of purpose. This aspect is the drive or tendency toward the re-establishment of a former balance in interaction. To trace this aspect to a focus in consciousness which transforms it into purpose is to observe the interaction, of which it is a quality, attain a sufficient complexity of organization to be called consciousness, intelligence, or thought.

One cannot conceive of conscious purpose as existing in separation from thought. To have a purpose means to be aware of the direction in which one's activities are moving, that is, aware of the future condition of integral activity which present action is operating to instate. But this awareness is the essence of thinking. Thinking is precisely becoming aware in advance of the consequences of one's activity, thus permitting the future to come into the present situation to modify interaction. What is involved throughout an adjustive act on the level of consciousness is an interaction of the organism with more than the present environment; the future consequences of the interaction as it proceeds also enter the present situation to guide and determine interaction. But the past is involved in the process. Consciousness, that is, becomes then the phenomenon in which past experience enters present experience in the guise of an anticipated, and therefore guiding, future. To be conscious means that the drive to equilibrium has resulted in behavior involving such an organization of available patterns of action as to include patterns which would otherwise be activated only later as a

[4] *Educational Issues and Unity of Experience,* Contributions to Education No. 357, Bureau of Publications, Teachers College, Columbia University, New York, 1929, pp. 92–93.

consequence of intermediate organism-environment interaction. Guidance or control of the drive is thus evolved; the latter is no longer blind. This is the operation of the past in the present, but it is also the operation of the future in the present. Consciousness, as this quality of past-present-future organization of activity, is thinking, and purpose is the quality of propulsiveness in adjustive activity when it is thus organized. Adjustive activity cannot exhibit one of these qualities in separation from the other. Thought and purpose are integrally related, and both are qualities of adjustive activity.

125. "The Psychology of Purpose" [5]

H. L. Hollingworth

Before leaving the topic of motivation we must consider another topic that is sometimes inexcusably confused with it — namely, the concept of *purpose* or *plan*. Thus it is sometimes loosely said that the motive of the hungry kitten is to eat; the motive of the fearful soldier is to get away from warfare. This is a hopeless confusion of the actual motive with the technique that will alleviate it. But the two things are quite different. The motive is the initial irritant that leads to activity. If the activity to which it leads is effective, that is, if it eliminates the irritant, then this effective act may be referred to as the technique. That is, it is the *proper way* to act in the face of such a motive. But the act and the motive, being different events, should not be confused or identified.

Thus the motive of a boy's activity on a particular occasion may be the prickly feeling of heat which he locates in his skin. This irritant sets up activities, and if the boy has already had considerable experience, either one or another of quite a number of alternative adjustments may be resorted to, in the light of previous learning. This particular distress may be relieved by quite a number of different techniques.

The boy may be relieved of his motive, for example, by lying immersed in the bathtub for awhile; by opening the windows; by turning on the electric fan; by going swimming; by falling asleep; by drinking cold beverages. Whichever one of these acts (determined by other cues from the present situation which reveal the feasibility of these various adjustments) the boy should adopt, it would be incorrect to refer to it as his motive. It would be instead, simply a method of relief, a technique of alleviation, a response that

[5] From *Educational Psychology*, D. Appleton-Century Company, New York, 1933, pp. 71–72.

might have for its effect the elimination of the motive. The motive is the persistent feeling of prickly heat.

However, in individuals capable of what we call *thinking*, an act may be *contemplated* before it is actually executed. To contemplate an act is to have some plan of it, some symbolic representation of it. This symbolic plan may, in well-trained and thoughtful people, be the very first reaction to the motive. Thus the boy in question might find " in his mind's eye " a visual image of the brook and of himself standing in the water. Or he might find himself repeating the names of his favorite soda fountain beverages, dismissing each until one came to mind upon which he lingered fondly.

Any such picture, representation, or symbolic reference to an act may be called a plan of that act, a *thought* of it. When such a plan occurs in connection with a motive, the two together constitute a *purpose*. A purpose then is the symbolic representation of a mode of eliminating a motive. It is a technique of relief, a plan of salvation, tentatively mapped out and considered before its execution. Since purposes play so large a part in human life, it is important to be clear about their character. A plan without a motive is inert. But a motive without a plan is likely to be futile. A purpose requires the joint occurrence and synergy of a motive and a plan.

126. Psychological Basis of Purpose [6]

Edward Chace Tolman

A purpose is a condition in the organism (analyzable presumably, if we knew enough, into physiology and then into physics and chemistry) whereby acts which lead to (or from) given types of end-situation persist and get learned, whereas those which fail in such gettings to (or from) drop out, get unlearned. This is a remarkable phenomenon. But it is not a supernatural or spiritualistic one. It is a perfectly objective feature which appears in behavior. And one of the chief tasks of the behaviorist is to note and record its appearances. To observe the range and distribution throughout the animal kingdom of such contingencies of acts upon their ends and the limitations and combinations of which such contingencies are capable, is one of the main jobs of the psychologist. He must, to be sure, explain such contingencies as soon as he can in physiological terms, but this need for a physiological explanation does not mean that he can deny or ignore the contingencies themselves. And the further fact that introspecting organisms do not always have to wait to act

[6] From " Purposive Behavior," *The Psychological Review*, 35:525–526, November, 1928.

in order to discover that their behavior is probably going to be in this way contingent — the fact, in short, that they can often correctly report purposes before those purposes appear in gross behavior is, of course, an even more remarkable phenomenon. It needs much study and explanation. But the existence even of this phenomenon is a testimony not to an essentially mentalistic character in purpose but merely to the complexities of the behavior-situation.

127. THE EXPERIMENTALIST VIEW OF PURPOSE [7]

John L. Childs

Thus two basic conceptions in the philosophy of experimentalism point alike to the same general conclusion for education. As we have already seen, the experimentalist sees man living in a world that is a mixture of the regular and the changing, of the fixed and the uncertain, of the stable and the precarious. In short, man lives in a world in which the character of existence is such that intelligent, purposeful activity is demanded if he is to achieve a satisfying experience. In the second place, the experimentalist also believes that the nature of experience is such that the necessary condition for learning to behave intelligently is the freedom to engage in purposeful activity. By purposeful activity is not meant mere random activity in response to fleeting impulse. Purposeful activity is controlled, experimental activity. But the primary controls inhere in the subject-matter of the situation of concern rather than in externally imposed influences. Purposeful activity is activity freely initiated by the agent in response to a situation whose difficulties have a challenging grip in his present experience. He frames his ends in the light of the resources and difficulties found in the actual problematical situation. Normally the motivation and the interest are intrinsic in the process itself, because the person dealing with the situation is awake to its bearing on his experience. In purposeful activity the learning is more sure because the whole individual is attending to what is developing. He is alert to see connections between transitive events, and between his acts and the consequences that flow from those acts.

In attempting to introduce the principle of purposeful activity into the school, the experimentalist is not concerned merely to add one more technique by which children can be induced to learn desired subject-matter. Purposeful activity as the foundation for school procedures is the natural outgrowth of his whole philosophical

[7] From *Education and the Philosophy of Experimentalism,* The Century Company, New York, 1931, pp. 81–82.

position. It is the educational correlative of his understanding of the world in which we live, and of the nature of the process by which experience grows intelligent. As such it is the fundamental principle in his entire program for education.

128. BEHAVIORISM DENIES PURPOSE [8]

Zing Yang Kuo

In the first place, the concept of purpose does violence to the stimulus-response formula. Behaviorism, as I understand it, cannot be anything more than a science of mechanics dealing with the mechanical movements of those physical structures (or electron-proton-aggregates according to Weiss) which the biologists have called organisms. The S-R formula of behaviorism is directly derived from the basic principles of physics. Hence, in describing behavior, no behaviorist should make any assumptions which are not in harmony with the fundamental concepts of the physical sciences. Now, in physics, every movement is considered as a direct functioning of some environmental stimulus; no modern physicist will assume a third term or third factor — be it mental or otherwise — to explain physical behavior. Why, then, should the behaviorist be required to do so? Is not the behavior of the organism also a direct functioning of environmental stimulation? Do we really need such concepts as motive, purpose, drive, impulse, determining tendency or what not, to explain behavior? If we accept the S-R formula as our scientific motto, can we allow any third factor — purpose, drive or what not — to be a causal factor of behavior? In other words, have we a right to assume any factor other than stimulus as the directing and determining agency of response? Indeed, to the behaviorists, every action of the organism is a passive or 'forced' movement — to borrow J. Loeb's expression — passive in the sense that the organism does not initiate movements by itself except being compelled by environmental forces. The difference between the action of a man and the movement of a stone is merely a difference in complexity, primarily due to the differences in the complexity of structure. With the advance of the behavioristic technique such a difference should become capable of mathematical treatment. The basic principles that have been employed to explain the behavior of a stone should be sufficient to explain human behavior. The behaviorist need not assume an inner motive in the case of human behavior any more than the physicist needs to assume spiritual influence in the case of stone movement.

[8] From " The Fundamental Error of the Concept of Purpose and the Trial and Error Fallacy," *The Psychological Review*, 35:416–417, September, 1928.

129. THE CONNECTIONIST VIEW OF PURPOSE [9]

Edward Lee Thorndike

It is a general law of mental action that the response to any external situation will depend upon the condition of the person as well as upon the nature of the situation. If the situation is itself an inner one, that is, a part of the person's mind, the response will depend not only on it but also on the rest of him. What a person learns as a consequence of any situation is a consequence of his nature as well.

The condition of the person is conveniently considered as consisting partly of rather permanent and fixed mental sets such as are commonly referred to by the words *instinct, temperament, purpose,* and *ideal,* and partly of more temporary and shifting sets such as are named fatigue, sleepiness, the disposition to add rather than subtract, and the intention to be as unfriendly as is consistent with good manners.

The general fact that the status of the person at the time influences his response is sufficiently obvious, being illustrated by almost every moment of any person's life. More careful and systematic evidence of the choice and direction of connections and the determination of responses by the set or attitude of the person, as influenced by the instructions given him or by the general nature of the task, has been reported by the psychologists who have studied the thought processes.

Equally obvious are the influences of those more permanent attitudes or sets of mind in a person which belong to him as Frenchman or German, Christian or Jew, teacher or physician, father or son, optimist or pessimist, realist or romanticist, extravert or introvert, hard-boiled or sensitive, energetic or inert.

The attitude or set or adjustment of a man is a chief determiner not only of what he thinks and does but also of what he will welcome or reject — of what will satisfy or annoy him. If you are set to speak French, you are discomforted by the thought of an apt English phrase which would have rejoiced you under ordinary conditions. If you are a beginner at golf, you are content with a drive which in later expertness may be intolerable to you.

Every connection is made by a particular person or mind or brain in a particular status. Every after-effect of every connection is an effect upon a particular person or mind or brain in a particular status. Expectations, intentions, purposes, interests, and desires refer to dynamic factors as real as the situation-response connections

[9] From *Human Learning,* The Century Company, New York, 1931, pp. 119–122.

PUPIL PURPOSES

between hearing *four times five* and thinking *twenty*, or seeing *c a t* and saying " cat."

Some of you have perhaps thought or felt that the view of learning as connecting which I have presented in the previous lectures is too mechanical and fatalistic, leaving no room for the control from within by purposes of the man's own making. Some of my fellow-students of psychology and education certainly think so.

What I have just said concerning the ubiquitous and potent influence of mental sets or dispositions, including the total make-up of the person so far as it may be active in any given case, seems to meet these criticisms.

The influences which coöperate with the situation to determine the response are as complicated, variable, purposive, and spiritual as the learners themselves are. The chief rôle in the drama of learning is not played by the external situations, but by the learner. The reason why I have said much about frequency of connections, satisfyingness of connections, identifiability of situations, availability of responses and the like, and little about the purposes or mental sets or total minds which direct and organize them is not that I belittle the latter. It is rather that the general importance of the latter is obvious, and that the variations of individual idiosyncrasy do not seem specially fruitful for study. So far, then, there should be no quarrel between an honest connectionist or associationist and an honest purposivist. Both equally believe that individual attitudes, adjustments, dispositions, sets, interests, and purposes work with the situations of each moment to determine what connections these shall make.

The quarrel, if any, will be over the connectionist's account of the constitution and development of these attitudes, sets, purposes, or selves.

What is any given set or attitude or disposition of mind made out of? More broadly, what are a person's interests and purposes made out of? Still more broadly, what is his *total mind* or *self* or *entire system of tendencies* that may coöperate with the external situations? The answer which I must in honesty give, though aware of the difficulty which I should have in defending it, is that all these are in the last analysis made out of connections and readinesses, original or acquired, including those multitudinous connections whereby satisfyingness and annoyingness are attached to certain events in the mind.

If I observe any special set or purpose, such as the tendency to divide rather than multiply, or the desire to give opposites rather than meanings, or the lust for fame, or patriotism, or general benevolence, and list what I find in it, the list contains ideas, connections with totals and with elements, readinesses to connect, interests, and the like — all produced by original tendencies or past connectings and rewardings. If I attempt to analyze a man's entire mind, I find connections of varying strength between (a) situations, elements of situations, and compounds of situations and (b) responses, readinesses to respond, facilitations, inhibitions, and directions of responses. If all of these could be completely inventoried, telling what the man would think and do and what would satisfy and annoy him, in every conceivable situation, it seems to me that nothing would be left.

I read the facts which psychologists report about adjustments, configurations, drives, integrations, purposes, tensions, and the like, and all of these facts seem to me to be reducible, so far as concerns their powers to influence the course of thought or feeling or action, to connections and readinesses. Learning is connecting. The mind is man's connection-system. Purposes are as mechanical in their nature and action as anything else is.

130. A Criticism of Thorndike's Theory of Learning [10]

J. F. Brown and D. D. Feder

In Thorndike's classical theory of learning all the phenomena of learning, from the modified avoidance reaction of paramecium to the general relativity theory of Einstein are explained by the three laws, (1) the law of readiness, (2) the law of exercise, (3) the law of effect. Concerning the finality of these laws we let Thorndike speak for himself. " One form of misunderstanding these laws consists in supposing the necessity of additional factors." The wide experimental and theoretical criticism that the above laws have received is already familiar to most students of psychology to-day. But despite the criticism the laws remain the corner stone of the vast structure of American educational practice and theory.

In his recent book, " Human Learning," * Thorndike casts aside his dictum concerning the finality of his laws and presents a decidedly modified theory, which we briefly outline:

(1) The law of readiness receives practically no consideration at all in the new book.

(2) The law of exercise, or at least its sub law, the law of use, is almost completely abandoned. Mere repetition is declared to be of no avail.

[10] From " Thorndike's Theory of Learning as Gestalt Psychology," *Psychological Bulletin*, 31 :427–432, June, 1934.

* E. L. Thorndike, Human Learning, New York, Century Co., 1931. Our criticism is chiefly concerned with this book. Unless otherwise specifically stated all future page references refer to it.

" Repetition of a connection in the sense of mere sequence of two things in time has then very, very little power, perhaps none, as a cause of learning " (p. 28). This is shown in a series of rather ingenious group experiments on humans in the first and second chapters of Thorndike's book. That mere repetition could not carry the whole burden of animal learning has been clear to Thorndike for some time. He makes, however, no reference to the broad literature on this problem. While the omission of the many well-known papers on animal learning available in English is perhaps to be understood, the present writers consider it a bad oversight on his part not to have mentioned the work of Lewin on humans. Lewin's experiments, performed in a more systematic theoretical setting than Thorndike's, gave identical results and forced Lewin to identical conclusions. Incidentally they were performed some ten years ago.

(3) The law of effect also receives considerable modification. " Satisfyers " retain their potency in the new theory, " annoyers " have limited power. Important as it is for the theory of learning, however, we will not attempt to deal with Thorndike's theory of motivation in a paper of this length.

Not only has the validity of the old laws been modified, but we find five distinctly new concepts postulated as necessary to explain human learning. They are (a) belonging, (b) identifiability, (c) availability, (d) trial, (e) system. It is our contention that these conditioning factors, which in Thorndike's presentation are so many *ad hoc* hypotheses, functioning somewhat as the psyches of the vitalist, are logically prior to his other laws. We further believe ourselves able to show that these factors are the properties of organized wholes, in fact, the basic postulates of Gestalt psychology. As we criticize each one we will give at least one reference to papers by Gestalt psychologists in which the property under consideration was previously investigated in terms of Gestalt psychology.

A. *Belonging.* The chief new factor that conditions learning according to Thorndike is " belonging." Thorndike describes it as follows: " a sequence carrying with it a sense that the second thing belongs to the first or such a sequence plus the *sense of relatedness* or *belonging* " (p. 18, italics ours). Belonging, to Thorndike, is obviously not given in the stimulus as physically defined. It is therefore either something that accrues to two independent psychological events, or it must be a primary property of certain events. It seems to us that Thorndike is not clear on this point. But, if it is something accruing, through experience or anything else, it need not have been handled as a new postulate but could be treated by the old laws. Since Thorndike does not so treat it, he must admit it as a primary property of certain psychological events. Then our argument is simple. " Belonging " or sense of relationship implies organization (*i.e.*, Struktur, Gestalt), a property of wholes and only of wholes. Wholes cannot be treated as additively formed sums of parts. " Belonging " cannot be inherent in the parts as such. Thorndike and the Gestalt psychologists are talking about the same sort of thing.

The chief tenet of Gestalt psychology is simply this: *There are events in nature where there is organization and this organization is primary, so that the properties of wholes can not be understood as a resultant of the activities or properties of the individual parts.* This is *not* mysticism, it is *not* vitalism, it is *not* mentalism. It is simply a proposition about experience, possessing, until it is refuted, equal probability and equal epistemological validity with the opposite statement that the events of nature are composed of individual independent parts. This has been difficult of comprehension to many people because most students of science have had the atomistic approach drilled into them without any questioning of the epistemological validity of the atomistic assumption that wholes are made up of the summation of their parts. The Gestalt psychologists in their investigations came upon certain psychological events that could not be explained by treating these events as additively formed sums of parts. In most cases, since they too had received the regular atomistic training, they tried at first to do this. But is was impossible. Thorndike has apparently recently come upon events of this nature.

It is enlightening to read Wertheimer's 1912 paper on apparent movement carefully to see what led him to set up the Gestalt hypothesis. Strange though it may seem to readers without first-hand knowledge of this paper, the fact is that Wertheimer discovered nothing. But, of far greater importance to the history of psychology, he thought through to their logical consequences the several existing atomistic theories regarding apparent movement and then he subjected these hypotheses to a series of brilliant critical experiments. He found that no existing theory could by the summation of independent local events explain apparent movement. He found out further that the likelihood of any further theory doing so was extremely slight. Hence he was *forced* to postulate the existence in nature of at least one psychological event in which the structure or organization or Gestalt is prior to the parts. After finding one such event he and his colleagues naturally enough began to look for others. They found many. Such in skeleton is the history of Gestalt psychology.

In learning, Koehler found " belonging " an essential factor for learning in apes; Lewin found it equally essential for humans. Numerous other investigators have since made use of it.

" Belonging " then refers to the fact that certain psychological

events exist as structures (Gestalten, configurations), irrespective of experience and prior to it. Learning occurs easily (i.e., without repetition) when the subject experiences such an event. If we have made ourselves clear concerning " belonging " we may deal more briefly with Thorndike's other factors.

B. *Identifiability* refers to " the qualities in a situation which make it easy to connect something with it, and the qualities in a response which make it easy to connect it with something " (p. 82).

In the Gestalt psychology it has long been recognized that certain structures are very stable and can be broken down only under certain conditions. Others are less stable. Considerable research has already been devoted to this property of Gestalten. Let us consider here only the work of K. Gottschaldt. Gottschaldt demonstrated about eight years ago that the recognition or non-recognition of the simplest and most commonly experienced geometrical figures was conditioned by the whole in which these figures were imbedded. Furthermore, he showed that the stability of certain structures could not be modified, no matter how great the experience. It is very instructive to compare Gottschaldt's experiments with those of Thorndike (pp. 82–89) concerning " identifiability." Such a comparison convinces us that Gottschaldt and Thorndike were investigating the same thing.

Under certain conditions the relation of " belongingness " between two elements appears where it was previously lacking (Thorndike's nomenclature), or new structures emerge or are differentiated from existing structures (Gestalt nomenclature). This we call learning. *" Identifiability " refers to the fact that since structures vary in their stability, parts in certain structures are more readily differentiated into parts of new wholes than in others. Learning occurs easily when the task set for the subject is to " form a connection" between parts of less stable structures.*

C. *Availability.* " Consider now the principle of availability or get-at-ableness of the response, which is that, other things being equal, connections are easy to form in proportion as the response is available, summonable, such that the person can have it or make it at will " (p. 89). So far as we can see no really new principle is here involved. The problem of availability again hangs together with the stability of structures. Particularly interesting in this connection are the experiments of Schwarz. Schwarz showed that the " availability " (i.e., whether or not a part of a structured whole occurred) of a response depended on the structure of the whole in which the response in question was imbedded.

" Availability " of a response refers to the fact that as structures vary in their stability, certain responses can be differentiated from

the wholes in which they occur into new wholes more readily than others. The stability of structures conditions the appearance of new responses and so conditions whether in a given situation learning or habitual response will occur.

D. *Trial.* By trial Thorndike refers to the utilization of the incorrect or inadequate responses on the way to the goal. This is a problem of motivation and lies without the limits we have set for ourselves in this paper. One quotation, however, will show how very close Thorndike has come to certain basic Gestalt concepts. " For example a boy confronts the situation — Find the product of 435 and 721. . . . Find the product of 435 and 721 not only starts him on the first step of writing 435×721 or 721×435, but also remains a pervading element and controlling factor during the remainder of the chain, until some status is attained which announces that the required result is attained and bids him turn his mind to other things " (p. 93). Surely we have clearly here " perception of remote goals," leading to " resolution of tension " and hence " equilibrium." These are basic concepts of the Gestalt theory of motivation.

E. *System.* System concerns " the tendency to make the connections or links or bonds or associative habits which I have represented as the fundamental dynamic features of mental life subservient to certain logical and conventional systems " (p. 94). " On the other hand these systems, from the humblest, such as the alphabet, to the proudest, such as a science or a philosophy, are themselves constituted out of connections." Here Thorndike infers (without any experimental basis at all) that systems are built up of connections. If connections in themselves depend on belonging, identifiably, etc., it should be obvious again that system implies organization.

We have attempted to demonstrate that Thorndike has unwittingly adopted the basic concept of Gestalt psychology. In his book, however, he devotes a considerable section to criticism of Gestalt psychology.

131. A CRITICISM OF THE STIMULUS RESPONSE VIEW OF BEHAVIOR [11]

Hilda Taba

Selective choice and self-determination in human personality seem to be concepts that do not exist in the vocabulary of behaviourists, and to a great degree in the vocabulary of most of our contemporary psychologies. Personality is supposed to be devoid of any such determining capacity. It is left to the mercy of chance conditions in

[11] From *Dynamics of Education,* Harcourt Brace and Company, New York, 1932, pp. 86–88.

external stimulation. It is not the product of stimulation by meaningful things in our environment, but is a result of an elementary atomistic stimulation of our senses. Statements like the following are very frequent in present-day writings in educational psychology:

" All forms of human behaviour, whether muscular activities such as those of grasping, striking, or speaking; glandular activities, such as the secretion of tears, saliva or gastric juice; or mental activities, such as perceiving, imagining, remembering, thinking or reasoning, are reactions to definite stimulation." *

The statement that all our forms of behaviour are reactions is a very true one and cannot be emphasized enough. The trouble is that the reaction to a " definite " stimulus has come to mean a definite reaction to a stimulus that is but an abstracted element of the total stimulating situation.

Are the reactions to isolated, elementary, and meaningless sense stimuli the characteristic aspect of human behaviour? Can behaviour be understood only in terms of these? And if so, what are the consequences?

There is no doubt that reactions of this type — the type Watson and Gates have selected for their examples — occur in human behaviour, but as studied by them they occur only under conditions of controlled experimentation; that is, in artificial situations. They do not occur in normal experience. And even in those experimental situations, one may question the possibility of the existence of purely single and isolated reactions to single stimuli. These stimuli are part of a larger stimulating situation, and what psychologists are able to observe for themselves is largely an abstraction made for the sake of proving a theory, formulated beforehand. If such reactions occur under normal conditions, they are so rare that an attempt to use the principles culled by observation of such cases for the explanation of all human behaviour is highly unjustified. Experimentation with abstracted stimulus-response patterns is desirable for certain limited purposes, but a clear distinction should be made between what happens in experimentally controlled situations and what takes place in reality. Psychologists should not substitute abstractions for real human behaviour, or from the former deduce principles for the latter.

Organic behaviour is of a totally different character from the one constructed by such psychologies. Humans as well as lower organisms react to objects and to meaningful situations in their environment, and do so in the course of, and by the direction of, some activ-

* Gates, *Psychology for Students of Education*, p. 24.

ity initiated by themselves. Biological investigations have definitely proved that even organisms as simple as those able to make only two different types of responses are capable of behaviour differentiated to some degree, which cannot be fully understood by such mechanistic conceptions. The behaviour of such organisms does not occur in terms of an isolated and immediate stimulus but is a function of objects and complex situations in environment, including elements like position, direction, degree of concentration, of stimulating matter, rates of change, and so forth. This, of course, does not mean that these elements are grasped by lower organisms as such. It only means that when different stimuli are demanding more than one reaction, these several simultaneous reactions organize themselves so that the total reaction is different from and more than their sum when appearing separately. Such organized reactions make possible a behaviour specifically directed towards some phase of the environment, and thus add to the apparent purposiveness and intelligence of the organism's behaviour.

132. " SATISFACTION: ITS SOURCE AND FUNCTION IN LEARNING " [12]

H. B. Wyman

To state the case in non-technical language, the " Laws of Learning " rest upon the basic conception of reflex-arcs in the nervous system. That the elemental neurone structure with connecting synapses in the central nervous system are microscopically verifiable should be understood from the first. While the neural structure upon which the " laws " are based must be accepted as *fact,* it should be remembered that the psychology founded upon this structure is *theory.* Because the one is verified by recognized neurologists, the theory of human behavior built upon it is accepted as being equally valid. The reader is reminded that most of the theories of human learning were fabricated from facts observed in the study of animal behavior. Why not? If we explain behavior on a simple neural structure made complex by adding a great many such structures together, then animal behavior and human behavior would be fundamentally alike. It is logical, then, to study animals, where much greater freedom is to be had, and then apply the findings to man.

So it is that the stimulus-response explanation of human behavior (derived as indicated) is a theory attempting to explain the everyday facts of experience such as memory, intelligence, learning, on the basis of neurones and synapses known to exist in the nervous system.

[12] *Progressive Education,* 12:224–229, April, 1935.

The *sine qua non* of all experience is the ability to learn, hence it is of vital import in any psychological theory. It is for this reason as well as the bearing upon schoolroom practice that the "Laws of Learning" have been singled out for discussion. They may be briefly stated in the following terms:

For a synapse ready to conduct, to do so is satisfying; not to do so is annoying. For an unready synapse to be forced to conduct is probably annoying. This law is followed by the Law of Effect which asserts that if a bond or synapse responds with satisfaction, the connection or bond is strengthened; if a bond functions with annoyance, the bond is weakened. The third law holds that the more frequently a ready bond acts, " other things being equal," the stronger the bond becomes and the more likely one will be to repeat this experience. Conversely, the more frequently a bond functions with annoyance, the weaker the connection in the synapse and the less likely one is to repeat the act. There are some elaborations of these laws but the essence as paraphrased here in non-technical terms will meet our present needs.

All human experience, from the building of a simple reflex to the highest form of creative thinking can be explained, so this theory holds, on a simple " strength of synapse " basis. If learning takes place, it is because the bond which brings that response has been strengthened. Such a simple bit of learning as 3+2=5 will serve the purpose of illustration. When presented with the stimulus 3+2, the response, " 5," is made to follow. If the child is in an arithmetic class or other situation favorable to learning, he will have a set of bonds in readiness for such stimulation, and the response " 5 " will give a measure of satisfaction as a result of this readiness and subsequent action of the synapse involved. If this is done on several occasions of a similar nature, the bond will become stronger with each use and eventually becomes " fixed." Over-learning is explained by a bond that is much stronger than need be to produce the desired response.

The agreement of the facts of everyday experience with the theory is striking. There are, however, some points at which the theory seems inadequate if the teacher, relatively unfamiliar with the obliging nature of psychology, becomes critically minded. One question likely to arise in the mind of such a teacher is, " How does one learn from an annoying situation? " Simple enough! In the bond which functioned with annoyance, actual weakening resulted; but, at the same time, other bonds function and it is in these that the learning occurs. To illustrate: In this part of the country it is a favorite trick to initiate the " tenderfoot " by proffering a very attractive-looking ripe olive. As you may surmise, the experience is downright annoying, and one " learns " from it despite the fact that the bond for eating fresh ripe olives has been annihilated. But the bond for withdrawing or saying, " No thank you, I am very fond of them, but I've just had some," has become relatively strong and it is here that learning has taken place.

The difficulty is that one of the most common facts of experience (namely, that certain things are satisfying and certain things annoying) has been rationalized into a psychological theory that leaves too many vital facts of life inadequately accounted for. In the first place, satisfaction and its counterpart, annoyance, are concepts that are out of place in a mechanistic interpretation of life. We have no reason to think that purely mechanical forces experience either satisfaction or annoyance. It should also be noted that many situations from which learning accrues are neither satisfying nor annoying. True, one may indulge in further rationalization to the effect that these situations may be only mildly satisfying or annoying, but that all experience must be placed somewhere on the scale ranging from extreme satisfaction at one end to extreme annoyance at the other. This helps but little except as it is used to further the theory.

What has happened is that the concomitants of an act have been mistaken for the effective elements in all behavior. The " Laws of Learning " ascribe to a feeling of satisfaction or annoyance a peculiar function which makes one or the other of them primary in all learning. Kilpatrick refers to the Law of Effect as the basic law. If learning is to take place, satisfaction must ensue. This postulates readiness on the part of the neurone. This readiness when involving a relatively large number of synapses is spoken of as " set " or " purpose."

It is easy to see why Dr. Kilpatrick has gone to extremes in this matter of child purposing. If purpose is " set," " set " is readiness; and readiness is absolutely indispensable in learning. It is therefore evident that purpose is the crucial factor in learning. Dr. Kilpatrick believes in the significance of activity in learning, and rightly so. The combination of these two factors accounts for his characterization of the project as " wholehearted purposeful activity of the child's own choosing." It is readily seen why it is regarded as futile to carry on with an activity when the child's purpose lags. It means that no more learning takes place when readiness has gone. Pushed to its logical conclusion, it becomes an absurdity.

Another difficulty presents itself. If the bond is strengthened by satisfying experience, it is difficult to explain how this can be.

If the satisfaction comes some hours or (as is frequently the case) some weeks later, we are also in a real difficulty to explain how the bond could be effected by this subsequent satisfaction. However, we do know of the undisputed effect upon our subsequent behavior. What has been said of satisfaction and the strengthening of bonds could also be said about annoyance and the weakening of these connections.

What is the true source of satisfaction and annoyance and how do they affect human behavior? No experience takes place in isolation but is a part of a total situation in which it is for the moment focal. It gets its qualities from the situation fully as much as from the particular thing under consideration. Change the situation and you have changed the particular, because this part gets its qualities from the whole. Satisfaction and annoyance are among the many qualities of an experience. If the experience fits smoothly into the pattern of behavior which one has set up — one's purpose, if you please — satisfaction accompanies and follows the action. In order to have this satisfaction, the experience must give a nicely integrated picture as it moves to completion. If a certain action results in an outcome that is counter to the aims and purposes of the individual, then the pattern is distorted and the purpose is temporarily or permanently thwarted. This results in annoyance. It is readily seen how an experience that was originally satisfying, because it fitted in with the purpose of the moment, may be a gnawing cancer at a later date because it is not in line with the later purpose. For example, the satisfaction which comes from giving one " a piece of one's mind " may later cause frequent annoyance and embarrassment because it is not in accord with an avowed purpose of remaining calm under all sorts of trying circumstances.

How strange that we should seek such a subtle answer where conditions are relatively simple? A flat tire is satisfying to the repair man and annoying to the owner of the car; a fine job of safe-blowing is highly satisfying to the burglar and highly annoying to the owner of the safe. So we might continue indefinitely. The effect of a given action is contingent upon the pattern of behavior in which it is functioning.

On the surface this may seem to be a restatement of purpose as " set." " Set," which is a condition of neural pathways, can never be one with purposive activity which is characterized by projecting goals, selecting among them and setting up means of attaining them. On the one basis, what happens is a matter of accident. You do what you do because at the moment that particular pathway is strongest owing to the inherent strength of the bond or to the conduction unit in which it is functioning. If it proves satisfying, we have assurance that the bond must have been ready and will be even stronger the next time. A set of synapses would have difficulty in arranging the necessary readinesses to result in a particular system of orderly responses. What the whole organism can do functioning as a unit, and what the synapses might do working in machine-like fashion are entirely different.

The point is that we tend to do a thing or not do it, not because its previous insertion into a behavior pattern strengthened or weakened a bond, but because it appears to further or hinder the activity in progress. It hinges upon the meaning that the activity has for the prosecution of the purpose in hand. Inherently, satisfaction or the lack of it has nothing to do with whether or not we learn. The vital thing is that the individual re-acts to what has happened, which is to say that he sees the relationship inherent in the whole situation and the significance of each partial situation for the activity which he is striving to promote. That these meanings will be interesting to him is most likely true; to say that they are either satisfying or annoying is not in accord with the facts.

What are the educational implications of the foregoing statement of the case? In the first place, the " Laws of Learning " are founded upon an hypothesis that is of extremely doubtful validity. If this foundation is unwarranted, the laws are wiped out at once. In the second place, the laws are responsible for all kinds of abuses in education. Some of these have been mentioned. Rewards and punishments play entirely too important a rôle in learning so conceived. Exercise, drill, and habit formation become of paramount importance, and the genuine significance of true purpose is lost. Finally, it obscures the real source and value of satisfaction, which is an emotional quality of experience resulting from an activity that promotes the end sought and adds new zest to life.

Annoyance resulting from activity that falls short of achieving the purpose set up may be, and frequently is, the most dynamic factor in the new activity engaged upon with the same general purpose in view. Any layman knows that a feeling of satisfaction may be the most deadening influence in the experience of the individual. Instead, then, of being the sine qua non of all learning, satisfaction proves to be a generally valuable after-effect of learning. Rather than the cause of learning, satisfaction and also annoyance are the result of learning. There can be neither without learning, which may be restated as " seeing the meanings inherent in a whole situation." One cannot be satisfied or annoyed by an action unless one sees the significance of that action for what he wants to do. That he will tend to repeat those actions that are satisfying and to fail to repeat those that are annoying is true only when he is engaged upon an activity directed toward the same end as before. In some cases, the teacher wants one effect; in other cases, he wants the opposite one to follow a given action. The teacher wants a large measure of satisfying experience because he desires a large amount of success, measured in terms of promoting worthwhile experience, to attend the student's efforts. Plainly the emphasis must be placed upon meanings and understanding, and not upon drill and the formation of fixed habits. The learner tends to continue to do the things from which he gets some meaning; i.e., from which he learns. Both satisfaction and annoyance, among other values, are important because they furnish positive proof that meanings have come out of the particular learning situation. Exercise is important only in so far as old meanings are re-ëstablished, and new and more extensive meanings are discovered. After the meaning of 3+2 is understood, repetition can do little beyond keeping it in one's stock of meanings. This gives a valuable clue to the importance of spaced learning over unspaced.

One of the regrettable features of the " Laws of Learning " in practice is the piece-meal conception of human nature and human action. The stimulus-response psychology is an atomistic view of human nature which attempts to build up the behavior of man by an additive process in which countless fixed bonds are alleged to give the elaborate flexibility and complexities of human action. The parallel theories in biology and physics are the cell and atomic theories respectively, with their gene and electron-proton elaborations. When one attempts to explain the functions of the human body by the relatively simple properties of a cell (namely, vegetative, reproductive, and response to irritation) he attempts the impossible. The behavior of man transcends the properties of the cells that make up his body. The organism explains the cell, not the cell the organism.

Education based on such a psychology becomes an atomistic sort of affair consisting of a multitude of simple reflex-like responses that are expected to serve the needs of an everchanging situation. Thorndike's contention that " all learning is analytic " means that each element in a learning situation must be analyzed out and " fixed " by building the corresponding bond by exercise or drill. The true essence of learning is not analysis but synthesis, without which there can be no point to analysis. We meet situations as wholes and any picking out of constituents should serve to give a truer conception of the whole. It must not be overlooked that these constituents get their qualities not from themselves alone but from the whole in which they are to be found. Furthermore, this new learning experience gets its meaning from previous experience and adds new meaning to it in return. Thus education is a continuous reconstruction of experience. On the one hand, we have addition of responses; on the other, integration and reorganization of experience.

The piece-meal conception of education manifests itself further in its effect upon pupil-teacher relationships. The teacher is forced to place the major emphasis upon a fixed stimulus and a fixed response. The child is a passive organism in whom the proper response may be built if the stimulus is presented a sufficient number of times under the proper conditions of readiness. Subject matter constitutes the stimulus, and subject matter the response. The child, the soul of the educative process, is likely to be lost to the teacher's view. The textbook becomes a mass of facts to be learned; the teaching procedure degenerates into drill; the teacher becomes an arbitrary drillmaster; and the child, the unsuspecting and unsuspected victim of the system. Thinking is reduced to the minimum and becomes a dangerous thing for the child to do. Thinking begets knowledge and understanding, but understanding is an impostor where satisfaction and annoyance are the only means of learning.

Much more could be said concerning the deleterious effect of the " Laws of Learning " upon education. One problem has been singled out as being worthy of special mention. This treatment will permit of reference to only one. Certainly one of the major objectives of any system of education should be that of enabling the student to evolve an adequate philosophy of life. Without such a philosophy, a goal toward which one moves, the educational process has failed. The " Laws of Learning " tend to interfere with and to stifle this vital phase of education because they fail to supply satisfactory goals.

An adequate philosophy of life is one that influences the individual to seek out the relationships that are to be found in every situation. By so doing, it enables one to see every item of behavior in its proper perspective. So long as the well-spring of behavior is the stimulus and one's conduct is determined by a combination of the strength of the stimulus and the condition of the synapse, there is little that can be done about establishing and pursuing goals. Man is purely a victim of circumstances. In reality, before one can determine a course of action he must see the situation in all of its ramifications or relationships, and select those stimuli to which he will respond. He determines, furthermore, just what he shall do with them; i. e., whether he shall ignore them, be spurred to more determined action in the opposite direction, or incorporate them into his behavior because they further the activity upon which he is engaged. In other words, the effect of the stimulus is contingent upon how he *sees* it in the light of its effect upon his immediate program or his inclusive pattern of behavior summed up in what has been referred to as " a philosophy of life."

The difference hinges upon the conception of purpose. In the one case, purpose is " set " which, being interpreted, is a rather widespread condition of readiness involving many synapses. Let the reader imagine what kind of philosophy of life this kind of a purpose would supply. In the opposing view, purpose is in terms of ends to be attained which implies that these ends must be translated over into means. This demands that every item, every possible course of action, must be viewed in terms of how it effects this end. Applying the facts to a philosophy of life, it is evident that all conduct, all situations, must be viewed in terms of their relationship to the dominating goals of the individual's life. This makes for a life that moves steadily forward on a program which, properly conceived, strives for the ennoblement of man. The implications of this conception for the moral, economic, political, international and other phases of human experience may occur to the reader.

133. MECHANISTIC PSYCHOLOGY AND MOTIVATION [13]

Raymond H. Wheeler

. . . No problem pertaining to the school system needs critical inspection more than the problem of motivation. Here again the prevailing practice is a direct outgrowth of the mechanistic point of view in science, and the natural atomism of the everyday mind. Motivation, it has been assumed, is a process either of stamping in or of stamping out of specific responses in a mechanical building-up process, or, it is assumed to be the intensification of an instinctive urge or drive obtained from heredity, or resident in some particular set of nerve paths. Recent developments in biology, neurology, and psychology demonstrate the absurdity of both conceptions. Moreover, conventional practice in motivating the pupil assumes that pain and pleasure are the goals of life and have some mysterious power to regulate and stabilize behavior patterns. It is now known that if this procedure is carried out consistently, behavior patterns suffer disastrous atomization, if not out and out disintegration. The personality of the learner is warped and his sense of values irrevocably distorted. Our conventional psychology of motivation is based on a great hypocrisy. The goal of mastering subject-matter must be its own reward. In other words, unless nature is assumed to be idealistic instead of hedonistic, adequate education is impossible. All the new facts in science, disclosed within the last several years, point indisputably to the idealistic character of nature's laws. This means that insight, not the feeling of pleasure or pain, is the primary factor to emphasize in education. It means further that in so far as the feelings and emotions are to be developed in the pupil they

[13] From "The Crisis in Educational Objectives," *Educational Administration and Supervision,* 20:22–23, January, 1934.

are to be developed in the course of appreciating permanent values and the laws by means of which nature approaches states of perfection.

Fourth, the mechanistic point of view, under which mental development is now promoted, prevents the pupil from understanding the importance of remote goals. His mind is trained to see immediate goals and to plan means of reaching them regardless of future consequences. In short, the pupil is not trained to develop foresight. He never learns to postpone his immediate wants so that when he becomes an adult, he cannot see the importance of long time planning for himself and for society as a whole. He cannot see the value of conservation, he lacks perspective in understanding current events and has a distorted conception of what is practical.

134. MENTAL DISCIPLINE [14]

Thomas H. Briggs

Psychology has also exploded the old belief, long potent in practice, that the mind should be " disciplined " — that is, trained by long exercise in doing the difficult and the disagreeable so that it will joyously content itself with such work later when it has to be done. Once again common sense should not have needed psychology to disprove so silly a belief. If discipline exists in perceptible amounts, experienced educators should be expected reasonably to agree on what subjects give it; but, as Thorndike has shown, they are far from agreement. Moreover, if any person actually believes in a specific, he applies it for his own benefit; but no sensible individual can be found who is persevering at some difficult, disagreeable, and otherwise useless task that his disposition may be sweetened or his character strengthened. And yet hundreds of thousands of youth in secondary schools are encouraged or required to stick at such tasks with the promise of some mythical personal benefit. It should be obvious that such a " discipline " damages rather than helps. Certainly it prevents the expenditure of time on studies of assured value. The only discipline worth striving for is that which comes from intelligent application of powers for clearly conceived and appreciated objectives. The courses of study and the methods of teaching in secondary schools need much modification to align them with sound discipline.

[14] " The Changing World and the Curriculum," *Teachers College Record*, 35:54, October, 1933.

135. " AVOIDANCE OF THE TERM PURPOSE "[15]

Percival M. Symonds

Modern psychology is particularly concerned with avoiding the terminology of purpose and consciousness, not because purpose and consciousness are unrealities, but because they imply a point of view which does not yield to the scientific approach or is fruitless for control. There is no need to deny purpose. It exists and is a most powerful force. But the psychology which admits purpose as an explanation is a beaten science. It admits failure. It proposes to adopt an unanalyzable concept because it is too lazy to adopt the slow and painstaking experimentation necessary to make the analysis. When psychology falls back on purpose as an explanation of behavior, it stops advance. It says that we have reached the ultimate. Modern psychology holds a different hypothesis. Purpose must fall into line with other behavior phenomena. At present the most hopeful clues are that purpose involves the phenomena of delayed reaction, and that purpose is a conditioned reaction, the stimuli including the great organic processes such as hunger, sex, and other organic, muscular, and glandular processes. This is now little more than a hypothesis, but it has the advantage of stimulating experiment and thought, whereas the concept of purpose deadens scientific activity. Purpose as a psychological concept is also useless as a control of conduct. Since purpose resides within the man, we are not told how to form or stimulate it. But a concept of conditioned response, to use one hypothesis of modern psychology, leads immediately to a method of control. Such a concept provides education with a technique.

136. PLANNING BASIC TO PURPOSIVE BEHAVIOR [16]

Ellsworth Collings and Milbourne O. Wilson

1. *Pupil Planning.* Purposive behavior contemplates pupil planning in every instance. It does for at least two reasons. In the first place, purposive behavior involves the functioning of a series of interrelated aggregates of stimulus-response mechanisms, and, as such, involves the response of boys and girls along their drive in this step, for stimulus-response mechanisms function in this manner. Pupil

[15] From *The Nature of Conduct,* by permission of The Macmillan Company, publishers, New York, 1928, pp. 8–9.
[16] From *Psychology for Teachers,* Charles Scribner's Sons, New York, 1930, pp. 285–287.

planning is, in this sense, demanded in every instance for without it purposive behavior would be impossible. Second, planning is one of the lines of growth. Growth of boys and girls is, as we have seen, change in drive and response and it takes place in this step through the boys and girls responding along their drive. It is in this fashion boys and girls grow in planning — in finding means necessary in the attainment of a particular goal. Pupil planning is, in this sense, the basis of growth in this phase of conduct. Such growth is desirable for the success of an individual in a democracy depends very largely upon ability to formulate effective plans for the attainment of chosen goals. If the teacher does the planning growth in this step is thwarted. The resultant change is in the teacher's drive and response since it is her stimulus-response mechanisms that function in planning. Teacher planning blocks, in this sense, the functioning of the stimulus-response mechanisms of boys and girls along this line and in so doing prohibits growth in planning. Pupil planning thus is basic in purposive behavior and growth. Without it purposive behavior, on the one hand, is thwarted, and, on the other hand, growth in this phase of conduct is blocked.

2. *Procedure in Pupil Planning.* Planning involves, as we have seen, three interrelated steps. First, it includes the initiation of means. This involves boys and girls suggesting means for the attainment of a chosen goal. Luetta's suggestion of James for Governor Bradford's part in the First Thanksgiving story is an instance. Second, it involves evaluation of means. This involves discussion of the desirability and practicability of the suggested means. Frank's explanation that James would be a good manager is an illustration. Third, it involves choice of means. This involves preference for or against particular means. Donald's decision to have James for Governor Bradford's part is an example. The functioning of each of these steps in this constitutes the procedure of pupil planning.

PROCEDURE IN PUPIL PLANNING

I. Initiation of Means
II. Evaluation of Means
III. Choice of Means

3. *Successful Pupil Planning.* Planning involves, as we have seen, the initiation of means, evaluation of means, and choice of means. These are the traits of planning. The functioning of each trait includes the pupil's response along its drive, for stimulus-response mechanisms involved in each trait function in this fashion. The functioning of the initiation of means, for example, involves the pupil responding along its drive in suggesting means for the attain-

ment of the chosen goal. The same is equally true of the other traits of planning. Successful planning is, in this sense, the pupil responding along its drive consecutively in the initiation of means, evaluation of means, and choice of means. It is, in other words, the pupil itself performing each of these steps in this order.

4. *Guidance in Pupil Planning.* Pupil planning involves, as we have seen, the response of boys and girls along their drive in the initiation of means, evaluation of means, and choice of means, and as such, involves guidance, for pupil response along their drive depends upon stimulation and direction. Guidance in planning, for this reason, is along two lines. In the first place, it provides stimulation of pupil response along their drive in the traits of planning. It provides stimuli capable of stimulating pupil response along their drive in each of these steps. Guidance in planning includes, in this sense, stimulation and direction of pupil response along the drive in the initiation of means, evaluation of means, and choice of means.

137. Child Purposes Do Not Provide Educational Objectives [17]

Stephen S. Colvin

The second implicit assumption is: If we understand child nature we shall discover not only the methods to be followed but the aims to be sought. This second assumption, I believe to be largely false, and generally misleading. The child's interests must be appealed to if he learns properly and economically. This is a self-evident statement. It is not true, however, that in the child's immediate interests the objectives of the educative process can be found and formulated. Again, in all learning self-expression is desirable, but it does not follow from this that self-expression as such is a supreme educational objective. Neither does the truth of the statement, " Purposive activity is one of the greatest motives in leading the child on in his studious endeavors," justify the further statement that the aim of education is to lead the child on eternally from one purposive activity to another, or that purposive activity is the final goal of the educative process.

Neo-Rousseauism finds its chief exemplification to-day in the project-method (the supreme expression of purposive activity, as some would have us believe). This apparently is the goal of all teaching, if I understand the words of some of its most ardent supporters. If the project method is present, if the pupils work with interest and purpose, then all is well, according to some theorists.

[17] From " The Source of Educational Objectives," *School and Society,* 17:508–510, May 12, 1923.

It doesn't matter much what you do if you only do it with a purpose.

What has happened here is not difficult to understand. It has been clearly seen that the project, the purposive activity, is an important if not a necessary means in many instances of reaching worth-while educational results, and then all of a sudden results have been forgotten in the insistence on means. What has taken place is that means have themselves become ends, methods have become objectives, and the sum total of the educative process is expressed in a type of activity that in itself is both method and aim, means and objective. I wish to make my point here clear. I believe it to be fundamental and essential. Perhaps an analogy will serve:

When the uses of the sail, rudder and keel were first understood and embodied in a boat a revolution in navigation was accomplished. There was no more the necessity of laboriously pulling the oars to drive the unwilling boat over the rough and opposing sea, or of waiting for a friendly breeze to waft the craft to a distant port. A *method* of navigation was found that was to accomplish untold results in the succeeding ages. The sailor must study his craft in order to guide it in safety, and speed it to the harbor he sought. But this harbor of his seeking was not determined by the nature of his boat or the method of his sailing. What port he was to steer for was not indicated by his rudder or his sails. The rudder must be turned, the sails must be set, the boat must be pointed by the helmsman, and *how* this was to be done must first be decided by where the boat was to go. True, the boat could not be sailed anywhere. It could not be driven straight into the wind. If the quarter was adverse it might take skill and patience; the craft must tack back and forth, it could not hold its course straight from shore to shore, but still at length it could reach the port of destination in the very teeth of contrary gales. You can not by the study of the boat determine what port you should sail to, you can determine only how you are to sail to that port.

Truly the child must be interested in what he is to learn, but what he is to learn is not revealed by his narrow and immediate interests. Purpose is an aid to learning, but the purposes of the child are not the ends of the educative process; they are means by which desirable ends may be achieved. The skilled teacher uses interest and purpose to get results, but the results to be sought are not identical with interest and purpose; sometimes they are quite opposed to these when interest and purpose are immature and fleeting and when the result is important and enduring. Child nature tells how to guide the pupil; it does not tell us in any satisfactory way whither we should guide him. Look into the child's spontaneities and purposes as much as you will, you will never find reading, writing and arithmetic immediately revealed, nor anything else that is a major objective in school-teaching.

Child study has served to accomplish great results in our methodology, but it has been barren in giving us any ultimate educational objectives. Sometimes its results when translated into terms of objectives have been not only barren but strange and misleading. In the days when the Recapitulation Theory held sway it was thought by some that the child must go through all of the real and fancied experiences of his savage forebears and his pre-human ancestors in order to be properly educated. To-day we are sometimes led to believe that pure spontaneity is in itself the educational goal, irrespective of where that spontaneity leads. The ship set adrift will catch the winds in its sails, will set for itself a brief and ever-changing course, but at length it will lie stranded on the beach or grind itself to pieces on the jagged reef. The child must be understood in order that he may be guided.

138. RELATION OF INTEREST AND PURPOSE [18]

John Dewey

We have already noticed the difference in the attitude of a spectator and of an agent or participant. The former is indifferent to what is going on; one result is just as good as another, since each is just something to look at. The latter is bound up with what is going on; its outcome makes a difference to him. His fortunes are more or less at stake in the issue of events. Consequently he does whatever he can to influence the direction present occurrences take. One is like a man in a prison cell watching the rain out of the window; it is all the same to him. The other is like a man who has planned an outing for the next day which continuing rain will frustrate. He cannot, to be sure, by his present reactions affect to-morrow's weather, but he may take some steps which will influence future happenings, if only to postpone the proposed picnic. If a man sees a carriage coming which may run over him, if he cannot stop its movement, he can at least get out of the way if he foresees the consequence in time. In many instances, he can intervene even more directly. The attitude of a participant in the course of affairs is thus a double one: there is solicitude, anxiety concerning future consequences, and a tendency to act to assure better, and avert worse, consequences.

[18] From *Democracy and Education*, by permission of The Macmillan Company, publishers, New York, 1916, pp. 146–150, 152–153, 155–156.

There are words which denote this attitude: concern, interest. These words suggest that a person is bound up with the possibilities inhering in objects; that he is accordingly on the lookout for what they are likely to do to him; and that, on the basis of his expectation or foresight, he is eager to act so as to give things one turn rather than another. Interest and aims, concern and purpose, are necessarily connected. Such words as aim, intent, end, emphasize the *results* which are wanted and striven for; they take for granted the personal attitude of solicitude and attentive eagerness. Such words as interest, affection, concern, motivation, emphasize the bearing of what is foreseen upon the individual's fortunes, and his active desire to act to secure a possible result. They take for granted the objective changes. But the difference is but one of emphasis; the meaning that is shaded in one set of words is illuminated in the other. *What* is anticipated is objective and impersonal; to-morrow's rain; the possibility of being run over. But for an active being, a being who partakes of the consequences instead of standing aloof from them, there is at the same time a personal response. The difference imaginatively foreseen makes a present difference, which finds expression in solicitude and effort. While such words as affection, concern, and motive indicate an attitude of personal preference, they are always attitudes toward *objects* — toward what is foreseen. We may call the phase of objective foresight intellectual, and the phase of personal concern emotional and volitional, but there is no separation in the facts of the situation.

Such a separation could exist only if the personal attitudes ran their course in a world by themselves. But they are always responses to what is going on in the situation of which they are a part, and their successful or unsuccessful expression depends upon their interaction with other changes. Life activities flourish and fail only in connection with changes of the environment. They are literally bound up with these changes; our desires, emotions, and affections are but various ways in which our doings are tied up with the doings of things and persons about us. Instead of marking a purely personal or subjective realm, separated from the objective and impersonal, they indicate the non-existence of such a separate world. They afford convincing evidence that changes in things are not alien to the activities of a self, and that the career and welfare of the self are bound up with the movement of persons and things. Interest, concern, mean that self and world are engaged with each other in a developing situation.

The word interest, in its ordinary usage, expresses (*i*) the whole state of active development, (*ii*) the objective results that are foreseen and wanted, and (*iii*) the personal emotional inclination. (*i*)

An occupation, employment, pursuit, business is often referred to as an interest. Thus we say that a man's interest is politics, or journalism, or philanthropy, or archæology, or collecting Japanese prints, or banking. (*ii*) By an interest we also mean the point at which an object touches or engages a man; the point where it influences him. In some legal transactions a man has to prove " interest " in order to have a standing at court. He has to show that some proposed step concerns his affairs. A sleeping partner has an interest in a business, although he takes no active part in its conduct because its prosperity or decline affects his profits and liabilities. (*iii*) When we speak of a man as interested in this or that the emphasis falls directly upon his personal attitude. To be interested is to be absorbed in, wrapped up in, carried away by, some object. To take an interest is to be on the alert, to care about, to be attentive. We say of an interested person both that he has lost himself in some affair and that he has found himself in it. Both terms express the engrossment of the self in an object.

When the place of interest in education is spoken of in a depreciatory way, it will be found that the second of the meanings mentioned is first exaggerated and then isolated. Interest is taken to mean merely the effect of an object upon personal advantage or disadvantage, success or failure. Separated from any objective development of affairs, these are reduced to mere personal states of pleasure or pain. Educationally, it then follows that to attach importance to interest means to attach some feature of seductiveness to material otherwise indifferent; to secure attention and effort by offering a bribe of pleasure. This procedure is properly stigmatized as " soft " pedagogy; as a " soup-kitchen " theory of education.

But the objection is based upon the fact — or assumption — that the forms of skill to be acquired and the subject matter to be appropriated have no interest on their own account: in other words, they are supposed to be irrelevant to the normal activities of the pupils. The remedy is not in finding fault with the doctrine of interest, any more than it is to search for some pleasant bait that may be hitched to the alien material. It is to discover objects and modes of action, which are connected with present powers. The function of this material in engaging activity and carrying it on consistently and continuously *is* its interest. If the material operates in this way, there is no call either to hunt for devices which will make it interesting or to appeal to arbitrary, semi-coerced effort.

The word interest suggests, etymologically, what is *between*, — that which connects two things otherwise distant. In education, the distance covered may be looked at as temporal. The fact that a process takes time to mature is so obvious a fact that we rarely make it explicit. We overlook the fact that in growth there is ground to be covered between an initial stage of process and the completing period; that there is something intervening. In learning, the present powers of the pupil are the initial stage; the aim of the teacher represents the remote limit. Between the two lie *means* — that is middle conditions: — acts to be performed; difficulties to be overcome; appliances to be used. Only *through* them, in the literal time sense, will the initial activities reach a satisfactory consummation.

These intermediate conditions are of interest precisely because the development of existing activities into the foreseen and desired end depends upon them. To be means for the achieving of present tendencies, to be ' between ' the agent and his end, to be of interest, are different names for the same thing. When material has to be made interesting, it signifies that as presented, it lacks connection with purposes and present power: or that if the connection be there, it is not perceived. To make it interesting by leading one to realize the connection that exists is simply good sense; to make it interesting by extraneous and artificial inducements deserves all the bad names which have been applied to the doctrine of interest in education. . . .

Interest represents the moving force of objects — whether perceived or presented in imagination — in any experience having a purpose. . . .

The problem of instruction is thus that of finding material which will engage a person in specific activities having an aim or purpose of moment or interest to him, and dealing with things not as gymnastic appliances but as conditions for the attainment of ends. The remedy for the evils attending the doctrine of formal discipline previously spoken of, is not to be found by substituting a doctrine of specialized disciplines, but by reforming the notion of mind and its training. Discovery of typical modes of activity, whether play or useful occupations, in which individuals are concerned, in whose outcome they recognize they have something at stake, and which cannot be carried through without reflection and use of judgment to select material of observation and recollection, is the remedy. In short, the root of the error long prevalent in the conception of training of mind consists in leaving out of account movements of things to future results in which an individual shares, and in the direction of which observation, imagination, and memory are enlisted. It consists in regarding mind as complete in itself, ready to be directly applied to a present material.

139. THE NATURE OF INTEREST [19]

Frank N. Freeman

In the first place, interest means following one's interests. In this sense, interest is closely related to freedom. Freedom is thought to be necessary because insistent interests press for realization. Interests are thought to be inherent drives which develop and mature within the individual relatively independently of external circumstances. They come to fruition at definite stages of development in childhood and youth and demand realization as the price of sanity and vigor of mind.

This doctrine, emphasized by G. Stanley Hall, is widely accepted in modern theory. It is an excellent example of a half truth. A distinction should be made between interests and drives. Interests are specific, whereas drives are general and largely not specific in human beings. The drives, as for example, the hunger drive or the sex drive, may lead to a great variety of particular activities. They become specific according to the circumstances and education of the individual. They do not dictate particular educational activities but allow for great variety in the way they may be expressed. Interests on the other hand are specific. Being specific, they are determined not only by the nature of the individual, but also, and in very large measure, by his environment and training. Interests are very largely acquired, and may be cultivated. The cultivation of interests, starting with the relatively undifferentiated human needs and drives, is one of the chief functions of education.

According to a second usage, interest means very much the same as intellectual curiosity. It is the thrill which goes with finding out things and the impulse which prompts the activity of finding out things, of exploring the environment. It is strong in children and apparently in the young of the higher animals in general. Unfortunately it tends to die out in the adult as he becomes acquainted or thinks he becomes acquainted with his surroundings. But it can be fostered and can remain fairly vigorous thruout life. It is particularly valuable because it combines almost unalloyed pleasure with practical usefulness.

The mistake that is sometimes made about this intellectual curiosity is to suppose that it is very highly selective, and that the child is curious only about certain specific things, and that education must rely wholly or chiefly on the lead of the child to find out what he is

[19] National Education Association, *Major Issues with Reference to Proposed Reforms*, Department of Superintendence, Official Report, Washington, D. C., 1933, pp. 64-65.

interested in. The objects of any person's curiosity are, of course, restricted in a measure by his abilities, his previous experience and his stage of development. But the teacher has a very wide range of choice within these restrictions, and the lines of curiosity cannot be used as specific guides in the development of the curriculum. Curiosity is an appetite which thrives on feeding and languishes from starvation; but it is not, unless pampered, a finical or highly selective appetite which demands just certain viands at certain times. It creates no obstacles to the formulation of a general dietary.

The third type of interest is suggested by one use of the term in everyday life. We say a person has an interest in a business when he has a practical stake in the business thru the fact that he has invested labor or money in it. His interest in this case is not intellectual curiosity. It is a demand upon his thought and energy due to the fact that his practical fortunes are bound up with the success of the institution. In similar fashion a child has an interest in an enterprise if he has committed himself to carrying forward the enterprise. Such an enterprise is commonly called a project. If the child engages in a project his interest in the completion of the project as a whole is diffused over the subsidiary activities or forms of learning which are instrumental in the total activity. Thus the child may learn arithmetic because he needs to use its operation in building a bird house or laying out a garden. What we may call the scientific activity is motivated by the practical activity.

That theoretical interest may thus grow out of practical interests is beyond question. That it is wise to make use of this relation to develop desirable academic interests, particularly in the case of backward children, or children and youth in whom practical interests seem to be strong and theoretical interests weak, is doubtless true. But that theoretical interests are regularly subordinate to practical interests either in the development of culture and science in the race or in the experience of the individual, or that practical enterprises should furnish the chief framework for the organization of the curriculum of the school, is, I believe, a conclusion contrary to sound psychology and pedagogy. Rash as it is to question the analysis of such a preeminent thinker as Professor Dewey, his account of interest in his early book, *Interest and Effort in Education*, has, in my judgment, by its one-sided emphasis on the practical origin of interest, misled a whole generation of educators. The child is motivated to a greater degree by a relatively disinterested desire to know than is the adult. This desire is a precious thing which we should foster rather than discourage.

140. " THE LEARNER'S INTEREST " [20]

George S. Counts

The major controversy appears to center in the question of interests. Much is said concerning the need of organizing the curriculum about the child's interests. That curriculum-making must have regard for these interests is obvious; but that this means an uncritical incorporation into the school program of any activity in which under any conditions the child may display an interest is clearly an indefensible article of faith. Yet the principle that the child's interests should be recognized is often given this interpretation. Any interest that the child may manifest is then regarded as a safe, and an almost sacred, pedagogical guide. The logical implication of such a doctrine is that the curriculum-maker has no function and should abdicate his office in favor of the interests of the child! The learner is made the artisan of his own educational program.

The chief cause of misunderstanding and error here resides in the widely current notion that the term *interest* carries a specific, rather than a generic connotation. From some of the discussions one gains the impression that the child's interests are fixed and predetermined modes of behavior which he has brought with him into the world, that they must always and everywhere be the same, and that they can be as definitely numbered and catalogued as the organs of the body. As a matter of fact, children's interests are potentially as many as the activities of mankind, as varied as the patterns of human culture, and almost as fluid as the passing fashions. They adapt themselves to the most diverse situations and assume both the color and form of their surroundings. The Eskimo youth displays an eager interest in acquiring the technique involved in the construction of the kayak, the Igorot boy longs to become expert in the war and festival dances of his tribe, and the American child of favored parentage covets an initiation into the mysteries of the art of reading. At best the term ' *interest* ' is but a loose and general category under which may be grouped innumerable activities possessing the quality of a measurably perfect union of subject and object. Even the food and sex impulses assume many forms and accommodate themselves to circumstances.

In educational discussions the adjective ' *spontaneous* ' is often used to qualify the term interest. To this word educational theorists

[20] " Some Notes on the Foundations of Curriculum Making," National Society for the Study of Education, *The Foundations of Curriculum-Making*, Twenty-Sixth Yearbook, Part II, Public School Publishing Company, Bloomington, Ill., 1927, pp. 77–80. Quoted by permission of the Society.

seem to be extremely sensitive; but while some are attracted, others are repelled, by it. One will argue that in constructing the curriculum the interests, but not the spontaneous interests, of children should be recognized; while another will maintain that only as the interest is spontaneous can learning be carried on effectively. Undoubtedly, in many instances the strength of the controversy is merely a gauge of the degree of misunderstanding. The parties to the dispute attach different meanings to the same labels. Let us, therefore, see in what senses the word ' spontaneous ' is used. We shall then be in a position to determine the measure of guidance which the interests of children can give us in curriculum-construction.

All interests are ' spontaneous,' in the sense that they spring from the individual's own nature; and, if the environment is made to include both the internal state of the organism as well as the external surroundings, all interests are ' conditioned,' in the sense that they are provoked by the environment. Interests are always products of the union of the organism with circumstance. If environing conditions are changed, existing interests undergo modification or are displaced by other interests. The term ' spontaneous ' is sometimes applied only to those interests which are aroused by an unplanned environment and which arrive unheralded on the educational scene. To certain minds these unanticipated interests which appear in the absence of an environment purposefully arranged to call them forth take on a peculiar authority and sanctity. They are thought to be the instrument of a mysterious revelation of the nature of the child. In actual fact, they may throw less light on the problem than a series of carefully controlled exposures to a succession of different situations. They may be the pure product of chance, the fruit of unknown causes. This fact, of course, does not condemn them as unworthy. They may be good or evil; but whether they are the one or the other is not to be determined by their spontaneous or accidental appearance.

There is another use of the word ' spontaneous ' which is of much more value to education. The appeal which a particular situation makes to the learner may be either direct or indirect, unmediated or mediated. The learner may feel an interest in an activity because of its own intrinsic worth, or he may feel an interest in it because it is instrumental to the attainment of some desired end. Interest of the first type may be legitimately styled "spontaneous." Since it provides the conditions for most economical learning, its value to education is almost beyond measure. Learning is prosecuted most effectively when the individual identifies himself most completely with the thing to be learned. Only under these conditions is there neither dispersion of attention nor dissipation of energy. Yet, that the purposes of education can be achieved wholly through interest of this type. is a fatuous deception. A fair measure of the work of any productive life and a large share of the work of the world must be performed under the conditions of derived interest. Much of civilization itself may be regarded as an instrument of mediation between human desires and their satisfaction. Social life may be so organized in the future that the more arbitrary and cruel incentives to labor will disappear, but the hope of making all activities necessary to the life of society intrinsically interesting to those who engage in them is an idle dream. Moreover, the only freedom that man knows in this world is that freedom which comes to him through the intelligent ordering of conduct, not on the basis of the appeal of the immediate moment or situation, but in response to environment spatially, temporally, and socially extended. In this power of self-discipline and intelligent self-direction the individual should constantly grow; and an education that has failed to promote this growth has failed at a critical point. Increasingly as the child matures, he should be expected to assume obligations and to adopt purposes which require the definite subordination of the personal and the immediate to the social and the remote. Only as the individual gains this power to stand alone in an enlarged world will he be able to direct the course of his own life.

What guidance, then, can the curriculum-maker derive from a study of the interests of the child? If learning is to proceed at all, the attention of the learner must be secured. And his attention can be secured only through a direct or indirect appeal to his interests. These interests must be utilized to the fullest possible extent, but they cannot be accepted as positive and trustworthy guides in selecting the content of the curriculum. They constitute the raw materials and determine the conditions of education, but they cannot furnish its goals. They reveal the present psychological position of the learner; they do not indicate the direction in which he should move. Until we have found the child's interests we have not found *him* — he is still lost in the educational woods. Only as his interests set limits to the educational possibilities may they be regarded as guides in the choice of the objectives of education. In the selection and validation of the content of the curriculum they should serve as negative, rather than as positive factors. *Nothing should be included in the curriculum merely because it is of interest to children; but whatever is included should be brought into the closest possible relation with their interests.*

141. Extrinsic Interests Effective [21]

Edward L. Thorndike

The notion that the mind will not learn what is alien to its fundamental vital purposes is attractive and plausible but definitely false. In order to earn a little money or to make a good impression on the experimenter intelligent adults will learn the most trivial and useless things, such as lists of nonsense syllables, irrelevant numbers attached to words, locations on meaningless and futile maps, tossing balls over one's head at an unseen target, and typing words backward. They have spent four hours (and probably would spend forty) at such a task without losing the ability to learn it, and without any obvious and striking diminution in the learning. In the experiments with learning by adults which we have done over a period of nine years, we have worked sometimes with such learning as might be desired or required in real life, sometimes with learning which, though not of much use to the learner, was interesting as a game and test of his powers, and sometimes with learning which no sane person would undergo except for some ulterior reward. We never failed to get learning.

As the representative results described above show, the rate of learning does not suffer greatly even when what is learned is utterly valueless to the learner. Extrinsic interests are adequate to maintain learning when intrinsic interests are not available or require an undue expense of time, labor, or skill on the part of the teacher.

On the whole, we may conclude from the experiments that when certain unpalatable mental medicines need to be taken, too much time and pains should not be taken to disguise them. If a stretch of dull learning can be learned as it is in ten hours, it will usually not be profitable to spend five hours in making it so interesting that it can be learned in seven.

142. Child and Adult Interests [22]

Ernest Horn

There is often found the assumption that children are not interested in the activities of their elders. This assumption is unwar-

---

[21] From *Adult Interests*, by permission of The Macmillan Company, publishers, New York, 1935, pp. 52–53.

[22] From " Discussion of the General Statement," National Society for the Study of Education, *The Foundations of Curriculum-Making*, Twenty-Sixth Yearbook, Part II, Public School Publishing Company, Bloomington, Ill., 1927, pp. 100–101. Quoted by permission of the Society.

ranted. It flies in the face of the most obvious conclusions of commonsense and of scientific analysis. For the boy to have it said that he acts like a man is to him the greatest compliment that can be paid. It has been pointed out elsewhere that the overlapping between the needs of the child and the adult is very great, not only with respect to the actual activities in which he engages, but also with respect to his needs for understanding and appreciation. Many adult activities in which he can not yet engage and in which he may never engage are, nevertheless, from his point of view, worth understanding and appreciating.

It has been said that schools in the past have imposed adult values upon the child. The fact is that children suffer not so much from the imposition of unquestioned adult values in their natural setting as from the imposition of subject matter which either is unrelated to life or is formally arranged according to the interests of the subject specialist. But even the artificialities which attend the academic organization of subject matter are to be preferred to the pettiness and disorganization found in curricula built upon fallaciously assumed children's interests. Many of those who have written and spoken most voluminously about making the school vital to children have sinned most grievously in failing to build the curriculum according to the child's actual needs and interests in life outside the school.

Indeed, formalism, and verbalism arise, not primarily because the child's interests are neglected, but because instruction is divorced from the needs and interests of life outside the school. This separation is scarcely more complete between instruction and the needs and activities of children, than between instruction and the needs and activities of adults. In other words, formalism and verbalism tend to arise when subject matter becomes academic. Nor is such formalism limited to the " three R's." It is found as truly in other subjects.

143. ORIENTATION TO CHILD INTERESTS AND ADULT LIFE [23]

Harold Rugg

The . . . issue which should be brought out boldly is: To what extent shall the content and arrangement of the curriculum be determined by the interests and natural activities of children or by the criterion of preparation for adult life.

[23] From " Curriculum-Making: Points of Emphasis," National Society for the Study of Education, *The Foundations of Curriculum-Making,* Twenty-Sixth Yearbook, Part II, Public School Publishing Company, Bloomington, Ill., 1927, p. 151. Quoted by permission of the Society.

Since the time when Francis Parker first scandalized the Puritan scholastics that has been the nub of educational controversy.

I can make my own position clear at the start, perhaps, by pointing out the *coördinate* position of these two factors. An extreme emphasis upon either one of these two fundamental elements of the educative process will constitute merely an inadequate basis for curriculum-construction. The orientation of the curriculum-maker must be comprehensive enough, therefore, to include in its perspective both institutional life and the growing child.

Which of the two should be named first, which shall precede, is a question that is impossible of answer. For neither one nor the other precedes. Neither alone can dictate the curriculum.

An orientation, however, which will encompass child interest and adult society will produce a sound foundation for the school curriculum: a synthesis as broad as all of human living. Indeed, as the General Statement says (Par. 8): " The curriculum-maker is compelled to decide what use he shall make of the present needs, interests, and activities of children, on the one hand, and of the results accruing from the scientific study of society on the other."

Now, to me, the real nub of the matter is expressed in the next sentence: " The data from adult life will go far to determine what is of permanent value; the data from child life will go far to determine what is appropriate for education in each stage of the child's development."

144. TECHNIQUES FOR SURVEYING PURPOSES [24]

William A. McCall

There are three methods of discovering what are the purposes which actuate men, women, and children. There are the methods of self-analysis, of self-observation, and of alter-observation.

The method of self-analysis is a simple, expeditious, and practically valuable method of sampling human purposes. To test the method I have recorded the chief motives, wants, or purposes which actuated me yesterday, which was a holiday. Most of these purposes were followed by an immediate and complete or partial realization of them. A condensed list follows: (1) To perform morning toilet properly. (2) To adorn myself as becomingly as possible. (3) To eat an appropriate and enjoyable breakfast while discussing bungalows with my wife. (4) To give my salary received the day before to my wife. (5) To think out and describe for others the proc-

[24] From " My Philosophy of Life and Education," *Teachers College Record,* 35:567–569, April, 1934.

ess of making a curriculum. (6) To display proper manners at a dinner to which I was invited by a group of ladies. (7) To discuss both intelligently and entertainingly the following topics which arose during and after dinner: (a) Coöperative housekeeping, (b) Appreciation of nature, (c) Poetry of Wordsworth, (d) Maine coast as a summer resort, (e) Life in France during the war, (f) Conditions under which a President of the United States should temporarily retire or be retired, (g) The accuracy of character-reading by means of palmistry, phrenology, and physiognomy, (h) Correspondence courses for training the memory, (i) Advertising methods, (j) The book, *Education of Henry Adams*, (k) Mental and physical effects of coffee, (l) The difference between the language of the Kentucky mountaineers and the surrounding lowlanders. (8) To read the newspaper so as to separate fact from rumor and editorial bias and attempt to arrive at some conclusion regarding such matters as the: (a) Fate of Peace Treaty in United States Senate, (b) Success of the League of Nations, (c) Dispute over Fiume, (d) Motives actuating the various foreign countries in their attitude toward Soviet Russia, (e) Probable effect of turning railroads back to private owners, (f) Significance of development of new parties in America and the worth of their programs, (g) Wisdom of whether to and in what to invest some savings at this time, (h) Chances that Lewis, Stecher, or Caddock would be the next national wrestling champion. (9) To appreciate some poems in the Oxford *Book of English Verse*, and to sing the old ballad of Barbara Allen found there. (10) To enjoy, entertain, and educate a twelve-month-old baby. (11) To dictate to the mother certain changes in her method of caring for the baby. (12) To button and unbutton clothes, tie and untie shoe strings, open and close doors, use elevators, dodge automobiles, and keep footing on icy street, etc. (13) To enjoy phonograph records of *Ave Maria, Wilhelm Tell Overture,* Lalo's *Melody,* Wagner's *Evening Star,* and Massenet's *Twilight.* (14) To retire with the hope that I had made no enemies during the day. It is evident that the method of self-analysis conscientiously applied by many individuals for several days at various times in the year would give a set of varied purposes.

The method of self-observation has for its function to reveal not all the wants which ask to be satisfied but all the wants that are finally approved by the individual and thus result in activity. Thus this method means an observation and tabulation by an individual of those of his motives which produce mental or physical activities or both.

The method of alter-observation is the observing of an individual, not by himself but by another. A keen observer can often infer from a given activity what motive prompted it. Trained observers could thus discover the chief purposes which prompt human activity.

Each method has its advantages and disadvantages. The method of self-analysis is superior in that it reveals desirable purposes which are not acted upon because it would be unwise to try to satisfy these wants in a society organized as at present. There must be numerous cravings which ten generations hence will be virtues but which at present are crimes. Educators should know these wants in order that they may be able, if possible, to develop in pupils an ability to so reorganize the old order as to give opportunity for the gratification of these desires.

The method of self-analysis is inferior in that it will reveal some purposes which adequate racial experience has abundantly shown to be undesirable. These purposes must not get into the curriculum.

The method of self-observation is superior to the method of self-analysis in that it reveals what wants are adjudged by the individual to be, among all his wants, the most practical and, all things considered, the most worth while. For, psychologically, each individual proceeds to satisfy that want which, in the light of all deterrents, promises the greatest satisfaction. Among my list of holiday wants there is one which I did not gratify for obvious reasons. Previous attempts at domestic dictation had not paid in terms of satisfaction. Domestication is to the home what socialization is to society. The socialized individual is one who has learned to discipline his wants in such a way as not to come into violent conflict with the wants of others. He has gained skill in balancing competing wants in the optimum fashion. This is why no special survey of social interests apart from individual interests is necessary. The method of self-observation is the best of the three.

Self-observation is inferior only in that it fails to reveal those purposes which the individual does not know how to take even the first steps toward realizing, and those cravings which are unnecessarily or unjustly thwarted by the existing social organization. It is specially important that these latter cravings be revealed because it is in their hidden recesses that the red flower of revolution takes root.

The method of alter-observation is now superior only in cases where it is suspected that self-analysis or self-observation is being done by an individual who is incompetent as, for instance, an infant, or dishonest. Except in such instances its value is not at present very great. Much of what is significant in life goes on beneath the surface. Many of our strongest purposes are satisfied through subtle and relatively invisible activities. Each year sees progress in the development of a measuring technique which will make visible these invisible activities and will make inferences from them to purposes surer. But for some time to come, at least, the curriculum of purposes must be discovered mainly by the use of the methods of self-analysis and self-observation.

145. Methods of Studying Pupil Interests [25]

Gertrude Hildreth

There are several alternative methods of obtaining pupil interest and attitude data. One method is that of personal interview with the pupil. Another is observation of the individual while he is engaged in a variety of activities in and out of school. A third method is that of asking the pupil to record on a suitably arranged blank statements concerning his activities and preferences. If there are many cases to study or if information for a large proportion of pupils is required, the first method, used exclusively, is almost out of the question unless the school has a large staff for guidance work. Aside from the amount of time consumed there are the additional problems of pupil reticence during interviews and the recording of results in objective form, uncolored by the preferences and biases of the interviewer.

The second method is even more time consuming and just as dependent upon highly trained observers for reliable work. It avoids the factor of embarrassment to the pupil, provided he does not discover that he is being observed. Either of the two methods represents a highly specialized activity. The third method, that of having pupils record in some objective fashion information concerning their personality traits, interests and habits, though not in all respects free from objectionable features from the standpoint of reliability and validity, nevertheless is a time saver, gives the pupil a part in the undertaking, and affords permanent records in convenient form for filing. When time and adequate personnel staff are available such records may profitably be supplemented by data obtained through methods one and two. A record blank filled out by the pupil constitutes a natural starting point for an interview since it releases tension on the part of the child by centering attention on his paper rather than on himself. The complete " blocking " which even the expert interviewer encounters when he puts such questions as " Now tell me which subjects you have most difficulty with " is in decided contrast to the situation when the interviewer can say " Now, let's see what you wrote down about your school work. Here you have

[25] From " An Interest Inventory for High School Personnel Work," *Journal of Educational Research,* 27:11–12, September, 1933.

the names of the subjects you like best, and here the ones you do not like so well." At this point the pupil will usually volunteeer more information about his success in school work.

The objection to the questionnaire method when the record is made by the child and is unchecked by other methods is that the child may be unable to give an accurate picture of himself with respect to the traits in question or he may intentionally falsify his record to make it fit the picture he wants his teachers and advisors to have of him. Other things being equal, the pupil who is older and more mature mentally is more capable of giving an accurate picture of his personality. Whether, even though he is more capable of giving an accurate picture, he is more apt to do so, depends upon several factors: the morale of the school and the sportsmanship of the pupils, the use that pupils feel is to be made of their records, the purposes for which the information is being collected, the pupils' attitude toward the person who is directing the study, and the extent to which pupils are momentarily influenced by companions or " heroes " among their classmates. Results will be more satisfactory if pupils are convinced that they are to be helped in their problems rather than to feel that someone is trying to " get the goods " on them. The request that pupils fill out interest inventories should come from a person with whom the pupils are in satisfactory rapport.

146. A Technique for Studying Interests in Play [26]

Harvey C. Lehman and Paul A. Witty

The present chapter will include a description of a technique used for disclosing: (1) the play activities most commonly engaged in by representative persons from five to twenty-two years of age residing in certain communities; (2) the play activities best liked by these individuals; (3) the games and other play activities consuming the greatest amount of time; (4) the extent to which a given child participates with other children in his play activities, and (5) the effect upon play behavior of such variables as age, sex, race, season, intelligence, community, etc.

In the case of children old enough to read, the plan employed was to place before each individual a comprehensive list of 200 play activities, having him check each one in which he had engaged of his own volition during the week preceding the date of the investigation. In addition, each pupil was asked to indicate the three activities which had given him the most fun or which he liked best. He was

[26] From Lehman and Witty's *Psychology of Play Activities.* Copyright 1927 by A. S. Barnes and Company, New York, pp. 35–37.

asked also to indicate the one activity to which he thought he had given the most time. In the last of a series of six investigations the children were asked to identify and indicate those activities in which they had participated alone.

The development of this plan proceeded slowly. The general procedure was decided upon only after long deliberation. The plan of having the children check a printed list was adopted since it seemed the most feasible manner of obtaining significant data.

The questionnaire method was discarded because of the obvious limitations set forth by Thorndike; the observation method was eliminated as it was thought to be too time consuming to permit securing sufficient data to make the results highly significant.

Some of the items of the list were obtained from the studies of Croswell and McGhee. A few more were procured from the Cleveland Survey. Several competent persons were asked to supplement the list. Since play is so subjective a phenomenon, it is impossible to compile a complete list. At the end of the list finally assembled spaces therefore were provided in which items omitted could be added.

A preliminary investigation was made at Hibbing, Minnesota, in Sept. 1923, for the purpose of determining whether the proposed technique would procure satisfactory results. The resultant data indicated that some of the children had checked all the activities in which they had participated at any time. Subsequent studies were made at Linwood, Eudora, and Tonganoxie, Kansas. During this preliminary work the following improvements were made in the technique:

First. The list of play activities was increased from 140 to 200 items. Certain of the activities at first included in the list were found to be indulged in only rarely. If two or three per cent only of the children were found to engage in an activity during the course of a week, the activity was removed from the list unless it was thought to be highly seasonal in character. The activities added were those most frequently indicated by the children in the blank spaces provided for that purpose.

Second. The alphabetical arrangement of the items of the list was abandoned. It was found that with alphabetical arrangement the first items of the list, i.e., " Anty-over," etc., were relatively unfamiliar to certain children and caused confusion and delay. As a means of enabling the children to comprehend the directions more readily the well-known activities were placed at the head of the list. These included such activities as " Football " " Basket ball," and " Baseball."

Third. The list of activities was found to be too long to be finished at a single sitting by third and fourth-grade pupils. Provision was made therefore for children in these grades to spend two days at the task.

Fourth. The directions to the teachers were changed repeatedly during the preliminary work and those finally used were as specific as those ordinarily employed for the giving of mental tests. Separate sets of directions were made out for teachers of the third and fourth grades. In these greater emphasis was placed on the fact that the play activities engaged in *during the past week only* were to be checked. The teachers of these grades were instructed to *read aloud* the list of activities to their pupils to insure comprehension.

CHAPTER IX

ACTIVITIES FOR REALIZATION OF PURPOSES

147. Life, A Continuity of Activities [1]

Franklin Bobbitt

LET us remember that a human life is 100 per cent behavior. Life is doing things. For abundance of human living we need to do a great number and variety of things. For success in human living we need to do these things reasonably well. We shall use skills as *means*, and knowledge as *means*, but the *end*, or objective, is the living itself — successful, abundant, humanistic, continuous, now, tomorrow, next year, and on through the allotted span of years.

Rightly to look at this matter, we need to have before us a list of the activities which constitute this continuity. In the more enlightened life of today these are of vast number and variety. For example, an individual observes the things, persons, and actions of his environment. He ponders meanings, values, uses, and relations. He talks over his observations and experiences with his associates. He listens to the accounts of their experiences. He reads newspapers, magazines, and books and thus indirectly, through language, extends his observations outward to all the world, backward through history, and inward to the essences of things. He reflects on his observations and readings. He discusses problems with his associates. He plans procedures and carries them into execution. He carries on the numerous activities of physical living. He associates with his fellows. He engages in numerous leisure occupations. He participates in the activities of family life, brings up his children, and performs numerous unspecialized work activities about the home. As a public-spirited member of the community, he helps to maintain an enlightened public opinion. He makes intelligent demand on the innumerable social groups and agencies which are supplying his needs. He evaluates their offerings; he accepts and rejects on the basis of merit. He carries his share of the social burden in the labors of his vocation. He does his share in creating, sustaining, and overseeing his governmental agencies. These forms of behavior constitute the good life.

[1] From "The Trend of the Activity Curriculum," *Elementary School Journal*, 35:261–262, December, 1934.

An individual's activities, variously classified, are physical, social, intellectual, emotional, practical, economic, civic, political, religious, domestic, recreational, vocational, and the like. In the balanced life every wholesome phase of human living finds its proper place and amount, though varying, of course, according to the individual's nature and situation.

The term " activity " must be defined in a way to cover the intangible activities of the subjective life. An individual's intellectual activities, even though invisible to the eyes of sense, are just as real as his muscular activities. As a matter of fact, a person's outward behavior is but an externalization of what goes on first in the mind. Intellectual and physical activities are equally portions of human living.

148. " THE LEARNING PROCESS CHARACTERIZED BY ACTIVITY " [2]

Walter S. Monroe

From the standpoint of the problems of methods of teaching, the most significant characteristic of the learning process is the activity of the learner. Children acquire motor skills, memorized facts, knowledge, ideals, and other controls of conduct as the result of perceiving, thinking, doing, feeling. A child's mind is not a blank tablet on which the teacher may directly write the things which he wishes the child to learn. The child educates himself by participating in such activities as reading textbooks, doing exercises in algebra, solving problems, writing themes, listening to explanations by the teacher, observing what goes on about him, describing what he has done or seen, answering questions orally, asking questions, writing examination papers, making a chair in the shop, preparing a meal in the laboratory, playing in the school orchestra, and listening to concerts and other entertainments. It is only through engaging in such activities that the child learns. The teacher cannot communicate skills, ideas, facts, principles, and ideals directly to the student; knowledge is not transferred from a textbook to the learner's mind. Learning is a process of growth. The child is not something to be moulded by the application of external pressure, but is rather a living thing whose mental growth is to be directed largely by the school.

The preceding paragraph is not presented as a definition of the learning processes, but rather to provide a point of view. . . . The reader should endeavor to master this point of view, which is sometimes referred to as the " principle of self-activity in learning," be-

[2] From *Directing Learning in the High School,* by Walter S. Monroe, copyright 1927, by Doubleday, Doran & Company, Inc., pp. 1–3.

cause it furnishes the only rational basis for the consideration of problems relating to instructional procedures. The principle of self-activity is generally accepted in theory but not infrequently it is violated in practice. Our pedagogical vocabulary includes many words and phrases whose meanings retain traces of the concept of learning as a passive process in which the teacher rather than the pupil is the active agent. It is not unusual to read that a teacher "imparts" knowledge and is responsible for "making his subject interesting," that he is expected to "explain" or "demonstrate," that his function is to "communicate" what he knows to his students, that the teacher "adds new knowledge," that the teacher must "prepare" his students for a new topic and then conform to certain principles in "presenting" it. Even such terms as subject-matter, content, textbook, and curriculum are frequently used in a way which implies that learning is at best a process of passive absorption. It is, of course, improbable that any person who has studied modern psychology would agree with these implications if asked explicitly concerning them, but contacts with students in education courses and with teachers have convinced the writer that the blank tablet theory of learning still functions in the thinking of many persons and in much of our educational practice.

149. THE NATURE AND FUNCTION OF ACTIVITY [3]

John Dewey

It is obvious that the term ' activity ' is exceedingly broad. It does not lose this breadth in connection with educational programs. It runs a whole gamut. Of itself it says nothing about kinds of activity, and of itself it says nothing about the source of activity or about its locus and residence. It decides nothing, for example, about the ratio of physical, emotional, and intellectual factors. It says nothing about who or what starts the activity going, or whether its residence is collective or individual; evidently solo and chorus singing are both activities. Of course many of these ambiguities are mitigated, if not eliminated, in educational matters by the context, by the actual things that the word is used to denote. But a survey of literature, including the various definitions reported in this volume, shows that the term is elastic enough to cover dissimilar affairs in education. Hence different judgments as to the value of an ' activity ' program

[3] From "Comments and Criticisms by Some Educational Leaders in Our Universities," National Society for the Study of Education, *The Activity Movement*, Thirty-Third Yearbook, Part II, Public School Publishing Company, Bloomington, Ill., 1934, pp. 81–86. Quoted by permission of the Society.

are more or less connected with the different views as to what is meant by the term.

It has consequently occurred to me that perhaps the most helpful thing I can do is to set forth some of the conceptions that, in their extreme forms, are opposed to one another, and to indicate the problems that these oppositions give rise to. The statement of the problems may both clarify the situations by showing how differences of view arise and indicate the general directions in which their settlement is to be looked for.

1. To some minds the term ' activity ' suggests doing something overt, something sufficiently gross or macroscopic to be readily perceptible by others. Such persons might not deny that a child engrossed in reading a book or listening quietly to music is active, but they would not take the clue to an educational activity program from such ' inner ' acts. Since it is bodily activity that is gross and easily visible, while thinking is an implicit action, the educational equivalents of such a conception are evident without amplification.

The cause of the educational movement that emphasizes the importance of overt doing is not far to seek. It is primarily a reaction against the bad consequences of the externally enforced passivity characteristic of the traditional school with its imperative demand for quiet, silence, immobility, folded arms, set positions. When the reaction was positively supported by carrying into the school the results of child study, which showed that the young child is predominantly motor, the doors were thrown wide open to an activity program in the sense of emphasis of perceptible bodily activities, of doings and makings, of play and work. The educational problem that emerges is to discover, with different individuals and in the same individual at different stages of growth, the part played in the whole scheme of growth by the factor of doing.

With respect to chronological growth, a scale or spectrum exists. Speaking generally, the younger the child, the greater the rôle of overt, as distinct from implicit, activity. Upon the whole the infant when awake is *doing* something with sense organs and muscular equipment. With increasing maturity, the ratio of implicit activity increases. But there are also great individual differences. In adult life, we all recognize the distinction between the executive and the inquiring and artistic types. Persons of the first sort think for the sake of doing; those of the second type act (in the sense of doing and making) chiefly for the sake of directing and enriching emotional and intellectual experience. Differences show themselves early in life. Some children are distracted and confused by the amount of doing that is a stimulus to others, while the latter are benumbed by conditions that are suited to the former.

In short, there is nothing in the bare concept of activity that gives helpful direction to the educational program. There must be the kind and amount of doing that conduces to health and vigor, that produces observation and reflection, that clarifies and tests ideas, that tempers while it expresses emotions. No set program can be deduced from these generalities. They define a problem to be met by continued observation and experimentation, the solutions never being twice alike with different individuals or different groups. The settled point is that activity as doing is a means rather than an end.

2. Activity may be judged and evaluated according to its concrete and tangible results or according to the contribution it makes to a relatively intangible personal development. In theory, it may be measured by both without their conflicting with one another. In practice, one or the other so tends to predominate that different, almost opposed, types of educational procedure may result. Measurement in its quantitative, statistical, form fixes attention upon near-by, fairly direct results of action. Personal development is a thing of much longer time-span and lends itself to qualitative rather than quantitative judgment. It is open to the objection that it is 'subjective.' On the other hand, the more mature and experienced the teacher, the less will he or she be dependent upon tangible, directly applicable, external tests, and will use them, not as final, but as guides to judgment of the direction in which development is taking place. The more fully the processes of long-term growth are studied, the more objective will be the estimates of what is going on in particular individuals, while too much reliance upon special tangible tests tends to prevent attention to the conditions and laws of general growth.

What has been said applies directly to the mooted question of educational ' ends ' and ' objectives.' The valuation of activity on the basis of close-by, tangible results tends toward formation of one type of ends and objectives; namely, those that are specific and externally definable and measurable. Consequently, acceptance of this view will dictate a program that will, although it is an activity program, differ radically from the activity program in which concrete tangible results are subordinated to an enduring long-span growth. While my own philosophy leans decidedly in the latter direction, I am here concerned more with pointing the distinction that will explain differences in so-called activity programs and aid in clarifying thinking and decision on the subject than in settling the question. From the standpoint of activity as itself a continuing growth of the whole being (not divided into inner and outer, or into doing, thinking, and emotion as separate things), ends and objectives are not so much things to be definitely achieved by students as they are points to be borne in mind by the educator in surveying the progress of individuals to make sure that it is fairly balanced.

While space will not allow of the development of the points, it should be noted that the conflict between activity directed at acquiring skill and acquiring definite bodies of formal knowledge, and activity growing out of and expressing the existing state of experience belong in the category just discussed. Again there is no opposition in theory. There cannot be general growth unless skills and information are acquired and retained. But practically, educational systems differ as to where the emphasis is placed. Are skills and special modes of knowledge made the specific goals of activity, or are they treated as means for carrying on and enriching experience as a going concern? If the implications of this question are borne in mind when examining actual or recommended forms of activity programs, it will be found, I think, that ambiguities are cleared up, and special points will fall in place as members of an inclusive scheme. In that case, choice will at least be more conscious and intelligent.

3. Probably the point on which there is the greatest amount of controversial difference concerns the opposition often set up between the child's desires, preferences, and experiences on one side and social values and demands on the other. According to some, an activity program must grow directly out of the existing attitudes and contacts of those under instruction. To others, this course appears to be antagonistic not only to acquisition of subject matter in any organized way but also to preparation for meeting the inevitable requirements of later life. Others still evade the idea by setting up forms of activity that are practically uniform for all, so that the habit of conforming individual activity to that of others is established.

This problem, as far as theory is concerned, arises because a false antithesis is set up. There are multitudes of active tendencies in the young and a multitude of nascent preferences and dawning interests. There is a great deal of elasticity within an individual; individuality is rather a *direction of movement* than anything definitely formed. Selection and arrangement have to occur anyway unless everything is carried on at haphazard according to the caprice or pressure of the moment. The problem is therefore to discover *within* present experience those values that are akin to those which the community prizes, and to cultivate those tendencies that lead in the direction that social demands will take. If emphasis is put upon these points of community, not all clashes of personal desire and social claim will be avoided, but in the main there will be growth toward harmony.

The very dependence of the young establishes within their own make-up response to social demands. A good instance in the life of

the preschool child is the learning of language. Ability to understand the language of others and to speak coherently is an imperative
social claim. But no crisis of antagonism arises with the young child
because within the active tendencies of the child there are already
operative the desire and the tendency to communicate and be communicated with. By taking advantage of them the problem of
reconciling present experience with social values and with preparation for future social requirements is met almost without consciousness that there is a problem.

Much of the practical difficulty and conflict that exist is due to a
false idea of the definiteness and fixity of the desires and interest of
childhood. When children are asked in an overt way what they
want or what they would like to do, they are usually forced into a
purely artificial state and the result is the deliberate creation of an
undesirable habit. It is the business of the educator to study the
tendencies of the young so as to be more consciously aware than are
the children themselves what the latter need and want. Any other
course transfers the responsibility of the teacher to those taught.
Arbitrary ' dictation ' is not a matter of words or of form, but consists in imposing actions that do not correspond with tendencies that
can be discovered within the experience of those who are growing
up. The pupil also makes an arbitrary imposition on himself when,
in response to an inquiry as to what he would like, he, because of
ignorance of underlying and enduring tendencies and interest,
snatches at some accidental affair. On the other side, those who
strongly insist upon the priority of social claims and values to present
experience usually overlook the leverage they might find in the latter
for an uncoerced approach to their end, and they also exaggerate
the fixity of social demands. There is nothing that society itself
needs more than self-reliant personalities with habits of initiative,
re-adaptability, and inherent decisiveness.

From the brief survey of these three points, the conclusion follows
that the mere concept of activity *in general* no longer has any definite
educational value. It did have when it stood in marked contrast with
quiescence and passive absorption. But we have now reached a
point where the problem is to study in a discriminating way from
a variety of points of view various modes of activity, and to observe
their respective consequences when they are employed. Otherwise
an activity program will be in danger of being a catchword used to
justify all sorts of things of greatly diverging values.

There must be some kind and amount of overt doing. But in the
abstract this activity may be boisterous, rowdy, thoughtless, blindly
emotional, passionate, mechanical, and perfunctory, swallowed up in
doing what others are doing, or the opposite. Activity may consist

of a succession of more or less spasmodic, because brief and interrupted, performances, or of a consecutively developing occupation evolving over a long period. It may be suggested by external, and more or less accidental, occasions, or it may be based upon competent study of the conditions of growth and the laws of cause and effect in formation of mind and character. Let it be recognized that all existing tendencies are multiple, often conflicting; that present experience is complex, containing a variety of possible values; that it is a continuous and moving thing that can be understood only by taking long sections into account where what is done now has consequences far beyond immediate tangible and visible ones; that what can be seen is valuable only as a sign of a slow development not itself perceptible; and then the principle of activity will take its place in its just perspective within the whole educational scheme.

150. STRUCTURE AND NATURE OF ACTIVITIES [4]

A. Gordon Melvin

The doctrine that education is life has its partial counterpart in the idea that school life finds its rise in an organic complex of the conduct of individuals and groups. Life itself is a complex or matrix of acts, some of which are contemplated, some begun, many continuing and others nearing completion. At one given moment a schoolboy may be contemplating a visit to a baseball game on Saturday, while he is actually engaged upon the making of a churn to furnish a colonial house. Hundreds of other activities have been begun and are in abeyance, such as a book he is reading, a pageant he is writing, or a code of flag signals which he is practicing. So the group with which he works is engaged in many similar individual activities and in many which each shares with the others of the group, such as writing a play for assembly, going on a trip to a stained glass factory or planning an exhibit of hobbies. Thus when we say that education is life, we postulate some such active and developing series of inter-related acts and enterprises as that which has been discussed.

Mrs. Johnson has suggested this organic nature of the educative process by the use of a simple symbol. She has indicated the organic nature of her work at Fairhope by the use of a bit of pine branch. This is a similar figure to that used by Froebel when he named the Kindergarten, the Child's Garden. Each of these figures is intended to indicate education proceeding by means of the inner

[4] From *The Activity Program*, Reynal and Hitchcock, New York, 1936, pp. 23–25, 151–153.

dynamic force of a growing life expanding into a vital structure. The
pine branch emphasized the way in which, as each branch takes its

own path, and each pine needle develops radially into a newer something, so school life expands and grows. The name Child's Garden
implies the same outward expression of an inner force while at the
same time it emphasizes the importance of the good and true environment.

The idea may perhaps be better expressed in its completeness by
a diagram. Ultimately the pine branch takes its nourishment and
life from the branch and the branch from the trunk. So in the life
of the child and the school are certain trunk lines of experience which
branch forth and grow in many directions forming that veritable
complex which we have referred to as the matrix of school life.

The lines here indicate the interweaving and interlocking of the
activities and interests of the individual or group in a dynamic complex which is of such a nature that it may at any of ten thousand
points spring forth into new life, new pattern, new design. Such,
then is the organic life of the school from which true educational
activity may find its way forth in a thousand new experiences. . . .

Probably no aspect of modern school life has been more widely
misunderstood, incoherently written about, and actually misused in
the public school program than the activities which make up school
life. Lacking any thorough understanding of the meaning of organic living and learning teachers have allowed wide deviations
from good method to masquerade under the banner of the activity
program.

Numerous articles encumber magazines and books which relate
discursively a series of doings, actings and makings, inchoate in
origin, progress and outcome. One would gather from reading the
reports that the teachers who were directing the activities reported

had little real understanding of what they were desirous of securing by the activities they sponsored. They seem to have had small

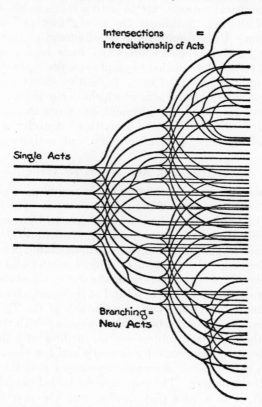

Intersections = Interelationship of Acts

Single Acts

Branching = New Acts

realization of the meaning of the activities themselves and their natural functional relationships to other activities and to life itself. They lack realization of the difference on the one hand between topics, themes, ideas, and subject-matter. On the other they do not understand the relationships of concrete physical acts, study, drill, and activity.

ACTIVITIES ARE NOT PHYSICAL

The confusion existing in current thought with respect to the relations of so-called " mind " and so-called " body " have led to an undesirable divorce in the elements of our thinking. We have been taught that some activities, for instance, the making of a sled, or the building of a log cabin, are physical in nature, while others such as the writing of an essay or group discussion of a social problem are mental. In reality every activity is an activity of the whole personality. In the making of a sled the mental aspects of our being, as well as the physical aspects, are in active relationship to the sled, the object of the act. Similarly the most "mental" act involves physical action. Unfortunately the development of the "manual" or "creative" activities in schools which have been stimulated by recent school reform has tended to emphasize the "physical" act at the expense of the "mental" one. In reality the two go together. Usually, however, only those acts which challenge the mental aspects of personality, as well as the physical, are from the point of view of the school desirably educative activities. Activity should never be thought of as mere physical activity, but activity of the total personality.

ACTIVITIES ARE NOT SUBJECT-MATTER

A very common misunderstanding of the meaning of activity confuses school activities with school subject-matter. The confusion is obvious in the work of teachers who profess to be carrying on an activity which they call *Astronomy*, or *Growth of the Thirteen Colonies*. Such a misconception leads to undesirable practices in the outcome. Confusing the meaning of subject-matter and activity the teacher teaches to secure mastery of the subject-matter concerned, rather than to secure mastery of a kind of living which involves such subject-matter. In dealing with the Growth of the Thirteen Colonies, for example, she might be vastly concerned with the children's mastery of the organized subject-matter dealing with this theme in a text. This, she might consider primary and her chief goal. Proceeding with this in mind, she might encourage activities branching from the subject-matter. The pupils might be led to make a growth map or chart, or to write a play dealing with the sanctioned theme. Thus activities would be made subsidiary to and servants of subject-matter. They would be regarded as a subterfuge to enforce the subject-matter, a device to make it more palatable and interesting. Fortunately, they do so operate, and upon this depends much of the speciousness of work carried on according to this plan. Children do find a relief from mere study of organized subject-matter in activities developed from it and based upon it. It is true, nevertheless, that programs of activity such as the giving of a Pageant on American Life for a school festival, or building of a pioneer home, should be primary, and the involvement of subject-matter should come as a supplement to and buttress for the development of the primary activities. Activities do not exist to facilitate the mastery of subject-matter. They stand alone as a part of life. Because we cannot live adequately without subject-matter, we pursue it as a necessity for the activities we are engaged upon.

151. GROWTH A DIRECT RESULT OF ACTIVITY [5]

Charles W. Waddell, Corinne A. Seeds, and Natalie White

We believe that each teacher should realize that growth is a direct result of activity — that the power to act, to respond to stimuli, to satisfy inner urges, with which all humans are endowed to greater or lesser degree, makes growth in the individual possible. It is this activity on the part of man, his interaction with his environment in response to compelling drives or urges from within, that has built the world as it is found today and wrought changes within man himself which make of him a civilized being. These same forces at work in the child — his desire to play dramatically or live the lives of the adults about him on a child level, his urge to satisfy his curiosity, his desire to construct or manipulate, his ever-present drive to be physically " on the go," and his desire to share with others the fruits of his endeavors — all of these, bringing him for their satisfaction into the world of things and men, thus cause him to build his world — to grow, to fit into society as he finds it. Thus, activity — the satisfaction of felt needs, wants and desires — becomes the key-word in education. To grow, a child must act, and act with satisfaction. To plan for the release and for the utilization of these powers within the child which will insure the best and finest growth for each and all comprises the art and science of teaching.

152. CONCEPTS OF ACTIVITY IN RELATION TO THE ACTIVITY MOVEMENT [6]

William S. Gray

When the term " activity movement " was first used, it represented a revolt against the passive learning from books that characterized education in former decades. It emphasized the value of overt mental activity, such as making things, going on excursions, and playing games. These activities were in sharp contrast with those usually employed in learning to read, write, spell, and study content material from books. They were based on a clear recognition of the value in child life of physical freedom and play, self-activity, and concrete experience.

The chief issue arising from this definition of the activity movement relates to the relative emphasis that should be given to physical

[5] From *Major Units in the Social Studies,* The John Day Company, New York, 1932, p. 13.
[6] From " Controversial Issues Relating to the Activity Curriculum," *Progressive Education,* 11:334–336, October, 1934.

and mental activities. In former decades, the controversy was clear-cut and specific between the proponents and opponents of the activity movement. During recent years, the two groups have become far less sharply differentiated on this issue due to two facts: First, the growing recognition by all educators of the values that attach to each type of activity; and second, the expansion of the activity concept which has brought to its support those who hold radically different views concerning the relative value of physical and mental activities. Striking evidence of such differences is found in the forty-two definitions of the activity curriculum reported in the *Yearbook*. For example, some activists give large emphasis to physical activities; others advocate " useful, vigorous, mental and physical effort on the part of the child "; a majority give major emphasis to the intellectual effort of children.

The fact that proponents and opponents of the activity movement are no longer sharply differentiated on the general issue under discussion makes it no less vital and significant. As a profession, we need to know more accurately than in the past the effect of various types of activities upon the physical, mental, and emotional life of the child. We need to know also the relative emphasis that should be given to different kinds of activities at each stage in the development of various types of children. In other words, the fundamental issue which we face today does not relate to the validity of either physical or mental activities, nor to their relative importance, but rather to the wisest use which can be made of both types in promoting child development.

A second definition of the activity concept is as specific as the one just presented but carries with it much broader implications. It is based on recommendations made by Dewey more than thirty years ago and represents, in a sense, a vigorous criticism of the methods employed at that time in acquiring information and in promoting mental growth. Believing " that ideas arise in the definition of activity and serve to direct that activity in new expressions," Dewey advocated " a pedagogy that shall lay more emphasis in securing in the school the conditions of self-expression and the gradual evolution of ideas in and through the constructive activities." *

Two points merit special emphasis relative to this concept of activity: First, it was concerned chiefly with the intellectual life of the child and with the means of promoting mental growth. This fact is often forgotten by some who quote Professor Dewey in defending their activity programs. Second, supplementing his emphasis on the need of self-activity were clearly defined intellectual and social aims

---

* All quotations in this paper are from " The Activity Movement," National Society for the Study of Education, Thirty-third Yearbook, Part II.

which contributed to his total philosophy of teaching. As will be pointed out later, many current proponents of the activity curriculum have failed either to define corresponding aims of their programs or to differentiate clearly between the activities included and the objectives toward which they are directed.

The chief issue arising from the foregoing definition of the activity concept relates to the value of activities as means and as ends. The function of the activity as defined by Dewey was perfectly clear. Owing to the divergent views held by current activists, such is not the case today. Some maintain that in activity there is growth and that the important consideration is that the child shall be active, mentally or physically, or both. A majority of the activists, however, maintain that " an activity begins with something that pupils have already experienced and through their desire to enjoy or interpret the experience more fully, it is pursued vigorously. As the activity continues, difficulties arise. Through the effort of the pupils to overcome them, new interests develop, new problems appear, and so on." With respect to each of the views presented, it is pertinent to ask, What are the intellectual and social objectives which they aim to serve? A third group of activists believe that activities may be used at times in preparing for and in stimulating the purposeful study of a unit of subject-matter. In this position, they are supported by many opponents of the movement. Here, then, is a very definite and specific area of controversy. There is need of much critical study and experimentation to determine the most valuable purposes which activities serve, the conditions under which they can be used best as means and as ends, and the objectives to which they contribute when used in either of these two ways.

153. ACTIVE DECISIONS RELATIVELY INFREQUENT IN LIFE SITUATIONS [7]

Guy M. Whipple

It is asserted that life is a continuous series of active responses. " The individual . . . faces at each moment some situation that is making demands upon him and to which he responds with preferences and with efforts," etc. Now, years ago when I taught psychology at Cornell, a group of forty or fifty students undertook to keep exact records for one week of every situation, trivial or significant, in which a definite decision or active resolution of a difficulty had to be made by them. The results were really astonishing;

[7] From " The Activity Movement From an Adverse Point of View," *Progressive Education*, 11:342, October, 1934.

they showed that active decisions about situations were relatively infrequent in their lives, either inside or outside the classroom. Minutes and even whole hours go by without such experiences. Discount this report, if you wish to, by fifty per cent. I still contend that neither children nor adults are forever responding to situations in the alert and almost chipper manner that the activists seem to regard as a normal condition of existence.

154. PLACE OF ACTIVITY IN THE SCHOOLROOM [8]

E. H. Cameron

The newer type of schools is characterized by the fact that the pupils are much more patently moving their arms and legs and making more audible sounds with their larynxes than they do in the old-fashioned school. The proponents of the new schools say they base their views on the " new " psychology, one of which seems to be born every few years. They say that modern psychology teaches that the very purpose of the mind is to govern and control action. An older psychology thought of the mind as something, to be sure, connected in some way with a body, but in nature so different that it must be thought of as apart from the body and treated and developed as an end in itself. The child's body was for the teacher a necessary evil that got in the way and hindered the true purpose of education, which concerned the mind alone. It cannot be doubted that this view of mind has been of weight in connection with traditional education. The apostle Paul thought of his body as a drag on the aspiring soul and.writes, " I keep my body under." When I began teaching, the first question asked of a teacher looking for a position was " Can you keep order? " Keeping order consisted largely in the task of keeping the pupils' " bodies down." We have departed a long way from this tradition even in schools that do not describe themselves as " progressive " or " activity " schools. But it is a far cry from the doctrine that mind and body are correlative functions of a single basic unity and from the now generally accepted psychological view that the mind's proper and unique function is to guide and direct activity, to the educational corollary that the advocates of these newer schools have deduced from the doctrine. Instead of being called activity schools, these schools should be called

[8] " Psychology and Recent Movements in Education," *Proceedings of the Annual Conference of the Faculty of the College of Education, University of Illinois, With the Superintendents of the Schools of Illinois,* University of Illinois Bulletin, Vol. 28, Bureau of Educational Research, College of Education, No. 26, Bulletin No. 54, Urbana, Ill., February 24, 1931, pp. 13–16.

movement schools. Now there is a vast difference between movement and activity — or at least between moving limbs and active muscles. William James in expounding the functional point of view of mind in his *Talks to Teachers* over thirty years ago — a point of view which as I have said is now generally accepted — was very careful to make this distinction, and I doubt not for the very reason that he feared some exaggeration as a consequence of his statements. Listen to what he writes in concluding his argument that all consciousness leads to action.

" The reaction," he says, " may often be a negative reaction. Not to speak, not to move, is one of the most important of our duties in certain practical emergencies. ' Thou shalt refrain, renounce, abstain '! This often requires a great effort of will power, and physiologically considered is just as positive a nerve function as is motor discharge."

The fact is, of course, that just because mind and body together in their intimate relationship constitute an organism whose function it is to act, it follows that this organism is always active, though not necessarily moving about or even kicking with feet and legs or moving hands and arms. The fact is, of course, that there are no schools in which the pupils are not all active. Death is the only condition in which pupils are not active.

I would not have labored so long to bring about a conclusion that is so very obvious if the leaders in the so-called activity-school movement did not base their views on some such logical formula as this:

Psychology teaches that the mind functions through bodily activity; ∴ in school, children should be moving about and doing things with their hands.

Having cleared the ground in this way we are ready to perceive more readily the real problem concerning activity in the schoolroom. The problem that we have to face is that of determining the really desirable kind of activity to be pursued. Shall the schoolroom be a place where the activity engaged in consists in movements of legs and arms and oral language, or is it more desirable that there should be activity unaccompanied by outward movement, in the form of silent language rather than of speech? Now the answer to these questions cannot be obtained from the psychology involved, as we have seen. Where shall we turn for an answer? So far as I can see, we must look to the results. One may have the opinion that the best consequences in life are those that occur in relation to nonmoving activity, and that, therefore, school is the place where children shall learn to perform this kind of activity. It is no proper answer to this point to say, as some one is bound to say, that it is not natural for little children to be active in this way, and that it is natural for them to be active as *in* play. It may be taken for granted that the reason for the existence of the school is that we desire in children some other outcome than that which develops naturally. The real point is whether the method of repression of muscular movement is the best for bringing about that intellectual and moral development which we conceive to be the goal of the educative process.

I am always suspicious of any argument used to advocate a method of school procedure on the ground that it is natural for the child to act thus and so. In my opinion more logical crimes are committed on the ground of the natural than on almost any other ground. If one defines nature as that which existed before man's corrupting influence was laid upon it, and if one thinks of the natural man as the primitive man who dwells in such an environment, it seems clear that a greater or less amount of time *is* spent in moving about. He has to hustle for his food. The amount of activity engaged in, however, is directly proportional to his hunger, and to the extent that he is satisfied, he remains relatively quiescent. When darkness comes on, he perforce ceases his roving and becomes relatively inactive. It is under these circumstances that his activity is thrown in on himself, so to speak. He begins to have ideas, memories of what happened in the chase, imaginations of what might have happened. At first these ideas may have been used merely to fill in the idle moments. They prompted no activity resulting in actual movement. Soon, however, primitive man began to respond to these ideas by making representations on the walls of caves, and thus art began and has continued, a sort of activity that is in no sense related to the direct procuring of food. By an extension of this same process — ideas became a means of indirect action with reference to the world that in time resulted in a making over of the environment — in a word, in those changes which we describe as civilization. Ideas represent delay in overt activity, and during these periods of delay we are preparing for overt action in a much more adequate way than when action is immediate and impulsive.

It would appear then that there is considerable justification for the relative lack in overt activity in the traditional schoolroom. Indeed, it may be held that the school exists, at least in part, for the purpose of training the young in that higher form of activity in which manifest outward movement is restrained and the process of deliberation engaged in.

On the other hand, there seems little doubt that the traditional school has too often made this restraint of outward movement an end in itself or has used it for purposes of mere discipline or order with the result that the atmosphere of the schoolroom is too artificial to be truly educative. It is incontrovertible that the experiences of the schoolroom should be as meaningful as possible to the pupil, and meanings are derived primarily from contact with an active manipulation and use of things. Wherever experiences outside of school have been inadequate to provide these meanings which are indispensable for the higher thought processes, the school itself should provide them. At all stages of education, therefore, means must be provided for this kind of direct contact with the world of things in preparation for the development of adequate and correct ideas. It is safe to say that the kindergarten and the earlier grades of our more progressive school systems have gone a long way in the direction of making schoolroom experiences meaningful to the young and in releasing them from artificiality and formality. Many schools have still far to go before this evil spirit of education is banished.

155. FUNCTION OF OVERT ACTIVITY IN EDUCATION [9]

Frank N. Freeman

This brings us to still another emphasis which is commonly made in modern progressive education. A practical enterprise may be carried on largely by study and thought, as for example a library project, or it may consist chiefly of overt bodily activity, such as gardening or shop work or folk dancing. A program which involves a large measure of these overt activities is called an activity program. It is the fashion to consider activity programs to be inherently and markedly superior in their educative effect to programs which contain comparatively little overt activity. In order to evaluate this view we must make a general survey of the function of overt activity in education.

As usual we must begin by making an analysis and drawing distinctions. We cannot evaluate activity unless we know what kind of activity we are talking about and the relation of activity to our educational aims. The value of activity for mental development is sometimes inferred from a misconception of the presentday psychological conception of the connection between thought and motor impulses or minute muscular contractions. It is true that when we think of words nerve impulses travel to our vocal cords and produce minute contractions, or that when we think of swinging a golf club

[9] National Education Association, *Major Issues with Reference to Proposed Reforms,* Department of Superintendence, Official Report, Washington, D. C., 1933, pp. 65–66.

there are similar nerve impulses followed by slight contractions of the muscles of the arm. All thought is probably accompanied by some movement tho it may be so delicate as to be beyond our observation.

But this hardly means that we must go out of our way to lead the child to engage in activity. It means that activity is so all pervasive that we could not stop it if we would. In fact we might turn the principle around and say that the way to train the child in activity is to induce him to think, because this will exercise the activities that go with thinking. But this is perhaps drawing too fine a line.

What we need to do is to conceive properly the development from overt or external activity to the internal activity which we call thought. Our responses to the external world are at first made in the form of moving about from one place to another, moving objects about and handling or manipulating them. In the course of these manipulations the animal or person notices likenesses, differences, and connections or relations. In the course of development the individual at the human level, at least, learns to think of resemblances, differences or combinations which are not actually made before his eyes but which he makes in thought. He also learns to use symbols which stand for objects and relations. That is, he learns to use some form of language. In other words, he has learned to think. Overt activity has become internal activity or thought.

It is the business of education to facilitate this development, not to retard it. Of course, adequate thought depends on adequate previous experience with the physical world. We cannot think soundly if we have not known the things we attempt to think about. This applies to activities as well as to objects. Well-designed education neither neglects the stage of concrete experience and overt activity nor tarries too long upon it.

Activity may be justified on other grounds than on its function in supporting thought. Some activities are useful in their own right. We learn to dress ourselves, feed ourselves, write, handle tools, play games of skill or drive automobiles, not because these activities give us the material for thought but because they yield us useful or pleasurable returns. If we teach a child to dance and play and observe the social amenities we may not make him intellectually brighter but we make him more competent in dealing with his social environment. We learn such activities by performing them. Activities which are useful in themselves and which fall within the province of the school should be put into the curriculum, not primarily because they promote intellectual growth but because they have direct value. In other words, we should not make activity a fetish. It is not a magic method of making geniuses out of morons. It has its own place in the scheme of education, a place which has not been accorded it in traditional education. But that place is not the dominant one. We shall not judge correctly what that place is if we think that the way to get children to think is to have them move their arms and legs. Moving the arms and legs is the way to get some things done but thinking is accomplished by a different technic.

156. LEARNING FROM BOOKS IMPORTANT [10]
Everett Dean Martin

There is a tendency among very modern educators to reduce book learning to a minimum. It is said that book knowledge is only hearsay, second-hand information. The student does not make a fact his own so long as he must take someone's word for it. What books tell you prevents your finding out for yourself. You know an emotion only when you feel it, a fact when you deal with it, a truth when you discover it. " We learn by doing." A leading progressive educator says, " The school of tomorrow is going to get away from mere reciting what has been got from books. That is, we are going to give up the notion that the school is the place where we assign certain set tasks and the child goes off and prepares those things and then comes back to convince us that he has done what was required. . . . In the school of the future, the child is going to live, really live. This means what he learns he learns because he needs it then and there."

This rather extreme form of protest against formal book learning is really an attempt to correct the opposite extreme. We all know persons, conventionally educated, who substitute reading for living, and the book for reality. There are those who never talk about events or ideas, but always quote what some book says about them, as if they believed that work, love, joy, pain, became fit subjects of contemplation only in print. The world of actions and things gives way to a world of words only. Human existence becomes a sort of grown-up children's game of authors. Education becomes an evasion of the challenge of real situations. Emotion and fancy are exhausted in doing nothing. It becomes preferable to read about things than to experience them. The individual thinks he has acquired wisdom; he merely has a taste for reading and a good memory.

In these days when educators are frantically striving to find some new method of teaching which will save democracy from mediocrity, it is the habit to blame the older education for any and all intel-

[10] From *The Meaning of a Liberal Education*, W. W. Norton & Co., Inc., New York, 1926, pp. 69–70.

lectual futility. I believe, however, that futile persons would be ineffective no matter what the method of instruction. The statement quoted above to the effect that in the schools of the future the children are going to live and are to stop reciting required lessons and learn what they need " here and now," is a little like the platitude that one can learn more out of life than out of books, a saying which always flatters the illiterate. It seems to be thoroughly modern to believe that the best way to get an education is to stop studying and just *live*, — whatever that is.

I am of the opinion, however, that anyone who can learn from life can also learn from books without spoiling his mind. There is a difference between learning from books and merely learning to repeat passages from them, and I had thought that in really learning from books one was learning from life. Whether one can get more information from books than from things depends somewhat on the books, also what it is one wishes to learn, as well as one's capacity to learn. Manipulation of objects — doing — has no more educational value than repeating words. Either may become a mere routine exercise. Education is the organization of knowledge into human excellence. It is not the mere possession of knowledge, but the ability to reflect upon it and grow in wisdom. It would seem that as few people acquire wisdom from practical experience as from books.

157. SELECTION OF ACTIVITIES IN EDUCATION [11]

Goodwin Watson

Perhaps there may be a tendency in some programs to rely too much upon activity *in response* to problems and difficulties. This is an important phase of educational activity, but it is not complete. Men and animals do not merely respond to situations — they go out and hunt for the kind of stimuli that arouse in them the kind of activity they like. Learning to create tensions that give zest to life is as important as learning to carry out processes of solution that will resolve conflicts, reduce tensions, and fulfill purposes. Starting with boredom is as important as starting from an assignment. Lower animals are adept enough at solving set problem situations, but a higher form of mental development seems to be involved in creating the purposes that create the problems to be solved.

One criterion that grows out of psychological analysis of ambi-

[11] " Comments and Criticisms by Some Educational Leaders in Our Universities," National Society for the Study of Education, *The Activity Movement*, Thirty-Third Yearbook, Part II, Public School Publishing Company, Bloomington, Ill., 1934, pp. 99–100. Quoted by permission of the Society.

tion is not emphasized in the discussion as I think it might be. An activity, to be appropriate to an individual, must fall within the fairly narrow range of tasks that are hard enough to test the individual's powers and easy enough to promise fairly frequent success. Success has no meaning when applied to activities so easy that there is no chance of failure, or to activities that lie beyond the powers of the individual concerned. A fairly persistent use of this criterion would exclude, it seems to me, very large numbers of activities now carried on in some activity programs. Suppose we ruled out all those enterprises, whether suggested by child or teacher, whether in response to immediate situations or longtime purposes, and so forth, that were either (a) so easy as to make success a foregone conclusion, or (b) so hard as to make failure inevitable. It seems to me that such a selection would add sting and vitality to programs apt to be insipid or burdensome.

158. STUDIES OF CHILDREN'S ACTIVITIES [12]

Ellsworth Collings and Milbourne O. Wilson

Meriam's Studies of Children's Activities. In the Experimental Elementary School at the University of Missouri, Meriam found that children normally engage in four lines of activities. They are handwork activities, story activities, observation activities, and play activities. Handwork activities include construction of various things in wood, textiles, metal, yarn, and raffia; story activities include story telling, reading, and dramatization; observation activities include study of industries and natural phenomena; and play activities include both indoor and outdoor games, contests, and sports. The following are typical illustrations:

(1) *Handwork Activities*
   Making a doll's dress
   Making a snow sled
(2) *Story Activities*
   Telling the Gingerbread Man story
   Dramatizing Little Red Riding Hood
(3) *Observation Activities*
   Study of the country post office
   Study of the flowers of the country
(4) *Play Activities*
   Playing tenpins
   Playing baseball

[12] From *Psychology For Teachers*, Charles Scribner's Sons, New York, 1930, pp. 194–203.

Professor Meriam conducted a study recently at the University of California of 150 children of random selection between the ages of 6 and 12. The total number of children listed was 2847, distributed in the following manner:

	Cases	Per Cent
Play activities	1219	42.8
Work activities (Handwork, etc.)	637	22.6
Observation	577	20.2
Communication (Stories, etc.)	414	14.5

This study indicates the distribution of children's activities among play, handwork, stories, and observation.

Dewey's Studies of Children's Activities. For some time at the University of Chicago Professor Dewey experimentally studied the activities of children. Dewey found that the children of his experiment engaged normally in four lines of activities. The first line consists of construction activities. He found boys and girls are always eager to construct something in either wood, cloth, metal, clay, yarn, or paint. The second line consists of communication activities. Children, he found, eagerly express themselves through reading stories, telling stories, singing, and dramatization. The third line consists of exploratory activities. Boys and girls are curious concerning the things about them and express a keen desire to study natural phenomena and country occupations. The fourth line consists of artistic activities. He finds children delight in attaining skill in such activities as folk dancing, drawing, etc. Dewey finds, after several years of study of children, that they engage continuously in four major lines as follows:

(1) *Construction Activities*
  Making a doll house
  Making a watch fob
(2) *Communication Activities*
  Telling the Three Bears story
  Dramatizing Rip Van Winkle
(3) *Exploratory Activities*
  Finding out the names of the flowers in the country
  Finding out how people in colonial times made their clothes
(4) *Artistic Activities*
  Painting a picture of the child's playhouse
  Engaging in folk dancing

Collings' Studies of Children's Activities. Collings conducted an experiment over a period of four years for the purpose of studying children's activities. In this experiment children were afforded opportunity to pursue activities of their own choosing. A record was made of the activities and it was found at the end of the four-year period that the children engaged consistently in four major lines of activities. The first line of behavior consists of Excursion Activities. It includes children's purposes to find out about things in life outside of the school, such as, for example, How to Know the Wild Flowers of the Country, How Our Ice Is Made, How People Travel in Egypt, etc. The second line consists of Story Activities. This line includes children's purposes to communicate things to each other, for example, telling the story of Boy Blue, singing Jolly Old Saint Nicholas, dramatizing The Three Bears, etc. The third line consists of Construction Activities. This line includes children's purposes to construct something, for example, a rabbit trap, a library table, an angel food cake, etc. The fourth line consists of Play Activities. This line includes children's purposes to compete in things, for example, Roly Poly, Bean Bag, Volley Ball, etc. This experiment indicates that children in the elementary school engage normally in the following lines of activity:

(1) *Construction Activities*
How to make a rabbit trap
How to make a sponge cake
(2) *Communication Activities*
How to tell the Story of the Three Bears
How to dramatize the story of Mother Goose
(3) *Excursion Activities*
How to know the birds of our community
How our ice is made
(4) *Play Activities*
How to play Roly Poly
How to play tennis

The University of Oklahoma Junior High School Studies of Children's Activities. During the past six years the Junior High School of the University of Oklahoma has been experimentally studying the activities of boys and girls. This experiment indicates that boys and girls of junior high school age engage normally in five lines of activities. The first line includes Construction Activity in which the purpose of boys and girls is to produce something. Its scope includes purposeful construction in wood, textiles, metal, art, etc. The second line includes Communication Activity in which the purpose of boys and girls is to communicate something. It includes purposeful participation in story telling, reading, dramatization, and writing short stories. The third line includes Exploratory Activity in which the purpose of boys and girls is to find out something. Its scope includes purposeful investigation of industries, occupations, and natural phenomena. The fourth line includes Play Activity in which the purpose of boys and girls is to compete in something. It includes purposeful participation in games, athletics, and contests. The fifth line includes Skill Activity in which the purpose of boys and girls is to perfect something. It includes purposeful practise in singing, instrumental music, drawing, typewriting, public speaking, debating, oratory, mechanical drawing, etc. The following are typical illustrations:

(1) *The Construction Activity*
How to make a radio
How to make an Indian flower vase

(2) *The Communication Activity*
How to dramatize Silas Marner
How to write a short story of the Yellowstone

(3) *The Exploratory Activity*
How wild animals live in Oklahoma
How we predict our weather in Oklahoma City

(4) *The Play Activity*
How to play tennis
How to play basketball

(5) *The Skill Activity*
How to write 18 on the Thorndike Handwriting Scale
How to play the piano according to the musical scale

Similarity of Studies of Children's Activities. There appears to be much similarity of the foregoing studies of Children's activities in spite of the fact that the studies were carried on by different educators working independently in different schools over the country. This might be expected since each study is the result of direct study of the activities of boys and girls. Kilpatrick's Problem Activity, Meriam's Observation Activities, Dewey's Investigation Activities, Collings' Excursion Activity, and the University Junior High School Exploratory Activity are practically identical in purpose. They all involve the purpose of boys and girls to find out something. The same is true of Kilpatrick's Consumer's Activity, Dewey's Communication Activities, Meriam's Story Activity, Collings' Story Activity, and the University Junior High School Communication Activity. The purpose to communicate something is the foundation of each of these lines. The Producer's Activity (Kilpatrick), Construction Activity (Dewey), Handwork Activity (Meriam), Hand Activity (Collings), and Construction Activity (University Junior High School) likewise are similar in purpose. Each includes the purpose of boys and girls to produce something. There seems to be some difference between the Play Activity, Artistic Expression, and Skill Activity. The Play Activity is included in three studies — Meriam's, Collings', and the University Junior High School. Artistic Expression is found in only one study (Dewey). The Skill Activity is listed in two studies (Kilpatrick and the University Junior High School). The following lines of activities occur in two or more of the five studies with a slight difference in terminology:

(1) The Excursion Activity
(2) The Communication Activity
(3) The Construction Activity
(4) The Play Activity
(5) The Skill Activity

The Excursion Activity. The distinguishing feature of the Excursion Activity is its purpose. It involves, as we have seen, purposes of boys and girls to find out something — to explore, to investigate, to discover. Its scope is wide and includes purposeful study of the activities and natural phenomena of community life. The following are typical illustrations:

How people travel in Egypt
How Mr. Smith manages our historical museum
How we make our laws
How to know the wild flowers of our community
How electricity produces our light
How modern inventions have changed our ways of living
How America became a nation

If, for example, the purpose of boys and girls is to find out the names of the wild flowers of the community it is carried on primarily outside of the school since it is necessary to investigate the flowers in the fields of the community. On the other hand, if the purpose of boys and girls is to find out how electricity produces light it is carried on primarily inside the school since study of this purpose demands laboratory equipment and experimentation. This is best provided in the school laboratory. Still, if the purpose of boys and girls is to find out how people travel in Egypt, it is carried on in the school library, for study of the purpose demands investigation of sources dealing with travel in foreign lands. The purpose is, in other words, the determining feature of the Excursion Activity and not its technique of study. It may be, and is, carried on outside of the school, in the school laboratory, and in the school library.

The Communication Activity. The Communication Activity involves, as we have seen, purposes of boys and girls to communicate something — to converse, to dramatize, to tell. It includes purposeful participation in a wide range of stories in reading, dramatization, story telling, and writing short stories. The following are typical illustrations:

Dramatizing Silas Marner
Reading the story of Tom Sawyer

Telling the story of Evangeline

Writing a short story of the Yellowstone

The Communication Activity is not limited to any particular type of story. It includes the following:

Fairy tales, myths, legends, and fables

Inventions, industries, and science

Animals and natural phenomena

Travel, exploration, sightseeing, and adventure

Hunting and fishing

Humor and fiction

History and biography

Poetry and drama

The Construction Activity. The distinguishing feature of the Construction Activity is its purpose. Its purpose is to produce something — to make, to create, to fashion. Its scope is wide, and includes purposeful construction in wood, metal, paper, textiles, yarn, leather, cardboard, raffia, reed, rope, clay, paint, water colors, crayola, and foods. The following are typical illustrations:

How Jane made her Chinese flower vase

How Luella made her leather hand bag

How Nadine made her angel food cake

How John made a painting of his father's farm home

How Jim made a clay statue of Daniel Boone

How Tom made his radio

How Jane made her spring dress

How James made his library table

How Wilbur made his fireplace andirons

The Play Activity. The Play Activity involves, as we have seen, purposes of boys and girls to compete in something — to win, to vanquish, to master. Its scope is broad. It includes purposeful participation in a wide range of games and contests. They may be classified as follows:

Indoor Games — Indoor baseball, basketball, checkers, etc.

Outdoor Games — Volley ball, tennis, football, etc.

Indoor Contests — Debating, typewriting, etc.

The following are typical illustrations of play projects:

1. How to win the Kansas football game
2. How to win the basketball championship
3. How to win the tennis tournament
4. How to win the checker championship

The Skill Activity. The Skill Activity involves, as we have seen, purposes of boys and girls to perfect something — to excel, to exceed, to be proficient. Its scope is wide. It includes purposeful practise of a wide range of activities. The following are typical illustrations:

a) How to use the understroke in swimming
b) How to use the punctuation marks correctly
c) How to play America on the piano
d) How to write a short story according to the rules of composition
e) How to typewrite according to the touch system
f) How to sing alto in the glee club
g) How to be a public speaker

CHAPTER X

SELECTION OF SUBJECT MATTER

159. THREE CONCEPTS OF KNOWLEDGE [1]

Ernest Carroll Moore

THERE are three kinds of schools which grow out of these three conceptions of education. According to the first kind, the great thing is knowledge. It is stored up in books, in courses of study, and in the minds of teachers and other learned folks. Schools exist to retail it to young people, to pass it on from the places where it is to the places where it is not. That it may be passed on easily, it must be prepared in little carefully molded cubes or accurately weighed doses. That is the work of textbook makers and of manufacturers of methods. Teaching, according to this view, consists in seeing to it that the learner takes the proper number of pellets of knowledge each day, and the object of the recitation is to find out whether or not he has done so. Since what he has taken is knowledge in its essential form, he must retain it in the form in which he took it. To see that he has done this and is continuing to do it, there must be periodical inspections of his stock of knowledge. These are called examinations. They occur at regular intervals, since the amassing of a fixed amount of knowledge and the retention of it in its original condition is thought to be necessary before one can safely amass further knowledge.

The object of education according to this view is knowledge. The business of teaching is to put it where it is not. Textbooks are to provide it. Recitations are to find out whether or not it has been taken. Memory must retain it, and examinations must be given to test the knowledge state of pupils. Since knowledge is the one thing needful, the quantity of knowledge which can be compressed into the memory of a school child becomes a matter of vast importance. Courses of study are written chiefly, in many cases, to indicate the quantity which every good retailer of knowledge must succeed in lodging in the memory of each child. To cover the prescribed amount of work is the mark toward which the teacher is made to

[1] From *What Is Education?* Ginn and Company, Boston, 1915, pp. 18–24.

press and toward which she is usually, in such a system, overpressed. That the directing authorities may know that teacher and pupils are handling the required stint of knowledge, that teachers may know that pupils are stocking themselves with it and retaining it in undiminished state, that parents may know that their children are amassing the fixed heaps of prescribed facts, that the children themselves may know how much they know, great reliance is placed on examinations. They are given with great regularity. Their results are carefully tabulated. Children are weighed and measured by them, are encouraged or discouraged, are promoted or demoted by them. As soon as one is over, everybody settles down to prepare for the next one. This is called an examination system of schools.

It is conceivable that either a university or a kindergarten might be conducted in this way. Fortunately they are not, but elementary schools, secondary schools, and colleges, not a few, are. The method is of long standing. Dr. McLean, formerly the head of the Pacific Theological School, once told me how he was taught theology at Princeton fifty years ago. He said: " Each day the professor brought our meat into the classroom cut up into neatly prepared little cubes, all of the same size. He then proceeded to insert the proper number of these into the stomach of each one of us. Two days after he looked into our stomachs to see if we were retaining them in the exact form in which he had given them to us."

The second kind of school tends to regard knowledge as something common and unclean. It claims a loftier mission. It sets out to sharpen and perfect the mind by putting it to work not on matters that it will have to work on as long as its possessor lives, but on special teaching disciplines, valuable not because of the opportunities for knowledge-getting which they provide, but for the mental exercises which one can perform in pursuing them. What you manipulate, they say, does not count. That you manipulate is the great thing. The best mental exercises are those which have been used so long that a perfect technique of using them has been developed. There are certain studies which are made much of in this type of school because they train the students not in the *object* matter with which they profess to deal but in ratiocination in general. They provide hard work and plenty of it. They demand exactness. They enable teachers to assign fixed lessons of graduated difficulty, to require a system of recitations and examinations which tell exactly whether the student is meeting the requirements of the assignment or no. It makes little difference that the student after six or seven years of such labor will seem to himself to have learned nothing. The fact is that his mind will be a much more flexible and ready instrument because of this gymnastic. These are the mind-training schools. They make use of all the machinery which the others employ except the important element of knowledge.

The third kind of school believes both in knowledge and in mental training, but it holds that they go together and cannot possibly be separated. It asserts that knowledge is inner conviction, organizing experience in terms of vital need, and that, while mind can be trained specifically to organize experiences, since different experiences call each for its appropriate form of reaction, mind cannot be trained in general to make them. This school looks upon knowledge not as a fixed and immutable thing but as a useful tool which men have shaped to meet their needs in living. It is not at all finished or final. Men made it by thinking, and men will improve it by thinking, and before anyone can use it, or any part of it, he must remake it through his own thinking for himself. What Moses thought or Plato thought or Euclid thought will never do me any good until I succeed in thinking it for myself. The great thing then for this school is not knowledge, but learning to use one's own mind upon matters which men have found to be important by using their minds upon them. Textbooks are important because they suggest to us some things which the race has found it important for us to think about. Teachers are important because they stimulate us to think by surrounding us with problems and reasons for solving them and such help in going about the matter in profitable ways as we stand in need of. They help us to look at things and study things and talk about things and repeat things and memorize things which can best be thought about in these ways. And from time to time, to make both us and themselves better acquainted with the success which we are achieving in our thinking, they set specific pieces of work for us to perform and examine our performance of them with somewhat greater care than they can give to our day-by-day thinking. It is not the amount of ground which we cover or the number of courses which we "take" which decides whether or no we are getting an education, according to this conception. Education is determined by what the student does. A single subject which has been pursued in such a way that he has learned to stand on his own feet and use his own mind in the getting and solving of its problems provides a more real education than a whole college course in which one has merely endeavored to appropriate the thoughts of other men or tried to become a thinker without thinking about anything which seemed to require thought. The first kind of school seeks to put its students in possession of results without allowing them to go through the processes of getting them. The second kind of school seeks to develop processes apart from the context of reality which gives them meaning. Its instruction goes on in a vacuum. It produces "thoughtless thinkers"; while the first kind does not set out to make thinkers at all, and is rarely disappointed by having them develop.

160. "Erudition or Information" [2]

Henry C. Morrison

No doubt the theory which is, and always has been, most prevalent in actual practice is that which implicitly holds that knowledge and information are synonymous with education, that the more an individual knows in the sense of erudition the better educated he is. The view is reflected in most courses of study. It prevails in the ardent commercial exploitation of schools, in the interest, or supposed interest, of easy methods of imparting information.

Very likely the natural history of the idea goes back to the day when it was easily to be seen that the "learned" — chiefly clerics — were in actuality the only free men outside the nobility, and that there was a pathway to greatness along that line which the sons of the common folk could follow. Ideas persist, long after their meaning has disappeared, and to this day organized knowledge has very great prestige, indeed, despite the fact that we rarely elect an academician to be President.

Not a little pessimism regarding the possibility of education as a transforming and regenerating influence owes its origin to this mistaken view of what education is.

Unhappily, we sometimes find out-and-out rascals among men who have attained distinction in college. Education is therefore a delusion. Were not these men educated? Of course they are what they were born to be. So the argument runs. Those who can see in Man nothing more than a sort of organic machine find in such cases data for their theories. . . .

Practically speaking, the eruditional theory as applied in schools signifies becoming informed about science instead of acquiring the insights upon which intelligence is founded; becoming familiar with literature and the products of the fine arts instead of taking on the tastes which ought to arise from these sources; being informed what one ought to believe and like in the place of conviction and preference themselves.

The theory retains its predominant influence largely by weight of tradition and partly, no doubt, as an expression of vested interest. If one qualifies himself to teach an academic subject in high school, it is hard for him to believe that his subject is anything else than in itself an integral part of education. More than that, granted the

[2] *Basic Principles in Education*, Houghton Mifflin Company, Boston, 1934, pp. 338, 340–341.

theory, it is easy for people to appear with new subjects which they would like to teach, on the ground that pupils " ought to know," and thus the program of studies expands indefinitely. If the high school can be held to instructional efficiency only by way of preparation for college, the professional interests of academicians will dominate the high school and be transmitted to the elementary school. If one has invested capital in enterprises set up for the production of apparatus designed to make the getting of information easy and school life entertaining, it is easy for him to believe that his wares are themselves an essential part of education.

161. RELATION OF SUBJECT MATTER TO NEED OF INDIVIDUAL [3]

Ephraim V. Sayers

It may be said that educational procedure, if it is regardful of the unity of individual and environment that has been emphasized in this discussion, will make the individual's successful reduction of disturbed relationships, both on and below the level of thought, its chief concern. Put negatively, there will be no arbitrary presentation of race experiences to be learned in separation from a disturbance normally needing such ways of behaving for its reduction. Education will be cautious in increasing the number of disturbances already within the experience of the individual lest failure of reduction result. It will endeavor to work as much as possible within experience as it is, introducing more and more control. Other individuals, as events in the environment, will be utilized to the fullest in the coöperative reduction of common individual disturbances and in the development of coöperative patterns of control. Control will be assumed to be control of the environment, that is, power to reconstruct the environment to meet the demands of a dynamic and expanding complacency. These are a few indications of the course education will pursue if it accepts, and is guided by, the conception of unity of individual and environment that has been developed.

162. DEVELOPMENT OF THE RACE HERITAGE [4]

Ross L. Finney

The exigencies of our argument suggest some elaboration of the phenomenon of cumulative racial learning; to which end a few illustrations will prove helpful. The technique of so simple and

[3] From *Educational Issues and Unity of Experience*, Contributions to Education No. 357, Bureau of Publications, Teachers College, Columbia University, New York, 1929, pp. 90–91.

[4] From *A Sociological Philosophy of Education*, by permission of The Macmillan Company, publishers, New York, 1928, pp. 32–34.

commonplace a thing as making bread harks back through a long
series of inventions and discoveries to the very dawn of human life
upon the planet. Modern methods in milling, recent improvements
in baking, the method of lightening dough, the original devices for
cooking, the first cracking of the kernels, the domestication of wheat,
the initial discovery of the plant, are among the steps in the long
series. Meat getting has had an evolution quite as interesting. It
is a far cry from our modern ranches, feeding pens, packing plants,
storage, transportation, and marketing facilities, back to the naked,
barely human savage, sallying forth into the forest in the precarious
hope of making some chance killing — with great risk of being himself the killed! Our modern inventions are none of them so wholly
modern as they seem. Among the prerequisites of the airplane were
the mathematical discoveries of Euclid and Pythagoras, who in
turn built upon the foundations inherited from Crete, Egypt, Phœ-
nicia, and Babylonia. The wheel is so old that the mind of modern
man runneth not to the contrary, although reckoned in terms of
social evolution it is a relatively late invention. The steam loco-
motive is but a recent assembling of ancient elements. The har-
nessing of steam is recent; but the taming of fire, by which the steam
is produced, was the achievement of naked savages in the long-
forgotten past. To whom shall we give the more credit for the steel
rail, Bessemer or Tubal Cain? Almost all the plants and animals
of modern agriculture have been in use throughout the historic
period, while many of the materials used in modern manufacture go
back to a vanishing past. But in their day these earlier contributions
were quite as epoch making as those of our own.

Similarly, all our institutions and cultures have evolved; and
there is no intellectual exercise more enlightening than to trace that
historic evolution in the various social fields. Political scientists,
for example, find the genesis of our Constitution in Colonial and English precedents, which in turn they trace back to their origins in the
Roman Empire and in primitive Teutonic life. Much factual material has been brought together recently to throw light on the origin
of the state in the conflicts of early tribal society. Professor Ely
specifies an industrial stage, a handicraft stage, an agricultural
stage, a pastoral stage, and a hunting-fishing stage in the evolution
of industrial society. Other writers make different divisions. To
understand our own school system we trace its evolution back step
by step through modern and mediæval Europe, to ancient Greece
and Rome; and then infer its prehistoric origin from the practices
of primitive peoples now living. Westermarck has written the history of the human family, and corrected our notions about its primitive forms. Every moral code has a history: our own has derived

contributions from pioneer conditions, from Puritanism, from chivalry, from ancient Roman law, and from the still more ancient Hebrew ethics, which in turn were rooted in the code of Hammurabi, and thence back to prehistoric times. In the long, slow sifting of the ages those forms of conduct which society has decided are harmful, have come to be socially disapproved, while those that are adjudged harmless or helpful have come to be approved. Even the Christian religion has evolved; and the study of its evolution takes us back not only to the Jahveh cult of ancient Israel, but to the religions of Egypt and Babylonia, with prehistoric savagery in the ultimate background. Science has a history of the utmost fascination, surpassed in interest, if at all, only by the history of art: for the relics of primitive art carry us back to an even remoter past. And so it is in all fields. Little by little the race has learned; and the findings of racial experience have been transmitted and accumulated. Thus do we now possess that vast, mental heritage by the use of which we conduct our social life on the present high level of civilization.

163. Basis of Selecting and Organizing Subject Matter [5]

Hilda Taba

Education that seeks a continuous reconstruction of the total social and individual experience through self-directed activities cannot rest content with a development of the individual which treats as incidental the activities and phases of learning that are paramount in building and directing experience in its wider and non-academic sense. It not only has to emphasize those phases of learning which are not directly connected with the mastery of academic subject matter, but it is compelled to go beyond this, and subordinate the whole process of educational practice (including its subject matter) to the demands and needs of developing experience. In other words, the liberation of the powers and capacities for a rich, wide, well-integrated experience, the growth of interests and of motivation for further learning and of methods of inquiry and good reasoning, should be the determining standards for the organization of the educational processes and its materials.

This means that the form and sequence of educative activities should be determined by their effects on the growing individual, and that subject matter should be selected and organized to serve as an adequate means for the cumulative, consistent, and continuous growth of this experience.

[5] From *Dynamics of Education,* Harcourt Brace and Company, 1932, pp. 223–226.

The hitherto dominant methods of curriculum construction have paid little heed to this demand. Like educational aims, so also the sequences of educational experiences and the selection of subject matter is effected not on the basis of what is essential for the development of educands, but what follows the logic of external and objective values — and the growth of experience is subordinated to those values. In this respect the logic of the sciences represented by the academic subject matter and the demands of adult life furnish the most widely applied standards. What to teach, in which way to do it, how to organize and relate facts and ideas, how to interpret phenomena, and in which channels to lead the awakening intelligence and thought — all these problems are solved not on the basis of what is most fertile in the way of self-directed, well-organized, and wide as well as qualitatively diversified and rich experience, but what best preserves the values, the logic, and the method of thought of the formulated knowledge and accepted moral and social institutions, and best transmits the ideology of the research specialists in their respective fields. Or else the practical demands of adult life are given the deciding role in the selections of educative subject matter and in the organization of educational activities.

In both these cases the integrity, fruitfulness and self-direction of developing experience from within are sacrificed to some ulterior purpose, are subordinated to the externally derived values, and a superimposed logic of organization governs the process and content of education.

The conflict of policies regarding the central principles of the organization of educational processes and content is a comparatively old one. The discussion of it has taken the form of a conflict between the psychological and the logical organization of the subject matter of instruction.

The general position of those standing for the priority of the logic of the subject matter as a basis for the organization of educative materials, as against the proponents of the so-called psychological organization, is that there are binding principles of thought, leading ideas, and compelling generalizing concepts in the bulk of our formulated race experience which are absolutely necessary for a consistent and intelligent way of looking at the phenomena of life. If these fundamentals of race experience are neglected, the developing experience, it is claimed, inevitably becomes futile, fragmentary, incidental, lacks an organizing centre of outlook, and is not able to grasp the fundamental relations, the fundamental principles of thought and inquiry, is poor in content, powerless in its functions, and subjective.

The assumption underlying such a position is that the experience of the layman, when allowed to take a normal course of development, is not able to achieve a closely-knit network of interpretations, that it is not capable of seeing the logic of facts, events and ideas, and that it is not capable of intellectual organization and of intelligent re-adjustment in meeting problems. It is supposed that if education were to abandon the logic of the systems created by the different sciences, the resulting experience would be chaotic, unorganized, incompetent and blind.

To a certain extent this position is a correct one, especially when viewed in the light of the present prevailing attempts toward the psychological organization of the educational process and its subject matter. The present practices of using the individual as an educative unit, around which and according to the demands of which the educational process is to be organized, are frequently based on a narrow and one-sided conception of that individual, who is conceived only as a psychological phenomenon, with subjective drives, interests and motives for action, and with definite, and to a certain degree fixed patterns of conduct. The individual is viewed apart from his relation to the objective world of facts, ideas, concepts, and so the latter's structure is seen independently from the effects that that relation would or could have on the structure of his experience. As the interests and trends of activity of the individual do not carry within themselves the patterns for their growth and development the organization of education around the individual conceived in such terms leads to the incidental, fragmentary, one-sided and narrow development of experience. Education in such terms is apt either to neglect or to deform the fundamental logic of ideas, events, the inherent relations between facts, points of view and interpretations. It is also likely to fail to understand and follow the logic of the objective world around us. The organization of education in such terms is certain to lead to the disintegration of race experience into fragmentary, incidental, and unrelated knowledge, interpretations, and outlooks.

But this position is based on the erroneous supposition that the logic of the objective world and ideas is identical with the logic of distinct isolated sciences, organized around specific principles of thought and dealing with specific groups of facts. It is also a mistake to suppose that the logic of the research specialist is the natural logic for every type of experience, and that the unity of segregated fields of knowledge *eo ipso,* when followed and mastered, assures the unity of total experience. It fails to draw a definite distinction between the logic of subject matter, as specialized and scientifically organized bodies of knowledge, and the general logic of fundamental relations, sequences, and implications of the facts, meanings, concepts and events. The former is the logic and organization of the scientist within his own field; the latter is a logic from the standpoint of intelligent experience, not limiting itself to any specific field, but seeking relationships within the totality of experiential material. The former would be a coherence of settled and systematized deposits of all experience, the latter that of experiencing; the former is specialized, the latter general.

164. Selecting and Organizing Subject Matter in the Social Studies [6]

1. In the selection and organization of the materials of instruction in the social sciences the educational statesman should be guided by five controlling principles or considerations — the purpose of education, the powers of the child, the time allotment of the school, the life of the surrounding community, and the obligations associated with professional competence.

2. The great purpose of the American public school . . . is to prepare the younger generation for life in a highly complex industrial society that is committed to the ideal of democracy and equality of opportunity for personal growth, that places its faith in intelligence rather than force in the achievement of social ends, that is in rapid transition from an economy based on individual enterprise and competition for private gain to an economy essentially co-operative and integrated in character and dependent for efficient operation on careful planning and co-ordination of production and consumption, that is marked by innumerable conflicts and contradictions tending to place in jeopardy its inherited ideals and to block the full utilization of its energies and talents, and that now, because of its rich natural endowment and its advanced technology, is capable of inaugurating an era of reasonable security and abundance for all, of freeing the human mind from material worries and of devoting its varied resources to the tasks of cultural advance.

3. The achievement of this far-reaching purpose requires the introduction into the school curriculum of materials which will equip the younger generation, as fully as possible, to understand, to appreciate and to evaluate the great changes under way and to act intelligently and in the common interest in facing the innumerable issues that lie ahead.

4. The materials and activities selected must be within the range of the capacity and the experience of the learner and so graded as to

[6] Commission on the Social Studies, American Historical Association, *Conclusions and Recommendations,* Charles Scribner's Sons, New York, 1934, pp. 46–49.

insure a steady progression in understanding and power to deal effectually with social data and situations.

5. In view of the revolutionary expansion of the secondary school enrollment during the past generation and the general reduction in opportunities of employment, this gradation of materials may be undertaken with little reference to the factor of elimination and on the assumption that the ordinary pupil will remain in school through the period of adolescence and will even have opportunities for continued education in adult years.

6. The critical character of the present epoch in American and world history, with its social stresses and strains, makes especially imperative the organization of a program of social science instruction coherent and continuous from the kindergarten through the junior college and the articulation of this program with a program of adult education.

7. The program of social science instruction should not be organized as a separate and isolated division of the curriculum but rather should be closely integrated with other activities and subjects so that the entire curriculum of the school may constitute a unified attack upon the complicated problem of life in contemporary society.

8. The program of social science instruction, along with the rest of the curriculum, should be as intimately articulated as possible with the life, the activities, and the institutions of the surrounding community, the fact being fully recognized that the advance of industrial civilization has been attended by an enormous extension of community boundaries and an equally altered relationship of community to regional undertakings and possibilities.

9. In the selection and organization of social science materials the teaching staff of the country, co-operating with the social scientists and the representatives of the public, should assume complete professional responsibility and, resisting the pressure of every narrow group or class, make choices in terms of the most general and enduring interests of the masses of the people.

165. Criteria for Selection of Materials [7]

Mildred English and Florence Stratemeyer

The desired activities, including investigation, problem solving, comparison, judging, conferring with the teacher and with other pupils, require a new use of old materials as well as the use of many

[7] From "Selection and Organization of Materials of Instruction," National Education Association, *Materials of Instruction*, Department of Supervisors and Directors of Instruction, Eighth Yearbook, Bureau of Publications, Teachers College, Columbia University, New York, 1935, pp. 133–140.

previously unused materials. Rather than being used to create interest only, maps, charts, the bulletin board recording current happenings, cartoons, poems, songs, fragments of inscribed clay or stone, source extracts, and the like, are fundamental and necessary tools to problem solving.

It is a point of view which suggests as a *first criterion, the selection of instructional materials in terms of their bearing upon experiences or problems being considered by the group.* The agreed-upon goals in terms of the problem or situation at hand become the focal point of selection. It means material (1) selected to give fuller meaning to daily experiences, and (2) selected because it contributes naturally to the development of the experience or situation without imposing that which is unrelated.

The goals as thought of by the teacher holding the educational point of view just suggested demand that a *second criterion* be coupled with the first standard: *the selection of material to lead to an understanding of fundamental concepts, generalizations, and principles — controls based upon facts and experiences which give power to meet new situations.* It means the selection and use of instructional materials in a way to assist the learner to see relationships among facts, to use materials in the solution of problems, to apply principles arrived at inductively to new data and new situations. The " handy bag of facts " without understanding and recognition of relationships is of little worth in solving new and different problems. Contrariwise, the real understanding of such a basic idea or generalization as " True freedom is based upon order and organization " is fundamental both in the school situation and in civic and social activities. Likewise, a recognition of such a principle as " Species have survived only through adaptation to environmental conditions," derived from watching bird migrations and the storing of the winter food supply by the squirrel, helps in understanding the hibernation of bears, the habits of the Eskimos, and the plans and methods of the Byrd expedition. It is a criterion which is directed toward the selection and use of materials in a way to help the learner to push his thinking forward and to open doors ahead. The following questions may serve as more specific checks in applying the second criterion:

1. Are the materials such that meaning, significance, and understanding of the use of principles and processes are emphasized?

2. Are the materials so organized as to point to relationships between problems and processes and give opportunity for selection and application of processes appropriate to situations?

3. Does the material take cognizance of the need for (a) exact repetition of materials for mastery, (b) repetition of essential meanings in new situa-

tions to functionally exercise recall, and (c) repetition of meanings in new situations for the purpose of enlarging the concept?

The *third criterion* places emphasis upon children as the active agents in the learning process. The abilities as well as the interests and needs of the pupil group become the starting point and indicate the direction of movement toward the achievement of the goals set up. Just as two points determine a straight line, every experience selected for the curriculum has two points of reference — the goals to be achieved and the present conditioning factors of the learner. Only as we consider the two in relationship do we have any sound basis in going forward. Thus our *third criterion* may be stated: *selection of materials within the range of understanding of the group — selection from real situations on the level of the child's understanding and in accord with pupil interests and needs.* It is a criterion which leads one, when evaluating materials, to ask such questions as:

1. Do the materials present real situations as they actually occur and in a manner realistic to children?
2. Is the material within the experience and understanding of the children at the given stage of development?
3. Are the pupils prepared by previous experience to react appreciatively and understandingly to it?
4. Is it of a degree of difficulty that enlists the children's abilities fully and yet provides for at least a measure of success?
   a. Does it provide for the principle of increasing difficulty?
   b. Do the children have the background necessary to carry it out with satisfaction?
5. Is it sufficiently flexible to permit of adaptation to changing circumstances — to take into account the environmental conditions of the children?

For the values of the vividness and the reality of materials for the given pupil group, we are just beginning to recognize the possibilities of the use of the excursion and the value of first-hand contact with persons and things through attendance upon political discussions, contacts with public welfare agencies, study of the local community and its problems, visits to museums, visits to commercial and manufacturing establishments, and the like. So conceived, much instructional material is found outside of the school building. For many schools the community is essentially the laboratory offering a wealth of direct contacts, as well as such printed materials as reports of city departments, legal and commercial forms, copies of ordinances and ballots, accident and fire-prevention pamphlets and posters, health pamphlets, and other publications.

Another interesting area in this connection is that represented by the increasing tendency to use the various phases of art as means both of presenting materials and as expressions of reactions to and interpretations of ideas and attitudes. Art materials in the hands of pupils may become effective, first, as sources of desired information; second, as stimuli to the learner's own creative powers; and third, as a means of acquaintance with age-old racial activities. Art materials, whatever may be their nature, not only provide data needed in working on problems and afford acquaintance with age-old racial activities, but supply also the visual imagery which the junior high school child is constantly seeking as the vehicle for his own expression. Portraits, contemporary views (including cartoons), reproductions of paintings, imaginary scenes from the professional illustrator, views of historic sites, buildings, models, graphs and diagrams of comparative facts, dramatizations may all be included in the pictorial arts. They suggest a definite relationship between art and the social sciences.

Let us carry this thought a step further to see its possibilities. Information may be the single purpose of a child's careful study of art records. The words of medieval manuscript are beyond his interpretation, but the vellum with its precision of lettering and the illumination which often accompanies the text help him to reconstruct monastic life as well as the manners and customs of the Middle Ages. Similarly the arts of the carpenter, the spinner, and the iron worker reconstruct colonial life for pupils whose units of study are the traditions upon which some of the present social ideals are founded.

The *fourth criterion* is suggested as a corollary of the third, namely: *the selection and use of materials to provide for individual differences in ability, interest, and need — providing for individual growth within group activity.* This is a criterion which in its implications suggests such questions as:

1. Is the material sufficiently comprehensive to " demand a variety of responses from different children and permit each to go at it and make his contribution in a way which is characteristic of himself? "
2. Is there provision for differentiating experiences for different ability groups?
3. Does the material provide for *continuing* growth and development, suitably graded to the growing needs and widening interests of pupils?
4. Is the manner of presentation clear and understandable to children?
5. Does the language correspond to the reading and speaking vocabulary of the children (non-technical, real, interesting)?
6. Does the material provide for the use of local data?
7. Does the material provide for the utilization of pupils' experiences — the environment used a source of direct interest and approach?

The *fifth criterion* is directly related to the goals set up (see criteria 1 and 2): *the selection and use of materials of instruction to help children in turn to grow in self-direction in the choice and evaluation of materials.* This criterion rests upon the belief that the teacher's place in the educative process is that of a member of the group who, on the basis of larger experience, is a recognized leader, whose function it is (1) to assist in selecting the influences which shall affect the learner and (2) to assist him in properly responding to these influences — responding in a way to develop independent power on the part of the pupil in the selection, evaluation, and judgment of materials.

The fifth criterion suggests several others as corollaries to its best use. *Sixth criterion: the selection of materials noting basic purposes for which the material has been developed and testing its validity in the light of known truths and facts.* There is a rapidly developing body of print materials being issued for purposes of advertisement or propaganda. It is significant that both teacher and pupil grow in power to test such material for its true worth. Frequently the selection and use of such material means testing the scientific basis of the data presented — *a check on authenticity.* In other cases it means *sensitivity to varied points of view and the continued search for materials to make the several viewpoints available.* In still other situations it is the *recognition of propaganda as propaganda* — a distinguishing of the sensational, the partisan, that based only upon an appeal to the emotions. It means the review of materials, asking such questions as:

1. Are checks made on the claims of an advertisement before using?
2. Are the essential meanings and understandings included so presented as to give accurate and correct information?

The import of this criterion is noted in the area of films, pictures, and slides. Commercial pictures, as well as those appearing daily in newspapers and magazines, furnish a definite fund of material. Pictures in themselves frequently show history in the making and suggest data needed in solving problems. Charts and diagrams can graphically illustrate such topics as the tariff, the fluctuation of railway rates, resources of different sections of the country, immigration and movements of population. Pictures may well tell the history of the development of transportation facilities on land and on sea, or of the changes brought about in agricultural methods. Many other excellent illustrations are available through slides. The more recent explorations in the field of the motion picture make it possible for children to follow in a unique and impressive way the unfolding of a series of related episodes. The dramatic element of historic episodes especially has lent itself to the production of many historical films by commercial companies. Unfortunately, these episodes are not always " filmed " in such a way as to tell the truth.

The fifth criterion suggests also as a corollary *a seventh standard: differentiation in the selection and organization of materials between those having permanent values and those concerned with temporary or passing interests.* Differentiation should be made both in the emphasis given to the contextual idea or ideas and to the manner in which the material is filed.

As an *eighth criterion* it is suggested that *selection should provide for balance and variety in types of material.* This standard is significant by way of (1) acquainting pupils with a wide variety of sources, (2) recognizing basic factors conditioning interest, (3) stimulating new interests through different media, (4) allowing for individual differences, (5) providing stimuli to the learner's own creative powers, and (6) providing for the all-round development of the individual. It is a criterion which raises such questions as:

1. Is the material varied enough to meet the requirements of the activity or experiences — will it contribute to the ideas desired through a variety of avenues?

2. How often and how recently have similar materials been used?

3. Is the material such that it " opens up a new field, raises new questions, arouses a demand for further knowledge, and suggests what to do next on the basis of what has been accomplished and the knowledge thereby gained? "

4. Does it provide for needed recall of past learning experiences (repetition of vital facts when needed)?

5. Does it introduce and emphasize essential elements (eliminating unnecessary, artificial, and forced repetitions)?

Lastly, attention should be given to *selection of materials having appropriate mechanical make-up.* Other things being equal, those materials are to be preferred that rank high as to

1. Clearness and conciseness (vocabulary, sentence structure, style) and interest value.

2. Attractiveness, usableness — suitability of type, form, size, margins, quality and finish of paper, spacings, illustrations, etc.

3. Mechanical durability and suitability.

4. Proper methods of emphasizing important phases of work (i.e. use of italics, illustrations for heightening interest, etc.).

5. Convenience — completeness of table of contents and index, definite page arrangement, etc.; usability under existing conditions.

An abundance of potential material is available for the using. Let it not be said that we are poor in our wealth — poor either in the use of meagre materials or, more significant, poor in the way we use such materials to help children grow in power to envisage desired human relationships and to participate actively in their realization. The criteria serve as guides for (1) the selection and use of available instructional materials and (2) the development of new and the enrichment of old materials as needed by selected groups. Pupil and teacher should share the work — selecting, organizing, and filing materials, referring to materials, adding new materials — the pupils to push forward experiences and problems in which they have a real interest, the teacher to assist pupils to carry these experiences forward in ways to arrive at desired goals set up.

166. THE SUBJECT CURRICULUM [8]

Sir John Adams

The French are the typically tidy-minded people of the world; so we are not surprised to find that they are the first to rebel against the confusion that prevails in our theory and practice in connection with the use of knowledge as an instrument in education. It is generally admitted that education consists in the deliberate guiding of the educand by means of communicating knowledge. But too often this knowledge comes to be regarded as an end in itself, and not as a means. It gets to be treated as the aim of education, instead of merely as its instrument.

The knowledge that we admit is part of the educator's business to communicate, is too often resolved into a thing of shreds and patches. Curiously enough the systematic way in which we have classified the subjects to be taught in school, is one of the chief causes of the scrappiness of which complaint is made. The subject-matter to be taught by each specialist — the *docendum,* as De Quincy used to like to call it — is in most cases exceedingly well organised, but each specific *docendum* has been split off from the big river of knowledge in general, and is therefore separate from the broad stream, and reduced to an eddy. Each of the eddies tends to remain shut off from the rest: they cannot be entirely isolated, but they are sufficiently cut off to lose wholesome touch with the big palpitating flowing mass with which they should be in intimate and responsive connection if they are to function in a healthy way.

Dropping metaphor, let us look critically into this classification into " subjects," to which we have become so accustomed that we are apt to regard it as of the very essence of " the nature of things." Time was when philosophers, the teachers of that distant period, could calmly take all knowledge to their province. Even as late

[8] From " The Teacher as Integralist," *The Kadelpian Review,* 14:5–7, November, 1934.

as the times of Francis Bacon this claim could be made without arousing ironical laughter. But, though it took centuries to get knowledge so divided up that specialism (*departmentalism* is the American equivalent) became an absolute necessity in schools, the classification of the different branches of knowledge went back farther still. It is commonly admitted that the beginning of what we now call school " subjects " may be traced back to the fifth century A.D., though, as usual, if we turn back to that arrant anticipator, Plato, we find this classification suggested in a rudimentary form of the seven liberal arts. You will find three of these arts of a literary kind in the *Trivium*, to wit, Grammar, Rhetoric, and Dialectic: and four of a somewhat scientific kind in the *Quadrivium* — Music, Arithmetic, Geometry, and Astronomy.

But while these seven arts are thus separated from one another, there was nothing to hinder the teachers of the fifth century A.D. from instructing in the whole of them. When Varro, Capella, Cassiodorus, Boethius, Isidore and the rest of that learned company had set down all they knew about things in general, they had plenty of room for an appendix. They wrote encyclopedias on such a small scale that they could themselves read almost at a sitting all that they had put down.

Since specialism has set in all this has been changed. Each individual marks out his own area, and scrupulously keeps within it. The whole realm of knowledge has been staked out, and each plot bears an unmistakable notice against trespassing. So rigid did this become that, in the schools at any rate, a reaction was inevitable. People with a pansophic tendency, who wanted, like old Amos Comenius, to claim a universal lordship over learning, began to preach the oneness of all knowledge. But they took the wrong tack by trying to treat all knowledge as common ground for humanity, and humanity was not big enough to make good its claim. It was not till the latter part of the nineteenth century that in the schools a really effective revolt was developed. It took the form of what became popular under the name of *Correlation*. This plan was to bring into their proper relations all the subjects of the curriculum. History was to be persistently correlated with Geography. This could be done without any undue strain or distraction. But Arithmetic had also to be connected up, and it was not easy to make a convincing correlation here. Dates of battles, heights of mountains, populations of cities made rather poor material for systematic teaching of arithmetic. When literature, nature-study, music, economics, and algebra had all to be dragged in and correlated it is not surprising that deputations of " parents and others interested " began to wait upon school authorities to protest against this new system that seemed to block the way to the teaching of anything fresh. Pupils were kept so busy correlating old material that there seemed no room for anything new.

The scourge sank down to the youngest classes, as appears from the somewhat profane remark of the little boy in the Kindergarten who got so fed up with the *primulacea* in all its relations to reading, arithmetic, spelling, drawing, modelling, story-telling that when at last his mistress produced a specimen in connection with a color game, he remarked in stark desperation: " Oh! damn that primrose! "

The natural re-action came, with a falling back upon an increased rigidity of " subject " teaching. Had it not been for what we have just described, it might not be easy to account for the sentence in Professor Johnson's book on *The Teaching of History:* " The business of the History-teacher is to teach History." The casual reader might be inclined to say: " Well, of course; but why take the trouble to say so? " The now discredited Correlationists could, if they cared, give a convincing answer.

But we have kept our French critics far too long in the ante-room, though, if they could have heard our criticism they would not have objected very much, since the discussion has prepared the way for the complaint they now proceed to make. Their grievance is that our whole instructional system is so divided up that it has lost all unity; it has got organised into a smooth-working machine in which everything appears to go very well, but nobody seems to know what it all means. The boy in one of the higher grades in a French *Lycée* goes to class after class during the day, does this, that, and the other thing, and finally goes to the dormitory or to his home, without at all realising, or seeking to realise, what it is all about. This is bad enough, the critic thinks; but worse is to follow, for the masters do not seem to be in any better plight. They come to their classes, open their *serviettes*, as their lecture-cases are called, deliver the lecture — usually, it must be confessed, an admirable one — and then pass on to another class. It is as Ernest Lavisse, the former Recteur of *L'École Normale Supérieure* of Paris, remarks: " The case of a fragment of an educator that addresses itself to a fragment of a pupil "; and he might have gone on to add, " about a fragment of a subject."

167. Disconnected Subjects a Source of Inert Ideas [9]

A. N. Whitehead

Culture is activity of thought, and receptiveness to beauty and humane feeling. Scraps of information have nothing to do with it.

[9] From *The Aims of Education and Other Essays*, by permission of The Macmillan Company, publishers, New York, 1929, pp. 1–2, 10–11.

A merely well-informed man is the most useless bore on God's earth. What we should aim at producing is men who possess both culture and expert knowledge in some special direction. Their expert knowledge will give them the ground to start from, and their culture will lead them as deep as philosophy and as high as art. We have to remember that the valuable intellectual development is self-development, and that it mostly takes place between the ages of sixteen and thirty. As to training, the most important part is given by mothers before the age of twelve. A saying due to Archbishop Temple illustrates my meaning. Surprise was expressed at the success in after-life of a man, who as a boy at Rugby had been somewhat undistinguished. He answered, " It is not what they are at eighteen, it is what they become afterwards that matters."

In training a child to activity of thought, above all things we must beware of what I will call " inert ideas " — that is to say, ideas that are merely received into the mind without being utilised, or tested, or thrown into fresh combinations. . . .

The solution which I am urging, is to eradicate the fatal disconnection of subjects which kills the vitality of our modern curriculum. There is only one subject-matter for education, and that is Life in all its manifestations. Instead of this single unity, we offer children — Algebra, from which nothing follows; Geometry, from which nothing follows; Science, from which nothing follows; History, from which nothing follows; a couple of Languages, never mastered; and lastly, most dreary of all, Literature, represented by plays of Shakespeare, with philological notes and short analyses of plot and character to be in substance committed to memory. Can such a list be said to represent Life, as it is known in the midst of the living of it? The best that can be said of it is, that it is a rapid table of contents which a deity might run over in his mind while he was thinking of creating a world, and had not yet determined how to put it together.

168. LOGICAL AND PSYCHOLOGICAL ORGANIZATION OF SUBJECT MATTER [10]

Boyd H. Bode

There is reason to think that much of the onesidedness and confusion in our thinking could be eliminated by a more careful consideration of the nature and function of what we sometimes call the " logical organization of subject matter." It is not claimed that such a consideration will furnish a solution to every problem, but it is indispensable for the formulation of an adequate educational program.

[10] From *Modern Educational Theories,* by permission of The Macmillan Company, publishers, New York, 1927, pp. 46–54.

Many of our troubles are due to the fact that we have reacted indiscriminately against the abstract, lifeless organization of subject matter which we are becoming accustomed to call a " purely logical organization."

The meaning of this term can easily be exemplified by an inspection of textbooks, particularly those of an earlier day. A physicist, for example, is tempted to begin an exposition of physics with definitions of such concepts as matter, force, and energy; while a historian naturally follows a chronological order which is designed to trace out, step by step, the causal connections by virtue of which the present grew out of the past. This statement is not intended to imply a criticism; there are certain purposes for which an organization of such a sort is proper and required. The point just now is that such an organization is not intended primarily to furnish a record of racial experience, but rather to present what is in a sense an artificial arrangement of the fruits or results of racial experience. In a cut-and-dried account of physics the " human " element is obviously left out entirely; we learn nothing of the trials and disappointments that were involved or of the hopes and issues that were at stake. Stated in its lowest terms, what we get is a sort of catalogue of results, together, it may be, with a marshaling of data to show that the inferences are sound. Less obviously, perhaps, but in a very real sense, our histories may likewise leave out the human element. They do not stir our imagination or our partisanship in the way that is done, for example, by a good novel, because the material is not organized in such a way as to stimulate the pupil to reinterpret and dramatize the account in terms of his own experience. In other words, abstractly scientific forms mean a logical rather than a psychological organization of subject matter.

It is sometimes supposed that logical organization is just a peculiarity of the scientific mind or a convenient device which the research specialist finds useful for his purpose. That it is not a suitable form, without modification, for teaching purposes is doubtless true. But this does not decide the question whether " logical organization," in the sense just indicated, is something which concerns the research specialist and no one else. If we take this position, we are at once committed to the view that such organization should not be permitted in the curriculum, except in so far as we are training prospective scientists. On the other hand if we hold that scientific organization of subject matter is important for the purposes of general education, it becomes necessary to make clear why this is the case.

As a preliminary to a discussion of the question at issue let us first try to draw a contrast between the knowledge of the practical man and the knowledge of the scientist or research specialist. If we

compare the two we find a significant difference in type of organization. As an extreme illustration, let us take the case of a man who is
lost in the woods. Such a man is quite likely to develop a keen interest, for the time being, in geography. He is much concerned to
discover the location of the towns and rivers and the position of the
North Star, but all the while his interest is confined within narrow
limits. He is not concerned at all with the size of the Sahara or the
location of the north magnetic pole. He cares only for those facts
which will help him find his way back home. The facts of geography
which he requires are selected and organized with reference to a further end; he requires, as we say, a practical knowledge of geography.
It represents an attitude that is obviously very different from that of
the specialist in geography, who is interested in geography " for its
own sake," and consequently organizes his facts on a very different
basis.

This difference in attitude, it will be observed, does not mean that
science alone has organized knowledge; it means that there is a difference in the principle or basis on which the organization is made.
Even the humblest rag-picker organizes his knowledge. He classifies
the different kinds of rags; he knows where rags can be found most
abundantly or most cheaply, where and at what prices they are sold,
and he may even know in some detail what is done with them after
they have passed out of his hands. In the same way a plumber may
know a great deal about water; yet his knowledge may be very different from that of the chemist. To the plumber it is important to
know that water freezes at a certain temperature, whereas the chemist seems to be more interested in the fact that water consists of
H_2O. Either of these traits might appropriately be offered as a definition of water. The plumber would naturally prefer his own definition, because the freezing of water has an important bearing on
plumbing. This peculiarity of water brings in much new business
and must be borne in mind when new plumbing is installed. The
chemist, on the other hand, attaches a greater value to the chemical
definition because of its importance for the analyses which must be
made in order to extend the field of chemistry. When knowledge
is so organized as to make it effective for the acquisition of more
knowledge, we call it pure science. When it is organized for some
purposes other than the accumulation of more knowledge, we call it
practical or applied knowledge.

To put it differently, theoretical or scientific knowledge is particularly concerned with deduction. For practical purposes the proposition that the earth is round is hardly an important part of
geographical information. The average individual can get his bearings quite well and can secure abundant information about climate

and change of seasons without reference to the shape of the earth. From the standpoint of science, however, the shape of the earth is a matter of great moment. By introducing the proposition that the earth is round we can make many other geographical facts appear in a different perspective. If the earth is round, then it is possible to explain deductively such facts as difference in time, differences in season, the possibility of the sun shining into a window with northern exposure at this latitude, and a multitude of other facts which to the practical man are merely empirical observations. Scientific geography shows why these facts are as they are; it shows that they could not be otherwise. The goal of scientific organization is serviceableness for purposes of deduction. The facts and discoveries that are of supreme importance to science are those which knit together a body of facts so as to facilitate deductive procedure. The law of gravitation and the principle of evolution are conspicuous examples. Still another case is the law of atomic weights in chemistry. A law of this sort might be of little practical importance and yet be supremely important to the chemist. Scientific knowledge is " pure " in proportion as it approaches this form of organization.

From his own standpoint the scientist is abundantly justified in exalting this kind of knowledge. In the first place, when knowledge fits together so as to form such a system, it constitutes perfection of method and proof, because a wide area of fact is made to converge upon a single point. From an empirical standpoint, a traveler's report that the sun rises later every morning when we go west is an isolated, uncorroborated bit of evidence. But from the standpoint of scientific geography a great mass of observations that have been accepted as fact stands and falls with this assertion. Secondly, the scientific organization of knowledge makes this body of achieved knowledge a peculiarly effective instrument in the acquisition of further knowledge. This is shown impressively by the prevalent use of mathematics in a great variety of fields. The application of mathematics shows that the development of the sciences is in the direction of facilitating deductive inference.

The distinctive character of such organization is emphasized if we contrast it with what has been called the " psychological " organization of subject matter. As was said just now, a logical organization aims to arrange knowledge in such a way as to show the relation of premise and conclusion. In geography it begins with the earth as a globe and works progressively toward details, so that the particular facts take their place in a system, which means that we do not merely find these facts empirically but are able to explain them after they have been found or perhaps to predict them before they have been found. Geographers, for example, tell us that at the poles the year is divided into a single day and a single night, although no geographer has ever been at either pole long enough to verify the fact. They can tell the length of day at any given place for any given date and can show how arctic explorers starting at different places on the earth gradually move toward a common point if they proceed due north from wherever they happen to be.

As contrasted with this, a " psychological " organization is a very different affair. This kind of organization lacks the purely objective, detached, impersonal quality of " pure " knowledge. Its center of reference is the individual learner. We have often been told that geography must begin with the locality in which the pupil lives in order that he may see his own surroundings in a wider spacial context. The idea is that the actual process of learning must be more empirical and less deductive than the final organization which we call scientific. The question that confronts us just now is whether the final organization that is achieved by a pupil should be " scientific " in character or should be of a different and more " practical " sort.

This question has been an underlying issue for a long time. It is involved, for example, in the long-drawn-out struggle over the professional training of teachers. The stiff-necked traditionalist who sees no need for a professional study of education takes for granted that " logical " arrangement, plus a reasonable amount of common sense, is all that a teacher needs. He suspects that all this " psychologizing " is inspired mainly by sentimentalism. As someone once put it, there are two kinds of teachers: those who love their pupils and those who know their subject. If the teacher knows his subject thoroughly, his procedure is all laid out for him. He must have some skill, of course, in simplifying and illustrating his material so as to bring it within the comprehension of the pupils, but the aims or " objectives " and the order of steps are determined for him. They are inherent in the subject matter itself. A knowledge of the technique of teaching " is necessary mainly to make the subject ultra-patent in order that the dullards in school and college may get something out of education." A knowledge of technique " is not of great importance, except in dealing with the backward pupil. Knowledge of the subject, spontaneity, character, personality, must be held as the principal items in the qualifications of the teacher. In some of the good old days these were estimated at their true value." *

This view has a certain plausibility until we raise the previous question. Why should any of the subjects at present in the curriculum be studied at all? The dyed-in-the-wool traditionalist is dis-

* Tait, W. D. — " Psychology, Education and Sociology "; *School and Society,* January 10, 1925, pp. 34, 35.

posed to treat this question cavalierly. Knowledge is worth while
on its own account. This is apt to be the substance of his reply,
somewhat adorned, perhaps, by allusions to " culture," to the joys
of intellectual pursuits, and to the desirability of cultivating the
mind.

All this may be granted, however, without disposing of the question. Life is more than scholarship. There are additional claims
that are entitled to consideration. It is fairly certain that there are
further reasons why schools are maintained in civilized communities.
Society is concerned to make provision for its own perpetuation. The
world's work must be done somehow, and so we must give heed to
vocational interests: There are certain ideals or common purposes to
be fostered which we call by such names as character and citizenship.
What is called the logical organization of subject matter is concerned
with one interest to the exclusion of these others. There is no justification for this exclusion, nor for the assumption that if the ideal of
professional scholarship is protected, these other interests will take
care of themselves.

169. BOOKS AND SUBJECT MATTER IN THE ACTIVITY PROGRAM [11]

William H. Kilpatrick

. . . The question . . . arises as to what use the activity program
will make of books and specific subject matter. The answer is unequivocal. We are concerned first with each child that he grow as a
person and into proper human relationships. We wish to use books
and subject matter but only as means to continuous child growth
and living as an end. And we are not apprehensive as to results.
Under the activity program, intelligently directed, more books will
be used and more subject matter will be acquired than under the
older program. We wish our children to become intelligent about the
world around us, while they learn to enrich life and also (so some of
us at any rate are thinking) learn to criticize our institutional life
so as the more intelligently to control it. All of this we desire, as
previously stated, for the sake of and on the bases of simultaneous
growth in intelligent self-direction and appropriate social outlook.
Therefore, as children undertake any enterprise and try to deal with
it intelligently, they will need help from various sources. Books
will furnish one valuable aid. Most of our pupils will come from
homes where reading is at least expected of them. The teachers,

[11] From " The Essentials of the Activity Movement," *Progressive Education*, 11:356, October, 1934.

also, will expect reading and encourage it. The danger is that parents and teachers alike may too quickly advise books, forgetting that these are valuable not as the signs of an education but as the means to life. In this as in many other matters, appetite should not be forced. If books are used because they are needed they will more likely be appreciated accordingly. In this the teacher and the brighter pupils can set a tone which will help others to give the books a fairer chance. Once the mind is willing and the teacher wise, most pupils will come readily to the use of books. The appetite for reading easily grows. We must not expect that all will become great readers, but we can easily improve over what now obtains.

The discussion for books holds also for subject matter. By " subject matter " we mean here simply knowledge conceived as instrumental to thought and endeavor. If the school be successful and pupils live in fact rich and varied lives, there will necessarily arise many and varied demands for knowledge. Here, as usual, the teacher and the better pupils will lead the way and set the growing standards, but the others may truly share the life and its inherent demands. If knowledge and standards thus be not forced from the outside, but are shown not only to fit into life but actually to inhere in it to enrich it, then the attitudes of pupils are favorable and the seeking of knowledge and the building of appropriate standards are both natural and easy. True it is that home and community standards will continue to exercise their influence (thus setting a serious problem for a new and wider adult education) but the procedures here advocated indicate promising lines of school endeavor. Collings' experience in the Missouri rural schools, to quote a carefully recorded instance, bears out the promise.

170. "THE ROLE OF SUBJECT-MATTER AREAS IN AN INTEGRATED CURRICULUM " [12]

Traditional systems of subject-matter have developed largely without recognition of their relation to other systems of study. This fact is apparent when we realize that the introduction of a new area of learning to a curriculum does not ordinarily call for any reorganization of other areas, or systems of study. Consequently, a curriculum which endeavors to provide an integrated experience will frequently find itself in conflict with the rate and the content of traditional courses of study, logical though they may be. The following statements concerning special areas and interests are representative of the changed attitude which the integrated curriculum has devel-

[12] *Educational Research Bulletin*, 15:53–66, February 12, 1936.

oped in the minds of subject-matter specialists at the University School. The reader should note that the resulting concepts are more inclusive than those necessitated by a conventional curriculum. It has been the experience of the staff that integration has stimulated and extended the teacher's concept and study. The specialist loses his prejudice but finds ample need for his best attainment.

THE ARTS

In the arts program in the University School, music, home economics, and the industrial and fine arts have a double function, for the pupils in the school have the opportunity to elect to work in one or more of the arts areas on the same basis as they choose to join a foreign-language class or a special science or mathematics group. Distinct from these special arts activities with the pupil-teacher planned programs is the contribution the arts areas make to the whole school program. In the seventh, eighth, and ninth grades the unified-studies faculty includes a representative of one of the arts fields, and arts teachers or members of arts groups are frequently called upon to make their contribution to social science, science, language, or mathematics classes.

It is important that in the specialized arts work which is being carried on in the various well-equipped laboratories, the whole school philosophy is the chief factor in determining the approach to subject-matter, the procedure involved in planning and carrying out activity, and the pupil-teacher relationships. A growing understanding and agreement between the teachers in the various arts fields has enabled the arts to become more and more an integrating factor in the whole school experience of the child. The arts teachers are thought of as general educators rather than as specialists in art. They believe definitely that no one type of art experience is an equivalent for all others and that for the child such experiences should be as varied as possible with emphasis on one or more of the arts fields.

For the work in the arts laboratories the time reserved in the schedule varies with the grade-level and with the individual within the grade. Thus those children who learn most satisfactorily through the arts experiences may be able to spend several hours a day in the workshops, while others may have one period or less each day of this individual or group arts activity.

Among the chief factors in the integration of the child's school experiences are school assemblies, Christmas pageants, games, and May festivals. The interest and abilities of each child in the school are utilized in creating the spirit of these natural social situations.

The relationship between the arts and the seventh-, eighth-, and ninth-grade unified studies may be perhaps best explained by examples of different activities. Pupils wrote and sang songs which were instigated by their work; they used all available reference material in planning; they wrote creatively about their interests and feelings during this period; they experimented in science with the materials they used in painting the walls, building the furniture, and making the cushions and draperies. In the spring of the year they opened the room with a music program and luncheon. This does not mean to indicate that the arts usually stand at the center of the work of these groups, for the programs vary with the specific needs and abilities of each group of faculty and pupils.

The whole spirit of the period between the Civil War and the present day was instilled in eleventh- and twelfth-grade social-science units when they called in school singers and instrumental groups to illustrate what the music of that time was like. They had the opportunity to relive the past with the old-time band and minstrel. They saw the symphony develop. They recognized the relationship between the grand opera and the latter part of the nineteenth century, which led to a better understanding of each. They caught the spirit of the " Bicycle Built for Two " song, and, what is more important, they began to realize how modern music, the airplane, and the automobile are among the products of our age which will serve best to determine for future generations how we feel about things and what we are interested in.

In similar ways the language, the science, and the mathematics classes welcome the contribution the arts can make to a better understanding of particular subjects and the seeing of the relationships between all phases of past and present living. Thus it is a rare occasion for a period to pass when members of almost any class in the school cannot be found hard at work in the arts laboratories clarifying and turning to practical application elements of every type of school experience.

We have an unqualified conviction that the satisfaction and enriched experience which have come to pupils through the various arts have meant a better understanding of all experience and an emotional and intellectual release.

PHYSICAL EDUCATION AND HEALTH

The very term " physical education " is a misnomer for it implies a philosophy of dualism which is inimical to the facts of the unity of the organism. " Health education " is an equally noxious term for it implies a special course in hygiene or " how to be healthy " where health concepts are taught frequently from a book. Evidences of integration might best be sought in the behavior of children. We try not to ask ourselves, " Do children understand health concepts? " but rather, " Do children act as if they understand health concepts? " Emphasis, therefore, is not on health instruction but on activities which introduce health concepts when they are related to the child and his environment.

Our concept of health includes harmony of function, vigor, and quiet joy, and emphasizes the unity of the organism: the integration of the personality where children are not fighting bodily discord, on one hand, and the liabilities of social existence, on the other. An effort is being made to honor " *Mens sana in corpore sano* " in practice as well as quotation.

Teachers, for example, understand that a child's whole physiology may be affected by a change in his social status in the group; that suggestion sometimes works curative wonders; and that deficiency in the activity of the thyroid may cause arrest of mental and physical development. Such phrases as " curative pedagogy " and " diagnostic and remedial teaching " must become everyday realities in practice.

When the aims of good education and hygiene become the same, the education of the " whole " child can become a reality. Good education then becomes a condition of normal development, both somatic and mental, and teachers become as concerned about the quirks of the personality as they do about deviations from the normal body.

Health, therefore, is not the responsibility of a few specialists but of all teachers. The specialists, however — the school physicians, the psychologist, the school nurse, the physical education teachers — are present in the school set-up and constantly focus the attention of the staff on important facts concerning individuals and situations. In this way they help staff members and students to see new relationships and make new interpretations, thereby assisting the process of integration. The school program for health might be said to stand on three legs:

Health protection is concerned with adequate health examination and elimination of the strains and drains of remediable defects. It is also concerned with the control of the school environment in the interests of health.

Health teaching refers to the use of ideas, philosophy, and practice of that personal conduct that conserves and promotes health. The emphasis here is not in telling children how to act but in giving them opportunity to act. It is here that the dining room, the science laboratory, the health office, and the playground become places where much systematic incidental health teaching takes place. No health " course " as such is taught.

Physical-education activities form the chief motives for following those health practices which make for greater efficiency. Children are not interested in health as an abstraction but are tremendously interested in activity. Illness prevents activity and attainment of vital individual and social goals. Children will therefore often follow a Spartan regimen to attain them, especially if guided by good leadership.

The integrated efforts for the health of children come to a focus before the Health Committee, composed of the school physicians, the psychologist, the school nurse, the dietitian, a representative of the lower grades, the teachers of physical education, and the assistant director of the school who acts as chairman and is the chief contact with the parents.

This committee meets on alternate weeks and takes for its chief functions the following responsibilities: to act as a clearing house for considering the specific problems of individual students who show evidence of maladjustment; to carry each case through to some definite conclusion with the aid of parents, teachers, and family physician; to check the health examination and make recommendations to parents and teachers; and to work hand in hand with parents and counseling teachers by assisting with records, tests, and in interpretations of medical and psychological experience.

LANGUAGE — ENGLISH AND FOREIGN

The language program in a progressive-school curriculum is a most difficult matter to analyze. Language develops as a function of normal living. Reading and writing, which are merely extension of language activity, are necessary to progress in all areas of study. The question therefore has been raised at the University School as to whether special courses in English were necessary. While it has been apparent that little progress in foreign language could be made without a special class, study was made of the entire program to determine whether the English teacher might not best function in classes with teachers of other subject-matter areas. In the unified-studies courses, as noted previously, such a plan has been followed. On some days the discussion concerns especially the leisure reading and the writing of the children, but the major problems of writing, reference reading, organization of oral and written reports, and effectiveness of speaking are considered as they arise in the process of the general problem. English is, consequently, an integral part of the curriculum, the English teacher merely a member of the class faculty whose special duty it is to be sensitive to the matter of language development in reading, writing, speaking, and listening. As reading of literature and creative writing come to present more complex problems and require longer periods for discussion and investigation, special classes in English are organized. There is always, however, as has been noted in discussion of the unified studies for the upper grades, time for the teacher of English to work in the science or social-science class itself.

Special avenues of language, however, develop at various stages. The field of mathematics has such a specialized vocabulary that it may be and sometimes is, called a language. Such special vocabularies do not grow gradually, but some times, at least, are acquired hurriedly. Similarly there may come a time when the most profitable expansion for language may come through an added tongue. Care must be taken to make certain the development is a necessary one. Moreover, since in America one teacher of a foreign language and a few books must take the place of a social group, the necessity must be strong enough to overcome these unnatural difficulties. At the University School the study of French, German, or Latin is carried on in separate classes, but, as is seen from the foregoing, is related to development in English. Since the study of a foreign language thus appears as an extension of interest in a foreign culture and also in use of language, the teachers of English and of social science confer with students who desire to begin such work. They consider not only the child's background of general social understanding, but his development in reading and writing his native tongue. It seems doubtful that the individual who reads little in his own literature will ever read the literature of France, Germany, or Italy except under constraint. It appears more advisable for him to use his energies in reading material which does not offer serious vocabulary and structural difficulties. Consequently pupils at University School read extensively in English before attempting a foreign-language class.

Examination of criteria developed in the eleventh and twelfth years by students in the English classes reveals the integration of the reading program with the content of other language courses and with less closely related fields. The criteria follow:

1. Is my reading free as to types? That is, do I read all types — drama, poetry, fiction, essay, biography — with ease and understanding which are unhampered by the form?

2. Is my reading varied as to subject-matter? Can I read a book on science, social problems, art?

3. Is my reading varied as to the social culture presented? That is, can I adjust myself to a setting other than my own?

4. Is my reading varied as to nationality of the writer? (Note: Matter read may be in either translation or original, depending on development of the individual)

5. Is my reading varied as to the historic background of the writer? Can I read material written from the standpoint of a previous culture?

It may be noted that many of these criteria themselves involve understandings developed in areas other than English or foreign language. It is the province of the teacher of literature, however, to see that those understandings apply in the reading of the child. Music and graphic and plastic art are also factors in the study of the various literatures. Pupils compare techniques in these related fields. Biological, psychological, and social concepts are basic to interpretation of books. Great responsibility rests with the teacher of the vernacular. The English class becomes a strong integrating factor in the program, and a test of the ability of the individual to integrate his experiences.

MATHEMATICS

In mathematics there are two phases of demonstration. The first is quite applicable to the junior-high school levels of maturity, and is that of indicating, directing toward, assisting to discover through experience. This is the method of experiment which sums up and generalizes. The second method is quite applicable to the senior-high school levels of maturity, and is that of the nature of proof: " of logical reasoning from premises assumed to possess logical completeness." *

The junior-high school program is concerned with the concepts of number (whole, fraction, decimal fraction, directed, irrational), estimation and measurement, geometric forms, verbal problems, formula, equation, table, graph, and their relationships applied to such areas as industrial arts, physics, chemistry, home economics, biology, physical education and health, social science, fine arts of drawing and music, and administrative practice.

Examples from the seventh level —

1. Two boys determined how to arrange seats and tables for 200 persons, in a room of given size, for a program of known content. This project involved estimation, measurement, geometric form, whole and fractional numbers, addition, subtraction, division, and multiplication with application to and relationships with administrative and committee practices, home economics, and industrial arts.

2. Two girls determined how many pounds of seed were needed to resow an area of the physical-education playground. The application was to an actual problem and relationships were set up with the needs of the physical-education program.

3. Two boys constructed a device to determine the value of, and two devices to determine the area of a circle. This project involved number, estimation, measurement, geometric form with application to wood and relationships with industrial arts and science.

* Dewey, John, *Nature-Experience*, pp. 10–11.

4. Four boys constructed graphs recording the data of heights and weights of their seventh-grade group. This involved measurement, number, geometric form, table, graph.

5. Two girls in their study of a social science problem constructed a graph involving addition, division, and percentage.

Examples from the ninth level —

1. The group began their study with the development of the formulas for such figures as triangle, rectangle, trapezoid, and circle; then the application of these in combination to common objects in the environment such as lamps, thumb tacks, and saws for both areas and volume formulas. This was followed by a trip to the mechanical-engineering laboratory to observe how such forms as gear teeth, axles, cylinders of engines, and cones of metal were always comprised of the basic geometric forms. The unit developed with uses of the forms in building construction, in sciences like physics and chemistry, in fine arts, industrial arts, and home economics. The work was further developed to the point where pupils were creating their own application of the basic geometric forms to common objects of their observation.

2. The group studied the concepts of verbal problem, formula, equation, table, graph, and their relationships; how to derive from four of the concepts given the data for the fifth concept; and which of these concepts, with what degree of precision, were applied to such areas as physics, biology, social science, and fine arts. Again this unit was developed to the point where individuals carried on with their own creations of formulas to different problems of their choice.

3. The group studied the concept of balance in an equation; how to manage the quantities in an equation without destroying the balance represented through the sign of equality; the application of the concept of balance to levers, bridges, personality traits, body balance, food balance, oxygen- and carbon-dioxide balance, in areas such as home economics, fine arts, industrial arts, and science.

4. The group studied the concept of directed numbers; the reading of numbers from left to right or right to left, and the meaning of zero; the applications of directed numbers to directed forces, automobiles, football, street cars, elevators, bank accounts, temperature, elevation, achievement-test scores, height and weight values, calendars of different peoples, social-science issues, fine-arts productions.

These illustrations indicate a definite effort to select types of materials closely correlated to a definite end. That end is integration of the concepts of mathematics among themselves and their application to various areas of reality.

One of the most important concepts as well as one of the most basic to modern life is the nature of proof. While it is possible to emphasize this concept in all areas where abstract thinking occurs, mathematics is peculiarly qualified to develop a pupil's understanding of just what is involved in proving something. Demonstrative geometry is the means through which we attempt to accomplish this purpose, but we can find no justification for requiring the pupils to prove a certain number of theorems determined in advance. Furthermore, the emphasis is not placed on the conclusions reached but rather on the method of thinking by which they are established. These conclusions are not absolutely true. Their truth depends on the definitions and assumptions from which they are deduced, and any change in one or more of these definitions and assumptions will change the conclusions. It is thus possible to extend the study of proof beyond the narrow confines of geometry and to examine some of the countless propositions which are found in other areas of life; as, for example, the kind of advertising to which students are daily exposed is a fertile field in this connection. Behind every advertisement is a multitude of assumptions, and the pupils have become greatly interested in listing the assumptions made by the person who buys the advertised article through the influence of the advertisement. On the whole, the experience has had a decided influence on their ability to detect these assumptions, and in many cases the pupils have stated that they are becoming more resistant to advertising and are looking for proof of the facts stated. Many of them have voluntarily submitted their analyses of advertisements which they have found in their reading, with a further statement concerning the assumptions which they accept and those which they reject. This illustrates how their thinking about matters involving proof has been changed. If we accept the fundamental assumption that " mathematical thinking occurs wherever inferences are drawn logically," we have a key which opens the mathematics classroom to all phases of human activity. One of the most far reaching developments in man's eternal search for truth is the realization that all the conclusions of mathematics, regarded for so long as being absolutely true, depend in the final analysis on a series of assumptions. This indeed is true of the conclusions reached in any area of thought and to make pupils conscious of this tremendous fact is to equip them with a powerful method of thinking about the problems of modern life.

SCIENCE

The experiences of the last three years of science teaching in the University School have led us to a number of policies and procedures, conclusions which apparently could never have been achieved by philosophizing alone but only through working in actual situations that challenged us to intimate co-operation with the other areas. Our provision of a continuous fourteen-year experience in science has been thoroughly justified, we feel, in practice, and we have been able to draw up tentatively the following statement of the total content of the area:

1. Scientific thinking (not to be considered as particular to this area nor as a unit of study) but rather as applicable to all problems, its limitations and its possibilities; as evident in the classical achievements of scientific investigators; as a socially necessary function; as learned (among other ways) by the devising, executing, and interpreting of controlled experiments or observations.

2. Maintenance of the individual's original curiosity about the world and himself through the translation of that curiosity from naïveté to an intellectual compulsion.

3. The scientific world-picture (from electrons to galaxies, without dogma, but rather with a real understanding of the 1936 A.D. relativity of human knowledge) for the purpose of the individual's achievement of perspective.

4. Those scientific principles necessary to intelligent behavior from the point of view of individual and community health, physical and mental; the social responsibility of the " good life," a new morality predicated in terms of effectiveness and integrity in social relationships.

5. The adventure of civilization: the social conquest of natural materials and forces through the application of scientific principles (from metallurgy and dynamos to medicine, radio, and aircraft).

6. Science and human relations: scientific thinking and principles of the present political, social, and economic disintegration of the species.

Every one of these divisions of the content is pertinent to the intellectual and emotional growth of the child at any level of his school experience. This is not to say that the organization of the work or that the nature or scope or implications of the specific problems arising can possibly be the same on one level as on another. In the elementary-school and junior-high (Grades VIII–IX) program, science is studied at any time when it is necessary for the solution of individual or group problems. These experiences are organized by the group. A science problem can become at any time the central emphasis in the unit of work; it may be a profitable, temporary digression; it may be one of the divisions in the study of a larger, possibly a " social science " unit. The one science unit which has demonstrated its worth and its appropriateness within this level of growth during the last three years, is the " science of human reproduction." That this intimate need of children in the early years of adolescence has been expressed and has achieved the recognition of the school community is a healthful indication of integration between the school experience and the life of the student.

At present it seems to be in the ninth-grade year that the science area emerges as one of several particular fields of experience which the students recognize as including the consideration and, in one degree or another, the solution of certain significant and long-term problems necessitating the setting aside throughout the year of a regular time within their weekly program.

These areas do not actually lose sight of one another in the ninth, tenth, eleventh, and twelfth periods. The three- or four-year science program that emerges for each student group as it passes through these levels of experience, remains flexible in its organization. We have achieved the elimination of the traditional, formal division of the area into biology, chemistry, and physics and have provided instead opportunity for meeting the significant demands of our young people, by this time experienced in planning (with the guidance of the teacher) their own educational experiences. The content of such a sequence of experiences cannot be identical for any two successive levels of children, but it has already been possible for us to chart the general divisions of scientific experience and the large, significant concepts that have demonstrated their urgency and value. A group problem arising in some other area in the school or community life can at any time have precedence over the scientific problem in hand.

We have found that a reference library with a variety of textbooks and the organization of work with division of the labor and responsibility have every advantage over the use of one book with its predetermined organization and regimented assignments. The function of the science laboratory is consistent with its historical, research significance; nothing can prove much more valuable to the student than an experience involving his own solution of a problem.

We feel that there is no justification of a science experience which has no implications beyond its alleged factuality. Unless science has implications in the thinking and living of the students, at the time and afterwards, the science program has evaded its responsibility and its challenge. In the need of our time, there can be no defense for the neglect of the implications of scientific discoveries and thinking as an intelligent procedure.

SOCIAL SCIENCE

The quest of the modern educator is for unified experiences which will be life situations. In the social sciences the educator came somewhat nearer to ideal education when he achieved the welding of history, geography, economics, and sociology into a single whole. In the high school this unification of several related subjects has been called social science. The high-school course in social science has come increasingly to be taught as a unit, and the several subject fields of the social sciences have contributed that information necessary for the solution of social problems of vital concern to the students.

University School has of course recognized since the inception of the school this intelligent union. Social science, organized in this manner, is one of the areas of learning within the school. University School, however, has gone some pioneering steps beyond integration of several disciplines into a co-ordinated course. In the seventh, eighth, and ninth grades, as described in other articles in this report, social science is one of the areas co-operating in the " core " or uni-fied-studies program. Here, when a problem is attacked, social science sheds what light it can, science supplies information, techniques, or materials desirable for the solution of the problem, the arts make their particular contributions, and the English area assists with the problem of the resulting reading and writing of students. In the tenth, eleventh, and twelfth grades where interests and needs have become more specialized with increasing maturity, the areas are no longer amalgamated but separate areas of learning emerge. This does not imply that there is no further integration between social science and the arts, to cite one example. It does imply that integration can arise only from a felt need for co-operative action within either area.

An interesting co-ordination was recently achieved with a tenth grade. In social science the project embarked upon was a study of the Elizabethan period. After individual investigations of life in that age had been conducted by the students there was an expressed desire for the translation of this study into an art form. The students felt that they might perpetuate their findings, that they might make a permanent contribution to the school body, that they might express their understanding of the Elizabethan age through a more appropriate medium than merely the unfeeling written report. The social-science teacher appreciated the students' attitude and, in addition, felt that such an undertaking involving manual work and physical co-operation might help the group to achieve a fine solidarity, that such an art experience with a group which used the art laboratories only infrequently would be revealing to many students. The co-operation of the art teacher was enlisted, and the major part of the group worked on a series of eight panels depicting phases of Elizabethan life. A few individuals worked in the shop on the construction of ship models or with the home-economics specialist in costuming dolls in period clothes. The completed panels were installed in the social-science room as a base for the operations of this tenth grade.

Another example of co-ordination of the gifts of specialists occurred within an eleventh grade when the group commandeered the services of teachers of fine arts, mathematics, and music, as well as the aid of a veteran archaeologist of Ohio State University in order to understand better the cultures of the Indians of ancient America. These specialists were simply requested to illustrate in whatever ways they thought desirable the contributions of Indian civilizations to the fields of experience they represented. The fine-arts teacher delivered a lecture accompanied by lantern slides on Indian art and architecture, and explained Indian art symbolism through elaborate designs on the blackboards. The mathematics teacher demonstrated the Inca *quipu* or string of knots which served the Peruvians as a measuring and counting system, described the development of the number systems, and talked of astronomical advance of American primitives. The music teacher described the rhythms of Indian music and presented samples of Indian music through various instruments. The archaeologist described the science of digging and the significance of archaeology for students of society. In a later investigation of specific phases of Indian types, the students examined the literature of the Indian peoples and read upon the scientific and medical development of the Indian.

In another eleventh-grade section the music group worked in a close relationship with social science. In a study of the period of the Civil War, group discussion of songs and group singing provided an enjoyable and educative part of class work. When the study dealt with the turn of the nineteenth century, the ideas, inventions, and spirit of the time, as reflected in the popular songs, formed a part of the general inquiry.

A twelfth grade studying the distribution of wealth in the United States found their most reliable source of information in the recent study made by Brookings Institute — *America's Capacity to Consume*. Desiring to express some important data graphically in order to understand the social structure of America, the group found it valuable to work in close touch with the mathematics and fine-arts specialists. In testing the ability of the class to draw logical conclusions from graphs and data, techniques in " the nature of proof " first worked out by a mathematics specialist were utilized. As described elsewhere in this summary, a study of psychology had its inception in the confused beliefs as to human nature manifested by students in attempting to interpret the significance of America's maladjusted distribution of wealth.

Limitations of space forbid the citation of further examples from the upper grades. That integration is inherent in the schedule and school set-up of the seventh, eighth, and ninth grades should be apparent to the careful reader. The home-building experiences of these grades have, typically, afforded opportunities for children to test materials of many sorts in the science laboratories before purchasing equipment, for construction of furniture in the industrial-arts laboratories, and for such home-economics work as planning tasteful furnishings and decoration. Opportunities for integration in the education of children are legion; in University School these opportunities which arise through social science are capitalized, and unified experiences eventuate in situations approximating life.

171. SUBJECT ORGANIZATION IN THE HIGHER GRADES [13]

Laura Zirbes and Lou LaBrant

As the children grow older, the problem of selection [of knowledge] becomes more complicated. Many educators who have, at least in part, accepted the ideals of progressive education for the lower grades, have rather suddenly discarded them for the higher grades. Here they have introduced formal education with subject-matter divisions, justifying the change on the ground that the body of knowledge which the children now face calls for organization if it is to be interpreted, and that since there must be selection from possible knowledges the only possible selection must be through these subject-matter organizations.

There are several inconsistencies in such a change of viewpoint. In the first place, children do not, at age eleven, become markedly different from what they were at age ten. There is no age at which one can say that here a certain characteristic begins. It has been popular to use the term " oncoming of adolescence " to suggest some mysterious and unusual differentiation, with the assumption that here we have something which suddenly appears and changes the world for the child. The best knowledge we have on the subject indicates that adolescence is marked by a complexity of characteristics, just as early childhood is also complex; that these characteristics are not suddenly assumed, but are developments of the organism; that the various traits, if they do change, do not all change markedly at one time. In other words, there is no reason to suppose that the child cannot gradually develop from what he is at eleven to what he is at twelve or thirteen. There is also no reason to believe that children of the same chronological age or grade are identical in their physiological and psychological development. To use adolescence or high-school entrance as an excuse for a radical change in educational philosophy, therefore, becomes an absurdity.

A second much used excuse is that, now that knowledge has become

[13] From " Social Studies in a New School," *Progressive Education,* 11:92–93, January-February, 1934.

complex, some formal system is necessary. Here again we are likely to find a considerable amount of rationalization. We ourselves met college-entrance requirements; we met these through formal courses in five or ten subjects. We are able to see the child develop through a progressive school program while college is a long way off, but, when we begin to consider the junior high-school child and to realize that he is only five or six years from college, our hearts fail. If we go much farther, we may find ourselves in an impossible situation, where, without time enough to cram or catch up, we take refuge in the conventional high-school program. It is at least possible that some such process of rationalization is responsible for the lack of continuity between elementary and high-school levels. The seemingly inescapable entrance requirements for college have, until recently, reduced us to inconsistency.

Certain fallacies are apparent. We say that knowledge has become complex. It has always been complex. The simplicity of the child's understanding has limited the choices he has had, but they have been varied unless the school has deliberately set limits. It is as though one were beginning to work out from the center of a circle. Although the horizon becomes larger constantly, so does the known area become larger. Learning is made more difficult *at any level* if the school attempts to teach material which is not contiguous to known or experienced matter.

Related to the foregoing is the objection so frequently raised that, when children are allowed to pursue a program built of their needs and interests, and work together to accomplish some desired result, there are bound to be large gaps in the children's knowledge. There seems to be, on the part of these objectors, a feeling that life itself does not provide relations; that only as some super-teacher relates information does it become integrated. Examination of the situation shows that, in contradiction to the objectors, knowledge is typically related everywhere, except in the departmentalized programs of formal learning in schools. In learning which grows out of group living, there is always a connection between the individual's old experience and the new; that is, there is no gap between the *information* and the *child*. Relationships are experienced more vividly and convincingly than they can be taught in formal courses.

It is a contradiction when we say that the younger child must have experience which is an integral part of his life, but that the older one may find his education in a study of facts not related to experience. It is contradictory because, the older the child, the nearer he is to the necessity of recognizing subject matter in its life contexts. In the actual business of responsible living, his activity must be purposeful and functional. Shall the school, then, as he approaches this responsible and unified living, emphasize a world apart from living? It is thinkable that the very small child might be taught (if he could learn) information which he could not find in a normal day's living. He would have some time in which to recover, in which to supply meanings. But we have developed an educational system in which the opposite theory seems to be at work. We begin the child's schooling with meaningful experiences, but more and more provide him with school work which holds only theoretical relation to what he terms " real life." In fact, so great has the inconsistency become that we are not even mildly amused when a commencement speaker, addressing a group of young men or women who have ostensibly been gaining new experiences through schools for sixteen years, says, " When you get out into life you will find — ." We accept the statement as normal, forgetting that education should be thought of as developing a desirable *way of living*. Nor are we duly critical of the school's failure to educate in this sense.

172. ORGANIZED SUBJECTS SHOULD BE TAUGHT [14]

William C. Bagley

I shall discuss at this time the current widely heralded proposal to abandon entirely all efforts to present learning materials in the form of organized bodies of subject-matter, such as arithmetic, geography, physics, or geometry, and to bring to the learner from these and other fields materials that he may need from time to time in solving the self-recognized problems of his own life or in realizing his own immediate purposes. To put it another way, it is proposed to deny to the learner any advantage that may lie in utilizing in the learning process the *internal* relationships of learning-materials — logical, chronological, spatial, causal — and to retain only that method of learning which consists in applying learning-materials in a present situation to meet an immediately-felt need.

This is not a new proposal by any means. It has been made repeatedly in the history of education. It was even carried out consistently and on a large scale over a number of years in the world's largest national system of education, with results to which I shall refer later. Recent studies show that a large majority of the leaders in public education in this country subscribe to the theory and would put it into practice if they could.

The situation has now reached a stage where it is difficult to discuss the matter rationally. At a recent meeting a prominent dean

[14] From " Is Subject-Matter Obsolete? " *Educational Administration and Supervision,* 21:401–404, September, 1935.

of a university school of education accused teachers (and I quote his words) of "hurling chunks of subject-matter" at pupils to be "merely memorized." Another member of our guild complains that some of his colleagues are still "subject-matter conscious." He denies that anyone ever learned by logical or chronological or causal relationships, with the implication that to attempt to get anyone to learn anything through a recognition of such relationships is an act that involves no small degree of moral turpitude. In short, with thousands of American teachers and students of education this theory has become essentially a religion, and when an issue reaches this stage its discussion on a rational basis and in terms suitable to a university lecture-room becomes very difficult.

Now no one would contend that there is not a very important place for the kind of learning that is represented by the solution of immediate problems of learning and the realization of immediate purposes. This pattern of learning should dominate the earlier school years and should be abundantly provided for throughout the school and college programs. But to rule out all other types of learning (except perhaps in schools for the feeble-minded) is a proposal which, if carried out consistently, would be a very serious injustice to the normal learner for it would deprive him of many important elements of a liberal education.

Two fallacies are implicit in most of the discussions which protest against utilizing in education subject-matter organized in terms of the internal relationships of the materials learned.

The first fallacy is represented by the assertion anent " chunks of subject-matter hurled " at the learner " to be memorized." The implication is that the only way in which organized subject-matter can be mastered is by the parrot-like memorizing of words. There is such a thing, of course, as learning through understanding. In many cases, indeed, there is no need for " memorizing "; the proper development of a true understanding may give it a permanent place in mind with a single " insight," as certain of the Gestalt experiments clearly prove. Even if some repetition is essential to mastery it need not and should not be a meaningless repetition. To assert that it must necessarily be the latter is an unjustified and unworthy appeal to ignorance and prejudice.

The second fallacy is more insidious. It is the assumption that in the individual life knowledge has only one function. If it is useful at all it is useful because it can be applied in a direct, overt fashion to a situation that confronts one. I accidently cut my hand. I recall my knowledge of antisepsis and run for the iodine. I find mosquitoes in abundance at my summer home. I apply my knowledge of biology and make an effort to locate the stagnant water. I must compute my income-tax, and I apply my knowledge of and skill in addition, and, if possible, my knowledge of and skill in subtraction.

If on an average day you will count all instances of this direct and overt application of knowledge you will find that the range of applications is extremely narrow, unless your vocation is of such a character that it involves numerous direct uses of specialized knowledge, as in engineering or medicine or navigation. Let us take, for example, your knowledge of geography. In what overt, practical applications have you ever used even a small fraction of it? As you have boarded a train you may have wished to choose a seat on the shady side, and to this end you may have reconstructed in your mind a map of the region you were about to traverse and so have been able to "reason out" which side of the car would be in the shade. But have you ever used in this direct, practical way your knowledge that the earth is a sphere? Or the fact that this sphere revolves around the sun? Or the relationships of the earth's rotation to the laws of storms? And yet what do you think of an educational theory which, if consistently applied, would have limited your learnings to those materials that had a direct instrumental function? What do you think of a theory which holds that, in the absence of an immediate "real-life" problem or purpose as a motivating stimulus to learning, ignorance becomes a virtue? There is no psychological justification for the contention that effective learning can only take place in the context of a problem or a purpose. In the report of his latest experiments in adult learning published only a few weeks ago Thorndike says, "The notion that mind will not learn what is alien to its fundamental vital purposes is attractive and plausible but definitely false." *

You may say, of course, that most of those who advocate learning through the solving of problems exclusively have in mind other uses than those that I have illustrated. Probably they do, but if so, their proposals will not justify a complete rejection of learning through recognizing internal relationships — causal, chronological, spatial, logical. You may say that you will need history in order to understand current politics, or that you will need geography in order to read newspapers intelligently. Granted; but the kind of history that will help you most here will be that which you studied in systematic and sequential courses based on time-relationships that enabled you to get a time-perspective upon present problems; and the kind of geographical information that will help you most is the kind which, in a well-organized system, has Peiping, tea, opium, coolies, sailing junks, poor land communication, illiteracy, ancestor-worship, intensive farming, periodic famines, and a number of other significant

* Thorndike, E. L.: *Adult Interests.* New York, 1935, p. 52.

understandings associated with China. Fragmentary learnings incident to the solution of an immediate problem, in the first place might readily be forgotten once the immediate problem was solved; or, if remembered, might not include the very thing that you need when you wish to interpret properly a newspaper dispatch. The principle, "Learn with intent to remember," has been experimentally established. It is well illustrated by the advice that Dean Pound is said to give his students of law, "Read every case as though you were certain that all records of it were to be destroyed immediately after you finished your reading." Learning merely for the sake of an immediate (and very likely, an unimportant) application, unless accompanied by this "intent to remember," would seem likely to be a superficial learning.

173. Schools Should Teach Complete Bodies of Facts [15]

Richard Robinson

There is a certain principle, obvious enough when once stated, that is largely overlooked in modern American education. This is that we should not be taught in school things that we shall learn anyhow, without much waste of time, in our experience in after life. What the school should give us is that which is necessary and yet can not be got easily anywhere else. This principle should often be applied in opposition to the principle that education should fit us for our vocation; it is a waste of opportunity to teach us in school things that the first two years of our vocation will teach us anyhow, and educators should seize every opportunity of throwing the work of merely vocational training on to the employers themselves. The further application of it is as follows. The few years that we spend at school can not compete with the rest of our lives in the *volume* of the information they teach us, but they can very easily do so in its *systematic* character. Our school-time is the best opportunity we have to learn organized and complete bodies of facts. For example, at school we can learn the whole outline of the history of a given people in a given time. In later life we shall pick up more historical facts than we ever learned at school; but they will not be concentrated; they will not belong to the same people and the same period. In later life, again, we shall pick up what can be learned on the run, but not what requires constant exercise and practice. These considerations indicate that we ought to learn at school that which, being necessary to cultured persons, requires drudgery and is not learned in later life.

[15] From "The Paradox of American Education," *School and Society*, 31:60–61, January 11, 1930.

The most desirable results can not be obtained without drudgery. The present tendency, therefore, to cut out the element of drill, to reduce education to the imparting of titbits about the modern world (such as "human geography"), and thus to produce young people who are superficially sophisticated but fundamentally ignorant, is contrary to our best interests.

174. "The Place of School Subjects"[16]

William S. Gray and Adelaide M. Ayer

The discussion thus far has pointed out divergent views concerning the place of subject matter in the curriculum. Similar differences exist concerning the place of school subjects. At one extreme are many who believe that pupils will learn most effectively if the work of the school is organized in terms of subjects representing the great fields of human interest and activity. In such cases, whatever activities are introduced are subordinated to the major purposes of the units taught. As such, they are means of motivating learning. At the opposite extreme, school subjects are entirely eliminated and subject matter used only as it contributes to the immediate needs of the pupils. This view is represented in such statements as the following: "An activity curriculum is a series of individual and group experiences growing out of the needs of the children and guided on the basis of the meanings, processes, and standards that are reflected in the environment and that give significance to the activities." Those who take this view claim that more subject matter is needed to meet the interests and needs of children than is included in the traditional curriculum.

Various intermediate positions have been identified. Some would retain subject organization during a period of transition. For example, "although the major divisions of the complete curriculum organized on an activity basis might well be designated by entirely new terms, there is certain value in retaining the old during a period of transition. To illustrate for the third and fourth grades, I should classify the major divisions comprising the entire curriculum as follows: (a) social science; (b) language and communication; (c) healthful living and enjoyment; (d) natural science; (e) arts and crafts; and (f) music and literature" (Definition 1). The effort to organize specific subjects into related fields, however, has been vigorously criticized. "The mere rearrangement of familiar subject mat-

[16] From "Controversial Issues," National Society for the Study of Education, *The Activity Movement*, Thirty-Third Yearbook, Part II, Public School Publishing Company, Bloomington, Illinois, 1934, p. 176. Quoted by permission of the Society.

ter in the form of general science, general mathematics, and the like, assumes only a continuance of the archaic subject-storage conception of education. The compositing movements, therefore, as such, are really no part of the modernization of the curriculum. They are merely new ways of doing the old things . . . Merely to juggle the arrangement of academic subject matter is to make *changes* but not necessarily to make progress. It may even be retrogression." *

175. "CHANGING CONCEPTIONS OF LEARNING AND OF THE SUBJECT MATTER OF THE CURRICULUM "[17]

In times past, and too largely in present school practice, the curriculum has been conceived primarily as formal subject matter (facts, processes, principles), set-out-to-be-learned without adequate relation to life. The pupil has too frequently been required to repeat words, express ideas which he does not understand, and to accept, adopt, and use materials which have been furnished him ready-made and completely organized by the teacher. " Learning " was thought of as the ability to give back upon demand certain phrases and formulas which had been acquired without adequate understanding of their meaning and content.

In recent years, however, we have come to recognize that there are many different forms of memorizing and learning. Some of these are permanently advantageous; others are fruitless for the development of the child. The forms of learning which should be encouraged are those which lead on the intellectual side to generalization, on the habit side to the cultivation of useful skills, and on the side of attitudes and appreciation to the recognition of those relations which are most permanently satisfying. Advantageous learning affects favorably the individual's behavior. Meaning grows only through reaction. The term " true learning " therefore, is applied to any change in the control of conduct which permanently modifies the individual's mode of reacting upon his environment. Advantageous learning is never guaranteed by mere formulation of subject matter which is used in instruction. The teacher must patiently strive to bring the pupil to the point where the best arrangements of subject matter are made his own for actual conduct through the process of true learning.

Increasingly, " subject matter," likewise, is taking on a different

* Franklin Bobbitt. *Twenty-Sixth Yearbook* of this Society, Part II, p. 55.
[17] National Society for the Study of Education, *The Foundations of Curriculum-Making*, Twenty-Sixth Yearbook, Part II, Public School Publishing Company, Bloomington, Ill., 1927, pp. 17–19. Quoted by permission of the Society.

conception, correlative with the changed conception of learning. The essential element in "subject matter" is probably now best conceived as "ways of responding," or of reacting. From one point of view, "subject matter" will be conceived as the best mode of behavior that the race has discovered; from another point of view, the actual ways of responding that the learner is building into his own character.

New subject matter is brought into the curriculum as race experience, therefore, to provide patterns of response which the learner needs at any stage of his growth. Learning, for the educator, however, is not satisfactory until the new way of behavior (that is, the new mode of response) has been so built into the learner's nervous system that it may be reasonably expected to function efficiently when the proper time comes. The final test of learning is the emergence of appropriate conduct.

The curriculum should be conceived, therefore, in terms of a succession of experiences and enterprises having a maximum of lifelikeness for the learner. The materials of instruction should be selected and organized with a view to giving the learner that development most helpful in meeting and controlling life situations. Learning takes place most effectively and economically in the matrix of a situation which grips the learner, which is to him vital — worth while. Traits learned in a natural, or lifelike setting, give promise of emerging definitely in appropriate conduct. It is the task of the teacher and the curriculum-maker, therefore, to select and organize materials which will give the learner that development most helpful in meeting and controlling life situations. The method by which the learner works out these experiences, enterprises, exercises, should be such as calls for maximal self-direction, assumption of responsibility, or exercise of choice in terms of life values.

The learner must, in general, as regards any particular problem, conception, or solution of a problem, approximate the best available form of racial organization through his own personal mode of assimilation. In helping the learner to reach this approximation, the intelligent teacher will use the methods which have been proved by previous educational experience to be most effective. No formulated scheme of assimilation, made in advance, and handed out complete by the curriculum-maker, can, of itself, be sufficient. To be truly functional for him, the process of assimilation must be the pupil's own. This does not, however, deny the effective part that the good teacher or other expert may have in assisting the pupil. The curriculum-maker should arrange activities and materials so as to give the learner carefully planned assistance.

CHAPTER XI

GRADE PLACEMENT AND TIME ALLOTMENT

176. Implications of Universal Education for Grade Placement [1]

A. C. Krey

It is assumed that universal school enrolment up to the age of sixteen, if not also beyond this point possibly even to the age of twenty, will continue and that this will be accompanied with an administrative policy approaching automatic promotion. Each grade of school, therefore, will present nearly the whole range of mental ability as well as of previous scholastic achievement. The problem of grade placement of material is therefore not a matter of one grade after another but rather within each grade.

To satisfy the conditions imposed by universal school enrolment and automatic promotion, an effort has been made to use concrete material drawn from actual human experience as a base for the work in every grade. Nowhere is the work purely abstract or descriptive. Thus for example, in the senior high school grades principles of economics, government and sociology are developed only in connection with actual human experience with the problems involved. Most of these experiences are drawn from the American scene, both contemporary and past, but significant variations in the rest of the world are also considered. Geography and history continue to furnish the concrete material, and social science supplies the principles of selection and suggests the significance of the materials. Thus, for example, Valley Forge may mean nothing more to the dull pupil than a small army of ill-clad, poorly fed soldiers huddling with Washington around the fires in the Pennsylvania valley, while it may be made a means to the understanding of governmental efficiency, national, and even international finance, for the brighter pupils. Or Addis Abbaba at the present time affords both the engrossing drama of military campaigning as well as an avenue to international diplomacy and the balance of international alliances. That is what is meant by serving the whole range of ability at one and the same time.

[1] From "An Experiment in Local Curriculum Construction," *Curriculum Journal*, 7:10–11, March, 1936.

177. Ripeness as a Criterion for Placement [2]

Carleton Washburne

There comes a time in every normal child's life when he is ripe for doing certain things, for learning each of the things he needs to know. To try to teach him before he has reached this ripeness is not only inefficient and wasteful, but may permanently blight his learning. Yet not only traditional schools, but many progressive schools, continually and painfully struggle to teach to unripe children things which, a little later, the children would learn easily and satisfyingly.

Everyone, of course, recognizes the gross differences in readiness — no one tries to teach tap dancing to a one-year-old, or Latin and algebra to a kindergartner. In a general way, all schools arrange their programs in accordance with the increasing ages of the children. But they use calendar age as a measure of ripeness; they have not learned the relative difficulty, from the child's standpoint, of many of the things they teach; they ignore the wide range of differences in maturity among the children in any class.

Progressive schools do less forcing than do traditional ones; they seek more actively to enlist the child's interest and sense of need for what he is learning, and to interrelate the various parts of his school work to his life outside the school. But they often sin as badly as traditional schools when they assume that because a class activity calls for the learning of a skill, all children in the class are equally ready for that skill. They, like traditional schools, frequently measure maturity and readiness by chronological age, and work in ignorance of the degree of maturity that is necessary for learning any given thing.

Over forty years ago, some of the followers of Stanley Hall recognized the importance of the doctrine of ripeness. But it is only during the past few years that people have begun to turn the light of research on the problem of how to determine a child's stage of readiness, and how to determine at what stage a given skill, or habit, or set of ideas can most effectively be acquired.

Most of the still meager research has had to do with physical habits and skills, and intellectual skills. The fields of physical, biological, and social sciences, and those of the arts are still almost wholly unexplored. But they could better afford to wait, because in these fields there is less attempt on the part of schools and homes to force growth. It is in the habit-training of little children, and in the teaching of reading, spelling, arithmetic, and other intellectual skills

[2] "Ripeness," *Progressive Education*, 13:125–130, February, 1936.

to older ones, that most of the damage is done. For it is damaging to try to force on a child a learning for which he is not yet ready. The data gathered by Dr. Wm. E. Blatz in Toronto concerning the toilet habits of infants afford a good illustration.

Blatz found that children whose parents tried to train them too soon were seriously retarded in their learning of bladder and bowel control. He was able to set definite ages at which each of these controls could be effectively learned. Parents who waited for this degree of readiness were rewarded by children who easily acquired and retained desirable control. Those who failed to wait were in for years of difficulty and for repeated relapses on the part of the children.

The situation is just the same with intellectual learning. A child whose teacher tries to teach him to read too soon is foredoomed to failure. This failure is not the relatively harmless one of the child not learning to read until he is ripe for reading. It often results in an emotional reaction against reading which may persist for years. A child who tries, under the urgence of blindly-conscientious teachers, to learn fractions before he is ready, has developed an attitude toward fractions that inhibits his learning of them even when he has reached the necessary maturity. All through our schools are children who, in spite of honest effort, in spite even of " felt need " and " integrated programs," have failed, have built tottering superstructures on shaky foundations, have developed dislikes when we want them to have a love of learning.

Progressive education has gone a long way toward making children's lives happier and their work more meaningful. Its cardinal principle is the study of the living, growing child first of all. But in its reaction against subject matter divisions, against considering subject matter as an end in itself, it has failed to analyze the actual learning that must take place, whatever the setting, whatever the motivation and interrelations. And in its study of the child, it has centered its attention on his interests, to the partial exclusion of a study of his ripeness for what it would have him learn.

Strange that one should almost have to apologize for writing to progressive teachers and parents about the teaching of the three R's! One feels that one is in danger of losing progressive respectability in doing so. Yet every progressive school does attempt to teach these things; practically all have times in the day when the children are engaged in a definite attempt to learn sight words or phonics, multiplication facts, or spelling. The children may have got their first impetus from an activity; they may have had at least an inkling of the need for learning these things; but, for the moment, they are engaged in the actual acquisition of a skill or of subject matter.

Every progressive teacher knows that this happens in the classroom, but we don't quite like to talk about it. It is a skeleton in the progressive closet. It makes us look as if we still were part of *hoi polloi* of traditional schools.

I think it is this attitude that has kept us from doing as good a job as we should do in utilizing what research has been done in the field of fitting the curriculum to the child's stage of maturity, and from contributing experience and research to this field. In this article, therefore, I want boldly to talk about some of the research that has been done in regard to children's ripeness for certain types of subject matter — partly in the hope of encouraging the application of such research in our work with children, and partly to stimulate thinking among us as to what we can do to ascertain the maturity-stages necessary or desirable for all kinds of activities — artistic, physical, social, and intellectual.

When should children learn to read? For three decades Marietta Johnson has cried out against too early a beginning of reading. But most of the American educational world has gone right on starting children in their reading when they enter first grade — at the age of six or a little before. About a third of first grade children fail — far more than in any one other grade — but teachers seem not to have questioned whether or not they were attempting the impossible. Or if they questioned it, they feared the pressure of parents. At no point — unless perhaps at the time of passing college entrance examinations — do parents insist so strongly on a child's learning a given thing as they do on his learning to read when he first starts to school. A mother doesn't worry much if a child's first tooth is a little late in appearing, if he creeps a little longer than the average, or if his first speech is somewhat delayed. She knows that, in the long run, he will chew and walk and talk as well as the child who begins earlier. But let him be slow about beginning reading and she and the father criticize the child, the teacher, and the school system. We have probably fostered this attitude, unwittingly, by our own assumption that all children at six are ready for reading.

My own attention was forcibly called to the harmfulness of this assumption several years ago by two incidents. One was the case of a boy, sitting among his contemporaries in the fifth grade but unable to read second grade books. All sorts of tests and remedial methods had been applied in vain. Then our psychiatric social worker took on the case. After weeks of building up *rapport* with the boy she got his story. He had tried to learn to read when he first went to school in another city. Our tests showed that his mental age at that time must have been about five and a half. He was unsuccessful, and the teacher, discouraged by his failure, tried making fun of him. " I decided right then," he said, " that I'd *never* learn to read! " Then he burst into tears and added: " And now I wish I could and I can't! "

That same year a first grade teacher, new in our schools, seemed very much discouraged. As she talked with me one day, the tears sprang into her eyes as she said, "I'm a failure, and I wanted so badly to succeed! There are three children in my room whom I just can't teach to read." Tests of those children revealed that mentally they were not quite six years old.

We resolved to find out at what mental age children really could satisfactorily learn to read. So the next year all first grade children (seven classes of thirty each) were given intelligence tests; careful records were kept of their progress, objective tests were given to reveal their achievement. The results were striking. Those who were mentally six-and-a-half years old in September had, in the large majority of cases, learned satisfactorily. As we went below this mental age level, the proportion of children who succeeded dropped off precipitately.*

The next year we repeated the experiment with different teachers, different children, and different tests, but got identical results. Experiments in Los Angeles gave similar conclusions. Nowadays each first grade teacher in Winnetka has a chart showing when each of her children will be mentally six-and-a-half, and is careful to avoid any effort to get a child to read before he has reached this stage of mental growth.

Mental age is not the only factor to be considered, however. There is the whole question of physical readiness of the eyes, on which Dr. Emmet Albert Betts has done so much work and on which more work is needed. There is the matter of the child's experiential background on which Mrs. Johnson has so long laid stress. And there is specific reading readiness as measured by some of the new reading-readiness tests. All these things must be taken into account if we are not to force open a bud not yet ready to bloom.

But should we have children begin as soon as they are ripe? I don't think we know. A carefully controlled experiment, but one involving a relatively small number of children, was carried on for three years in Winnetka recently, to see the effect of longer postponement. One room full of children was given no regular training in reading, writing, or arithmetic until the middle of the second grade, but had many and varied activities and experiences. Each child in that room was matched against several (usually three) children in other first grades, of the same mental and chronological age — chil-

---

* " When Should Children Begin to Read? " by Mabel Vogel Morphett and Carleton Washburne. *Elementary School Journal*, March, 1931.

dren who began reading and number work as soon as they were ripe, and had, of course, a rich activities curriculum as well.

By the middle of the second grade the experimental group had made much less progress in reading and number work, on the average, than had those who were receiving systematic training. Then the experimental group began to have systematic training too — supposedly just the same amount as the children with whom they were compared. By the end of the third grade the experimental group had caught up to the others and gone a little beyond them in practically all subjects. They also proved to have more eagerness to learn and to have more spontaneity in their academic work.

This experiment is too small to be conclusive. The third grade teacher probably did an over-conscientious job with the children. But certainly it would seem to indicate the possibility that little or no harm is done, and perhaps considerable good is achieved, by waiting beyond the stage of minimum ripeness.

After a child begins to read, the question arises as to what books are suitable to each successive stage of his ability. To give a child a book for which he is not yet ready does just what any other too-early learning does — it develops distaste where we want to develop liking. It retards the child when we want to advance him. It forms bad habits.

When a child tries to read a book that is too difficult, he loses interest and becomes discouraged. Without analyzing the cause, he begins to dislike not only the particular book, but reading itself. Not liking to read, he reads less and fails to get that fluency which comes from much reading and is necessary to the enjoyment of reading; and his eyes, struggling over unfamiliar words in sentences that to him are difficult, become habituated to many fixations and backward movements to the line, instead of learning to swing rhythmically along the line with not more than three or four pauses.

It becomes, then, necessary to know just how hard a book is, and what degree of reading ability a child must have if he is to read it easily and with enjoyment. Grants from the Carnegie Corporation, the coöperation of the American Library Association and of many teachers, and work in the Research office of the Winnetka Schools, have combined to enable any teacher or parent to select for any child books which fit his reading ripeness.

After a long study of what some 37,000 children of measured reading ability read and enjoyed,* these books were carefully analyzed, and the differences were found between those that children of one level of reading ability like and those liked by children of higher and

* *What Children Like to Read* by Mabel Vogel Morphett and Carleton Washburne. (Rand, McNally & Co.)

lower reading abilities. Years of research resulted in a formula by which the vocabulary and sentence structure of a book can be analyzed, and by which one can predict, with reasonable accuracy, what degree of reading ability a child must have if he is to read that book with fluency and ease.

A committee of the American Library Association then selected the fifteen hundred best children's books available, and these were all analyzed as to difficulty. The resulting list, fully annotated, makes up a sizable volume,* to which a supplement through 1935 has just been added. Any teacher or parent or librarian, knowing a child's reading level (as shown by standard tests) can, with the use of this book list, offer the child a wide variety of reading that fits his stage of reading growth. With such books his interest in reading will usually increase, and his facility and skill will increase proportionately.

Spelling is more prosaic and less important; so we'll dismiss it with a few paragraphs. But the doctrine of ripeness holds here, too.

There is evidence (and common sense supports it) that systematic work in spelling can wait harmlessly until a child has at least third grade reading ability. By this time the child has already learned, incidentally, to spell a number of simple words, and he is mature enough to read and study others. The main point of caution is to avoid giving him words to learn that are so hard for him as to be discouraging. The mere fact that he is sitting in a room with other children is no indication that his spelling-readiness is the same as theirs. It is as absurd to give all children in a room the same spelling words to learn as it would be to give them all the same book to read. Just as their reading levels spread over three or four years in any grade, so do their spelling levels.

A child's spelling level can be gauged by classification tests, by standard spelling scales, or by his score on a fifty-word pre-test on a given grade's spelling list. Such tests will at once show the list to be so easy for some children as to make it a waste of their time to study it, while for others it is so hard that an attempt to learn it will cause discouragement and loss of interest. There are two essentials in teaching spelling — first, letting a child work on words which fit his ability so that he may taste the success that comes from work at his own level; and second, closely related to this, arousing his interest in the words and how they are built. All of us learn far more words through our reading and through analogy with words we have studied than we do through direct attack. But there is, I believe, ample evidence that direct study of some words helps decisively in this incidental learning.

* *The Right Book for the Right Child* by Mary S. Wilkinson, Vivian Weedon, and Carleton Washburne. (John Day Company.)

Above first grade, arithmetic is the chief cause of school failures, and is probably the most frequently disliked subject in the curriculum. There are a number of reasons — the abstractness of much of it, the unrelatedness of much that is in the textbooks to the child's daily experiences and needs, *and* the fact that our arithmetic curriculum and the child's assignments are so often completely out of keeping with his psychological readiness.

The work of the Committee of Seven in this field during the past ten years is fairly well known * and is beginning to affect curricula and textbooks in even traditional schools. The Committee of Seven, however, has only made a beginning on the studies that should be made in this field. It has shown that certain topics, as ordinarily taught, cannot be successfully completed by most children until a certain mental age is reached and until the children have an adequate foundation. Its results make it clear that the same arithmetic assignment to a whole class, with the ever-present spread of at least three or four years in mental ages and equally wide spread in foundation knowledge, is bound to result in many failures. And they make it clear that, if we will ascertain the child's readiness for a topic by getting his mental age and by testing his concepts and his knowledge of pre-requisite arithmetic topics, we will remove one of the major causes of discouragement and failure.

There is probably no one subject for which we have such a mass of data indicating the importance of the right degree of maturity to the learning of each topic. And there is probably no subject (except perhaps beginning reading) in which there is as much gross violation of the child's right to wait until he has grown to the proper mental stature for coping with each learning problem.

These four examples indicate the line our thinking should take if we are to give children work for which they are ready. A number of analogous studies have been made in connection with children's physical development. At least two very interesting studies have been conducted to discover their interests in play materials. But in most fields we are still confined to conjecture and trial and error. Even this is not so bad, however, if we are conscious of the fact that there *is* a period of ripeness for each thing a child undertakes, be it in the field of music or art, of games or discussions, of science or academic skills. When a child is not succeeding happily with any type of undertaking, let us immediately raise the question as to whether, perhaps, we have not given him something to do for which he has not the necessary ripeness.

After all, what is the hurry?

---

* " One Reason Children Fail in Arithmetic " by Carleton Washburne, *Progressive Education,* March, 1932, for example.

178. SUMMARY OF EXPERIMENTS OF THE COMMITTEE OF SEVEN ON GRADE PLACEMENT [3]

Carleton Washburne

The experiments of the Committee of Seven indicate very clearly the need for taking into serious account the mental level and the arithmetical foundations of each child before attempting to teach him any given arithmetic topic. Not to do so is to doom many children to failure; to do so adequately is to insure reasonable success to the large majority of the children.

Recommendations are given in terms of mental age and arithmetic ability rather than in terms of school grade because there is such a wide range of mental age within each grade, and so much difference between grades having the same designation in different school systems, that grade levels have comparatively little meaning. The data on graphs, however, were the first obtained, and were treated by grades and chronological ages; results for this one topic, therefore, are given by median chronological age in the summary.

To use the Committee's results satisfactorily, superintendents and teachers will want to give group intelligence tests and arithmetic foundations tests to determine the approximate level of each child as to mental age and ability in arithmetic. The following summary table indicates the mental-age levels and arithmetic foundations scores children should first attain if at least three out of four of them are to make the very modest mastery represented by a retention test score of 80 percent in the various topics herein reported:

Topic	Minimal Mental-Age Level	Minimal Arith. Foundations Test Score (in Percent)
Addition Facts		
Sums 10 and under	6 yr. 5 mo.	—
Sums over 10	7 yr. 4 mo.	—
Subtraction Facts		
Easier 50	7 yr. 0 mo.	84
Harder 50	8 yr. 3 mo.	96
Subtraction Process	8 yr. 9 mo.	57
Multiplication Facts	8 yr. 4 mo.	
	or 10 yr. 2 mo.	96

[3] "The Grade Placement of Arithmetic Topics; A 'Committee of Seven' Investigation," National Society for the Study of Education, *Report of the Society's Committee on Arithmetic*, Twenty-Ninth Yearbook, Public School Publishing Company, Bloomington, Ill., 1930, pp. 669–670. Quoted by permission of the Society.

	Minimal Mental-Age Level	Minimal Arith. Foundations Test Score (in Percent)
Simple Long Division		
1- and 2-place Quotient	10 yr. 9 mo.	81
Meaning of Fractions		
Non-Grouping	9 yr. 0 mo.	—
Grouping	11 yr. 7 mo.	—
Graphs, Simple Bar	10 yr. 5 mo.	—
Percentage, Case I	12 yr. 4 mo.	
	or 13 yr. 11 mo.	100

179. Basis for Determining Time for Beginning Reading [4]

Arthur I. Gates and Guy L. Bond

The determination of the optimum time of beginning reading seems to be a problem of determining the maximum general and social returns from learning to read at any given time. We believe that investigations should be made to determine the time at which reading ability will be of more general, social, and educational value than other activities which would be pursued if reading were not taught. We believe that the reading program can be organized to enable children to learn to read at this time whatever it may be. This implies that the optimum time of beginning reading is not entirely dependent upon the nature of the child himself, but that it is in a large measure determined by the nature of the reading program. We think there is no ultimate justification for assuming that materials and methods of teaching must remain forever fixed as they are, waiting upon nature to change the child through maturity until he reaches a point at which he can proceed successfully. We think, on the other hand, that techniques and materials of reading can be adjusted to teach children successfully at the time when reading is, all things considered, of optimum value to them. At least, we think that to determine the best time to begin reading, it is quite necessary to conduct investigations designed to produce the best possible adjustment of the program to the child beginning early and later; and not merely to determine children's success at different times of beginning in a standardized program. To do the latter may merely tell us how difficult the materials and methods are rather than when, all things, especially social and educational values, being considered, it is best for a child to learn to read. Although there is little to indicate that constitutional or physiological factors require a postponement of

[4] From " Reading Readiness," *Teachers College Record*, 37:684–685, May, 1936.

reading to later than the usual ages, there is evidence that physiological, especially sensory handicaps, may interfere with beginning reading at any time. The remedy is correction of the difficulties or adjustment to them rather than merely waiting for time to cure them. Preparation for reading consists in part in discovering and correcting or adjusting to various constitutional handicaps.

180. "GRADE PLACEMENT IN THE SOCIAL STUDIES" [5]

The question of grade placement has two major aspects: that of sequence or vertical articulation, and that of adaptation to the maturity of the learner. By sequence is meant the need for planning the order of experiences so that the learning is most efficient. Altho some learning does occur regardless of the sequence, it seems reasonable to suppose that one sequence may be distinctly more advantageous than another, other things being equal. For example, two sequences may afford very different distributions of repetition or drill. If the findings of educational psychology in other fields apply to the social studies, it is clear that two such sequences may differ greatly in effectiveness.

The other aspect of grade placement — adaptation to the maturity of the learner — is the meaning usually attached to the phrase. By this is meant the allocation of experiences in social sciences to the particular age or grade group which is at the stage of development where the new experience will be most meaningful and educative. Assuming that some understanding of the conditions of colonial life in America is to be included in the program, are the experiences to develop such understanding provided best in the fourth, seventh, or some other grade? Again, in what grade is housing to be considered? Is the Constitution of the United States to be studied in the sixth or the eleventh grade? Such questions seem unanswerable in any definite sense except as they are rendered far more explicit. On the face of it, at least, colonial life may be a theme of educational value in almost any grade, depending on the particular aspects treated and the form of presentation to pupils. Indeed, many if not most of the major themes of the social studies appear to have educational potentialities in any and all grades if properly presented. One reason why grade placement in the social studies is so difficult is the fact that the body of experiences constituting these studies is not as readily and universally organized in standard patterns and subdivisions as, for example, the content of arithmetic. Nothing in the social studies quite corresponds to the series of skills making up

[5] National Education Association, *The Social Studies Curriculum*, Department of Superintendence, Fourteenth Yearbook, Washington, D. C., 1936, pp. 165–166, 168, 170–171, 173–174, 176–177.

ability to add columns of figures: knowledge of individual combinations, ability to add a seen number to a number in mind, ability to carry, ability to keep place in column, and so forth.

It may be well to call special attention to the distinction between concepts and materials. In general, the first question to be settled is the grade to which will be assigned concepts such as respect for the will of the majority, consideration for minority views, the significance of money as a medium of exchange, or the characteristics of life in mountainous regions. Existing studies show but few objective approaches to this problem. Such work as has been done has dealt with the grade allocation of reading materials, graphs, maps, and time lines. The placement of such materials is important but subordinate to the question of placement of concepts.

It should be noted also that there have been great differences in views as to the size of the unit to be assigned to particular grades. The recommendations made by the Committee of Ten in 1892, the Committee of Seven in 1898, and the Committee of Five in 1911 all related primarily to the assignment of a whole course to a grade, as, civics to the eighth grade or ancient history to the ninth grade. Obviously, any final solution of the problem of grade placement involves the choice of the optimum grade or age at which major concepts in each field shall be presented. Furthermore, the apparent trend toward integrated courses emphasizes the need for grade placement of smaller units in the various fields to be included.

METHODS OF DETERMINING GRADE PLACEMENT

Broadly speaking, there are three ways in which the problem of grade placement may be approached: (1) present practise; (2) opinion of individuals or groups; and (3) evidence of ease of learning, child interest, and utility to pupils. In every aspect of public education present practise has been and still is a potent factor. Grade placement is no exception to the rule. But, unless one is thoroly convinced that whatever is is right, one can scarcely accept present practise as an adequate basis for decision in matters of grade placement. The second approach — opinion of individuals or groups — has been used in the social studies very commonly during the last half century, especially in the form of committee recommendations. The third approach — thru objective evidence of the interest, learnability, and immediate use as far as pupils are concerned — has affected the curriculum greatly in some subject fields but thus far has influenced the social studies program relatively little because scarcely any objective evidence has been gathered.

The three methods proposed relate to the problem of assignment to different grade levels in general. Such allocation is important from the point of view of the school system as a whole. Another problem, however — the question of appropriateness for a particular group of children in a specified grade at a particular time — is of considerable importance to the teacher of that group. The fourth-grade classes, for example, in any rural or city school system differ greatly in maturity and capacity. The teacher of a particular class may need to modify the grade placement of experiences in the light of the needs of his pupils. School systems should use the methods suggested to determine general grade placement, but supplementary studies should be made by every teacher to adapt appropriately for his own class.

Opinion of individuals and groups — In 1936 it is unnecessary to review the recommendations of the earlier groups of experts which made rather definite recommendations as to the chronological organization of the course in social studies. Suffice it to name the more influential groups — the Committees of Ten, Fifteen, Seven, Five, and Eight.

In recent years every curriculum committee has needed to formulate some general pattern in accordance with which the pupil experiences will be organized by grade or age. Very rarely, however, is any explanation given of the bases which determined the decision as to pattern. Apparently the plan adopted is the result of consideration in the group responsible and represents majority judgment.

The recommendations of national committees with reference to grade placement have evidently become much less specific and definite, as judged by the comparison between the report of the Committee of Seven in 1898 and the report of the Commission on the Social Studies in 1934. The change may be due in part to the growing trend toward some type of integrated social studies program with the attendant growth in complexity of the area represented at each grade level. Another factor may be the growing realization that the allocation of specific experiences to particular grades calls for precise knowledge of the characteristics of pupils in those grades rather than armchair philosophizing and committee discussion. Yet there is need for interpretation, especially by groups who represent different educational interests, of the data secured about children's interests, activities, and abilities in relation to objectives that seem important in the social studies. In reality, the approaches of expert opinion and objective facts complement each other.

Child interest — Concepts and materials may be assigned to grades on the basis of child interest by either of two methods: the discovery of child interests at each grade in the field under consideration, and the trial of actual materials in several different grades to discover the point of greatest interest. In general, both methods will be found to be of value. The former gives leads as to the concepts and types of material that will be most significant to pupils in a particular grade; the latter supplies a means of grade placement of instructional materials after they have been prepared.

Ease of learning — The proportion of pupils who can perform successfully any particular activity is important information in determining its grade placement. There is a question, however, concerning the decision as to the percentage of success which signifies proper grade placement. Clearly if 0 percent of the children are successful after teaching, the activity is too difficult for the grade. If 100 percent of the children are successful, the activity is too easy for the grade and should be assigned to a lower grade. Under an ideal, individualized procedure, each pupil would enter upon a new learning task at the earliest time when he could achieve mastery in a reasonable period of application. Since classes are not homogeneous, some figure less than 100 percent probably represents the optimum grade placement. Mathews * raises the question but does not answer it finally. He suggests 50 percent, 67 percent, and 75 percent, and presents data for these three points.

Meltzer † studied the development in the minds of children of some concepts whose understanding makes some important situations of contemporary life more intelligible. Understanding of 31 concepts was tested by interviewing over 300 pupils from Grade IV thru Grade XII. He found a steady gain from grade to grade (perfect score — 248; mean — Grade V, 27.4; Grade IX, 86.0; Grade XII, 138.9) but the pupils tested showed wrong meaning or no understanding concerning about half of the concepts tested. It should be noted, however, that Meltzer made no attempt to develop understanding of the concepts; he only tested the development under existing conditions.

Lacey ‡ studied the social concepts of 450 children in the first three grades by means of tests based on pictures. She found that these children had little conception of such abstract terms as " thrift," " patriotism," " industry," and " courtesy." She found also that concepts involving personal relations are more difficult than those involving objects.

* Mathews, C. O. *The Grade Placement of Curriculum Materials in the Social Studies.* Contributions to Education, No. 241. New York: Teachers College, Columbia University, 1926. p. 23–42.

† Meltzer, Hyman. *Children's Social Concepts; a Study of Their Nature and Development.* Contributions to Education, No. 192. New York: Teachers College, Columbia University, 1925. 91 p.

‡ Lacey, Joy Muchmore. *Social Studies Concepts of Children in the First Three Grades.* Contributions to Education, No. 548. New York: Teachers College, Columbia University, 1932. 89 p.

Mathews * investigated children's understanding of specific instructional materials at different grade levels from the fourth to the twelfth. The materials used were three types of reading: episodes, descriptions and expositions, and newspaper articles; five kinds of charts and graphs: bar graphs, line graphs, circular graphs, time lines, and pictograms; and maps. He tested comprehension by questions with objective answers. He found that ability to understand the selections used increases gradually from the fourth to the twelfth grade. He discovered also that the episodes were better comprehended than the other types of reading material, and that circular graphs were most readily understood, bar graphs next, and line graphs least easily understood. For each of his samples, he suggests the proper grade placement, assuming 50, 67, or 75 percent comprehension as the standard of difficulty. He concludes that the types of materials in the social studies are placed from one to three grades too low.

Thomas † tested the ability of 355 children in Grade IV thru Grade VII to read different kinds of graphs. She found that above the fourth grade children can read graphs of simple types if the graphs are adapted to their attainments in the tool subjects. Her seventh-grade pupils averaged 75 percent of correct responses. She concluded that "with the proper instruction and explanation, children in the seventh grade can interpret all simple graphs." Her findings concerning the greater difficulty of line graphs supported those of Mathews.

Aitchison ‡ tested the understanding of the zones possessed by 1110 pupils in the sixth, seventh, and eighth grades and 860 college students. The widespread and lasting misconceptions which appeared led him to urge the elimination of all mention of zones from fourth- and fifth-grade geography and substitution of the terms "low, middle, and high latitudes."

Thorp § investigated the ability of pupils to use various geographic tools, including globes, maps of different types, and graphs. She tested regular classes in Grade IV thru Grade VIII and also an

* Mathews, C. O., *op. cit.*, 152 p.
† Thomas, Katheryne Colvin. "The Ability of Children To Interpret Graphs," in *The Teaching of Geography*, Thirty-Second Yearbook, National Society for the Study of Education. Bloomington, Ill.: Public School Publishing Co., 1933. p. 492–94.
‡ Aitchison, Alison E. "'Torrid, Temperate, and Frigid Zones'—Sources of Error in Children's Thinking," in *The Teaching of Geography*, Thirty-Second Yearbook, National Society for the Study of Education. Bloomington, Ill.: Public School Publishing Co., 1933. p. 483–85.
§ Thorp, Mary T. "Studies of the Ability of Pupils in Grades Four to Eight To Use Geographic Tools," in *The Teaching of Geography*, Thirty-Second Yearbook, National Society for the Study of Education. Bloomington, Ill.: Public School Publishing Co., 1933. p. 494–506.

experimental sixth-grade class which had received intensive drill in the use of the tools. Altho the general results were not very satisfactory from her point of view, the experimental class showed considerable power and she concluded that the work was easily within the comprehension of the average sixth grade. This interpretation raises the question as to the amount of time to be devoted to developing such abilities. Presumably almost any ability can be developed if time enough is given the task. The proper grade placement of any item must always take into consideration other contestants for inclusion in the curriculum. Thorp suggests Table 24 for grade placement of geography tools, based on the findings of her study.

Shaffer * studied the ability of pupils in Grade IV thru Grade XII to interpret cartoons. He concluded (1) that such interpretation improves markedly between ages twelve and fifteen and (2) that cartoons are desirable curriculum material for the junior high school.

SUMMARY

Present practise and expert opinion are undoubtedly the major factors determining the placement of an item in a particular grade in most school systems. Indeed, the factual evidence for placement of social studies items in one grade rather than another is pitifully meager and inadequate. Yet assignment to correspond with present general practise can scarcely be defended. The only alternative left is opinion, as expert as possible. Judgments based on group opinion probably can be improved by securing opinions concerning the degree of pupil interest, the likelihood of immediate utility to the pupil, and the probable proportion of pupils who can attain the desired outcomes in a reasonable period of time. These are the major factors that should influence the decision.

The evidence presented does hold out some possibilities of direct usefulness in the gradation of teaching materials. Clearly the reading difficulty of most social studies materials is too great for the grades for which planned. Some information is available also regarding the proper grading of certain other skills, including the interpretation of cartoons, graphs, and maps.

It is perhaps significant that objective studies have been addressed largely if not entirely to the question of adapting the teaching to the maturity of the learner. Relatively little appears to have been done regarding the problem of optimum sequence in learning the social studies.

* Shaffer, Laurance F. *Children's Interpretations of Cartoons; a Study of the Nature and Development of the Ability To Interpret Symbolic Drawings.* Contributions to Education, No. 429. New York: Teachers College, Columbia University, 1930. 73 p.

It should be noted also that little attention appears to have been given thru objective study to another problem that has become increasingly significant in recent years. That is the question of the particular aspect of major subjects that should be dealt with in particular grades. For example, there seem to be no objective studies that indicate just what should differentiate the treatment of housing in the third grade from the treatment in the seventh grade or in the eleventh grade. At the present time topics like housing appear thruout the grades. What are the distinctive functions to be served in each grade where it appears?

Decision as to optimum grade placement will always involve both the collection of objective evidence and its interpretation by competent persons. The facts are meaningless apart from the other elements in the situation; experts are needed to interpret the facts, relate them to the whole situation, and arrive at judgments that will affect practise favorably. Similarly the experts cannot work without facts; they need to base their recommendations on experience that includes as much objective evidence as possible.

Perhaps the most practicable procedure in grade placement is the experimental trial of units at various grade levels. This approach is available in every school system. Teachers who try out a unit in several different grades for several terms can readily discover where it is most appropriate.

Another practical suggestion is that units be used interchangeably in adjacent grades, since there is no convincing evidence for fine discrimination in grade placement. This suggestion is particularly important in rural schools and in the large number of small schools in which a teacher has an entire grade or two entire grades. In such schools a one- or two-year cycle of units may well be used with all the pupils in the room. Until there is much greater certainty than at present regarding optimum grade placement, general observation would indicate that the precise order of a series of experiences for one pupil or a group of pupils within a grade or two is relatively inconsequential.

181. " A PLACEMENT STUDY IN SECONDARY SCHOOL ECONOMICS " [6]

F. G. Macomber

NEED FOR PLACEMENT STUDIES IN CURRICULUM MAKING

It is generally recognized by progressive educators that subject matter is of value only as it contributes to certain educational aims

[6] *The Journal of Experimental Education,* 4:353, 357–358, June, 1936.

or objectives. These aims are now usually stated in terms of pupil development such as the ability to solve problems scientifically, the ability to perform certain tasks, the ability to appreciate the finer things of life, and the development of certain attitudes and understandings.

Curriculum makers have given most of their time to the determination of objectives and the selection of subject matter and teaching techniques, but have done very little in the scientific placement of the materials of the curriculum. In the past placement has been made chiefly on the basis of so-called expert opinion. While this is necessary in getting a curriculum to functioning, this method should be followed by scientific studies to determine the degree of correctness of placement.

Placement, however, cannot be made by grade alone. We know that all children of the same grade or chronological age are not equally capable of gaining the same understandings or of developing the same abilities. Consequently, if placement studies are to be of much value to curriculum workers they must produce data which will aid in developing a curriculum adjusted to the abilities of the individual pupils. Our problem is not to determine at what grade level a certain concept can be taught but rather to determine the mental ability and other factors essential to the understanding of the concept under given learning conditions. At the present time there are very little scientifically derived data to aid in placement of the materials and activities of the curriculum.

STATEMENT OF THE PROBLEM

The purpose of this study was to determine the extent to which high school juniors and seniors of different mental age levels could gain an understanding of certain economic concepts and problems; namely, those of price, money, and banking.

PROCEDURE OF THE STUDY

Problems of price, money, and banking were selected chiefly because they were very closely related; they formed the chief topic of conversation at the time the experimental teaching was being done during the winter of 1933–34; and are important parts of every secondary economics curriculum and text. Numerous other topics in the social studies field could have just as well been chosen.

The writer believes the following general conclusions and implications are justified by the data derived from this study:

1. Taken as a whole, the concepts involved in this study are

entirely too difficult for the high school students of Group III and for large numbers of Group II. This study is broad enough in its scope to cast considerable doubt on the advisability of attempting to teach economics to any but students of better than average ability without greatly modifying the content, procedures, and time allotments of the course.

2. The amount of overlapping in the scores between the high school students of Groups I and II and between those of Groups II and III on the tests over the units is proof of the inadvisability of segregating students in economics on the basis of their mental ability as determined solely by intelligence tests. Their ability in economics should be an important factor. This is in line with the findings of numerous studies made to determine the effectiveness of the I.Q. or M.A. as an indicator of probable success in a given academic field. There is some overlapping between Groups I and III, being between 10% and 20% on most final tests. The overlapping in the case of the college students is much greater than in the case of the high school students. This is especially true of Groups I and II where the lines of the percentile graphs cross on several occasions.

3. Most of the concepts taught in this study are within the understanding of the high ability high school student as taught, although at some points especially in the banking unit, the time for study needs to be lengthened if it is felt that understanding is essential at these points.

4. The fact that on the great majority of the tests the high school students of Group I made better scores on the pre-test than did the Group III students on the final test is evidence of the need for truly differentiated courses in economics with different content, teaching procedures, and time allotments. After several weeks of study the students of Group III still lacked the degree of understanding of most of the concepts possessed by Group I students at the beginning of the study.

5. The high ability high school students are at least as capable as the college students of Group I in the field of economics, and can study with understanding any of the concepts that can be included in the curriculum for high ability college freshmen and sophomores. The same is not true for the students of Group III where the performance of the college group was considerably better than that of the high school group. However, neither the high school nor the college students of Group III demonstrated ability to understand economic concepts as they were taught.

6. Taken as a whole, the concepts involved in this study are within the understanding of the majority of college students of Group I, but entirely too difficult for the students of Group III. No general-

ization can be made for the Group II students. Each area must be considered individually.

7. There is a growing demand on the part of many outstanding educators and laymen that the public schools develop, on the part of the students, an understanding of the more important economic, social, and political problems faced by the American people. The results of this study raise grave doubts as to the possibility of doing this without fundamental curriculum changes. The teaching procedures used in this study, while probably superior to those of the average high school economics class, were still largely representative of the subject-matter approach. Under these procedures and time allotments few students of average and less than average mental ability gained what could be called an adequate degree of understanding of most of the concepts of the units taught.

Whether the development of a well articulated social studies core based on real life problems and taught by teachers committed to the philosophy of the activities curriculum would result in a higher degree of understanding will be known only after careful experimentation covering a period of several years. The writer is confident that we could, at least, come much nearer the desired goal than we are now doing.

8. The present study indicates that most of the economic concepts of the units taught are of too great a degree of difficulty for any but the higher ability students of the high school and the lower division of the college, given present teaching procedures and time allotments. This raises the question as to the possibility of the average man voting intelligently on the many complex social, economic, and political questions placed before him at every election. Experimental studies of the abilities of adults to understand such problems need to be made. The present long-range tendency in our democracy has been to increase the responsibility of the voting population through the use of the initiative and referendum. Certainly this study, based as it is on the more or less artificial conditions of the classroom and utilizing high school and lower division college students, should not be used as conclusive evidence that the average adult is incapable of understanding many of the questions on which he is called to render a decision. It does indicate, however, that our present educational program is not developing such understanding of our major economic issues, and raises considerable doubt as to the ability of a large number of the persons gaining a degree of understanding essential to intelligent voting directly upon such issues.

182. "Objective and Subjective Grade Placement of Supplementary Readers" [7]

W. G. Bergman

In order to supplement the regular reading texts used by the children of the Detroit public schools, two copies each of seven additional titles were made available in February 1934 to Grades II B thru VI A in all schools. These books were selected and assigned to their respective half grades on the basis of the judgment of the subject supervisors. After these supplementary readers had been in use for a year, an appraisal program was initiated by the supervisory staff in cooperation with the department of research to determine, upon both subjective and objective bases, the suitability of each book to the grade in which it had been placed.

Subjective judgment on the suitability of the grade placement was obtained by questionnaires to the teachers. This questionnaire inquired into the popularity of the books, the methods in which they were used, the subjects with which they were correlated, etc. All of these questions had significance in the choice of reading material. The one question from this questionnaire, however, which is considered in this paper is the question concerning the proper grade placement of the various titles.

The objective method used was the measurement of the vocabulary and sentence structure of the books. This is the method which was developed by the Research Department of the Winnetka public schools.

Three items are taken into consideration by this method in determining the grade placement of a book. The first is the total number of *different words* which occur in a random sampling of 1000 words. The second item is the number of *uncommon words* in the same sample. (An " uncommon word " is here considered as one that does not occur in Thorndike's list of the 1500 most frequently used words.) The third item is the number of simple sentences occurring in a random sample of seventy-five sentences. These three items are combined into a formula * which gives the grade placement of the book. (In the following paragraphs " vocabulary-sentence burden " will be used to designate the basis for the determination of grade placements by the technic just described.) A book which received a grade

---

[7] National Education Association, *Reconstructing Education Thru Research*, American Educational Research Association Official Report, Washington, D. C., May, 1936, pp. 263–267.

* Grade placement of a book = .00255 × number of different words + .0458 × number of uncommon words − .0307 × number of simple sentences + 1.084.

placement of 7.4 is approximately equal in difficulty of vocabulary and sentence structure to the books most frequently chosen when pupils of seventh-grade reading ability are allowed to select their own reading material freely.

Table 1 presents the two types of information concerning each of the seventy books: grade placement on the basis of vocabulary-sentence burden, and grade placement on the basis of teachers' judgments. The reading of the table may be illustrated best by taking the first line. *Kitten Kat* is at present used in the II B. The vocabulary-sentence burden indicates that it is of 1.1 difficulty and therefore the difficulty of the book is slightly less than the average for books in Grade I B which is designated as 1.2. (Since the difficulty at the beginning of Grade I B is 1.0 and at the end 1.4, the average for I B is taken as the mean of these two figures, 1.2. Similarly the midpoint of I A is taken as 1.7. The same interpretation will be followed in the other grades, 2.2 as average of II B, 2.7 as average of II A, etc.) On the basis of teachers' judgments, *Kitten Kat* was 2.1, that is, slightly easy for grade II B in which it is used.

From observation of this table it is seen that the range of grade placements on the basis of vocabulary-sentence burden is far greater than on the basis of teachers' judgments. This can be seen more clearly by the summary which is included in Table 2.

TABLE 1

SEVENTY BOOKS NOW USED IN GRADES II B–VI A IN DETROIT PUBLIC SCHOOLS WITH VOCABULARY-SENTENCE BURDEN AND TEACHERS' GRADE PLACEMENTS

	Present Usage	Vocabulary-Sentence Burden	Teachers' Judgments
Kitten Kat	2B	1.1	2.1
F–U–N Book	2B	2.3	2.2
Elson Basic Primer	2B	1.1	2.1
Childhood Reader I	2B	2.4	2.3
Squirrel Tree	2B	1.5	2.4
Our Book World Primer	2B	1.5	2.3
Number Stories I	2B	1.6	2.4
Real Life Reader I	2A	2.2	2.6
Elson Basic Book I	2A	2.4	2.6
Good Times Book	2A	1.2	2.3
Little Eagle	2A	1.2	2.7
Our Book World I	2A	3.8	2.5

	Present Usage	Vocabulary-Sentence Burden	Teachers' Judgments
Do and Learn Book II	2A	5.3	2.7
Science Stories I	2A	3.6	2.6
Elson Basic Book II	3B	3.1	3.2
Skags, the Milk Horse	3B	2.4	3.0
Childhood Reader II	3B	5.1	3.2
Our Book World II	3B	4.8	3.2
Shorty	3B	4.2	3.4
Real Life Readers II	3B	3.7	3.4
Pleasant Pathways	3B	7.3	3.6
Elson Basic Book III	3A	5.2	3.5
Do and Learn III	3A	6.4	3.6
Little Wooden Doll	3A	4.9	3.7
Our Book World III	3A	6.2	3.6
Indians in Winter Camp	3A	3.2	3.4
Music Appreciation Reader II	3A	4.7	3.6
From Hunter to Herdsman	3A	3.0	3.6
Children's Own Reader III	4B	6.0	4.1
Peppi, the Duck	4B	3.9	4.2
Jean and Jerry's Vacation	4B	5.0	4.2
Judy's Ocean Voyage	4B	4.8	4.2
Red Feather's Adventure	4B	4.4	4.3
Susanna's Auction	4B	3.9	4.1
Taming the Wild Grasses	4B	3.0	4.3
Little Pear	4A	4.2	4.5
Cat and the Captain	4A	5.2	4.3
In Wooden Shoeland	4A	4.9	4.4
Winding Roads	4A	6.4	4.4
American History for Little Folks	4A	5.6	4.5
Music Appreciation Reader III	4A	5.4	4.3
Pathways in Science III	4A	3.2	4.6
Abe Lincoln, Frontier Boy	5B	3.6	5.3
Real Life Stories V	5B	8.3	5.3
Peggy in Her Blue Frock	5B	4.8	5.1
The Museum Comes to Life	5B	6.2	5.3
Little Fox	5B	4.1	5.2
Far-Away Hills	5B	8.1	5.3
Robin and Jean in England	5B	6.8	5.2

TABLE 1 (continued)

SEVENTY BOOKS NOW USED IN GRADES II B–VI A IN DETROIT
PUBLIC SCHOOLS WITH VOCABULARY-SENTENCE BURDEN AND
TEACHERS' GRADE PLACEMENTS (cont.)

	Present Usage	Vocabulary-Sentence Burden	Teachers' Judgments
Poppy Seed Cakes	5A	3.1	5.2
Treasure in the Little Trunk	5A	4.3	5.3
A Child's Life of Washington	5A	4.1	5.4
Our Neighbors Near and Far	5A	5.5	5.4
Music Appreciation Reader IV	5A	6.7	5.6
Christopher Columbus	5A	7.0	5.6
Pathways in Science IV	5A	4.1	5.6
Real Life Stories VI	6B	8.7	6.2
Little Princess	6B	6.9	6.2
Toby Tyler	6B	7.7	6.2
Boys and Girls of Modern Days	6B	8.8	6.3
Stories of American Explorers and Settlers	6B	5.9	6.3
Story of the Earth	6B	5.9	6.3
How the Present Came from the Past — Book I	6B	4.8	6.3
Arkansas Bear	6A	5.8	6.3
Heidi	6A	5.2	6.3
Heights and Highways	6A	8.2	6.4
Health School on Wheels	6A	9.7	6.4
Music Appreciation Reader V	6A	7.2	6.4
Pathways in Science V	6A	5.4	6.5
Europe, the Mother of America	6A	7.2	6.6

The reading of Table 2 may be illustrated by the first line. The mean for Grade VI A is 7.0 on the basis of vocabulary-sentence burden. The easiest book is 5.2, the hardest 9.7. The range is 4.5. The fifth column shows the mean minus the grade. In this case the mean is 7.0 and the value of the middle of Grade VI A is taken as 6.7; therefore, this value is given as +.3. This indicates that the seven books in Grade VI A are, on the average, .3 of a grade harder than those freely chosen by pupils in Grade VI A. The next five columns give the same information on the basis of teachers' judgments.

Probably the outstanding difference between the teachers' judgments and the objective measurements is the much greater variation in the range of grade placements according to the objective method.

In no half grade did the teachers think that the most difficult book was more than .6 of a grade more difficult than the easiest book, while the objective method indicated that in the same half grade the easiest book was almost five grades easier than the most difficult book.

The correlation of the subjective judgment of the teachers and the objective measurement of vocabulary-sentence burden is .69. However, the reluctance of the teachers to place any book much out of its grade placement probably makes this correlation an indication of agreement between objective procedure and the judgments of the supervisors who originally placed the books, more than an agree-

TABLE 2

SUMMARY OF GRADE PLACEMENTS GIVEN TO THE SEVEN BOOKS OF THE VARIOUS HALF GRADES BY THE TWO METHODS
As Assigned by Supervisors' Judgments

| | VOCABULARY-SENTENCE BURDEN | | | | | TEACHERS' JUDGMENTS | | | | |
Grade	Mean	Easi-est	Hard-est	Range	Mean-Grade	Mean	Easi-est	Hard-est	Range	Mean-Grade
6A	7.0	5.2	9.7	4.5	.3	6.4	6.3	6.6	.3	−.3
6B	7.0	4.8	8.8	4.0	.8	6.3	6.2	6.3	.1	.1
5A	5.0	3.1	7.0	3.9	−.2	5.4	5.2	5.6	.4	−.3
5B	6.0	3.6	8.3	4.7	.3	5.2	5.1	5.3	.2	.0
4A	5.0	3.2	6.4	3.2	.3	4.4	4.3	4.6	.3	−.3
4B	4.4	3.0	6.0	3.0	.2	4.2	4.1	4.3	.2	.0
3A	4.8	3.0	6.4	3.4	1.1	3.6	3.4	3.7	.3	−.1
3B	4.4	2.4	7.3	4.9	1.2	3.3	3.0	3.6	.6	.1
2A	2.8	1.2	5.3	4.1	.1	2.6	2.3	2.7	.4	−.1
2B	1.7	1.1	2.4	1.3	−.5	2.3	2.1	2.4	.3	.1

ment between the teachers' judgments and the objective determination.

The correlation given above is influenced by the range of grades in which the books were used. If correction for this is made by correlating the deviations of the objective and subjective judgments from the normal expectancy of the various half grades, the correlation drops to .32. Therefore it appears that the differences between the objective and subjective judgments are not merely in amount, but that many books are called easy on one basis and difficult on another.

A study of the scatter diagram from which this correlation was computed shows that of the thirty-eight books which were called easy by the teachers themselves, twenty were easy for the half grade in which they were used according to the objective judgment and eighteen were difficult. Of the fifteen considered correctly placed by the teachers' subjective judgment, four were called easy and ten difficult by the objective method. (One book was called suited to the grade by both objective and subjective methods.) Of the seventeen that were called difficult by the subjective methods, seven were rated easy and ten difficult by the objective.

The tendency thruout seemed to be for teachers to assume that a book used in any *half grade* was appropriate for that *grade* at least. In the " B " sections, books were generally considered to be too difficult and in the " A " sections to be too easy for the half grades to which they were assigned. This tendency occurred with no other exceptions than the two half grades in which the books on the average were considered to be properly placed. However, the objective determination showed the books in eight of the ten half grades to be too difficult. In the " B " sections the books were found to be .5 of a grade too difficult while in the " A " sections they were only .2 of a grade too difficult.

183. " DETERMINING BASIC READING MATERIALS THROUGH A STUDY OF CHILDREN'S INTERESTS AND ADULT JUDGMENTS " [8]

Herbert B. Bruner

What do children like to read? What reading materials do teachers think most appropriate for children? Should children be encouraged to read only that which catches their fancy, or should they be exposed to materials adults think worthwhile? These and similar questions raise a network of problems concerning reading materials. Solutions to many of these have been sought by course-of-study makers, textbook writers, research workers, and individual teachers.

That course-of-study makers, during the past five years, have generally placed a greatly increased emphasis upon the use of engaging child experiences is indicated by a recent survey of 15,000 elementary school courses of study published during the period 1915–28.

Although it is almost universally admitted that children enter with more happiness and a higher degree of success into those activities which them are intrinsically appealing, few would be willing to accept child interest as the sole criterion for determining all curriculum materials. The present trend would seem to be in the direction of approving materials which are not only interesting to children but receive also the sanction of competent adults.

In an attempt to prepare and select reading materials measuring up to this twofold standard — interest and appropriateness — the

[8] *Teachers College Record*, 30:285–286, 304–309, January, 1929.

experiment briefly described in this article was set up and carried through Grades 1 to 6 by Mary E. Pennell, formerly Assistant Superintendent of Schools, Kansas City, Missouri; Alice M. Cusack, Primary Supervisor, Kansas City, Missouri; and the writer, with the coöperation of 1500 teachers, 50,000 children, over a hundred student critic teachers and some interested parents.

In applying the results of this experiment to the problem of selecting a well-balanced list of reading materials, various assumptions might be made, depending upon the answers given to such questions as: Shall all types of materials — most and least frequently used literary selections, story-dramatic, story, and descriptive informational selections — be used? If so, what proportion of each type should be placed in each grade? Should a balance be maintained between longer and shorter selections? Should informational selections of the descriptive type be completely eliminated regardless of the amount of this type of material which must be read in life? And the like.

In selecting reading materials for the fourth, fifth, and sixth grades the following assumptions would seem reasonable:

1. It is educationally desirable that selections of the informational type as well as both most and least used literary material be included. That new life is needed in the reading materials presented to children is almost universally accepted. Since none of the most used literary selections found its way into the list of the highest 10 in this experiment, there seems to be sufficient evidence that appropriate new materials can and should be found.

2. Some balance, consisting of, for instance, 30% of selections most used in textbooks and courses of study, 40% of selections least frequently used in textbooks and courses of study, and 30% of informational selections, should be maintained. This assumption is set up because of a belief in the desirability of improving and making more interesting the reading of children by adding new and fresh materials while retaining the best of the old. Since a large proportion of the reading a child or an adult has to do in life is informational, it is particularly desirable that materials of this type be included.

3. Only those informational selections should be utilized which ranked in the upper 80% as shown by the results of the experiment.

4. An attempt should be made to raise the interest element in the descriptive type of informational selections by changing the form, where advisable, to the story type, and, in some instances, to that with a high dramatic element. Although a sufficient number of informational selections ranked in the top 80% to make up the 30% assumed desirable in assumption 2, the high ratings given informational selections of the story-dramatic type, such as " The Swing Over the Swim-

ming Pool " and " The Red Sweater's Service," would argue for the value of changing the form of some of the selections of the descriptive type. Although the scores accorded the selections marked † in the following lists were sufficiently high to warrant their inclusion, a re-writing along the lines suggested would doubtless add to their *interest* element.

5. No literary prose selections of the 108 utilized in the experiment should be chosen which ranked in the lower quartile or received a percentile score of less than 25.

In striking the 30-40-30 balance suggested in assumption 2 it would be necessary in some cases to place a selection in a grade where it did not receive its absolute highest rank, but in no instance should the conditions of assumptions 3 and 5 be violated. Where grade changes have been made in the following recommended lists of reading materials, a selection so changed received in most cases almost as high a rank in the grade in which it is placed as in the grade in which it received its top rank; for example, " The Snow Battle " ranked 7 in the fifth grade and 8 in the fourth grade. It is placed in the fourth grade in the recommended list in order to maintain the suggested 30-40-30 balance. For similar reasons, " Daniel Boone and the Founding of Kentucky," which ranked 16 in the fourth grade, 27 in the fifth grade, and 28.5 in the sixth grade, was placed in grade six. In shifting selections from one grade to another on the basis of the criteria used, it is probable that some changes in vocabulary, sentence structure, and the like, will be found necessary to fit the material to the abilities of the children of the various grades.

The following lists of reading materials for grades four, five, and six are recommended as a result of applying the conclusions of the experiment in the light of the foregoing assumptions.*

RECOMMENDED LISTS OF READING MATERIALS FOR GRADES 4, 5, AND 6

GRADE 4

INFORMATIONAL

Name of Selection	Rank
The Swing Over the Swimming Pool	2
Barbara's Basket of Fruit	29
The Fire Engine That Lost Its Way #	63
Pioneering In The Air	72
The Man Who Said, " What Can I Do? "	93

* Selections marked # were chosen for these lists from materials originally presented in grades three to seven. It will be noted that in accordance with usual practice, and because of the need, more material has been placed in the sixth grade than in the fourth and fifth.

Name of Selection   *Rank*

LEAST FREQUENTLY USED LITERARY SELECTIONS

MOST FREQUENTLY USED LITERARY SELECTIONS

GRADE 5

INFORMATIONAL

Grade 6

informational

Name of Selection   *Rank*

The Happy Prince	9
The Race for the Silver Skates #	12
The Magic Prison	13
Molly in Her Element	16
The Charcoal Burner	20
A Silent Heroine	22
Sergeant York of Tennessee	26
Daniel Boone and the Founding of Kentucky	28.5
The Challenge of Fujiyama #	39
The " Great White Doctor " of Africa	44
Hunting With a Camera	54.5
On the Farm	59
Clever Companions #	65

MOST FREQUENTLY USED LITERARY SELECTIONS

The Porcelain Stove	10
Gulliver's Travels	17
Ali Baba and the Open Sesame	19
The Adventure of a Mason #	23
Moni, the Goat Boy	31
Sinbad the Sailor	33.5
Rip Van Winkle	33.5
A Dog of Flanders	38
Where Love Is, There God Is Also	46
Damon and Pythias	57

In choosing the literary selections which were sent to the classrooms for experimentation, 2742 were considered in the fourth, fifth, and sixth grades alone. Through the judgment of carefully selected committees and reference to outstanding courses of study, this list was reduced to 108 for further experimentation. In preparing the material for the informational selections an effort was made to include that which would not only satisfy the ascertained interests of children but would also be accurate in every detail. Considerable attention was devoted to the form of this material in order to determine the relative ranking of the descriptive, story and story-dramatic type. The unusual care given to the preparation of the informational selections was due to the belief that the need for this kind of selection in basic reading programs is great. The aim sought in placing the experimental books in the hands of children and teachers, therefore, was to determine from an already highly selected list of materials those which seemed to be most interesting and most appropriate when presented in actual classroom situations. The foregoing lists contain the selections which most nearly measure up to this twofold criterion on the basis of the assumptions made.

184. Time Allotment in a Daily and a Weekly Program of Studies [9]

Jesse H. Newlon and Others

Chicago public schools have recently issued a "time allotment schedule which is to be followed in the schools of the city as closely as circumstances will permit. Variations from this schedule may be made by the principal in consultation with and by the consent of the district superintendent." Such time schedules serve their purpose in assuring a balanced weekly program. Too often, however, they serve to delimit worthwhile experiences which can only be brought to fruition if sufficient time is allowed for the continuance of the activity at the time when the pupils are most interested in it. Time schedules in a school should have the same underlying principles as time schedules which we make in our daily lives. It is true that the housewife and the business man have schedules, but they do not often allow the schedule to prohibit them from completing an important task in which they are engaged. Certain matters of routine nature should be taken care of daily at stated times and only a certain time allotment should be given to these activities. The majority of our daily tasks, however, cannot be confined to predetermined time limits. This same principle applies to the schoolroom. It is inconceivable that a profitable excursion to the neighbouring post office or an excursion to an art center can be put within the time limit of a half-hour. Neither is it possible to finish many tasks in fine arts, in construction, in manual training, and the like, in the daily time periods or even in the allotment for the week. There should be such flexibility both in the daily and in the weekly program that the teacher and the pupil will have opportunity to complete those activities which promise to give the greatest educational results. Instead of making it necessary for the principal in consultation with the district superintendent to pass on variations in schedule, the classroom teacher should be made responsible for so adjusting her work that children will get the most out of their school experiences. The courses of study for the elementary schools should contain illustrations of changing time allotments in accordance with the type of work being undertaken in a classroom, noting the longer periods necessary for excursions and larger investigations as against the shorter periods which are needed, for example, in drill.

[9] "The Curricula of the Schools," *Report of the Survey of the Schools of Chicago, Illinois,* Vol. III, Bureau of Publications, Teachers College, Columbia University, New York, 1932, pp. 41–42.

185. The Daily Program and Time Allotment in Florida [10]

However, as adjustments are made, care should be taken that reasonable time allotments are maintained. Very often teachers give an excessive amount of time to those subjects in which they are particularly interested. There is no mandatory time allotment for the State; however, the following may be suggestive: approximately thirty per cent of the school time should be devoted to the mastery of skills and items of information that promise to be of permanent worth; approximately twenty per cent of the time should be devoted to health, physical education and recreational activities, and the remaining time should be planned directly to develop understandings and attitudes. Suggestions are made in the Table below for the several subjects to assist teachers who organize their programs more strictly on the subject basis. These allotments are based upon the judgments of recognized experts in the fields where such experts have stated their opinions. In other fields the allotments are based on a survey of best current practice and study of the material in this course of study.

TABLE

Approximate Time Allotments Suggested for Florida Schools

Subject	Grade	Minutes per Week
Reading, Language and Grammar	1	500
	2	400
	3	400
	4	300
	5	300
	6	250
Arithmetic	1	Incidental
	2	125
	3	175
	4	200
	5	200
	6	200
Writing	1	70
	2	70
	3	70
	4	70
	5	70
	6	70
Spelling	1	Incidental
	2	75
	3	75
	4	75
	5	75
	6	75

[10] Florida, *The Course of Study for Florida Elementary Schools, Grades I–VI,* State Department of Public Instruction, Tallahassee, 1933, pp. 25–27.

TABLE (*Continued*)

Subject	Grade	Minutes per Week
Social Studies	1	200
	2	200
	3	200
	4	300
	5	300
	6	300
Elementary Science	1	100
	2	100
	3	100
	4	150
	5	150
	6	200
Art	1	125
	2	125
	3	125
	4	125
	5	125
	6	125
Music	1	125
	2	125
	3	125
	4	125
	5	125
	6	125
Physical and Health Education	1	300
	2	300
	3	300
	4	300
	5	300
	6	300

186. " TIME TABLES " [11]

George C. Kyte and Robert H. Lewis

Beginning with Payne's study of time allotments in the elementary school subjects in 1904, surveys of this nature have been made at ten-year intervals. The present investigation constitutes the survey of 1934–1935 practices. We endeavored to include in this study the data from all cities reporting in one or more of the previous investigations by Payne, Holmes, and Ayer. Usable replies were received from sixty-three representative school systems, named at the end of the article.

OBSTACLES TO INVESTIGATOR

The reports indicate the increasing difficulty of conducting studies of time allotments. The integration of subject matter and the devel-

[11] *The Nation's Schools,* 17:23–25, January, 1936.

opment of activity programs are educational movements minimizing the guidance to teachers with respect to the distribution of school time. Three pertinent quotations illustrate the problem confronting the investigators and forecast the probable greater obstacles which will confront an investigator in 1944. The statements also indicate attitudes toward time allotments in the light of the trends in teaching.

" We are making an effort to deformalize our classroom procedures. Therefore, we are not adhering to any specific time allotments. The teachers are endeavoring to utilize the time so as to secure the best results for the individual and the group."

" An arbitrary statement of the time allotment to the various formal subjects would be quite misleading. . . . In the primary grades, it would be impossible to give anything like a satisfactory report based on the separation of the day into formal subject matter periods."

" We have no definite requirement as to time allotted; but the recommended portion of time given to each of the subjects in the elementary curriculum is indicated on the enclosed schedule."

Table I contains the data with respect to the grade placement of each subject or some other item regularly assigned school time. When courses in the junior high schools entitled English are taken into account, it is evident that language, reading, physical training, art and music are generally placed in all eight grades. There is some tendency to omit spelling and arithmetic from grade 1 but to assign the former to all other grades through the sixth and possibly seventh grade and the latter, through the eighth grade.

Penmanship is placed in the first six grades by practically all of the school systems and also in the seventh and eighth grades by a majority of them. All the cities list the social studies or various phases of them in grades 4 to 8, almost all include them in grade 3, and a majority also present them in the first two grades.

Seventy-five per cent of the school systems place health education in the first six grades and 60 per cent continue it in the next two grades. In grade 3 to grade 6 inclusive, 83 per cent of the systems indicate instruction in phases of health education.

ALL GRADES TEACH SCIENCE

Elementary science is placed in all grades by a large majority of the school systems, 64 per cent listing it in the first grade and 83 per cent, in the eighth grade. A majority set aside time for opening exercises in all grades. These activities take various forms such as flag salute, morning inspection, reading of notices and scriptural reading.

More institutions include handwork of various sorts in the first six grades than the percentages would seem to indicate. Often it is implied under art but without sufficient definiteness to warrant tabulating it under handwork. Industrial arts and household arts are widely placed in the seventh and eighth grades. There is a marked tendency to place the former subject in the sixth grade also.

RECESS IN FIRST SIX GRADES

Three tendencies characterize the inclusion or the omission of recess. At least 75 per cent of the systems make provision for it in the first six grades. When junior high schools are organized, there is a

TABLE I

GRADE PLACEMENT OF SUBJECT MATTER ACCORDING TO 63 SCHOOL
SYSTEMS REPORTING IN THE FALL OF 1934

Subject	Percentage of Systems Listing Subjects in Specified Grades							
	I	II	III	IV	V	VI	VII	VIII
English.................	...	...	...	...	...	...	36	38
Language..............	97	100	100	100	100	100	64	62
Reading...............	98	100	100	100	100	100	57	58
Spelling...............	56	98	100	100	100	100	61	56
Penmanship...........	97	100	100	100	99	99	57	52
Arithmetic............	68	100	100	100	100	99	95	96
Social studies.........	29	29	27	22	22	22	27	25
History...............	27	31	42	57	70	73	68	73
Civics................	36	37	35	47	50	50	34	48
Geography............	22	25	52	78	78	78	68	48
Science...............	64	66	67	73	70	68	70	83
Health education......	75	78	83	83	83	83	61	60
Physical training.......	93	93	95	97	95	95	96	98
Recess................	83	83	82	80	75	73	43	40
Industrial arts.........	17	17	20	25	42	52	88	83
Household arts........	2	2	3	7	22	35	73	69
Art..................	97	97	97	99	99	97	96	88
Handwork............	22	20	22	20	18	17	4	4
Music................	100	100	100	100	100	100	98	98
Opening exercises......	68	66	63	63	65	63	54	52
Miscellaneous.........	54	63	62	62	62	55	73	81
Total Number of Systems	59	59	60	60	60	60	56	52

Explanation of Terms: Language includes composition, grammar, drill on English usage; reading includes oral and silent reading, phonics, literature; science includes nature study; health education includes hygiene, physiology and health study but not physical training; physical training includes athletics, gymnastics, calisthenics, folk-dancing and directed play but not recess; civics includes citizenship, government, safety education, thrift and morals; art includes drawing, painting, modeling and picture study; handwork includes paper cutting, primary weaving, construction by young children but not industrial arts and household arts; recess includes scheduled recess periods, relief or rest periods; opening exercises include flag salute, reading of notices, scriptural reading and morning inspection; "miscellaneous" includes secondary school subjects or any subjects or activities for which time is allotted regularly but which are not listed elsewhere.

general tendency to omit the recess period, the time consumed in changing classes supplanting it. A significant number of cities indicate that, in all or in some grades, the physical training period is assimilating recess time.

The average amount of time allotted per week to each subject in every grade through the eighth is shown in Table II. The totals indicate that reading is assigned more time than is any other subject. From 508 minutes in grade 1 the average amount of time decreases irregularly grade by grade until it reaches 154 in grade 8. Marked reductions occur at four points: between grades 2 and 3, 3 and 4, 4 and 5, and 6 and 7.

The social studies are assigned the second largest amount of time largely owing to the allotments in grades 4 to 8 inclusive. There is also a distinct tendency to give the subject considerable stress in grade 3. In the highest four grades, the number of minutes per week per grade allotted to the social studies, approximating 300 minutes, exceeds other subjects.

Although arithmetic receives a total amount of time which places the subject in third place in this respect, in the average amount of time allotted per grade it ranks second in all grades except grades 1, 4 and 5. The small amount of time assigned to the subject in the first grade is due to the number of systems allotting no time to it in this grade and to others providing for only incidental instruction in the subject. This latter reason accounts for the smaller amount allotted in grade 2 than that in grade 3 but its continued omission by some of the cities affects the average.

Language clearly ranks as the fourth subject in terms of the total amount of time allotted to it. From this standpoint, however, it ranks second in grade 1 and third in grades 2, 3, 7 and 8. Beginning with an average of 129 minutes per week in the first grade, the amounts gradually increase until the average weekly allotment is 212 minutes in grade 7.

The small weekly time allotments per grade assigned to spelling and to penmanship indicate the general tendency to follow the conclusions obtained from the various research studies regarding drill. The small averages for spelling in grades 1 and 8 and for penmanship in grades 7 and 8 are due to the number of school systems omitting these subjects from the specified grades. Increments of time allotted to spelling in grades 3 and up used for dictionary drill and word study constitute the primary cause of the average amount per grade for spelling exceeding that for penmanship.

Omission of health education and of science by some school systems causes the average amount per grade for each subject to be small. But the tendency to include these subjects incidentally and often as part of reading and language instruction is the more prominent factor affecting the time allotted. As they are actually taught, therefore, they occupy more time in the instructional program than the averages would seem to indicate. The introduction of general science in junior high schools accounts for the increased time allotments in the grades above the sixth.

The time allotments per grade for art and music disclose the tendency to set aside about 90 minutes per week to each of these subjects in every grade. The number of cities tending to allot 100 minutes per week to art and 75 minutes per week to music affects to some extent the differences in the two sets.

Physical training is assigned average time allotments which vary only slightly from grade to grade, approximating 110 minutes per

TABLE II

AVERAGE NUMBER OF MINUTES PER WEEK ALLOTED TO ELEMENTARY SUBJECTS IN 1934–1935

Subject	Number of Minutes per Week in Specified Grades								Total
	I	II	III	IV	V	VI	VII	VIII	
Language........	129	131	155	173	184	187	212	212	1,383
Reading..........	508	456	382	282	227	201	157	154	2,367
Spelling..........	29	82	92	92	88	86	84	77	630
Penmanship......	76	78	84	81	74	74	55	50	572
Arithmetic.......	62	145	197	215	219	219	232	236	1,525
Social studies*....	79	88	139	228	282	297	323	297	1,733
Science..........	43	46	53	48	48	49	73	109	469
Health education..	29	26	31	35	38	38	34	35	266
Physical training..	109	109	111	109	109	112	110	110	879
Recess...........	104	107	103	93	86	82	52	44	671
Household art...⎫ Industrial art and ⎬ handwork.....⎭	23	21	23	27	42	57	136	118	447
Art..............	98	87	85	89	89	91	91	82	712
Music...........	82	82	85	86	87	90	85	82	679
Opening exercises .	43	43	43	42	41	38	28	26	304
Miscellaneous.....	67	74	67	63	65	61	112	150	659
Total Number of Minutes........	1,481	1,575	1,650	1,663	1,679	1,682	1,784	1,782	13,296

* Includes history, civics and geography.

week per grade. The time assigned to recess periods averages a little more than 100 minutes per week in each of the first three grades. The average amounts decrease in successive grades until they reach only 44 minutes per week in grade 8.

For the total period of eight school years, 48.7 per cent of the time is devoted to the subjects commonly described as the Three R's —

reading, penmanship, spelling, language and arithmetic. The content subjects, consisting of science and the social sciences, are assigned 16.6 per cent of the total time. The special subjects, including all of the rest, are given 34.7 per cent of the time. Naturally, the relative amounts differ markedly from grade to grade, as may be seen by an inspection of the data in Table II.

187. QUESTIONS REGARDING STANDARDS FOR TIME ALLOTMENTS [12]

1. Has a statistical standard, as presented in the preceding studies, any value except that it shows the trend of opinion and practice?

2. Do community conditions explain why in one elementary school one of the fundamental subjects is allotted time during one-half year, and in another school during eight years?

3. Do individual differences of pupils offer a reasonable explanation?

4. Do differences in length of school course or of school year explain this great divergence in time allotments?

5. Does the subjective influence of school administrators, either their indifference or enthusiasm for the value of a certain subject, explain the great variation in time devoted to it?

6. Have propagandists had any influence in determining school schedules?

7. Have most elementary school curricula developed largely by the process of accretion, including legislative enactments which provide new subjects and specific time allotments for them, without first evaluating previous schedules?

8. How may we determine definite standards of attainments for the various subjects and for the various grades?

9. Will it ever be possible to determine in fourth-grade arithmetic, for example, whether to give twenty or thirty minutes time a day until it is agreed officially as to what knowledge and skill in arithmetic we may expect the fourth-grade child to have?

10. Gradually, will it be possible for individual opinion to give way to scientific knowledge on such questions as the following: What subjects should be commonly taught? What is the relative social value of each stated in some objective form? What is its essential content? What are reasonable standards of accomplishment?

[12] National Education Association, *The Elementary School Curriculum*, Department of Superintendence Second Yearbook, Washington, D. C., 1924, p. 172.

188. Time Allotments in Arithmetic [13]
R. L. West, Charles E. Greene, and W. A. Brownell

DESIRABILITY OF OPTIMAL TIME ALLOTMENTS

Theoretically it should be possible to set up optimal time allotments for arithmetic in the various grades. Obviously, however, such time allotments are dependent on such items as the objectives of arithmetic, the relative value of arithmetic in the total curriculum, the efficiency of teaching, and evidence from careful studies to determine the relation of accomplishment to pupils' capacities. Much time must elapse before any of these items are determined with any degree of certainty. Meanwhile time allotments must be prescribed and schools must operate.

SUGGESTED TIME ALLOTMENTS

From the studies analyzed, the following schedule of time allotment is suggested in Table IV. The median time reported by Mann is added for comparison.

TABLE IV
Suggested Minimum and Maximum Time Allotments in Minutes per Day and per Week for Arithmetic (Grades I–VI) Compared with Median Time in 444 Cities Reported by Mann

Grade	I	II	III	IV	V	VI	Total
Per Day.........	15 to 20	25 to 30	35 to 40	40 to 45	40 to 45	40 to 45	195 to 225
Per Week........	75 to 100	125 to 150	175 to 200	200 to 225	200 to 225	200 to 225	975 to 1125
Mann........... (Per Week)	80	146	196	211	215	215	1063

In interpreting these recommendations it should be noted that the time given means the total time devoted by a pupil in a day or a week to all forms of arithmetic activities, either in individual or in class work.

[13] "The Arithmetic Curriculum," National Society for the Study of Education, *Report of the Society's Committee on Arithmetic*, Twenty-Ninth Yearbook, Public School Publishing Company, Bloomington, Ill., 1930, pp. 74, 77–78.

School systems that are spending much less or much more time than these amounts should examine their achievements carefully to determine whether more time is needed to produce satisfactory results or whether excess time is being accompanied by wasteful or inefficient teaching.

189. CURRENT PRACTICE IN TIME ALLOTMENT TO SCIENCE TOPICS [14]

Wilbur L. Beauchamp

An attempt was made to discover any agreement in the amount of time which should be spent on different topics. Twenty-seven courses indicated the time allotment for each unit. Because of the diverse nature of the units, it was difficult to get a comparison over a comparable body of material. The results obtained from an analysis of courses in which the number of periods per week were identical are shown in Table 4.

TABLE IV

NUMBER OF COURSES REQUIRING A SPECIFIED TIME ON CERTAIN UNITS

Unit	Number of weeks									
	1	2	3	4	5	6	7	8	9	10
Weather	1	1	..	3	..	..	..	..	..	..
Electricity	..	..	1	3	..	..	..	2	..	..
Heating homes	1	..	..	..	1	..	..	..	..	..
Foods	..	1	1	..	1	1	..	..	..	3
Machines	1	3	..	..	..	..	1	..	..	..
Lighting homes	..	..	2	..	..	..	..	..	..	..
Transportation	..	..	..	..	2	..	..	..	1	..
Communication	..	..	..	..	..	..	2	..	1	..
Clothing	1	..	1	..	2	..	..	..	..	..
Air and its use	..	1	1	1	..	..	..	2	..	..
Heavenly bodies	..	1	..	1	..	1	..	1	..	..

It is evident from the results that either the outline of the topic does not indicate the extent to which the details are covered or there are different standards of attainment in different systems. Owing to limitation of space it is impossible to show the grade placement and sequence of topics in the courses. This analysis was made and the results of the study show, however, that a given topic may be

[14] *Instruction in Science,* National Survey of Secondary Education, Bulletin No. 17, Monograph No. 22, Government Printing Office, Washington, D. C., 1932, p. 31.

included as the first topic in the seventh grade of one course and as the tenth topic in the ninth grade of another course. In other words, grade placement and sequence of topics evidently rests upon no established principle of organization. Such a principle must take into account the complexity of the ideas presented and the intellectual maturity of pupils at different levels.

CHAPTER XII

TEACHING PROCEDURES

190. CONTEMPORARY EMPHASIS ON METHOD [1]

1. FAITH in method, divorced from knowledge, thought, and purpose, has long been the besetting sin of pedagogy in the United States. Whether in the sphere of classroom teaching, curriculum construction, testing procedures, or school administration, the consideration of substance and values is all too often subordinated to method and technique.

2. This devotion to method and technique *per se* is revealed in the interest aroused by the invention of a new or the rediscovery of an old pedagogical device, in the heated discussions at educational meetings over the relative merits of competing " methods," in the spread of various techniques for the " objective " determination of programs of civic training, and in the time, energy, and money consumed in the construction of tests, scales, score-cards, outlines, units, and stereotypes of one kind or another.

3. This obsession with formalistic methodology has also manifested itself very generally in the programs of teacher training institutions. During the past generation these institutions have tended to overload their curricula with courses in the mechanics of instruction and administration, have directed their attention too largely to the refinement and super-refinement of techniques, have neglected the more fundamental problems of purpose, thought, value and content and have lamentably failed to co-ordinate training in teaching procedure with scholarship in subject matter. Being absorbed in improving the mechanics of the educative process, they have unwittingly accepted social conceptions and purposes inherited from the past.

4. The traditional and generally current emphasis on a narrowly conceived methodology requires correction, and is actually being corrected in certain schools and teacher-training centers. It is totally out of harmony with the conception of education outlined in this

[1] Commission on the Social Studies, American Historical Association, *Conclusions and Recommendations,* Charles Scribner's Sons, New York, 1934, pp. 69–73.

volume; it violates the principle here maintained that the validity and adequacy of the school program depend both on the adjustment of its content and procedures to the nature of the pupil and on the correspondence of its purposes with the unfolding fortunes, potentialities, and hopes of society.

5. In the measure that method is dissociated from appropriate content or knowledge of pupil growth, education becomes shallow, formal or capricious, or all three. There is no procedure that can render substance unnecessary; there is no technique of classroom legerdemain that can take the place of scholarly competence; there is no device of instruction that can raise the quality of the educative process above the purpose, the knowledge, the understanding, the vision of the teacher who employs it.

6. When the nature of the social sciences, as system and flow of thought, is taken into account, it becomes evident at once that methodology, however useful and indispensable when developed in relation to content and purpose, is utterly incompetent in itself to organize, control, and direct the teaching process. Even in the mind and work of the purest methodologist some frame of reference, not method, dominates organization and emphasis. These considerations are particularly applicable to teacher-training institutions, curriculum makers, and persons engaged in the supervision of social science instruction.

7. Since methodology, if considered intrinsically, is inseparable from the content of thought in the field involved, it cannot be organized successfully into a separate discipline and be made the peculiar possession of a teacher, a supervisor, or even a teacher-training institution.

8. Methodology, if it revolves around its own center, becomes an intellectual operation akin to that of the Sophists of ancient Greece or of the minor scholastics of the Middle Ages; if it advances to the center of the substance with which it deals, it becomes a relevant aspect of purposeful activity.

9. In concluding this criticism of the contemporary emphasis on formalistic method the Commission would point out that this emphasis . . . represents in some measure a reaction from an equally formalistic emphasis or knowledge in the colleges and universities and a widespread disregard of the psychological problems involved in the teaching and learning processes. Many a college education has been filed away in a drawer of notes and notebooks, there to gather dust and be forgotten. Knowledge, like method, if ineffectively related to significant purpose, is sterile.

191. Teacher Activities Essential to Effective Use of Curriculum Materials [2]

Florence Stratemeyer

Activities Which Teachers Would Like to Carry Forward in the Effective Use of Curriculum Materials. It is a truism to say that that which is now carried forward need not be representative of desired performance. The several groups of teachers and supervisory and administrative officers were asked not only to report present performance, but to indicate the activities which in their judgment were essential to the effective use of curriculum materials and which they accordingly would like to perform, were no difficulties present. As an additional check and as a further basis for determining and selecting those activities which would seem to be most important in the effective use of curriculum materials, a jury of nine experts working in the field of the elementary school and cognizant of its present problems were also asked to indicate the activities which in their judgment were most significant.

A study of the reports . . . reveals slightly more total agreement among the several groups in terms of desired activities than in the case of present practices. Again we find that some teachers within each group would like to carry on each activity, while there seems to be no item which all would like to perform. The jury of experts, on the other hand, find themselves in complete agreement with respect to the desirability of elementary teachers performing twelve of the activities. Like the teaching group, some think it desirable to carry on each activity of the check list. The activities agreed upon by the experts are as follows:

I 4a. Utilizing the pupil inventory as a basis for selecting objectives or goals of instruction.

I 4b. Utilizing the pupil inventory as a basis for selecting subject matter or units of work.

II 6a. Using the objectives as bases for selecting subject matter or units of instruction.

III 11. Selecting subject matter from among the materials in the pupils' environment and the resources of the community, with reference to pupils' abilities, interests, and needs.

III 15. Determining pupils' interests.

IV 7. Determining the organization of materials and method

[2] From *The Effective Use of Curriculum Materials*, Contributions to Education No. 460, Bureau of Publications, Teachers College, Columbia University, New York, 1931, pp. 33, 42.

of procedure as the work of the class period develops (i.e. immediate planning in terms of pupil reactions).

IV   9. Selecting methods of instruction so as to provide for the abilities, needs, and interests of the individual pupil.

IV   15. Providing for pupils to assume adequate responsibility in activities.

IV   19. Selecting effective illustrative materials (e.g. diagrams, specimens, visual aids, etc.).

IV   22. Adapting assignments to the needs and abilities of the pupils (e.g. determining scope and difficulty of assignments, best time for making, etc.).

V   7. Following up diagnosis (indicating means of improvement, selecting proper remedial measures, etc.)

VI   3. Noting deficiencies in the course of study, looking to desired revisions.

192. The Basis of Adequate Teacher Guidance in Developing Large Units [3]

The attitude of the teacher is very important. He should understand the point of view concerning education held by the Raleigh schools which is, in a sense, based on modern trends in this and in other countries. The teacher should read widely, not only professional books, but the best literature of the day. He should read the daily newspapers and be informed about world events in order that he may be able to discuss with the children the happenings of the day as they hear them discussed at home, or elsewhere, and as they read the papers for themselves.

In undertaking work with large units, the teacher should have convictions about the work. He must believe in the possibilities of this type of work and he should be open-minded as the work develops, ready to discard those leads that are not worth while and take others that may offer greater possibilities.

In assembling materials and information for the development of a unit of work, the teacher will need to learn to judge the value of what he finds in terms of the child's interests and the growth level of the group. This means that the teacher must keep an experimental attitude toward the work. In working out a toy shop, a second-grade teacher, after trying the unit with two different groups and checking closely on the results, was convinced that the unit was too difficult

[3] Raleigh, *Statement of the Aims and Educational Program of the Raleigh Public Schools,* Curriculum Bulletin, No. 2, Raleigh, N. C., 1928, pp. 39–44.

for the children of this grade, and noted the points wherein the group failed to get the learnings that might have been secured by an older group. It is only by such an attitude toward the work that the teacher will be able to grow in the ability to guide the children in selecting centers of interest out of which units will come that will be within their grasp.

The teacher should be keenly alive to the educative possibilities of any experience of the individual child or of the group, ready to direct such experiences along lines that will produce growth in knowledge, skills, attitudes and habits of the child at this stage of his development.

Care should be taken to provide for the development of all sides of the child's nature. No one unit of work will furnish all of the experiences that should come into the life of the child. Provision should be made for those phases of the program that are not taken care of in the unit of work. The child should grow, daily, in knowledge, in the necessary skills for carrying on his work, in his appreciations, in health habits, and in right attitudes. It is only by keeping careful record of the outcomes of each unit and checking with the attainments set forth in the " check list " section of the course, that the teacher will be able to know the progress the pupils are making.

It goes without saying that the personality of the teacher is important. He should be the guide, not the master, of the group and at all times he should be a member of the working group, ready to give the help or suggestion necessary for the child to take the next step. Some times this may be done by asking a question or by directing observation. At times it may be necessary to face the self-satisfied child with something better than he has done, to stir him to greater achievement.

The teacher should strive to create an atmosphere in the room that will encourage each child to do some creative work. It is his problem to set up conditions and provide experiences for the group that will call for activities that will result in learning. Opportunities must be given for the children to have first-hand contact with real situations, for them to investigate, to experiment, to deal with actual life situations. Tools and materials must also be furnished or made available for the children to express themselves without having to depend on facts handed out to them or on thinking by other people. No subject is worth much for children, however much it may interest them, if they are not able to find materials and opportunities for first-hand expression. It is the teacher's place, then, to find situations and tools that will give the children opportunity for first-hand intake and at the same time to see that media are available for first-hand output.

ACQUAINTANCE PERIOD

In addition to these general and fundamental requirements, the teacher needs to know the interests, tendencies and abilities of the group. In taking a class, the teacher will want time to sense and define the problems that face the group. This period we call an *acquaintance period*. The length of this period will vary with the group. No definite time can be assigned for it. It may take two or three weeks. The children should not be rushed into an activity or encouraged to undertake a unit of work unless it has drive enough to hold the interest of the group and give enough experiences for growth of the individual pupil along many lines. At the same time, the work should not be allowed to drag, the children turning from one thing to another as their interests may direct.

There are several things that may be done to help the teacher get acquainted with the group.

1. *Records*

A very careful record is kept of each child as he goes through the Raleigh schools. This will furnish much that will help the teacher understand the pupil, for it gives a complete statement of his health equipment, his growth in knowledge, in habits, in attitudes, in skills, the places where he is deficient and needs definite help and encouragement and his strong points, as his special interests and attitudes.

2. *Centers of Interests*

It is well to have in the room several centers of interest that may attract the attention of the children as they enter the grade. Growing plants, a bird, an aquarium, collections of nature materials brought in by the children will prove stimulating.

A reading table should hold interesting and attractive books and pictures, suited to the growth level of the group — some easy reading materials, more or less familiar to the group, some that is entirely new. Children's magazines will find a place on the reading table, also.

Drawing materials, paints and brushes, an easel, clay for modeling, will form another center, inviting the children to express themselves graphically.

A piano, a phonograph and records, and other musical instruments will stimulate the interest of the children in music.

Construction materials, pieces of wood of different lengths, blocks, a work bench, tools, will appeal to those who wish to build.

Pictures, drawings, booklets made by a previous grade will often prove stimulating and suggestive.

As children turn to these centers of interest, the teacher will join the different groups, note their interests, answer questions and give suggestions as to the use that can be made of the different materials supplied. By watching the children as they find themselves in these different centers the teacher will learn many things that will help her plan the work for the groups. Often units of work will grow out of the children's activities during this period of orientation.

3. *Conference Period*

Discussion is the tool we use to help the children interpret what they have seen, to help them express themselves. Very important in this period of getting acquainted with the group is the hour in which the teacher discusses with the children the things in which they are interested — their homes and the members of the family; how they come to school; the things they bring to school, as flowers, butterflies, caterpillars, and so on; the stories they like and want to share with the group; the games they enjoy; the trips taken during vacation or at other times; collections made during the summer; the things they are doing in the individual work period. The teacher may read to the group, or tell them stories, giving opportunity, also, for them to read or to tell stories to the group.

As the children have opportunity to share their experiences with the group, questions will be asked and the teacher should keep a very careful record of the interests and the needs of the individual child and work from the beginning to have every child a member of the group.

Out of this period will often come the leads for the units of work to be undertaken, the questions to be answered, the problems to be solved by the group. For example, in a third grade the books for the use of the children were kept on the teacher's desk, as no reading table had been placed in the room. The children read these books and wanted others. They decided that they needed a library in their own room. This brought up the question of what they wanted for the library. The principal was asked for a reading table. When she told the children that she had none to give them, they decided to make a table, some chairs and a set of shelves for the books. Letters were written to the principal and to the superintendent, asking for books. It was found necessary to have some rules governing the use of the library and the care of the books, as some of the children were careless with the books and allowed them to get very soiled and torn. A group worked out a set of rules for the use of the library and submitted it to the entire group for adoption. They wanted to know how to catalogue the books and how to keep a record of the ones taken out over night or over week-end. A trip was made to the city library, where the superintendent of the children's department showed them how to catalogue their books and what kind of a record to keep.

193. Procedures for the Teacher in Guidance[4]

Paul B. Diederich

There are three typical procedures in setting up a counseling system. One is to assign a certain number of pupils to each teacher — after much debate as to whether it is better to assign girls to women teachers and boys to men teachers or mixed groups to both, and whether to assign groups of the same age and grade or to have several grades represented. All this debate misses the point that the counselor should first of all be a friend, and one cannot assign friends. The second procedure is to allow pupils to choose any teacher as their counselor. A second choice is usually requested in case too many pupils choose the same teacher, or in case the teacher does not feel *en rapport* with the pupil. This procedure has the advantage of putting together people who have confidence in one another, but it has the disadvantage that pupils often choose teachers with whom they will have no further classroom contact, and it is very difficult to follow and understand a pupil's development without this contact. The third procedure is to allow pupils about a month in which to get acquainted with the teachers with whom they will work throughout the year and then to choose one of these as their counselor for the year, indicating a second choice for the reasons given above. This procedure is more likely than the previous ones to distribute the burden of counseling unequally, but it is well to recognize the fact that some teachers are more effective than others in this relationship. One may compensate for the extra load by freeing them from other work, as will presently be explained.

If counselors are to put their records to work, it is absolutely indispensable that they have some time free for counseling within the school day. If the pupil's free periods happen to coincide with the teacher's, this is easy to arrange, but nowadays teachers do not have free periods. The typical administrative procedure for arranging conferences is as heavy-handed as the assignment of counselors. They set aside a short period a day or a week as a home-room period. In these periods one is confronted with from twenty to forty youngsters who have nothing in particular to do, and one has to exert all one's ingenuity to keep them out of mischief. Hence the effusion of May baskets and endless discussion of school politics. To tell them to study their lessons and then to call one after another to the desk for short conferences is exactly like calling a soldier out of his company and discussing his personal problems with him for

---

[4] From " Evaluation Records," *Educational Method*, 15:432–440, May, 1936.

five minutes on the reviewing stand. It is as public as a goldfish bowl and as insecure as the edge of a volcano.

A much cleverer device which is useful for a variety of purposes is to eliminate the home-room period and substitute for it an " overflow " period, preferably directly after lunch every day. This period has to be thoroughly sold to pupils, with the understanding that the moment they get out of hand, regimentation will be resumed; but when it is finally in operation it looks something like this: Pupils who are nervous, high-strung, weak, or convalescent go to darkened, quiet rooms and lie down. They will object, but it is up to the physical education people to convince them that for the sake of their health they simply must do it. If the school has no cots, pupils can bring rag rugs or blankets and learn to relax fairly comfortably on the floor. Other pupils will want to go to the library to read, to the laboratory to perform individual experiments, to the studio to draw or paint, to the music room to sing or play phonograph records and instruments, or to the shop to make things. Much of this activity can be supervised by older students appointed by the school council. Still others will want to dance, and if one can only furnish the room, they will be glad to furnish the music. Other rooms can be fitted up for simple indoor games and for conversation. Some meetings and rehearsals can be held at this time, but definitely scheduled activities over any long period of time should be discouraged. The boys will want to go outdoors and play games. This problem will have to be handled by the physical education people. We don't want violent activity immediately after lunch, with no opportunity for a shower afterward. If pupils will accept a ban on strenuous organized games, however, the fresh air won't hurt them.

Some of the teachers, especially those with light counseling loads, will have to supervise these activities, but if a limited number of activities is provided, each involving fairly large groups, some of which can be supervised by responsible older pupils, the number of supervising teachers can be cut down to a minimum. Teachers not on duty should use this period for counseling conferences. As many as possible of these conferences should be requested by pupils, but definite appointments should be made. These appointments should have precedence over all other activities in the overflow period.

The administrator will probably spend the period walking the corridors in an agony of apprehension, or darting across the street to round up the boys who will inevitably slip over to the drug store for refreshment and a smoke. The idea of a period within the school day when pupils are not in a particular classroom, responsible to a particular teacher, and solemnly at work, threatens the foundations of an administrator's universe. The people in the school who are interested in education may have to help him make the adjustment. Two devices for this purpose may be suggested. The first is to build him a large filing cabinet in which he can keep the boys he catches in the drug store. The second is to sell him the idea by listing and describing the activities that will be available during the overflow period on a mimeographed sheet, and having pupils indicate which activities they will attend each day for at least a week in advance. Attendance can then be taken at these activities and the little pink or green slips can be collected in the usual manner. This will make the administrator happy, but it will be well to wean him away from this red tape as soon as possible. Can't there be one period in the day when a boy can go outdoors and lie down under a tree if he wants to?

The value of such a period for the release of tensions, for the development and pursuit of individual interests, for training in the intelligent use of leisure, and for counseling can hardly be denied. Time can be found in the daily schedule by eliminating the home-room period or recess, by slightly lengthening the school day, or by curtailing some academic requirement: for example, by the rule that no student may take more than one foreign language at a time. It is better to provide too little rather than too much time at first. It might be initiated by providing a lunch period one hour long, and expecting lunch to be eaten in the first, second, or third twenty minutes of the hour according to the number of groups to be served. Teachers can take turns supervising the activities of this period according to a schedule which takes into account their counseling load. Some teachers may not have to supervise at all; others from one to four days a week.

So much for the organization of the school which will permit records to function. We now have a counselor, chosen by the pupil from the teachers with whom he is working, who is responsible for following, interpreting, and directing his all-round development. We have a period within the school day when all of the pupils and (in their turn) all of the teachers are available for conferences, while the other pupils have something interesting and worth while to occupy their time. When pupils and their counselors get together after this elaborate preparation, what will they talk about?

They may talk about anything they please, of course, but the ultimate purpose of their discussion will be to ascertain, clarify, and direct the pupil's progress toward the objectives of the school. This implies that the school has thought out, expressed, accepted, understood, and taken seriously some statement of its common, central objectives. In order to reduce the multitude of specific objectives to a form which can easily be held in mind, it is a good idea to group these objectives under such headings as mental and physical health, methods of thinking, social living, esthetic appreciation, scholarship, interests and purposes, special aptitudes, and the like, each with appropriate sub-heads. Each teacher will be responsible for gathering such evidence as will be described later of his pupils' progress toward these objectives. As he gathers the evidence it will be helpful if he can make some tentative, preliminary interpretation of its significance, at least classifying the evidence according to the objectives to which it relates. If the school has an official list of objectives, this can be done very easily by writing down the number of the objective and the appropriate sub-head, supplemented when necessary by a written statement. For example, if a test, anecdote, or written paper clearly shows good thinking in its aspect of awareness of problems, this may be indicated by classifying the evidence as " 1.1 " before sending it to the counselor. This preliminary interpretation is important because the teacher who observes the original situation in which the evidence is gathered is naturally in the best position to interpret its significance. This device also prevents the accumulation of evidence that has little or no relevance to the objectives of the school.

For the sake of administrative convenience, all such evidence can be dumped in a chute in the central office at the close of the school day, and some clerk can sort it out and have it in the right counselor's mail box by the following morning. The counselor will read the evidence as it comes in, noting the interpretation made at the time of its collection, discussing possible variant interpretations with the teacher concerned, taking or recommending whatever remedial or other educational measures are necessary, and filing the evidence in the pupil's folder.

At intervals of varying length the evidence will be discussed in conference with the pupil. This may be because he has done something thoroughly admirable which should be praised and followed up, or something which casts doubt upon his integrity and good sense, which should be explained and corrected. Or it may be because there is no evidence at all of certain aspects of his development, and the counselor wishes to fill in the gaps in his information. The counselor may or may not refer to the evidence in his possession, but the pupil will have to accept the fact that the counselor is in pretty close touch with what he is doing in every department of school life. He will not resent this if it is clear that the counselor is sincerely interested in his development and anxious to help.

After sufficient evidence has accumulated, the counselor should endeavor to summarize and interpret it, presenting a coherent, meaningful picture of individual growth toward the objectives of the school. This summary should not be in code symbols or in any stereotyped classification of evidence, but should be written in paragraphs, immediately available for professional use, endeavoring to preserve as much of the force and flavor of the original data as possible. This may be done by references to typical incidents, quotations from written work, citations of test scores in terms of percentiles, etc. The summary should retain as much concrete material as possible, abstracting from the original data more by selecting the typical data than by describing behavior in terms of character traits. For example, instead of saying that a pupil is generally dependable, one might say that he almost invariably prepared his assignments satisfactorily and on time, as evidenced by the fact that he had presented during the past three months only two excuses for incomplete or unsatisfactory work, while the average for his class was fourteen excuses. The summary should normally be organized in terms of the central, common objectives of the school, supplemented if necessary by a section on other aspects of development not covered by these objectives. Each summary should be written with the previous summary in mind, reconstructing it, and keeping the record up to date with the pupil's development. Summaries may be clipped as face-sheets over the material summarized in the pupil's folder.

The summary should be written in terms which will be immediately available, with as little translation as possible, for any reports which the school may be called upon to make to other agencies. It should not, however, be copied *in toto* for these reports. It should contain the whole truth about the pupil, as frankly and accurately as the counselor can report it, to be used only for professional purposes within the school. Reports to outside agencies should transcribe only such portions of this report as are necessary and suitable for their particular relationship with the pupil. Reports to parents would include material not reported to colleges, and vice versa. Economy would dictate, however, that the counselor's summaries should be written in such terms that these other reports may easily be drawn from them, without having to re-read the original data.

The pupil's academic history, in terms of subject-matter experiences and achievement, may be kept somewhat distinct from counselor's summaries, inasmuch as individual teachers would be in a better position than the counselor to summarize data of this kind. Interim reports covering various aspects of progress in subject matter may be sent to counselors for purposes of guidance, reports to parents, etc., but many schools prefer to make the final report on a given course or activity the responsibility of the teacher in charge. Such reports are usually made at the end of every course or extra-curricular activity. They may take the form of a mimeographed description of the nature of the group, the activities in which all participated, and the average gains in the most significant measures of outcomes, followed by an individual typed statement of the pupil's significant variations from the activities of the group, his gains in the measures of outcomes reported for the group, and any comments or recommendations for further study that the teacher cares to include.

When an important report is to be made to any other agency, the counselor will abstract from his most recent summary the materials pertinent to this report and present this statement in writing for discussion by a " case conference " of three or four teachers who know the pupil well and of someone who knows the conditions to be observed in this particular kind of report. Such a conference will correct possible eccentricities of individual judgment, check possible misinterpretations, and reveal other implications of the evidence than the counselor may have understood. On the basis of this discussion the counselor will revise his statement until it is approved. In the interest of economy in discussion it is important for the members of the conference to have duplicate copies of the counselor's statement long enough before the conference to consider it carefully. It is the height of folly to expect a case conference to meet without preparation and produce a satisfactory report. Its function is rather that of criticism and amplification of a report already prepared by the counselor. It is also helpful in exchanging professional information about a student, in bringing fresh insight to bear upon his problems, and in directing his education at various crises in his development. We should expect as a beginning at least one case conference on every senior before his final report is approved and sent to college, and we hope to extend the practice gradually to at least one case conference a year on every student. Since normally no more than four teachers need be present at a case conference, and since, after practice, and with the counselor's written statement in advance as a basis for discussion, the conference usually will not take more than ten to fifteen minutes per student, this should not be an impossible standard to maintain in small schools with an adequate faculty.

In all summaries and interpretations the chief danger to be avoided is that of disregarding the evidence and writing a character sketch of the pupil based on personal impressions alone. Such reports reveal more about the teacher who wrote them than about the pupil. This tendency may be corrected by encouraging references to the original data, documenting each point by the evidence, and by having the summaries read by the principal or by a central committee, alert to challenge unsupported statements. This will not rule out subjective evidence, but it will maintain a salutary amount of pressure to take the objective evidence into account.

Let us now list and describe briefly the kinds of evidence of progress toward the objectives of the school which may gradually be made available as a basis for counselors' summaries and conferences:

1. *Personal Pattern of Goals.*

Since the school exists, at least in some measure, to help the pupil achieve the goals he sets for himself and to lead him to formulate ever clearer, more consistent, more attainable, and more socially valuable goals, it is important to ascertain what these goals are and to record progress toward them. This requires a carefully planned conference technique in which the counselor discusses with the pupil such areas of goals as his life work, school work, school life, home and friends, sports, hobbies, the arts, reading, and other recreational activities. Under each of these headings the pupil writes out anything he would like to do or to be, indicating as far as possible or desirable when he formed these interests or purposes, and why. Thereafter at intervals of perhaps once a week or once a month he records anything he has done or experienced which he feels is significantly related to the goals he has set down, whether helping or hindering. In this way one can tell which goals are really controlling behavior, which are merely paper goals, and which are thwarted by circumstances over which he has no control. Goals may be added or dropped from time to time. The collection and interpretation of such materials is of the very greatest importance, not only in assisting pupils toward a new orientation in life but as a fundamental basis for the revision of the secondary school curriculum.

2. *Records of Significant Experiences.*

The personal pattern of goals may be supplemented by a record of the experiences of sample weeks which seemed to the pupil most interesting or important. These experiences may reveal other goals which are implicit in behavior but not consciously formulated, and they constitute an important source of evidence on developing interests and sensitivities.

3. *Reading Records.*

The pupil's record of free reading is perhaps the most significant index we have of his general intellectual maturity. It has been found best to limit the continuous record to free reading in books, leaving magazine and newspaper reading to periodic sampling through tests or check lists, and assigned reading to a record kept by teachers. Quantity, quality, variety, understanding and emotional response seem to be the most important criteria for interpreting the reading record, when taken in conjunction with the other facts known about the pupil. A report on these factors may be sent to the counselor by the English teacher after periodic conferences on reading, designed to assist the pupil in his selection and understanding of further reading.

4. *Records of Cultural Experiences.*

The reading record may be supplemented by records of other cultural experiences such as plays, concerts, movies, radio programs, visits to museums, travel, music lessons, scientific investigations, religious experiences, and the like. Such a record is fairer and more helpful to the non-verbal student than the reading record.

5. *Records of Creative Expression.*

Records of creative expression — any product which represents the pupil's own ideas and feelings as distinguished from a practice exercise — are an important index of developing interests, attitudes, work habits, and the like. If we are to be fair to the creative expression of all pupils, we should include in this category not only creative writing and the space arts but dramatic and musical performances, political achievements, new laboratory experiments, original problems in mathematics, etc. Since we have had so little experience with records of creative expression, it is well for teachers to experiment with a variety of such records and to compare their usefulness. Some common elements of such records might be: the names of pupil and teacher, the date, the name, title or subject of the creative product, the medium or materials, the approximate number of hours of work represented, and a statement by the pupil of the purpose or central idea of his product, what he learned or tried to express in creating it, interesting circumstances connected with it, and how successful it was in achieving his purposes. The teacher's interpretation and evaluation of the product or of the process of creating it should be included, if only in a phrase. If the product is visible, a small photograph, even by a miniature camera, is very helpful in recalling it to mind and in giving concreteness to the interpretation. Probably different record forms have to be developed for the different kinds of creative expression. A collection of such records from every department of school life should reveal a great deal about students' relative fertility, imagination, creative power, work habits, interests, and attitudes.

6. *Anecdotal Records.*

These are brief records of observations, interviews, comments, quotations from written work and the like, which reveal significant tendencies in pupil development, especially toward the objectives of the school. They contain a short, clear, objective, accurate account of something the pupil said or did that throws light on some aspect of his development. Any necessary interpretation of the incident is rigidly separated from the account of what happened otherwise teachers tend to substitute their impression for the evidence. For samples of good anecdotes, consult the four Gospels. Anecdotes are difficult to obtain from teachers in the limited time at their disposal, but progress toward many important objectives can as yet be evaluated only in this way. Fortunately many schools are assisted by apprentice teachers, and the anecdotal record is an excellent teacher-training device for focusing attention upon individual needs and problems. Once the habit of writing anecdotes is acquired, it is not easily discarded because it has such a stimulating effect upon the teacher's awareness of his pupils as individuals.

7. *Records of Conferences.*

In a modern program of education individual conferences play such an important part, both in coming to understand the pupil and in directing his development, that some record should be kept of their important outcomes, conclusions, and unsolved problems. The form of this record should be extremely flexible to suit the nature of the conference, but if anything of importance was uncovered, the teacher should write it down as soon after the conference as possible. Experience indicates that what transpired in the conference cannot be remembered accurately over a long enough period of time to reveal change and growth. Conferences with parents are extremely important in this connection.

8. *Records of Excuses and Explanations.*

Some schools have the practice of requiring some form of excuse or explanation in writing for misconduct, incomplete or unsatisfactory work, tardiness, absence, or any other unfulfilled obligation. If such statements are consistently required, sympathetically handled, and properly interpreted by the teacher who secures them, they form an excellent record of the reaction of the student to his difficulties and enable many possible maladjustments to be nipped in the bud. The record of incomplete and unsatisfactory work, when put together from every area of school life, forms the most objective evidence we have of the development of good work habits in the academic setting.

9. *Records of Tests and Examinations.*

After every important test or examination, whether standardized or home-made, the teacher would do well to prepare a brief report covering the nature of the group which took the test, the nature of the test and how the group was prepared for it, the highest, lowest, and middle scores, and the national norms if they are available. This statement might be mimeographed and one copy put in the folder of each pupil who took the test. On these copies should be typed or written the pupil's score or standing in the test, what this meant, if anything, with relation to the objectives of the course, and some comment as to strengths and weaknesses shown, progress or decline, and possible reasons. Such statements should not take long to prepare, and they would be immediately valuable in counseling. Perhaps no other occasion in the normal processes of school life offers such rich opportunities for helpful counseling. If tests and examinations are worth giving, they are worth recording and interpreting in a form which will enable those responsible for the pupil's education to act intelligently upon them, and to draw sound conclusions from them.

10. *Health and Family History.*

This is the indispensable foundation of all school records; all other records must be interpreted in the light of the pupil's health and family background. It is usually based upon an annual or semi-annual physical examination with additional data secured at registration, in times of illness, in conference and correspondence with parents, and during health instruction and physical education periods. It usually includes various indices of physiological maturation, a record of illnesses and their effects, present physical condition, deformities, defects in eyesight, hearing and speech, glandular deficiencies, physical strength and vigor, health habits, attitudes and understandings, and as much as the school can discover of the home environment as related to mental and physical health. The record is kept by the school nurse or physical education department, but significant developments which have a bearing on the student's relationships in school should be reported at once to the counselor.

11. *Oral English Diagnoses.*

Since effectiveness in oral communication is one of the pupil's most valuable assets, many schools are at great pains to secure an accurate and comparable record of its development. In this connection it is helpful to have one or two teachers who are particularly sensitive to speech problems present at the annual or semi-annual registration conference. This is a fairly uniform, lifelike and important situation in which the pupil has to do a good deal of talking. Since the room is likely to be fairly busy, the presence of one or two extra teachers who seem to be absorbed in their records will not falsify the situation. These teachers have the records of the previous conference before them and take notes of progress and difficulties under such headings as pronunciation, enunciation, quality of voice, diction, usage, force, fluency, poise, handling of the situation, general effectiveness, etc. This record is used in subsequent work in speech without revealing the source of the information.

12. *Minutes of Student Affairs.*

Records kept by students of their handling of their own affairs are often highly illuminating with respect to the development of good citizenship. The students who had the ideas, who made their points, and who did the work stand out clearly, as do those who failed in their responsibilities. The inclusion in the record of the reports of committees is an especially fruitful source of evidence. Without violating the spirit of the student government, the counselors can gain much valuable insight into the development of their pupils by reading through these records, if they are well kept — and it is the business of the school to see that they are well kept.

13. *Personality Ratings and Descriptions.*

Personality ratings are in disfavor because the traits studied usually have no consistent meaning from one teacher to another, their ratings are notoriously unreliable, and they encourage thinking in terms of symptoms rather than in terms of the underlying causes of behavior. When other evidence of progress toward an important objective is unavailable, however, they may serve a useful purpose. Care should be taken that each trait is clearly defined in terms of behavior, and that each step on the scale is defined in terms of characteristic patterns of behavior. The situation in which the behavior was observed should also be recorded. A pupil may be thoroughly reliable on the playground and quite the reverse in the classroom.

14. *Questionnaires.*

Under this heading may be included all of the more formal personnel data secured from pupils. These may include personal inventories, family background, scales of interests and preferences, statements of opinion on significant leading questions, and the like. Their character is well known and needs no comment here. Such information should be read and interpreted by the counselor and filed in the pupil's folder.

15. *Records of Courses and Activities.*

These records have already been described. . . . They are mentioned here for the sake of completeness. Interim reports on progress in courses and activities, other than the records already mentioned, may be sent to the counselor from time to time when any new development requires his attention, or for purposes of guidance and reports to parents.

16. *The Administrative Record.*

All odds and ends of official records may be included under this heading: entrance data, correspondence, adjustments of program, assignments to sections, disciplinary action, acceleration or retardation, awards and honors, offices held, etc. This material may or may not be significant for the evaluation of progress toward objectives, but it is often important for the interpretation of other records, so a place should be made for it in the pupil's folder.

It is not suggested that any school attempt to install all these forms of records at once. They are only intended to present alternative possibilities among which schools may choose, and to illustrate the richness and variety of types of evidence which are available for the evaluation of even the more intangible outcomes of progressive education if schools are willing to develop, collect, and interpret them.

194. "SECURING INFORMATION AND STUDYING THE GROUP — A PREREQUISITE TO PLANNING INSTRUCTION" [5]

GUIDANCE IN PLANNING

Getting Acquainted — the Teacher and the Group. One of the first things that each teacher must do if she is really to help children plan worth-while experiences is to get acquainted with the group which she finds in her charge, learn as much as she can about each boy and girl — about their past experiences, their interests, their prejudices, their viewpoints. She needs to learn to see the class, not as a group alone, but as individuals working together (sometimes not working together) on enterprises of common and of individual interest. She needs to help children understand and solve some of the problems which are always caused when people are closely associated — working in the same room, using and sharing tools and books, sharing cloakrooms, lockers, and what not, drinking from the same drinking fountains, playing together in the same yard. She

[5] Los Angeles County, *Teachers' Guide Intermediate Unit, Courses of Study,* Los Angeles County Board of Education, 1931, pp. 34–37.

will be eternally faced with the challenging problem of helping little human beings get along one with the other, to give and take, to assume their part in undertakings and responsibilities, to use materials and time suitably and thriftily, to have consideration and respect for the other fellow, to learn to take care of and put away their belongings. Endless life adjustments! There will be everlasting problems of adjustment which the teacher will need to help the child make with growing effectiveness. The personal equation — the friendship of the teacher and the child — is of great importance in this daily-living together. The teacher's attitude toward the child must be one which will command his confidence and his respect if she is to exercise her function of helping him in his purposing, his planning, his executing if necessary, and in his evaluation of the work which he is doing.

Securing Data Relative to the Physical Abilities and Health Status of Members of the Group. Before attempting to solve any problem, we must first of all ascertain the nature of the problem which is to be solved. This is true in planning a health program for children, *or any other phase of an educational program, which must, of necessity, consider the physical abilities of the individual to be educated.* A teacher's problem, then, is to ascertain the physical status of the particular children in her group.

Every school keeps, or should keep, cumulative records pertaining to the children's welfare. If such records are complete, a teacher may be able to secure her information from them. If such records are not complete, a study or survey of the situation will be necessary. The nurse, or the health advisor, as we prefer to call her, and an examining physician, should help obtain this information and analyze it. Any survey which attempts to ascertain the physical status of children should endeavor to find out how many and which children have defective vision, defective hearing, cardiac difficulties, nervous disorders, apparent malnutrition, incipient tuberculosis, defective permanent teeth, abnormal tonsils, defective speech, and the like. Such a survey should be made by an examining physician and a nurse. The teacher and the parent of the child being examined should be present.

The teacher will have as much need of definite facts relative to the vision, the hearing, the cardiac difficulties, and so on, of each child in her room as she has of knowing the child's I. Q. or his achievement quotient. The information pertaining to the child's physical welfare, like any other data which may condition instruction, should be a part of the working possession of each teacher. She should study health records along with achievement records as a basis for planning instruction. Classroom work must be adapted to the physical abilities of the children in each class, and the procedure must be modified to meet specific problems at hand.

Securing Data Relative to the Race, Age, and Progress of Members of the Group. Most teachers will find that they have in their rooms pupils of widely differing abilities, interests, experiences, ages, and capacities. All of these factors condition instruction. We have discussed in the preceding paragraph the necessity of getting acquainted with members of the group. Aside from this important social situation, this getting acquainted, it is necessary for the teacher to secure certain significant data pertaining to the children in her group — more or less statistical in nature, but usable information, on the age status, the grade-progress status, the health status, the race status, and on the achievement and conduct of pupils as shown from records. These data should be secured and reduced to usable form for study and analysis. A chart, similar to the one on page 147 of *The Classroom Teacher*, by Strayer and Englehardt, will be decidedly helpful in giving you a graphic picture of your group, although the picture is incomplete. You will find this device more usable if the names of the children instead of numbers are used in the squares. Such graphic pictures of your room will reveal the necessity for further investigations to ascertain the causes of the distribution and the causes of known facts, and will give you a fair idea of the necessity for varied activities and of the types of experiences which may be most valuable to different small groups within your room. You will recall that one criterion in planning work is that " a unit of work must stimulate many kinds of activities and so provide for individual differences." It is imperative, though it should scarcely be necessary to mention it here, that each teacher, *before planning work for any group, should know what kind of group she is planning for, what she is supposed to accomplish, and the best means of doing those things which need to be done.*

A SUMMARY OF THE BASIC CURRICULA FOR CHILDREN IN THE FIRST, SECOND, AND THIRD GRADES

We are including for your convenience a summary of the basic experiences which boys and girls in the primary grades have had, the summary made from the basic curriculum for primary grades as found in the primary unit published in July, 1930. You will need to consider this in planning.

Health

Experiences conducive to building and maintaining good health habits, and a wholesome, joyous attitude toward play and the out-of-doors. Experiences in simple team work, in playing hunting games, in relay races, in stunts, in using playground apparatus, in rhythmical activities, and in playing various games.

Social Studies

Experiences involving the home and home life, and such people and agencies as directly contact the home and the child; people and agencies in the community. Experiences involving learning about the Plains Indian, the Pueblo Indian, the Eskimo, the Mexican, the Japanese.

Reading

Experiences in reading simple stories and books. Listening to poems and stories read by the teacher. Learning poems and rhymes in which they are particularly interested. Dramatizing. Experiences which will help them acquire reading skills.

Language

Experiences in informal discussions, in planning, in explaining, in evaluating, in narrating, in coöperative story-making, in dramatizing. Creating bits of prose or verse. Practically all of the work is oral.

Art

Experiences involving the expression of ideas in a simple way through various media: paper, cloth, clay, paint, wood, etc. Art and social-studies experiences are correlated.

Music

Experiences in singing happily and appreciatively many songs. Listening to much beautiful music. Experiences involving a rudimentary knowledge of music symbols.

Arithmetic

Incidental number experiences necessary to meet their own needs. Children in the third grade have experiences in learning to add and subtract accurately and quickly.

Writing

Learning to write clearly, legibly, and with reasonable speed the words for which they have particular use.

195. Factors Involved in Pupil Study [6]

PROBLEM I. THOROUGH INITIAL AND CUMULATIVE INVESTIGATION OF CHILDREN'S INDIVIDUAL NEEDS

" ' How old are you? ' inquired the visitor of his host's little son.

" ' That is a difficult question,' answered the young man, removing his spectacles and wiping them reflectively. ' The latest personal

[6] California, *Teachers' Guide to Child Development,* California State Department of Education, Sacramento, 1930, pp. 435–436.

survey shows my psychological age to be 12, my moral age 4, my anatomical age 7, and my physiological age 6. I suppose, however, that you refer to my chronological age. That is so old fashioned that I seldom think of it any more.' " *

This story amusingly suggests the difficulties which modern teachers and principals encounter when they begin to study in scientific fashion the children for whose development they are responsible.

Adequately to understand the needs of their pupils requires knowledge of all these factors (not listed with intention to indicate their order of importance):

1. Physical condition of child.
2. His chronological age.
3. His home environment.
4. His previous training.
5. Nationality and language difficulties of child.
6. Social attitudes and habits of child.
7. Work attitudes and habits.
8. His emotional development.
9. His characteristic interests.
10. His special abilities.
11. His mental age.
12. His intelligence quotient.

A careful consideration of *all* these factors is the only satisfactory basis for grouping children in relation to their individual needs. For this reason it is important that a study of the child be made from the very beginning of his first school year, and that the record of this study be supplemented during each year of his life in school with all the relevant facts which can be accumulated. Only by access to such complete records may teachers hope to form accurate judgments of children's needs.

196. COMMUNITY ANALYSIS [7]

H. Gordon Hullfish

Thus though the curriculum (and teaching method) will move off from the community that surrounds the school, it will do so only as this is an effective means of bringing the student through to the end desired. It is here that the concept of analysis in education may be of high value, not to set the objectives for the subject as has so often

---

* *Childhood Education*, V:268. January, 1929.

[7] From "Critical Considerations in Curriculum-Making," The National Council for the Social Studies, *The Social-Studies Curriculum*, Fourth Yearbook, McKinley Publishing Company, Philadelphia, 1934, pp. 28–30.

been assumed but to locate the points of contact with the thought and action of the community which will serve as means in shaping the educative process. The number and kinds of gainful employment available; the unemployment present, and its causes; the educational and recreational facilities; the agencies that prevent crime, or the forces that foster it; the safe-guards arranged to protect the health of the individual; the physical conditions of homes, and their control; and the like. In these ways the community may be surveyed in an effort to discover those points of study that will lead to a kind of understanding of, and participation in, community life which shows intelligence at work creating more wholesome and equable standards of living, and that will provide the opportunity for the organized materials of the social studies to lead to this understanding and guide the participation. In short, the subject matter with which we are prone to start will be placed in relationship to activities in which it is a necessary factor if those activities are to be carried on in educative terms. Incidentally, but quite significantly, the social studies may right at this point take the lead in building fruitful relationships of knowledge by having the teachers of other subject materials cooperate as the study of these problems goes forward. If, for instance, the physical condition of homes within the community is a matter of study, the contributions from science and art may well loom large. And so with other problems.

An analysis of this character, to be sure, is nothing more than a starting point in an approach to the curriculum. Equally important is an analysis that discovers the attitudes and preferences of those individuals whose total activities make up the community life. Again, it is important to scan the particular community in which each school is placed. Especially must this be a consideration of those who teach the social studies. The teacher needs to be aware of the conflicts in attitudes that are inevitable in the life of the student, and this may be achieved only as the attitudes of those agencies which play forcefully upon the student (the family, the church, the corner gang, the special groups to which he and his friends belong, the clubs in which the parents participate, the local press, etc.) are understood. From a purely protective point of view this is important information for the teacher. From an educational point of view, however, it is of higher value, making it possible to arrange activities, and to organize materials, that force an objective and thoughtful consideration of those conflicts that get established through the mere association with the customs of a group.

Naturally, the actual conditions of the situation immediately surrounding the school, together with the attitudes cherished by the members of the community, will but reflect the character of the larger social situation. Thus, this analysis, local in character, will have to be viewed in the light of those forces which, as we noted earlier, are pushing us in the present toward new social patterns. Educative experiences will then be selected, and arranged progressively, in order that orientation in the community will serve to illuminate the forces with which intelligence must reckon as it works in the present. The same principle of selection will serve as the fund of knowledge which the teacher of the social studies has available is brought into play. Here historical materials, the forms that set the duties and obligations of citizenship, the sociological records of man's attempt to organize to conserve particular values, the literature that shows man aspiring to values that are compatible, or incompatible, with our day and time, the materials that reveal the ways in which natural conditions and resources have influenced man's actions and motives — all of the organizations of knowledge that may be classified under the social studies will be meaningful as they are used appropriately to bring the student to ever higher levels of social understanding and appreciation.

197. SUGGESTED PROCEDURES FOR STUDYING ENVIRONMENT [8]

Fannie W. Dunn

INVENTORY OF AVAILABLE RESOURCES
WAKE COUNTY, N. C.

I. How assembled.

The Seventh Grade Teachers' Organization undertook to make such an inventory, and set up an Environment Investigation Committee to compile reports. Each seventh grade teacher undertook: (1) to send the chairman of the committee a list of all educational resources discovered in his or her community; (2) to plan and take one trip for the purpose of using environmental resources; (3) to report in detail how one resource was used; (4) to report all uses made during the year of available resources; and (5) to plan a list of interesting places for summer visiting.

II. Compilation of all lists of resources.

Occupational activities: dairy farm, game preserve, pet farm, animal farm; creamery, tobacco warehouse, cotton gin, sorghum making, canning clubs; cigarette factories, cotton mills, soap factory, saw mills and saw mill camps, power plant bakeries, chair factory; rock quarry; log trains, freight office, express office, ticket office, airport, trains, highways, county roads, broadcasting station; photographer, home and farm demonstration agent;

---

[8] From " The Environment as a Primary Source of Materials of Instruction," National Education Association, *Materials of Instruction,* Department of Supervisors and Directors of Instruction, Eighth Yearbook, Bureau of Publications, Teachers College, Columbia University, New York, 1935, pp. 32–33.

general, grocery, hardware, and dry goods stores, city market, curb market; gas stations, janitor, carpenter, house being built, school gymnasium being built, lunch room, cafeteria, hotel.

Institutions: church; state agricultural college, with its textile department, experimental farm, observatory, ceramics department and library; state laboratory of hygiene; dog and cat hospital; local Junior Red Cross; state historical association; state museum; library with children's and adults' departments; school for the blind; Soldiers' Home; Old Ladies Home; state capitol; county courthouse with offices of board of education, auditor, sheriff, clerk and register of deeds; state weather bureau, local post office; state naval office, state highway department; highway patrol; banks.

Recreational opportunities: state and community fairs; theaters, log cabin theater at Ebenezer School; Folk Players; flower shows in fall and spring; dogwood festival; library facilities; picnic places on local lakes; interesting gardens; community music night; fiddlers' convention; community play night; local bands, local fiddlers; music stores; local swimming pools; nature trails; zoo; amateur photography.

Historical resources: Indian relics found in community, folklore society; Miss ——'s collection of colonial pitchers; Mrs. ——'s quilt exhibit; Mr. ——'s old guns; Mr. ——'s old money; historical names in the community; names of streets in nearby city; antique shop; replica of Mount Vernon; colonial costumes in one of the schools; location of old stage road; historical homes — W. H. Page, Andrew Johnson.

The cultural heritage: collection of folk tales at Duke University; Dr. Odum's collection of Negro work songs; Mr. ——'s collection of folk tunes; Christ Church as an example of fine architecture; other resources already listed under other categories.

Individuals of community: Mrs. W. —— has photographs of state, which she will lend; Mr. —— is a good P.T.A. speaker; Dr. —— is a connoisseur of books; Mr. —— knows pottery; Miss —— has lived in China; Dr. —— knows rocks; Mrs. —— has visited in Holland; etc.

198. Procedures Employed in Developing a New Type Instructional Program [9]

Roberta LaBrant Green *

During the last five or ten years, accounts of progressive practices in private and public schools have become increasingly common.

[9] From " Developing a Modern Curriculum in a Small Town," *Progressive Education*, 13:189–193, March, 1936.

* Mrs. Green's article deals with two definite movements in the high school at Holton, Kansas, in which she teaches. The first is the gradual break with the conventional curriculum. The second is the attempt of the school to gain the support and coöperation of the community without which " any school program becomes temporary and unstable, collapsing with slight changes in school staff." That these efforts were successful is attested by at least one unusual sequel — an invitation to the students to work on the local housing program.

For the most part, however, these accounts seem to come from institutions which have special privileges in the matter of equipment, numbers and training of teaching staff, freedom from customary dictation of state departments of education or, in some cases, selection of students. Because of these facts, it may be that an account of the introduction of a progressive program into a small conventional school, including all the students in the community, where no additional equipment or especially trained teachers have been available, may be of interest. It may to a degree answer the questions so often raised following discussions of progressive practices in experimental or demonstration schools: How can such things be done where there are no extra funds? Where can teachers be found who are able to do such teaching? How can the ordinary school, especially in a small community, find materials? How can such teaching be done in spite of required texts and state courses of study? And last, but certainly important, what will school patrons say of such a departure from tradition and precedent?

This report concerns the six-year high school in Holton, Kansas, a county-seat town of three thousand population. Holton is located ninety miles west of Kansas City in what has been one of the richest agricultural sections of the state, but in what was one of the driest of all the drought areas of Kansas during the three years ending March 1, 1935. It is a town in which all of the four banks failed or were forced to close during the first four depression years. A large, well-equipped building, built and bonded for $139,000 in 1929–30, did provide better than average housing, but caused a heavy financial load when property valuations suddenly dropped, taxes on the new valuations became nearly thirty per cent delinquent, and twenty-five per cent of the county population became dependent upon relief. If the cultural background of the town in which, until fifteen years before, there had thrived a small denominational college, was of better-than-average quality, this was balanced by a belief in tradition and the eternal rightness of formal teaching of Latin and the classics. So it can be seen that when the present program began to be formulated in September, 1932, there was little about the situation which was unusually propitious.

Because the change in program began in the English department, an attempt will be made to trace those changes first, and then discuss various new practices which developed in other departments.

During the first year, under a new head of the English department, the previous formal plan of teaching composition and literature was replaced by more personal, functional work. Literature classes became laboratories for broadening the reading interests of students, for forming improved reading habits, and for learning to evaluate and select reading materials. Composition, including speaking, writing, listening, and thinking, was also put upon a more personal basis, first requirements being those ideas which the student wished to express. Correct forms and structures were discussed only when need for improvement arose in the pupil's speech and writing. By the end of the first year, it was decided to replace some of the textbooks by library materials. Students were to pay a semester fee of fifty cents. The first purchase from this fund was to be a set of state texts. Thereafter the money was to be used to add to library equipment. This plan was proposed to students, who almost unanimously favored it. They in turn explained the proposal to their parents in writing, each student making his explanation in terms of his understanding of his own parents. Response from parents was almost identical with that of students when they fully understood the reasons for the change. . . .

As a basis for the work in composition in the seventh and eighth grades, the staff proposed to set up a simple social studies program closely related to the lives of the students. When school opened in the fall, a joint meeting of the two grades was held. The pupils were told that they might choose between studying English composition from a text in the customary way, or basing their composition upon a study of their homes and home community. Free discussion followed concerning possible ways in which this could be done, and the advantages of one plan over the other. The vote, when taken, was unanimously in favor of the newer plan. Little explanation was made to parents at the time and little was said about the change, for it was felt that the new plan, if sound, would eventually speak for itself better than theorizing at the beginning would do.

The first question to confront the hundred students then was: How can we best begin a study of our homes? Let it be clear at this point that the composition class was not to take the place of the social science class, so the special requirements of that department did not need to be met. Any sound study of the children's environment which would call for a wide variety of composition experiences was held acceptable. Moreover, the benefits to be derived from students' planning and directing their own study seemed of great importance. Accordingly, considerable time was given to hearing suggestions and discussions as to how the work should begin. It was finally agreed that the students should begin with their own homes because that was what they, supposedly, were most interested in; and that the first step should be making a list of all the materials that went into their houses. Homes were examined from cellar to attic, and there resulted great jumbled lists of materials ranging from India rubber to chromium, from lacquer to fish ponds. It was easy for students to see that order must be brought about from this chaos. Perusal of any list showed that certain materials fell naturally under the same classification: brick, cement, plaster, marble; tin, copper, chromium; cedar, plaster board, pine; trees, shrubs, grass, bulbs, etc. So came the idea of classifying for convenience of study, not for the sake of making outlines. Six groupings emerged: landscaping and grounds; woods and wood substitutes; metals; finishes; lighting and plumbing; and materials of masonry. Lighting and plumbing, the students decided, would be a bit too complicated for anyone but a science teacher to direct, so that list was laid aside. Because of the relationship between woods and finishes, those two groups were combined, leaving but four.

Each pupil was then invited to choose the group of materials he preferred to study. A few who had no preference were arbitrarily assigned in order to make a fairly even division. The home economics teacher, with the physical science background, was given metals; landscaping and grounds went by choice to the physical education teacher, who had training in biological science; the superintendent chose to direct work with woods and finishes; and the masonry group went to the English teacher.

The work in all four sections followed much the same plan so far as making use of materials at hand in the community, individual and group work bearing on the general project, individual and group reports, interviews, and securing materials through advertisements was concerned. However, each class worked out its own plan of procedure. Teachers kept a close check upon the kinds of English composition activities which resulted. As composition needs became evident, special teaching was done. In all the groups the following types of composition work were found to be needed and were accordingly taught, but always with reference to the problem at hand and with recognition by the students that here was something which they needed to know in order to carry on the particular study:

1. Using library and reference materials, including the keeping of bibliographies and the taking of notes on materials read.
2. Learning by listening to reports by members of the class and by adults.
3. Personal interviews.
4. Letter writing.
5. Organization of materials, including formal outlining where needed.
6. Informal discussion.
7. Manuscript forms.
8. Formal oral and written reports. This included such specific items as use of personal pronouns, function of verbs as related to sentence sense, correct forms of common irregular verbs, end stops, simple capitalization practices, spelling of words used in writing, and pronunciation and enunciation.

In order to show how local materials were used and how wide a variety of actual experiences ensued, the following account of what transpired within the group studying masonry is here presented. This is used merely as exemplifying the types of work carried on in all four groups.

When the masonry group assembled as a unit, the first thing for consideration was how to begin their study. As they had no text with which to explain the year's work, they agreed that each person should keep a written report of all his work, including accounts of individual as well as of group work. After some little discussion, it was generally agreed that because brick and cement were the most used masonry materials, study should begin with them. First came an examination of all library materials, including magazines as well as books. This included such things as an account of the Egyptian sun-dried brick made from sediment along the Nile, the Biblical account of the making of brick by the Israelites, the art of tile-making as developed by the Dutch, and present-day brick manufacture. Students also turned to local contractors and to old residents of the town, with such questions as why the town had so many poor and old brick walks; the different kinds of brick commonly used, their special uses and values, and relative costs; and what were the advantages of solid and veneer walls. All these topics, of course, presented occasions for oral and written reports as well as for interviews and class discussion.

A similar procedure was followed in studying cement, although something of the chemistry of cement was investigated as well as the Kansas industry of cement-making.

199. PROCEDURES FOR PUPIL ORIENTATION AND SETTING THE STAGE [10]

I. PERIOD OF ORIENTATION

If the curriculum is to make use of child activity and child experience, if it is to be constantly enriched by the group, a period of orientation must be provided. Understanding between teacher and pupils must be secured. And it takes time to find out what any particular group of pupils is like. It takes even more time for pupils to find out what a particular situation is like. This period of orientation, of the sensing and stating of problems which have a common interest for the group, must not be hurried. Pupils will tell about what they have done in the vacation time, about trips, about things they have seen, and about their association with other people in group work. They will recall some of the outstanding work of

[10] From *Curriculum Making in an Elementary School,* Lincoln Elementary School Staff, Ginn and Company, Boston, 1927, pp. 45–50.

preceding years. The teacher sometimes learns in this period of orientation what the pupils are yearning for or are playing or working at outside of school, and thus helps them carry it over into school and make it a more fruitful and satisfying piece of work. If the teacher enters into this and gives from her experience, the work of the new year begins to emerge.

II. SETTING THE STAGE

The teacher probably has known all along that she would like a particular kind of work done. But she wishes the pupil to feel his own worth and his own problems in any undertaking. So she has set the stage to call for the statement of the problems as she wishes her class to feel them. This means, of course, systematic planning but equally systematic willingness to wait until pupils can take over the plan or can present one which has equal value.

The setting of the stage may take place before the beginning of school through placing books, wood, boxes, paper, paints, animals, or other materials in the classroom. Pupils explore the material. They begin their own pieces of work. They draw others into them. The teacher may, however, have to modify or perhaps completely discard her prearranged plan and make an entirely new approach, better adapted to the special needs and interests of the group. One teacher had planned to approach beginning reading through the use of children's summer experiences on the farm and at the seashore. Two bulletins had been prepared with these headings: " Fun in the Country " and " Fun at the Seashore." Pictures and questions about gardens, chickens, cows, haying, swimming, digging in the sand, and boating were placed under the appropriate headings to stimulate the children to tell stories of their summer fun.

One group was to tell their summer stories while the other explored and looked at books. When it was gathered together, however, not a child seemed eager to share his experiences with the others. Those who were looking at books soon grew restless and, one by one, began to go back to their work of making boats, trucks, and wagons, painting pictures, and playing with farm animals and blocks. Those who were telling stories were eager to join the other pupils in their activities and were allowed to do so. The teacher saw that her group of children was much interested in the present and not in the past, in manipulative and play activities and not in oral expression. The work she had done in making her set-up for stories had gone for nothing, but she began anew and made other bulletins. The reading that she had in mind came not from the summer stories but from bulletins about what the children were making and playing.

Was the teacher wise to make a change? The interest in reading and oral expression which later resulted showed that she accomplished her purpose more effectively. The teacher was just as well satisfied, for her aim had been to stimulate interest in reading through the use of real experiences.

If the class, however, shows at once what it wishes to do, that is the place to begin, and the teacher's task for the time being is only to direct it so that it is growing.

But suppose that the group does not have well-defined notions or any notions. Suppose it has done only what some teacher or parent has said must be done, that it is accustomed to wait to be told; then the method to be followed in starting the work is to be found in one of these suggestions.

1. The pupils with the teacher make a survey of what they have to do during the year. They note the daily programs and the school set-up. What can be done about it? They talk over the work of previous years; they make suggestions as to things they would like to have or would like to do. Perhaps a little planning arises in connection with the rearrangement of the daily program or in connection with the smooth running of the school and the part which this particular group can take in it. This is the method of approach which will have to be made if the daily program is set in advance. When a first effort is being made in a school to make more use of pupil initiative and responsibility, this preliminary discussion of the school program and general method of work may supply the entering wedge. The skillful teacher begins here to show the pupils that she values their suggestions highly.

2. Leads for the center of interest may develop out of the experiences of the pupils during the summer. Pupils bring in their summer exhibits. They sit together and discuss what each individual has done, and through that others may get an inspiration. The farm unit in the first grade had its beginning in that way. A study of blue prints and one of fossils started from summer exhibits.

3. It is generally possible for the teacher to set the stage so that a particular unit of work is sure to arise. The list of available units for each grade should be large so that individual differences in teachers and children may show themselves. The teacher must wait until the pupils have time to adjust their ideas and their plans to any piece of work. Time is not wasted if plans are being made, considered, rejected, or accepted. This time of consultation, of trial, of apparently no headway, is often the most valuable part of the whole year's work, for then the pupil begins to understand the teacher and the group, then he begins to lose himself in finding something to do; he begins to see that his ideas are valuable, and that a premium is

put upon thinking. The teacher should not be drifting during this time. She should be watching for usable leads into the particular units or projects which she wants to have the class undertake. She will know whether the leads are usable from her knowledge of children, from her understanding of the demands of education, and from criteria which have been set up for the selection of units. Only if that is true may she set the stage for the development of particular units. The teacher then can set the stage, may do so, but she must not control all the thinking of the child or all the doing of the child.

How to set the stage for any particular unit of work will be determined by its content. It is self-evident that a unit centered around banks will be very different from one centered around milk or the farm. Each will require its own material, its own specialized room equipment, its own peculiar set-up for trips, exhibits, and organization of the class.

4. Still another method of setting the stage is for the pupils, with the teacher, to make a complete survey of the available school equipment. Library, books on shelves, tools, shops, opportunities for work of various sorts, playgrounds, wood, clay, paper — indeed, any of the equipment which the school may have — will be examined and talked about. Its use will be explained and suggestions will be made about it by the teacher and by the members of the class. The best method to use in this exploring of the equipment will be to let the pupils work with it. Put a supply of wood, tools, clay, paper, paints — anything which is available — in the classroom and let the children go to work. They may at first make useless things. But something of value will begin to take form: a house, a boat, an engine, a toy, a bookcase — the list is interminable if the material is of sufficient variety. From some one of these the teacher or the group takes a special lead. Comments on the piece of work, its workmanship, its possibilities, its value as something for them to consider as a part of their own project, will be secured from the pupils. Time must be taken for this. And the teacher must not be the only one to make suggestions. Whatever the pupils say may become bases for further plans. Out of the equipment and its use may arise the center of interest, or unit of work, with all its growing details.

200. THE QUESTION AS A TEACHING PROCEDURE [11]

Frank W. Thomas

In the traditional form of the recitation, consisting almost exclusively of question and answer, the teacher's success in directing it

[11] From *Principles and Technique of Teaching*, Houghton Mifflin Company, Boston, 1927, pp. 272–274.

depended upon his skill in questioning. As the recitation gradually evolved toward a less formal type, the means by which the teacher guided the discussion assumed more varied forms, but the term "questioning" was still kept to cover them all. Consequently, it has not been unusual for books on methods of teaching to give elaborate classifications of the kinds of "questions," good and bad, with discussions of the relative merits of thought-questions, topic-questions, fact-questions, alternative questions, drill-questions, direct questions, leading questions, and similar variations. Since the tendency of the unskillful teacher is to ask too many questions, and to be more concerned with his own questions and the answers desired than with the real mental processes of the pupils, it is doubtful if the detailed treatment mentioned above has much corrective value. A certain amount of questioning is necessary in any recitation. If the questions used serve effectively to reveal, both to the teacher and to the pupil, the adequacy of the latter's knowledge for planning and carrying out some investigation or other undertaking, or if they successfully direct his mental efforts into profitable lines and keep them there until the pupil arrives at some goal with an unimpaired sense of personal achievement, the questions are probably good, regardless of their designated place in the classification. If, on the other hand, the questions of the teacher dominate the recitation, if they interrupt or confuse the pupils' thought, or if they allow the pupil to shirk responsibility for constructive effort and give fragmentary bits of the information which the teacher seems to have in mind, the questions are certainly poor.

The tendency of most teachers to use too many questions is one of the common faults against which a warning should be given. Stenographic studies of actual recitations, such as those made by Stevens, prove that the majority of teachers fire questions at their pupils with such frequency as to preclude thoughtful consideration of a topic. The result is a series of monosyllabic replies, with the teacher doing, as Stevens proved, 64 per cent of all the talking, and the pupils playing only a defensive rôle in the proceedings. Other practices which are regularly to be avoided are those of asking vague questions, repeating questions, and repeating answers. The first of these usually reveals a lack of definite thinking on the teacher's own part. For example, a question such as "What about the Monroe Doctrine?" is a characteristic example, and merely means a hint to the pupil to repeat any fragments he may recall from his reading of that topic. A realization of the mental state from which such questions spring should require no further arguments to condemn the practice. Repetition of either questions or answers is a time-wasting performance which encourages carelessness and inattention among the pupils.

The writer made it a practice for a time to interview young teachers who showed these faults, in an effort to discover their line of thinking during that part of the recitation. Most of them admitted that they were intent on getting from the pupils certain answers which they had in mind, rather than on trying to discover and redirect the pupils' thought. Their attempts to improve their own recitation purposes brought a marked decrease in their former faults. A systematic experimental study in regard to the causes of all such faults in questioning might prove extremely valuable.

Good teachers do not rely on questioning alone in directing class discussion. Sometimes a brief suggestion or direction, now volunteering some pertinent information, now calling attention to facts which have been overlooked, occasionally a few words of criticism or appreciation — all these are effective means of equal value with questioning in furnishing effective guidance in the recitation.

201. " A Supervisor's Check List of Criteria of a Skilfully Conducted Class Period " [12]

Francis D. Curtis

It is platitudinous to state that the old-fashioned " recitation " is no longer considered good classroom practice. Progressive teachers and supervisors have long recognized the futility of the procedure by which the teacher assigns " the next five pages," then spends the following class period in quizzing the pupils to find the extent to which they have " covered " the materials assigned. Yet this practice is probably followed in an overwhelming majority of classrooms. Many teachers employ it because they have been " brought up on it," because it is the easiest way to teach, or because they have no specific training in any other ways of conducting class work.

In schools too small to provide a corps of supervisors for the various subject-matter fields, the task of supervision inevitably falls to the principal or the superintendent. However well trained for his position he may be, he cannot be expected to have had specific training in all of the courses included in the program of studies of his school. Yet if he is to fulfill his major function, namely, to improve the quality of instruction throughout his school, he must be able to offer constructive criticisms in all the classes he observes, whether or not he is specifically trained in the fields they represent.

Needless to say, there is no one " best way " to teach. The more gifted and ambitious the teacher, the wider is the variety of ingenious and effective devices and techniques that he employs. A complete

[12] Educational Administration and Supervision, 20:578–582, November, 1934.

catalog and description of these devices and techniques if obtainable would fill volumes. The general supervisor would doubtless find such a catalog bewildering if not relatively useless. There are, however, certain criteria of a well-conducted class period, of which at least some should probably characterize every such period which is devoted wholly or in part to socialized activities.

1. *Does the Period Begin with Adequate Orientation of the Day's Work with That of Preceding Periods?* — Does the teacher take pains to insure an understanding of the relation of today's tasks to the preceding work? Such orientation may be effected by beginning the period with brief class discussions of such questions as these: " Who will state several important principles or ideas which we developed in class yesterday? " " What portion of yesterday's work do you consider most interesting or important and why? " " Our work today deals with ————. In what previous discussions was this topic mentioned? What topics which we have previously discussed seem to you related to this one? " A number of pupils should contribute answers which the teacher or the pupils should then summarize.

2. *Is There Evidence as the Work Proceeds, That the Teacher Has Carefully Planned the Activities?* — By careful planning is not meant here the preparation of a highly formalized and voluminous written lesson plan of the type which unfortunately has been sanctioned and stressed in some courses in education and in some of the pedagogical literature. There are, however, certain unmistakable " hallmarks " of a carefully planned class period which should be evident to even an inexpert observer:

(a) *Are All Materials Which the Teacher or the Pupils Need to Use during the Period Ready at Hand?* — By leaving the classroom in search of an outline, a book, or a missing piece of apparatus, or by encountering any avoidable obstacle in the work, the teacher is confessing to insufficient forethought for the activities to be carried on.

(b) *Does the Teacher Progress from Activity to Activity with Assurance?* — Hesitancy or uncertainty of teacher activity or of class direction betrays inadequate teacher preparation.

(c) *Are the Activities Carried Through with Due Economy of Time?* — Careful planning of the period prevents unprofitable wandering from the subject and insures arriving at a desired goal by the end of the class hour.

3. *Do Interest and Attention Remain High Throughout the Class Hour?* — These factors are more often manifested by the postures of the pupils, the nature and direction of their gaze, and the nature of the responses to questions and problem situations than by the wild waving of hands or the blurting out of answers. It is true, of course, as every veteran teacher knows, that some pupils become adept at

simulating interest and attention when their thoughts are remote from classroom activities. Nevertheless the teacher who has acquired the habit of " watching the fringes " of the class, or who has " cultivated the roving eye," is alert to detect and to revive flagging interest and attention.

4. *Is the Nature of the Activity Changed with Sufficient Frequency?* — Much otherwise effective classroom technique becomes monotonous and unprofitable if too long continued. The skilful teacher usually makes two or three major changes of activity during a class period. Illustrations of major changes of activities are shifting from teacher demonstration or explanation to pupil writing of a report or a theme; from a period of directed study to one of general class discussion; from a search by the pupil for supplementary materials to a pooling of this material in groups or committees; and the like. The skilful teacher makes minor changes of activity every few minutes during the hour. Appropriate minor changes include shifting from one technique of directed study to another; from one type of question to another; from one type of manipulation to another; and the like. Sometimes, however, pupil interest is maintained at a high level for most of the period without the necessity for a conscious attempt on the part of the teacher to change the activities frequently — for example, during the progress of a major activity such as individual pupil experimentation; the reading of an interesting supplementary book; the display of projects; or the like. In such cases the nature of the major activity is such as to provide an abundant variety of minor activities.

5. *Is There Much Problem Setting through Skilful Questioning?* Skilful questioning is fundamental to skilful teaching. Indeed, it is probably true that the pupil achieves little real learning unless he uses in the solution of various thought questions or problems the facts he has memorized. The art of making good thought questions is one which any teacher should be able to master; yet there is evidence which indicates that an overwhelming majority of teachers confine their questions chiefly to the types that involve only observation or merely the recall of memorized materials. Cunningham * lists twenty-two types of questions; Monroe and Carter † list twelve

---

* Cunningham, Harry A.: " Types of Thought Questions in General Science Textbooks and Laboratory Manuals." *General Science Quarterly*, Vol. IX, January, 1925, pp. 91–95; also, Curtis, Francis D.: *Second Digests of Investigations in the Teaching of Science.* Philadelphia: P. Blakiston's Son and Company, Inc., 1931, pp. 84–86.

† Monroe and Carter: " The Use of Different Types of Thought Questions in Secondary Schools and Their Relative Difficulty for Students." Bureau of Educational Research, *Bulletin* No. 14, University of Illinois Bulletin, Vol. XX, No. 34, 1933, pp. 6–7; also Burton, William H.: *Nature and Direction of Learning.* New York: D. Appleton and Company, 1929, pp. 472–474.

types of thought questions. These valuable lists are by no means exhaustive; there are probably at least forty types of questions appropriate for class use. Few teachers will probably use all of these types, but it is not unreasonable to expect a classroom teacher to make habitual use of at least ten different types of thought questions.

The art of skilful questioning involves not only the use of a variety of types of questions but also the ability to state the question at the first trial in exactly the wording desired. The teacher who habitually restates his questions not only advertises a lack of precision in his attack but also inevitably causes confusion in the minds of the pupils.

6. *Does Every Pupil Take Part in the Thinking and Contribute to the Group Discussions?* — To attain this goal, the teacher must not only vary the attack frequently but must also provide questions and problems of appropriate difficulty to challenge individual interests and abilities. One practically unfailing means of getting everybody to participate is to require all the pupils to write an answer to a question or to write a summary of a discussion. If during such an exercise the teacher patrols the class, directing, helping, and encouraging, he can insure a high percentage of participation.

7. *If the Teacher Demonstrates an Experiment, Is This Demonstration Performed Skilfully?* — This criterion would apply chiefly to class periods in science, industrial arts, and perhaps mathematics. A demonstration has little justification unless it is skilfully performed. Skill in demonstrating is usually manifested in

(*a*) The teacher's indicating unmistakably at the start exactly what the problem is which the demonstration is designed to solve. This purpose is most certainly achieved by stating the problem as a direct question.

(*b*) The way in which the actual manipulation of apparatus is carried on. Is this manipulation deft and assured? Is it performed without needless motions and with economy of time? Does it proceed directly to a clearcut solution of the problem?

(*c*) The ability of the pupils, when the demonstration has been completed, to formulate a direct answer to the problem.

8. *Does the Teacher Show Skill in Capitalizing Such Spontaneous Interests as May Arise during the Period?* — Such interests may offer opportunities for motivation which the planned materials of the period may not provide to anything approximating an equal degree. On the other hand there is a danger that the pursuit of spontaneous interests may lead into seductive bypaths along which the class may wander interminably and unprofitably. Therefore, spontaneous interests offer valuable auxiliary opportunities for teaching; but they

do not in themselves provide a desirable substitute for carefully planned, sequential activities.

9. *Does the Teacher Indicate the Principles or Other Learning Goals Which Are of Greatest Importance?* — The teacher may find his background of subject-matter and experience a handicap in sensing the difficulty which the pupil who lacks this background of knowledge and experience may have in recognizing the high points of the class discussions. He must therefore be careful to focus attention upon these high points as they emerge during the discussion, in order to insure that the pupils may obtain a clearcut distinction between a desired outcome and its developmental materials.

10. *Is There an Adequate Number of Summaries during the Period?* — Following a class discussion it is appropriate for the teacher to halt the progress long enough to enumerate and organize the important points. Sometimes the pupils are able to make acceptable summaries of such materials; but probably it will prove more profitable for the teacher to summarize first and then to allow the pupils to recapitulate the summary; or to add to a teacher's partial summary, which the pupil restates, such additional points as the pupil thinks important. Or perhaps the teacher may first encourage the pupils to summarize the discussion, and from the various pupil contributions he may make a final summary which he then asks the pupils to recapitulate orally, or to write in their notebooks or on the margins of their textbooks.

11. *Is There Adequate Drill upon Essentials?* — Sometimes this drill may consist appropriately of mere recall of factual material; but probably more frequently it should consist of requiring the pupils to use previous material in new problem situations.

CHAPTER XIII

EVALUATING THE OUTCOMES OF INSTRUCTION

202. Evaluation in 1826 [1]

Elizabeth . . . hath been engaged, during her attendance at this school, in storing her memory, that strong and capacious storehouse of mankind, with useful ideas, lessons and information generally.

Pursuant to this end, she hath deposited in her memory for future use the multiplication and other arithmetical tables.

She hath repeated the principal divisions, oceans, islands, etc., and answered 109 questions on the map of the world.

She hath recited the principal divisions, lakes, rivers, bays, gulfs, etc., and answered 41 questions on the map of North America.

She hath defined the boundaries of 12 of the United States and repeated 95 of the chief towns and 33 of the principal rivers belonging to these 12 states and answered 86 questions corresponding to the geography of that fine country.

On the map of South America, she hath committed to memory the different countries belonging to that great peninsula and repeated 58 chief towns and 33 of the principal rivers and answered 39 questions corresponding with its geography.

Let no one say, hereafter, that females cannot learn, for that is an assertion without foundation. Elizabeth is a living proof to the contrary and she merits the approbation and encouragement of her parents and friends.

203. The Historical and Present Limitations of Measurement [2]

Orlie M. Clem

The history of the measurement movement indicates that it should not make too extravagant claims. Accepting the S-R system and the intelligence test, measurement early emphasized original nature.

[1] " Certificate Issued in 1826," *Progressive Education*, 13:26, January, 1936.
[2] From " Dare Professional Education Be Sensible and Attempt to Evaluate the Contributions of Measurement to the Public School Situation? " National Education Association, *Reconstructing Education Thru Research*, American Educational Research Association, Official Report, Washington, D. C., May, 1936, pp. 197–201.

Later, it gave more consideration to the claims of nurture. At first, measurement deified norms and standards; now, it is recognized that medians and sigmas are often delusions and snares. It is what happens to each individual child that is important. Similarly, measurement exalted the normal curve in marking; but today revolt against the dictatorship of the curve is marked. Paradoxical as it may seem, measurers have emphasized the unreliability of teachers' marks, and yet marks have constituted the most common criterion for determining the validity of all types of tests: intelligence, achievement, and personality. Measurement early claimed that intelligence test measured innate intelligence exclusively, but abandoned this position. It is now generally agreed that tests measure what they measure. Measurement hailed the achievement test as an instrument for universal comparison of schools. Today the rigid comparison of school systems and teachers on any basis except the minimum essentials of learning is recognized as a possible menace. With considerable assurance, measurement sought a quantitative determination of character, but now makes far less extravagant claims. Measurement reported that new type informal examinations measured achievement just as well or better than conventional essay examinations. Some curious psychological workers on the clean-up squad are now asking, What kind of achievement? Measurement demonstrated that pupils achieved as much or more in large classes as in small. Little experimentation was reported in which a different technic was used with the two types of class, nor was there any measure of personality or attitudinal outcomes.

Measurement in the curriculum field has been the father of " scientific analysis." Such a point of view holds that the test of all curriculum materials is need. Many accept this theory for minimum essentials of elementary-school subjects, but consider it inadequate above this level. Bode has remarked, " No one can prove scientifically that anyone ever needs anything." A deep-seated conviction prevails generally that scientific analysis reveals merely what is, not what ought to be, with the inference that whatever is, is right. Hence, it appears inconsistent with a broad, social philosophy which should be concerned with the remaking of standards. Advocates of a broad, liberal culture in education recognize in scientific analysis too much emphasis on vocation and too little on " sweetness and light." They reject emphasis on education for efficiency conducted on such a cash register basis as scientific analysis. Critical thinkers who interpret the purpose of education as growth, the reorganization and reconstruction of experience, find the scientific analysis theory inadequate.

Scientific analysis has given to teacher training the well-known

Commonwealth Study. The plan proposed by this study is too simple; it assumes that the whole is equal to the sum of all its parts; that the knowledge of one thousand and one duties represents a teacher. It reduces a teacher to the role of a semiskilled mechanic turning out rather mechanical products. It disregards a dynamic theory of teacher preparation. It makes little provision for what Bagley has called "emergent idealism." Such a conception of teacher preparation is piecemeal and inadequate.

Professional education would render a distinct service if it should admit the historical and present limitations of measurement. Measurement should admit, first of all, the fragmentary nature of its past achievements. Rugg said in 1929, "Less than one-twentieth of our recent research products are truly experimental studies." If Rugg's statement were checked it would reveal that many studies do not control a single variable, or involve equivalent groups, or determine the significance of the difference. Other studies would involve questionnaires in which the ignorance of one thousand persons is no better than that of one; many would be incapable of verification; few of practical value. Experiments on nonsense syllables, maze learning, ball tossing, and target shooting appear fragmentary to the practitioner. He has a growing conviction that measurement has not come to grips with real educational problems. The scientific worker is familiar with the fragmentary character of experimentation on such problems as the whole-part method of learning. Yet frequently sweeping generalizations are made from fragmentary research or from a study of an infinitesimal part of a general problem. For example, an experimenter concludes that method X is superior to method Y. He fails to specify "superior in the thing measured by Z." Measurement should frankly admit of innumerable experiments: "This study ought never to have been made; having been made, it ought never to have been accepted; having been accepted, it should never have been published." The fragmentary character of educational research has been stated by Courtis: "We have no science worthy of the name and no prospect of developing one so long as we refuse to face the inadequacy of our present results and the nonscientific character of our many generalizations."

Measurement should admit its apparent lack of direction. It utilizes interminable mechanisms, technics, analyses, computations, tabulations. It has engaged in excessive adventuring; has produced more facts and used less than any other profession. By fragmentary and invalid procedures some enthusiasts have attempted to prove and disprove almost anything and everything. It is fitting to ask, What is all this worth? Waddell says, "As yet the scientific measurement specialists have contributed almost nothing in the way of tests or measures of the more significant and real elements of true education." Briggs says: " By reference to our shelves groaning with published technical studies, we can find the number of identical twins born of Caucasian parents with I. Q.'s between 100 and 123 who fail to pass second-year Latin in the ninth grade of the junior high schools of Arkansas with the A. D., P. E., and sigma, all neatly tabulated and charted. But what of it? What do we do with it? " Matthew Arnold, in his essay on *Literature and Science* set forth the proposition that in evaluating elements of education, the question should be asked, " What does this element have to contribute to the sense in us for conduct and to the sense in us for beauty? " Does society not have the right to ask some such question of measurement? No one could deny that the individual experimenter has the right to an ascetic juggling of quartiles, percentiles, P. E.'s, ogives, sigmas, and regressions. Like unto the ancient sophists or medieval scholastics, he may gain real satisfaction from endless computations of the P. E. of the P. E. But when millions of dollars of hard money and millions of human hours are spent, society has the right to inquire, What does this proposition have to contribute to the integration of human values, to the release of human energy in conduct, or to some recognized social ideal? Measurement without the guidance of a social philosophy is barren.

Measurement should admit that its most worthy achievements have been concerned with the formal aspects of education. Also, the major part of this work has been on the elementary-school level. Difficulty of number combinations in arithmetic, mechanics of reading, frequency of word use in spelling, errors in language; these are representative of the narrow types of research in which reasonable success has been attained. Recognizing the limitation of research to the formal aspects of learning, Washburne has said, " Provision for individual differences in the mastery of knowledge and skills; means of socializing children; the full use of the children's natural interests; the discovery and cultivation of children's specialized interests and abilities; the integration of their social and individual life; these are the problems demanding research rather than an exclusive concentration on the relative effectiveness of borrowing or equal additions on subtraction and such like separate elements."

Measurement should beware deadening uniformity which may result from standardization and mechanization by quantitative research methods. There are some schools in America manned not by teachers but by interns, " efficiency experts," with card index types of mind. To them experimentation implies a cold, impersonal treatment of any and all methods by a skeptical scientist. Meticulous measurements and records are the fruits by which they are known.

The classrooms and corridors of these schools bristle with charts and graphs, tables of percents, diagrams of all sorts, all types of data showing the whichness of the what. There are in filing cases questionnaires and tests of every known type containing measurements of everything and everybody on the place, measurable and immeasurable, temporal and spiritual. Teachers in these schools are objectively measured, and it is axiomatic that they strive to attain the goals by which they are measured. Pupils do little adventuring in these schools, lest they affect the tune and rhythm of the machine.

Measurement should frankly admit that it cannot solve all educational problems. The conviction grows that exact science in education has proved a " false messiah." Critical thinkers recognize that research cannot tell us what is the " good life." Science in education can tell us what is, but not what ought to be. Raup has well stated the limitations of the scientific method: " We have been trying to crowd the whole of vital human thought thru the cold and cramped channels of the method of exact science. We are coming to realize that human thought eventually forges out its beliefs not in the coolers of exact science, but in the crucible of vital, interacting human desires and preferences." Buckingham has shown that statistics are no substitute for thinking, and that the gifted researcher knows when to quit figuring. There must always be an interpretation of statistics. Buckingham shows that if an educational survey is conducted of a mill town, the use of the data may vary much. One policy-maker may be a realist and conclude that since 70 percent of the pupils are going into the mills, they should be given vocational training. A second policy-maker may be a humanist and conclude that since the majority of these pupils are destined for narrow industrial lives, they should be given cultural materials. Universal salvation does not lie in bare statistics. It is better for professional educators to recognize this truth than to have it revealed to them by others. Rugg has recently recognized that some educational products cannot be evaluated by exact science: " It is my confident judgment that the designing and construction and use of scales in art, in composition, in poetry, has in the past and will in the future continue seriously to retard the development of truly creative processes in our schools." There should be a reconciliation of science and sanity. Educational statistics cannot short-circuit to solution all the complex problems of human nature. Machine-run society seldom duplicates all the controlled conditions of the laboratory.

204. "The Ultimate Influence of Standard Tests" [3]

L. M. Terman

A hundred years from now the educational historian will probably characterize the present era as the one which saw the birth and development of the testing movement. From a half-dozen points of view the introduction of standard tests of intelligence and of school achievement must be regarded as of capital importance, for these devices are already leaving their mark upon school organization and administration, instructional methods, curricular content, textbooks, and even educational ideals.

Thus far, the influence has been most marked upon school organization — including classification of pupils — and methods and curriculum. The purpose of this editorial is to voice a prediction that in the next two or three decades the chief influence will be upon educational aims and ideals.

Why is this prediction made? Do not tests which measure capacity and achievement necessarily place the emphasis upon methods of insuring the mastery of a subject rather than upon the aim or purpose that guides the choice of school activities?

For the initial period of the test era the answer is, Yes. It is true that, up to the present time, tests have acted chiefly to heighten our concern about ways and means of advancing the pupil's achievement as measured by scores on achievement tests. In the investigation of this problem, however, we are beginning to stumble upon some very significant facts — facts which suggest that possibly the emphasis has been wrongly placed.

The evidence which is accumulating suggests, for example, that a lot of factors which we have always regarded as important determinants of pupil achievement probably have, taken separately, relatively little influence upon the child's accumulation of knowledge and skill in most of the school subjects. Several studies published in the 1928 yearbook of the National Society for the Study of Education give evidence to this effect. One of these fails to find any statistically significant difference between the subject-matter achievement of pupils taught by " best " teachers and the achievement of those taught by " poorest " teachers. Another fails to find a significant correlation between the achievement of the pupils and school expenditures. Another investigation, a rather extensive one, fails to find more than a negligible correlation between achievement of unselected ten-year-olds and the total number of days these pupils

[3] *Journal of Educational Research,* 17:57–59, January, 1928.

have attended since entering school. This finding is confirmed by another investigator in another state. Another study indicates that the remedying of physical defects has little or no effect on achievement. Still other investigations, previously reported in educational publications, have shown that achievement is affected to an astonishingly small extent by size of class or by the use of widely different methods of instruction. Thus it seems to make little difference in ultimate achievement whether a pupil is taught phonics or not; whether he is taught reading by the word method, the sentence method, or some other method; whether he is taught spelling as a separate subject or not; or whether 12 percent or 25 percent of the total school time is given to arithmetic.

It is not asserted that these assumed influences count for nothing at all. Probably a sufficiently thorough investigation would show that all of them do count, a little. It might show that all of them together exert in the course of several years a fairly considerable total effect. Even so, the suggestion remains that they are less important than we have commonly thought them to be in their influence upon achievement. The evidence that is accumulating seems to indicate that the mastery of the subject which a pupil of twelve years has attained probably depends more upon his mental level than upon all of these other factors combined, assuming at least a fair amount of educational exposure in schools of the sort commonly found in typical cities of this country. I have little doubt that more searching investigation will confirm this tentative conclusion. If so, what follows?

It would not follow that the testing of the achievement of pupils is futile. The findings reviewed do suggest that the testing of ability is probably even more important than achievement testing, but we are still justified in regarding both as necessary. They are necessary for school grading and for both educational and vocational guidance.

It perhaps would follow that we ought to reconsider our educational aims. Probably we have been laying too much stress upon the mastery of subject-matter. Probably moderate deviations in achievement, either above or below the "norm," are educationally less significant than we have thought. It has certainly been proved that ability to do certain work, say of the ninth grade, or of the freshman year in college, depends less upon the subject-matter that has been mastered than it does upon general intellectual ability. This is probably true of every grade.

If the present exaggerated emphasis upon subject-matter achievement is lessened, however, what is to take its place? The possibilities are: first, that we shall in time place more emphasis than we do now upon the ethical and social ends of education and care more than we do now about making the school a wholesome place in which to live; second, that we shall stress, to a greater degree than we now do, the child's attitudes and interests as contrasted with his scholastic achievement; and, third, that we shall be more concerned than we now are about the significance of intelligence — both general intelligence and special abilities — for educational and vocational guidance.

205. RELATION OF TESTING TO THEORY OF LEARNING [4]

Hilda Taba

Between methods of testing learning and theories of learning, there exists a twofold connection. In the first place, testing devices are usually formulated in terms of what a theory of learning considers as important results. Every theory of learning has tended to develop means of testing learning that are in harmony with its basic trend. Thus, the traditional theory of learning that stood for the mastery of subject matter by memory was accompanied by examinations, the main purpose of which was to test this mastery. The scientific school, with its emphasis on habits, skills, and the formation of response connections, has devised " standardized tests " that express the basic principles of this school in the form of the tests as well as in their content.

On the other hand, this twofold connection reveals a converse aspect in that the methods employed for testing, and the results revealed by testing, in turn affect the concept of learning responsible for these tests by tending to dictate what is important in that learning. It is obvious that different ways of testing emphasize different types of results and allow the others to go by unnoticed and unmeasured. This selectiveness or bias is productive of a programme for further learning elaborated in terms of the possibilities and shortcomings of the tests themselves.

The position of testing is consequently of such importance that this subject cannot be viewed with indifference by thinkers in the general field of educational theory. This is apparent when it is realized that success in the application of any theory, and the formulation of that theory itself, depend greatly on the form of testing employed. Educational tendencies, striving to realize some specific aims of their own, are endangering their positions and thwarting the achievement of these aims by unthinkingly accepting systems of testing that are alien to their thought. Almost as important as the de-

[4] From *Dynamics of Education*, Harcourt Brace and Co., New York, 1932, pp. 174–178.

velopment of a philosophy is the establishment of devices of control that are in harmony with that philosophy and which further learning in terms of that philosophy. To the degree that a theory of learning utilizes ways of testing formulated in terms different from its basic principles, the theory is incomplete and impractical in its fullest sense, and is unwittingly working to defeat its own ends.

One of the chief requirements of adequate testing, both as a check on results and as a guidance for further learning, is that there be a positive correlation between what is considered as important learning and what the testing methods emphasize or reveal. Such a harmony existed between the aim of learning as a mastery of subject matter and the examinations that test this mastery. It also exists between the theory of learning as an acquisition of fixed skills, responses and habits, and the testing of these achievements by standardized tests. But in the case of the theory that views learning as a reorganization of ways of behaviour and as the acquiring of more intelligent and more appropriate patterns of behaviour, results as yet cannot be adequately tested because testing methods compatible with the theoretical basis have not been evolved, and testing has been done largely with devices borrowed from other, and often decidedly antithetical, systems.

The discrepancy between theoretical bases and testing procedure is particularly evident since the spread of standardized tests. Standardized tests have of late become an almost universal means for testing learning, and progressive education has adopted these devices in spite of the fact that its theory of learning differs radically from the one that produced such tests.

While standardized tests are an invaluable tool for scientific education, they possess their limitations and shortcomings. An uncritical usage of this tool can result only in harm and will also serve to defeat the good points it may possess.

What can the standardized tests test, and how far can they help that education the main aim of which is to foster a creative reconstruction of behaviour, to produce personalities with well integrated outlooks, and to promote the development of ever increasing abilities to deal with new problems?

Let it be first of all admitted that standardized tests have rendered most valuable service to the teaching of fundamental skills, such as reading, arithmetic and spelling. They have also been helpful in guiding training in certain skills and habits. There is no doubt that they far surpass the old-time hit and miss judgments of teachers in their accuracy, objectivity and diagnostic value. Furthermore, as the acquisition of elementary skills, habits, and emotional responses is a very important part of learning under any theory of education, anything that renders more accurate information as to achievement in these fields of activity is of definite assistance to the conscious guidance of learning. Possessed of the ability to test skills, habits and elementary attitudes accurately, education has been in a position to know more clearly what it seeks and to construct more consciously means to achieve its aims.

But it is also true that for evaluating or studying appreciations, general abilities, emotional factors, and the motivation of behaviour standardized tests have proved a much less reliable tool. A wholesale and uncritical adoption of these devices is fostering practices and concepts that are decidedly not in harmony with the aspirations of progressive education. An examination of some of these salient discrepancies will not be amiss.

In the first place, standardized tests are atomistic and mechanistic. They test single responses, isolated habits and skills, and segregated bodies of information. Their method is that of the compilation of the whole from single items evaluated in separation from the whole. They proceed on the assumption that experience is an aggregate of various functions and acts that can be treated mechanistically. They assume that an improvement of behaviour can be brought about by effecting changes in its isolated elements, and that this improvement can be adequately evaluated by the simple process of adding up the discrete achievements.

Diametrically opposed to this is progressive education conceiving behaviour and learning as a unity of activity, where the whole organism is participating to the extent that in every partial act the total organism is involved in one way or other. Consequently, to test isolated elements of that behaviour as units unto themselves is not only insufficient but is even detrimental to the furthering of learning in terms of organized, unified behaviour. For this one must judge the elements of behaviour in their connection with the whole, one must start with the whole and proceed from that to the elements. The method employed by standardized tests is precisely the opposite: from the elements, considered independently, the whole is compiled, which in this case is not a whole, but an aggregate.

Progressive education, furthermore, works on the assumption that many different learnings are taking place simultaneously with any specific act of learning. The acquisition of one habit tends to modify other habits, as well as other emotional and mental reactions. The learning of one fact has its influence on the reaction to other facts. It is therefore held impossible to evaluate learning by measuring just one single learning at a time and by itself, as standardized tests necessarily do. Learning is an organic process and proceeds by laws governing organic processes, whereas such testing is mechanistic and evaluates learning by following mechanistic laws. Learning proceeds by patterns, in which partial functions are subordinated to the total behaviour pattern. In testing with standardized tests, partial functions are judged as if they were independent functions.

It is precisely this atomism and mechanism that has made standardized tests accurate evaluators of skills, habits, and informations, yet at the same time has made them incapable of coping adequately with attitudes, emotional reactions, choices and values. These latter are patterns of behaviour that inherently do not express themselves in single isolated elements of behaviour. They are produced by, and can be seen only in, larger meaningful wholes.

206. Position of the Curriculum Committee of the National Society for the Study of Education on Measurement [5]

One of the most potent forms of curriculum-control is measurement by means of uniform examinations and standardized tests. Teachers and pupils will inevitably work for the elements represented in the instruments by which their success is measured; therefore, it is of the utmost importance that changes in goals and methods be accompanied by the development and use of new tests and examinations corresponding in type to the advances made in the curriculum. To serve a useful purpose, tests must be fitted to the requirements of the curriculum and to the requirements of method. They must be determined by the purposes set up in the curriculum for the group of children being tested.

This Committee condemns emphatically the evaluation of the product of educational effort solely by means of subject-matter types of examinations now prevalent in state and local school systems. We have reference specifically to the rigid control over the school curriculum exercised by those administrative examinations which over-emphasize the memory of facts and principles and tend to neglect the more dynamic outcomes of instruction.

The foregoing statement is not to be construed as interfering in any way with tests of any character given intelligently for general scientific research.

[5] National Society for the Study of Education, *The Foundations of Curriculum-Making*, Twenty-Sixth Yearbook, Part II, Public School Publishing Company, Bloomington, Ill., 1927, p. 25. Quoted by permission of the Society.

207. Developing More Comprehensive Means of Evaluation [6]

Ralph W. Tyler

The chief problem in the minds of most teachers and administrators is how to evaluate effectively. In the past, the results of educational experiments have commonly been judged in terms of the marks received by pupils, of scores made by pupils on standardized tests, of success in college-entrance board examinations and other school examinations, or of marks received by students while in college. I think it is fair to say that these methods have not given sufficient evidence. Most examinations and teachers' marks measure only a limited aspect of the educational development of boys and girls. They may indicate quite accurately the facts or ideas which the pupil has memorized, the pupil's familiarity with the technical vocabulary of the school subjects in which he has been working, or the acquisition of such skills as those involved in reading and mathematics. Progressive schools, although interested in these outcomes, are also concerned with other phases of the pupil's growth. Some schools are concerned with the development of habits of social responsibility, and of more discriminating taste in the selection of reading material and in dramatic or art productions. They hope to influence and guide the development of abiding interests so that the lives of the young persons will be fruitful and happy. These are but illustrations of the fact that the purposes of progressive schools include effects upon development of the boy and girl which go considerably beyond the kind of behavior ordinarily covered in our usual marking systems. An adequate evaluation of the effectiveness of these progressive schools must furnish evidence as to the progress the pupil is making in these various directions. One cannot evaluate the school solely in terms of a few aspects of development.

If we accept the importance of these various purposes or objectives of progressive schools, we must enlarge our concept of evaluation. An adequate evaluation involves the collection of appropriate evidence as to the changes taking place in pupils in the various directions which are important for educational development. This evidence is not limited to that obtained from paper-and-pencil examinations. It may include records of observations of young people, the collection of products of their work, records of their reading and of the dramatic and musical productions which they have attended, and evidences regarding other purposes which progressive schools are attempting to realize.

[6] From "Evaluation: A Challenge to Progressive Education," *Progressive Education*, 12:553–556, December, 1935.

This concept makes it apparent that no one uniform program of evaluation can be used in all schools which call themselves progressive. In so far as the purposes of individual schools differ, the plan of evaluation will differ correspondingly. That is to say, an adequate evaluation will indicate the degree to which each school is achieving the purposes which it has set out to accomplish. Evaluation in this way becomes a responsibility of the individual school and requires a series of individual programs. This clearly necessitates the development of instruments for getting evidence of the achievement of each of these important purposes so that each school may choose those instruments which are appropriate for its purposes. Some schools will want, for example, instruments practicable for them to use which indicate the developing interests of pupils, which show the discrimination pupils are learning to use in the selection of their reading, musical, and dramatic experiences, which picture their habitual modes of reaction in social situations, and which indicate their developing attitudes toward social problems.

Recognizing this need, the Committee on Reports and Records of the Progressive Education Association's Eight-Year Experimental Study had proposed a coöperative program for developing more comprehensive means of evaluation. Thus, progressive schools have an excellent opportunity to develop the needed instruments to improve educational evaluation. These schools have had unusual experience in clarifying their own purposes and objectives. In developing their experimental programs and in their concern for the individuality of their pupils, they have learned to consider not only the intellectual development of children, but their social, emotional, and physical development. These experiences are of inestimable value in the development of better methods of evaluation.

There are various ways in which this coöperative effort may be directed, but I should like to outline one possible program which seems to offer great promise for making evaluation more adequate. The first step, which will serve to direct effort, is for each school to formulate in a clear and understandable fashion the purposes or objectives which it is trying to realize. This proceeds on the assumption that education is a means of bringing about changes in young people and that these purposes or objectives represent a statement of the kinds of changes in its pupils which the school hopes it may help to bring about. These objectives will indicate the variety of aspects of pupil development which needs to be considered in a satisfactory program of evaluation. This statement of purposes will probably include statements of certain understandings to be developed, certain attitudes to be acquired, certain skills and habits to be realized. Together, they should represent major changes in young people toward which the effort of the school is directed.

The second step in this proposed procedure is for the staff of the school to go through the list of purposes or objectives and indicate after each objective any methods which it thinks practicable for obtaining evidence of the degree to which this purpose is being realized. In making this notation three kinds of statements are possible. The staff may state that valid evidence about the attainment of this purpose is already being gathered by means of some particular procedure. For example, a school which includes among its purposes the development of facility in rapid silent reading might state after this objective that evidence could be obtained through the use of the Iowa Silent Reading Test and that this was already a part of the plan of evaluation in the school. In the case of certain other objectives, the staff might be able to indicate ways of getting this evidence which are practical and can be immediately followed, but which had not heretofore been a part of the school program for evaluation. For example, one of the purposes of the literature course may be to develop discriminating taste in the selection of reading materials. The staff might indicate after this purpose that such evidence could be obtained by having the pupil keep a reading diary which would indicate what books or magazine articles he had read in school, and he would be asked to indicate his own reaction to each selection read. There will be a third group of objectives or purposes after which the staff will probably put question marks indicating that they do not know any practicable methods which can be used in the school for collecting evidence about the attainment of these programs. We might expect to find such question marks after objectives concerned with the development of certain attitudes, habits, or interests, or with the acquisition of methods of reflective thinking. The points where question marks have been entered indicate the kinds of evidence which are needed for satisfactory evaluation, for which we do not now have practicable instruments. Undoubtedly, there will be certain kinds of evidence needed by several schools. A dozen schools, perhaps, might be concerned with ways of determining the degree to which their pupils were developing the habit of assuming responsibility in the social group. Many schools may be concerned with the development of a scientific attitude; that is, a tendency to look for evidence with reference to an important problem, rather than jumping to an immediate conclusion. At these points where there are common needs for practicable methods of obtaining evidence of pupil progress, we can organize a coöperative attack upon the common problems. A committee of interested teachers, for example, may be working upon methods for determining the development of the habit of social responsibility; another committee may be concerned with means for discovering growth in social attitudes; a third committee, with methods for determining pupils' interests. Each committee will be attacking an important problem in the development of instruments for evaluating progressive education.

At this point, the question of the practicability of this coöperative attack may be raised. What hope is there that this attempt to develop new instruments will be fruitful? The experiences of Ohio State University and the Rochester Athenæum and Mechanics Institute, during the past six years, indicate clearly that many of the areas which are now called intangible and incapable of evaluation can be appraised and that this appraisal can become more and more accurate and valuable. The first problem is to get some evidence with reference to these so-called " intangible " objectives. A later problem is to refine this evidence and make it more exact. There is no use to attack the second problem first. We cannot develop refined measures until we have first devised ways of collecting some objective evidence, even though they are crude.

One reason for believing that a coöperative attack is likely to be fruitful is that a clarification of educational purposes, stated in terms of changes which we hope will take place in boys and girls, directs the attention of the teacher and parent in a way that makes intangible changes more and more tangible. That is, clarifying our own purposes makes it more easily possible to recognize the desired changes in young people when they are evidenced. Another reason for hope that practicable methods may be developed is due to the possibility of sampling. By a careful study of boys and girls and a record of their behavior in a variety of situations, it is often possible to discover a few indicative situations in which one may get a clear picture of the development of that boy or girl without having to study him in all the possible situations of life. Binet, for example, in devising a test of the general mental development of young children, found certain situations which he used that were especially indicative of the mental reactions of children in a wide variety of life situations. As a part of the coöperative attempt to develop needed instruments, we shall make some careful studies in an effort to locate indicative situations which would enable us to judge the changes taking place in boys and girls without having to follow them around with camera, dictaphone, or notebook all day long.

A third reason for believing in the value of this attack in developing new measures is due to the possibility of indexes of change in people. In many cases, we have found certain changes in students which are difficult to measure directly, but which can be appraised rather accurately through other types of behavior that have been found to serve as satisfactory indexes. We are, of course, familiar with the use of an index in physical measurement. Ordinarily, we do not measure the temperature of the air in a room by direct measurement. To do so would require the determination of the average mass of the molecules of air and their average velocity. Instead, we use a thermometer. A thermometer does not measure temperature directly. It measures the amount of expansion of a column of liquid. Nevertheless, the thermometer can be used as a valid index of temperature because it has been found again and again that there is a high correlation between the change of temperature in the air in a room and the expansion of the liquid in the bulb of the thermometer. In this coöperative study, we shall be looking for and trying out promising indexes of educational development which may not in themselves be the purposes of an educational program but which we may find are highly related to desirable purposes which are difficult or impracticable to measure directly.

A fourth factor which gives promise for the success of this program is the fact that a clearer understanding of the changes in young people which are significant educationally enables the school to secure wider assistance in obtaining information about these changes. At the John Burroughs School, for example, parents have coöperated in reporting information about pupils that has been of value in making educational endeavors more effective. Playground supervisors and city librarians are potential collectors of helpful data. Coöperatively, we may get a much more comprehensive picture of the growth of boys and girls in the schools.

Through the clarification of objectives, through the careful study of boys and girls in terms of these objectives, through the search for indicative behavior, through the trial of indexes, through wider community coöperation, I think it is very possible to continue to extend our instruments of evaluation so that more and more of the important changes in young people will be recorded. During the coming year, it should be possible to develop instruments appropriate for at least four or five major purposes, for which we do not now have practical means of measurement. Each succeeding year might well result in similar expansion of our facilities for evaluation. This development of new instruments is possible and of tremendous significance. It is not a technical problem alone. The continuing improvement of progressive education depends upon the development of means for evaluating each promising effort of progressive schools in terms of its major, important purposes.

208. Relation of Evaluation to Purposes of School [7]
Rollo G. Reynolds and Cecile White Flemming

A program of evaluation must involve a continuous program of research, measurement, and record keeping. It must have its founda-

[7] From "The Evaluation of the Horace Mann Program," *Teachers College Record*, 36:699–701, May, 1935.

tion in the philosophy and objectives of the school. Never more than to-day have American schools been challenged to think honestly and clearly of their purposes and objectives; never more stimulated to improve steadily their curriculum and procedures; never more obligated to consider the results attained and to evaluate the total program as it involves teachers, children, and society.

. . . We [Horace Mann School] have been attempting constantly to learn to what extent our purposes are being realized. We have scrutinized and investigated our procedures, measured our product with the best available instruments, sought evidence of our outcomes in new ways where existing means of measurement are inadequate; and thus we have attempted an evaluation of our total coöperative effort.

The evaluation of the results of education is not easy, however, especially when teachers are sincerely and thoughtfully directing their efforts to insure coöperative service by their grown-up pupils in a democratic society and their maximum contribution to human welfare and progress. Our program of evaluation cannot be completely adequate and final in its judgment until we have some agreement as to what are the ideals of democracy, and what attitudes and activities are essential and socially approved. This is a serious concern for American teachers, since attitudes and interests are inevitably being developed in boys and girls by the school. What attitudes and interests are to be stressed? How much of each and in what relationships for a given child with his particular total make-up?

The Horace Mann School has recognized a second aspect of its responsibility in helping to educate for a democratic society. This purpose is the fullest possible development of the whole nature of each individual, so that he may live richly and happily as an individual in terms of his own special aptitudes and abilities, and yet function consistently as a social person, seeing critically the possibilities in coöperative effort and working with an impelling desire to utilize orderly processes in bringing such coöperative effort to fruition.

We have been giving the best thought which we could command to the aspects of growth which we wish to assure our children in terms of physical development and emotional control, knowledge, skills, habits, and attitudes. All the specific results desired in each of these realms of growth must be sought and their acquisition judged in relation, first, to the child's whole nature, his capacities, aptitudes, needs, and potentialities; second, in relation to the social requirements of his own childish environment; and third, in relation to the demands of adult living in a democratic society.

It is when we begin to clarify our objectives with respect to specific learnings, skills, habits, and attitudes that we realize how little we know that is really definite and precise. When we try to analyze, to break these general categories into definite elements, we cannot yet even define with precision such traits as dependability, accuracy, open-mindedness, or spirit of coöperation. We have no definite analysis of levels of maturity, or concrete meaning for degrees of excellence or success at successive stages of development. Even with the progress of the last twenty-five years in analysis and measurement, we have made but a beginning with these intangible personality traits. Much research is needed. The Horace Mann School is participating in such research.

The effectiveness of any program of evaluation must be conditioned to varying degrees in individual situations by the extent to which the staff can take account of, measure, or otherwise evaluate and control the many elements of the complicated situation called a school. These contributing and conditioning elements include:

1. The pupils themselves, their equipment for learning and growth, and our knowledge of this pupil material.
2. The organization of the school with respect to size, classification of children; the type and scope of the program as to activity, variety, instruction, recreation, and social emphasis.
3. The quality of teacher direction.
4. The methods of instruction.
5. The quality and variety of materials and equipment.
6. The home conditions.
7. The relations of home and school.
8. The relations of community and school.

All these basic elements demand varied and adequate methods and instruments for the evaluation of an educational program.

209. "The Problem of Measurement Involved in Integration" [8]

L. Thomas Hopkins

Recently attempts have been made to improve measurement: (1) by obtaining a more comprehensive list of teachers' objectives; (2) by stating these objectives in such clear and definite terms that they can serve as guides in the making of examination questions; (3) by analyzing subjectmatter topics in relation to these objectives; and (4) by selecting only such items from topics as will relate to the objectives to be achieved.

[8] National Education Association, *Reconstructing Education Thru Research*, American Educational Research Association, Official Report, Washington, D. C., May, 1936, pp. 203–205.

While this is a distinct improvement over the old methods of dealing solely with the analysis of subjectmatter for obtaining test items, it still stems from the traditional concept of education and follows the assumptions underlying traditional measurement. Such refinement may tend to fix more surely the old type of education and make more difficult any transition to newer or different conceptions.

To understand how the traditional conception of education and measurement will not satisfy the increasing emphasis upon integration, we must first see what integration means. In the literature on the subject it is used in at least four ways:

First, integration refers to the internal aspects of the behavior of the individual as he faces the situation without. When the internal aspects of the movements are characterized by wholeness, that is, when his physical, emotional, intellectual movements are in organic relationships that make for the maximum functional use, he is said to be integrated. This internal integration is not something apart from external behavior either preceding or following it. Rather, it is the internal state of functioning of the individual concomitant with overt behavior processes.

Second, integration refers to the kind and quality of the relationship of the individual to his environment. When an individual makes many contacts in a wide environment, resolves the ensuing disturbances with the best thinking of which he is capable at that time, and builds dynamic drives and cumulative technics for use in acting more intelligently in meeting subsequent disturbances, he is said to be integrated with his environment. Since the individual and his environment cannot be segregated as they are both part of the unit experience, there must be a relationship between the integration of the individual within himself and with his environment. Desirable overt behavior is a result of internal unity and balance.

Third, integration means the guidance of intelligently selected pupil experiences around some large indigenous unifying relationship. Perhaps the most effective way to achieve this is to assume fundamental meanings which are important in the adjustment of all individuals to environment and to explore meaningful experiences so that pupils may come to recognize and practise such meanings. Subjects disappear, fixed subjectmatter is abolished, minimum standards of attainment are eliminated, and teacher-domination of the learning situation is merged into shared control and direction by teacher and pupils. For those who believe in the first two conceptions of integration, this conception is only a means or a device to the end of better attainment of the other two. For others, this may become an end in itself, similar to the perpetuation of the traditional curriculum.

Fourth, integration is relating or putting together in larger wholes the specific subjectmatter already selected and taught in the traditional curriculum. This means the retention of existing subjects and subjectmatter intact but combining the elements of reading, social studies, language, history, and geography by rearrangement and redistribution wherever such adjustments can be made within the existing framework. It differs from the third conception in that it assumes the validity of the old material, while the third rejects it. To curriculum-makers this is correlation and not integration.

As one examines these conceptions of integration it becomes increasingly apparent that the assumptions underlying the technics of traditional measurement will not satisfy them. These assumptions contain no relationship to the internal balance of the individual; they do not consider the adjustment or maladjustment of the individual in his environment; they are not applicable to a variable learning situation in which uniformity has been removed both from the materials and the controls; and they are not even applicable to the very minor attempts in the subject curriculum to bring together in some more unified form for better teaching the subjectmatter which has long been emphasized by the traditional school.

The problem of measurement in integration now becomes reasonably clear. It is to build new assumptions and technics that center measurement in the interaction of the individual with his environment and recognize desirable changes in each. When the interaction is satisfactory, the individual finds integration within himself and with the environment. When the interaction is unsatisfactory for a variable period, the individual becomes disintegrated within himself and maladjusted with his environment. Whether the interaction will tend in one direction or the other depends upon a number of crucial and strategic aspects of the movement of the individual in the experience. Some of these are:

1. *The purpose of the individual* — How purposefully is he engaged? How clear is his purpose? Does it become more refined as the experience continues? Does his expanding purpose control and direct the experience? Is he happy in the pursuit of this purpose?

2. *The interests of the individual* — Do new and dynamic interests result from the development of the experiences? Are the interests such as to lead the individual into greater scope and depth of the social heritage? Do they include increasingly all aspects of a well-rounded life? Can they stand the test of open and shared criticism of the consequences? Do they become specialized only in later years as a result of normal development?

3. *Criticized values* — Are individuals constantly developing a series of long-time values which relate both to desirable social and individual ends? Do they see the helpfulness of values in dealing with certain recurring experiences? Are they continuously reformulating and revising these values consistent with their own growth?

4. *Acting on thinking* — Are individuals increasingly taking more aspects of an experience into account? Are they constantly thinking better about the values which are considered? Is their behavior increasingly becoming

more thoughtful? Are they growing more confident in their ability to utilize thinking as a basis for their behavior?

In the light of these strategic aspects of experience, validity and reliability take on new meaning. A measuring instrument is increasingly valid either as to source or function when it relates better to the actual experience of a learning group in relation to its changing purposes. That measuring instrument is most reliable which best takes into account the largest number of strategic aspects in experience integrated around the purposes of the learning group. To meet this need for the measurement of the total process of learning thru its most strategic aspects with emphasis upon personality adjustment as the center, new forms of measurement must be given far greater weight than in the past. Some of these are:

1. Teacher's observations of the general behavior of pupils
2. Diary accounts of the development of complete experiences
3. Records of work proposed and accomplished by individuals
4. Teacher's records of instances of emotional instability or stability of individuals
5. Teacher's records of lack of cooperation
6. Teacher's records of instances of lack of social stability or control of social adjustment
7. Records of how children contrive new responses to meet unforeseen aspects of experiences
8. Performance of children in cooperative group activities involving the utilization in modified form in a new setting of the learnings acquired in some previous experience
9. Accounts of how children explore and direct experience with emphasis upon the relationships of wholes to aspects, how ends and means merge together, how meanings are refined, and how behavior becomes even more intelligent.

For life and learning the individual and his environment are inseparable. Traditional measurement has assumed them to be distinct and separate. Testers have stressed certain demands in the environment apart from the individual and have expected the individual to conform. Possibly they feared the effects of thoughtful individual behavior on the environment. Many critics of measurement have accepted the same dichotomy but have centered upon the child and his growth to the almost complete neglect of the environment of which he was a part. They feared the oppressive effect of cultural uniformity which the traditional school imposed. The new measurement must see both the child and the culture as one inseparable unit of experience. It must center study upon what happens or should happen in the interaction. Herein lies integration. The problem is to discover a correlative means of measurement.

210. " Developing a Comprehensive Program of Evaluation to Cover the Social Studies Curriculum "[9]

In listing a series of possible objectives of the social studies and in
suggesting various means by which the degree of attainment of these
objectives might be appraised, the reader may be left with the impression that any comprehensive evaluation of the social studies
curriculum is impossible because it involves the appraisal of so many
types of behavior and the use of such a variety of instruments as to
make it too cumbersome for the classroom teacher to employ. The
appraisal program must be workable or it fails thru its own weight.

*A comprehensive program of evaluation can be made practicable,
however, when certain major considerations govern it* — In the first
place, when appraisal is made an integral part of the learning process,
it is not necessary to set aside separate blocks of time for testing.
The activities of learning and of evaluation go hand in hand and the
record of the pupil's activities in learning, the products of his activities, the results of his own efforts and experiences, are frequently
records for appraisal. In the second place, when the pupil realizes
the significance of evaluation for him and is encouraged to make
self-appraisals, it is possible for him to collect much significant evidence of his own development without placing an undue burden either
upon him or upon the teacher. The self-evaluation records being developed in the Denver high schools under the direction of Guy Fox
illustrate the practicability of this procedure as one major aspect of
appraisal.

In the third place, considerable economy of effort is made possible
by the fact that many situations can be used for evaluation in which
the reactions of the pupils throw light on their development in several
directions. For example, an inventory of the resources and needs of
the local community by a seventh-grade pupil threw light upon his
attitude toward the functions of social and economic processes, his
ability to use certain types of social science information, his ability
to understand and to use some technical terms in the social studies
field, his facility in written expression, his understanding of certain
significant social and economic relationships, his ability to construct
and to interpret certain kinds of maps and charts. Test situations of
this sort make it possible to collect significant evidence relating to
several desired outcomes of the curriculum without consuming a relatively large amount of time in the mere process of appraisal. More

[9] National Education Association, *The Social Studies Curriculum*, Department of Superintendence, Fourteenth Yearbook, Washington, D. C., 1936, pp.
341–343.

analytical evaluation procedures can then be used for diagnosis only with those pupils whose satisfactory progress is not revealed in these complex situations, and only at those points where difficulties are encountered. This is similar to the procedure employed by the physician who makes elaborate diagnoses only of patients whose general health is in question and only at those points, such as the lungs, the heart, the digestive tract, where general deficiences are evidenced.

A fourth consideration in the development of practicable methods of evaluation is the possibility of developing indexes of pupil progress in those aspects of his growth which are difficult to appraise directly. . . . Some types of human behavior which are difficult to appraise directly can be practicably tested by certain indirect evidences which serve as indexes of the desired behavior.* To develop such indexes is usually a task for research workers in the field of evaluation but as these indirect measures are developed and validated they become useful appraisal instruments for teachers whenever they provide a practicable means for evaluating certain pupil changes which cannot be practicably appraised by direct methods. One important caution needs to be observed when using indexes of behavior. An indirect measure should not be used unless it has been shown by actual comparisons that this indirect measure does give results similar to those which are obtained from the direct measures of the desired behavior. It is not enough for the indirect measures to be practicable; they must also be valid.

The difficulties involved in developing a practicable program of evaluation can be overcome. By making the appraisal an integral part of the learning process, by encouraging the pupil to make his own evaluations, by utilizing situations for evaluation which throw light upon the pupil's development in several directions, and by employing indexes of pupil development at those points where the collection of direct evidence is highly impracticable, a comprehensive program of appraisal which is also practicable can be developed.

In planning a comprehensive appraisal program it will be helpful to list the major objectives which are being emphasized for the particular class in question — Then, in connection with each of these objectives, the teacher will list the opportunities which he will have for collecting evidence of this type of behavior. In many modern schools learning situations are provided which are sufficiently lifelike so that they give an opportunity for the teacher to learn something of the pupil's attitudes, something of his work habits and study skills, something of the information which he has acquired, something of his skill in interpreting data, something of his concern for the well-being

* Tyler, Ralph W. " A Generalized Technique for Constructing Achievement Tests." *Educational Research Bulletin* 10: 199–208; April 15, 1931.

of other pupils, something of his habits of working cooperatively with other people. As the teacher lists these opportunities which he will have for collecting evidence on each of these objectives, he will find that the number of special evaluation instruments which he will need to use beyond those which would normally be used in the day-by-day activities of the classroom is not large. He will probably want to have a daily record of the reading done by pupils, he may want to give special tests involving interpretation of data, he may want to give separate tests on the technical vocabulary of the social studies, he may want to test the acquisition of the more important facts, but these instruments may be administered periodically and so planned that during any one week only a small portion of the time may be used for such appraisal purposes.

Continuous evaluation is too important to dismiss by the easy explanation that it is impracticable — Continuous evaluation is essential to determine the degree of effectiveness of the social studies program and to obtain an intelligent basis for curriculum improvement. An adequate program of appraisal provides evidence of the degree to which all of the important purposes of the social studies are being realized. To this end, teachers will increasingly use a variety of evaluation methods instead of limiting themselves to written examinations. A comprehensive plan of appraisal also involves cumulative studies of pupils and cumulative records of their behavior beyond the years of formal schooling so that the relative permanency of these educational experiences may be determined. Evaluation is necessary, it is practicable, but it involves a new conception of methods of appraisal which modify radically our present procedures.

211. " CONSTRUCTION AND APPLICATION OF NEW MEASURES FOR THE SOCIAL STUDIES " [10]

J. Wayne Wrightstone

Evaluation and testing usually follow new and experimental practises in education, but sometimes a controlled appraisal does develop concurrently with new curriculum practises. The modern mood of scientific and pragmatic thought demands that experiments in all areas of curriculum and method shall be tested and evaluated before the new practises are widely accepted. In experimental and progressive educational practises, educators generally ask for objective

[10] National Education Association, *Reconstructing Education Thru Research,* American Educational Research Association, Official Report, Washington, D. C., May, 1936, pp. 164–167.

evidence to support the claims of experimenters. The activity movement and especially the social studies unit of work practises of progressive education have been the topics of claims and counter claims for the values which developed from such programs. What are some of the new tests for evaluating the alleged newer and less tangible values?

Progressive compared with conventional education has arrived at a stage of development both in curriculum practises and in testing where new objectives and practises of instruction have created a need for new tests. The project technic and the integrated activity unit of work have opened up entirely new kinds of classroom behavior and objectives both in elementary education and in secondary education, especially for social studies. Teachers, however, have not devised instruments to measure these important objectives.

What are some of the new needs and values for which new tests and measures must be devised in progressive education? In both the elementary and secondary school the correlation of various subjects around a center of interest or a problem, usually arising from social studies content, has been stressed in the integrated activity units of work. Under such a changed curriculum and conditions of learning some of the important objectives to be achieved are: (a) the ability to obtain independently information about a problem from various sources: (b) the ability to interpret information; (c) the power to express creative impulses and experiences in various media; (d) the development of constructive interests and attitudes; (e) the growth of concomitant factors in the educative process, such as initiative and cooperation; and (f) personal and social adjustment which have definitely won for themselves a place in mental hygiene as it is related to the school curriculum and environment. These, then, are some of the significant new needs in the progressive schools.

CONSTRUCTION OF NEW TESTS FOR SOCIAL STUDIES

Let us examine, one by one, some of the newer needs and values of progressive educational practises for which we need new tests, for example, the ability to obtain independently from various sources information about a problem. Analysis of the behavior of the pupils in a functional school situation shows the following skills and powers are used. When John Jones or Mary Smith has chosen a problem for study and investigation, each has to possess abilities to obtain facts and information from narrative, descriptive, tabular, statistical, graphic — viz., bar, line, circle, or picture-graph — sources. Each must have skills and abilities to locate the data in libraries, books, magazines, newspapers, etc., as well as ability to use an index, bibliography, and the like. A test for such an integration or constellation of skills and abilities will cut across conventional subjectmatter lines and will be based upon a functional analysis of the curriculum and behavior in which pupils engage to develop their own interests and problems. Thus a test of working skills in obtaining information, if its content and behavior factors were classified according to traditional subjectmatter lines, would represent reading, English, social studies, science, arithmetic, and library instruction.

A test on the " Working Skills in Social Studies Research " was constructed. This test consists of five major parts: Part I tests the ability of the pupil to read and interpret narrative descriptive material; Part II tests ability to read tabular statistical material; Parts III and IV, ability to read the various types of bar, line, and picture graphs; Part V, ability to locate data in books or the library, encyclopedias, etc. It was supposed that such a test might provide a good index of the pupil's ability actually to understand the printed materials from which he must secure his facts as well as a test of his knowledge of certain library technics. Several pencil-and-paper tests * at the elementary- and secondary-school levels have already been prepared in provisional form to test this new need of the new education. Much additional work is necessary to make sure the tests are valid measures of actual pupil behavior.

Another new need arising from the new curriculum practises is the skill and ability necessary for sifting, evaluating, and organizing facts and information gained from various sources into a form of presentation — in other words, a test for organizing facts and data which pupils have obtained. When John Jones or Mary Smith has collected information, it is necessary to separate irrelevant from relevant facts in their running notes; to sense the logic, unity, and coherence of a topic; to coordinate and subordinate appropriate data; and to organize an outline. Again, a test for such a constellation of functional behavior and abilities of pupils will disregard subjectmatter lines, and various parts of the content of the test might be classified under the conventional subjects of reading, social studies, language activities, etc.

Such a test was devised in an attempt to measure the ability of the pupil to organize the facts or data which were collected in the library, laboratory, or classroom investigations. This test of " Ability To

---

* Pirtle, Mrs. Lela N. *Library Test — 6B.* Thomas Jefferson High School, San Antonio, Texas, 1932. ¶ Barnes, Emily Ann, and Young, B. M. *Children and Architecture.* Lincoln School Curriculum Studies. New York: Teachers College, Columbia University, 1932. p. 259–61. ¶ Rogers, J. L., et al. *Iowa Every-Pupil Tests of Basic Skills in Reading, Study, and Language.* University of Iowa, Iowa City, Iowa.

Organize Research Materials " included measures for such abilities as: (a) separating relevant from irrelevant materials; (b) sensing the logic of complete ideas; (c) coordinating and subordinating materials; and (d) outlining ideas under a stated topic.

A third important new need in a progressive social studies curriculum is the measurement of power to interpret, to infer, or to generalize from facts and information. This is distinctly different from memory, recognition, and recall of facts. What do the stated facts mean? What inferences, conclusions, or generalizations may be drawn from the facts? These are the questions asked and answered in such tests as those developed by Ralph W. Tyler * and associates for the natural sciences. A test for interpreting facts in the social studies was devised to measure the ability to draw inferences from prescribed facts and data.† Social studies facts in the test are presented in verbal, tabular, and graphic form; in content they are statistical and non-statistical. This new need grows from the emphasis of the progressive school upon thinking about and thru facts rather than remembering and reciting them.

A fourth new need is the emphasis in the progressive schools upon interests, attitudes, and beliefs. Thurstone and others at the University of Chicago have developed some new tests, especially for civic and social attitudes. Further measuring instruments will undoubtedly develop for these objectives of education. Another test, a " Scale of Civic Beliefs," was constructed which measured the beliefs and attitudes of pupils in described situations. This test is divided into four parts and purports to measure civic attitudes and beliefs in the fields of (1) race attitudes toward negroes, Indians, Chinese, Japanese, and others; (2) international attitudes toward the League of Nations, immigration, tariff, Philippine Islands, and the like; (3) national political attitudes toward the Constitution, political parties, laws, etc.; and (4) national achievements and ideals in morals, economics, education, and the arts and sciences. The total score of the test presents a composite index of a person's tendency to favor liberal positions on controversial issues. For validity as to liberalism the items were checked against editorial opinion in liberal magazines, such as the *Nation* and the *New Republic*. For a consensus of liberalism versus conservatism the items were checked by social scientists of admittedly liberal points of view.

A fifth major objective of education in progressive schools is the

* Tyler, Ralph W. *Constructing Achievement Tests*. Columbus, Ohio: Ohio State University, 1934. 102 p.

† Wrightstone, J. W. " Measuring Some Major Objectives of the Social Studies." *School Review* 43:771–79; December, 1935. ¶ Clark, Marion G. *Exercises in the Use of Historical Evidence*. New York: Charles Scribner's Sons, 1935.

continuous growth of concomitant factors as initiative and cooperation. Measurement in the field of these social performance factors
has usually employed observational technics. The " time-sampling
method " defines a unit of behavior in terms of observable overt
activity. The occurrence of such defined behavior is recorded over
a stated period of time. Anecdotal or observer-diary records are
methods of recording significant pupil behavior, and contribute
toward evaluation of these performance factors in the educative
process. Such records provide a qualitative rather than quantitative
analysis of behavior. The following observer-diary record illustrates this point:

John Jones: March 15 — Brought in clippings from newspaper on farm
loans in the U. S. March 20 — Brought in some charts of commodity
prices, constructed from a table of figures in a magazine which he consulted
in the library. March 23 — Made a report on topic of exports; gave data
gathered from several textbooks. April 2 — Volunteered to act as leader
of a class group to investigate recent government reports on exports.

Scoring — The scoring of the limited anecdotal records has been
attempted by using the equal-appearing-interval technic. When
notes about each pupil have been classified into the defined categories of behavior, the cumulative record is rated by several judges
for the quality of the acts. The scale on the basis of which the judges
make their ratings is an eleven-point scale from zero to 10 and may
be represented graphically as follows:

```
 0   1   2   3   4   5   6   7   8   9   10
 |   |   |   |   |   |   |   |   |   |   |
```

The examples of cumulative records of initiative which have been
cited may be used to illustrate the rating technic. Three independent
raters might assign to the record of John Jones the value of 8, 9,
and 8, which would average 8.3. The same raters might assign to
the record of James Smith the values of 5, 5, and 6, which would
average 5.3.

212. " STANDARDS OF ACHIEVEMENT FOR THE JUNIOR HIGH SCHOOL " [11]

Edgar G. Johnston

Mr. Gradgrind wanted facts, " nothing but facts. Facts alone
are wanted in life. Plant nothing else, and root out everything else.
You can only form the minds of reasoning animals upon facts:

[11] *Junior-Senior High School Clearing House*, 9:215–218, December, 1934.

nothing else will ever be of any service to them. This is the principle upon which I bring up my own children, and this is the principle upon which I bring up these children. Stick to facts, sir! " You will remember the schoolroom scene in which Dickens portrays the practical Mr. Gradgrind inspecting the quality of instruction.

" Give me your definition of a horse."

(Sissy Jupe thrown into the greatest alarm by this demand.)

" Girl number twenty unable to define a horse! " said Mr. Gradgrind, for the general behoof of all the little pitchers. " Girl number twenty possessed of no facts, in reference to one of the commonest of animals! Some boy's definition of a horse. Bitzer, yours."

" Quadruped. Graminivorous. Forty teeth; namely, twenty-four grinders, four eyeteeth, and twelve incisive. Sheds coat in the spring; in marshy countries, sheds hoofs, too. Hoofs hard, but requiring to be shod with iron. Age known by marks in mouth." Thus (and much more) Bitzer.

" Now, girl number twenty," said Mr. Gradgrind, " You know what a horse is."

Frequently, parents, laymen, and even teachers unfamiliar with the purpose of the modern school and the consequent reasons back of its organization of curriculum and methods of instruction ask rather apprehensively what standards the junior high school undertakes to maintain. The criterion by which " standards " are to be judged is usually drawn from their own experience in the common school of an earlier day and either consciously or unconsciously takes much of its color from a point of view towards education not far different from that of Mr. Gradgrind. A good many of us were brought up on the dictum that " knowledge is power."

In all probability the average high-school youngster of today knows many more facts than did his predecessor of a generation ago. It is equally probable, however, that exactly the same facts will not be common knowledge to all of the group and that their factual background may omit specific items of information for which high-school youths of an earlier day had developed an exaggerated respect. The following questions are selected at random from tests given to pupils of the seventh grade in a modern junior high school.

ENGLISH

1. (true-false) The Romans came to England in 55 B.C.
2. A word which was introduced into the English language as a result of the Roman invasion is ....
3. To find out what e pluribus unum means, I should look in the section of my dictionary that explains ....
4. When I look up a word I can find out the following four things about it:
   1. .... 2. .... 3. .... 4. ....

5. (true-false) Bob Cratchit is the name of the old man in *Saddle to Rags* who outwitted the highwayman.

MATHEMATICS

1. In this space draw an angle of 37°.
2. How many degrees are there in the third angle of a triangle if one angle is 40° and another angle is 65°?
3. Write as a common fraction reduced to its simplest form 12½ per cent.
4. Mr. Adams found that 8 per cent of his apples were not good enough to sell. Out of 35 bushels he had . . . . bushels of good ones.

GENERAL SCIENCE

1. Under what conditions will a siphon operate? Make a diagram of a siphon, and explain its action.
2. What causes an artesian well to flow? Make a diagram to explain.
3. Trace back to the sun the energy which we obtain when we eat a piece of beefsteak.

SOCIAL STUDIES

1. The principal contribution of the Phoenicians was . . . .
2. Apollo was the Greek God of . . . .
3. Our present calendar of 365 days was made by . . . .
4. With the help of your definition blanks, define each of the following words: government, astronomy, temple, pottery, culture, Pharaoh, acropolis, time line, civilization, irrigate.
5. Draw a scale of miles and use that scale to draw a map of Greece, locating the following places on the map: Athens, Marathon, Sparta, Delphi, Mount Olympus, Olympia, the Gulf of Corinth, Thermopylae, Piraeus harbor, and the Acropolis.

FRENCH

1. Write le, la, les, or l' before each of the following words:

_____ boîte	_____ plume	_____ règle
_____ élève	_____ encre	_____ pupitre
_____ fenêtres	_____ cahiers	_____ maison
_____ carte		

2. Draw a map of France with 4 rivers, 4 cities, and 4 mountain ranges.

FINE ARTS

1. Draw connecting lines between the style of chair in the first column and the set of characteristics in the second column which corresponds:

Jacobean	Shield-shaped back
Hepplewhite	Spindle arms and back connected by rail
Italian Renaissance	Heavy straight back, spiral or twisted legs
Adam Brothers	Slender straight legs — inlay
Windsor	Heavy boxlike straight carved back
Queen Anne	Vertical grooves, oval back — often light in
Sheraton	color

William and Mary	Pierced back, straight or cabriole legs
Chippendale	Curving forward and backward spread in legs
Duncan Phyfe	giving extra stability — frequent use of lyre back
	Inverted bell in legs connected by stringer
	Cabriole legs, high round-shouldered back — feet with claw and ball

INDUSTRIAL ARTS

1. Show how you could divide a board into three parts (width) and describe how to do it.
2. Give the composition of common solder, pewter solder, brass, and bronze.
3. The strength of an electromagnet is determined by what factors?

It may be said that all of the items here presented are ones with which some seventh-grade pupils are familiar. It is probable that few well-educated adults could score the entire list correctly. There are some items which you have known at one time but have forgotten because you did not use them; there are probably others you never had occasion to learn. It is far from my purpose to suggest an extension of this list as an adequate measure of junior-high-school achievement. Standards are not so easily determined. I hope, rather, to present a number of considerations which must receive thoughtful attention if any statement of standards is to be realistic.

I. *Standards can be determined only in terms of the goals towards which achievement is desired.* These goals must include more than " book learning." An ideal based on information alone demands too little, rather than too much, of the school. Habits and skills, information and understanding, attitudes and ideals, all represent outcomes of learning for which the school must accept responsibility. The efficient junior high school will provide thorough but intelligent drill for the attainment of essential skills and will administer objective measures to determine the degree of attainment. In the selection of skills to be taught, it will take into account probable future use and relative importance. For instance, the junior-high-school pupil of today will not be compelled to wrestle with cube root; learning to read graphs will play an important part in his mathematical training.

Pupils should acquire much information, but facts will be chosen for their significance to the learner and will be used as instruments to understanding rather than as ends in themselves. In the eighth grade of a traditional school, I learned that Popocatepetl and Iztaccihuatl were mountains in Mexico, that Mexico was bounded on the north by Texas, New Mexico, and Arizona, and on the east by the

Gulf of Mexico, and that it was a purple spot on the map. I got no appreciation of the Mexicans as a people, nor any understanding of their peculiar problems, their struggles, their achievements, and their national ideals. I learned that Reykjavik is the capital of Iceland. It was never suggested to me that the people of this small island had made early and signal development in orderly democratic government and have at the present time the oldest parliamentary body on the face of the globe. Facts are important, but only as they are assimilated, related to each other, fused with significance, and made a basis for developed understanding. In striking and desirable contrast to the unrelated fact gathering that was too frequently characteristic of history and geography, physiology, and civil government in the grades now comprised in the junior-high-school years is the approach to learning provided in well-planned excursions to points of interest in the local community or neighboring localities. The junior high schools of Ann Arbor have demonstrated an unusually effective program of such educational trips functionally related to the various departments of the school and making distinctive contributions to a first-hand understanding of social institutions.*

Particularly important (and difficult to achieve) is the development of desirable attitudes, an objective which should permeate the work of the school. Attitudes are not something which can be assigned and tested for; they can be assured only by setting up the kind of situation in which desirable results are likely to occur. In terms of happy adjustment to his social environment and of effective contribution to the life of his community, no outcomes of learning are more important to the pupil of today than attitudes of self-reliance, of responsibility, of tolerance, and of coöperation. No adequate measure of the success of a school or the growth of an individual can leave out the outcomes of learning which fall within this category.

II. *Standards must be set up in terms of individuals and adapted to individual needs, interests, and abilities.* Pupils are not all alike. Not all of them can or should learn the same things nor can they learn with the same speed. Through the use of standardized tests with nation-wide norms, it is possible for us to determine achievement in specific fields of learning with a considerable degree of objectivity. These norms, however, should not be used as standards. Such a procedure is an injustice both to the superior student who should accomplish far more than the norm for his grade or age, and to the pupil whose abilities do not make the achievement of the norm

---

* *Helping Children Experience the Realities of the Social Order* (Ann Arbor, Michigan: Ann Arbor Board of Education, 1933), 307 pp.

a reasonable expectation for him. Some children of the seventh grade ought to achieve tenth-grade norms in reading. For others, a fifth-grade level may represent commendable achievement. Every child has a right to succeed. The responsibility of the school is that of keeping the pupil working up to *his* capacity — the child of exceptional ability doing exceptional work, reading widely, exploring new fields of interest, building up a substantial foundation for later work in school and for adult life; the child of meager academic ability discovering the satisfaction of success in work adapted to his capacity. Obviously, the problem which confronts the teacher is a much more complicated one than that of assigning to all pupils the same selected list of tasks and expecting from all of them the same results. To the teacher of vision and humanity, however, its solution should prove vastly more satisfying.

III. *Standards should pertain to symmetrical development of well-rounded personalities, not to the accumulation of unrelated specific abilities.* Growth of the individual is the ultimate measure of achievement in the junior high school. Acceptance of this point of view means a balanced relationship between the various phases of development, not overemphasis on one aspect (e.g., acquisition of information) to the neglect of other important attributes. Furthermore, it carries important implications for the organization of the school — provision of adequate machinery for guidance, avoidance of overdeveloped departmentalism, freedom from emotional strain, sympathetic study of cases showing maladjustment, recognition of every worth-while achievement. For each pupil development should progress in terms of his powers, abilities, and interests. The school should provide rich and stimulating experiences as a basis for growth, wise guidance among the choices offered the pupil, and accurate estimates of progress made. It should establish a close working partnership with parents since neither home nor school can achieve its purposes without coöperation and understanding on the part of the other. The aim of this partnership, however, should be to promote child development, not merely to enforce scholastic achievement. Furthermore, there should be consistent growth of the pupil in self-reliance and responsibility. He should be led to evaluate his own achievement with increasing accuracy and honesty.

The considerations presented here may be termed a sort of "preface to standards." Such a basis will prove disappointing to some. It lacks the definiteness and ease of administration which characterize a formula of names and dates and figures. Unfortunately — or fortunately — children are not fixed and definite and do not fit readily into predetermined formulas.

213. Evaluating the Outcomes of Instruction in Los Angeles County [12]

The fundamental steps which we have stressed throughout the program are: purposing, planning, executing, evaluating. Teachers take precisely these steps in solving their own problems. In diverging from traditional paths, we must take every means at our disposal to reassure, by objective evidence, the fearful and the doubting, and to evaluate for ourselves the program of education in terms of acquired knowledges, increased skills, and improved habits of behavior. The world at large is prone to measure education outcomes to a large extent in terms of knowledges and skills. Likewise it is prone to criticize if children have acquired *only* the knowledges and skills without having acquired good habits of work and of conduct. This situation must be met with good judgment. It behooves us to plan and evaluate sanely, to weigh values, to know exactly what we are doing.

Will you remember in evaluating your teaching that *we must consider not only the knowledges and skills which have been acquired, but also to what extent the conduct and actual thinking of the children have been modified.* Acquisition of knowledges and skills, no matter how satisfying, is not enough. In this respect a progressive program demands more than any program yet proposed.

We are giving you a rating scale to be used in evaluating the outcomes of instruction by means of observing the activities of pupils. This scale is a carefully devised list of the specific outcomes of instruction in terms of performance and attitudes. It should be of real help to you in discovering whether or not one of the fundamental objectives of education — a desirable modification of conduct — is being realized.

We shall discuss briefly the standardized achievement test as a means of measurement, emphasizing the value of tests for educational diagnosis and the improvement of instruction.

The third means of measurement to be discussed will be that of tests devised by teachers. This phase will be discussed rather largely from the standpoint of determining the effectiveness of instruction which the teacher presumes she has been giving to the class, i. e., of determining the actual knowledges which have been gained by the group in carrying on a specific unit of work.

[12] *Teachers' Guide Intermediate Unit, Courses of Study,* Los Angeles County Board of Education, 1931, pp. 53–55.

EVALUATING THE OUTCOMES OF INSTRUCTION BY OBSERVATION OF
PUPIL ACTIVITIES

The best scale which has come to our attention for purposes of
helping teachers evaluate the outcomes of instruction is the *Kenosha
(Wisconsin) Self-Rating Scale for Teachers.* The major portion of
the scale is quoted below. You will find a complete discussion, as
well as the scale, in *Visiting the Teacher at Work,* by Anderson, Barr,
and Bush.

1. The pupils are the aggressors in purposeful activity.
   a. They believe in what they are doing.
   b. They continue their work voluntarily when opportunity offers.
   c. They do more than is required of them.
   d. They bring in outside materials unsolicited.
   e. They volunteer information.
   f. They ask questions as a natural way of gaining information.
   g. They move about naturally as their work demands.
2. The pupils are learning that which is worth while.
   a. They are using subject matter to solve worth-while problems.
   b. They gather data because they have a *present* use for them.
   c. They are improving oral and written language through natural use
      of English as a tool in thinking.
   d. They are learning to coöperate by coöperating.
   e. They are learning to be courteous and thoughtful of others.
   f. They are learning their civic responsibilities by engaging in civic
      activities.
   g. They are learning to enjoy and understand good music, art, and
      literature.
   h. They can distinguish between fun and unwarranted disturbances.
   i. They are building strong bodies.
   j. They are gaining in their desire to learn that which is worthy.
3. The pupils are acquiring right habits of study.
   a. They read intelligently or are consciously trying to improve their
      skill.
   b. They raise questions of their own.
   c. They are learning how to gather data, using pictures, exhibits, mu-
      seums, references, indexes, card catalogs.
   d. They are learning how to select matter which is of most worth to
      them.
   e. They are learning to suspend judgments.
   f. They are learning to respect authority of ideas.
   g. They are learning economical ways of memorization.
   h. They are learning to think in terms of their own experiences as well
      as of the experiences of others.
   i. They are tolerant of the views of others.
   j. They finish what they begin.

4. The pupils are interested in their own progress and feel responsible for their own success.
   a. They voluntarily try to maintain their efficiency in the tool subjects.
   b. They are given opportunity to work up to full efficiency in the tool subjects.
   c. They estimate their own progress, utilizing standard tests, graphs, etc.
5. The pupils are a vital part of the school as a whole.
   a. They meet people naturally and politely.
   b. They are responsible for their conduct on grounds, in hallways, to and from school, and in their classrooms.
   c. They play fair with their associates and teachers.
   d. They are ready to coöperate in school activities.
   e. They are loyal to their school.

214. School Marks Inadequate Basis of Evaluation [13]

William Bruce

Many of us have encountered a marking system in which one hundred per cent was the perfect mark, while perhaps seventy per cent was passing and sixty-nine per cent or below meant failure. Such marking systems have descended upon us from the days when the exact recitation of the textbook was the standard for one hundred per cent perfection. It was easy for the teachers to mark spelling, arithmetic, geography and history papers upon this percentage scale because each answer was regarded as either wholly right or absolutely wrong. Other school work, such as skills in writing and oral reading, and even "deportment," were forced into the percentage mold in spite of their non-mechanical character and the evident impossibility of reaching "perfection." Such criticisms of the percentage system resulted in many schools abandoning it. As educators have moved on to adopt other marking schemes, they have left the demand for "one-hundred-percenters" in the hands of certain perfect politicians.

Scientific measurement in education shifted the standard for marking from the perfect recitation to the normal or median performance of the group. Standardized tests were devised to assist the teacher especially in those areas, such as writing, oral reading and English composition, where the assessing of numerical percentages had proved most difficult. The measurement movement seemed to place still greater emphasis upon competition because distribution according to the normal curve over a wide range was demanded.

[13] From "School Marks and Confusion in Education," *Educational Administration and Supervision*, 22:275–281, April, 1936.

This gave plenty of room to work for a higher score than one's neighbor. Furthermore, since a medium grade was given to the average paper each individual's interest, if he only knew it, lay in having his neighbor's mark relatively low. In addition, the perfection possibility was abolished by making all tests so hard that even the brightest pupil would fail in power or speed before the end was reached. Indeed, the measurement movement seemed to fit neatly with the assumption that competition is the life of the school.

Another type of marking system which appears at first glance to be quite different from percentage and numerical scores consists of a series of letters. One common form runs from A, representing excellence, through B, C, and D down to E, which stands for failure. This device differs from the percentage scheme by reducing the number of passing marks from the thirty-one between seventy per cent and one hundred per cent to a mere four. The plan still permits the teacher to assume that the pupils will all be competing strenuously for A's, thus apparently assuring maximum progress. Although the letter system seems on the surface to be different from numerical marking, it has proved necessary to reduce letters to numerical equivalents before they will function in the school systems where pupils are " passed " and " honored " upon the basis of " averages." It appears, then, that this kind of letter marking system is closely related to its predecessors in having a range of numerical values which imitates a worker's wage scale.

Are not the three systems mentioned above built upon the common assumption that a wide range between the lowest passing mark and the highest mark will produce strong motivation through competition? Examination of the actual effects of the marking system upon the children in the public schools shows that only a few pupils near the top of the class, who are already interested in the work itself, compete for honors. Near the bottom of the class may be found those who struggle for the social security of " staying with the gang." The majority of the class who are between these two extremes pursue their work in the comfortable assurance that they are " with the crowd." In other words, the main source of motivation *transferred* through marks is the guarantee that the pupil will not be thrown into a new and less mature social group. This statement applies to the public-school youngster who is not yet motivated by a foreseen probability that getting high marks now will mean more money later on, and thereby more things then desired. In contrast, mature students in a teacher-training institution may feel quite differently about the range of marks. The practical student may foresee quite clearly the advantage of B's over C's in obtaining a position from a schoolman who still takes marks seriously. But the student of education should avoid the psychological slip of inserting in the minds of youthful pupils his own mature, money-using motives. Marks do not motivate children as a salary range does adults, because marks are of use chiefly for continuance in the work and with the social group.

The public schools, then, need a marking system which accords with these two fundamental motives of childhood and youth: (1) An interest in pursuing an activity for its own sake, (2) a desire to continue comradeship with the members of one's working group. But it may occur to the reader that for neither of these motives do we need a marking system at all. Youngsters pursue activities in social groups outside of school without benefit of marks. Indeed, marks are a bit dangerous because they divert attention from the activities and may also produce anti-social attitudes. Before we cast marks aside, however, we may well remind ourselves that a definite standard is still needed to indicate when the pupil is *ready* to go on into more difficult work. The psychological moment for advance into the new level of activity must be marked. With this consideration before us, let us look at other marking proposals.

The "mastery" mark is one proposal which meets certain needs of the school pupil. This plan merely gives an M for each task mastered. The M indicates that the pupil is really ready for the next task. In general, the mastery scheme has been connected with individual-instruction procedures which have permitted the learner sufficient time actually to master the task rather than merely "passing" with a seventy-five per cent or D standard, still ill-prepared for the next task. The mastery mark appears to be especially appropriate in a subject like mathematics in which mastery of certain skills may be measured with relative ease, and in which the units of work seem to follow each other in a logically supporting sequence. The idea of mastery is not so clearly applicable in a study like history or literature, in which readiness for the next activity depends upon a quality of interest and insight that many teachers would hesitate to label " mastery." Perhaps it would be helpful to replace the M with the mark R, meaning " ready " for the next school activity.

Another letter mark which has been used to avoid the competitive emphasis of the A to E scale is the S for " satisfactory." The intent apparently is to indicate to the parent and pupil when satisfactory progress is being made. There arises considerable misunderstanding, however, concerning the standard upon which " satisfactory " progress is determined. The parent is likely to assume that his child who brings S marks from the fifth-grade teacher is achieving the educational norms of the fifth grade. The teacher, on the other hand, may merely mean that this pupil is making " satisfactory progress " considering his low intelligence or physical handicaps. The child may make " satisfactory progress " throughout a whole year in the fifth grade and still not be " ready " for sixth-grade work. We suggest, again, that an R mark will more clearly designate what the pupil, the parent and the teacher need to know; namely, when the youngster is ready for the next educative step.

It is evident that neither the R mark nor any other kind of mark is a neutral symbol for an exchange value which can be used in a variety of ways like currency. In our economic system the employer does not mark the dollar bills in the employee's wage envelope with symbols to indicate that this one goes to the grocer and that to the landlord. In the school, however, the teacher who gives the R mark must attach to it a quite definite statement of what the pupil is ready *for*. In some cases the R will mean ready for the next unit in the particular subject. In others it may mean ready for the next grade. At the end of the high-school period a large R may stand for readiness to enter a wide range of institutions of higher learning. In a teacher-training institution a certain R might be required before the student was permitted to begin supervised teaching, while a still more significant R might be the sign of certification for public-school teaching. In other words, the fundamental use of a school mark is to point the way quite specifically into further educative or vocational activity. The teacher who gives the R mark, or any mark for that matter, needs to look forward clearly and definitely into the pupil's future as well as " examining " his present school achievements.

The R or " ready " mark is not an entirely novel proposal, for many schools have been moving in this direction. That is, the teacher's emphasis has shifted from the mere distribution of low and high marks toward diagnosing the specific weaknesses of individuals and providing effectual remedies so that the pupil may have an adequate basis for further work. Even when the child is " passed " by the second-grade teacher, she sends to the third-grade teacher plain statements of the pupil's skills, knowledges, habits and attitudes which indicate how fully he is " ready " for the third grade. To prepare such statements the second-grade teacher must look forward intelligently at least into the child's probable third-grade experiences. The lower elementary grades have made considerable progress toward the substitution of the " ready " type of statement for the range of competitive marks; but beyond these early grades the great mass of elementary and secondary pupils are assigned marks upon a competitive scale, and are passed upon averages. This crude device of averaging percentages or the equivalents of letter marks permits teachers to evade the question whether the youngsters are really " ready " for anything. This fundamental question comes up only in extreme cases when a pupil is on the edge of " failure." Then, if several teachers are concerned, they may get together and talk over how unready the pupil is for anything. Will the time ever come when the attitude aroused by the crucial case will be applied more widely? Some signs point in that direction. Although experimentation with non-competitive marking systems has only begun, here and there a shift is occurring from preoccupation with the distribution of marks over the normal curve to the careful guidance of each individual toward goals appropriate for him.

As teachers and pupils alike come to see that marks, of whatever kind, are more like the mileage markers along a highway than like dimes and dollars scattered in the road, they will concentrate their attention, like sensible tourists, upon the road ahead rather than stopping to criticize every mileage marker. Several significant changes follow from this shift in attention. In the first place, an immense amount of nervous energy which has been wasted upon competitive marks by both teachers and pupils will be turned into more wholesome and educative channels. The interests of teachers and pupils will become more nearly mutual interests. The most important result, however, is bringing into focus the question: What are we getting ready *for?* This does not imply preparation for remote goals. It means primary emphasis upon " continuous growing " — going ahead into new activities — contrasted with mere competition for marks.

Whether or not the analysis we have made of marking systems is valid, and irrespective of the practicality of the " ready-mark " suggestion, the writer believes that an attack upon this problem is a feasible first step toward clearing the way for the investigation of fundamental social and educational contradictions. Whether a shift from the misuse of marks for competitive motivation to their use as " ready " mileposts will eliminate all conflict between productive workmanship and mark-chasing must be answered through intelligent experimentation by skillful teachers. How the conflict between money-chasing and productive workmanship in the business world can be resolved lies in the hands of those economists who have social insight. The degree of relationship between the economic conflict and the school marks problem will become more evident as changes are promoted in both areas. Although these problems may arise again and again to plague the economist and educator, the clarification of the school marks issue will free the student of education for further delving into the contradictions of our common thinking. When he sees that teaching is not primarily a task of distributing marks over a scale, his mind will be more open to the opportunities that lie ahead. As the teacher sees more clearly the purpose of marking, he will take a positive attitude toward making whatever marks his school administration uses serve this purpose. He will throw his influence, no doubt, toward a gradual modification of the inherited marking scheme in accordance with the needs of the pupils. When teachers are freed from the vacillation and retreat caused by the school marks bugaboo, they will have energy and courage for the construction of a forward-looking school program even though this involves the exposure of deep-cutting contradictions in our culture. Indeed, fundamental problems can scarcely emerge until our conception of the school rises above the level of a competitive game.

215. "REPORTING PUPIL PROGRESS" [14]
William H. Bristow

In helping school, parents and pupil to evaluate growth, it is essential that a plan of reporting be developed which not only will further the positive objectives of the school but will also prevent conflicts. Conflicts occasionally grow up around competition, satisfactory and unsatisfactory work, inability of individual pupils to adjust themselves, and strained pupil-parent-teacher school relationships. At best it is difficult to interpret in meaningful, comparable, concrete and objective terms what goes on in connection with the learning of an individual pupil.

WHAT REPORTS SHOULD ACCOMPLISH

In all of his work the pupil should constantly gain in ability to solve his own problems with the help and cooperation of his teachers, his fellow pupils and his parents. He should learn to face problems squarely, to evaluate impartially and to discover solutions to his problems. The most valuable outcomes in education cannot be expressed in terms of subject matter covered; they are dependent rather upon the development of emotionalized attitudes.

A reporting system should aid the pupil to develop wholesome attitudes toward himself and his work. It should give him the feeling of security that comes from a realization that he is actually making progress. It should develop in him an objective impartial attitude toward his own development so that he may clearly see in what directions it is necessary to make improvement. It should further create a desire for such improvement.

[14] *The Nation's Schools*, 17:23–24, June, 1936.

Reporting should contribute to group growth by making sure that the individuals in the group are not placed in a highly competitive and emotionalized situation in which the only way to secure the recognition is through " beating out the other fellow." The responsibility of each individual to help other members of the group should be recognized and the powers possessed by each will be made a contributing factor to group success.

Reports should aid the parent to understand the strength and weaknesses of his child, his aspirations, the types of activities in which he has natural interest and ability and the ways in which the home can contribute more effectively to his growth. They should foster mutual confidence and partnership between parents and children.

FOUR GUIDING PRINCIPLES

The reporting process should bring to light both individual and group difficulties and should establish that mutual respect and determination so essential for satisfactory learning. Likewise a helpful relationship between home and school should be fostered. The responsibility of the school cannot be discharged by merely reporting that the child is doing unsatisfactory work.

A reporting system based on the foregoing principles will (1) avoid situations in which the pupil can most easily solve his problem by any form of dishonesty; (2) create a situation in which the home and the school will spontaneously cooperate to further the social, emotional and intellectual well-being of the child; (3) be so drafted that the child will exercise to the fullest extent his several abilities through the removal, as completely as possible, of harmful competition with other children in his environment, and (4) constantly encourage the pupil to excel his own previous record.

The following are characteristics of a satisfactory reporting system:

1. Delineations of traits should be stated positively.

2. Individual differences should be recognized.

3. The system should foster cooperation between home and school.

4. It is important that school and parents learn to recognize evidences of growth.

5. Items reported on should be pertinent and meaningful.

6. Accuracy demands that school data be objective.

7. Much educational data are essentially confidential and should be used only in a personal interview.

8. The report should consider the whole life of the pupil rather than academic achievement only.

A report card is usually a card, folder, booklet or any other form, except a form letter, that is or can be used by a school in reporting pupil success to the parents.

The report card is given to the pupil who takes it home for parental inspection and sometimes " approval." One of the greatest difficulties now apparent is the fact that there is often no understanding as to what the marks mean. This sets up conflicts between pupil and parents, and frequently between parents and school.

It is usual to issue reports at regular intervals. This practice delays until the regular report period the making of a report rather than giving it at a time that would, in an individual case, be most effective.

Practically every report card that can be drafted will be one of two kinds. It may be brief, concise and objective but the entries on the card are not items which constitute a " report "; instead, they are items of a confidential nature which, properly used, serve as the basis of a judgment or report rather than a report itself. In this category belong all percentile grades, rankings, percentage marks and even some of the symbolic grades.

The folder or small booklet type of report card, which couches the report in terms of accurate observations about the learner, his habits and character traits, must of necessity become a much larger booklet or folder than is now in ordinary use. A report card alone is not adaptable to the requirement that home-school communication is essentially a " two-way " system.

216. "Long-Time Tests in Curriculum Planning"[15]

Edgar Dale

The title of this paper is prompted by a strong conviction of the lack of important, long-time test data necessary for adequate curriculum planning. It will be assumed that the word " test " means any method of gathering evidence. In curriculum planning we are concerned with two sorts of evidence, To what extent are the curriculum objectives being reached? and To what extent is the behavior that is implied the life behavior of the students for whom the curriculum is being planned? The words " long time " will be used to show that the evidence is collected continuously or after a period.

Three important problems must be faced in any adequate type of curriculum planning: First, what facts are available concerning

[15] *Educational Research Bulletin*, 14:145–149, September 18, 1935.

the mobility of the high-school or college students for whom this curriculum is being prepared? In other words, will these students spend their lives in their home towns, counties, states, or are they likely to move to other states? Second, to what extent are high-school and college students utilizing the fields for which they were technically prepared? In what respect do the beginning jobs vary in their requirements from those held after ten years in the field? Twenty years? How effective was the school training in enabling each individual to meet the vocational and citizenship demands put upon him? Third, what losses in needed skills, interests, attitudes, and information occurred between the time of learning and the time of use? How much relearning was necessary to bring these skills and abilities up to a satisfactorily functioning standard? If we are to have national planning as far as human resources are concerned, it is clear that we must have far more data on such questions as these than we have had in the past.

In 1932, Hamlin found that only 43.2 per cent of 5,368 Iowa high-school graduates were located in the counties from whose high schools they had graduated seven to eleven years previously. Thirty-one per cent were living in Iowa counties other than those in which they had secured their high-school education; 25.8 per cent were living outside the state. Further, although 74.6 per cent of these persons lived on farms and in villages during their high-school years, only 47.1 per cent of them were living on farms or in villages in 1932. The percentage living in cities had increased from 25.4 per cent to 52.9 per cent. Also, more than two-thirds of all the city children had moved to other communities in comparison with 59.1 per cent of village children, and 48.5 per cent of farm children.*

A number of other studies of mobility on the high-school level have appeared. These show a high degree of shift from city to city, country to city, and state to state; less dependence can be given to a curriculum which is highly localized, assuming of course, that such training offers few possibilities for general transfer. An important long-time test in curriculum building is, Where will these graduates or students make their homes?

The second question is the extent to which the vocational and non-vocational training of students is utilized. Are the occupations followed those for which the students prepared? Can the general types of jobs to be held by these students be predicted and can more adequate curricular provision be made for them? Thorndike in a notable study published last year points out that the values of certain

---

* Hamlin, Herbert M. " Residence in 1932 of Iowa High-School Graduates 1921 to 1925," *Journal of Educational Research,* XXVII (March, 1934), pp. 524–28.

items of the school record and test scores for educational prediction and guidance are great. The grade reached at the age of fourteen, fifteen, or sixteen, taken together with the age to which the family plans to keep the boy or girl in school, will predict the grade which the individual will reach at any age with substantial accuracy.* Thorndike also discovered that the school record and other test scores, alone or in combination, were nearly valueless as means of forecasting success at mechanical work.

These data do have important curriculum implications. The curriculum maker can put to substantial use the fact that under certain circumstances he can discover accurately the number of grades which a student is likely to remain in school. The boy who is likely to drop out in the early years of the high school probably needs a different kind of curriculum than the boy who will remain in school for several additional grades.

The Thorndike study is also of interest to the curriculum worker who plans to carry on such long-time tests. Numerous difficulties will confront the investigator who tries to get in touch with students after they have left school. In the Thorndike study some had changed their names; forwarding addresses had not been left by others at their previous addresses since addresses are useful to bill collectors. Still others had moved out of town. Thorndike lists a number of ingenious devices by means of which his investigators tracked down the students who had been tested at the age of fourteen.

There is an increasing number of studies in reference to occupational and professional adjustments, but almost nothing appears in terms of the competency of the individual as an intelligent citizen. Smothers and Hamlin report that

the fact that considerable numbers of graduates of vocational and college-preparatory courses failed to realize their objectives with respect to occupation and college attendance emphasizes the need for giving attention in courses of both types to the general values which may come from education in addition to the special values which each type of course has to offer.†

A number of excellent studies have appeared which deal with commercial training in the high school. Significant improvements in such training could be made if supervisors of these courses availed themselves of these data or made similar studies in their own communities.

The most glaring lack of important curriculum data of a long-range type relates to the non-vocational objectives of high school

* A correlation of .90 or higher is given. See Thorndike, E. L., et al. Prediction of Vocational Success. New York: Commonwealth Fund, 1934. p. 113.

† Smothers, Homer I., and Hamlin, H. M. "Occupational Careers of High-School Graduates," School Review, XL (April, 1932), p. 306.

and college. Relatively little is known concerning the reading interests, tastes, leisure activities, political leanings, and religious interests of graduates and students who drop out before graduation. Whitlow in a study of graduates of smaller high schools makes it clear that

the type of reading reported most frequently by the graduates was distinctly at variance with the type to which the average high school gives attention. The book reading, as was the periodical reading, was predominantly in the field of fiction. Less than 18 per cent of the favorite books mentioned were outside the fiction field. About 5 per cent preferred biography, slightly over 5 per cent, history or religion or philosophy; approximately 2 per cent science and the remaining 6 per cent was scattered over the fields of travel, professional books, sociology, and drama. Not once was the reading of poetry mentioned.*

Superintendent Moseley, of the schools of Meriden, Connecticut, completed a study last year which gave significant data about the reading activities of adolescents and other members of the community. At the present time, Waples and Wert are making an extended study of the reading activities of various case groups. This should be an aid in curriculum planning.

The third problem is, What losses in important skills, interests, attitudes, and information occurred between the time of learning and the time of use? One of the most important recent studies of permanence of learning is that made under the direction of Ralph Tyler, of Ohio State University. Most studies, with the exception of this one, suffer from the defect of a composite score which covers up significant parts of the data. Mr. Tyler, however, classified the forgetting in terms of the differing objectives in one field, that of zoölogy. Eighty-two typical students who had taken no course in zoölogy in the interim were retested after fifteen months. The losses and gains were as follows:

Per Cent
Gain

1. Naming animal structures pictured in diagrams .... −77
2. Identifying technical terms .... −26
3. Recalling other types of specific information ...... −21
4. Applying principles to new situations 0.7
5. Interpreting new experiments .... 25 †

We may conclude from this study that highly specific information is most quickly forgotten, that information of more general application

<hr />

* Whitlow, C. M. "Graduates of Smaller Schools," *Junior-Senior Clearing House*, VII (October, 1932), p. 112.

† "Permanence of Learning," *Journal of Higher Education*, IV (April, 1933), p. 204.

is relatively permanent, and that in the important fields of applying principles and interpreting new experiments there were no losses but a significant gain especially in interpreting new experiments.

It is generally true that we tend to retain well those things which we are regularly using. Does this mean, then, that we should decrease the amount of specific information which we are presenting in our courses in geography, history, and arithmetic? Possibly this is true. It is quite likely that the method of attack, the development of principles, ought to be emphasized more and the learning of specific information emphasized less. One must always have the reservation, however, that losses occur because the individual has not become sufficiently interested in the subject to pursue independent reading or other activity in it.

At this point, the question of the development of attitudes presents itself: How permanent are they? How are they best taught? Information highly valuable to curriculum workers is found in the studies of Thurstone and Peterson dealing with the influence of motion pictures in the development of attitudes. Their technique was to give attitude tests to children and youth, take them to certain motion pictures selected because of assumed power in changing attitudes in reference to war, gambling, peace, Germans, prohibition, Chinese, and to give retests after viewing. One of these groups was retested on their attitude toward Chinese after nineteen months. The group started at 6.61 on the scale, were at 5.19 after viewing the picture and after nineteen months had returned to 5.76. In the case of all other films except one, residual traces of the exposure were in evidence at the end of periods of two and one-half, six, and eight months. The problem of a control here is, of course, important, but the data are extremely suggestive.* Certainly, such findings have important curriculum bearings.

These studies yield a number of implications for curriculum planning. Certainly, adequate, valid, and reliable tests given over periods of time to the same individuals are needed. Records of such tests must be carefully preserved. There must be national co-ordinating of studies relating to the activities of graduates and drop-outs. The appropriateness, adequacy, and permanence of learning must be studied on a national scale. This evaluation of long-time trends is especially valuable when radical educational changes are being made. Further, they are indispensable in any survey of the actual or potential human resources in this country.

* Thurstone, L. L., and Peterson, Ruth C. *Motion Pictures and the Social Attitudes of Children.* New York: Macmillan Company, 1933. pp. 39–72. (Motion Pictures and Youth — The Payne Fund Studies).

CHAPTER XIV

ORGANIZING INSTRUCTION

217. School Should Be a Form of Community Life [1]

John Dewey

In the theory of the school, the first factor in bringing about the desired coördination was the establishment of the school as itself a form of community life. It was thought that education could prepare the young for future social life only when the school was itself a coöperative society on a small scale. The integration of the individual and social is impossible except when the individual lives in close association with others in the constant and free give-and-take of experience, and finds his happiness and growth in processes of sharing with them.

The idea involved a radical departure from the notion that the school is just a place in which to learn lessons and acquire certain forms of skill. It assimilated study and learning within the school to the education which takes place out of school when living goes on in a rich and significant social medium. It influenced not only the methods of learning and study, but also the organization of children in groups, an arrangement which took the place occupied by ' grading.' It was subject-matter, not pupils, that was thought to need grading; the important consideration for pupils was that they should associate on the terms most conducive to effective communication and mutual sharing. Naturally, it also influenced the selection of subject-matter for study; the younger children on entering school engaged, for example, in activities that continued the social life with which they were familiar in their homes. As the children matured, the ties that link family life to the neighborhood and larger community were followed out. These ties lead backward in time as well as outward in the present; into history as well as the more complex forms of existing social activities.

Thus the aim was not to ' adjust ' individuals to social institutions if by adjustment is meant preparation to fit into present social ar-

[1] Quoted by Thomas Woody, in "Historical Sketch of Activism," National Society for the Study of Education, *The Activity Movement*, Thirty-Third Yearbook, Part II, Public School Publishing Company, Bloomington, Ill., 1934, pp. 35–36. Quoted here by permission of the Society.

rangements and conditions. The latter are neither stable enough nor good enough to justify such a procedure. The aim was to deepen and broaden the range of social contact and intercourse, of coöperative living, so that the members of the school would be prepared to make their future social relations worthy and fruitful.

It will be noted that the social phase of education was put first. This fact is contrary to an impression about the school which has prevailed since it was founded and which many visitors carried away with them at the time. It is the idea which has played a large part in progressive schools: namely, that they exist in order to give complete liberty to individuals, and that they are and must be ' child-centered ' in a way which ignores, or at least makes little of, social relationships and responsibilities. In intent, whatever the failures in accomplishment, the school was ' community-centered.' It was held that the *process* of mental development is essentially a social process, a process of participation; traditional psychology was criticized on the ground that it treated the growth of mind as one which occurs in individuals in contact with a merely physical environment of things. And, as has just been stated, the *aim* was ability of individuals to live in coöperative integration with others.*

218. Instructional Organization Must Be Based on Interests [2]

H. Gordon Hullfish

It is reasonable to expect the school to encourage the development of independent interests, intellectual, esthetic, or practical, on the part of the students.

Thus far we have called upon the school, as it reconstructs its procedures, to place a major emphasis upon the orientation of the individual in his world and upon the integration of his thought in order that he may act more and more intelligently in the social situation. These emphases throw into relief the fact that education must move forward from the interests of the individual. There can be no argument about the soundness of this approach to the educative process. Interest is central. The point that is here important, and especially when there is an active movement away from subjects as the educational hub, is that this admission of the force of interest in initiating and carrying forward educative activity need not place the school

* From Dr. Dewey's statement in the history of the school, by Katherine Camp Mayhew and Anna Edwards.
[2] From *The Educational Frontier*, Wm. N. Kilpatrick (ed.), D. Appleton-Century Company, New York, 1933, pp. 185–186, 190.

in the position of catering to sudden fancy and shallow whim. Orientation and integration, both leading to increased social insight, provide a sense of direction which ensures that the consideration of interest will not lead to the glorification of mere caprice.

The purpose involved in the educative process as thus described, the development of individuals loyal to a scheme of action that puts intelligence to work in social affairs, suggests that provision be made for carrying forward the emerging interests of the students to the point where genuinely independent interests have been established. As such interests develop and the individual gets knowledge put together in those relationships that provide control and make possible the further extension of knowledge, a deepened social insight is made increasingly possible. It has hitherto been our educational habit to start the individual out with knowledge organized by the specialist, and as knowledge has been increased, it has been our further habit to let him work with ever smaller segments of it. Always, however, the specialist's organization has been the point of introduction for the student. The impoverished and inept educational product of such an approach is all too familiar, and it is little wonder that a violent reaction occurred leading to the exaltation of interest. What is now needed, and is here suggested, is that as individual interests are encouraged they should lead on to the point where the student finds in organized knowledge those materials that make it increasingly possible for him to move about independently.

Under these prior conditions subjects would be studied properly, namely, in a way to bring the individual, already deeply interested in the field, to make such an organization of knowledge therein as would lead him to live ever more intelligently. This seems the sole excuse that the school has for the presentation of subjects; and in terms of this purpose the school may, as it is thus found appropriate, continue to present knowledge organized into subject-matter divisions. That is to say, subjects should be available as instruments for which particular students have use as they follow interests whose warmth urges them to such action. Subjects should not be required as vehicles in which all must ride regardless of where they desire to go. The school has discovered that it is futile to present the same organization of knowledge to all students, even within limited divisions of that knowledge; it needs now to permit the student to discover the exhilaration that follows upon the realization that one is building up an organization of knowledge which widens understanding and makes increasingly possible the intelligent control of social forces. Indeed, if some are so disposed, the school ought to encourage them to seek the joys that may be theirs as they organize knowledge for the fun of organizing it.

219. Characteristics of a Desirable School Organization [3]

Elementary schools differ widely in the type of school life which they foster. Some are so organized and administered as to provide a wide variety of worth while educational opportunities for children. Others provide a very limited number of such opportunities. Some provide for the all-round development of the child, while others give attention to a very limited aspect of development. Some are so organized as to have all activities of school life contribute to desirable educational goals. Others embody conflicting types of activities in which certain practices encourage outcomes of a highly undesirable type. Development of an adequate instructional program is conditioned directly by the general type of school life for which provision is made. This makes it desirable in approaching the problem of curriculum improvement in a given school to give consideration first of all to the general type of school life which is fostered by the school organization.

Variations in the kinds of activities in which children engage and in the ways in which activities are carried on in different schools may be accounted for to a considerable extent by the concepts teachers, principals, and superintendents have of what is a desirable type of school life. It is important, therefore, for teachers and administrators in a particular school to give consideration to this matter as a preliminary step to curriculum improvement. Materials which follow should aid in this regard.

First, consideration is given to certain major characteristics of a desirable school organization. Numerous ones might be mentioned. Among the more important are the following:

The school should be organized on a democratic basis.

The school should be an integral part of the community.

The school should provide for the development of social understandings and for the participation of its pupils in the social affairs of the community.

The school should provide a balanced and varied program of activities for its pupils.

The school should provide an attractive physical environment in which the children enjoy living.

The school should provide for the cultural enrichment of the teacher.

The school should be organized on a democratic basis. It would

[3] The Arkansas Cooperative Program to Improve Instruction, *A Teachers' Guide for Curriculum Development*, Bulletin No. III, State Department of Education, Little Rock, Arkansas, 1935, pp. 14–20.

seem to be a truism that schools which are designed to perpetuate democratic ideals should be organized on a democratic basis. In the schoolroom should be found the same type of freedom, responsibility, and control that characterize the operation of a desirable type of democracy in everyday life. The ideals of democracy should control and direct all the activities and experiences of the children. It becomes the duty of school officials to organize the school so as to contribute to the realization of such ideals.

Very often, however, we find our schools operating under an organization that is not in keeping with democratic ideals. Such schools still cling to the idea of teacher domination and pupil subjugation. The principal is often autocratic and austere, a stern disciplinarian in whom little sympathy or consideration of pupils is manifested. Orderliness, outward quiet, apparent concentration, and little physical movement may prevail when actually there exists an inner spirit of restlessness, a continual mutiny against the school, which only the iron rule of the teacher or principal can control. In such schools children are suppressed and fear dominates. Obviously, there can be little growth in such desirable qualities as leadership, responsibility, creative self-expression, and social participation.

The ability to govern oneself is developed only through the practice of self-government. If the school is to be a laboratory for democracy the pupils must share in their own government, in planning the program, in administering the curriculum, and in conducting the life of the school. When this type of organization is employed children become interested in every phase of school activity, they work hard, develop original ideas, initiate new enterprises, and evaluate their own work constructively. They grow individually and collectively in the capacity to govern themselves. In brief, by engaging in democratic practices in school they come to know democracy as a functioning type of social organization and control.

The school should be an integral part of the community. If the school is to assume the responsibility for training citizens for the community it must become a community institution. As such it will be a center of community activities, it will utilize the entire community environment, and will work directly with other community agencies in carrying out its educational objectives.

The school should be a center of community activity just as it is a center of child activity. Developed at the expense of the community for its children, its actual use by them represents only a part of the total utilization possible. The educational materials and physical equipment may be used to the fullest advantage by extending their availability to the community for adult education and general public activities.

The school should extend its activities beyond the classroom walls in order to secure needed contacts with the community environment. Such first-hand contacts are most valuable means of education. Schooling is only one phase of the total educative process that affects the individual. Various other community agencies and institutions contribute as well. Optimum growth and development take place when the objectives of all such agencies are compatible and coordinated, and each works directly with the others to provide wholesome and healthy expansion of the children's capacities and abilities.

The school should provide for the development of social understandings and for the participation of its pupils in the social affairs of the community. Schools are established for the perpetuation and improvement of the society which maintains them. If they are to discharge this function effectively they must provide for the participation of pupils in such activities as will develop intelligent conceptions of the social life of the community.

Intelligent understanding of the various aspects of social life is best derived from first-hand experience with the factors involved. The pupil coming to school from the average home knows little of the fundamental social and economic life in which he participates. It is the function of the school to orient the pupil in his social setting by providing social experiences adapted to his level of development. As he experiences successive contacts the individual will progressively develop a deeper understanding of the life about him and the relationships that exist between the various aspects of his social environment.

The school should provide a balanced and varied program of activities for its pupils. There has always been activity in the classroom and there always will be. However, the variety of activities in the usual classroom in the State is extremely limited. If the school is to produce a well-rounded individual, its activities should be so varied as to provide for the all-round development of the individual, and so balanced as to make the development orderly and sequential. Each activity should be subjected to evaluation as to quality, content, aim, and meaningfulness. When this course is pursued, the child will not only read, write, listen to lectures, work problems, and take examinations; but will engage in activities such as, constructing, discussing, interviewing, modeling, surveying, experimenting, making excursions, painting, drawing, building, dancing, playing, singing, observing, debating, and carving.

The school should provide an attractive physical environment in which the children enjoy living. One's surroundings play an important part in his development. Consequently, the classroom should be a place where children can live and work happily and effectively.

It should be characterized by homelikeness, charm, simplicity, and restfulness. The classroom should provide for freedom, opportunities to develop initiative and independence, the practice of cooperation, and the development of creative impulses. By such standards the traditional room is generally found to be woefully lacking. Pupils are required to sit in fixed rows of desks for most of the school day. The physical setting, such as, lighting, cleanliness, temperature, pictures, furniture, and other items, is generally not adjusted to meet the needs of the child. Frequently the room is colorless and bare, and materials are meager.

Teachers can do much to transform such classrooms into desirable places in which to live and work. A little courage, a little ingenuity, and a large amount of energy can accomplish wonders in this regard. With interest aroused on the part of the pupils, equipment can be made if necessary, school grounds can be beautified, and conditions generally can be materially improved. The children will enjoy their room even more when they have helped to improve it because it is theirs both in fact and in spirit.

The school should provide for the cultural enrichment of the teacher. The desirable school offers to the teacher the same things which it demands for the child — the same freedom, the same opportunity for individual development, and the same latitude for initiative and originality. It transforms the teacher from the deadening routine of hearing and directing lessons to a position of guiding children in undertakings that involve the spirit of adventure and the enthusiasm which accompanies highly purposeful activities. Each experience offers a new challenge to the teacher as it opens up new vistas for the pupils. This challenge leads the teacher to study and reflect in order to deepen his insights and understandings. It leads him to increase his appreciation of child nature and to broaden his capacity for sympathetic guidance. It results, in brief, in a teacher who grows and develops.

Opportunity for teacher growth is perhaps as important in the long run as opportunity for child growth, for teachers who lack such opportunity make poor provision indeed for the growth of children. Their influence many times may be positively harmful. Provision in an elementary school program of opportunity for teacher growth is therefore a characteristic of primary importance.

ORGANIZING THE INSTRUCTIONAL PROGRAM

The instructional organization in many schools is rigid and permanent; a scheme of narrow compartments through which children are moved at definite intervals on the clock; a time schedule arranged to consume an exact ration of subject matter each day at the same time; a sort of nurse's schedule for doses of intellectual medicine. It is apparent that in order to achieve the desirable characteristics previously discussed in this section fundamental change must be made in the organization of the instructional program. The program of work should be flexible and tentative, a provisional plan for the work of the class. General guide lines should be followed as to time just as we follow them in life activities, but children should not be required to work by fifteen- and twenty-minute intervals in rigid order. They should be allowed to work through one task into another. The schedule thus is adaptable to the changing needs of the group, according to the judgment of the teacher. Schedules will vary according to the experience and maturity of groups. Needs for physical activity and the time needed for specialized routine activities will be given consideration. The details of each day's program will evolve from study and consideration of the tasks that must be accomplished that day. Children will be allowed a part in planning the details of the day's schedule, such planning being looked upon as a valuable educative activity.

There are four general points of emphasis that should receive consideration in planning a program of work. First, provision should be made for children to engage in undertakings of complex, lifelike qualities that involve the development of fundamental social understandings and provide opportunity for participation in socially significant activities. Undertakings of this type give opportunity for the child to develop desirable attitudes and appreciations in such a way that they will be highly generalized and will function in his regular life activities and relationships. It is to provide for this desirable point of emphasis in the instructional program that units of work are developed which involve subject matter from many fields and which are organized around the dominating purposes of children. The phase of the instructional program which makes provision for this desirable emphasis may be referred to as the unit of work phase of the program.

Second, provision should be made for the mastery and organization for effective future use of habits and knowledge. Attitudes and appreciations, as is pointed out in the section on aims of education, function as the individual has adequate mastery of various habits and knowledge. In many cases special emphasis is necessary to provide for this mastery. Consequently, a well-conceived program of work will provide for such mastery. In the past, inappropriate emphasis has many times been placed upon this aspect of education. Frequently it appears that teachers have pupils engaged in drill activities merely to keep them busy. Often the skills or facts emphasized are of little significance and represent mere memorization by pupils. This obviously is undesirable. But even though the emphasis on mastery of habits and knowledge has thus been distorted in many cases, it remains an essential point of emphasis in a well-rounded program of work. This is sometimes referred to as the drill phase or the direct teaching phase of the instructional program.

Third, provision should be made for wide participation in creative and recreational activities. Many creative and, upon occasion, recreational activities will be employed in units of work. However, there is need for further provision of these types of activity in a well-rounded instructional program. Children should play games, organize clubs, take hikes, write stories and poems, read magazines and books, paint pictures, do woodwork, make collections, and do many similar things in addition to the activities of this kind that they carry on in organized units of work. An adequate program of work will provide free time in which children may follow their individual interests in activities of these types. Such provision must be based on individual choice and interest. It must be free from the hampering influence of the school regimen of marks and tests. The teacher must be an interested friend and not a taskmaster. Through this phase of the instructional program the child should have special opportunity to strengthen his individual interests and aptitudes, to engage in activities that provide for wise use of leisure time, and, in many cases, to lay a basis for later choice of a vocation.

Fourth, provision must be made for routine activities of the school. Like any other organization which involves many persons, the school must have a certain routine which provides for the effective functioning of the group enterprise. Provision should be made in the program of work of the school for these routine activities. Included will be such items as health inspections, assemblies, care of wraps and lunches, care of school equipment and materials, supervision of lunch hour, and management of school traffic. Other more or less routine activities for which definite time allotments may be required are such periods as may be needed by special teachers and for work in the shop, laboratory, gymnasium, and library.

220. "Organized Teaching and Theories of Teaching"[4]

Gerald Alan Yoakam and Robert Gilkey Simpson

Organized teaching is systematic instruction of the young in a selected environment. In some communities this environment is hardly better than the community in which it exists; but in most cases, the school brings the child into contact with an organized way of life, specially prepared for children and involving contact with

[4] From *An Introduction to Teaching and Learning,* by permission of The Macmillan Company, publishers, New York, 1934, pp. 8–10.

selected experiences which the race has had in the past and which are believed of worth in training the child for his place in the adult world. This point of view of teaching has obtained for a long time. Recently it has been changing under the influence of a new philosophy which insists that education is not merely preparation for adult life and that the best type of education for the young is that which best meets the needs of children at each particular stage of their development. The group propounding this philosophy also insists that the child must be active in learning and that the time-honored principle of pouring in information and repressing childish impulse to action is fundamentally wrong, chiefly because it does not educate. The child-centered school is one in which the emphasis is upon better ways of living for children and upon activities which engage the interest and effort of children because they have value to them here and now. In such a situation teaching becomes a process of arranging the environment so that in it children purpose, plan, collect, organize, assimilate, report, reproduce, create, and carry on activities that are natural and valuable for them. The environment includes contacts with subject matter of the formal type; but all the experience of the child is subject matter, and teaching is a process of guiding him in experiencing things worth while in the modification of his attitudes, ideas, skills, habits, and appreciations through active experience. The most promising results from the application of this theory seem to the writers to be those in which organization of these experiences constitutes a reworking of such fields of human experience as literature, history, science, social studies, art, music, etc., from the standpoint of the child. The least promising are those concerned with the development of fundamental skills — reading, language, writing, and numbers and certain technical aspects of art, music, and industrial arts. There is one notable exception to this in a system of beginning reading which seems to develop adequate skill in reading in an environment of activities which takes due account of the interests of children and provides for an abundance of activities which make the development of skill certain. It is through such experiments that an adjustment between the old education and the new will eventually come about.

221. Instructional Organization and Generalizations and Ideals [5]

Generalizations and ideals — The fact that the character of younger children has been found to consist of specific responses to specific situations, without much reference to general principles for

[5] National Education Association, *Education for Character,* Research Bulletin, Vol. XII, Washington, D. C., March, 1934, pp. 78–79.

guidance, does not mean that children are incapable of generalizing. Generalization is possible for many children, but like habit formation, it proceeds in accordance with certain principles. Among the conditions essential to effective generalization are these: (1) situations in which it is desired that the same type of response be made must have a prepotent element in common; (2) the learner must begin with responses to specific situations, and proceed therefrom to the development of general principles; (3) the learner must have sufficient intelligence and experience to appreciate the similarity of important elements in different situations which call for the same type of response; and (4) the learner must have a desire to generalize from specific experiences.

Children cannot develop general traits or ideals merely by talking, hearing, or reading about them in general terms. Loyalty, obedience, fairness, and similar terms are given real meaning only thru specific experience. Moreover, two or more principles or ideals may conflict with one another in a given situation, and when this occurs the requirements of the situation must be given precedence over the demands of any particular principle. For these reasons the learner's attention should be forcused first of all on situations rather than on generalizations.

Any procedure for teaching generalizations needs to take into account also the wide differences among children in the capacity to generalize, due to differences in maturity, native intelligence, and previous training. Children in whom this capacity is limited need special training in regard to a large number of specific situations before they can be expected to generalize wisely and effectively.

Altho it seems wiser to approach character education thru specific situations rather than thru generalizations, the latter become increasingly possible and important as the child's experience increases. As rapidly as possible he should be led to draw general conclusions which, allowing for exceptions, will help him to meet similar situations in the future. One must, of course, guard against generalizing from insufficient evidence, and against the blind application of principles in situations for which they are not appropriate. However, in spite of the problems involved, the effort to develop the child's generalizing ability is likely to be more fruitful than a program which is limited to the teaching of specific habits alone. The situations which the individual will encounter during his lifetime are far too numerous and unpredictable to be taught separately and effectively during childhood.*

* For additional discussion bearing upon the question of generalization, see such references as: Benson, Charles E., and others, *op. cit.,* p. 177–87. Hollingworth, H. L. *Educational Psychology.* New York: D. Appleton and Co., 1933.

222. "CAN TEACHERS CREATE THINKERS?"[6]

Ben D. Wood and F. S. Beers

The question whether teachers can create thinkers is an interesting one. In many of the hortatory appeals mentioned earlier an affirmative answer to this question is either implied or overtly stated. The denunciation of facts and knowledge and the plea for making thinking universal in the rising generation seem to go hand in hand, and to emanate from the same sources. It is a curious association of errors which might inspire a Freudian devotee to talk meaningly if not meanly of wish-fulfillment, and the practiced politician to suspect academic logrolling. But the attempt to make all or any considerable fraction of the population in our high schools, or even in our colleges, *thinkers* is at least anomalous in view of the obvious fact that it has been and is impossible, by any teaching or coercive methods thus far discovered, to make them *knowers,* even of a mediocre sort. The hortatory pleas for intellectual conversion, like the outcry against facts and knowledge, may be noble in motivation, but they add one more example in a long list that might be cited to show that piety no less than thinking becomes effective if not nobler when informed and directed by a little ordinary garden variety of facts and knowledge. The obvious and widely known fact that college graduates are not educated is not owing to lack of heroic efforts on the part of teachers to " train " students in pure thinking, but rather to the fact that their magic, even when learned at the feet of the most notorious leaders of the thinking cult, is not sufficient to perform the miracle of turning muscle and proper academic allegiance into cerebral cortex.

Neither Galileo nor Kelvin nor any other real and disinterested thinker ever suggested that all laborers, stable boys, shoe menders, and kitchen maids could or should be made into thinkers by " trained teaching skill," the rules of logic, the laws of inference, or any other legerdemain of the craft. It should be remembered that very few of the real thinkers had the advantages, or otherwise, of teachers (trained or untrained), or of carefully constructed curricula, or of the amenities of the school and classroom rituals. In this country, Franklin, Washington, Lincoln, Edison, the Wright brothers, and others, had no teachers to " make them think " or to save them from storing their minds with useful information.

Chapter 18, " Transfer of Training and Formal Discipline," p. 405–30. Kennedy-Fraser, David. *The Psychology of Education.* New York: Boni and Liveright, 1924. " Results of the Learning Process," p. 165–83.

[6] From " Knowledge versus Thinking? " Teachers College Record, 37:492–494, March, 1936.

It is an old and very plausible oratorical trick to demand that teachers shall make over all their pupils into thinkers and responsible philosophers; and it is an older and even more plausible trick to suggest ways and means of achieving this miracle in terms that are so broad as to be meaningless and in generalizations that are so inclusive as to be empty. These tricks are the common recourse of those who are sensitive to the dangers of information and facts, and who exalt thinking, even in a vacuum, above the power that Bacon associated with knowledge. It is quite another trick, however, to suggest ways and means in terms of concrete curricula and teaching procedures which will enable teachers to convert pupils who are incapable of making the simplest associations in elementary courses into paragons who can evaluate social institutions, formulate generalizations, apply them to novel situations, and make inferences with unerring acumen.

The advocacy of thinking — thinking inspired by teachers, and undefiled by facts or knowledge — as a panacea for present ills in education, and in society generally, is, in some quarters at least, reminiscent of appeals formerly heard from unauthorized exhorters for more and better " sanctification " as a cure for all sin and as a prelude to vaguely but eloquently defined rewards in the next life. " Sanctification " is as vague as " thinking," and it has, therefore, been a favorite shibboleth in primitive rites, just as thinking has become a verbal talisman in certain school rituals. The rewards of these two states of blessedness have been vaguely but attractively and convincingly sketched, while the cost of achieving them has been dismissed quite cavalierly as a mere nothing. The plea for the vulgarization of thinking assumes two doctrines — " perfectibility," and the power of teaching to achieve perfection. That both doctrines are at least half wrong is obvious.

There is, however, fairly convincing evidence that information can be taught, and that it will be retained and used if it is appropriate to the needs and lives of students. Information that has little or no relevance to later life, like old telephone numbers, is quickly and fortunately sloughed off. Numberless experiments have shown that such forgetting is the rule rather than the exception in American schools. But such evidence does not impugn the value of knowledge, either intrinsically or as a basis for fruitful thinking. It merely shows, among other things, that the pupils have been taught wastefully, and that the curriculum is highly disjointed.

223. EDUCATIONAL THEORIES AND INSTRUCTIONAL ORGANIZATION [7]

W. C. Bagley

The most salient characteristics of American educational theory have been summed up in four sentences by an Australian educator who spent several months in a nation-wide study of American schools: (1) " An experience which is not of immediate value to the child has no place in the schoolroom." (2) " All schoolroom situations should arise from the learner's felt need of the moment." (3) " The training (or disciplinary) value of a subject can no longer be used as a criterion in curriculum making." (4) " The walls between subjects must be broken down completely in order that the school work may be properly ' motivated.' " . . .

In my opinion, American educational theory as I have defined it has an important but a quite limited field of application. Carried beyond this field, its results, I am confident, will be little short of disastrous. To be concrete, let me take the so-called activity programs. These, I believe, should dominate the earlier stages of education. I have held for many years, too, that throughout the elementary and secondary schools there should be abundant opportunities for the learner to follow the learning " leads " that his interests suggest. Fifteen years ago I called such opportunities " free-project periods." Next I called them " free-activity periods." Now I shall have to call them, I suppose, " free-areas-of-interest periods," and there will doubtless be another name for them next year — but they all mean the same thing.

Now, to recognize a limited place for free activities is one thing; to maintain that all learnings should be of this type is quite another; and it is the latter tenet that comes inevitably as a corollary from the fundamental premises of our dominant theory. This is nothing more or less than a downright negation of one of the most important human characteristics; the ability, namely, to work systematically and persistently in the face of immediate desire, interest or impulse. It is this capacity that has enabled mankind to climb upward from the plane of the savage and the brute. As Graham Wallas pointed out long ago, this ability has been a *sine qua non* of social evolution as contrasted with biological evolution. To attempt to nullify this factor, whether by official fiat or otherwise, suggests Huxley's famous epigram, " What has been ordained among the prehistoric Protozoa can not be altered by act of Parliament."

It is because this capacity for sustained effort is normally weak in young children that I believe our current theory to have a legitimate

[7] From " Modern Educational Theories and Practical Considerations," *School and Society,* 37 : 409–411, April 1, 1933.

place in the earlier stages of education. I shall grant, too, that there are some unfortunates who never get beyond this stage; volitionally they never grow up, and for them activity programs and other appeals to immediate interest may be needed indefinitely. For normal children in the later pre-adolescent years, however, and throughout adolescence, the assumption that they can not and should not learn unless they have an immediate yearning for learning is not only an affront to their intelligence, it is a gratuitous denial of their grit, their courage — in short, their will-power. An educational theory which encourages the belief that there is no difference between the work attitude and the play attitude not only flies in the face of the plainest facts of experience, it is also charged with social dynamite. Of course many workers find their work fascinating, more fascinating sometimes than play, and most fascinating perhaps when, by effort and struggle, they have reached a high plane of endeavor. But to identify work and play under the same psychological rubric is fatal. I would maintain, furthermore, that the higher-order interests are attained in no other way than through an initial period of struggle — of effort to do initially uninteresting and sometimes distasteful things. An educational theory which says, not merely in effect but in so many words, " If you do not have an immediate interest in a task you are justified in evading it " — such a theory is about as debilitating in its probable influence as can be conceived. And yet it is just such a theory which has been weakening the fiber of American education for a generation and which is now being preached and, so far as possible, applied, in a most extreme form on a nation-wide front. . . .

224. Implications of Gestalt Psychology for Instructional Organization [8]

R. M. Ogden

In his recent lectures at Chicago on " Nature and Life," Whitehead writes:

Every special science has to assume results from other sciences. For example, biology presupposes physics. It will usually be the case that these loans really belong to the state of science thirty or forty years earlier. The presuppositions of the physics of my boyhood are today powerful influences in the mentality of the physiologists. Indeed, we do not need even to bring in the physiologists. The presuppositions of yesterday's physics remain in the minds of physicists, although their explicit doctrines taken in detail deny them.*

We must admit, I think, that many psychologists and most edu-

[8] From " The Gestalt Theory of Learning," *School and Society*, 41:531–533, April 20, 1935.
* 1934, University of Chicago Press, p. 5.

cators operate with obsolete conceptions of physical fact and law. Just as modern physics denies its earlier type of mechanistic positivism, so physiology and psychology must cease to make their assumptions on this basis. To me, it has always been an interesting and intriguing thought that learning, as such, found no place in the psychology of my two eminent teachers, Titchener and Külpe. Only latterly have I come to understand the reason. Both were positivists. Function had no place at all in Titchener's psychology, and it acquired a place in Külpe's system only as a static, and never quite as a dynamic, concept.

I am not contending that the Gestalt theory has arrived at a complete and satisfying explanation of the self-regulating improvement of behavior which we call learning; much less that it has rewritten the laws of physics. I do say that it offers a means of approach to the problems of growth, maturation and learning more consonant with modern physics than are the pathway-hypotheses of unit-acts which seem to underlie the usual mechanistic interpretations still current in psychology and education.

Let us take as a concrete instance the learning of mathematics, which begins with counting. First comes the pupil's observation of one, another one, and another one, to which the arbitrary names *one, two, three,* etc., are attached. Some educators seem to suppose that is all there is to arithmetic: the conditioning of this unconditional behavior with units, by graphic and linguistic terms, to which the pupil becomes inured by repetition and success. But the discovery of the cardinal number creates a Gestalt, the unit-members of which lose their identities as named units, and acquire a systematic meaning from which the whole scheme of measurement is derived.

Can we suppose that no significance really attaches to this discovery; that it is built up out of parts which have no intrinsic meaning; that the arbitrary " bonding " or " conditioning " of one unit-act with another could ever yield a science of mathematics? Such would seem to be the positivistic conclusion.

The Gestalt theory of learning begins at the other end. The organism is from the beginning a fully integrated unit. Its meanings are its integrated provocations, endurances and searchings. From an already organized beginning, search and endurance under provocation define and refine the patterns of behavior. The persistence of these patterns, once they are found, constitutes learning. A thing is learned when it is incorporated into a way of behavior, and in this process the organism and its environment are one. Persistence follows incorporation and depends upon the degree and kind of incorporation that takes place. Some ways are learned at once, and for all time. Others are temporary, and readily forgotten.

A brief description of the functional process of learning might run as follows:

Learning is any persistent improvement of behavior.

Improvement means facility in achievement.

Achievement means two things: positively, the attainment of an end, which is the completion of a behavioral pattern instigated by an organic need. Negatively, achievement involves avoidance and retreat from disaster, or any disruption of the integrated pattern which the organic need has motivated.

Thus, motivation is in the first instance self-regulation. Only secondarily, and as a result of an internal state of readiness, is it subject to involuntary arousal by appropriate stimulation from without — as when a flash of light occasions the winking of the eyes.

Learning is promoted in two ways (1) by the acquisition of skill, and (2) by the acquisition of knowledge. Skill, the more primitive of the two, is the improvement of a biological pattern of response in terms of its general conformity to the environmental situation. One learns skilful behavior, individually and socially, by discovering the right rhythm of performance. The experiential criterion of such acquisitions is esthetic. One feels one's way through a skilful or tactful performance without the necessity, or even the possibility, of distinguishing the partial patterns of behavior which are employed. Skill is always to some extent blind. The artist knows best after the completion of his work what he has been about, and what he was after. The skilled artisan need give little or no thought to the logic of his successive manipulations. It is the rhythm of a self-regulating development of a pattern fully integrated from the start which holds him to his task until his achievement is complete.

But in addition to primitive skill, behavior is also improved by knowledge. This means discernment of the partial patterns involved. It means abstraction of their salient features, such as weight, measure, shape and quality. These features can be named, numbered, graphed, that is, abstracted and dealt with as surrogate behaviors. They, too, can be felt rhythmically and their development can be followed esthetically. But they can also be placed and dated, recorded and compared, as the background of their concrete total behaviors can not.

Thus, the realm of abstraction grows out of concrete total behavior as partial patterns emerge which qualify themselves as quasi-units, or the dimensions of things.

In dealing with discernible units or things we enter the realm of logic and learn the principles of order which made blind skill possible. We learn to follow directions of orientation, impulse and differential sensitivity. We learn to individuate partial patterns and to regard their internal structure and constancy; to identify a person or thing in varying surroundings. We learn to assimilate one thing with another, one event with another, when, to begin with, these were learned separately as partial patterns in different contexts. Finally, we learn to redefine one thing or event when it is capable of functioning as another thing or event in a different context. That which had one use is found to have another, as well. Versatility and the so-called transfer of training are thus explained.

In brief, a Gestalt theory of learning posits a completely integrated behavior which can be improved by the elaboration of partial patterns within the whole. These patterns remain under the domination of the whole organism. Any undue dominance of a partial pattern leads to abnormality or perversion. The positivist's view of this process is not only naïve; it also leads to abnormality and perversion of behavior, whenever it leads his pupil to identify operations or facts as independent units or entities. Radical behaviorism insists that in order to learn any subject, be it linguistic, mathematical, scientific or historical, the pupil must incorporate it in his behavior as something he wants. The satisfaction of his adjustment is the criterion of his achievement. He learns the subject when it belongs to him as one of his ways of behavior. This notion of behavior underlies the Gestalt theory of learning.

225. IMPLICATIONS OF PSYCHOLOGY FOR INSTRUCTIONAL ORGANIZATION [9]

Hollis L. Caswell

A third point at which the implications of the two psychologies [Mechanistic and Organismic] appear to suggest different procedures is in connection with the organization of instruction. The difference comes in the focal point of organization. Instruction organized on mechanistic principles tends to have its focus outside the learner. The controlling idea appears to be that the pupil is aroused to activity of the desired type by external factors. As Bode suggests, the implication is that " The pupil is just so much raw material awaiting the manipulation of the teacher." The result is that the curriculum maker tends to concentrate on external forces which he believes he can bring to bear on the child in such a way as to secure the desired type of activity. The problem, in brief, is to provide stimuli which cause the learner to act in certain desired ways. It is

[9] From " Practical Application of Mechanistic and Organismic Psychologies to Curriculum Making," *Journal of Educational Research*, 28:21–23, September, 1934.

the task of the teacher to provide situations involving such stimuli. This can be done most easily and effectively if the various responses that are desired are arranged in order of difficulty and organized by subject fields. It can be achieved most economically if the child is required to react to each stimulus a certain number of times at given time intervals. Consequently, the problem of organizing instruction is that of arranging for the application of stimuli at suitable times and in proper order. As a result we have arithmetic organized in a logical sequence which carries the pupil through a planned series of stimulus-response situations. A given response is required a given number of times at specified intervals. In geography we have levels of difficulty measured by the intricacy of concepts and the requirement of successful completion of one level before proceeding to another. In history and literature we have chronological development with emphasis on each item of information which is to be added to the preceding items, thus gradually building an understanding of history or literature. The unit of instructional organization becomes the immediate stimulus-response situation. One instructional unit is tied to the next because of its logical relationship. In brief, the ideal organization of instruction from the mechanistic point of view seems to be achieved when the teacher knows in advance precisely what activities the pupils are to engage in, what stimuli will produce the desired activities, and the order in which it is desired that the activities be carried on. Thus, the teacher assigns, grades, groups, questions, rewards, punishes, and urges in order to get children to react with the desired activities at the proper time and in the desired sequence. If the particular activity to which attention is directed is engaged in, the teacher has successfully conducted her work.

Curriculum making from this point of view has the task of indicating for the teacher the particular responses that are desired, and the order and frequency of these responses. As the specific abilities to be developed are thus defined, experimental procedures may be employed to discover the most valuable materials for developing given abilities. Once discovered, these materials become relatively uniform in use until further experimental work has revealed possible improvements. In this way a definite base is provided for selecting and organizing instructional materials.

From the organismic point of view this concept of stimuli relatively external to the learner, applied on schedule by the teacher, is not acceptable. Rather, learner and environment are considered one. The learner in the situation becomes the focal point of consideration and his experience the means of education. Educational possibilities are present as felt wants or goals arise for the individual.

Activities take on meaning as they are thrown into peculiar relationships as means to the desired goal. Thus, the intent, or goal, or purpose of the individual becomes a major point of reference for organizing instruction.

For curriculum making this means that instructional organization cannot be set up in rigid form in advance. The precise stimuli and responses cannot be anticipated in full for they are complex of relationships and seldom take the same form. Since this is the case, the teacher must have freedom to deal with these complex situations with all their peculiar elements as they arise. This suggests that the restrictions of prescribed pages in textbooks, sequential organization of subject matter, restrictions within narrow subject fields, and strict time allotments must be lessened, and that instruction cannot be organized in advance as it is to be given. Instead, the teacher must be furnished with raw materials of instruction. He must employ these materials in the relationships dictated by the intent, or goals, or purposes of the children he is teaching. He must, in brief, look to the learner, in the particular situation in which he finds himself for the focal point of organizing instruction.

Another phase of curriculum making upon which the organismic point of view appears to have distinct bearing is in connection with courses especially designed to relate or integrate facts and skills mastered in other courses. I refer, for example, to such phases of instructional programs as the auditorium work in platoon schools. Case states of the function of auditorium work that " it is here that the pupils learn to interpret the classroom activities in terms of life and social situations, . . ." * The concept evidently is that activities are first carried on in the classrooms in such a way that they are unrelated to life and social situations, and later are brought together or integrated. This appears to be an effort to build a whole by combining a variety of more or less discrete parts. By assuming that learning is carried on effectively by securing some information in one place and some in another, all of which is to be brought together finally in organized form by the auditorium teacher, the basic concept of the organismic point of view appears to be violated. Similarly, the organismic point of view leads us to question the organization of special courses for character education, for health education, and for the purpose of summarizing, rounding out, or terminating work of specialized nature.

* Case, Roscoe David. *The Platoon School in America,* Stanford University Press, 1931.

226. QUALITIES OF A GOOD PROJECT [10]

John Dewey

Bare doing, no matter how active, is not enough. An activity or project must, of course, be within the range of the experience of pupils and connected with their needs — which is very far from being identical with any likes or desires which they can consciously express. This negative condition having been met, the test of a good project is whether it is sufficiently full and complex to demand a variety of responses from different children and permit each to go at it and make his contribution in a way which is characteristic of himself. The further test or mark of a good activity, educationally speaking, is that it have a sufficiently long time-span so that a series of endeavors and explorations are involved in it, and included in such a way that each step opens up a new field, raises new questions, arouses a demand for further knowledge, and suggests what to do next on the basis of what has been accomplished and the knowledge thereby gained.

227. PROVISION FOR DRILL [11]

W. H. Kilpatrick

Closely connected with subject matter in the minds of many teachers is the question of drill. Because meaningless drill has proved so repellent, many teachers fear any sharing of decisions regarding this with pupils. The crux lies in the word " meaningless." Let the actual situation of any child call to him for drill and there seems no lack of willingness to engage in it, as we see in the case of small boys with their first roller skates or of larger boys with their catching and batting. Even clearer, perhaps, is the case of very young children with their repetition of words and phrases and noise-making operations, often to the great annoyance of unsympathetic adults. One could without difficulty make out a good case that the child is a " natural " repeater. But learning is far from being mere repetition. Let but the experiences of the child arouse sufficient interest in and regard for consequences, and repetition as such retires into the background. Felt connection is the best basis of acquisition. We used to think that much mechanically repetitive drill was necessary to learning such things as spelling, writing, and number com-

[10] From " Progressive Education and the Science of Education," *Progressive Education*, 5:202, July-August-September, 1928.

[11] From " The Essentials of the Activity Movement," *Progressive Education*, 11:356–357, October, 1934.

binations. Now it appears that bare repetition, without any supporting connection or check, carries no learning effect; while, for the normal child, a sufficiently varied and interesting school life will by its inherent use of spelling, for example, teach ninety per cent of what may be needed. And similar conditions appear to hold in the case of most, if not all, the so-called mechanical operations. The remaining ten or more per cent seems best cared for on the basis of individual treatment, the teacher studying each case on its merits and helping the individual child to map out his own remedial treatment. Here, as elsewhere, the building of a common standard of accepted ideals is a great help. The main point of the whole matter is that everything done be meaningful to the doer. Let drill come only after the need has been set up and the meaning connection made clear. In the degree that these be attained, the rest becomes easy.

228. "ORGANIZING INSTRUCTION FOR MASTERY OF SKILLS" [12]

We now turn to the second general type of instruction, that is, directing children in the mastery of skills and information that promise to be of somewhat permanent value. This phase of the instructional program is important and should receive the careful attention of the teacher.

The experience of the race has accumulated a number of skills and a body of information which are applicable to many situations in life. It is economy for the use of these to be made automatic so that they do not have to be learned anew for each situation. The skills and the information to be mastered should be conditioned by (1) the immediate need of the learner, (2) the probability that the skill or information will be of value in other situations, and (3) the ability of the learner to master the skill or information economically. A teacher should give attention to each of these considerations before deciding that it will be advantageous for her pupils to make automatic the use of particular skills or items of information. In the past, too much time has been given to developing skills and learning facts that do not meet the present needs of the children and that give little promise of being of permanent value. Such material should be eliminated from the curriculum. The outlines by subjects in this course of study will help the teacher discover what are the important ones for consideration.

Not only have many skills and much information of little real worth received undue attention in the past, but the methods of teach-

[12] Florida, *The Course of Study for Florida Elementary Schools, Grades I–VI*, State Department of Public Instruction, Tallahassee, Florida, 1933, pp. 19–21.

ing and fixing skills and information have often been wasteful of the time of both teachers and pupils. This has resulted in a severe limitation of the educational offering, for little time has been available for developing understandings and appreciations, and for creative self-expression and recreation. We may summarize our discussion on this point thus far by saying that it should be the ideal of every teacher to discover what skills and information her children need, which of these promise to be of permanent worth, which may be learned effectively by her pupils and, having discovered these things, to make automatic the use of these skills and items of information with the greatest possible economy of time and effort.

In realizing this ideal the following steps should be taken:

1. Make the process clear to the pupils and be sure that each one is employing it correctly
2. Have the pupils repeat the process for short periods with intervening intervals of increasing length
3. Test the pupils to see what progress they make
4. Examine the process employed by those making unsatisfactory progress, have pupils correct errors that have developed during drill, and resume practice
5. Retest, examine process, and have the pupils continue practice until the skill or item of information is fixed satisfactorily

A correct start is most important. Very often children are drilled on incorrect processes rather than on correct ones. Some methods that may be employed by the teacher in getting a correct start is to demonstrate the process, explain the process, and have children try the process. If the latter method is employed the teacher should analyze each step to see that it is done correctly.

Repetition is the dominant feature of learning when fixing skills is the aim. Practice should conform to these standards:

1. The repetition should be satisfying or pleasurable to the learner. Interest in drill can be maintained with relative ease because the objectives are tangible and the results are apparent. The following are suggestions for getting pupils to engage happily in drill:
   a. Set up definite objectives.
   b. Inform the pupil of his progress from time to time.
   c. Foster pride in accomplishment.
   d. Avoid dullness and monotony. Make the drill exercise energetic. Begin promptly, with snap and vigor. Make the period short.
2. The learner must give strict attention to the task. Repetition without attention is useless.
3. The repetitions must be correct. Every error tends to establish a false association. It requires greater effort to break a wrong habit than to form an entirely new one.

4. The repetitions must be sufficient in number to make the process automatic or to attain the degree of skill that is desired. To study a word to the moment when it can be spelled is not sufficient. Attentive repetition must be continued until a reasonable degree of over-learning has taken place.

5. Short, intensive drill is most effective.

6. Small units should be used as drill material and mastery of each unit attained.

Permanent learning is possible only at the price of frequent relearning. When matter has been learned only to the point of the first correct recall, there is little likelihood of permanent retention if it is not kept in use. But after the first learning, the relearning takes place in much less time and with more permanent results. Review drills in skills once learned can be given at lengthening intervals. For example, an arithmetical table that was learned yesterday should be reviewed today, again in two or three days, then again in a week, in a month, in three months, and at the end of the year.

Numerous aids for the teacher in conducting drill are now available. Flash cards, games of various kinds, graphs and charts showing individual and group progress can be used effectively. Excellent work books in nearly all fields of study in the elementary school are available. Teachers should keep themselves informed about the best drill materials that are to be procured and should use all possible means to make drill effective. Such materials now available are suggested in the subject outlines in this course of study.

229. INSTRUCTION IN A CONVENTIONAL AND AN INTEGRATED CURRICULUM [13]

L. Thomas Hopkins and James E. Mendenhall

To interpret successfully the data presented [Academic Test Results], the reader should have in mind some of the important underlying educational principles upon which the elementary department of the School operates. Perhaps these can best be introduced by contrasting the conventional subject curriculum with the integrated experience curriculum of elementary schools. The subject curriculum is characterized by a large number of subjects which are organized more or less independently of each other. The subject matter is selected in advance of learning by traditional procedures, arranged in logical order, and emphasizes primarily the learning of informa-

[13] *Achievement at Lincoln School: A Study of Academic Test Results in an Experimental School,* Bureau of Publications, Teachers College, Columbia University, New York, 1934, pp. 3–4.

tion and the development of skills by a relatively passive learner. For each grade there are uniform learnings as well as minimum standards of attainment, objective examinations, grade organizations, credits, marks, promotions, and other administrative devices. The pupil is advanced or retarded according to fixed standards of achievement for each grade. The " education " of the individual is selected, organized, and presented to him by the school. The control is external to the learner and the learning process. Apparently, education is conceived of as the accumulation of subject matter, skills, promotions, and credits within subjects.

The integrated curriculum, on the other hand, is organized around fundamental and abiding interests and experiences of the learner. Subject matter is fixed in advance only in broad outline. Selection is made from this broad outline on the basis of greatest social worth and immediate functioning in the learning experience. The learner is active, since he is within the educative process, seeking to develop and direct it better. Emphasis is placed upon meanings, insights, understandings, and broad techniques. Grades represent years in school. Standards of achievement from year to year are variable and related to the individual group and the individual learner. Objective subject-matter examinations are infrequently used, since their validity for such a curriculum is seriously questioned. The control of learning rests primarily within the group composed of teacher and pupils, all of whom are considered learners in a new situation. Education, then, becomes a process by which the individual increases the area and depth of his experience and becomes better able to direct its subsequent development.

230. " The Cooperative Group Plan of Organization " [14]

James F. Hosic

A typical unit in the cooperative plan is made up of a group of children and their teachers. In a school in which there is one teacher for forty pupils, two hundred children and five teachers might constitute such a group. Each teacher would be responsible for one fifth of the program of the group and the five would plan their work together under the leadership of one of the number acting as chairman. Furthermore, each teacher would have a room equipped for the kind of activities to be carried on in it. Thus one room might be a library room, for English work; another, a museum, for social studies; a third, an arts and crafts room; a fourth, a laboratory, and a fifth, a recreation room. Each class of pupils would spend an hour

[14] *School and Society*, 31:6–7, January 4, 1930.

with the teacher in her own room. One class would be her special care and would meet her on coming to school in the morning and say good-by to her on leaving in the afternoon.

Such a plan of organization is already in operation in several widely scattered places. That it can easily be worked seems to admit of no question. In order to put it into operation, however, the principal must recognize certain essential facts. Negatively speaking, this is not specialization or departmentalization as those terms are commonly used. The writer scrupulously avoids employing these terms, for the reason that they are sure to be misleading. The teachers are grouped not by subjects but by pupils. Those teachers are together who have the same children in their care. This is distinctly different from the high-school tradition, which ought not to be carried into the intermediate schools, to say nothing of the earlier years. No teacher in the cooperative group plan is permitted to give her whole time and attention to a single subject. Horizontally her range is less than is now common. Vertically it is less than in the case of special teachers of — let us say music. No teacher, moreover, works alone. Much has been said of isolation in the school. Here is a remedy for it. No new buildings are demanded, nor need additional expense be incurred. As can easily be seen, this plan will provide better facilities at less cost than the one-teacher-to-one-class arrangement which it is proposed to displace.

Positively several benefits are assured. Among the more apparent of these are the following: Strong teachers in a school have the opportunity of making their influence felt. The process of spreading through the school the procedures of the most skilful is greatly accelerated. Every teacher, also, has put within her reach the possibility of being something of an expert in certain closely related fields of work. Concentration on history and civics in grades four, five and six, for example, will get results that spreading attention over twelve or fourteen subjects never can. Initial liking, too, will help, though most teachers like to do what they can do easily and well.

Unification of the child's experience is provided for, and a proper distribution of emphasis. If large projects or units are wanted, the mechanism is at hand to plan them and carry them through. Good plays in the adult theater usually command the services of several persons, each a master in his own line. School plays and other school projects will be better when two or more competent persons have charge of them and there is a room suitable for presenting them. Modern "activities" in conventional classrooms, with ordinary general equipment, in the hands of regular teachers who are trying to do what they were never trained to do, would frequently be funny if they were not so pathetic.

231. " General Provisions for Program Construction in the Transitional School " [15]

Cyrus D. Mead and Fred W. Orth

In listing guiding principles in good program construction, this summary should prove to be of considerable value. The work of schools where schedules for all grades were based upon these principles was personally supervised by the authors. These principles will be found to be in harmony with the essential requirements of modern progressive education.

1. Provision for long periods which are conducive to related activities rather than a series of short periods are advisable.

2. The opening exercises of the day should be brief, stimulating, and interesting to all.

3. The morning periods should, in the main, be given over to the acquiring of the more formal tool subjects, such as arithmetic, spelling, language, etc., and the practicing of skills; the afternoon, to the pursuit of freer activities, such as nature study, domestic science, and industrial arts. It is expected, however, that the work of the morning periods will necessarily absorb much from the work of the afternoon activities. Much of the arithmetic, language, spelling, etc. will grow out of these afternoon activities in a most natural manner.

4. Free time during the course of the day or week for individual activities of a creative nature should afford opportunity for mediums of expression not frequently developed under the ordinary schedule.

5. Ample time should be provided for play and physical activities. The play period should always be considered an end in itself. The formal subjects should enter into the games only when they are conducive to the improvement of the games. In other words, play should be developed through education.

6. In programming the subjects, it is probably best to place arithmetic as the first of the more formal studies. An easier subject, such as reading or spelling, should follow, after which a period of recreation is advisable. After the relief period one of the more difficult of the remaining subjects should follow, perhaps history or language.

7. Subjects, such as drawing or writing, which require considerable muscular control should precede rather than follow a recreation or physical-education period.

8. Periods devoted to the more formal studies, such as arithmetic, history, spelling, etc., requiring close mental work, should be inter-

[15] From *The Transitional Public School*, by permission of The Macmillan Company, publishers, New York, 1934, pp. 66–67.

spersed with recesses and a physical-education period but the latter should precede or follow a recess.

9. Subjects which are similar in character or which correlate readily, such as writing and spelling, reading and literature, or phonics and word study, should follow one another.

232. Characteristics of a Good Daily Program [16]

Many teachers will find that an instructional organization of the type implied by this course of study will require changes in their daily programs.

The daily program should provide for flexibility in time allotment. The teacher and the children may need very long periods for an excursion, for construction, or for research in connection with the unit of work while at certain other stages in the development of the unit, a much shorter period will suffice. All periods during the day, therefore, should be lengthened or shortened according to the time required for the children to carry out their purposes. Thinking in terms of balancing the work over a period of a week will aid in securing flexibility.

The daily program should provide for long, uninterrupted work periods. The children should be given ample time for getting out materials, for using them long enough to get some satisfaction, and for putting them away in an orderly fashion. The children may work in groups or alone while the teacher moves among the workers guiding by questioning where help is needed, by encouraging, or by challenging. The teacher should make note of the needs of the children or of habits and attitudes which are being formed. Notes which the teacher makes concerning the needs of the children should be used in selecting material for the direct teaching period.

Time should be reserved for the direct teaching program. The length of this period will vary from day to day with the needs of the children. This time should be used in helping the children develop abilities which they have found necessary in carrying out their plans.

The program should be so arranged that each group of children will have some undirected time each day. This is a " choosing " time for the child. He may work on something which he has started for the unit, he may read a book either for pleasure or to get information; he may draw or paint a picture; he may work on a story or poem he wants to write; or he may experiment with materials in the classroom. This is not a time for aimless wandering. Each child must work with a purpose.

[16] Virginia, *Tentative Course of Study for Virginia Elementary Schools, Grades I–VII,* State Board of Education, Richmond, Virginia, 1934, pp. 28–29.

Time should be reserved at the beginning of the day for an informal planning or conference period. During this period there should be a discussion of work accomplished the day before and plans made in light of previous accomplishment. At this time, children should have the privilege of presenting their problems to the group for suggestions. They should also share information with the other members of the group. Sometimes it is best to have a short conference period before and after the work period. This plan provides for a discussion of ways of working and also for a period of evaluation at the close.

The program should provide for the unrelated general activities. The group may sing songs, play games, dramatize stories, or engage in numbers of other worth while activities which are not related to the unit of work or to each other.

Routine activities should be included in the daily program such as washing hands before lunch and putting on suitable clothing before going out-of-doors.

It is felt that this discussion of the characteristics of a daily program is a sufficient guide for the teacher and makes it unnecessary to include samples of schedules in the course of study.

233. THE DAILY PROGRAM IN THE CHILD-CENTERED SCHOOL [17]

Harold O. Rugg and Ann Shumaker

What real differences in the daily lives of the children do these two types of programs [representing old and new educational philosophies] signify?

The first difference is one of flexibility. The program of the formal school is rigid, permanent; that of the child-centered school is very flexible, tentative. The former is a scheme of narrow pigeonholes: spelling from 9:20 to 9:35, penmanship from 9:35 to 9:45, oral or written composition from 9:45 to 10:00, and so forth.

A day in a child-centered school, however, is a much more flexible affair. It is, indeed, merely a provisional plan for the work of the class. Certain intervals in the day must be arranged for in advance — those, for example, that make use of special teachers in shop, laboratory, gymnasium, music room, and library. But the preponderance of the day in a child-centered school is left relatively unprogrammed. Note the frequent occurrence in Mr. Tippett's schedule of long starred intervals in which he refuses to fix in advance the content to be studied, the skill to be mastered, the arts to be practiced.

[17] From Rugg-Shumaker's *The Child-Centered School.* Copyright 1928 by World Book Company, Yonkers-on-Hudson, New York, pp. 72–73.

Flexibility! Schedules so tentative that educative units may be developed, " rich in group and individual activity; in opportunity for developing responsibility, initiative, coöperation, and scientific attitude; in the need for information and skill; and in social meaning."

A daily program planned in part by the pupils themselves; partially evolving from the newly discovered interests and needs of pupils, and partly planned, in skeleton only, in advance by the teacher. Finally in scheduled details is it compatible, therefore, with both the aims and the content of the new education.

A program for maximum child growth? A second characteristic of the new programs shows how the child-centered schools are trying to provide for this — the periods are longer, less uniform, and adapted to the changing needs of the work of successive days. The formal school pigeonholed the child's day into thirty minutes of arithmetic, fifteen minutes of composition, twenty minutes of language, and so on. The plan in the child-centered school, however, abounds in hour-long periods, forty-minute assemblies, a half hour in the gymnasium, an hour and three quarters for individual, self-initiated undertakings.

These longer intervals of the new school program have been made possible, of course, by the greater activity and variety in the work. The child's day in the formal school is exceedingly bookish; it is verbal; it requires acquiescent attitudes and emphasizes listening and memorization. Very little provision is made for constructive, creative activities in connection with the learning of the subjects. To hold the child's waning attention, to whip up fading interests, ten- to twenty-minute exercises became the necessary order of the day.

But the new schools are governed ever by the slogan of activity. They recite the catechism of spontaneity rather than that of conformity. Child initiative and many-sided growth are the goals. Naturally, therefore, a day in such a school is subdivided into fewer compartments than in the verbal, passive school. Periods can be longer because of the great scope and variety of activities crowded within any one.

CHAPTER XV

THE UNIT BASIS OF ORGANIZING INSTRUCTION

234. TYPES OF UNITS [1]

H. B. Bruner

CLASSIFICATION NUMBER I

Units of Unplanned Experience

THIS type of unit cannot be written up in advance since it represents the expression in action of the thing in which the child is most immediately interested. There is little, if any, teacher guidance when this type of experience is considered in its purest form. This does not mean, however, that a clever and understanding teacher may not so manipulate environmental factors as to surround the child with a wealth of alluring situations which invite him to create and to live. Pure creative activity falls under this classification. A child wants to sing and he bursts into song, not utilizing necessarily the songs in the adopted music book, but singing things his own heart most desires and often creating for his own pleasure his own song, words and music. The activities in this classification will vary from those actuated by sudden impulses to those lured out into the open by the wise and child-loving teacher. They are always, however, the child's own. To write them up in advance for any large group of children is obviously impossible although case after case can be recorded indicating what may be expected when conditions are appropriate and enticing. . . .

CLASSIFICATION NUMBER II

A Unit that Starts With an Adjudged Worth-While Wholehearted Purposeful Experience and Is Allowed to Eventuate in Whatever Subject Matter It Will

The teacher's primary concern in this type of unit is in having the children involved in interesting experiences which have promise, socially and individually, experiences that will lead on to an en-

[1] From *The Place of Units in Course of Study Construction*, South Dakota Curriculum Revision Program, Bulletin No. 2, State Publishing Company, Pierre, South Dakota, 1930, pp. 4–8.

riched life and to a finer understanding of self and others. She is not concerned as to the field of subject matter from which the content may be drawn, but she is vitally interested in whether or not the experience engaged in will make for happy and enriched living on the part of the individual and for the improvement of society through such living. What she wants is living and growth, but being a practical individual she knows quite well that she must have content — accurate buoyant content consisting of materials every element of which will be one hundred per cent pertinent in advancing the wholeheartedness and value of the experience. She desires to create an opportunity for the child to express himself because he wants to, even though she has been careful to find guarantees that the experience would secure the approval of at least advanced-thinking adults. The experience may eventuate in subject matter from industrial arts, social studies, mathematics, English, or a number of other subjects. The teacher doesn't really care as long as it fully meets the criteria of social and individual promise. The content of the unit must be accurate and appropriate, but what does it matter from what field it comes so long as the child is growing? . . .

CLASSIFICATION NUMBER III

The Theme or Generalization Unit

Under this heading would fall the unit in which a teacher has selected a pivotal issue, theme, or generalization, the understanding of which would be most valuable for the individual and society. The first and most important task in building this type of unit consists of choosing from all the possible themes those which if understood would be most strategic in the life of the individual and would eventuate in the most good to society. Content is absolutely necessary in this type of unit, but only that content which contributes directly to the understanding of the theme or generalization chosen. For example, if a teacher should decide that it is important that children have an understanding of the theme that " Men move from place to place in search of better living conditions," it would not be necessary to include all the facts of Roman history but only those concerned with the migrations of the people in and out of Rome as they attempted to find easier and better living conditions. This might mean that out of a thousand facts ordinarily taught in Roman history only fifty would be used in the development and understanding of this theme. It is quite possible that fifty or a hundred more facts of Roman history would be used in developing an understanding of a theme which would deal with the forces that have developed communication.

This conception of a unit breaks down the idea that all subject matter which has formerly been considered necessary to an understanding of Roman history or that of any other country must be presented at one time or together. It would seem that it would be far more effective to select only those elements of subject matter that are pertinent to the understanding of those generalizations or themes which are under consideration. Moreover the teacher will not include all types of activities or approaches in such a unit but only those which will involve the content through which an increasing understanding and interpretation of the underlying theme can be secured.

This is the approach which seems at the present time to offer, especially in such subjects as social studies and science, an optimum opportunity for most successfully combining the two extreme notions of unbridled children's interests and adult chosen subject matter set out to be learned. The theme is chosen by adults out of the rich racial experience and after due consideration of the present and future problems with which children and adults are and may be confronted. The interests of children are elicited and held through a discriminating selection of those activities and materials which are most effective in developing an understanding of the selected theme.

CLASSIFICATION NUMBER IV

A Unit in Which the Teacher Determines in Advance the Informations or Skills She Thinks the Pupils Need and Consciously Plans Activities Which Will Eventuate in the Desired Ends

In units falling under this category teachers have decided in advance that pupils need certain subject matter such as the multiplication tables, spelling words, history facts, map locations and the like, and consciously plan to lead pupils through the kinds of activities that will eventuate in the adult-desired subject matter in which the pupils are lacking. It is a type of motivation. While it is a species of sugar coating, it is entirely legitimate, especially if resorted to after wholehearted purposeful activity has not proved successful in securing the valuable aspects of subject matter. Here the teacher purpose is dominant, but it is the aim of a teacher who realizes that it is far more effective in the long run to capture the interest of the child than to force subject matter on him when the only reward consists of grades or teacher approval. In the unit illustrated below the teacher realized that her pupils were lacking in skill in simple operations with United States money. Hence she felt that it would be profitable to set in motion an activity which would require pupils to engage in simple operations with United States money so that skill might be gained.

She decided that the cafeteria offered an opportunity for the development of such skill and hence led children into a general discussion of such problems as the kinds of food to be sold; the amounts of each which should be kept on hand; the necessary materials and equipment and the like.

She read to and with them reports about food, how we are fed, the best kinds of food to buy, etc. Many pupils made price cards. Signs were painted, cashiers and clerks were selected, the cost of certain articles was determined, facility in making change was secured; and the like. Through most of these activities the children gained skill in simple operations in United States money, the teacher goal set in the beginning.

This type of unit, while frowned upon as " devicy " by the ultra Dewey-Kilpatrick advocates, represents a level far beyond that existing in many classrooms today where the whole procedure is consciously or unconsciously based upon the slogan, " You need to know how to add and divide so I am going to see that you get it by sheer repetition regardless of whether you like it or not."

CLASSIFICATION NUMBER V

Subject Matter Units Involving Correlation

Under this classification will fall units devised by teachers who are more interested in subject matter than in activities or experiences but who are quite willing to cross subject matter boundaries in an endeavor to bring in all of the material pertinent to the topic under consideration. These units might be named units of correlated subject matter. In constructing and teaching units of this type a teacher is not limited by platoon organizations or subject matter fields but feels free to draw from any field any content which will contribute to the logical development of her topic. An example of a ridiculously wrong use of correlation is the case of a teacher who attempted to center everything fifth grade pupils needed to know about all subjects around the topic of Africa. She secured the map location facts rather legitimately by placing Africa in relation to other parts of the world. When she wanted to teach certain facts about government in the United States she called to their attention the war of the Barbary coast indicating that the United States government sent vessels to the northern coast of Africa. This, she reasoned, gave her the necessary entree to a discussion of the three divisions of government — executive, judicial and legislative, and from there on out she felt sure that she was entirely justified in discussing any phase of the work of these three divisions because she had finally gotten them connected in some fashion or other with Africa. This type of artificial correlation is all too frequently indulged in and a unit so constructed is consequently loose and unappealing.

The correlation approach, however, even when it is not used to optimum effectiveness, indicates at least that the teacher has the feeling that subject matter lines are not absolutely sacred. The right type of correlation unit is one in which only that subject matter is drawn from the several fields which is appropriately related to the topic being discussed.

CLASSIFICATION NUMBER VI

The Drill or Topic Unit

Under this classification would fall units developed for the sole purpose of teaching pupils certain skills and subject matter facts. The pupils must know fractions and the use of maps, therefore we shall teach these in the most economical fashion possible. All too often this type of unit employs the memoriter method only; sheer repetition under compulsion is the only instrument employed. The practical administrator, supervisor, teacher, or course of study maker, while recognizing the fact that some of the inescapable essentials may never be gotten through any of the five types of units mentioned above, would still revolt at this procedure. They would enthusiastically urge an optimum use of the laws of learning with special emphasis upon readiness in relation to those skills and informations which might not have been secured through the methods employed in the five other classifications. They would agree for example that in the seventh grade children need to know the use of maps and would advise teachers consciously to plan units which would give children this skill.

This type of unit will have to be employed in many subjects such as geometry, and the formal portions of English, manual arts, music, and art, but should be resorted to only after every legitimate and economical attempt to start with a vital absorbing pupil interest has been exhausted. All too often, especially in the senior high school the assumption is made that subject matter is sacred and that the logical organization dictated by tradition must be strictly adhered to. This assumption is accepted most readily by teachers who are trained to present it in no other fashion. To break the habits of years is difficult and the urge to keep the status quo through the laissez faire attitude is too great for the nerves and ambitions of some.

235. "The Unit of Instruction and Study" [2]

R. B. Raup

For human beings life is made up of events or units. In some instances these events become so complex, interwoven, and varied that they seem to blend into a steady stream or process, but this is probably only a seeming, or an illusion. The stream or process in a person's life appears rather, upon closer scrutiny, to be a complex series of these interconnected events or units. One's observation of everyday life makes this evident. We do not start in the morning and go in a steady, unbroken motion till evening, or better, we do not start when we are born and go with one steady stream of life till death. This steady stream or process is really a matter of innumerable interconnected units or events.

Each of these units has a beginning and an ending, or an opening and a closing. The very use of the term unit or event implies that there is a starting and a stopping, marking some amount of duration. Some events prove to be much more enduring than others, that is, they reach over a much longer period. Their stopping points are farther removed from their starting points than in the case of other units. For instance, a person might set out to raise a crop of wheat. Such a unit in that individual's life would extend over a period of months, but note immediately that when we speak of a period we have to divide it into units, in terms of months, and a month in terms of days, and so on down to fractions of a second. The same would be true in any line of our life's activities which we might choose to investigate. What investigation means is just this delving into the nature of the units that give character to the thing which we are investigating. Whatever way we start, we find that life thus divides itself up into these start-stop affairs which we are now calling events or units.

It quickly becomes evident that there is interconnection between these units in any individual's life. Suppose that a person goes to a restaurant to get his lunch. There is a starting and a stopping of that event as a whole, but that entire event is itself made up of a great number of other events which are shorter in duration but which are none the less of this same start-stop nature. For instance, one puts on his hat. This act starts and stops. He goes from where he is to the restaurant. This also is a start-stop affair. Between these first acts and the very last one of paying his bill as he leaves the restaurant, the affair is one of units. We could analyze them in almost endless detail if we so wished. The interconnection and interde-

[2] *Journal of Educational Method*, 7:112–115, December, 1927.

pendence of the units in this case is evident. The long series that we have described is held together as a larger unit which we have called " going to a restaurant to get lunch." The little events would be merely helter-skelter if they were not thus held together as a larger unit, and the larger unit would not be realized if it were not for its connection with the smaller units. Life thus seems to be made up not only of units as such but of units in a great variety of interconnections. One might advisedly think of such a case as the one just described as a hierarchy of units, and of what we usually call the life process as a great number and variety of such hierarchies in all sorts of relationships.

When a teacher thinks about the problems that come up in dealing with a child, he thinks in terms of units. There is no other way to think except in these start-stop, open-close, begin-end affairs which we are calling events or units. When a curriculum committee sets out to draw up a curriculum, it deals with units or events; it can deal with nothing else. Such units are what are usually known as units of subject matter to be covered in a given time. Some persons have lost confidence in these units of subject matter as the way to conceive and draw up curricula. They think rather in terms of units of child activity, or units of experience. There is a wide difference of opinion today as to what kind of units should be employed in the constructing of curricula and just as wide a difference as to the manner in which they should be originated. But with all these differences, the differing persons and groups must think, if they think at all, in terms of some kind of units.

One constructive avenue of attack on the problems of education must therefore be by way of examination of this start-stop affair, or unit. Why has this not been done before? Probably just because the unit is so common and so prevalent throughout all of our living that we take it for granted, much as we take for granted the phenomenon of breathing. Sometimes, however, these common, diffuse factors which we consider so much a part of us that we do not even observe them, greatly repay careful examination. This is particularly true in the case of this matter of units. It is possible that some of our wide differences of opinion with regard to what should constitute a curriculum for education awaits a careful study of the nature of the units which people have in mind when they speak on the subject.

Can we know enough about the nature of these units to make the study of them constructive for those who are concerned with education? Probably just being aware that they do exist and that learning does take place in such a setting is of worth to educators. We are not so limited, however. There are a few things about these units of which it is possible to be reasonably certain, and these few things should be genuinely fruitful to a student of how we live and learn.

In the first place each unit is an affair of interaction. For our purposes this interaction is to be seen as between the individual and some object, or part, in his surroundings. In fact all living is interaction. What we call the body and the mind are just different forms of interaction. When analysis is made of either it is found to be made up of great numbers of units of interaction, which in turn are interrelated in larger units. Our study cannot get us away from or out of these affairs of interaction, and, as has been seen above, we cannot find anything in our experience which is not articulated in units of some kind. These units are the ways in which interaction occurs. There is a starting and a stopping, a beginning and an ending of this give and take in the almost countless interrelationships which constitute the human individual and his conduct. Living is made up of interrelated units and each unit is one of these start-stop affairs of interaction.

How does this point have meaning for education? First, it is particularly fertile in suggestion as to the nature and function of subject matter. Our common practice keeps repeating the expression "units of subject matter," "units for instruction," and "units for study." If what has just been said about units is correct, this common practice is prone to overlook the most important part of any unit, that is, the individual whom the particular bit of interaction involves. When a scholar in physics writes a textbook on his subject, the units in which his thinking takes form are his own ways of relating with these phases in his surroundings. The larger as well as the smaller units of organization are his own. To neglect this fact in regard to textbooks or to any course of study is serious. To speak of a course of study in geography, for instance, is misleading. It would always show much less conceit and much more consideration for the learner if the form of reference were somewhat as follows: "Mr. A's Course of Study in Geography," or "The Ways in which Mr. A Handles and Organizes His Geographical Relations." Mr. A has no human right to assume anything more generalized than this for any course of study he may draw up.

The same would be true of a curriculum committee. No group can attempt to substitute its own units of interrelation for those of some other one or group without doing violence to essential human values, for it is impossible to predict, especially within any narrow time limits, such as, "the third week in March," or "10:30 to 11:00 A.M. on Wednesdays and Fridays," that the interaction units of any child or group of children will correspond with those of Mr. A or of the curriculum committee as they have been reported in their courses of

study. Mr. A and the committee coöperate with the school system
to deprive the child of his wholeness and integrity. Integrity is
never more clearly at stake than when some one would deprive one
of the ownership of his acts. No one can inject his own units of experience into another. When he so endeavors he is stupid and brutal.
Much less can one organize the products of another's experiences for
him in advance. The only functional, genuinely owned organization
of experience anyone ever has is that which he has worked out in
his own right. It is not identical with any other. Compare, for instance, the functional organization of geographical relations or of
principles of physics and chemistry which we as adults now have
with the organization in which we were supposed to learn it. Unless
one has kept up the particular study, for example, for purposes of
teaching, he will find there is scarcely any likeness between the two
organizations. There is wasted effort somewhere in the scheme, and
wasted vigor of living, a result which is traceable unmistakably to
this failure to recognize the fact that a unit is always some *one's* unit
and can belong genuinely to no one else. A unit is an affair of interaction between an individual and his surroundings.

This same fact of interaction throws light on the unit of study.
A person never studies a thing as such. What he studies is what he
can do with that thing. In other words he is concerned in his interrelation with that object, and what is being striven for is some sort
of effectiveness in that connection. When a child finds placed before
him a " unit " of subject matter, he becomes interested in his ways
to effectiveness with it. His attention to it may be described as his
endeavor to discover what he can do with it. Usually what he can
want to do with it is widely different from what the author of the
course of study wanted to do with it. This vicious situation is due to
the mistaken notion that it can be foreseen what an individual or
group will want to do at some stated time in the future. In a large
majority of cases what the pupil finds he can do with that unit is to
come sufficiently into speaking acquaintance with it to get by and
keep peace with the system. We take advantage of his acquired
willingness to be thus at peace with authorities — to get over a certain amount of some one's subject matter as a condition of this peace.
The pupil is brought up to give hostages to society in the form of
his most sacred possession, that is, the integrity of his own thought
and conduct, and society through its organized education has been
none too considerate in its treatment of the precious trust. All that a
child, or anyone, ever can study is how he can relate up with the object before him, or what kind of unit he can achieve in connection
with it. If this is kept in mind our curriculum making is bound to be
more flexible, adaptable, and humane.

236. UNIT OF EXPERIENCE [3]

John. L. Childs

A typical unit of experience would include the various phases of an activity, which starts with the need occasioned by a disturbance in the equilibrium relationship, which continues through the various efforts made by the organism in overcoming the disturbance, and which ends with the restoration of the state of complacency. Such an experience is a developing affair. The control of the organism is generally indirect. The activities of the organism have to modify the direction of independent changes taking place in the environment. To secure such redirection takes time. Hence the reference of activities of the organism is always toward future outcomes. It acts to modify things in the given present so as to bring about an eventual situation which will yield satisfaction. Thus, life may be said ever to " live forward." Activity projects itself into the future. In fact, experience may be described as " a future implicated in a present." As has already been said, it is inherently experimental in character, because " all invasion of the future is a risk, an adventure." Experience is primarily an active affair. It is " a process of undergoing: a process of standing something; of suffering and passion, of affection, in the literal sense of these words. The organism has to endure, to undergo, the consequences of its own actions." [*] By its very structure experience is adjustive in character, even if not always intelligently purposeful.

237. " FUNCTIONAL VERSUS SUBJECT UNITS " [4]

Will French

My problem in this discussion is to illustrate the difference between subject units and what are here called functional units, as a means of indicating something of the difference between a program of secondary education of the traditional type and a program more in keeping with our best educational philosophy.

First let us examine a unit as we find it existing in classrooms today. Not to be unfair, I shall use a unit upon which much time has

[3] From *Education and the Philosophy of Experimentalism*, The Century Company, New York, 1931, p. 73.

[*] John Dewey, *Creative Intelligence* (Henry Holt and Company, 1917), pp. 10–11.

[4] From *Curriculum Making in Current Practice*, A Report of Conference Held at Northwestern University, October 30–31, 1931, School of Education, Northwestern University, Evanston, Illinois, 1932, pp. 154–158.

been spent and upon which a careful, check has been made by the teacher who built and taught it. It is one of a series of carefully planned units in botany the general purpose of which is plant classification. I submit this as a good subject unit. If you could examine the "Analysis of the Unit" prepared for the teacher's use, the guide sheets for pupils and the illustrated keys you would all agree. Considering it as a unit in a required subject, however, I should like to ask a few questions. Laying aside the question of a school mark, to how many of the students who were required to do the work did it make any difference whether it was done with success or not? In what way will they be benefited by success in it? In what way will they now or in the future realize that failure in this unit made a real difference? How will society be recompensed by those who did succeed? What penalty will society pay because some were unable to master this unit? The answer is that the unit has none of these things in mind — it isn't intended to make any difference. The purpose of the unit is to teach pupils some things about botany that are needed by those who study more botany. Anything else learned during the study of the unit was purely accidental concomitant learning unconsciously included by the teacher and untested at the end of the study. Now we come to the crux of the issue. Is secondary education to be devoted to a study of units written for the purpose of getting students ready to study more units of that subject, or is secondary education to be a period in which adolescents undergo selected experiences which contribute to understandings and attitudes, skills and abilities of use and value in superior living under the conditions which a complexly organized social structure lays upon us all?

The contrasting type of unit is here referred to as a functional unit because it is to be a unit directly devoted to building such useful and desirable understandings, attitudes, skills, or special abilities as are necessary to the superior living on the part of students which our objectives indicate us to be committed to. It is functional too in that it proposes to include subject matter only to the extent to which, and in the order in which, it functions in the accomplishment of the objectives of the unit and of secondary education. Obviously, there will be quite a difference in a unit in biological science, say in zoology, in which subject matter is included and arranged primarily to lead to further proficiency in the study of zoology and a unit designed to improve some condition of health and physical well being and which, therefore, utilizes needed subject matter from all the science fields, from the social studies field, and elsewhere in order that students may have the understandings, attitudes, skills, and special abilities needed to cope with the situation.

Two points of view seem to me to be important in gaining an adequate concept of the content and organization of these units: First: Even an enlarged unit as compared to our present and past ideas of units cannot expect to justify an objective as a whole. As I stated previously the understandings of, attitudes toward, skills or special abilities in an objective not the objective itself as a whole ought to be in the minds of teachers when planning instruction. Simply to fire off a unit in the general direction of the health objective, for instance, won't bring down many birds. An enlarged concept of health is not acquired all at once by one experience any more than one gets a complete understanding of Lake Michigan by making one trip to one spot on the beach. If each of the units having health as an objective enlarges upon previous experience in an important new area we do not need to worry about whether the ultimate concept of the whole field of health will be attained. We may be sure that it will be attained in this way or not at all. Each unit must not only be focused upon one of our present socially valuable objectives but it must be the microscope by which a particular socially important area of the ultimate objective is enlarged for purposes of study. Second: The selection of these areas brings me to the next point. I contend that the desired ultimate concept of any objective will be approached most rapidly if at each level from the junior high school through college we select our areas largely on the basis of the immediacy of the problem to the experience of the individuals who are to study the unit. These are the points at which interest concentrates like white corpuscles around a point of infection. Here is the point of greatest felt need. Here is the point therefore, at which new material for the solution of the problem will most quickly be utilized. In other words, this is the point of learning.

Unfortunately, I cannot present today a sample of a functional unit. I shall, however, undertake to show what one might be like. In a vocational agriculture class in Winfield, Kansas, in which each student has the use of a small field and gets the income from it, the immediate problem is, " How can I increase my income? " Part of the answer to this is to be found in maximum yield; this in turn depends in part upon fertility, which in turn is a matter of chemistry, geology and biology. Therefore, the " subject matter " of these three fields is studied in so far as it bears on the problem. I do not want to risk the inference that this technique can be utilized only in vocational education and so I shall undertake to show what a unit might be like in a more academic area. Let us start with the health objective. Underlying the general health concepts are some relating to food. Beneath these are some having to do with the *care* of food — others having to do with its *use*. Let us say that we shall have one unit to be known as *The Care of Foods* and another entitled *The Use of Food*. Today we are going to use a part of the unit on care of foods to show how subject-matter would be utilized in such a unit. One of the items which we should consider is how refrigeration helps in caring for food and in connection with this we should study mechanical refrigeration as the newest and therefore least commonly understood development. The typical American family today does not know why its refrigerator is cold. Here, therefore, is a point in experience at which learning can begin. Around this point of need for information we shall gather all the subject matter which can help. Material now assigned to chemistry, physics, manual arts, history, civics, home economics, and biology will all be needed before we shall have an adequate comprehension of, an understanding attitude toward, and some skill in the use of this most recent " end product " which stands in the place of the now discredited old family ice-box.*

The same use of subject matter as needed in respect to every other worthwhile aspect of the problem of the care of food might be developed. When we have finished we shall have combed the fields of knowledge for all the significant items which would contribute anything of consequence in relation to the care of food. They would be included in the order of use, and of need in relation to our unit — not in a logical order as needed for the further study of any subject. But some one will say that some of the science involved in this unit cannot be understood unless the student has had a course in chemistry. I challenge that statement. I admit only that there would probably be a small amount of material included in the unit as " knowledge for the sake of gaining more knowledge " — explanatory material providing the tool facts needed in doing the work of the unit. This scheme is used by every encyclopedia from the most recent set for children's use to the most profound Encyclopedia Britannica. They all rely upon their ability to provide understandable information as needed. Cross references are inserted for those who care to go deeper into the matter. I am but proposing that we utilize these techniques. Nowhere in life except in school is it assumed that learning cannot go on except with a logical arrangement of subject matter.

Then we may say that the content of these units will fall within the general areas covered by the objectives of secondary education with more particularized areas as the topics for the related sub-units. The order of these units would be largely determined by the needs and interests of different educational age groups. The theory here is that if the educative possibilities of each age are utilized at that

---

* This item is used here, not because it is the most significant part of the unit but because it is objective and specific, hence easy to use as an illustration.

age, the students will be able to cope successfully with the problems of successive ages as they arrive. Subject matter will be utilized in each unit as needed irrespective of its present logically determined assignment to some department or subject or grade.

238. "ANALYSIS OF TRENDS IN AN INFORMAL UNIT TEACHING PROGRAM" [5]

Claire Zyve and Marie Merrill

During 1932–1933 teachers of New York State sent to the Informal Teaching Committee and to the State Education Department descriptions of 452 units which had been or were then in progress in their classrooms. Data from 788 additional units were obtained through questionnaires. With the help of a committee of classroom teachers [*] the manuscripts were read and analyzed to discover the trends in classroom procedure which seemed to be accompanying the unit program which these teachers were describing.[†] The trends and tendencies listed below are those which appeared in a majority of the descriptions and could be illustrated in about equal degree. In the complete description and discussion of these points [‡] 350 excerpts from the manuscripts are used in illustration. In the presentation given here the tendencies are listed with very brief discussion and are followed by a somewhat general analysis of the significance of the trends.

I. OPPORTUNITIES FOR SOCIAL EXPERIENCES

The most conspicuous among the trends observed in this analysis is the increase in opportunity for social experience among children. This trend is revealed in:

1. Children's expression of their own individuality in the arrangement of their classrooms.
2. Flexible use and arrangement of furniture.
3. Ingenious uses of materials.
4. Encouragement of informality in social relationships through coöperative room activities.
5. Provision for coöperative activities within the school as a means of producing informal social relationships among children of different ages.

[5] *Teachers College Record*, 35:293–303, January, 1934.

[*] Margaret Batten, Bronxville; Helen Hultz, Scarsdale; Mildren Striker, Greenburg.

[†] The grades and the number of units from each are as follows: — Kindergarten, 36; I, 47; II, 56; III, 56; IV, 74; V, 58; VI, 63; VII and VIII, 26; whole school, 31; unclassified, 5.

[‡] Bulletin No. 4, "Cardinal Objectives in Elementary Education," edited by J. Cayce Morrison. The State Department of Education, Albany. In press.

6. Teachers' recognition of the need for varied activities carried out by small groups in the classroom as well as for those which include all children; and their recognition of the fact that the length of time which an activity runs must be governed by the needs of the children in carrying it out.

The classroom of the elementary school of to-day appears to be one in which children are able to live normally. They make it so by expressing in it their own needs and ideas of beauty. It is not unusual to find them painting furniture or cupboards, making curtains and decorative hangings, or building tool chests or library furniture as each need arises. They care for and arrange flowers; they keep aquariums and herbariums. Their play life is expressed in playhouses and stores. They bring in their vacation exhibits or exhibits from other lands.

We find children making many attempts to fit classroom equipment to the varied program which normal living in a room demands. They need furniture which is flexible enough to permit their group projects to advance unhampered. We find them removing extra desks to provide room for a reading corner, or rearranging them to provide space for their sand table, aquarium and easel. One class turned the corner of its room into a printing shop. Ordinary folding screens may enclose a section for a playhouse, furnish curtains for a play or bulletin board space, or they may be used as an easel for large paintings.

It is especially interesting to note the wide variety, the inexpensiveness, and the diverse uses of materials. We find classes making their own Easter egg vegetable dye, painting on the back of discarded wall paper when their drawing paper is exhausted, or doing their block printing on old sheets. They sift the sand from the river bank for their sand-box, bring in clay from a natural claybank for their modeling, and catch fish in the creek for their aquarium. Mechano sets illustrate principles of bridges, while grocery store discards are convertible into anything from a medieval castle to the library corner furniture.

Coöperative room activities furnish many opportunities for learning acceptable ways of acting in a group. In some cases, such as a meeting to plan the work of the day, to discuss an assembly program, or a class trip, the whole group is working for the same end. In other cases, such as the writing of a play, the publishing of a class newspaper, or the reading of poems to other groups, a few children with similar interests are learning to work together.

These group activities frequently extend outside the classroom and include children of varied ages. We find an eighth grade boy advising a group of fourth graders in making model airplanes or a fifth grader skilled in the use of a ditto machine making the outline maps

needed by a third grade. The school reporters for the month may
" cover " interesting activities or exciting happenings in many rooms.
Numerous activities or centers of interests, such as the building of
a barn for a calf or informal singing in the hall before school, draw
children of different ages. Room stores specializing in a particular
product bring customers from many rooms, while community welfare
work, garden, dramatics, science, music, or poetry groups all serve to
eliminate age and grade barriers. Assemblies, long accepted as a
reason for bringing many children together, are sharing a place in
the school with an ever-increasing number of less formal and more
flexible activities based on working interests not limited to one age
or grade.

There seems to be an increasing variability in the extent to which
all children in a room are expected to participate in an activity and
in the number of different interests which may be in progress at one
time. Data on about 800 units in addition to the 452 analyzed were
obtained through a questionnaire sent to the teachers who had contributed reports on the original units. The report on 757 of these
units showed that 271 had been carried out by small groups of children without the whole group's participating in any way; 371 others
had been interests of the whole class; in the remaining 115 the children had worked on the same big unit with small groups working on
different problems within the unit. Of 156 teachers reporting, 104
said that usually several different activities were in progress in the
room at one time, while in 52 rooms there was ordinarily only one
activity carried out by the whole class. This technique which breaks
up the large groups into smaller groups with varied interests develops
the resourcefulness, independence, and social responsibility of the
children in each smaller group.

The range of the length of 788 units on which teachers reported
was from two days to forty weeks. Of these units 495 had a range
of one to seven weeks, while the range of 693 fell between one and
twelve weeks. The median length of time spent was five and eight-
tenths weeks. This tendency to base the length of time to be spent
on a unit on the needs inherent in it or on the interests of the children
results in many different interests appearing for fairly short intervals
during the year rather than in one interest continuing for a long time.
Nearly a third of the units ran three weeks or less, and slightly less
than another third between four and six weeks; 25 per cent ran between six and twelve weeks, leaving about 12 per cent continuing
more than twelve weeks. Four per cent (29 units) ran the whole
year.

II. SOCIAL AND ECONOMIC INTERPRETATION OF THE COMMUNITY

Another trend of the units analyzed is an increasing emphasis on the development of the social and economic understandings which tend to unite the school and the community. There are several tendencies which afford evidence of this:

1. The replacement of vicarious with direct experiences in dealing with the child's immediate environment.

2. The inclusion of materials in the school which increase the child's understanding of social and economic life in the local community.

3. The free use of (access to) the community by children for materials and experiences.

4. The recognition of children's current interests and experiences as well as planned curriculum materials throughout the whole of the elementary school and of the legitimacy of the reappearance of an interest on different age levels.

A tendency toward first-hand experience finds expression in direct action in the child's own environment in such activities as setting a hen, helping the milkman deliver milk, or caring for and shearing a sheep. In visualizing distant places or happenings of the past, this same tendency toward direct experiencing is illustrated by the frequency of exhibits, in the writing of letters to children in other lands, in plays or visits to historic places.

We find children studying the social and economic life of their own communities. They may be surveying the nationalities and types of homes from which children in the school come, or they may be helping with the organized welfare work, or visiting community industries or the town's historic spots. More complete social understandings which will come at a later age have beginnings in such activities as a study of the town's municipally owned and controlled waterworks or an analysis of school rules for the sake of getting rid of " dead wood."

Children gain in social and economic understandings through utilizing experts, interested parents, materials and advice which are available for the asking. One finds an engineer who has lived in China, a father who is an expert on oil, or a boy scout each talking in the classroom. Children also work with the experts of the community: the local landscape gardener helps with the rock garden, the bookkeeper in the bank starts an accounting system for the class, the mothers play with their daughters on the baseball and soccer teams.

These tendencies to replace vicarious with direct experiences, to include materials of purely local interest, and to bring people from the community into the school to give advice has brought recognition of a place in all grades for current interests and experiences as well as planned curriculum materials. A description of the way in which children coöperated with the community agencies in protecting elm trees against an unprecedented pest of cankerworms is an illustration. The pest may not recur, but the school has a program flexible enough to meet some other problem when the need arises. Among 788 units which teachers listed by name, there were 140, or 18 per cent, which seemed obviously to come under the head of current interests or experiences rather than planned course-of-study materials. Examples of the titles are:

> Planting seeds to raise slips
> for a garden
> Making a balanced aquarium
> Studying the projection lantern
> Issuing and dealing in scrip
> Caring for a pig
> The cause of the solar eclipse

For some time it has been accepted that the school curriculum for the younger children should be based upon their experiences. There is a tendency now for this same type of material to be found in every grade of the elementary school. It is interesting to note that with this provision for children's current experiences, the same interest frequently occurs again and again in different forms with children of different ages. For instance, such an activity as a room newspaper may appear in a second grade and again in a fourth grade; children give plays in every grade from the first up. Care of animals and growing plants is of continuous interest to children. Obviously, with older children the interest assumes a more mature or more complex form. In one school, children of the third, fourth, and sixth grades were working out simultaneously a graphic explanation of the solar eclipse. The sixth grade children carried their investigation much further than did the fourth grade, both in the scientific explanations involved and in the history of astronomy. Instead of a problem's being forever closed after it has appeared once, there seems to be a tendency for the thread of many interests to run through the elementary school years and to be added to in a more mature form as the years pass.

III. THE DRILL PROGRAM

A third trend is revealed in the tendency to include with the activity only the drill which has a functional use.

1. The inclusion only of the drill necessary for the accomplishment of the activity: in other words, the viewing of the classroom activity as a motivator of needed drill rather than as a vehicle of drill.

2. A decrease in time spent on factual drill; the setting aside of periods separate from activity periods for the purpose of more permanent learning of needed facts.

There was a tendency in the early period of the activity type of program to choose activities because they included the need for certain skills. That is, the need for a skill proficiency predominated, not the suitability or value of the particular activity to the group of children in question. The point of view now apparent in these teachers' descriptions is that an activity may make a child aware of the need for acquiring certain skill processes but that it is in no sense chosen simply because it affords an opportunity for practice in drill subjects.

The tendency to include with the activity only the drill which is integrally necessary to its completion has resulted in another tendency to put into separate periods drill for fixing facts which the school believes should be the common knowledge of all children. Teachers are including in their programs short drill periods for the facts on which automatic correct response is expected. For instance, 136 of 156 teachers equally distributed from Grades I to VI who answered a questionnaire on the subject said they included short drill periods. The distribution of time for drill indicated by these teachers is as follows:

Subject	No. Teachers Reporting	Average Daily Time in Minutes on 136 Reports
Spelling	96	10
Arithmetic	111	23
Grammar	74	9
Writing	82	9
Reading	95	23

This report might indicate either that functional use of facts is decreasing the time which must be spent in learning them, or that the number of facts to be learned is decreasing, or that the drill in these schools is highly efficient. It is not possible to draw conclusions, of course, as to whether facts were over-learned in the past or are under-learned in the present.

IV. THE INTEGRATION OF THE SEPARATE SUBJECTS

The shift of separate subjects from isolated positions to an integral place as tools in the solution of problems is still another observable trend. This change in function of the subjects of the curriculum is evident in several tendencies:

1. A disregard for subject-matter divisions in carrying out activities.

2. The recognition of the real arithmetical situations existing within the unit, the school, or the community.

3. The use of special subjects, such as music, shop, or physical education, as tools inseparable from the accomplishment of classroom activities.

4. The realization that science serves in the solving of many problems and interests.

5. The recognition that English expression is a basic part of all activities.

The disappearance of separate subject names and the appearance of more indefinite time divisions of the day seem to be developing coördinately with the informal activity program. The emphasis is shifting from " subjects to be learned " to " things to be done or appreciated." In such a program, where direct experiences are frequently the basis for learning, subject-matter designations cannot be made so clearly. There were frequent examples, such as a trip through a milk plant, watching birds build their nests, cooking and serving a luncheon, making a quilt, or illustrating a story, in which children were doing or beginning to understand many things. It is easy to surmise wherein these activities arithmetic, history, written English, or science enters, but in the carrying out of the activity these subject-matter divisions are disregarded.

The tendency to judge a unit on the basis of its value to children regardless of the degree to which it is a carrier of drill is resulting in a changing function of the separate subjects. Arithmetic, for instance, is used whenever it furthers the enterprise at hand and helps in transacting the business of the day. We find children studying a thermometer, computing cost of a train trip, earning money for relief, buying bulbs, measuring and cutting blue print paper. These are a few of many problems of the classroom in which arithmetic appears as a tool in reaching a solution.

There is a very close relationship and in some cases a complete integration of the purposes and ends of the so-called special subjects with other classroom work. For the majority of elementary school children fine and industrial arts are skills needed primarily for the graphic representation of ideas or concepts — a need which seems to come especially in the social and natural sciences. We find a class of nine-year-old children illustrating ideas which people of various times have held about eclipses. They paint columns for an Egyptian play, reproduce Indian art, or decorate a store. Music, rhythms, and dancing are also closely allied to classroom activities. They seem to be used, however, for expressing emotion rather than ideas.

There appear to be two types of science teaching: that by the trained science teacher and that by the room teacher. These teachers are both discovering, however, that science is necessary to the progress of classroom units and activities and are in turn becoming sensitive to the science possibilities in room activities. Interests in growing plants, in animals, in freezing and boiling points, in weather conditions, in deep-sea life, in the planetary system, in magnetism, or in bacteria are only a few of the interests that appear as outgrowths of other units.

English is the one traditional subject for which there seems to be a need in all activities. We find children talking with each other in conversation periods, in school council meetings, in informal assemblies, or in class meetings. We find them reading to other groups stories or poems they have written, reviewing books for a list for their mothers, reporting happenings of the school council, making vacation guidebooks for other children. They tell " how " they wrote a play or they write books of their own for the satisfaction of expressing a feeling or for the fun of organizing ideas or information.

V. THE USE OF BOOKS FOR REFERENCE

There is a trend, evident throughout all the descriptions, for children to build up research attitudes and to use research techniques in obtaining the information they desire. They reveal tendencies to:

1. Refer to books as tools in the solution of problems.
2. Build up and use libraries as reference rooms.

As many books of as many kinds as possible seems to describe the tendency toward the use of books in the informal unit program. Texts were mentioned in connection with the drill subjects where identical facts were to be learned; otherwise they were referred to as reference books in which children searched for answers to their problems. This change in function of the textbook from a book to be learned to a reference book or book to be consulted is an outstanding feature of the descriptions.

There are many cases in which teachers and children work together in building up reference libraries either for general use or for the use of particular groups. There is much evidence of need for informational as well as recreational material in the libraries and for well-stocked general libraries so that the room libraries may be changed as the interests change. Much reference work is being done by individuals or small committees, thus implying a need for a free use of the school library by groups of children.

VI. GROWTH IN TEACHERS

Finally there is a trend for teachers to develop the techniques which they are encouraging. This seems evident through tendencies which they show in:

1. Analyzing their work critically.
2. Compiling lists of materials and supplies for future use.

Most teachers commented on the values of their units, and suggested ways in which they might be adapted to other groups. In some cases they told what they would do to achieve greater participation on the part of children if the units were repeated. Many of them stressed the importance of wider use of the materials of the immediate community. They commented on the age of the children whom they thought would profit most by a particular activity or suggested other leads which might come from it. They suggested changes in teaching technique which might bring better results. These teachers, interested in the informal activity program, seem to realize that there are many ways of reaching an end and many activities possible in addition to those taking place. In short, they seem to view these units as flexible, varying with the needs and interests of groups. Most teachers also included a bibliography. Children's materials and references were frequently listed separately from the teacher's with all the necessary detail given to effect a saving of time should the unit be repeated.

239. UNITS OF WORK IN COURSES OF STUDY * [6]
Henry Harap

On the basis of a somewhat careful analysis we found that about 60% of the courses were subdivided into clearly recognizable units of work. The rest may be said to be subdivided into parts which are too fragmentary to suggest the completeness or unity of the parts. The subjects that exhibit this tendency to a marked degree are social studies, science, practical arts, health and physical education, and commercial studies; the subjects in which this tendency was exemplified to the smallest degree are mathematics, language, music, and foreign language. From the point of view of size of the unit the courses divide themselves equally into those which contain large units and those which contain small units, a small unit being one which lasts less than two weeks. This is not a matter of great consequence when large units are broken up into coherent subdivisions which the pupil senses.

Of the courses that are divided into a series of coherent units only 30 per cent are based on a technical process or graded step which shows

* This report is based on an analysis of more than 300 courses of study from about 125 school organizations.

[6] From *A Survey of Courses of Study Published in the Last Two Years*, Western Reserve University, Curriculum Laboratory, No. 44, Cleveland, Ohio, May 20, 1935, pp. 6–9.

a marked trend away from the conventional organization of subjects in the last two years. On the other hand, the functional basis of the unit shows a marked increase. Of the unitary courses, the complete social experience is the basis in 31% of the courses; the theme or concept, in 25%; and the center of child interest, in 13% of the unitary courses. When all courses analyzed, unitary and non-unitary, are used as basis of comparison, we find that 40% have a functional basis, that is, they are based on social experiences, themes, concepts, and centers of interest. These courses represent a departure from conventional practice. This is one of the most significant trends revealed by the survey. Our data would lead us to believe that the number of courses of study that represent this tendency has doubled in the last two years.

This same conclusion was reached when the activities were examined to discover the degree to which they were life-like. We found that about a third of the courses contained activities which might reasonably be regarded as life-like to a moderate or large degree. In 36% of the courses the activities were life-like to a small degree, and 31% contained no trace of social reality whatsoever. When this criterion was applied to each subject group it was found that health, physical education, and the practical arts were very life-like; that the commercial studies were fairly life-like; that language and the social studies were average; and that mathematics, foreign language, and science were socially real to a small degree.

As we perused one course of study after another, we had the conviction that very few teachers and course of study makers had probed deeply into the bases of the unit of work. Indeed, we discovered that our ideas were not perfectly clear. Consequently, the many specific bases of the unit of work were recorded and analyzed, yielding the reclassification of the bases of the unit of work given below. We would not give the impression that it is something to be standardized. It merely serves to clarify one's thinking. In the broadest sense, the unit of work appears to us to be a complete and coherent learning experience having a purpose which is meaningful to the pupil and which is closely related to a life situation; an aspect of the social or natural environment; or a center of child interest. It may, also, under favorable learning conditions be based upon a generalization or class of things, provided they are real and meaningful to the pupil. A unit based upon a technical principle or graded step is likely to be an unreal basis for a learning experience.

In our opinion, the tendency to organize courses around a number of major concepts, as for example in the Des Moines, Iowa, course in elementary science, may result in making them adult minded and rather intellectualized. It should be pointed out that the introductory statement in this illustration explains that each unit of study grows out of child interests but the body of the courses of study does not bear out this statement. This confirms our belief that despite the best intentions, an abstract analysis of concepts or themes cannot be made to coincide with individual behavior and social experience.

The Virginia State course of study, among the most radical of the new programs, is based on centers of interest from grade 1 to 12. It is uncompromisingly functional in content. The material is very rich in suggestions involving considerable readjustment of habits and attitudes of teachers. In its foundations it is about as thorough as any program. There is a very conscious effort to be consistent in the incorporation of the basic centers of interest, the basic generalizations, procedures, and means of evaluation. We are, of course, here reporting only the huge academic labors of the participants in the construction of the document. Whether it will remain a contribution to knowledge or be converted into a contribution to practice only time will tell.

A TENTATIVE RECLASSIFICATION OF THE BASES OF THE UNIT OF WORK

1. A complete life experience or situation
    a. A life-like enterprise — home care of the sick (health) — chorus (music)
    b. A practical task — care of the kitchen (home economics)
    c. A job — constructing a stool (industrial arts) — filing (commercial)
    d. A game — golf (physical education)
    e. Personal behavior — habits of eating (health)
2. An aspect of the social environment
    a. A phase of business — insurance (commercial)
    b. A geographic unit — Arabian Peninsula (geography)
    c. A social institution — The Home (social studies)
    d. A phase of economic life — Money and Credit (economics)
3. An aspect of the natural environment
    a. A phase of the natural environment — weather (science)
4. A center of child interest
    a. A child theme — boats (social studies)
5. A generalization or theme or concept
    a. Social organization — man and his world (literature)
    b. Social policy — utilization of natural resources (social studies)
    c. Historical — territorial expansion (history)
    d. Social environment — living together (social studies)

    e. Physical — the changing earth (science)

    f. Biological — evolution (science)

6. An important class of things

    a. In the plant world — fruit, trees (science)

    b. In the animal world — bird (science)

    c. In the business world — negotiable instruments (commercial)

    d. In music — songs (music)

    e. In the geographic environment — hot, dry lands (geography)

7. A technical principle; or phase of a conventional subject

    a. A scientific principle — gravity (science)

    b. An artistic principle — form (art)

    c. A phase of science — cells and tissues (science)

    d. A graded step or process — decimals (mathematics)

NOTE: The problem occurs as the basis but it is not included because it refers to the psychological form of the unit and is applicable to all the above classifications.

THE FORM OF THE UNIT OF WORK

As heretofore we have classified the courses of study according to form in order to discover any changes in common practice. For purposes of the tabulation we have distinguished four types: 1) outline under several headings; 2) solid paragraphs under several headings; 3) parallel columns under several headings; and 4) informal descriptions. The analysis shows an increase in organzied outlines and the complete disappearance of the informal account. The data for the last six years are shown in Table III. These changes are undoubtedly in response to demands from teachers, although our preference is for the solid paragraphs because they make for a full and complete treatment of the procedure.

We have not attempted to study the recurring topical headings of units but have observed that they are becoming unnecessarily more numerous and complex. Three out of every four courses of study include procedures, that is, they describe how activities are carried on. In this respect the modern course of study is a very great improvement over that of fifteen years ago. Many courses of study contain the raw materials for the construction of units and not the connected account of an actual learning unit as it was experienced on a given occasion by the pupils.

TABLE III

COMPARISON OF FORM OF UNITS 1930, 1932 AND 1934

Per cent of Total

	1930 242 Courses of Study	1932 317 Courses of Study	1934 287 Courses of Study
1. Organized Outline	47	48	57
2. Parallel Columns	27	16	17
3. Solid Paragraphs	19	26	25
4. Informal Description	7	10	0

240. STEPS IN DEVELOPING UNITS OF WORK [7]

Approach. The first step in developing a unit is often referred to as the approach. The function of the approach is to get pupils to formulate a dominating purpose out of which the unit may be developed. Purposes result from interests, that is, if children or adults become interested in something they soon formulate a purpose that leads to activity. Hence, in developing an approach to a unit a teacher is first concerned with discovering interests which the children in her class already have or with developing new ones.

There are several ways of finding what interests the children already have. As a rule, this should be done indirectly. Some methods which have been used successfully by teachers are given here.

1. Ask the members of the class to answer questions somewhat similar to these: Why do you want to come to school? What do you want to learn this year? Have you seen something lately about which you have wondered but about which you could not find the answer? What do you like to do at school, at home? (The children in the first grade may whisper their answers to the teacher. The older children may write the answers. Have no names signed to their papers. This is done to make them feel more free to say what they really feel.)

2. Watch the children while they are playing or working during their free time. The books which the children use voluntarily, the objects which they make, the playthings which they choose, the groups which they join, and the free discussions — all give to the teacher an excellent idea of the things about which the children are concerned.

3. Talk casually to individuals and to small groups letting them take the lead in the conversation. Occasionally when questions are asked, the teacher may make mental notes without comment. As soon as possible these notes should be recorded for future reference.

[7] Florida, *The Course of Study for Florida Elementary Schools, Grades I–VI*, State Department of Public Instruction, Tallahassee, Florida, 1933, pp. 12–19.

4. Give the children an opportunity to tell the others about good times they have enjoyed, about the interesting things they are doing or have done, and about the things they would like to do. (Mental notes may be made of the things children talk about and these may be recorded and used later.)

5. Ask the children to collect pictures which appeal to them or which they think would appeal to some member of the group. (These pictures may be brought to school and classified by the teacher for her own guidance. Other objects of interest may be used in a similar manner.)

6. Distribute to small groups of children catalogs from large mail-order houses and give the pupils directions for using the index. The teacher may watch to see what the children look for and she may use this knowledge later.

7. Talk to the parents to find out how the child spends his free time at home and the interests which his parents know about.

In so far as possible, each child should be encouraged to follow his own interests and to develop the skills needed for carrying out these interests. However, each individual should learn to be a member of a group and to make his contribution toward solving the problems of the group. This means that group interests must be developed and that each individual should be a member of some group, and should have the opportunity to contribute to its welfare. The interests found to be common to several children may be the basis for organizing a few groups. In some cases, group interests may have to be developed.

There are several methods of getting interests common to groups of children. Some of these methods are given here.

1. Provide more fruitful and varied first-hand experiences for the members of the groups by:
   a. Bringing interesting materials into the schoolroom, as for example:
      (1) Toys with which children may build and make things.
      (2) Musical instruments with which children may experiment.
      (3) Pets; as, chickens, rabbits, canaries, white rats, and other animals.
      (4) Plants; as, growing tomato slips, pepper plants, rubber plants, palms, or other plants.
      (5) Vivarium with turtles or frogs.
      (6) Aquarium with gold fish, minnows or tadpoles.
   b. Performing experiments showing need of plants for light, air, and water.
   c. Making excursions to see phases of the environment related to some need of the children; as for example, a dairy, a green house, a poultry farm, a post office.

2. Providing rich and varied experiences which may be gained from second-hand sources; as for example, pictures, hearing others report their experiences, examining materials which illustrate other phases of life.

As a particular interest is stimulated by the teacher, she will find her pupils gradually begin to formulate a large purpose. This purpose should be made the basis for a careful plan developed by the pupils with the guidance of the teacher. This plan should embody a list of the things the children want to do, how they propose to do these things, materials they need, and a division of responsibility. Having agreed upon such a plan, the unit enters the second stage, that of development.

Thus far little has been said about the teacher's plans. Throughout the unit she must guide the children. If she is to do this successfully she must plan her work carefully each day. The first step in planning, which is to discover or develop pupils' interests, has been discussed. As soon as this step is undertaken, the teacher should start canvassing the educational possibilities of the interests of the children. This involves three steps, the first of which is to list the activities that the children most probably would engage in if the interests were followed up and they were encouraged to try to achieve their purpose. The teacher's skillful guidance in the selection of activities to carry out the purpose set up is of great importance. She must know what possibilities for growth are inherent in a proposed activity and whether or not her pupils have advanced to that stage of development which will enable them to make use of these possibilities.

Each activity undertaken should be constantly checked by certain carefully chosen standards. The following are suggested:

1. The activity must further the accomplishment of the accepted aim of education

2. It must help to accomplish the purpose for which the unit was undertaken

3. It must be related to the life of the children

4. It must be sufficiently within the range of accomplishment of the children to insure satisfactory degree of success, but must be difficult enough to challenge the best abilities of the group

5. The activities undertaken by the group must be varied enough to provide for all phases of development, physical, intellectual, and emotional

6. They must provide for progress in the use of essential tools and for the development of desirable habits and attitudes

7. Materials for carrying out the activity must be available.

Besides being ready to guide children in selecting activities, the teacher must be thoroughly at home with the subject-matter. This leads to the second step which is to list materials and subject-matter that could be employed by the children in the activities listed. It is usually well to review and assemble in outline form the subject-matter that most probably will be needed. Points that may offer difficulties or that may require special emphasis should be noted. The teacher should not confine herself to this outline, however, but should have such command of subject-matter that she can readjust herself, take a different line of thought, and even change her objectives if the interests of the children take another angle. At the same time, such materials as books, visual aids, arts-and-crafts materials should be made convenient. The teacher should visualize the development of the unit and be prepared to guide it to a satisfactory termination.

The next step is to list the educational objectives that the activities and subject-matter will help achieve. The objectives should be taken from the list presented in this course of study or from additional ones derived from the aim of education accepted by the State. Having listed the objectives, the teacher is in a position to decide intelligently whether or not the possible unit has sufficient promise to warrant its development. She also will be in a position to guide the children in planning the development of the unit.

Not all teachers recognize that pupils should take part in planning the unit. It is essential that pupils suggest activities and, with the guidance of the teacher, select those most likely to accomplish their purpose. They should aid in deciding what materials are needed and how to secure them. They should take part in selecting committees and leaders needed to carry out the unit. The planning should eventuate in an outline of the problems the children would have to meet in order to realize their big purpose, the methods to be employed in meeting these problems, and an assignment of duties to the various members of the class.

Development of unit. After the approach has been made and plans have been formulated, the teacher should continue to be an active member of the group. However, she should not dominate the situation unduly, but should allow the children to take the initiative, to assume responsibility and to exercise judgment as far as they are capable. Nevertheless, through suggestions, through arranging situations and materials, and through thought-provoking questions, the teacher may skillfully guide all the activities of the classroom.

The activities that may be employed in developing a unit may be roughly classified as, group discussion, individual study, construction, and excursions and interviews.

Discussion activities. When all members of the group freely ask questions and express their opinions the activity is classified as discussion. In this type of activity the children make plans, select facts most pertinent to the solution of the problem under consideration, evaluate and organize the materials and data presented, determine meanings, judge the validity of statements, and arrive at conclusions.

Such activities may follow the collection of materials, and data bearing on the solution of the problem may be used for planning the solution, may precede or follow an excursion, and may be used to evaluate work already accomplished. They should come at any time during the class period when needed and should be allotted as much time as necessary.

Discussion activities can be judged by whether or not there is a worthwhile, wholesome, social situation. Such a situation is evidenced when the children are interested, take part in a natural manner, and are courteous but frank in criticisms and suggestions. Also, the success of the activity can be estimated by such evidences of thinking and learning; as, making accurate statements, giving reasons for opinions, questioning statements and opinions, avoiding needless repetition, keeping the topic under discussion in the foreground, and demanding sufficient data before reaching conclusions.

Study activities. Study, in contrast to discussion, is an individual thinking and learning activity. The time employed in this type of activity is the research or finding-out period during which children search for information to answer questions that have come up. During such periods the teacher has an opportunity to work with individuals and small groups. She can explain what information is necessary to answer the questions raised, how to select facts that are pertinent to the problem to be solved, how to use reference books and the library, and how to organize for class reports the materials found. The skills required for study which the children do not employ successfully should be noted and should receive special attention in the drill period later in the day. The success of the study activities can be judged by whether or not children grow increasingly independent in their study.

Creative activities. Some activities that may be employed in a creative way are building, drawing, painting, modeling, writing, doing handwork, dramatizing, experimenting, singing, and playing musical instruments. Such activities are especially valuable. They give concrete, enriched experiences which make them interesting, purposeful, meaningful, and educational to the child. They provide an opportunity for self-expression which has long been lacking in schools. They may be judged only in terms of the satisfaction which the child derives from engaging in them. Adult standards should not be imposed. As each child evidences a desire for improvement he should be assisted to develop better techniques than he may employ.

Excursion and interview activities. Excursion and interview activities may be employed to secure data for the solution of problems which the class has raised. They should be planned with very definite purposes in mind. Such planning should be done by the pupils with the guidance of the teacher. Questions to which answers are desired should be listed and the method of recording answers agreed upon. At times it might be desirable to apportion the questions among the members of the class. Permission from proper authorities must be secured and careful arrangements made beforehand about going and coming and about other details.

A follow-up discussion of the excursion is very necessary and should have careful attention. A check should be made to see what questions have been answered. Opportunity should be provided for discussion of the most interesting things. Misconceptions and misunderstandings should be cleared up.

Whenever the teacher sees that the greatest value of a unit has been secured for her class she should be on the alert for a culminating activity. A unit may culminate in a review, summary, and test, or it may end with a play, a puppet show, an exhibit, an assembly program, or some other climax calling for organization and summarization.

As a part of the summary of the unit, the children should have a part in judging their work. Each activity should be evaluated according to its contribution toward the purpose set up in the beginning. The children may see that other activities might have been used to advantage and that those used might have been better developed. This part of the conclusion of the unit is very valuable, for it is through such reflection that relationships are understood and the real meaning and significance of the unit realized.

Outcomes. When the unit is concluded the teacher should go back to her original objectives to see how much has been accomplished toward realizing them. Seldom will she find that she has realized them completely. She has probably modified her objectives as the work has progressed. But the unit should show some definite outcomes in terms of the objectives set up for that unit and of the accepted general aims of education.

Form in which units are presented. Units may be reported in various ways. A degree of uniformity makes it easier to determine where in a report to find each step in a unit described. In order to secure this uniformity the same form is employed for all units reported in this course of study. This form may be modified by local systems in any way they consider desirable. The form follows:

TITLE OF UNIT

1. *Approach.*
      (Explain fully how the dominant purpose of the pupils was initiated and what it was that they purposed to do)

2. *Objectives.*
   (List the educational objectives which the teacher believes the unit will help to realize)
3. *Plan.*
   (Give a detailed description which includes pre-planning or stage-setting by the teacher and the planning of pupils and teacher after the purpose has been established)
4. *Development.*
   (Describe the development of the unit giving activities in which pupils engaged to solve their problem or problems. Also, list materials and subject-matter)
5. *Outcomes.*
   (List outcomes and show how they were tested)
6. *Leads to other units.*
   (Describe interests developed which promise to lead on to other units)
7. *Evaluation.*
   (Evaluate the unit by listing its strong and weak points and by describing how it might have been improved)

241. " PROVISIONAL CRITERIA FOR EVALUATING CLASSROOM ACTIVITY * " [8]

Florence Stratemeyer

A. *With respect to the recognition of purpose — the major educational goals accepted:*
  1. Is the experience (activity or subject content) directed toward meeting the needs of the children in their immediate adjustment to life conditions?
     a. Is it related to other activities of the children, both in and out of school?
     b. Will it give fuller meaning to the daily experiences of the children?
  2. Does it form a part of a *continuing* development?
     a. Does it provide opportunity for the growth of the individual? the group?
     b. Is it more difficult than previous similar activities?
     c. Does it furnish leads into other worth-while experiences, stimulating a desire for a continued widening of interests and understanding (foundations for later learning)?

* It is to be recognized that not all the criteria need be met in a single experience or unit of work.

[8] From *The Effective Use of Curriculum Materials,* Contributions to Education, No. 460, Bureau of Publications, Teachers College, Columbia University, New York, 1931, pp. 118–119.

3. Does it give promise of outcomes functional in meeting the larger demands of society (the needs of adult society)?
4. Does it provide for selecting, planning, executing, and evaluating experiences?
   a. Fostering an inquiring attitude?
   b. Developing initiative and self-direction in the ordering of experience and in carrying the activities forward?
   c. Evaluating the worth of experiences, the effectiveness of the plan used, etc. (i.e. judging relative values, organization of experiences in relationship)?
5. Has it inherent within it the necessity for the development of the tools — skills, habits, knowledges, appreciations — adjudged incident to the important aspects of human life? (Are the phases of subject matter content worth while?)
6. Does it provide opportunity for social living and coöperative action — group thinking and planning?
7. Does it provide for individual thinking and planning within the free, informal association of pupils?

B. *With respect to adaptation to the pupil group — is it opportune with this group?*
1. Is the experience adapted to the general level of development of the children?
   a. Does it provide for the recognition of individual differences in interests, abilities, and needs, making individual growth possible within group activity (through stimulation of many kinds of activities)?
   b. Is it suitably graded to the pupils' *growing* interests and capacities?
   c. Is it of a degree of difficulty that enlists the children's abilities fully and yet provides for at least a measure of success?
      (1) Does it provide for principles of increasing difficulty?
      (2) Do the children have the background necessary to carry it out with satisfaction?
      (3) Are needed " working conditions " such that it can be carried to a successful ending (available practical materials, equipment, time factor, etc.)?
      (4) Does it provide for checking progress and growth?
2. Is the experience significant to the pupil group — will it be accepted by them as worth while?
   a. Is it related to experiences familiar to the children? Does it come out of the children's previous experience?
   b. Is it related to other activities of the children (in school and outside activities)?

    c. Will it give fuller meaning to the experiences of the children?

    d. Does it provide for differences in environment and occasion which constitute the avenues of immediate and direct interest and approach (community, time, pupil group)?

3. Does it provide for proper balance and variety of experience?

    a. How often and how recently have similar activities been experienced?

    b. Does it provide for needed recall of past learning experiences (repetition of vital facts when needed)?

    c. Does it introduce and emphasize essential elements (eliminating unnecessary, artificial, and forced repetitions)?

4. Is it practical in the school situation?

    a. Are the needed practical materials available?

    b. Does the time factor permit it to fit in with the total program?

    c. Is it possible to carry it to a reasonable degree of completion in the school situation?

    d. Is adequate guidance available?

242. USE OF THE PHYSICAL ENVIRONMENT AS THE BASIS OF UNIT OF WORK [9]

Edna Bridge Leining

SETTING OF THE STUDY

Lincoln School of Teachers College is situated in New York City overlooking Morningside Park. At once the environment of the school is conditioned. One cannot fail to be aware of the massive pile of rock immediately overhanging the sidewalk. In winter, that section is roped off with " danger " signs prominently displayed. " Why is it dangerous to walk on that side of the street? "

Wandering through the park the concrete walk is interrupted by natural rock, much worn and grooved. Scientists believe the glacier made some of those scratches about thirty thousand years ago. " What is a glacier? " " Where did it come from? "

A tree is growing through a rock. A loose piece of mica schist is picked up. The mica glistens. It flakes off. You can see through it. Water is trickling over gouged surfaces of rock. A huge block of stone is poised ready to fall. Perhaps it will make a miniature avalanche. Not all the park is rocky. It drops suddenly to a low

[9] From *Millions of Years in a Winter*, Lincoln School Curriculum Studies, Bureau of Publications, Teachers College, Columbia University, New York, 1935, pp. 3–4, 6–10, 12.

flat plain, yet we are told it was once all the same height. " Why? "
" Where did the rest of the land go to? "

You look north on Amsterdam Avenue. It slopes down into a valley rising steeply on the farther side. It is believed that there was
once a river flowing through the depression which is now One Hundred Twenty-fifth Street. " Where is that river now? "

The Palisades form a wall of rock made by an igneous intrusion
or perhaps a " volcano that didn't erupt." " Why didn't it erupt? "
" Why haven't we a volcano for the Palisades? "

You see the Hudson River that really isn't a river but an estuary
— an arm of the sea that has come in and drowned the valley. The
glacier filled in the gorge of the old river. That is why the new
George Washington Bridge had to be built with the longest span in
the world.

Such is the physical setting of Lincoln School in a rich geological
and physiographical environment. In addition, there are museums
close at hand. The American Museum of Natural History has a
wealth of material to supplement a study of the earth materials and
forms. In the Metropolitan Museum of Art, the uses of stone in artistic expression are shown. The library facilities of the city are of
the best.

Not only is the neighborhood environment rich in suggestion, but
the school itself affords unusual opportunities. It is experimental in
character, and so allows freedom to develop the idea that is " different." The curriculum of the elementary school has not been definitely formulated. It is adapted to each particular group of children, following their interests, needs, and abilities. Experiences are
integrated through their organization around a unifying interest.
Trips are made possible and encouraged by a school bus service.
Frequently, parents generously lend their own cars for such excursions.

The school is equipped with a well-chosen library, an industrial
arts shop, a science room, art rooms, cooking laboratory, sewing
room, gymnasiums, swimming pool, roof playgrounds, and an auditorium with facilities for showing motion pictures and slides.

The appearance of the classrooms with their blackboards and
bulletin boards is not unusual. The desks are movable. Easels,
paints, work benches, and tools are part of the equipment for room
activities.

The classes are not large. They average about twenty to twenty-
five pupils, usually about evenly divided between boys and girls.

The pupils of the school are of superior mental ability. About
ninety per cent of them have a mental age beyond the average of
public school children of the corresponding chronological age in the

country at large. A few are gifted children, although many are of average ability. While some of them have unusual home backgrounds, there are scholarships which make possible a very democratic social atmosphere in the school. However, there is probably a tendency for only liberal-minded parents to send their children to a school that does not follow a traditional program.

ORIGIN OF UNIT

In the elementary department, it is customary to encourage the children to engage in some worthwhile activity or hobby during the summer. Much attention is given in the early part of the school year to reports of such experiences; assemblies are held and exhibits are arranged showing the objects that have been collected during the summer vacation and brought in. There is certain to be a rock collection or two among the treasures which fourth-grade pupils bring in. One year, Robert brought in pieces of water-worn driftwood, stones and pebbles mounted on cardboard bearing the heading, " The Work of the Waves." Alfred had found some obsidian or volcanic glass. The discussion that followed the display of these collections encouraged others to bring in rocks and minerals. There seemed to be much interest in knowing something about all the specimens. However, there was a continuous undercurrent of interest in rocks.

During the first part of the semester, the children engaged in a food study in connection with the use of the cafeteria and also in a study of bees. When the time came to decide upon a new unit of work, they clamored for a study of rocks and minerals. The teacher was not at all certain that it would prove a sufficiently rich field for a main interest at this grade level. However, she was willing to be convinced. The children were asked what they wished to know about the subject. Immediately, enough questions were asked to fill several blackboards. When the queries were organized, it was found that they covered many different subject-matter fields, science, geography, and industrial arts predominating. As few books on rocks and minerals and their uses written for children were then available, the teacher spoke of the difficulty of securing sufficient information for such a study. The children replied that not everything had to be learned from books. The teacher finally agreed that they might have the study if they could show that it would be worthwhile and that enough study materials and sources of information could be found.

The next day the children started bringing in more specimens of rocks and making suggestions for supplementary sources of information. The father of one of the children had a friend who owned a coal yard. The child suggested that it might be visited by the group. That child also promised to obtain an exhibit of the different varieties of coal. Another child promised to bring in samples of rocks and minerals used for building materials. Plans were made to write letters to commercial firms for exhibits of the processes and products of minerals such as asbestos, iron, graphite, oil, etc. There were suitable books and pictures in the homes of some of the children which could be brought to school for the use of the class. Almost at once it was found necessary to learn to use the card catalogue and children's encyclopedias in the library. A bibliography, correctly made on library cards, was started by the children in order to show the sources of information thus discovered.

There was soon no question as to whether we should engage in such a study for we were already deeply plunged into it.

The unit on " Rocks and Minerals " proved to be a fascinating one to the children and had a richness that showed the title to be quite inadequate.

During the conduct of the first unit, such possibilities were revealed that it was decided by the teacher to explore that field still further when child interest seemed to warrant it. The study appeared to offer unusual opportunities for developing concepts and large generalizations in science. The group that followed demonstrated no readiness for such a study so the further exploration of the field was delayed until the third year.

Unquestionably, the first unit on science came into existence as a direct outgrowth of the children's interests. It was definitely initiated by them. The second time it was taught, it presented another problem. In consultation with the Research Department it was decided to teach the unit again for experimental purposes, opening up the same field of experience to this new group of children, arousing their interest in such a way that they would make the unit their own and carry it on.

It was but natural that the area covered in the first study should furnish the teacher's preview for the next year's work. The following informal outline of the study was made by her for her own use:

THE TEACHER'S PLAN OR PREVIEW OF THE UNIT OF WORK

Science and Geography
    Theories of the earth's origin
    Planets, stars, moon
    Cause of day and night
    Change of seasons
    Gravity
    Magnetism

Volcanic action
Classification of rocks according to origin
Constructive and destructive land forms
Kinds of soil
Physiographical concepts: island, river, mountain, valley
Use of maps
Identification of rock specimens
History and Fine Art
Evolution of the use of stone shown through pictures
Industrial Art
Uses of rocks and minerals
Cooking
Minerals in foods
Language, Spelling, and Writing
Discussions
Reports
Lecture illustrated with lantern slides
Writing of business letters
Stories and labels for exhibit case
Reading
Stories and myths about stones and earth forces
Reference material
Pamphlets
Letters received
Use of card catalogue and encyclopedias
Making of a bibliography on cards
Arithmetic
Experience with pounds and tons in coal study
Individual and Small Group Interests
Fossils
Petrified wood
Glass
Brick-making
Experimenting with cement
Asbestos
Lead pencils
Building materials
Making a model of a coal mine
Casting in lead
Salt
Chart showing how rocks are worn away

The preview merely indicated what could be included in the second year's study to give the children a worthwhile experience in the selected field. It revealed the quality and, in a measure, the quantity of the possibilities; but essentially it had no limiting powers. The planning tended to insure organization, yet it did not mean that the study as pursued by the second group was to be cast into that mold. The preview was merely intended to trace a path that might be profitably followed up if a better course for those particular children did not appear. It was in that spirit that the preview was set up.

In order to prepare the stage for the second study, it was decided to show a film on Commander Byrd's trip to the North Pole. In the discussion that followed, one of the questions raised was, " How could Byrd tell when he had reached the North Pole? " That precipitated an interest in the sextant, in the compass, in magnetism, and in the earth as a terrestrial magnet. Consideration of the earth in space led to much discussion of the various theories of the earth's origin. At that point a particular interest in the solar system led this group to dwell on a study of the sun, moon, stars, and planets. In general, their concern seemed to be with three large questions:

How did the earth come to be?
How did the earth become so that it could support life?
How did life come to be on the earth?

It soon became a very different unit from the one of the preceding year. The interest was much broader; it lay very decidedly in " The Beginnings of Things," which was the children's way of referring to the study. The formation of rocks, their identification and uses, and changing land forms were important only as a phase of a larger interest. Although the beginning of life was stressed, it could not be followed through an evolutionary study because of the limitation of time. This unit drew less upon other subject-matter fields than the first, but it covered a far greater range within the field of science. To insure a rounded development, the children were given an opportunity to engage in many unrelated interests and activities which will later be discussed.

243. " Unit in the Area of Unemployment " [10]

Comments

During recent years there has been much community and school interest in many developments, which are related to unemployment, as C.C.C. camps, introduction of new machines,

One of the F.E.R.A. (Federal Emergency Relief Administration) projects recently in a medium-sized Connecticut town was the construction of a public playground and athletic field. This work was naturally watched closely by all who would enjoy it. Several organizations had been contacted for suggestions during the initial planning and numerous editorials had appeared in the local papers discussing the pros

[10] Connecticut State Department of Education, Office of Research and Finance, Hartford, Conn., pp. 1–11.

and cons of such activities. The town seemed to be divided into two rather distinct groups — the liberals who welcomed such improvements, and the conservatives who felt this was no time for experimentation and the expending of millions of dollars.

Federal funds for aiding construction, surveys, shutting down or closing factories.

The different groups also were found in the high school pupils who naturally reflected the home and community environments. Teachers of social studies could feel assured that both sides of every socio-economic question would be presented with equal fervor, often equally prejudiced. Their suggestions concerning clear, reflective thinking based on careful discovery and consideration of the facts had not been fully woven into a pattern of conduct for many. They felt the need of more practice in scientific thinking growing out of live, current problems which involved research, organization of data, presentation, group discussion, and evaluation.

Good teachers recognize that it is more important to help children learn how to think than teach them what to think.

Practice is necessary for learning how to think individually and as a group.

While discussing general plans for vacation one day in a social studies period, one class evidenced much interest in the F.E.R.A. playground project. The teacher, sensing the interests and seeing the possibilities, acted as a wise chairman and stimulated and guided the discussion into worthwhile channels by encouraging discussion and helping the group precipitate the issues involved. These were listed on the blackboard to guide the thinking and comments. As the period drew to a close, the teacher asked the group what they wished to do. They wanted to think over the questions and gather more information and continue the discussion the next period. The specific question which each pupil was to work on was carefully determined. The teacher pointed out sources of information such as contacting the local relief administrator, talking to persons working on the project, reading a copy of the approved project to find out exactly how many man-hours of work were anticipated and the nature and cost of materials, interviewing the local social worker to find out more about the characteristics of the persons employed, the amount which each person

Genuine interest such as this often may be developed into a valuable, comprehensive unit or project.

The work of the teacher here is very important and was well done.

The teacher did a good piece of work pointing out sources of data and seeing that each pupil had a definite job for the next day and knew how to do it.

Pointing out sources of data is very important and helpful.

The discussion and evaluation of the reports as done here was very significant.

Asking questions and raising problems helped the pupils see the possibilities and stimulated their interests.

The interests and questions of the pupils should be drawn out.

The teacher again did right to recognize the problem of finding out if the pupils were interested and also give them a chance to solve it.

earns, reading current literature found in practically all recent magazines and newspapers which would help explain the nature of such undertakings, looking at motion pictures and film strips, and making original surveys.

At the next class meeting the teacher continued to act as the chairman providing a chance for the students to report on their findings and discuss even more critically what they thought about them. In order to foster more careful consideration of issues, however, she continually challenged the students by asking them such questions as, What is the meaning of F.E.R.A.? Are the people doing work which should be done by the local skilled tradesmen who are being thrown out of employment? Would it not be cheaper to get this work done by the lowest-bidding, responsible contractor? Do other countries have such projects? How are these workers paid? Would it not be more desirable to offer direct relief in the forms of a Dole? Why are so many people out of work? Are people really starving because too much has been produced? Pupils also were encouraged to challenge all the statements made in the discussion and to raise questions which were carefully noted and recorded.

At the close of the period the pupils again decided they would like to gather some more data and continue the discussion the following day. They were already beginning to sense the need of having facts before they had opinions; also of drawing conclusions cautiously, keeping an open mind, looking at all sides of a question, and taking plenty of time.

At the next meeting it was clear that the students were genuinely interested in several of the problems or questions which had arisen and grown out of their other researches. The teacher, therefore, asked them if they would like to define and list main problems and questions again and spend enough time on each to consider it carefully in accordance with the facts. The answer being a strong affirmative, they began to make a record of all the things they would like to know. Each pupil listed them on a piece of paper. The teacher encouraged them to express themselves freely and raise as many questions as they liked. She also occasionally asked students pointed questions such as, Why would you like to know that? Is that a good problem? Do you think we can do that?

One of the most important steps in planning is to determine the individual interests and needs and record them carefully.

Many of the questions asked by the pupils naturally were the same as had previously been raised or implied but which had not satisfactorily been answered. New ones, of course, were also asked. The following is a list of some of the things which one or more members of the class wanted to know or do:

1. How many days work will be provided by the local F.E.R.A. project?

2. Are there any other projects in the local towns?

Raising questions is one of the best ways to stimulate pupil initiative.

3. How many such projects are there in Connecticut? In other states?

4. How many people are doing this type of work?

5. How are the people selected for these jobs?

6. Do other countries have people who cannot find work? If so, how many?

7. How are the unemployed people taken care of in other countries?

8. Will members of the class likely be able to get a job when they are graduated from high school?

The solution of these questions involved many activities like wide reading, visitation, interviews, collecting historical data, study of conditions in many foreign countries, much discussion, correspondence, research, and listening to lectures.

9. Why is it that so many people cannot get work?

10. How has the invention and improvement of machines affected labor conditions?

11. Would there have been such hard times if Hoover had not been elected?

Many of these questions were especially good because they touched pupils so personally.

12. What is the N.R.A. and how does it affect conditions?

13. What is the Dole system? Would it be more desirable than the present form of relief?

14. Why should the rich be taxed to take care of the poor?

15. Why is not a F.E.R.A. worker allowed to make enough to support a family?

The extent and range of these questions indicate the large amount of preparation previously done by the group and also make it possible to meet individual differences.

These questions indicate how important it is to have easy access to well-equipped library and have social-science work rooms as copious materials.

16. What are the trends in modern architecture?

17. How did they take care of the unemployed in medieval times? Ancient times? Colonial times?

18. How can unemployed persons keep up their confidence and spirits?

19. What factors such as laziness or poor physical condition make a person relatively unemployable?

20. What type of training can the members of this class attain so as to make them more likely to get a job when they are graduated?

Pupils were wisely given a chance to raise questions and express interests at the beginning of the next period in order to take advantage of their experiences since the last meeting. Soon, however, they were faced with the need of determining or planning how they should proceed or organize their work to take care of individual differences and insure thoroughness, timeliness, efficiency, and convenience. The teacher again gave them a chance to think by asking them what they wanted to do. Several suggestions were offered. One pupil thought everyone should choose a different problem and report to the group as soon as he or she was ready. Another suggested that the questions be divided among the class so that one or more persons are working on every question. A third thought that it would be better not to try to solve all the problems at once but to select ten questions and have a committee of three report on each question. Other pupils suggested various combinations of the foregoing procedures. In each case, the teacher carefully guided the group by helping them evaluate each plan thoughtfully. She felt that learning to discover individual differences and meet them properly was one of the most valuable parts of the entire unit. Enough time was taken for good thinking. She also assigned simpler problems to the slow-learning pupils.

The teacher wisely recognized the problem of planning the unit carefully and giving the pupils a chance to learn to plan by planning.

Evaluating the plans suggested gave the pupils a chance to think about their own problems.

After considering the merits and defects of the various plans suggested for the remainder of the

period, the group decided that it would be best
to try to adopt the third plan. They immediately
began to determine not only which problems it
would be most desirable to attack first, but also
the order in which the committees working on
them were to report. It was also necessary for
the pupils to group themselves into committees on
the basis of their interests. Each committee was
free to elect a chairman.

Pupils should be given a chance to form their own committees.

As would be expected, it took another period
for the class to decide upon the problems to be
taken up first, the order in which they were to
be taken up, and the personnel of the committees.
After having done this careful planning, however,
they were off to an excellent start because they
had already roughly defined the problem, learned
much about it, determined many sources of help,
and laid out a careful plan or course of future
action. They agreed that the general procedure
would be by individual or committee reports on
various problems but felt there could and should
be many deviations such as excursions or field
trips — to factories or other F.E.R.A. projects,
listening to informed persons called into the
school to discuss a situation with them, making
a class scrapbook of photographs depicting various aspects of their problem, collecting up-to-date
information from numerous sources and making
it available to everyone, providing appropriate
places for filing and displaying printed and other
materials which would need to be brought into
the room by members of the class, listening to
valuable radio addresses, conducting debates or
panel discussions on controversial problems,
showing many things graphically by pictures or
photographs, constructing a model of the local
F.E.R.A. project, and participating in the arts
and crafts activities especially suited for the unemployed.

More planning was desirable.

Participating in these varied activities is more desirable than memorizing factual information not thoroughly depicted and understood.

Since the first committee had a rather simple
problem, it was decided to allow them two days
to prepare their report. The intervening time was
devoted to research, informal discussions, and
committee meetings. The classroom was used for

It is commendable that the class did not meet until they were prepared to make it a worthwhile experience. Pupils cannot discuss intelligently unless they have done some work beforehand.

Reports should be more than factual accounting; they should reflect careful preparation and understanding.

Evaluating the report gives the pupils a chance to discuss and learn many important things.

The teacher did well here to put this problem up to the group.

It was desirable for the teacher to provide the group another chance to

research, group meetings, and individual study under the supervision of the teacher who advised with, and helped them.

Three days later the class assembled as a whole. The time was devoted to committee reports. After discussing a few matters which pertained to the whole group, the teacher turned the meeting over to the committee chairman. The report was rather pointed and brief. The teacher took an active part as a member of the group and constantly asked for the source of information and questions which stimulated vigorous discussion which sometimes almost got out of control of the chairman who was advised to encourage everyone to speak naturally without holding up his or her hand as so often is done.

At the end of the committee report, the teacher helped the group bring out and discuss the questions raised and to evaluate the methods of the committee and the effectiveness of the report. This proved to be a very valuable experience. Many suggestions were offered for improving the method of presenting their data, bringing out and discussing the main points, speaking to the group, finding more information on their subject, and getting help from others in the class. Several of the members pointed out facts which they had gathered and wondered why the committee had not found them. At the close of the period the teacher asked the group what they thought the committee ought to do next. Members of the committee quickly stated they were not satisfied with their report and wished to have more time to work on it and then appear before the class again. In the discussion many new points had been brought out which they wanted to study further.

The second committee reported the next day. They apparently had profited much from the experience of the previous committee and, therefore, avoided many errors. They also stimulated much discussion but it was of a more thoughtful, objective type. There were several suggestions for improvement, however, in the period of evaluation. The pupils also spent a few minutes evaluating the general plan of procedure of their unit. They decided it was working out satisfactorily.

The committee which had just finished reporting were divided in what they wanted to do next. One boy wished to join the committee which was studying a problem in which he was especially interested; the others wished to study one of the unassigned questions which they had touched upon in their previous work. Their wishes were granted.

The procedure of presentation, group discussion, and evaluation of committee reports thus was followed until the sixth committee report was due. This committee had noted that several members of the class always offered additional data and suggestions to each report. They decided, therefore, that they would like to have a sort of preliminary meeting or seminar in which they would report to the group what they were going to do and how they were going to do it. This request was granted. The results seemed to justify the belief that it would be desirable to have preliminary meetings in all cases in order to keep all the members generally informed and also profit from their ideas such as on sources of materials, methods, and activities to be carried out.

The teacher felt that it was again necessary to help the group evaluate critically their previous plans and plan a future course of action which would be suitable to their new and enlarged interests, needs, and capacities. This was done, new interests also were listed and discussed. Several interesting discoveries were made. For instance, they found that many of the new and remaining questions were so closely related they could be grouped together under one committee, that their interests had enlarged and shifted in some cases so they would rather pursue new problems than the ones previously indicated but not yet fully satisfied, and that it was very wise to keep in close touch with everyone else, especially to discuss things in detail with them.

By this time the pupils were much better ac-

Margin notes:

evaluate the report and go over the complete plan of their unit.

Notice how individual interests were again recognized and met.

This discovery of the pupils is good evidence of desirable growth.

Pupils should be encouraged to form hypotheses such as this.

Plans should be checked and revised periodically.

These are some of the most important goals of development.

quainted with the methods of committee procedure, the characteristics of good thinking, the technics of group discussion and the tools of research, the sources of data, and value of careful planning and preparation. It was relatively easy, therefore, to help them discover their interests and plan for a wise, future course of action.

This is a common occurrence when pupils are granted a chance to help initiate, carry out, plan and evaluate their activities.

The broadened interests also had reached into related social problems especially in public recreation, delinquency and crime, and unequal distribution of wealth since these are so closely related to unemployment. They decided however, that they would rather complete some of their previous problems and take up the new ones later.

It would have been desirable to have a large cumulative activity such as an exhibit of work done.

At the end of four more weeks, it was discovered that most of the group now were especially interested in various phases and problems of recreation and leisure time, as e.g., What are the leisure time activities in other countries? The teacher, therefore, helped them determine their major interests, analyze and discuss them carefully, plan a definite program of procedure, continue to carry out that plan, and evaluate results critically as they go along.

This unit naturally led into another unit as it should in accordance with the changed interests of the pupils.

244. "UNIT ON MAKING TOOTH POWDER"[11]

Charlotte Mapes and Henry Harap

While discussing health habits one day, it was discovered that there were a few children in the class whose teeth were not clean. Then followed a discussion of how to keep the teeth clean. Some of the pupils did not use a commercial tooth-paste or powder as they could not afford to buy it. One boy used a mixture of salt and soda. Several used just salt.

At the teacher's suggestion, the children thought that they would like to make some real tooth powder. They were given the names of the following ingredients to be used: bolted, precipitated chalk, baking soda, and oil of wintergreen. The pupils suggested the following proportions to be used:

Chalk: $\frac{3}{4}$, $\frac{2}{3}$, $\frac{1}{2}$, $\frac{5}{6}$, $\frac{4}{5}$.

Soda: $\frac{1}{4}$, $\frac{1}{3}$, $\frac{1}{2}$, $\frac{1}{6}$, $\frac{1}{5}$.

[11] *Making Household Preparations,* Western Reserve University, Curriculum Laboratory, No. 36, Cleveland, Ohio, October 15, 1934, pp. 2–3.

The first three suggested proportions were eliminated because of too much soda. The majority then voted for the combination of $\frac{5}{6}$ chalk and $\frac{1}{6}$ soda.

Several brands of commercial tooth-powder were brought in by the pupils. The most common size of can was two ounces. It was then decided that each child would make 2 ounces of tooth-powder. Therefore, for each pupil the following would be needed:

$$\frac{5}{6_3} \times 2 = \frac{5}{3} = 1\frac{2}{3} \text{ or } 1.66 \text{ ounces of chalk.}$$

$$\frac{1}{6_3} \times 2 = \frac{1}{3} \text{ or } .33 \text{ ounce of baking soda.}$$

Since there were 43 pupils in the room, the following amounts of ingredients would be needed:

1.66 ounces	.33
43	43

71.38 ounces or 5.94 pounds of precipitated chalk. Six pounds of chalk would have to be bought. ‖ 14.19 ounces or .88 pound baking soda. One pound of soda would have to be bought.

Since oil of wintergreen is highly concentrated, it was decided to buy $\frac{1}{2}$ ounce.

The cost of the three ingredients follows:

6 pounds precipitated chalk at 30 cents.... $1.80
1 pound baking soda at 10 cents.......... .10
$\frac{1}{2}$ ounce wintergreen at 72 cents............ .36
Total...................... $2.26

In order to save time, and make it more simple in measuring, table-spoonfuls were used instead of weight. The pupils weighed out 1 ounce of chalk and one ounce of soda. When measured it was found that one ounce of chalk made $10\frac{1}{2}$ tablespoonfuls. One ounce of soda made 3 tablespoonfuls.

One child would receive: $10.5 \times 1.66 = 17.43$ tablespoonfuls chalk.
$.33 \times 1$ or .33 tablespoonful soda.

Since there are 3 teaspoonfuls in 1 tablespoonful, each pupil would receive a full teaspoonful of soda.

The chalk and soda were divided and placed in three containers. Three groups of pupils measured at a time. About $\frac{1}{2}$ hour was needed for all pupils to measure their ingredients which were then placed in small mixing bowls brought by each pupil. Each then received 10 drops of oil of wintergreen. Each pupil, using a smooth stick, mixed his ingredients for about 20 minutes to be sure that the oil particles were thoroughly broken up and mixed with the chalk and soda. Each pupil bought the powder which he mixed, receiving the 2 ounces for 5 cents.

$$43)\overline{\$2.26} \quad \$.052$$

The following commercial tooth-powders were brought to class:

Name	Amount	Cost
A	2 ounces	$.29
B	2 ounces	.35
C	4 ounces	.39
D	1½ ounces	.39
E	2 ounces	.25

The pupils discovered how much cheaper it was to make their own tooth-powder. They decided to find how much they had saved. Several examples follow:

A............................. $.29
Our Own...................... .052
Difference in price............$.238

$$.052)\overline{.23800} \quad 4.57 \text{ or } 457\%$$

The class discovered that they could make a little more than 5 times as much as they could buy for 29 cents.

C............................. $.20
Our Own...................... .052
Difference in price............$.148

$$.052)\overline{.148000} \quad 2.846 \text{ or } 284.6\%$$

Almost 4 times as much of the class product as they could buy for 20 cents.

Several of the parents asked to buy more. They had tried the powder and liked it. Many of the pupils said that they were going to make their tooth-powder from now on. It was an experience enjoyed by all the pupils.

CHAPTER XVI

THE COURSE OF STUDY

245. THE RELATION OF THE CURRICULUM AND THE COURSE OF STUDY [1]

Hollis L. Caswell

THE *course of study is a printed manual or guide which has been prepared to assist teachers to direct satisfactorily the development of the curriculum.* The course of study may be likened to the plans and specifications for a building. Both are carefully developed suggestions for directing a process, the one a construction process with building materials, the other a growth process with human abilities. Just as the plans and specifications are not the building, neither is the course of study the curriculum, even though in both cases there is an intimate relationship between the two. Obviously, a good course of study is a valuable aid to the development of a good curriculum. However, it is entirely possible for a school to have an excellent course of study and a poor curriculum, or a poor course of study and an excellent curriculum.

If this concept of the course of study is held clearly in mind it will eliminate much confusion concerning the process of curriculum-making. It will be noted in the following discussion how the distinction in the meaning of these two terms is an essential basis for proceeding with work on the curriculum.

WHO MAKES THE CURRICULUM?

Much discussion has been given to the problem of who should make the curriculum. Especially has the question of the responsibility of teachers in this regard been a point of dispute. It has been contended by some that only specialists can perform the intricate tasks involved in curriculum-making. Others have contended that, since the teacher is closer to classroom situations than the specialist, she should have the larger part in curriculum-making. Discussions on this point are well illustrated by two articles in School and Society. Whipple takes the position that the cooperative plan of curriculum-making is highly undesirable. He states:

[1] "The Curriculum and the Course of Study," *The Peabody Reflector and Alumni News,* 7:8, 22, January, 1934.

. . . too much of present-day curriculum-making is amateurish, trifling and a sheer waste of time — nay, worse than that, an injection of pernicious confusion in what should be an orderly progress. The let-everybody-pitch-in-and-help method is ludicrous when applied to curriculum-building. It is too much like inviting a group of practical electricians to redesign a modern power plant.*

Whipple's statement is answered by Bauernfeind as follows:

Some of this work is doubtless amateurish; . . . but all of it has helped to focus the attention of teachers and school officials on the faults of the past scheme and on the present needs of the pupils and schools.

No, curriculum-making by the teachers, at its worst, has not torn down the educational structure; neither has it brought about the disorganization which the " viewers with alarm " would have us see as the sole result.

It . . . has served to turn the spotlight of scrutiny on the old methods and materials which were formerly used without questioning; it has motivated study in the field of the curriculum and has helped to reveal to teachers some idea of what the new may accomplish. . . . Rather than wrecking the machine, the teachers, in the process of curriculum making, are able to become acquainted with the mechanism which they are called upon to operate, to keep in repair, and to improve.†

Such disagreements often arise from different concepts of the curriculum. Applying the definitions set forth heretofore, we see that teachers must have a large part in making the curriculum since it is under their direction that the curriculum actually takes form. All teachers are curriculum-makers. They engage in curriculum-making either well or poorly according to their previous training, their ability, and the assistance that is rendered them.

WHO MAKES THE COURSE OF STUDY?

On the other hand, it does not follow that all teachers should participate in writing the course of study. This task may be undertaken by one person, a committee, or a large group of teachers under the leadership of a supervisor, principal, or teacher assigned the special responsibility of directing the work. A few illustrations will suggest how various plans may be employed to prepare a course of study. Many state courses of study have been largely written by a single person, usually a member of the state supervisory staff. An interesting plan is used by the Long Beach, California, schools. A supervisor, head of a department, or a classroom teacher who is re-

* Guy M. Whipple, " What Price Curriculum-Making." *School and Society,* 31:368, March 15, 1930.
† Howard K. Bauernfeind, " What Value Curriculum-Making." *School and Society,* 31:711–12, May 24, 1930.

leased from instructional duties, writes a tentative course of study. This tentative course of study is tried out by a selected committee of teachers. After trial, this committee, under the guidance of the person who wrote the tentative course, revise it, after which it is employed throughout the city. St. Louis selected small committees of teachers who were relieved from their regular duties during the time required to prepare the course of study. Many other cities have employed similar committees, but have found it impossible to relieve the members of these committees from their regular duties. The state program in Virginia places the major responsibility on persons selected as chairmen of state production committees. These chairmen secure materials from groups of teachers over the State who work on various parts of the program. Thus, all teachers in the State have opportunity to contribute materials for the course of study, although one person in each field has full responsibility for writing the course. All courses are being tried out in selected centers and revised by a committee composed of the chairmen of the production committees before being made available to all teachers in the State.

In deciding who shall prepare the course of study, a number of points should be considered. In the first place, because of the peculiar difficulties of the task, intensive work is required by small groups of persons who are well grounded in curriculum procedures and who have intimate knowledge of the problems of classroom instruction. Contributions from technical studies by specialists and from the general experience of teachers must be selected and organized in such form that they can be employed easily by teachers to direct instruction. At the same time, it is highly desirable that the course of study evolve from materials and procedures actually found valuable in the classrooms of the school system for which the course is being prepared. Thus, although teachers in general may not advisedly try to write courses of study, materials which they develop in their classrooms may be employed advantageously by the committee or individual who is doing the writing. Such a procedure makes possible the optimum use of both teacher experience and contributions of specialists.

A general guide in determining who shall perform given tasks in curriculum-making that is of assistance on this point, is recognition that it is neither feasible nor desirable to develop classroom teachers into specialists in curriculum procedures or in writing courses of study. Rather, the effort should be to increase the ability of teachers to employ the various sources of guidance available for their help in developing the curriculum. For example, it is not essential that all teachers know the various methods for deriving aims. The concern should be to develop the teacher's ability to employ aims to direct instruction. Efforts to acquaint all teachers with procedures for deriving aims and to have them participate in phases of curriculum-making not directly related to their work in guiding the development of the curriculum in the classroom are ill-advised and often lead to confusion. Such specialized tasks should be undertaken by individuals or committees specially prepared to perform the tasks. There still will remain ample opportunity for the entire body of teachers to participate in curriculum-making. For example, opportunity should be provided through a curriculum program for discussion, observation, study, and demonstration of curriculum materials and procedures as well as for well-conceived experimentation. A curriculum program should represent an organization of all such means of improving the curriculum in such a way that each will supplement the others. When this is done, writing the course of study will assume proper relationship to the larger program of curriculum-making. It will neither be considered a task to be carried out by a select group working entirely apart from the general teaching force, nor an undertaking to be achieved alone through general work and discussion by all teachers. Rather, a select group will assume the direct responsibility for bringing into organized form contributions from the general experience of teachers and from technical studies by specialists.

Writing a course of study, then, is but one phase of a well-conceived curriculum program, and when so considered, assumes proper relationship to the larger program of curriculum-making in which specialist, administrator, supervisor, and teacher must work cooperatively, each making his particular contribution to the development of an improved curriculum.

246. "Making the Course of Study"[2]

A. S. Barr

To analyze the political, economical, social, intellectual, and spiritual problems of the world today in terms of training needs, to group these needs into the several fields of learning — health, citizenship, language, etc. — and to select activities of graded difficulties, interesting and worth while for the development of these abilities, is the task of the curriculum-builder. Tremendous as this task is, the making of Courses of Study with their lists of objectives, standards of attainment, methods, references, visual aids, standardized equipment, type lessons, etc., require for their making probably an

[2] *Journal of Educational Method*, 3:371-374, May, 1924.

even greater outlay of human effort. There was a time when course-of-study-making was much simpler and less exacting than it is to-day. Present standards demand, however, materials that are exceedingly accurate as judged by the subject specialists, materials that are practical as demonstrated by actual classroom use, and materials that are pedagogically sound as judged by the best scientific principles of education. To produce such material requires the most painstaking detailed work of many people.

It will be the purpose of this discussion to give a general outline of the entire procedure of course-of-study-making, and to include a brief statement of curriculum construction for the guidance of those engaged in the coöperative development of materials for classroom use.

I. STEPS IN CURRICULUM CONSTRUCTION

1. Select from the major fields of human activities one or more divisions for study and analysis. The steps in scientific curriculum-making are of such an intricate nature that persons choosing to work in the field should be warned against the danger of attempting to cover a large range of human activities in any one study.

2. There are three accepted methods of determining educational objectives through social analysis: (1) *The method of analysis,* by which a given field of human endeavor is broken up into its numerous specific activities and the abilities essential to the performance of these activities; (2) *the method of errors,* a method of analysis by which the shortcomings of society are listed for specific training; (3) *the method of agreement,* the study of the lives of successful personages of successful institutions, etc., for the principles, practices, and knowledges essential to success.

3. An analyis of the individual for those mental characteristics, abilities, and interests that characterize human behavior. The qualities here referred to are psychological and individual as opposed to the sociological objectives derived from an analysis of society. They are the mental non-social, universally desirable qualities characteristic of human activities and fundamental to child training.

4. The determination of those universal personal qualities (ideals) that should characterize man's activities regardless of age, sex, race, vocation, social status, or nationality. These are the social standards for judging human action, such as honesty, open-mindedness, self-sacrifice, etc.

5. A study of the activities of child life. The aim of education is to train children to live well as children, not merely to live well as adults.

6. The listing of the objectives, that is, the specific abilities that

one needs in the performance of life's activities as discovered in the analysis of items 1, 2, 3, and 4 above. The body of information here developed, while essential to the curriculum builder, need not be detailed in the course of study. A summarized statement of these objectives for the several grade levels will serve all practical purposes.

7. The formulation of guiding principles. The course of study for any department should be guided by general assumptions and principles dealing with: (1) the local community; (2) the age and maturity of the children; (3) previous training; (4) probable life occupations; (5) the time allotment of the several subjects; (6) other subjects in related fields.

8. The selection from the entire range of abilities of those abilities to be developed in school. Many of the abilities essential to the performance of life's activities will be cared for normally in the great school of experience.

9. The selection of pupil experiences, that is, the activities to be used in the attainment of objectives. Since like experiences affect different individuals differently, that is, they affect no two individuals alike, the activities used to achieve desirable goals (objectives) must take into account the principle of individual differences. Lists of tried experiences with plenty of freedom for individual differences are desirable.

10. The selection and standardization of the needed materials, supplies, equipment, etc., essential to the course of study.

11. The grade-placement of materials. This involves the study of the mental processes involved in the successful performance of each activity. It is impossible properly to place curriculum materials without actual classroom use of such materials.

12. The organization of experiences into correlated instructional units. The organization of materials may be an activities organization, a subject-matter organization, or a combination of both. Each has its advantages.

13. The formulation of proper methods of teaching each unit. A detailed analysis of method will doubtless show that the same methods are not applicable to all activities. In addition to specific discussion of method the course of study should include a statement of the technique of knowledge development, skills development, attitude development, etc.

14. The determination of standards of attainment (grade by grade). There should be a definite statement of what can reasonably be expected in any field of instruction for each grade level.

15. The introduction of the various mechanical devices essential to the course of study.

16. The constant revision of the course of study in the light of experience and experimentation.

II. WHO SHALL MAKE THE COURSE OF STUDY?

A distinction should be made between curriculum making and the making of courses of study. The two fields are distinct and will probably be carried forward by two different groups of school people. It appears that the determination of the major objectives of education, the listing after experimentation of worth-while activities, the development of principles of grouping, is the work of an expert analyst — the curriculum builder. Scientific thought of this type is general in its application and usable the country over. The evaluating of subject matter, the gradation of subject matter, the adaptation of subject matter to teaching situations, and the organization of subject matter into courses of study are fields to which public school people — teachers, principals, and supervisors — can make their most valuable contributions.* This is the field of course-of-study building.

The problem of " Who Shall Make the Course of Study " has been carefully studied by the curriculum committee of the Department of Superintendence. The three quotations from the " Elementary School Curriculum," Second Yearbook, Department of Superintendence, 1924, to follow, summarize the prevailing practices in making courses of study:

1. " To get the best results in the making of a course of study, the combined wisdom of experts, administrators, and classroom teachers should be pooled. In other words, both national leadership and local leadership are required.

" *Nationally*, there is a place for the pooling of the ideas of experts in laying down broad general principles. A properly balanced group of experts can lay down general principles that will better guide all communities than any local community can formulate for itself. Even though this is done, large responsibility will still rest on the local community.

" *Locally*, there is a place for every member of the school department in adjusting the course of study to individual needs of pupils and community conditions. When the classroom teacher herself helps in the formulation of the course of study, she understands its purposes and content, and if she is not in complete sympathy with them, she has a feeling of freedom to criticize them and she is willing to bring her experience to bear in their revision.

* The Elementary School Curriculum, Second Yearbook, Department of Superintendence, February, 1924, p. 54.

" Finally, a course of study must be looked upon as a growing proposition [a thing] that will continue to grow as long as the human race continues to grow." *

2. " The best results have been secured when four groups of people, or representatives therefrom, have been used in due proportion. These groups are: (a) the administrative and supervisory group — those carrying responsibilities extending throughout the system or approximately so, and bringing to them an overview of the relationships within the system and a sense of the relative importance of things; (b) the classroom teacher who must finally execute the curriculum plans; (c) the subject-matter expert, or specialist — the scholar in the subject under consideration; and (d) the intelligent, interested lay citizen who has a constructive attitude toward the public schools."

3. " Experience shows that the organization employed must provide for: (a) Securing the right spirit throughout the process of curriculum development and improvement; (b) launching the problem or problems effectively from time to time; (c) insuring necessary detailed work; (d) providing for proper correlation between subjects; (e) properly dovetailing the course longitudinally throughout the elementary and junior and senior high schools; (f) bringing the work on any course of study to a completed state where it is tentatively acceptable administratively; (g) testing the satisfactoriness of the tentative result; (h) installing and operating the finished course satisfactorily in the system that it is to serve; (i) constantly improving the completed course of study." †

247. A Task for Specialists [3]

Harold Rugg

. . . The tasks of curriculum-making are manifold, difficult, and can be carried out only by professionally equipped specialists. These tasks include the determination of the ultimate and immediate objectives of education, and the experimental discovery of the most effective modes of selecting and organizing the activities of the respective grades of the school.

The tasks are indeed difficult. They can be managed only by persons of broad background, rich experience, and special training

* *Ibid.*, p. 120.
† *Ibid.*, p. 41.
[3] National Society for the Study of Education, *Curriculum-Making: Points of Emphasis*, Twenty-Sixth Yearbook, Part II, Public School Publishing Company, Bloomington, Ill., 1930, pp. 161–162. Quoted by permission of the Society.

in the human and physical sciences; hence the validity of the generalization in our General Statement that " curriculum-making will increasingly utilize scientific procedure."

. . . In selecting the activities and other materials of instruction, the curriculum-maker must have a critical understanding both of childhood and of society. As for the latter, he must be a student of the problems and institutions of the modern world and of their evolution. He must master the rapidly accumulated mass of quantitative data dealing with industry, business, government, international relations, immigration, and a host of fundamental relationships concerning the physical and natural world. Curriculum-making will be based upon the synthesis of the keenest insights that he can discover concerning the trends of modern society and the reconstruction of its institutional life. I say, therefore, that the curriculum-maker must become a thorough student of society.

But if the selection and organization of curriculum-materials is to be wisely done, he must also become a student of learning, a master of the principles of child development. In the last two decades, we have witnessed the growth of a new and increasingly objective science of educational psychology. The very basis upon which the materials and activities of the school must be reorganized will be the principles and findings from the scientific study of learning, interests, general and special abilities, retardation, probable changes in the pupil population, anticipated occupational interests, etc.

Likewise, the curriculum-maker must solve a host of puzzling problems of grade-placement and organization. What activities, readings, open forums, etc., will provide effective means of instruction at various ages? How can vivid reading interests be developed? How frequently should important concepts and generalizations recur? When should systematic practice in spelling, arithmetic, etc., be begun, and how should practice be distributed? These are a few typical examples from a huge array of difficult psychological questions which the curriculum-maker is called upon to answer. Certainly, they can not be answered except by persons of broad background, judgment, and through careful experimentation. Only by measured trial of alternative procedures can objective answers be produced to the questions of grade-placement and organization. The curriculum-maker must analyze and measure. He must be a master of the literature of the psychology of learning. In the present state of our ignorance concerning most effective methods of creating and organizing materials, it is imperative that the curriculum-maker base his tentative organization upon the best hypothesis which can be deduced from existing knowledge. The techniques of controlled experiment, measurement, and statistical condensation must constitute the equipment of those to whom is to be turned over the rebuilding of our school curriculum.

Finally, the curriculum must be made in the light of the known facts and principles of school administration — such matters as length of class exercise, size of classes, arrangements of school programs, range of individual differences, library facilities, laboratory and shop equipment, etc.

The General Statement, therefore, in my judgment should have made more emphatic the doctrine that curriculum-making demands the coöperation of several specialists. This generalization has hardly been grasped at all as yet. Nevertheless, each of the tasks is important. Each demands specialized equipment. The day is past in which a single individual — be he professor, teacher, administrator, psychologist, sociologist, or research specialist of whatever brand — can encompass all of these tasks singlehanded.

248. PREPARATION OF COURSES OF STUDY IN SCIENCE [4]

Wilbur L. Beauchamp

Examination of the courses of study indicates that the majority of courses were formulated by committees representing each of the different fields of science; that is, the courses in general science were made by teachers of general science, courses in biology were made by teachers of biology, and so on. No reference was found which might indicate that the course was formulated by a single committee representing the whole field of science. Administrators apparently regard each of these subjects as a special field, rather than a sequence of subjects having a common core, with overlapping aims, methods, and psychology of learning. Conversation with teachers of science leaves a like impression. Teachers usually refer to themselves as teachers of physics or teachers of botany, and rarely as teachers of science. This tendency to regard each subject as an independent unit rather than as a part of a sequence of courses, as will be pointed out later, has an important bearing on the courses of study in science.

The committees operate under a variety of conditions, which are reflected in the courses of study produced. Four general types of situations will be described in this report: (1) committees operating under a director of curriculum; (2) committees operating under a supervisor of science; (3) committees operating under the direction of outside talent; and (4) committees operating without supervision.

[4] *Instruction in Science*, National Survey of Secondary Education, Bulletin No. 17, Monograph No. 22, Government Printing Office, Washington, D. C., 1932, pp. 3–8.

Committees operating under a director of curriculum. — Many of our large cities have what is commonly called a department of curriculum. In some cities the department is small, consisting only of the director; in others the director may be assisted by a large staff. In the schools visited, the activity of the department of curriculum varied greatly with respect to its relations with the curriculum committees. Occasionally it offered only a perfunctory supervision of committee activity; in other systems it practically dictated the entire curriculum policy. Departments of curriculum assist in the construction of courses of study by assembling various materials, such as courses of study from other school systems, science textbooks, and professional literature on the teaching of science. In addition, they frequently formulate general aims, principles of organization, and a general scheme for the presentation of the materials in a printed course of study. In some schools, the members of the committees were relieved of class work during a portion of the school year and reported to the curriculum department offices where all available materials were placed at their disposal. This plan made possible frequent consultations with the director. In other schools, the teachers assisting were obliged to carry on their regular school work to which was added the burden of formulating a course of study. Under this plan, the majority of the committees met in some conveniently located high school after the regular work of the day was over. Little, if any, opportunity was possible for consulting the director or for studying the materials collected by the department.

A considerable difference appears in the courses of study produced by the two plans just discussed. The committees working during regular school hours under the supervision of the director produced courses of study, which, in the majority of cases, indicate a thorough understanding of the general principles of organization and the nature of the task which they were to perform. Committees working after school hours, with little or no contact with the director, produced a heterogeneous mass of material with few, if any, principles of organization apparent. In the situations where the form of organization was given to them by the director, many of the courses show that the form is conceived as a purely mechanical scheme to be followed arbitrarily. Examination of these courses indicates that the organization is entirely consistent. A more careful scrutiny shows that although the organization may be consistent in terms of its major divisions, these divisions may be purely artificial so far as the detailed material is concerned. No fault can be found with the committees who proceeded in this manner. They did the best that they could with the time and resources which they had at their disposal.

The fault lies rather with the administration and organization which did not provide the opportunity for a good piece of work.

Committees operating under a supervisor of science. — In some of the larger cities a supervisor of science who is a specialist in the field of science teaching is employed. In such school systems the formulation of a course of study or the revision of existing courses is usually carried on directly under his supervision. The influence, however, of the supervisor of science in determining the content of the course of study varies greatly. In one school system observed, the course of study was formulated entirely by the supervisor and his assistant. The material showed clearly that they had first set up certain principles of organization and criteria for the selection of the content. The result was a unified series of courses in the different fields. The courses were placed in the hands of the teachers who were asked to suggest changes for their improvement. The personality of the supervisor was such that suggestions for improvement were readily given. The original course is in a constant process of revision and is used enthusiastically by the teachers in the system. This method of procedure, however, is an unusual one and would certainly be opposed by teachers in many cities. As a rule, the courses are formulated by committees who are appointed by the superintendent or the supervisor of science.

A comparison of the courses of study prepared by committees under the direct active control of the supervisor with those courses in which the control of the supervisor was limited, indicates the superiority of those courses over which the supervisor had the greatest amount of control. This superiority is evidenced most clearly by a comparison of the junior high school courses with the senior high school courses. In the junior high school, teachers as a rule are accustomed to supervision. Many have had little specific training in the various sciences, and as a result they are eager for suggestions; they regard the supervisor as an expert in the field. Senior high school teachers have no such regard for the supervisor; in fact, their attitude is often antagonistic. The majority of the senior high school teachers are specialists in some field of science. If the supervisor's training and experience in teaching has been in the field of chemistry, his opinion has weight with the chemistry committee. The other subject specialists do not regard him as competent in their fields. In other words, the majority of senior high school teachers are not prone to recognize expertness in the field of science *teaching;* they recognize only expertness in the subject matter of a certain division of the field of science. This attitude operates as a distinct disadvantage in the construction of courses of study. The lack of a general viewpoint toward the teaching of science is usually exhibited in courses formulated by subject-matter specialists; the content of the course is dictated solely by the logical divisions of the subject. Neither the contributions of the subject to the general aims of education nor the psychological and pedagogical considerations are taken into account in determining the organization or the subject matter selected.

It must not be concluded from the foregoing statements that this lack of cooperation between the senior high school teachers and the science supervisor exists in all systems. Observation by the writer, however, leads him to believe that it is often the case. Examination of courses of study and observation of classroom teaching leads the investigator to believe that the majority of senior high school teachers would profit by more contact with the science supervisor.

Committees operating under outside talent. — Experts brought in from outside the system have also left their impress on courses of study. In some cases these experts have been specialists in the curriculum and in other cases they have been specialists in science education. In the judgment of the investigator (as determined by an examination of the courses), each of these types of specialist has contributed to the development of the courses of study in such a way as to produce in the courses of the respective cities a uniformity of viewpoint and organization which are notably lacking in courses prepared without supervision.

Committees operating without supervision. — In some school systems the course of study is prepared by committees appointed for each special subject. These committees usually work independently of each other and are left entirely on their own resources, the only condition being that by a certain date a course of study for the subject must be forthcoming. A committee of that kind was observed in operation. Since the method of constructing a course of study aids in interpreting the final product, a description of the work of this committee is included. It is probably typical of the operation of many committees. The first meeting was very short. Each member was asked to present his outline of the course at the next meeting. No mention was made of the general aims of education toward the attainment of which the course should be focused. No specific objectives of the course were decided upon. No principles of organization nor criteria for the selection of subject matter were formulated. At the next meeting, one member was called upon by the chairman to present his outline. This was promptly criticized by those members whose outlines differed from the first in some respects. The criticisms consisted of — " I think that this should go first "; " That isn't a unit "; " This topic is too large "; " We will never have time to cover all that," and other remarks of a similar nature. The whole discussion was based upon personal opinions, likes, dislikes, and prejudices of the various members of the committee. After seven meetings the committee, through the process of compromise, arrived at a series of topics which were duly printed and distributed to the other teachers in the system. Two of the teachers of this committee were visited some time later and they were not following the course of study they themselves had cooperated in preparing. Lack of expert direction such as may be supplied by a director of curriculum or by a supervisor of science frequently produces the type of situation just described.

Another common type of committee procedure is to meet and decide upon the topics or units which are to be included. Each teacher is then assigned to develop a particular unit. Many courses of study disclose evidence of this type of procedure by an entire lack of uniformity in the organization of the different units. One unit will present a statement outline of the important ideas, another a topical outline, and another a series of problems. Analysis of the units reveals that the individual teachers must have had entirely different conceptions of the nature of the learning products to be attained and of the nature of the learning process. One unit may be focused upon the accumulation by pupils of details relating to the topic under discussion. Another unit may consist of problems to be solved, in which the details are used functionally to supply data for their solution. Still another unit may consist of a " hit-or-miss " collection of projects with apparently no other idea than " whole-hearted purposeful activity " on the part of pupils. And there may be one or more units in which the important generalizations of science and their applications in life situations are stressed. It is even possible to find all these types of materials mixed within a single unit.

The influence of other courses of study is indicated by the widespread use of certain objectives, specific aims, and topics phrased in identical words. As a rule, no credit is given for quotations made and it is only through a comparison of the years in which the courses appeared that the sources of these materials can be determined. A common procedure of course-of-study makers is to assemble all courses of study they can obtain and then make a composite of the whole. The assumption underlying this procedure is apparently that by this method they may be reasonably sure that nothing has been omitted.

249. ASSEMBLING COURSE OF STUDY OUTLINES [5]

Edwin S. Lide

The plan followed in assembling the course of study reflects to some degree the permanency with which the product is regarded.

[5] *Procedures in Curriculum Making*, National Survey of Secondary Education, Bulletin No. 17, Monograph No. 18, Government Printing Office, Washington, D. C., 1932, pp. 49–50.

Replies from 140 of the schools on this question are presented in Table 30. The majority of the courses are printed or mimeographed, 31 falling within the former class and 73 within the latter. More of the printed courses are bound than are loose-leaf, while the reverse is true of the mimeographed courses. The large number of mimeographed courses may reflect an attitude on the part of school men that courses of study as published are tentative rather than final or they may reflect an effort at economy. Courses are printed more often in the larger than in the smaller cities.

TABLE 30

NUMBER OF SCHOOLS USING CERTAIN METHODS OF ASSEMBLING COURSES OF STUDY (140 SCHOOLS OR SYSTEMS)

Procedure	Population group				Total
	I	II	III	IV	
1	2	3	4	5	6
1. Printed in pamphlet form...........	10	8	4	1	23
2. Mimeographed and bound	9	11	7	3	30
3. Printed, loose-leaf................	2	1	2	2	7
4. Mimeographed, loose-leaf	7	16	8	12	43
5. Combinations of 1, 2, 3, 4..........	17	13	1	2	33
6. Typed...........................	..	2	..	2	4

Evaluation. — The practice followed was considered satisfactory in 43 of the schools, with no changes desired. In 19 cases the evaluations were not so final. Where printed courses are considered desirable, it is explained for the most part that this will be done only after considerable tryout, and, in some cases, blank pages will be included for teacher notes. In most cases school authorities seem careful to guard against a consideration of the course of study as a fixed or crystallized product.

250. MAKE-UP OF COURSES OF STUDY [6]
Clinton C. Trillingham

As a rule, the new curriculum materials produced for classroom use, are mimeographed, loose-leaf, in outline form, and contain a sufficient variety and amount of material for various mental levels. Table XIII indicates that sixty-nine cities, or 75 per cent of the

[6] *The Organization and Administration of Curriculum Programs*, University of Southern California Education Monographs, 1933–34 Series, Monograph No. 4, University of Southern California Press, Los Angeles, 1934, pp. 48–50, 51.

ninety-three cities with curriculum programs, mimeograph their courses of study, while twenty-nine cities, or 31 per cent, put their materials into printed form. The overwhelming practice in cities from 30,000 to 100,000 is to mimeograph their courses of study; in the middle population group, twice as many systems mimeograph their work as print it; and in the largest cities, about twice as many systems print their materials as mimeograph them.

Thirty-five cities, or 38 per cent, produce their courses in loose-leaf form, while thirty cities, or 32 per cent, bind their work. In the smallest cities, twice as many use the loose-leaf system as those that bind their materials, but as the cities become larger the trend is in favor of binding courses of study. Seven of the cities over 500,000 bind their course materials, while three of them keep their courses in loose-leaf form.

TABLE XIII

Make-up of Courses of Study

| Make-up of courses of study | Population of cities in thousands | | | | | | | |
| | 30 to 100 | | 100 to 500 | | Over 500 | | Total | |
	No.	Per cent	No.	Per cent	No.	Per cent	No.	Per cent
(a) Set-up:								
Mimeographed...	34	80.9	30	73.2	5	50.0	69	74.5
Printed.........	4	9.5	16	39.0	9	90.0	29	31.3
Loose-leaf.......	19	45.2	13	31.7	3	30.0	35	37.8
Bound..........	9	21.4	14	34.2	7	70.0	30	32.4
(b) Form:								
Outline.........	27	64.3	20	48.8	7	70.0	54	58.3
Textual.........	8	19.0	14	34.2	6	60.0	28	30.2
(c) Differentiation:								
One course of study flexible enough for various mental levels...........	33	78.5	31	75.6	10	100.0	74	79.9
Different courses of study for various mental levels.....	4	9.5	9	21.9	2	20.0	15	16.2

This table should be read as follows: Thirty-four of the cities between 30,000 and 100,000 in population, which is 80.9 per cent of the cities in that group which maintain curriculum programs, mimeograph their new courses of study.

Fifty-four cities, or 58 per cent of the ninety-three cities that have programs, organize their courses of study in outline form, while twenty-eight cities, or 30 per cent, produce them in textual form. As the cities grow larger, there is an increasing tendency to produce course materials in textual form, as the percentages of the cities in the three population groups, on this item, are respectively 19 per cent, 34 per cent, and 60 per cent.

Seventy-four cities, or 80 per cent of the ninety-three cities studied, provide for individual differences by producing single courses of study with a variety of content and method for the different mental abilities, while but fifteen cities, or 16 per cent, produce different courses for the various mental levels, at least in certain fields. The situation in each population group is similar to the trend in the total group of cities. It is evident that numerous cities often utilize both procedures for the above mentioned practices in setting up their courses of study.

Hamtramck explains that they set up courses of study in both bound and loose-leaf form, which may be either outlined or textual, depending upon the stages of development and completion of the courses. They later plan to set up different courses for the various mental levels. San Antonio, Texas, first mimeographs its course outlines, and after a period of revision it puts them into print. Rochester produces single courses of study in the elementary grades flexible for all degrees of mental ability, while in their secondary schools they have separate courses for the different levels of mentality. Grand Rapids has special courses for low mental abilities, and in Birmingham separate courses are set up for special classes. Trenton mimeographs its courses and after they have been tried and adopted they are printed. Baltimore follows this same plan, and then binds its courses separately. San Francisco provides special courses for its special schools. Pittsburgh prints its courses of study after experimenting with them in mimeographed form.

The general practice in American cities as to course of study make-up seems to be to produce mimeographed, loose-leaf materials in outline form for preliminary tryout, study, and experimentation. After courses of study have been revised, and subsequently adopted, thus receiving a degree of permanency, the larger cities are inclined to print and bind them, sometimes changing the form from outline to textual.

The author feels that school systems would profit through their own reasearch work in determining which practices should be employed in setting up local courses of study. Both practice and opinion seem to warrant the conclusion that, as a rule, new courses of study should be mimeographed, loose-leaf, and in outline form, with a sufficient variety of method and abundance of content to care for every mental ability. Such a type can be readily revised and modified as needed. Different curricula should be provided for the different interests of pupils, but courses of study should be sufficiently suggestive to meet the needs of a wide range of abilities. Even though a course of study should be suggestive rather than prescriptive, it is the responsibility of the curriculum director to see to it that basic requirements are specified for the committees, and made known to teachers using the courses.

251. Content and Organization of Course of Study [7]

Henry Harap and Alice J. Bayne

Ninety percent of the courses of study include an introductory statement which varies in length from two to thirty pages. In 61 percent of the courses of study the general objectives, the broader goals of the subject are given. The basic views underlying the learning of the subject are given in 50 percent of the bulletins. General suggestions concerning learning procedure are found in 48 percent of the courses of study. The basic views on formal education are set forth in 13 percent of the bulletins. A description or enumeration of the learning equipment and supplies is included in 10 percent of the courses of study. A discussion of the nature of a unit of work is found in 4 percent of the courses of study, although certain implications as to its meaning are to be found in the section devoted to fundamental educational principles. The topics of grade placement, time allotment, adapting instruction to individuals, and the criteria for evaluating units of work are found in a handful of courses of study. Thus the introduction consists mainly of the basic philosophy or theory of the course of study plus certain teaching or learning suggestions.

While it is not always true that the theory as set forth in the introduction and practice as described in the body of the course of study agree, every school system should have a philosophy of education. It is, therefore, surprising that nearly nine-tenths of the courses of study fail to include such a statement. Particularly important is a discussion of the nature of a unit of work or the criteria for evaluating a unit of work. Curriculum workers are groping for an understanding of the nature of the basic learning unit. It would be helpful if those who are dealing with this problem in a practical way would tentatively devote a paragraph to this important element.

Only 10 percent of the courses of study discuss equipment, room furnishings, and learning supplies. The physical setting is a factor

[7] From " A Critical Survey of Public School Courses of Study Published 1929 to 1931," *Journal of Educational Research,* 26:50–51, September, 1932.

in determining the learning atmosphere and is fundamental to a lifelike activity. Every classroom is a work-room, a laboratory — abundantly stocked with materials — among which printed materials are only elements. If this view is to prevail it must get itself written into courses of study.

252. PRINCIPLES OF SEQUENCE USED IN DETERMINING OUTLINE FOR STATE COURSES OF STUDY IN TEXAS [8]

Fred C. Ayer

THE PRINCIPLES OF SEQUENCE

Finally comes the important principle of sequence. This principle covers the need for articulation and continuity in the long series of curriculum experiences which confront pupils as they rise to higher and higher levels of educational opportunity. Whatever may be said for the need of greater freedom in the selection and organization of teaching units, the essential values of logical and organized sequence remain undisputed. Moreover, a considerable degree of basic uniformity is essential in a state program of curriculum revision which takes into account the common educational needs of different districts, the frequent shifting around of both pupils and teachers, and a state-wide system of teacher training, to say nothing of a state-wide system of textbook adoption. The details of sequence rest largely upon the various committees in charge of the construction of different courses of study, but there are several aspects of sequence and uniformity which may well be considered from the point of view of the entire curriculum. The first of these pertains to the necessity for some basic plan of grade or age levels upon which to hang the general distribution of curriculum materials. In this connection it is recommended by the Executive Committee of the Texas State Curriculum Revision Program that the materials of the elementary-school program (above the kindergarten) be organized on a six-year sequential plan. This contemplates a three-year primary period adapted to the ages six, seven, and eight; and a three-year intermediate period adapted to the ages of nine, ten, and eleven. It is further recommended that the secondary-school program be organized on a six-year sequential plan. This contemplates a three-year junior-high-school period adapted to the ages twelve, thirteen, and fourteen, and a three-year senior-high-school period adapted to the ages fifteen, sixteen, and seventeen. . . . Provision should be made for the completion of the entire school period in eleven years by all

[8] From " General Principles and Patterns of Construction in the Texas State Curriculum Revision Program," *The Texas Curriculum Revision Movement,* Curriculum News Bulletin, No. 4, 1:8, April, 1936.

qualified pupils. Subject promotion at the secondary level should provide opportunity to complete the new six-year program in five years. A tentative outline covering the general distribution and sequence of state courses of study is presented here as Chart II.

CHART II. TENTATIVE OUTLINE FOR STATE COURSES OF STUDY

I. Statement of objectives for general public school administrative units. (To be prepared by Executive Committee.)
   A. Elementary School Objectives (six-year period, ages 6 to 11)
   B. Junior High School Objectives (three-year period, ages 12 to 14)
   C. Senior High School Objectives (three-year period, ages 15 to 17)

II. Statement of general curriculum core area or trunk line objectives. (To be prepared by State Construction Committees.)
   1. Language Arts
   2. Social Relations
   3. Home and Vocational Arts
   4. Creative and Recreative Arts
   5. Nature, Mathematics, and Science

III. Statement of general curriculum core area objectives by public school administrative units (if different).
   A. Elementary School
      1. Language Arts General Objectives
      2. Social Relations General Objectives
      3. Home and Vocational Arts General Objectives
      4. Creative and Recreative Arts General Objectives
      5. Science and Mathematics General Objectives
   B. Junior High School
      (Similar to A)
   C. Senior High School
      (Similar to A)

IV. Special courses of study covering the experiential, technical, and cultural strands in a given curriculum core area (either as subjects or major phases) and including such introductory and explanatory material as may seem essential. Each course of study should indicate its general objectives and by units its:
   A. Special Objectives or Outcomes;
   B. Suggested Pupil Activities;
   C. Suggested Teaching Procedures;
   D. Pupil and Teacher References.

V. Optional integrating projects in which a unit covers more than one subject or phase in one or more core areas.

VI. Suggested curriculum devices of various kinds which may prove helpful to teachers.

253. Suggestions for Use of the Colorado Course of Study in Teaching Language Arts [9]

Pauline G. Staats

A careful analysis of recent courses of study reveals great changes in content and organization. Some courses give the teacher very little specific help and others are so idealistic as to be impractical for ordinary school situations. It is hoped that the Colorado Course of Study for Elementary Schools, with its five divisions in one volume, has avoided these errors. It is presented to the teachers of the State as being conservatively progressive in content, and understandable and definite in organization.

The major justification for including any one of the five divisions in the Course of Study depends on the extent to which each division helps children to participate more fully and efficiently in present life activities. An effective program in the Language Arts — the entire field of communication — is unquestionably fundamental to this purpose.

The new Colorado Course of Study for Elementary Schools has four major uses in teaching the Language Arts:

To form a basis for a unified program of elementary school education and for the improvement of instruction in the Language Arts in the State.

To serve as a standard for grade placement of habits, skills, and appreciations in reading, composition, spelling, and handwriting.

To provide a source book of suggestions in method.

To be a guide for integrating class and school activities.

To improve instruction in the State is an acknowledged goal of all schools. Because the Course of Study is the one volume possessed by all schools, it may easily be used as a basis for selecting the common experiences and for interpreting the minimum degree of development on each grade level for all elementary school children. This is not intended to impede or restrict the class that is capable of greatly enlarging on those experiences or surpassing the standards included in each of the Language Arts. It should mean that all children of a certain grade level will have engaged in at least the common experiences set forth. It will also simplify adjustment for children who transfer from one school to another within the State.

[9] From "The New Course of Study for Elementary Schools, How to Use It in Teaching the Language Arts," *The Colorado School Journal*, 51:14–15, May, 1936.

The most important year in the life of any child is the present year. The experiences he has, the skills he develops, the activities he helps plan and engages in, all are important only insofar as they enlarge his contemporary life. Goals are stated for each grade level in reading, composition, spelling, and handwriting. The teacher may use the Course of Study to plan instruction in the Language Arts in terms of goals and to determine the particular needs of the class. These goals should be checked often enough to allow time for additional work on some skills; to plan remedial work; and to give assurance of attainment by the end of the year. In this way, the tendency to over-emphasize some skills at the expense of other vital skills may be avoided.

The grade standards are flexible enough to allow for individual differences and to determine a child's standing in any particular skill. For example, some children in the fourth grade may read easily on the level of eighth-graders in some or all skills. Other fourth-graders need some special help to attain the goals of the first grade. A fifth-grade child may be a superior oral reader and be inferior when required to do silent reading. The Course of Study may also be used as a check-list for isolating certain Language Arts' skills that are often entirely overlooked.

It was, of course, impossible and perhaps inadvisable to include in the Course of Study even a wide range of suggestions in method. However, the " Suggestions for the Teacher " may prove valuable to many teachers in indicating a few specific ways of accomplishing desired ends. Only tested ideas are included in the methods presented. Some teachers will use these suggestions as they are stated; others will use them in modified forms. For example the sample letter forms in the composition program show rather generally accepted forms — others are correct. It is much less confusing to children if certain forms can be agreed upon by all the teachers in the school so that each year's program may build directly upon the previous year's learnings.

It is well known that handwriting varies in individuals. Much confusion results when the teacher uses one formation of letters in teaching handwriting and a personal form in presenting other subjects. To eliminate this difficulty the alphabets included in the Course of Study may be used consistently for all school purposes.

The method selected for teaching spelling should be that which more efficiently teaches the skill as a life tool; not merely for making the most perfect scores on the Friday tests.

Since an important duty that society has assigned to the school is the properly balanced and complete individual development of all children, one use that can be made of the Course of Study in teaching the Language Arts is to enlarge upon the suggestions made in it concerning the methods for teaching bilingual children.

We can no longer pigeon-hole the program of education as we do odds and ends in their respective holes in an old-fashioned desk. School is no longer considered a place apart from life but a part of life. The Colorado Course of Study suggests many ways of integrating all school activities. A flexible school program will necessarily and naturally provide for practice in some form of Language Arts in every class during the day. The Language Arts provide the means of learning social studies, science, health and physical education, and fine arts. These in turn offer the most vital and interesting materials for learning the skills, habits, and attitudes of the Language Arts. In this way school becomes a place for living and not merely a place for learning certain facts and skills that may prove important at some future time. In addition it should be remembered that it is necessary for children to engage in an effective language arts program commensurate with the demands made upon it by the rest of the school program.

In using the Colorado Course of Study to improve instruction in the Language Arts it is suggested that only the parts which are consistently meaningful and important to the teacher be followed. Only by reading all of the Course of Study, thus gaining a complete picture of its scope, may understanding of it grow. Only by using it constantly as a source book will it prove effective as a means of improving instruction and initiating a constructive program of curriculum study in the State.

254. LOCAL AND STATE COURSES OF STUDY IN MICHIGAN [10]

L. W. Keeler and Clifford Woody

The Bureau of Educational Reference and Research devised a questionnaire to use in gathering data on the status of curriculum development in Michigan. This questionnaire was sent to those in charge of public schools in cities and towns, to county commissioners of education and to the heads of private schools. The number sent out and those returned are as follows:

Schools	Distributed	Returned
Cities and Towns	561	313
County Commissioners	83	44
Private Schools	108	55

[10] *Curriculum Development in Michigan Schools,* Bureau of Educational Reference and Research, School of Education, University of Michigan, Ann Arbor, Michigan, pp. 2, 12–14.

Cities and Towns were classified into four groups on the following population basis:

Group A,   population under 1,500
Group B,   population 1,500 to 4,999
Group C,   population 5,000 to 49,999
Group D,   population 50,000 and over

COURSES OF STUDY NOW IN USE

Question 5 of the Questionnaire was devised to secure information concerning the courses of study now in use in the school systems of Michigan. Because of the small quantity and wide variations of the data received, it was not felt worth while to present all of the tabulations in table form in this report. Instead, a summary of the significant findings are enumerated.

ELEMENTARY SCHOOLS

Local Courses of Study

Use of Local Courses of Study:

1. Few class A cities use a local course of study, but the use of these courses increases as population increases until in the D group the range of the percentages of cities using them in the various subjects of the curriculum is from thirty to eighty.

2. In towns and cities the subjects in which local courses of study are used to the greatest extent are arithmetic, reading and language; local courses of study are rarely found in fine arts and music.

3. The rural schools use local courses of study to a far more limited extent than do the schools in towns and cities.

4. Tabulations show that private schools have the highest percentage of use of local courses of study. (This may be accounted for by the fact that parochial schools adopt as their own the ideal course selected as suitable for all of the parochial schools.)

Date of Publication of Local Courses of Study:

1. This information was tabulated on the basis of 5 year intervals, beginning with 1915 and continuing to the present, the last period including only the years 1935 and 1936.

2. Few local courses of study in use were reported as published before 1925, but a small number published from 1920 to 1924 were found to be used in rural schools.

3. The total number of local courses of study published for the elementary grades in 1935 and 1936 is larger than the number published in any of the 5 year periods. (This refers, of course, to those local courses of study used by Michigan schools at the present time.)

4. Private schools show little evidence of using local courses of

study published before 1925; most of the courses of study used by these schools were published in the period from 1925 to 1929.

Form of Local Courses of Study:

1. Towns and cities report that most of their local courses of study are mimeographed; some are printed, however, and some are typed.

2. Courses of study in arithmetic, reading and English appear to be printed, mimeographed and typed in the same amount.

3. Rural schools are limited almost entirely to mimeographed courses of study.

4. Most of the private school courses of study are printed; some are mimeographed.

Need for Revision:

1. Fifty per cent of the cities and towns using local courses of study feel that these courses should be revised.

2. The need for revision is evidenced in all subjects to approximately the same extent.

3. Rural schools feel a greater need for revision than do schools in towns and cities.

4. Private schools do not feel that the need for revision is as urgent as do the public schools.

STATE COURSES OF STUDY

Use of State Courses of Study:

1. The use of the state course of study decreases as population increases; in class D cities the state course of study is used only in the subjects of physiology, hygiene and physical education.

2. In towns and cities the average use of the state course of study is comparable to their use of local courses.

3. In rural schools the use of the state course of study greatly exceeds the use of local courses.

4. In private schools the use of the state course of study is very slight as compared to the use of local courses; in arithmetic, however, the state course is used to a moderate extent.

Date of Publication of State Courses of Study:

1. The period of 1925 to 1929 includes the dates of publication of the majority of the state courses of study used by towns, cities and rural areas; no state courses of study are reported to have been published as recently as 1935.

2. Private schools make scarcely any report on this question.

Form of State Courses of Study:

1. The printed form of state courses of study is used to the greatest extent.

2. Private schools report the use of printed forms only.

Need for Revision:

1. Towns and cities indicate widespread desire for the revision of state courses of study.

2. Among the rural schools which are using the state course of study, seventy-five to ninety per cent are in favor of revision in the various subjects.

255. Statement of the Characteristics of a Course of Study for Port Arthur, Texas [11]

III. We believe the Course of Study should:
  1. Be organized on the basis of race experiences.
  2. Provide for integration of subject-matter in order to develop these experiences and thereby eliminate the distinct separation of conventional subjects in school.
  3. Provide a great number of stimuli in order to produce the desired responses.
  4. Provide new situations to be met in order to prepare the child for adult life.
  5. Provide a wise choice in the selection of a wide variety of experiences within the range of the child's comprehension and background.
  6. Provide through social studies activities needed for other phases of study of experience.
  7. Provide means of making the child conscious of and interested in his immediate environment.
  8. Develop a need for and a desire to practice such skills and habits as will aid them in the solution of the problem to its fullest extent.
  9. Provide for all levels of thinking and be a challenge to the abilities within the group. It should provide for some degree of success to all.
  10. Develop an interest in other phases of the problem and lead into other worth while problems and experiences that will develop a higher level of thinking.
  11. Develop a sense of values, and a sympathetic appreciation and understanding of other people.
  12. Be related to other experiences in which the pupils have been engaged.
  13. Contain experiences as practicable under the school conditions and with available materials.
  14. Aid in ordering experiences and give many opportunities for learning to cooperate in living and in becoming efficient.

[11] Port Arthur Public Schools, *Social Studies, A Tentative Course of Study for Grade Six*, Port Arthur, Texas, 1935, pp. 19-20.

256. "Bases for Evaluating Courses of Study" [12]

WHAT IS A COURSE OF STUDY AND WHAT IS IT FOR?

What is a course of study? A course of study has been defined as a document which is intended to guide the teacher in his attempts to aid pupils in learning. The curriculum, on the other hand, is defined as the body of experience to be communicated. It is what the pupil learns and experiences.

What are the essential purposes of a course of study? Among the chief purposes of a course of study are these:

1. To provide teachers with carefully thought out and far-sighted aims and objectives of education. These should show the teacher what education is for and lead him to see the relation of his many detailed tasks to the development of child life and service to society.

2. To furnish teachers with specific aims and objectives in every subject for each grade — also with expected outcomes in terms of pupil knowledge, habits, skills, attitudes, and ideals.

3. To supply teachers with a definite handbook which will be a guide to them in teaching the various subjects. For example: It will offer suggestions as to the educational resources of the local community; and approaches to subject-matter in terms of children's local interests, experiences, and environment.

4. To offer a ready guide for teachers as to content and pupil activities best fitted to realize the general aims and objectives of education — as well as the specific aims of particular subjects.

5. To coordinate all the efforts of the school, i. e., to unify the work of the various grades of the school as to aims, principles, and, to some extent, procedure.

6. To enable each teacher to see the work of his particular grade, not as a separate unit, but as growing out of the work of the preceding grade, and leading to the next higher grade.

7. To provide a basis of classification and promotion, i. e., to make assignments of work to be completed within given periods.

8. To supply a wide enough range of content for each grade, so that each teacher may select material suitable to the varying abilities of different classes and individual pupils.

9. To indicate methods and procedures, which are recommended because of their proved value, together with illustrations of classroom achievement resulting from their use. At the same time it should permit the teacher to exercise his own originality and initiative.

[12] National Education Association, *Keeping Pace with the Curriculum*, Research Bulletins Nos. 4 and 5, Vol. III, Washington, D. C., September and November, 1925, pp. 179–181.

10. To set up definite standards of attainment that may be expected of pupils.

11. To encourage teachers to consider the development of civic and character education in every subject in every grade.

12. To encourage teachers to keep in mind as one of their chief aims, the fostering of superior abilities with which some children are endowed, so as to develop the power of leadership and to help those who possess such abilities to realize the responsibility of using them for the benefit of the social group.

13. To stimulate teachers and to give them the right attitude toward their work. To suggest sources for additional reading and study.

Keeping these thirteen purposes of a course in mind, it is possible to set up, at least tentatively, certain bases for evaluating courses of study when issued. Course of study committees may also use them as criteria as to what should be included in the courses which they are building.

CRITERIA FOR EVALUATING COURSES OF STUDY

Up to date no criteria for evaluating courses of study have been published. A review of several hundred recent courses of study shows the existence of wide divergence as to: (a) Recognition of objectives, (b) Selection and organization of subject-matter, (c) Adaptation to community and individual needs of pupils, (d) Helpfulness to teachers, and (e) Mechanical make-up. The question arises: How can one determine which courses are best fulfilling the thirteen purposes of a course of study listed above?

To answer this question, the following criteria are tentatively suggested because nothing better seems to be available. Some of the points raised are much more important than others. No attempt has been made to weight them, or to render them objective. There is some overlapping of the questions listed under the five main headings. It is suggested that each question raised be applied to the particular course of study at hand. Instead of answering the question, " Yes " or " No," the person reviewing the course may rate it on each point, raised by the questions, on whatever subjective scale he sees fit as: " Good, fair, and poor," or " Excellent, very good, fair, and poor."

A. Recognition of Objectives:

1. Are general aims and objectives set forth indicating the general purposes of each course?

2. Are specific outcomes in terms of knowledge, habits, skills, attitudes, and ideals set forth for each subject?

3. Have the objectives and desired outcomes, which have been set

up, functioned in the selection and organization of the content? In other words, is there a gap between the objectives suggested and the activities set up? The Elementary Science and Nature Study section, which will appear in the forthcoming *Fourth Yearbook* of the Department of Superintendence, shows how intimate can be the tie-up between objectives and statement of activities.

4. The aims and objectives set up are in conformity with what particular philosophy of education?

B. *Selection and Organization of Subject-Matter:*

1. Is it so written and organized as to be an inspiration to teachers in their work?

2. Is the content such as will function in practical daily life?

3. Is the form and language clear and adapted to teachers' use?

4. Does it include suggestive lists of pupil experiences which will enable pupils to achieve the objectives set up?

5. Does it include suggestive lists of materials needed in providing adequate experiences?

6. Is the approach to each subject through situations and material familiar to children — Does it build on the experiences of children?

7. Is the subject-matter organized according to one or more of these bases: (a) Logical development? (b) Projects or problems, organized around children's interests? and (c) Central topics having large social values?

Whether any one of these bases or a combination of them should be accepted is still an open question.

8. Does it indicate standards of attainment for each grade, which give a basis for classification and promotion?

9. Are the results of scientific research, whenever conclusive, used as a basis for the selection and arrangement of content and is the statement of method in agreement with scientific studies as to the learning of pupils?

10. Is the work of the several grades in each subject coordinated and unified?

11. Does it provide for correlations?

12. Does it emphasize civic and character education as an outstanding objective of instruction in every subject in every grade?

C. *Adaptation to Community Demands and Individual Needs of Pupils:*

1. Does the course of study make use of local material?

2. Does it aim to meet needs peculiar to the community?

3. Is it flexible with provision for adaptation? Does it supply a wide range of materials for each grade? Are the problems under the major topics of each grade classified into such groups as: (a) prescribed, (b) alternative, and (c) optional?

4. Does it provide for individual differences among children in the same grade by: (a) Grouping material according to difficulty; and (b) Appealing to a wide variety of interests and abilities. In other words, does it help all children to work to their capacity, including those with special abilities and disabilities?

D. Helpfulness to Teachers:

1. In offering suggestions as to methods and materials, is some choice given the teacher as to subject-matter and method, so that she may exercise some judgment, independence and initiative of her own?

2. Are suggestions made relative to possible correlations with other subjects of the curriculum?

3. Are illustrative and type lessons included? Illustrations of good work?

4. Are suggestions as to use of standard tests and remedial treatment included?

5. Does the course of study give sufficient references and suggestions for materials, i. e., bibliographies for both teacher and pupil for each grade?

6. Are directions sufficiently complete and definite to serve the inexperienced and untrained teacher?

7. Does the course of study stimulate the teacher and give the right attitude? Does it inspire her (a) by keeping before her the large ideals — the aims and principles that control education; and (b) by making her conscious of the practical help it gives her toward applying such aims and principles in class work?

E. Mechanical Make-Up of Course of Study:

1. Is the form of arrangement clear and concise? Is the type easily read?

2. Is emphasis given to major topics, by proper indentation, use of special forms of type, etc.?

3. For the teachers' convenience, are the pages numbered? Is there a table of contents? An index? Are blank pages included for teachers' notations?

4. Is the character of the make-up in conformity with the stage of development: mimeographed or printed on cheap paper in early stages and printed in attractive form on better paper after it has been tested out? Is it printed in one document or in separate manuals, covering related units of the whole course?

CHAPTERS XVII–XVIII

ADMINISTRATIVE CONSIDERATIONS AND ADMINISTRATIVE ORGANIZATION IN CURRICULUM DEVELOPMENT

257. ADMINISTRATIVE PRINCIPLES OF CURRICULUM MAKING FOR PUBLIC SCHOOLS [1]

Walter D. Cocking

I. Aims and Objectives.

1. There should be a conscious acceptance of a definite educational philosophy.

2. The fifty principles formulated by the committee of the National Society for the Study of Education as the foundation steps in curriculum making are the best and most usable aims and objectives so far set forth.

3. The general aims of public education should be scientifically determined, clearly stated, and well understood.

4. Sound administrative principles should be determined as one of the first steps in a curriculum making program.

II. Instituting the Program.

5. The term, " curriculum," may be best used as including everything which has to do with the instructional work of the school.

6. A program of curriculum making should include restatement of aims, revision of the program of studies and time allotment, revision of content, selection of books and supplies, use of objective instruments to measure results.

7. A given course of study should be composed of the following elements: aims and objectives, methods of procedure, suggested activities, probable outcomes, lists of books and supplies, type lessons, work divided according to the promotion periods of the system, and bibliographies.

8. The direct responsibility of the curriculum program should be fixed in some one individual specially competent for the particular job. In recognition of the truth of this principle, progressive schools are creating a position known as " Director of the Curriculum."

9. The cost of the curriculum program should be carefully deter-

[1] From *Administrative Procedures in Curriculum Making*, Contributions to Education No. 329, Bureau of Publications, Teachers College, Columbia University, New York, 1928, pp. 108–112.

mined, provision should be made for it in the annual budget, and the expenditures should be carefully accounted.

10. Money spent on the making of the curriculum is one of the best expenditures which can be made of public funds.

11. Provision should be made for necessary clerical assistance.

12. The curriculum should be set forth in a mechanical form which will be most practical and useful to those who are to use it.

13. The mechanical set-up of the curriculum should be such that new materials may be added economically, efficiently, and expeditiously.

14. A particular subject or teaching unit should find a place in the curriculum on the basis that it can satisfy certain aims better than any other.

15. The plan used by school systems is to provide for school subjects; however, the teaching of these subjects should be largely through activities suited to the needs and interests of the pupils.

16. The content of the curriculum should be determined as scientifically as possible. The means used should include judgment of committees, opinion of experts, best practice, research, and experimentation.

17. The relation of books and supplies to the curriculum is that they should serve as aids in interpreting the curriculum.

18. Provision should be made for a curriculum library containing all materials dealing with curriculum making, and useful to those working on the curriculum.

19. The attitude of the public toward the school curriculum and its problems should be considered.

20. Definite steps should be taken to interest the community and keep it informed of what is being done in revising the curriculum.

21. Curriculum making should tend to increase the morale of the entire system. The success of the program is largely dependent on harmonious relationships, established throughout the whole personnel of the system.

III. Participation in Curriculum Making

22. Boards of Education should have a definite responsibility to curriculum making through authorizing the program, providing necessary funds, and approving the recommendations of the superintendent. This is essential to any program which is scientific.

23. The relation of various groups to curriculum making should be as follows:

Superintendent . . . . General oversight of the program
Research Director . . . . Measuring and interpreting the results

Curriculum Director	In charge of program
Principal	Serve on committees and install new courses
Supervisor	Guide and advise committees
Classroom Teachers	Serve on subject committees
Board of Education	Authorize program and appropriate money
Community	Advisory
Psychologist, Sociologist, Philosopher, Economist, Subject Expert	Consultant

24. The responsibility for the various phases of the curriculum program should be placed as follows:

Planning the program	Central office
Determining aims, program of studies and time allotment	Central office principals, supervisors, and teachers
Determining subject matter	Teachers with assistance of principals and supervisors
Making objective tests	Teachers with aid of supervisors and division of research
Installing new courses	Principal with assistance of supervisors
Carrying on constant revision ...	Entire system
Editing courses of study	Central office

. . . .

IV. Committee Organization

27. Curriculum workers should be selected because of their particular *fitness* for a particular job. As far as possible, objective standards should be employed.

28. Those *primarily* concerned with certain school tasks or jobs should be the *responsible agents* for curriculum making dealing with their respective interests.

29. Those working on the curriculum should be definitely trained in the principles of curriculum instruction.

30. The size of a committee should be such that definite responsibility can be placed and efficient work secured. Judged by the standards now available it will not be less than three or more than nine.

31. In order to get efficient results, (1) jobs should be small and specific, and (2) responsibliity should be fixed.

32. General participation in the work of curriculum making is desirable.

33. There should be a definite progression of subject matter. Unification of the work should be sought.

34. There should be a conscious integration of the work of one unit with that of another.

V. Appraising Value of Curriculum Programs

35. The success of a curriculum program should be determined chiefly by its effect on the training received by boys and girls. Success should be determined through use of both subjective and objective measures.

36. The outcome from curriculum making should be twofold: those which result in better training for boys and girls and those which serve to make for a more enlightened, virile teaching corps.

37. A definite program of objective measurement should be a part of curriculum making. The object of such a program is to determine the effectiveness of the new courses, or such elements of them as can be measured.

38. Controlled experimental studies which have for their object the scientific determination of elements in the curriculum should be constantly carried on by every school system.

39. Appraisal programs which have for their object the definite determination of the value of curriculum revision should be formulated and carried on.

V. General

40. The particular local conditions undoubtedly make necessary the adaptation of the program to fit the exact needs.

41. Courses of study should always be considered tentative and should be modified whenever good reasons appear.

258. STATEMENT OF ADMINISTRATIVE PRINCIPLES FOR CURRICULUM DEVELOPMENT IN FORT WORTH PUBLIC SCHOOLS [2]

ADMINISTRATIVE PRINCIPLES

1. All teachers, supervisors, and administrators affiliated with the school system should have an opportunity to participate in the preparation of courses of study.

2. The curriculum shall be constructed by the teachers, supervisors, administrators, and the curriculum director.

3. The curriculum maker must become a student of the child, of society, and of the accumulated experiences of the race.

4. As far as possible materials for curriculum building must be secured as a result of scientific research.

[2] Fort Worth Public Schools, *Language Arts, A Tentative Course of Study for Grade Six,* Curriculum Bulletin No. 146, Fort Worth, Texas, 1935, pp. ii–iii.

5. Curriculum experiments and work carried on in other centers should be carefully investigated and practical results made available for local use.

6. Before constructing any part of a course of study the entire program for that field of work shall be tentatively determined so that each part may be in consonance with the complete program and with the aims of education.

7. The curriculum must be developed in the light of known facts and principles of school administration — such as length of class period, size of classes, arrangement of school programs, range of individual differences, library facilities, and laboratory and shop equipment.

8. There should be a positive justification for all materials that find a place in the course of study. Subject matter must make some significant contribution to the aims of education.

9. The curriculum should not be based entirely upon the traditions and customs of a community, but these should be accorded consideration.

10. All curriculum materials should be carefully tried out before final installation is recommended.

11. The curriculum cannot be made exactly in advance.

12. Activities and materials of instruction should be conceived as units in a total scheme.

13. Education must abandon the practice, long obsolete in science, of relying upon easily found traditional values as guides in the educative process.

14. In school systems which have excellent courses of study, textbooks and reference books must find a place in the educational process as tools to aid teachers and pupils in making the materials of the course of study more effective.

15. Definite steps should be taken to interest the community and keep it informed concerning curriculum revision.

16. Contributions and suggestions from lay groups should be encouraged and welcomed.

259. "Leadership in Curriculum Building in 168 Large City School Systems"[3]

Margaret Alltucker Norton

In less than a decade curriculum construction and revision have become a definite part of the regular work of well-organized, progressive school systems.

[3] *School and Society,* 33:17–20, January 3, 1931.

The movement began, in most instances, by an inservice program of teacher training, which varied greatly in extent and in usefulness in different school systems, and a revision of practically all courses of study from the kindergarten through the secondary school. This meant that scores of committees were working simultaneously. Research workers everywhere focussed their attention on the problem of selecting from each of the many subject fields content which seemed to have the greatest social value, and on studies of how children learn. Traditional objectives were evaluated and new ones set up. Content thought to be non-functioning in modern life was eliminated. Activities suited to the growth needs of children were substituted and were designed to develop those knowledges, habits, skills and attitudes which appear to be most needed for successful participation in present-day living. Faculties of entire school systems worked on curriculum problems. Thousands of new course of study bulletins were rushed into print, or were mimeographed and tried out on an experimental basis. Curriculum and course of study building was the theme of educational yearbooks and the topic most frequently discussed at educational conventions. Within the last year or two less has been said on the subject. Does this mean that interest in curriculum building has waned? No! It means that we now take it for granted that curriculum and course of study building is a part of the very warp and woof of every well-organized, progressive school system.

A general upheaval of curriculum building was necessary since many school systems had for a number of years done little or nothing to modernize their courses of study. After having undergone a more or less thorough overhauling, many courses now need to be carefully tried out, better adjusted to the needs of children and revised from year to year so as to be kept up to date. This revision is going on continuously, and new courses are also being developed, for many of the first revisions were far from satisfactory. This work is largely done by local committees of teachers and principals.

To discover who is directly in charge of local programs of curriculum building, the Research Division of the National Education Association recently addressed all superintendents of schools in cities over thirty thousand in population, asking for the name and title of the person or persons in charge of curriculum construction and revision. Out of 168 replies, 113 named one person who was directly in charge. The titles are summarized in Table I. Two or more persons were named by 55 cities. Their titles are summarized in Table II.

TABLE I

TITLE OF PERSON DIRECTLY IN CHARGE OF CURRICULUM CONSTRUC-
TION AND REVISION IN 113 CITY SCHOOL SYSTEMS
(In cities over 30,000 in population)

Title	Number of school systems
Superintendent of schools	42
Associate, deputy or assistant superintendent of schools	26
Director of research *	14
Supervisor or director of elementary education †	13
Director of curriculum ‡	6
Chairman of curriculum committee §	3
Supervisor of secondary education ¶	3
Supervising director or director of instruction	2
Principal	4
Total	113

* This title varies as follows: assistant superintendent and director of research; director of research; director of research and guidance; director of measurements and research; director of research and auxiliary agencies; director of research, guidance and child accounting; director of instructional research, and director of high-school research.

† This title varies as follows: supervisor; supervisor of elementary schools; supervisor of elementary education; supervisor of grades; elementary supervisor; director of elementary grades; director of elementary education; director of kindergartens and elementary education, and director of kindergartens and primary education.

‡ This title varies as follows: chairman, general revision committee of board of superintendents; associate superintendent in charge of curriculum administration; director of curriculum; director, department of curriculum; director of course of study; director of curriculum study, educational measurement and research, and director of methods and curriculum.

§ This title varies as follows: chairman, curriculum committee; chairman, committee on curriculum revision; curriculum chairman, and secretary of supervisory committee on curriculum.

¶ This title varies as follows: supervisor of secondary education; supervisor of junior and senior high schools; supervisor of secondary instruction, and supervisor of upper grades and vocational and educational guidance.

Table I shows that in 68 out of 113 school systems in cities over 30,000 in population either the superintendent of schools or one of his associate, deputy or assistant superintendents is the person directly in charge of curriculum construction and revision. According to Table II, even where two or more persons are in charge of this work, the superintendent of schools and his associate, deputy and assistant superintendents are among those most frequently in charge. This

TABLE II

TITLES OF PERSONS IN CHARGE OF CURRICULUM CONSTRUCTION AND
REVISION IN 55 CITY SCHOOL SYSTEMS
(In cities of over 30,000 population where two or more persons are
in charge of curriculum construction)

Title	Number of school systems
Associate, deputy or assistant superintendent of schools *	41
Supervisors or directors of primary and elementary education †	32
Superintendent of schools	22
Junior high-school principal	7
High-school principal	7
Elementary school principal	6
Director or supervisor of secondary education ‡	5
District superintendent of schools	4
Director of research §	4
Assistant principal, high school	2
Director of vocational and educational guidance	1
Director, course of study, elementary grades	1
Curriculum consultant	1

* This title varies as follows: assistant superintendent; deputy superintendent; assistant superintendent, department of research; associate superintendent in charge of high schools; associate superintendent in charge of elementary schools; deputy superintendent in charge of secondary schools; assistant superintendent in charge of junior and senior high schools; assistant superintendent in charge of high schools; assistant superintendent in charge of junior high schools; assistant superintendent in charge of primary instruction.

† This title varies as follows: supervisor; director of elementary education; supervisor of upper elementary grades; director of elementary schools; elementary supervisor; supervisor, elementary grades; grade supervisor; director of grades; general supervisor of grades; supervisor, primary grades; primary supervisor; grammar grade supervisor, and platoon-school supervisor.

‡ This title varies as follows: director of high schools; director of secondary education; supervisor of junior and senior high schools, and junior high-school supervisor.

§ This title varies as follows: director of educational research; director of methods and research; director of educational research and service, and assistant director, department of psychology and educational research.

fact indicates that the majority of public school administrators consider curriculum construction and revision so important that they either take charge of it themselves or delegate it only to their immediate subordinates. In some instances this means that they assume responsibility for leadership and detailed guidance of committees. In many instances it means that they appoint the committees, give some guidance, review the completed reports and recommend them to the school board for adoption.

When reporting the name and title of the person in charge of curriculum construction and revision in their local school systems, a number of superintendents added comments such as these:

The actual work is done by committees of teachers and principals who report to the superintendent or his assistant.

Committees of teachers appointed by the superintendent prepare revisions of courses of study. These committees work under the direction of the assistant superintendents in charge of the subject and report to the board of superintendents; the board of superintendents to the superintendent, and the superintendent to the school committee.

The superintendent of schools has chief charge of curriculum construction and revision. But he consults very closely his principals and supervisors.

All curriculum revision is done by supervisors, principals and teachers under the direction of the superintendent.

The superintendent and assistant superintendents review the work of the curriculum committees.

Judging from the titles listed in Tables I and II, seven city school systems have special permanent departments of curriculum construction in charge of special directors who give their entire time to this work. These cities and the titles of the person in charge of curriculum building are listed below:

Chicago, Illinois, director of curriculum
Denver, Colorado, director, department of curriculum
Kansas City, Kansas, director of curriculum
Long Beach, California, director of curriculum
Los Angeles, California, director, course of study
Pittsburgh, Pennsylvania, director of curriculum study, educational measurements and research
Kenosha, Wisconsin, director, methods and curriculum

While other school systems do not make the person in charge of curriculum revision the director of a permanent department of curriculum, some very nearly approach that title. For example, Detroit, Michigan, has a supervising director of instruction; Lakewood, Ohio, has an assistant superintendent in charge of curriculum construction; Minneapolis, Minnesota, has a director of instructional research; New York City has a chairman of the general revision committee of the board of superintendents; Rochester, New York, has a deputy superintendent of schools in charge of a central curriculum revision committee; Tulsa, Oklahoma, has an associate superintendent in charge of curriculum administration, and many other school systems have allocated the work of directing curriculum construction and revision more or less permanently to an assistant superintendent of schools, the department of research and the supervisory officers.

Tables I and II show that in many cities supervisors are the ones directly in charge of curriculum construction and revision. If an analysis were made of the personnel of the curriculum committees in these 168 cities it would doubtless show that supervisory officers are included in the majority of primary and elementary committees. This is to be expected since course of study building is one of the chief means of supervision.

Curriculum and course of study construction is now recognized as a continuous, cooperative enterprise engaged in jointly by teachers, principals, supervisors and superintendent, with the assistance of outside specialists. Its leadership offers one of the greatest opportunities for service in the whole field of education.

260. "PLANS FOR CURRICULUM-MAKING IN SECONDARY SCHOOLS"[4]

Edwin S. Lide

SCOPE OF THIS REPORT

One of the curriculum projects of the National Survey of Secondary Education involved an extended investigation of plans and procedures for curriculum-making on a city-wide, county-wide, and state-wide basis. The complete report, which will shortly be published, includes examples from individual schools and other details of practice which it is impossible to include in a brief article. The present statement includes only certain information related to the organization and the procedures through which the secondary-school curriculum in cities was made or revised within the five years previous to 1930–31.

Data for the study were secured on a special inquiry form, 20 pages in length, received from 162 towns and cities varying in size and location. Visits were made to some of these cities. Of the 162 returns analyzed, 129 were descriptive of plans followed in a city as a whole, while the remaining 33 described plans in operation in individual or independent secondary schools. The inquiry form provided space, not only for indication of plans followed, but for opinions as to the merits of these plans. Because of the methods followed in securing the list of schools solicited for information, the results

[4] *School Review,* 40:751–759, December, 1932.

secured are more characteristic of better-than-average than of average practices.

SPECIFIC PROCEDURES FOR CERTAIN MAJOR STEPS

The procedures best adapted in one city to the realization of a step in curriculum-making may not prove the most satisfactory in another city. The three procedures mentioned most frequently as those used in realizing certain steps together with the total number of respondents reporting each of these procedures are presented in Table II.

The procedures designated for securing co-operation and interest were those employed before the program of curriculum-making was launched. In addition to those indicated in the table, a few schools, mostly in large cities, conducted a preliminary survey of the work of the schools and made use of specialists from without the city to help determine the direction in which revision could best proceed.

A smaller number of respondents indicated the use of procedures for securing publicity and for organizing committees. Some respondents felt that the less publicity the work was given outside the school, the better. In many of the smaller cities all teachers within a department were assigned to the work of revision in that department, and no methods of selection were employed.

In a few schools careful efforts were made to provide conditions which would facilitate a thorough job of curriculum-making. In the majority of the schools, however, training for revision was secured only in connection with faculty meetings conducted by the local administration, literature was available only through trips to a centrally organized library, no regular schedule of committee meetings was provided, and no special quarters were arranged for holding meetings. Teachers assumed the work of curriculum-making in addition to their regular duties. Many schools, however, pointed to the need of more careful arrangements than those employed.

The largest number of respondents indicated that, in determining methods of selecting and organizing materials, they were most often governed by those employed in neighboring centers. A surprisingly large number, however, indicated the employment, to some degree, of local research. Representatives of the various committees most often arranged for special meetings to provide for continuity and to eliminate duplication in the work of separate grades and departments.

A large number of respondents indicated that tentative outlines of courses of study were submitted to actual classroom tryout and revised in the light of the results reported. The need of constant

TABLE II

THE THREE PROCEDURES MOST FREQUENTLY MENTIONED AS
THOSE USED IN REALIZING CERTAIN STEPS IN THE
CURRICULUM-MAKING PROGRAM

Procedure	*Frequency of Mention*

Securing co-operation and interest:
1. Group meetings with administrative staff 88
2. Individual discussions with curriculum-staff members 52
3. Checking practices against specific objectives 45

Securing publicity:
1. Local press 43
2. Parent-teachers' association 42
3. Local school press 36

Organizing committees — criteria determining:
1. Success in teaching 50
2. Character of professional training 43
3. Length of professional training 22

Organizing committees — agency determining:
1. Central office solely 49
2. Nominated by principal, approved by central office 44
3. Teachers solely 18

Providing conditions of work — training teachers for revision:
1. Faculty meetings 94
2. Local extension classes organized through higher institutions .. 50
3. Individual training by regular employees 36

Providing conditions of work — making literature accessible:
1. Centrally organized library 82
2. Materials mimeographed and distributed 40
3. Public and private libraries 35

Providing conditions of work — arrangements for meetings:
1. No regular schedule 76
2. Weekly meetings 26
3. Bi-weekly meetings 11

Providing conditions of work — housing facilities:
1. No special arrangement 75
2. Special quarters provided 38

Providing conditions of work — relation to regular duties:
1. No release from regular duties 65
2. Some release from regular duties 38

Selecting and organizing materials — influences having *most* weight:
1. Practices elsewhere 75
2. Committee discussions 58
3. Local research 47

Selecting and organizing materials — influences having *some* weight:

TABLE II — *Continued*

Procedure	Frequency of Mention
1. State department of education	68
2. Reported research	66
3. Committee discussion	64
Co-ordinating and correlating materials:	
1. Joint committee meetings	64
2. Conferences with director of program	53
3. Skeleton outline prepared by each department	46
Trying-out of course outlines before formal adoption:	
1. All teachers in the classroom	80
2. Teachers criticize without trying out	48
3. Experimental classes organized	35
Assembling results — form in which submitted:	
1. Mimeographed, loose-leaf	40
2. Mimeographed and bound	33
3. Printed and bound	24
Training teachers in use of new courses:	
1. Supervisory demonstration meetings	63
2. Visits of supervisors	60
3. Committee in charge of revision	28
Appraising results:	
1. Informal, by administrative and supervisory staff	72
2. Use of standardized tests	49
3. Use of specially prepared tests	37
Providing continuous revision — agency responsible:	
1. General revision committee	73
2. Research department	22
3. Curriculum department	20

changes in course-of-study materials was often given as a reason for assembling such materials in a manner permitting easy change. The greatest number reported that the outlines were mimeographed in loose-leaf form.

In the larger schools the supervisors, through classroom visits and special-demonstration meetings, assumed most of the responsibility for training teachers in the use of new outlines. In many of the smaller cities no further training was provided after the new outlines were reported, since all teachers usually had a part in curriculum-making.

Few respondents reported a careful plan for determining the extent to which the revised plans improved the work of the classroom. In most cases such appraisal was entirely informal. Although about a third reported the use of standardized and specially prepared tests, in many cases these applied only to one or two fields of instruction.

Whether as a result of little or much appraisal, the committee responsible for the first general revision was usually assigned responsibility of making changes from year to year.

GENERAL APPRAISAL OF PLANS IN USE

Many respondents, in appraising the plan followed, stated simply that it was satisfactory and that they would make no changes in the plan even if they were to undertake an entirely new program of curriculum-making. Because many conditions influence the specific plan which proves most successful in a given situation, it is attempted, in this connection, to indicate only general conclusions given by a large number of respondents.

1. In the first program of curriculum-making it is desirable to build the curriculum from the ground up, but lack of money and time often prevent this procedure.

2. The service of a capable director is essential, and he should have special training for the work.

3. It is desirable that the range of participants be as wide as possible.

4. Because of the values resulting through motivation and expert advice, contacts with outside specialists are desirable.

5. The principles on which the curriculum-making program is based need to be kept constantly before the teachers. Thorough instruction of teachers is necessary.

6. Special care should be given the choosing of the committees, in larger systems particularly. Many respondents, however, did not consider that the use of objective criteria, such as number of years of experience and training, was an essential procedure in determining committee membership.

7. Definite leadership is needed for research work and for the direction of experimental classes organized to try out new materials.

8. Additional funds should be provided for the employment of substitutes for teachers and for extra clerical help. If no release from regular duties is provided, a strain is often placed on those responsible for much detailed work.

9. A course of study should be mimeographed, rather than printed, until it has been through several revisions.

10. Continuous revision is an indispensable basis of procedure. The responsibility should be upon those in charge of the first general revision.

The largest number of respondents indicated the need of more careful procedures than had been used in the following steps: securing co-ordination and correlation of the work of separate committees; securing criticisms and suggestions resulting from actual try-out of tentative courses; training teachers in the use of new courses; appraising the results of revision; and securing the teachers' suggestions to be employed in a program of continuous revision. The lack of teacher preparation for curriculum-making, however, was emphasized as the factor which, more than any other, obstructed curriculum development, while the professional growth of teachers was shown to be the greatest benefit derived.

261. "California's Program of Curriculum Reorganization in the Secondary Schools" [5]

Walter R. Hepner

California's curriculum reorganization program is essentially a state-wide effort to improve teaching practice. In general, such comprehensive activities are approached from two very different points of view. One assumes that the best results will be accomplished by bringing together a relatively small group of experts who, with certain minor democratic activities, develop the provisions of the new plans, issue the needed publications, and attempt to establish the plans in practice. The other approach makes use of well qualified leaders, but virtually evolves the ultimate plan in the classrooms and schools of the state. California is committed to the latter approach.

The view held by most workers in our state is that more lasting and basically sound results are achieved in coöperative endeavor involving all workers, rather than in the attempts of a few selected persons to formulate more or less hastily a program and to put it into the scheme of things by executive order. Fundamental revision comes not through the formulation of plans, procedures, and policies *per se*, but rather through a process that modifies specific practice. Current practice in the secondary schools is conditioned by many factors, including traditional materials and subject organizations, methods based upon varying types of psychologies, and attitudes and habits acquired from training and experience. The feeling is that revision will come about more effectively if all workers are encouraged to analyze and evaluate their own practices and points of view, to strive for improvement, and to participate in the formulation of the program of the state as a whole. . . .

It has not yet been proved that civilization can survive the materialism and the artificialities that have come with the machine age.

[5] *California Quarterly of Secondary Education,* 10:75, 76, 77, 79–80, January, 1935.

We educators believe that it can. We have faith that, through education of the right sort, civilization and our own democratic way of life can be not only saved, but led to flower into ever increasing opportunities for human well-being and happiness. Our efforts in curriculum reorganization are to determine what "education of the right sort " is, and to make provisions for it in every secondary school of the state.

Consequently, our California program is one of stimulating renewed effort on the part of every secondary school worker, to the end that out of our total experience there may be evolved patterns of educational practice adapted to individual and social needs.

ADVISORY COMMITTEE ON SECONDARY EDUCATION

With these views held constantly in mind, the California program has been in process of development for some time. In February, 1934, Dr. Vierling Kersey, State Superintendent of Public Instruction, appointed an Advisory Committee on Secondary Education of twenty-six members, who represent all types of public secondary schools and public and private colleges and universities. . . .

This committee is charged with the responsibility for giving consideration to every phase of secondary education; for developing plans for evaluating current practices; for outlining a program of curriculum experimentation and improvement; for devising means for making available, directing, and coördinating the educational forces and resources of the state; for evaluating progress in the reconstruction program; and for developing new plans for further progress.

The underlying idea is that this committee, through individual contribution and through the process of group thinking, will develop points of view, policies, and plans, and incorporate them in recommendations which will serve to point the way in a comprehensive program of secondary school reconstruction, and also to guide the State Department of Education in the discharge of its duty.

The State Superintendent of Public Instruction has also appointed a Committee on Coöperating Schools. The ten members of this committee are members of the Advisory Committee on Secondary Education. The duties of this committee are centered about a comprehensive project in curriculum experimentation which involves certain selected secondary schools, and the schools below and above, which send students to, or receive students from, them.

This committee is giving consideration to (1) the general types and methods of experimentation to be undertaken; (2) the principles and procedures to be applied in selecting schools as experimental centers; (3) the technique to be used in the guidance, control, and evaluation of the project; and (4) the plan for securing the coördination of the curricula and procedures of all secondary schools, lower schools, and colleges and universities that are involved in the project.

REGIONAL COMMITTEES AND THEIR FUNCTIONS

Since the organization of the Advisory Committee of Twenty-six members in February, 1934, meetings have been held more or less regularly, one-half of the committee meeting in Oakland and the other half in Los Angeles. Under the general guidance of this committee the program thus far developed includes the following:

1. The state has been organized into nine regions. For each region a committee has been appointed and is now
   a. Collecting reports of curriculum revision projects under way;
   b. Planning regional conferences;
   c. Contacting workers in the various schools; and
   d. Evolving criteria for the evaluation of teaching, administrative, and guidance practice.

2. A Curriculum Revision Information Service has been organized to report a wide range of curriculum revision activities collected by regional committees. Two packets of these materials have already been issued to superintendents and to all secondary school principals. Other packets will follow at frequent intervals throughout the year.

In setting up this information service the Advisory Committee on Secondary Education is unanimous in urging the serious consideration of the following points:

   a. That the projects reported have not been critically evaluated in light of any generally approved set of criteria; no claim of perfection is made, either by those who are carrying on the activity, or by the Advisory Committee.

   b. That evaluation is left to the individuals who read the reports.

   c. That the projects reported are examples of some of the ways in which schools are proceeding.

   d. That the purposes of distributing these reports at this time are:
   (1) To provide current materials for individual, committee, and faculty study and discussions;
   (2) To indicate that many and varied activities are in progress, and to give clues to the activities and thinking taking place in the various secondary schools of the state;
   (3) To stimulate (a) a thoroughgoing statewide study of aims and objectives, (b) the creation of curriculum materials, (c) the improvement of school practices, and (d) the laying of a foundation for an ultimate program of secondary education to be developed coöperatively by the secondary school people of the state.

3. A set of sixty bibliographies has been prepared by fifty leaders in California in the various phases of secondary education. Each bibliography

contains approximately fifteen highly selected and annotated references. About fifty have already been issued, others will follow, and additional bibliographies will be developed.

4. Coöperative arrangements have been made with the California Society of Secondary Education whereby live and pertinent materials of immediate concern to the reorganization program will be given a prominent place in the Society's magazine, THE CALIFORNIA JOURNAL OF SECONDARY EDUCATION. The Advisory Committee predicts wide and comprehensive utilization of this magazine by administrators and teachers engaged in curriculum revision.

5. The committee looks forward to the development of a handbook on secondary education in California to carry some such title as " Adolescent Growth and Development." However, the committee considers it unwise *at this time* to appoint committees for the specific purpose of preparing materials for the contemplated handbook. The point of view held is that during this year every possible encouragement and assistance should be provided in order to stimulate *all* secondary school workers to greater and more fundamental curriculum revision activities than have thus far been undertaken. It is felt that out of the experimental efforts of many, eventually, through the pooling of experiences and creative endeavor, there will come the formulation and acceptance of a philosophy of secondary education on a statewide basis, together with comprehensive and specifically helpful teacher guides to the various types of activities in the secondary school curriculum.

6. An agreement is now virtually completed whereby all colleges and universities of the state will admit students from a limited number of selected high schools upon the recommendation of the principal and without requiring the students to have completed a prescribed subject pattern. This plan will permit a rather thorough-going and more radical reorganization of the curriculum than is possible in most schools. It is the expectation of the Advisory Committee that the schools involved may become observation centers in their particular areas. The principals of some high schools and the superintendents in some cities are now developing plans to try out this new freedom in curriculum making.

7. Further experimental plans are nearing completion for tying two California high schools, one in Northern California and one in Southern California, into the Progressive Education Association's experimental group.

8. A Parent-Teacher Association Handbook on Secondary Education has been prepared and is now in experimental use. The plan is to make necessary revisions and print the materials in the early spring. This handbook will be used by parent-teacher study groups for the purpose of developing lay understanding and support of the reorganization program.

SUMMARY

In summary, the California program of secondary school curriculum reorganization is concerned primarily with the improvement of opportunities for adolescent boys and girls to grow and develop in a changing world, and to increase the social contribution of the public school to our democratic society. We begin with no preconceived ideas concerning the organization, administration, teaching methods, or subject matter of the ultimate program. Our procedure is based upon the belief that every educational practice and all instructional equipment and materials, both old and new, should be critically analyzed and evaluated. Then, through the processes of experimentation, coöperative endeavor, and pooled judgment a statewide plan for secondary education should be outlined. This plan will involve the formulation of a statement of a philosophy of secondary education derived through democratic methods. Furthermore, in the course of a year or two the plan should result in the development of printed materials. These should be designed to aid all workers in their efforts to give adolescents vital and realistic experiences that shall effectively lead them to a fuller realization of the accepted aims and objectives of the educative process.

262. Procedures for Curriculum Improvement Suggested by a Survey Report of Cincinnati Public Schools [6]

The first step taken by the Director of Curriculum should be a general evaluation of the subjects taught in the Cincinnati schools. This may be carried on by a committee of principals and superintendents. The general objectives of education need to be formulated and each subject of the curriculum justified in the general setting.

Once this acceptable program of studies is established, certain subjects may be studied extensively. This may be done through committees acting under the general guidance of the Director of Curriculum, composed of teachers and supervisors of the subject. Each committee should lay out the general plan of the type of curriculum wanted. In connection with this there should be conferences of the committee with outstanding men in curriculum work in these fields.

The next step would be the appointment of one or two individuals to write the course of study. The Director of Curriculum and the supervisor of the subject or subjects immediately concerned should furnish direction and aid in this writing. After completion of a curriculum it should be considered tentative while it is being tried out for a year. The committee which supervises the preparation of a curriculum should also interpret it and see that it is given a fair

[6] Cincinnati, *Survey Report of the Cincinnati Public Schools,* The Cincinnati Bureau of Governmental Research, Report No. 64, Cincinnati, Ohio, July, 1935, p. 281.

trial. After a trial of a year, changes may be made and the curriculum be inaugurated for a definite or an indefinite period of time. The critical period in curriculum construction is not, as many would suppose, in the actual writing of any given curriculum but rather in the placing of it in the school system. This problem should be considered from the very beginning, and teachers educated to the new course of study.

The cooperative method of curriculum development as briefly sketched above allows for a great amount of teacher participation. In the end this is the best method, since the teachers are most likely to accept such courses not only because they have written them but because the courses will represent the teachers' viewpoint and are more likely to be a practical product for schoolroom use.

263. Plan and Organization for Curriculum Development Recommended for Chicago [7]

Jesse H. Newlon and others

1. A Continuous Curriculum Policy

Chicago should inaugurate a policy of continuous curriculum revision affecting all departments of the school system and involving the constant participation of the entire teaching staff of the schools.

2. A Curriculum Department Under a Qualified Assistant Superintendent

A curriculum department should be established as a permanent feature of the central administrative organization and placed under a director with the rank of assistant superintendent and responsible directly to the superintendent or to the deputy superintendent.

Qualifications of the assistant superintendent in charge of curriculum revision should include a broad general education, extensive study in the philosophy and practice of education and in the social sciences, and a genuine interest in the relation of education to social change. Some practical experience in teaching is essential, and some administrative or supervisory experience is a desirable though not a necessary qualification. This position will not be administrative in the ordinary sense of the word, but will require ability to work cooperatively with the staff and with the public, and to direct the work of individuals and of committees. The head of this department should be primarily a student of education in its broader social aspects.

[7] From "The Curricula of the Chicago Schools," *Report of the Survey of the Schools of Chicago, Illinois*, Vol. III, Bureau of Publications, Teachers College, Columbia University, New York, 1932, pp. 103–111.

The staff of the curriculum department should include:

A. One or More Assistant Directors. The qualifications of these persons should be, in general, similar to those of the assistant superintendent in charge of the department. An appropriate division of duties should be made in accordance with abilities and special interests, but all should work in close coöperation, viewing the problems of each division of the school in the light of a total educational program.

B. The Subject Supervisors. All of the subject supervisors in the Chicago public schools should act in an advisory capacity in the preparation of courses of study. The services of these supervisors can be utilized in either of two ways:

a. The majority of them at least might be released from all administrative and supervisory duties. They would then devote their energies, as members of the curriculum department, primarily to the improvement of teaching through curriculum study and revision. They would, of course, be available for conference and for visit to schools on the request of assistant superintendents, district superintendents, and principals. If this plan were followed, the assistant supervisors and special teachers in the various subjects would be transferred to the offices of assistant superintendents, district superintendents, or other general administrative officers, and would work under their direction.

It is obvious that in some instances, as, for example, in the case of physical education, the supervisor or director of a department will be charged with certain administrative duties so that no hard-and-fast rule can be laid down regarding the functions to be assigned to each such officer.

b. These supervisors might continue to exercise their supervisory functions somewhat as at the present time, but with relatively less time given to actual supervision and more time given to participation in the work of the curriculum department.

In any event, supervisors appointed in the future should be well qualified not only with reference to the subject matter and methods in their own fields, but also with especial reference to their grasp of general educational problems and the necessity of effecting a more highly integrated program of education.

C. Specialists. While consulting specialists would not be included in the regular staff of the curriculum department, it is essential that provision be made for obtaining from time to time the services of specialists in various aspects of the curriculum for consultation with curriculum committees and others with respect to important problems. It will be desirable to invite for consultation persons who have made notable contributions in their respective fields, for example, in the teaching of reading, in the reorganization of science instruction, in some aspect of the teaching of the social studies, or in other fields. This policy has already been inaugurated in Chicago and has been followed by many cities in recent years.

D. *An Adequate Secretarial Staff.* The curriculum department should be a service department. It should work coöperatively with teachers, principals, and administrative officers in the elementary and secondary schools and in all departments of the school system. The department would have no authority to require participation in curriculum revision or the utilization of materials prepared under its direction. The assistant superintendents in charge of secondary schools and elementary schools would be expected to assume the professional leadership in their respective divisions, and policies in these divisions would be under their general control, subject only to review by the deputy superintendent or the superintendent. The curriculum department would serve as an integrating factor. It would view education as a continuous process and not as a process broken sharply at the end of elementary education or at the end of secondary education.

3. Budget for the Curriculum Department

Adequate provision should be made in each annual budget for the support of the work of the curriculum department. The supervisors and some of the clerical assistants are already provided for in the school budget. The items to be covered by a minimum budget would be approximately as follows:

For the salaries of the assistant superintendent and general assistants	$16,000
Additional clerical assistants	8,000
For consulting specialists each year	7,500
For substitute teachers to relieve classroom teachers for full-time curriculum work	20,000
Printing	12,000
Supplies	3,000
Professional libraries	10,000
Total	$76,500

It should be pointed out in this connection that $76,500 is less than one-tenth of one per cent of the budget of approximately $82,000,000 which has been adopted by the Board of Education for the school year 1932–1933. This proposed appropriation, however, includes certain sums which would be expended anyway, so that the percentage of the total budget would be less than the above estimate. This money would be expended for the constant study and improvement of education in Chicago. It is approximately the cost of the plans and supervision of construction for a new building costing $1,500,000, or for three buildings costing a half million dollars each. Everyone recognizes the necessity of expert service in the design and construction of buildings. Planning what is to be taught in a building is of far greater importance than the design of the building. The Chicago schools of the future will not be as effective as they should be unless the people and the Board of Education are willing to expend a reasonable amount of money in the continuous study and revision of teaching. To accomplish this end an organization must be set up and continuous leadership of a high quality must be supplied. Curriculum revision cannot with safety be made a matter to be attended to entirely after school hours or as an extra job for otherwise busy executives. In this connection it should be pointed out that if the Chicago schools are 5 per cent less efficient than they would be with a curriculum better suited to individual needs and social conditions, the waste measured in money is $4,000,000 annually.

4. Teacher Participation

Constant city-wide teacher participation should be inaugurated as a part of the continuous curriculum-revision program. This will involve the services of teachers on curriculum committees, attendance upon conference, and the assignment of certain teachers for work for varying lengths of time in the curriculum department at the headquarters building. Committees should be appointed by the assistant superintendents in charge of the larger divisions of the school system with the curriculum department acting in an advisory capacity. It will be desirable, however, that the curriculum department be given freedom to invite any teacher or other member of the instructional staff to participate in its work. These relationships should be informal and coöperative rather than controlled too much by routine and red tape.

In numerous instances teachers should be made chairmen of curriculum-revision committees. The teacher membership on every committee should be large both in the elementary and in the secondary schools. Membership on committees, attendance upon conferences, and other forms of participation should be rotated so that over a period of years many leading teachers will be included. Methods should be devised for securing the reactions of all teachers to important curriculum problems. The printed course of study is by no means the most important outcome of this process of curriculum revision. The most important outcome of the process is the growth of the participating teacher, which is immediately reflected in classroom procedures.

5. *The Responsibility of the Principal in Curriculum Revision*

The principal of the school carries a heavy responsibility in curriculum revision. He should be conversant with the best thought and practice and with curriculum problems in every grade and department of his school. He should follow the work of every curriculum committee that affects the school under his direction. He should initiate and supervise the utilization of new courses of study, teaching materials, and methods. The principal should serve occasionally on curriculum committees, and ways and means should be devised for securing from him constant criticisms and suggestions with reference to curriculum problems. In this work the Chicago Principals' Club which has already accomplished so much for the Chicago schools can continue to coöperate in many important ways. The importance of a continuous program of professional study on the part of every school faculty should be emphasized. Leadership in this program must be supplied by the principal. It seems unnecessary to point out that forming curriculum committees entirely of principals is not a desirable procedure.

6. *The Participation of the Chicago Normal College*

The resources of the Chicago Normal College should be utilized in curriculum revision much more extensively than at the present time. The Normal College should be represented on many curriculum committees. Its faculty should provide much of the leadership for the in-service professional training of the teaching staff.

Certain posts should be created in the faculty of the Normal College with special reference both to the broader training of prospective teachers and to the continuous reconstruction of the curriculum of the Chicago schools. These professorships should include:

a. A specialist in the socio-economic aspects of education, whose qualifications should include extensive training in the social sciences, as well as in education.

b. A specialist in the principles and methods of teaching, whose qualifications should include an extensive study of the philosophy and theory of education with special reference to curriculum problems.

c. An educational psychologist, whose qualifications should include extensive study of the problems of learning and who should be concerned primarily with the practical application of the findings of psychology to school learning situations.

Doubtless one or more members of the present Normal College faculty would qualify for these positions. The importance of the fields in which these specialists would work needs no further emphasis than has already been given in this report. Each of these professors should give a course each semester to students in the Normal

College and to teachers in service, and should work with curriculum committees, but it is important that they be given time and adequate assistance to bring to bear upon the professional education of teachers and curriculum reconstruction the most authoritative findings in their respective fields. They should not carry more than one-fifth of the normal teaching load in the Normal College.

7. *Professional Study Program Necessary to Curriculum Revision*

The necessity for a continuous program of professional study involving teachers and all other members of the instructional and administrative staff of the schools must again be emphasized here. A good foundation for such study has already been laid in Chicago, but it must be very greatly extended. Staff meetings should be made possible in all schools. Where buildings are utilized throughout the day, it will be desirable to dismiss schools for a portion of the day once or twice a month in order that such meetings may be held.

The responsibility of the principal in conducting staff meetings in the school under his direction has already been discussed. Upon the assistant superintendent in charge of each major division, as, for example, elementary education, will, of course, rest the responsibility of organizing and directing this professional study. It will be the function of the curriculum department to assist in every way possible. The point is that such professional study is basic to the improvement of teaching.

8. *Professional Libraries*

A good working professional library should be maintained in the headquarters building as an essential to the curriculum-revision and professional study program. A very good beginning has already been made in this direction. The central professional library should maintain a bibliographical service for all departments of the schools.

It is obvious that one central library cannot meet the needs of 15,000 teachers, many of whom would have to travel long distances to reach it. Therefore branch libraries should be established in various parts of the city. Gradually professional libraries should be developed in all of the larger buildings. The supervisor of libraries should be the librarian of the headquarters professional library and should be given such assistance as is needed in this library. School librarians should have charge of the branch professional libraries in the various schools.

9. *School Libraries*

Chicago has made a beginning in the development of school libraries, especially in the secondary schools. These libraries are maintained jointly by the Board of Education and the Chicago Public Library. But few elementary schools have libraries, and the committee has been unable to find an adequate library in any elementary school. A good library is essential to the development of a good curriculum and good teaching in any school, whether elementary or secondary. School libraries should be established, therefore, in every school in Chicago and placed under the direction of competent librarians. Much larger appropriations should be made for books. The junior and senior high schools almost without exception have inadequate libraries, and the libraries both at Crane College and at the Chicago Normal College are woefully inadequate to the needs of those institutions.

To direct the policies of the school libraries a director of libraries should be appointed. He should also serve as librarian of the central professional library.

10. Character of Materials to be Developed Under the Direction of the Curriculum Department

Varied types of curriculum materials should be developed by the curriculum department. Its function should not be conceived primarily as that of developing logically arranged syllabi to govern teaching in various subjects and grades. Materials developed should include courses of study rich in content and suggestions as to method. No pattern can be set for these courses of study. The tendency to integration is very evident. It will be the function of the curriculum department and the committees to study all such problems and to develop policies.

Materials should include studies of the general attitudes, concepts, and generalizations, and of the type of mind and personality that the school should strive to develop in American youth, and suggested procedures with reference to teaching. The Chicago schools should look forward also to the development of teaching materials for actual use in the classroom. There is always a dearth of suitable teaching materials where the curriculum is being constantly modified and improved to keep pace with a changing society.

11. The Status of the City-wide Courses of Study

Utilization of the courses of study developed under the guidance of the curriculum department should not be made mandatory. Latitude should be given to schools and to teachers, under competent leadership, to deviate from general practice described in the courses. It is inevitable that there will be a very wide use of courses of study where a school system is organized for the continuous coöperative study of curriculum problems and the preparation of curriculum and teaching materials.

12. Experimentation

The maintenance of experimental schools is essential to the development of a vital educational program in Chicago. A good beginning has been made in the establishment of the Lewis-Champlin and Joyce Kilmer experimental schools, which are rendering a most important service. Experimentation is also being carried on in other schools. This program should be extended to include other elementary and secondary schools. The heads of these schools should be carefully chosen with reference to their professional preparation and general ability to direct educational experimentation. Faculties of the schools should be chosen on a similar basis. Service on these faculties should be on the basis of rotation. Few members should serve more than five years.

Under the leadership of the principal, each experimental school should be encouraged to work out its own experimental program. Every experimental program must be carried out with reference to some considered theory of purpose and method. Divergent views are held to-day with reference to learning and methods of teaching, and even with reference to the major functions of education. It will be desirable that some schools be exponents of particular theories with reference to curriculum organization and teaching. The adoption of an eclectic policy by an experimental school can be carried only to a certain point. For example, there may be a fundamental inconsistency in an attempt to organize an elementary school on an extensive use of techniques of individualized instruction and at the same time to utilize highly socialized methods of teaching.

A well-considered experimental program will accomplish almost as much as any single factor to promote better schools in Chicago, and its influence will extend far beyond the city itself.

13. The Coöperation of the Universities and Colleges Located in Chicago

Chicago public schools are unusually favorably situated by reason of the location in Chicago of two of the greatest universities in the world and of other important institutions of higher learning. These universities and colleges have long performed and are performing an invaluable service to the Chicago teacher. The survey staff finds the departments of education and other departments in these institutions anxious to serve the city schools in any way possible. These resources should be more widely used than at the present time, as should the resources of the departments of education of the state university and other universities.

14. Citizen Coöperation

Lay groups interested in promoting education should be invited to participate in the study of the problems of the curriculum. An excellent beginning in this direction has been made in citizens' committees that have been organized by the superintendent of schools. The organization and the work of these committees cannot be too highly commended. This lay participation should be extended.

15. *Education Conceived as a Dynamic Social Process*

The recommendation fundamental to all others pertaining to curriculum reconstruction is that education in a rapidly changing industrial civilization be regarded itself as a dynamic ever-changing social process. This means that the curriculum can never be a fixed thing. Some elements in it will be permanent. Other elements will be changing. There will necessarily be eliminations and additions to meet changing conditions. Our concept of the process of education itself and of the function of education in society will change with the advance in knowledge in education and related fields and with changing conditions of our contemporary world.

264. " TEACHER PARTICIPATION IN CURRICULUM CONSTRUCTION " [8]

Prudence Cutright

The most successful course of study is that course which is most instrumental in lifting teaching procedures and instructional materials to a higher educational level. The major purpose of a course of study is to guide teaching, more consistently and more certainly, to the best educational objectives. *Teaching practice in any school organization must be taken at its current level and through comprehensive curriculum revision guided toward a higher plane.* This transition to a higher level of teaching occurs in the classroom; it constitutes the true measure of the effectiveness of the curriculum construction program. Thus, the crucial test of curriculum revision can be observed only in teaching practice. One cannot determine by an examination of what is printed between the covers of a course of study the extent to which that course is being well used by the teachers for whom it was designed. However valuable we may consider a printed course of study which contains worthy objectives, life-like activities, and subject matter of social worth, they are but a part of the true evaluation of a curriculum. A course of study should leaven the teaching of at least the majority of the teaching group for which it is designed or it fails in its major function.

Those interested in the improvement of teaching and in curriculum construction have witnessed the development of several noteworthy curricula which seem to have failed to make any marked impression on teaching techniques in the school system where they were developed. Attention only to what is printed between the covers of a course of study may in part be responsible for the failure of some curricula to stimulate teachers to better teaching. It seems to be

[8] *Educational Method,* 8:404–407, April, 1929.

the practice, in some cities where curriculum revision is in progress, to withdraw from the teaching group some ten or twelve progressive teachers of the subject under revision and to have this small group of teachers work in coöperation with curriculum and subject matter experts in developing a course of study. *The training of the remainder of the teachers, who will some day be called upon to use the course of study, seems to receive but little definite attention at least until the course is ready for publication.* Undoubtedly such a scheme has certain advantages, chief of which is the rapid production of a course of study.

The disadvantages may, however, more than offset the advantages. The activities of the small committee may leave the major teaching group untouched and relatively uninformed. When the course appears, the majority of the teaching group will be lacking in the intelligent and sympathetic understanding which should attend the adoption of any course. Because of this misunderstanding or the lack of understanding, the course may fail in its major purpose however well it may appear to the outside reader. There are disadvantages for the curriculum expert in that he is relatively unaware, at least until the course is adopted, of the difficulties which the average teacher will encounter in the use of the course. A small group of superior teachers, working in more or less cloistered coöperation with the curriculum expert, does not discover the obstacles which the new curriculum will encounter when put to a practical test. These obstacles may be numerous enough or great enough to prevent teachers from ever accepting the course of study seriously.

Where curriculum development is not accompanied by teacher training, such activities usually follow the publication of the course of study. The acceptance and usage of a course of study may under such conditions be a very slow, difficult process if ever really accomplished. Such a course is, in a sense, superimposed, and teachers who have not actually grown with the development of the curriculum may be uninterested, indifferent, or, what is worse, unsympathetic to the changes which are proposed. Thus, the technique of developing courses of study by the use of small groups of teachers, without attention to the remainder of the teaching group until the course actually appears for adoption, and without close coöperation with supervisory agencies, may be responsible for the indifference or helplessness which many teachers display in a half-hearted use of new courses of study. Curriculum revision in some quarters has run away from supervision. New curricula are being published so rapidly that the average teacher is in danger of having the waters of curriculum revision close over her head without being given an opportunity to learn how to swim.

Where curriculum revision calls for a change in teaching procedures and materials, as it usually does, it would seem the better part of wisdom to have the teacher-training program incorporated into the actual program of curriculum construction in order that all teachers may participate, directly or indirectly, in curriculum construction. But few teachers are prepared to participate in curriculum revision without some knowledge of the problems involved. Group-wide teacher-training activities create a basis of understanding and a readiness which makes every teacher a potential participant in the research activities so essential to curriculum development. The activities of the teacher-training program and the activities necessary for curriculum revision should be so interwoven and dovetailed that the course of study, when it finally appears, is the product of group-wide participation — group-wide in this sense, that while the major responsibility for initiating and devising has been carried by the small curriculum committee, all teachers have given definite assistance. Under such conditions the teachers' acceptance and the use of a course of study is a foregone conclusion. The course of study is in use even before it appears in print. The initiation of teacher training and introduction of curriculum revision under such a plan are almost simultaneous.

Immediately it is evident that the activities or experiences which are necessary to the fulfillment of the major purpose of a course of study are more supervisory in character than curricular. However, schools as a whole are not concerned with cataloguing or departmentalizing the types of activities but with determining their effectiveness in securing the desired goal, namely, that of intelligent usage of the course of study. The problem of adequate curriculum development is twofold, first, the discovery of desirable technique and materials of instruction, and, second, the provision for a background of understanding an experience that will lead to their intelligent usage, in at least the majority of classrooms. If this twofold aspect of curriculum development is accepted, teacher-training activities cannot be omitted from the curriculum revision program.

Teacher training here is used in its broadest meaning. It implies the acquisition of subject matter, the study of the literature of pertinent research, and an understanding of the philosophy underlying the proposed changes, as well as the development of skill in the proposed teaching techniques. It includes not only the training of classroom teachers but also, as far as necessary, the development of an understanding on the part of supervisory officers. In a city where supervisory responsibilities are largely invested in school principals, principals must be acquainted with the techniques of supervising the new course of study. Thus, a training program includes supervisors as well as teachers.

To illustrate the dovetailing of teacher training and curriculum revision, I should like to present a portion of a tentative social studies program. Before presenting this program, it should be said that it is the product not only of the curriculum department but also of administrative officers, supervisory officers, including school principals, classroom teachers, and experts in the social studies. The curriculum director, as chairman, submits tentative plans, experimental materials, and proposed researches for the suggestions of the groups just mentioned. Administrative officers give assistance in setting needed administrative machinery in motion, supervisory officers give assistance in their field; classroom teachers contribute from their firsthand knowledge of classroom problems, and subject matter experts advise their special field. Thus, the various school forces are guided through comprehensive curriculum revision in achieving the common goal, namely, the improvement of teaching.

In no sense is this program presented as a model but merely as an illustration of the function of teacher-training activities in preparing all teachers to participate effectively in the activities of curriculum development. Some of the activities which I will mention have already been accomplished and others will be put into operation this semester.

The procedure presented will undoubtedly be varied in its detail as the program progresses but the major activities will remain primarily the same. New studies and new activities are being added as their need is made evident. Sufficient detail has been presented to illustrate the major thesis of this paper: namely, greater attention to *teacher* training at the time when a course of study is being developed is to achieve its true purpose — that of raising the teaching level to a higher educational plane. The program outlined is based on the proposition that curriculum development should be an outgrowth of teacher training.

The work of curriculum revision is strategically situated to bridge, at least in part, the chasm which has long existed between theory and practice. In order to lessen the gap, it must proceed on a more comprehensive basis than is frequently the practice. The curriculum expert and his chosen assistants cannot develop courses of study in a handful of selected classrooms and then in turn expect the supervisory group to superimpose this product on a group of teachers who have at no time been taken into the confidence of the small curriculum group. Curriculum revision must be built on broader lines. We must retain the services of the curriculum expert but he in turn must give greater attention to creating a readiness for the materials developed in his direction. This readiness is best created through group-wide teacher-training activities as contrasted with the training of a few.

The curriculum revision program should be so outlined that the publication of a course of study indicates that the majority of teachers, not a selected few, have attained the goals indicated in the course of study. The publication of a course of study under such conditions is but a tentative goal mark before teacher training and curriculum revision again renew educational efforts to reach a still higher instructional level. In cities where several courses of study are being developed simultaneously, the same theory of teacher training should hold true.

Comprehensive curriculum revision demands that supervision with its teacher-training activities get into the advance guard rather than the rear guard of curriculum revision programs.

265. A Plan of Teacher Participation in Curriculum Development [9]

Carleton Washburne

A . . . major type of participation is that of the administrative and supervisory staff and teachers in planning curriculum, method, and research. Each principal meets the staff of his own school at frequent intervals (once a week to once a month), to work out the problems of the individual school building. The superintendent meets the teachers in grade or subject groups once every two weeks. Thus on alternate Tuesdays, the first grade teachers meet with the superintendent from 3:00 to 4:30, the fourth grade teachers from 4:30 to 6:00. On Wednesday, it is the second and fifth grade teachers, and so on. Junior high school English teachers meet with the principal of the junior high school and the superintendent of schools on alternate Mondays. The junior high school arithmetic teachers meet with the principal and superintendent on alternate Thursdays this year. Next year, the superintendent will meet with different departments of the junior high school teachers, and so on. . . .

One would have to be present at a few of the meetings to get a clear feeling of the entire democracy that prevails. There is no domination by anyone, and teachers are most outspoken in their opinions. The superintendent or principal usually presides, and therefore does not vote except in case of a tie. Every question is settled either by majority vote or by reference to active research. The head of the

[9] From "What is Progressive School Administration," *Progressive Education,* 12:220–221, April, 1935.

Research Department frequently participates in these group meetings, and most research done in the Winnetka Schools has its origin
in the grade and department meetings and is in part conducted by
the teachers themselves.

The entire curriculum has been built up and is being continually
revised in these department meetings. While teachers have a great
deal of individual freedom as to the methods they use, these methods
are always discussed, particularly if they differ from the methods
used by most of the teachers. When there is a question regarding
the relative effectiveness of two methods, research techniques are
applied. At the present time, the grade meetings are concerned with
trying to find out how to make the arithmetic curriculum more vital,
how to make it tie in more closely with the children's lives; with
working out a new spelling method which will allow each child to
work on lists of words of a difficulty appropriate to his own spelling
ability; with eliminating from the grammar course all elements of
grammar which do not have a direct functional effect upon the child's
written or spoken language, and a revision of the method of teaching
grammar to place the entire emphasis upon this functioning. At
these meetings, of course, a variety of minor and comparatively
routine questions are also taken up.

Besides the building meetings of teachers and principals and the
grade and department meetings, there are general faculty meetings
(once every six weeks). There are also special teachers' groups,
meeting with the supervisors, principals, specially qualified teachers,
or with the superintendent. At the present moment one group is
working out a health curriculum for the whole school system. The
chairman is a member of the physical education department, and the
group includes the Village Health Officer, a school nurse, a principal,
a teacher, and the superintendent. A second group, working under
the teacher of children of the non-academic type, is rewriting children's classics in simple form so that twelve-, thirteen-, and fourteen-
year-old youngsters whose reading ability is of third or fourth grade
level will be able to read them with interest and fluency. A third
group is meeting with the supervisor of group and creative activities
and learning from her what she learned, in a recent world trip, regarding the lives of children in various lands and the interests common to children everywhere at various age levels. A fourth group,
meeting with the same supervisor, is working out a science curriculum for the lower grades. A fifth is meeting with the psychiatrist
to study mental hygiene and child adjustment, while a sixth is meeting with the school librarian to discuss recent books for children and
work out a curriculum in literature. And so on.

Many after-school meetings? Yes. They are, however, so organized that a teacher ordinarily has a grade or departmental meeting one week, and a group meeting the next. The building meeting may come in the same week with either the group meeting or the grade meeting, but on the week of the general faculty meeting there are no group or grade meetings. Usually a teacher has only one or two after-school meetings a week; although in the junior high school, where a teacher may be a member of two or three departments, the number of meetings may average a little higher. Most of the meetings are between 3:00 P.M. and 6:00 P.M. Some group meetings are held in the evening.

But there cannot be participation unless people get together to participate. Teachers who come into the Winnetka Schools understand that such participation is expected. And the teachers themselves have decided upon most of the meetings and have cooperated in making out the schedule of meetings. I think they all agree that it is by getting together in these various ways that they grow and have an opportunity to participate creatively in the entire educative procedure.

266. Releasing Teachers for Experimental Work [10]

J. E. Stonecipher

It is highly desirable that the experimental course hold the confidence of the patrons of the school and to assure them that there can be little possibility of their children losing ground in their progress toward graduation or college entrance. Partly for this reason, it was decided to limit the experimental curriculum to ten periods per week, or half the pupils' school load, exclusive of physical education. The content of the course is planned to cover enough of the same area of subject matter to justify school authorities in certifying credit as equivalent to the regularly available courses of the Des Moines schools. The pupil who finds it necessary to transfer from the experimental curriculum will not be penalized by being out of adjustment, but will rather be enriched and stimulated by his partial experience. Our required core curriculum has not followed the time schedule or the emphasis of the usual world history course, but it does deal with the history of civilization in the tenth grade and offers thorough justification for certifying a credit in world history to another school.

It was originally planned that the teachers working with the experimental groups should not be released from other duties. I feel that this decision has been the most serious mistake made in the plan-

[10] From "Experimental College Entrance Units. Practical Limitations of the Experiment," *North Central Association Quarterly*, 9:353, January, 1935.

ning of the experiment. Adequate planning was impossible without great sacrifice on the part of the teachers. Consultation time was difficult to arrange. It has almost been impossible to make adequate records of the materials and practices of the group. As a result, we have much less helpful material to use in initiating the course with a second group next September than should be available. This condition has been rectified by releasing each of the teachers directing the experimental groups from one-fifth of her teaching load and by providing clerical assistance for mimeographing and typing materials and records.

267. Participation of Lay Committees in Curriculum Programs [11]

Clinton C. Trillingham

Participation of lay committees in curriculum programs. Curriculum programs in approximately two thirds of American cities have not involved the participation of lay members of the communities. According to Table XXXIII, lay committees have had a part in some phase of the curriculum work in twenty-six cities which is 28 per cent of the cities that maintain programs, while there has been no such participation in fifty-eight cities, which is 63 per cent.

In the individual population groups, laymen have had some part in the work of about one third of the cities in both the smallest and largest population groups. In the middle group of cities, there has been some lay participation in slightly more than half of the cities reporting.

Lynchburg plans later to use lay citizens in their program to some extent. San Diego has some advisory lay members for one or two subjects. Boston uses the advice of lay committees in setting up their shop courses and commercial courses occasionally. At Baltimore local conferences are held with certain representative individuals in the community. Los Angeles sometimes considers the advice of selected laymen in setting up their trade work. Six other cities mentioned very slight or occasional use of lay members or committees in connection with their curriculum activities. It is significant that over two thirds of the cities have established and carried on their programs without the consideration of lay members of the community.

Bobbitt * suggests that expert services of specialized groups in the community should be utilized, particularly in the vocational fields.

---

[11] From *The Organization and Administration of Curriculum Programs,* Southern California Education Monographs, 1933–34 Series, No. 4, University of Southern California Press, Los Angeles, 1934, pp. 97–99.

* F. J. Bobbitt, *op. cit.,* pp. 38–39.

TABLE XXXIII

PARTICIPATION OF LAY COMMITTEES IN CURRICULUM PROGRAMS

Participation of lay committees in programs	Population of cities in thousands							
	30 to 100		100 to 500		Over 500		Total	
	No.	Per cent	No.	Per cent	No.	Per cent	No.	Per cent
Yes..................	11	26.2	12	29.3	3	30.0	26	28.1
No..................	28	66.6	23	56.1	7	70.0	58	62.6
Total..............	39		35		10		84	

This table should be read as follows: Eleven cities between 30,000 and 100,000 in population, which is 26.2 per cent of the forty-two cities in that group which have curriculum programs, afford selected laymen a degree of participation in their curriculum work.

Bruner * recommends that the purposes, values, and procedures of a curriculum program should be discussed by competent people from within and without the system.

H. B. Wilson † asserts that the intelligent citizen is capable of rendering service in curriculum making, for his own experiences afford him ideas of practical services the schools could render, and he brings the laymen's point of view to the course of study committee. Bankers, newspaper men, gardeners, and the like have their contributions to make. Their participation makes for a more practical and common sense school offering.

Hopkins ‡ contends that lay members should represent the major organizations in so far as is possible. Lay citizens should act only in an advisory capacity in all of their curriculum relationships.

The expert opinion and the evidence of the table indicate that many school administrators do not take advantage of the potential services of representative laymen. The utilization of this service should bring about not only a better educational offering for the pupils, but should also create a feeling of understanding within the community itself. Every school system that claims to maintain a definite curriculum program should investigate this opportunity. The advisory services of certain selected individuals in each community should prove valuable.

* H. B. Bruner, *loc. cit.*
† H. B. Wilson, Second *Yearbook,* National Educational Association, Department of Superintendence, 1924, Part II, p. 41.
‡ L. T. Hopkins, *op. cit.*, pp. 335, 372.

268. Non-Local Curriculum Organization Desirable [12]

Will French

So far, curriculum reconstruction in public schools has come forward under one of two general types of plan. They may be designated as local and non-local. Under the local plan, each separate school system sets up its own curriculum construction organization. Denver is the classical example of such a set-up. Hundreds of small and generally poor administrations are to be found throughout the country. Under the non-local plan a larger unit is utilized. Reconstruction programs initiated by state departments of education for the schools of an entire state are the best examples of non-local type. Horn, years ago, argued for a national curriculum commission, but the plan met with no favor, and as the years have gone by in which fear of federal domination of American education has increased the idea has continuously lost favor. Others have more recently advocated the wisdom of non-local organization, but have presented little in the way of a plan.

Experience with the local organization plan has brought to light some inherent weaknesses when considered as a program to be generally adopted throughout the nation. Briefly they are as follows: (1) The cost is prohibitive. Only large systems are able to carry the necessary overhead for such undertakings. Moreover this cost tends to increase rather than diminish as the difficulties of the problem become more widely understood. Some school systems which might have afforded simple, early-day programs, now realize that they cannot afford an organization adequate to the problem and, largely, therefore, left to the large communities who already have the most experienced and often the best teachers in their class rooms. Many small school systems with meager equipment and the less experienced teachers get only a secondary and diluted effect, resulting from reading what the larger school systems may have put into print. A program which is to have any large effect on American secondary school education as a whole must directly touch smaller school systems because the typical American high school is a small high school. The average size of a North Central Association high school is one of twenty teachers.

(2) Few school systems have adequate research facilities. The excerpts from the National Survey quoted by Dr. Loomis illustrate some of the intricate problems upon which objective data must be gathered on a large scale if curriculum reconstruction is to be soundly

[12] From " The Survey and Reconstruction of Curricula," *North Central Association Quarterly,* 7:229–232, September, 1932.

based. Few large schools and almost no small schools have research departments adequately staffed for this task, nor with influence enough to gather data from a large enough number of sources to make the results valid. Time has increased, not decreased, the complexity of this task and the local organization plan has, therefore, become progressively less sound as a system of administering curriculum reconstruction on a national scale.

(3) Few school systems have the technically trained workers. In addition to being short handed in the research staff few school systems have the other technically trained workers necessary to a first class reconstruction program. This is shown by the fact that school systems temporarily associate with their program, curriculum experts or consultants who give part time and long distance service to the local organization. Not every school system can command even the part time service of subject matter experts, even if all of *them* were well qualified to act as consultants. Local leadership is frequently not good and results in some of the conditions mentioned by Dr. Loomis. Therefore, local curriculum construction is likely to proceed under weak scholarship.

(4) The total amount of money expended is needlessly great. The local plan calls for a duplication of overhead expense which makes it a poor plan to consider in connection with a nation-wide curriculum reconstruction movement. The cost of administration, research and other technical service is about the same irrespective of the number of school rooms served. To duplicate this expense in every city from average size up puts an unnecessarily large charge on to the nation's bill for education and wastes money in duplication of effort which is needed elsewhere. If curriculum reconstruction is to go beyond mere sporadic, localized effort, the local plan is not well adapted to the problem.

Advocates of the local plan have argued that it is a great professional gain for teachers in each system to participate in a curriculum reconstruction program. If this argument were basically sound it would mean that each teacher ought to write her own curriculum. Theoretically that may be true, but practically it is not feasible. No local curriculum organization has ever believed in the theory beyond the point of selecting a few of the best teachers to act as a committee to do the work. Participation for the many other teachers in the system is only nominal. If the professional growth theory were sound, local schools should select the poorest teachers for curriculum committees, as they are most in need of professional growth. No local system does this — intentionally at least. The theory is that to be an intelligent user of the curriculum one should participate in its writing. By the same theory, to be an intelligent reader of a book, one ought to help write it; to be intelligently obedient to a law, one ought to participate in making the law; when as a matter of fact, there are other ways of becoming intelligent about these things beside participating in their development. School systems which have utilized the local curriculum construction method have been the quickest to develop other methods for making their teachers who did not serve on the curriculum committees intelligent users of the product. This argument then does not warrant the adoption of the local plan for a nation-wide program.

My argument, so far, is that to meet the wide-spread need for the large scale, high grade curriculum construction revealed by the national survey, we need an effective non-local program of curriculum organization. The impossibility of achieving a national organization is obvious. State department of education organizations usually have the weaknesses of the local organization plan as far as research facilities and ability to stand expense are concerned. Moreover, traditionally and legally, state departments of education usually offer minimum programs that are concerned with setting up the standards below which the state is unwilling to have its schools go. A minimum program of curriculum construction will not satisfy the needs of the host of schools willing to go further. The cost which a state department assumes in providing more than a minimum program invites legislative criticism. For most of us, a national plan of curriculum reorganization is beyond the range of possibilities, and the state plan is an artificial set-up which groups together schools with but a minimum of common interests. We do have, however, in our accrediting agencies a natural grouping of both secondary schools and colleges in organizations now already interested in problems closely affiliated with that of curriculum reconstruction. Therefore, the most logical and the most natural unit for curriculum organization on a wide scale would be to extend the functions of the accrediting associations to include a well developed attack on the problem of curriculum. Six of these accrediting associations practically blanket the United States. Each operates in a rather mutually exclusive geographical area. Each includes in its area a large number — often more than a majority — of the schools in its area. In addition to the secondary schools, each includes the higher institutions who are sharing the secondary schools' interest in the curriculum. Each of these associations includes colleges and secondary schools who *desire* to work together in harmony on the solving of the principal problems common to the schools of that area. Cooperation in curriculum construction in these associations would, therefore, be a natural, logical outgrowth of the present organization. No new groups would need to be formulated, no new machinery of administration would need to be developed to duplicate in some degree what now already exists. There is no reason why these accrediting agencies could not extend their function to include a program of curriculum construction for their member schools. Briefly, some additional advantages would be (1) that the overhead cost could be spread over a large number of schools. A nominal amount from each school would in most cases suffice. Present dues in some cases could be made to carry the cost. (2) The cost would be reduced by reason of the research facilities and other expert services available in the faculties of the college members of these associations. (3) The best scholarship ability available in the areas served by the association would be available for use and a high quality of out-put would thus be assured. (4) The materials developed would get a wide *spread* throughout the area of each accrediting agency. This would mean a more uniform improvement in secondary school curriculum over large geographical areas. Each agency could easily keep in touch with what other agencies were doing and a desirable amount of national uniformity with appropriate adjustments to each area represented by an accrediting agency easily possible. Taking everything into account, the most appropriate organization for a non-local curriculum construction program demanded by the size of the task is the accrediting agency.

269. "SOME PROBLEMS IN A STATE PROGRAM FOR THE IMPROVEMENT OF INSTRUCTION" [13]

Doak S. Campbell

Any attempt to improve instruction in the public schools, undertaken on a state-wide basis, involves a number of difficult problems. Whether such a program is projected on an experimental basis or is merely concerned with producing and promulgating new courses of study, some of the problems will be similar. However, the direction in which our discussion will lead will be determined largely by the fundamental concept of the curriculum that is accepted. If by developing the curriculum we mean the refinement of subject matter, whether in textbooks or in any one of a number of types of teaching units, the teacher's place is largely that of a consumer. If, on the other hand, all phases of the instructional process are included in the concept of the curriculum, the teacher's place becomes that of chief agent in the process.

Thus we see that the problem is one of fundamental import. As is always the case when fundamental issues are at stake there are

[13] *The Tennessee Teacher*, 3:7, 9–10, May, 1936.

broadly different points of view, each with its supporters. For example, it is maintained by some that only the specialist can perform the intricate tasks of curriculum making. Others hold the opinion that, since the teacher is closer to classroom situations than the specialist could be, he should have a major part in curriculum development. Dr. Bagley, for example, supports the former point of view and ridicules the latter. He regards curriculum study by committees of teachers as an educational fashion based on the silly and tragic idea that each community must have a curriculum of its own.

Such disagreements with cooperative curriculum development illustrate the conflicting concepts of the curriculum and of curriculum development. They indicate that teacher participation in curriculum development is conceived merely in terms of writing up materials for inclusion in a course of study. They do not take account of the type of teacher participation which has been developed in more recent years.

The development of suitable courses of study constitutes an important phase of the improvement of instruction. If a course of study is looked upon as a means of consolidating and organizing the advance or improvement in curriculum development, then it follows rather than precedes much of the work of improvement. Under the broader conception of curriculum improvement the mere task of providing courses of study or units for a course of study is a specialized task for selected groups of workers, but there are many other phases of the program to be carried on in which general participation by teachers is desirable, if courses of study are to be used effectively.

Conceived as a means of improving instruction in all the schools, taking each situation where it is and proceeding as far and as rapidly as possible, a curriculum program should include participation by every teacher in the school system. A few suggestions as to the nature of this participation are here presented.

1. *Developing a consciousness of need for improvement.* Regardless of the extent to which educational leaders recognize the need for improving instruction in any of its elements, consistent, intelligent effort will not be made by the teacher until he also becomes aware of the need. It is not enough merely to tell teachers that there is need for improvement and then hand them materials designed to supply the need. The education of a teacher is not fundamentally different from the education of a child in this respect. His experience must be the basis for any effective learning that takes place. The opportunity to compare one's experience with that of other teachers confronted with similar problems may be helpful.

Procedures may be developed which will facilitate such cultivation on the part of teachers. Suggestive reference materials may be made available to them. Simple techniques may be suggested for studying the needs of children, the aims and purposes of the school, the needs of the social group in which the teacher works.

2. *Sensitizing the lay public to school needs.* This is closely related to the previous suggestion and should proceed in very close relation to it. To assume that the lay public is not interested in the instructional program of the schools is not sound. To assume that any well-directed effort to enlist the intelligent cooperation of the layman will not yield highly beneficial results is shortsighted. As a matter of fact, many of the more important elements in our present program are there because of the pressure exerted by parents, often over the protests of teachers bound by conservatism. Who put music into our schools? Not teachers, because they were conservative, but interested laymen. And so with art, home economics, and other recent additions to our curriculum.

We recognize, of course, the dangers that may arise from the desire for precipitate action when laymen become aroused. It is the responsibility of teachers to see that progress along this line is orderly. It is my belief that participation by laymen in improving instruction is also a most effective means for improving financial support for the schools.

3. *Encourage teachers in exploratory work.* Many teachers feel bound by administrative practices which prevent their attempting to improve the instructional situation. Superintendents and principals would do well not only to give teachers freedom to explore and experiment with new procedures and new materials, they should go further and encourage them to do so. Rigid time schedules should be made flexible. Materials of instruction from the immediate environment should be utilized wherever possible. Cooperative planning among teachers should be encouraged. Means of passing on to other teachers the results of exploratory work should be provided.

4. *The program should be kept flexible.* Great inequalities exist in our school system today. These are reflected in length of school term, amount of money spent for instruction per child, training of teachers, local environment, etc. Such inequalities will tend to continue although we hope to reduce them. Regimentation will not bring about the desired equality. It has not done so after a great deal of trial. We must, therefore, endeavor to discover a better means. We must take each situation *where it is* and develop as rapidly and as far as conditions warrant. This means that a uniform program will not be attempted and a rigid schedule will not be followed. It also means that the program of instruction will continue to be considered as experimental and will not be permitted to crystallize.

There will appear from time to time, as improvement goes forward, the necessity of adopting certain points of view and certain procedures which will be uniform. However, such action will be taken only after they have emerged from the experiences of a large number of teachers.

Many other problems might be suggested, such as the improvement of the preservice training of teachers, but those we have mentioned suggest some of the major tasks that may be undertaken with the hope that improvement of instruction may begin at once. If we can keep teachers enthusiastically at work, with open minds, we shall develop instruction for the Tennessee child that will approach that which he has a right to expect of us.

270. ADMINISTRATIVE TENDENCIES INDICATED IN PUBLIC SCHOOL COURSES OF STUDY PUBLISHED 1929 TO 1931 [14]

Henry Harap and Alice J. Bayne

As the curriculum making movement grows, new and varied experiences in administration are reported. The head of the program, the consultants employed, the special departments created, and the coöperative arrangements with teacher-training institutions differ from place to place. In several cases in which the bulletin is the product of an extensive and elaborately organized program, the organization is set forth in a chart.

The most revealing conclusion from our analysis is the important rôle that the teacher plays in curriculum construction. Not only do teachers serve on most curriculum committees, but in 178 instances they also either headed the project or shared in the leadership with administrative officers. The teacher is the leader in the building of single courses of study more than three times as often as any other school officer and as frequently as all administrative and supervisory officers combined. The principal appears in the rôle of committee chairman only seventeen times which is the least frequent.

Curriculum revision is continuing to make headway not only because it is intrinsically justifiable, but also because it has developed into a most effective instrument of constructive supervision. Thus, a number of school systems have delegated the function of curriculum revision to an assistant superintendent among whose normal duties is that of supervision. Fifty-three of the courses of study analyzed were revised by committees headed by a superintendent; sixteen were headed by an assistant superintendent; and fifty-five were headed by supervisors. It is reasonable to assume that these

[14] " A Critical Survey of Public School Courses of Study Published 1929 to 1931," *Journal of Educational Research*, 26:49–50, September, 1932.

programs of revision had the function of improving instruction as well as modernizing the courses of study.

In several instances the assistant of the regular and extension departments of nearby universities has been enlisted. The University of Alabama furnished three lecturers and incidental supervisory assistance to the Bessemer, Alabama, Public School program of curriculum revision. The Little Rock, Arkansas, courses of study have been revised with the assistance of the State University Extension Service. The Department of Extension Teaching of the University of North Carolina assists schools in curriculum revision. The Tulsa, Oklahoma, Public Schools have sent groups of teachers to the University of Iowa and to Columbia University for the express purpose of building new courses of study. The University of Nebraska joined the State Department of Public Instruction in the preparation of a high school curriculum. The construction of the Worcester geography course of study was supervised by the Department of Geography of Clark University. Some of the Indiana state courses of study were prepared by teachers in seminars at the Indiana University. Both the South Dakota and Virginia State Departments organized study programs with printed manuals for several thousand teachers preliminary to curriculum revision.

The director of curriculum was the presiding officer in the revision of thirty-nine courses of study, representing nine school organizations. The following school systems have organized bureaus or departments of curriculum revision since our last survey: Chicago, Ill.; Sacramento, Cal.; Minneapolis, Minn.; Detroit, Mich.; Binghamton, N. Y.; and the South Dakota State Department. In all, there are about a score of school systems which report special bureaus of curriculum revision. In four school organizations, the Bureau of Research was wholly or partially responsible for curriculum revision. These were Hawaii; Cleveland, Ohio; New York, N. Y.; and Lynn, Mass. We reiterate our opinion that if the creation of a separate bureau effects a separation between curriculum construction and the regular supervisory program it is unwise. Supervisory officers should school themselves in the art of curriculum construction and should systematically devote a large part of their time to this work.

Large school systems find it to their advantage to retain general and special consultants to assist them in curriculum revision. Twenty of the courses of study analyzed report the assistance of general consultants; twenty report the assistance of subject specialists; and thirty report the assistance of both general and special consultants. Consultants serve their school systems from several days to several weeks and in some cases follow up their personal conferences by correspondence. Nearly half the school systems represented by the bulletins analyzed engaged consultants for one or more of their courses of study, showing that it is common practice to enlist the coöperation of specialists.

271. ADMINISTRATIVE TENDENCIES INDICATED IN PUBLIC SCHOOL COURSES PUBLISHED 1932 TO 1934 [15]

Henry Harap

In the administration of the program of curriculum revision, one discovers the almost universal practice of committee procedure. The production committee, that is, the group which actually constructs the new course of study is always found. In addition, the survey revealed the fairly common occurrence of the general or central committee, particularly in the case of programs that are elaborate and involve several subjects and grades.

The teacher continues to play the most important role in curriculum revision. During the last biennium the superintendent appears to have taken a greatly decreased direct responsibility for curriculum revision, at least according to the records. In order of frequency, curriculum committees were headed by the following: teacher, supervisor, superintendent, professor, director of curriculum, assistant superintendent, and principal.

Heretofore principally a consultant, the professor in teacher training institutions, appears for the first time as a significant participating leader in practical curriculum making. Fifteen programs were headed by a professor. The Oklahoma State course of study was the result of a committee procedure under the direction of a professor at the state university. In the state of Missouri the program of revision was carried out in graduate courses at the University of Missouri under the direction of a professor. In Florida, as well as in several other southern states, the curriculum program was conducted under the direction of the Curriculum Laboratory at Peabody College.

The number of curriculum programs headed by the curriculum director in the last two years has declined. Due to enforced economies this administrative office has been discontinued in a number of school systems. The practice of retaining general and subject consultants has been continued at the usual rate, twenty-two of the former and twenty-one of the latter being reported.

[15] From " A Survey of Courses of Study Published in the Last Two Years," *Journal of Educational Research*, 28:644–645, May, 1935.

INDEX